THE PARADIGMATIC STRUCTURE OF PERSON MARKING

OXFORD STUDIES IN TYPOLOGY AND LINGUISTIC THEORY

SERIES EDITORS: Ronnie Cann, *University of Edinburgh*, William Croft, *University of Manchester*, Anna Siewierska, *University of Lancaster*.

This series offers a forum for innovative work in language typology and linguistic universals. It aims to link theory and empirical research in mutually productive ways and at the same time to make available a wide range of cross-linguistic data.

Published

Indefinite Pronouns
by Martin Haspelmath

Intransitive Predication
by Leon Stassen

Classifiers: A Typology of Noun Categorization Devices
by Alexandra Y. Aikhenvald

Anaphora
by Yan Huang

The Noun Phrase
by Jan Rijkhoff

The Paradigmatic Structure of Person Marking
by Michael Cysouw

In preparation

Subordination
by Sonia Cristofaro

Double Object Constructions
by Maria Polinsky

Copulas
by Regina Pustet

To be published in association with the series
The World Atlas of Language Structures
edited by Mathew Dryer, Bernard Comrie, David Gil, and Martin Haspelmath

THE PARADIGMATIC STRUCTURE OF PERSON MARKING

MICHAEL CYSOUW

OXFORD
UNIVERSITY PRESS

Great Clarendon Street, Oxford OX2 6DP

Oxford University Press is a department of the University of Oxford.
It furthers the University's objective of excellence in research, scholarship,
and education by publishing worldwide in

Oxford New York

Auckland Bangkok Buenos Aires Cape Town Chennai
Dar es Salaam Delhi Hong Kong Istanbul Karachi Kolkata
Kuala Lumpur Madrid Melbourne Mexico City Mumbai Nairobi
São Paulo Shanghai Taipei Tokyo Toronto

Oxford is a registered trade mark of Oxford University Press
in the UK and in certain other countries

Published in the United States
by Oxford University Press Inc., New York

© Michael Cysouw 2003

The moral rights of the author have been asserted

Database right Oxford University Press (maker)

First published 2003

All rights reserved. No part of this publication may be reproduced,
stored in a retrieval system, or transmitted, in any form or by any means,
without the prior permission in writing of Oxford University Press,
or as expressly permitted by law, or under terms agreed with the appropriate
reprographics rights organization. Enquiries concerning reproduction
outside the scope of the above should be sent to the Rights Department,
Oxford University Press, at the address above

You must not circulate this book in any other binding or cover
and you must impose this same condition on any acquirer

British Library Cataloguing in Publication Data

Data available

Library of Congress Cataloging in Publication Data

Cysouw, Michael.
The paradigmatic structure of person marking/Michael Cysouw.
(Oxford studies in typology and linguistic theory)
Includes bibliographical references and indexes.
1. Grammar, Comparative and general–Person   2. Typology (Linguistics)   3. Grammar,
Comparative and general–Number   4. Historical linguistics   I. Title   II. Series.

P240.85 .C95 2003   415–dc21   2002192576

ISBN 0 19 925412 5

Typeset by Newgen Imaging Systems (P) Ltd., Chennai, India
Printed in Great Britain
on acid-free paper by
Biddles Ltd., Guildford & King's Lynn

Contents

Long contents	vi
Preface	xi
List of abbreviations	xiv
1. Introduction: Objective, Definitions, Method, and Some History	1

PART I. PERSON MARKING

2. One Among the Crowd: The Marking of Singular Participants	39
3. Group Marking: Redefining Plurality in the Pronominal Domain	66

PART II. PARADIGMATIC STRUCTURE

4. The Diversity of the Core: A Survey of Patterns of Singular and Group Marking	101
5. Compound Pronouns: Other Person Categories Disqualified	166

PART III. NUMBER INCORPORATED

6. Cardinality: Redefining Number in the Pronominal Domain	187
7. The Diversity of Restricted Groups: A Survey of Dual Person Marking	204

PART IV. COGNATE PARADIGMS

8. Connecting Paradigms: Person Paradigms through Time and Space	245
9. Cognate Paradigms Revisited: Connecting the Dual	269
10. Finale: Summary and Prospects	295
References	322
List of languages according to genetic/geographical distribution	351
Index of names	361
Index of languages	367
Index of subjects	373

Long Contents

1. Introduction: Objective, Definitions, Method, and Some History		1
1.1	The feat of Domingo de Santo Tomás	1
1.2	Definitions and delimitation	4
	1.2.1 Preamble	4
	1.2.2 Person and number	6
	1.2.3 Paradigmatic structure	8
	1.2.4 Specialization and grammaticalization	12
	1.2.5 Remaining delimitations	15
1.3	Methodology	20
	1.3.1 Preamble	20
	1.3.2 Typology versus cross-linguistic research	21
	1.3.3 Sampling in typology	22
	1.3.4 Crypto-diachrony	24
1.4	Previous cross-linguistic investigations	24
	1.4.1 Preamble	24
	1.4.2 Forchheimer and his critics	25
	1.4.3 Greenberg and his co-workers	28
	1.4.4 Mühlhäusler and Harré	31
	1.4.5 Laycock on New Guinean pronouns	32
	1.4.6 Conclusion	33
1.5	Outline of the book	33

PART I. PERSON MARKING

2. One Among the Crowd: The Marking of Singular Participants		39
2.1	Introduction	39
2.2	Possible patterns	39
2.3	Singular homophony	41
	2.3.1 Dutch-type homophony (Sb)	41
	2.3.2 Spanish-type homophony (Sc)	45
	2.3.3 English-type homophony (Sd)	48
	2.3.4 French-type homophony (Se)	51
	2.3.5 Summary	52
2.4	Singular homophony and pro-drop	54

			Long Contents	vii
	2.5	The distribution of zeros		57
		2.5.1 Zeros in homophonous paradigms		57
		2.5.2 Zeros for speaker or addressee		58
		2.5.3 Zeros for third person		61
	2.6	Conclusion		64
3.	Group Marking: Redefining Plurality in the Pronominal Domain			66
	3.1	Introduction		66
	3.2	Definition		67
	3.3	Terminology		68
	3.4.	Towards a typology of groups		72
	3.5	A partial typology: the first person complex		78
	3.6	Different kinds of 'we'		80
		3.6.1 Type (Pa): unified-we		80
		3.6.2 Type (Pb): no-we		81
		3.6.3 Type (Pc): only-inclusive		84
		3.6.4 Type (Pd): inclusive/exclusive		85
		3.6.5 Type (Pe): minimal/augmented		85
		3.6.6 Rare types		90
	3.7	Generalizations		95
	3.8	Conclusion		98

PART II. PARADIGMATIC STRUCTURE

4.	The Diversity of the Core: A Survey of Patterns of Singular and Group Marking			101
	4.1	Introduction		101
	4.2	Method of classification		102
	4.3	No inclusive/exclusive: split non-singular		106
		4.3.1 Preamble		106
		4.3.2 Latin-type paradigm		106
		4.3.3 Sinhalese-type paradigm		108
		4.3.4 Berik-type paradigm		110
		4.3.5 Maricopa-type paradigm		114
		4.3.6 Rare variants		118
	4.4	No inclusive/exclusive: homophonous non-singular		123
		4.4.1 Preamble		123
		4.4.2 1/2-homophony		124
		4.4.3 2/3-homophony		129
		4.4.4 1/3-homophony		134
		4.4.5 Unified homophony		136
	4.5	Inclusive/exclusive: split non-singular		138
		4.5.1 Preamble		138
		4.5.2 Maranao-type paradigm		139

viii   *Long Contents*

		4.5.3	Mandara-type paradigm	141
		4.5.4	Tupí-Guaraní-type paradigm	143
		4.5.5	Kwakiutl-type paradigm	145
		4.5.6	Sierra Popoluca-type paradigm	147
		4.5.7	Rare variants	152
	4.6	Inclusive/exclusive: homophonous non-singular		152
		4.6.1	Preamble	152
		4.6.2	Inclusive/2-homophony	153
		4.6.3	Inclusive/3-homophony	155
		4.6.4	Exclusive/2-homophony	156
		4.6.5	Exclusive/3-homophony	158
		4.6.6	2/3-homophony	159
	4.7	Generalizations		160
	4.8	Conclusion		165

5. Compound Pronouns: Other Person Categories Disqualified — 166

	5.1	Introduction		166
	5.2	From compound to pronoun		167
	5.3	The Bantoid compound pronouns		171
		5.3.1	Preamble	171
		5.3.2	The basic compound paradigm	172
		5.3.3	Two inclusives innovated	174
		5.3.4	One inclusive innovated	177
		5.3.5	The strange case of Ghomala'	179
	5.4	Generalizations		181
	5.5	The incorporative reading revisited		182
	5.6	Conclusion		183

PART III. NUMBER INCORPORATED

6. Cardinality: Redefining Number in the Pronominal Domain — 187

	6.1	Introduction	187
	6.2	A metalanguage for number marking	188
	6.3	Markedness reversals	193
	6.4	Other numbers	197
	6.5	Conclusion	202

7. The Diversity of Restricted Groups: A Survey of Dual Person Marking — 204

	7.1	Introduction		204
	7.2	Method and terminology		205
	7.3	Duals without inclusive/exclusive		205
		7.3.1	Preamble	205
		7.3.2	The dual-unified-we paradigm	206

		7.3.3 Vertical homophony	207
		7.3.4 Horizontal homophony	210
		7.3.5 Vertical and horizontal homophony	215
		7.3.6 Summary	216
	7.4	Duals with inclusive/exclusive: three times 'we'	216
		7.4.1 Preamble	216
		7.4.2 Inclusive/exclusive in plural only	218
		7.4.3 Inclusive/exclusive in dual only	220
		7.4.4 Dual in exclusive only	221
		7.4.5 Dual in inclusive only	222
		7.4.6 Summary	224
	7.5	Duals with inclusive/exclusive: four times 'we'	224
		7.5.1 Preamble	224
		7.5.2 The dual-inclusive/exclusive paradigm	224
		7.5.3 The partial-unit-augmented paradigm	226
		7.5.4 Homophonous paradigms	228
		7.5.5 Summary	232
	7.6	Duals with inclusive/exclusive: five times 'we'	232
	7.7	Generalizations	236
	7.8	Conclusion	241

PART IV. COGNATE PARADIGMS

8. Connecting Paradigms: Person Paradigms through Time and Space		245
8.1	Introduction	245
8.2	Cognate paradigms	246
8.3	Towards a theory of paradigmatic change	249
8.4	Up and down the Horizontal Homophony Hierarchy	251
	8.4.1 Preamble	251
	8.4.2 Interconnecting the small paradigms	252
	8.4.3 Up the hierarchy	254
	8.4.4 Summary	258
8.5	Up and down the Explicitness Hierarchy	259
	8.5.1 Preamble	259
	8.5.2 Minimal/augmented inclusive (or not)	260
	8.5.3 Inclusive/exclusive (or not)	264
	8.5.4 Vertical and singular homophony (or not)	265
	8.5.5 Summary	267
8.6	Conclusion	267

9. Cognate Paradigms Revisited: Connecting the Dual		269
9.1	Introduction	269
9.2	The typological hypothesis	270

9.3		Linking the major dual paradigms	271
	9.3.1	Preamble	271
	9.3.2	Different duals connected	272
	9.3.3	Duals lost and found	274
	9.3.4	Paradigmatic variation in Miwok	275
	9.3.5	Summary	278
9.4		Minimal/augmented and its variants	279
	9.4.1	Preamble	279
	9.4.2	The Australian hotbed	279
	9.4.3	Paradigmatic variation in Gé	281
	9.4.4	Summary	283
9.5		Dual-3we as an intermediate	284
	9.5.1	Preamble	284
	9.5.2	Links to regular dual patterns	285
	9.5.3	Links to minimal/augmented patterns	287
	9.5.4	Summary	290
9.6		Number marking incorporated	291
9.7		Conclusion	294

10. Finale: Summary and Prospects 295

10.1		Summary of results	295
	10.1.1	Preliminaries	295
	10.1.2	Person and number	296
	10.1.3	Paradigmatic structure	297
	10.1.4	Horizontal homophony	299
	10.1.5	Singular homophony	301
	10.1.6	Vertical homophony	302
	10.1.7	Pure person and the Explicitness Hierarchy	303
	10.1.8	Diachronic interpretation	305
10.2		Towards a theory of person marking	306
10.3		Prospects	310
	10.3.1	Syntagmatic questions	310
	10.3.2	Independent versus inflectional marking	311
	10.3.3	Asymmetry of affixation	315
	10.3.4	Gender in person paradigms	319
10.4		Wider application of results	320

Preface

Almost exactly fifty years after Paul Forchheimer published his doctoral dissertation, 'The Category of Person in Language', in Berlin, I am in Berlin writing this preface to my revised doctoral dissertation, which is in subject and spirit strongly related to Forchheimer's pioneering work. Over the past centuries, person marking has attracted much linguistic attention, partly because it is hypothesized to be a fundamental dimension of language, but probably also because it appears to be such a nicely limited sub-domain of linguistic investigation. In the spirit of Forchheimer, I have compiled a survey and typology of the linguistic variation of person marking, which is grossly underestimated by the traditional three persons and two numbers.

Many problematic aspects of Forchheimer's investigation have been recognized since its publication, which has given me the opportunity to avoid many a pitfall—hopefully not stumbling upon too many new ones. The central characteristic of my approach is to investigate person marking within the confines of the paradigm—and to be very strict about what counts as a paradigm. In this way, the resulting typology of person marking is resistant to the problem of Eurocentrism: I do not just amass linguistic devices alike to European-style personal pronouns from anywhere in a particular language, but explicitly restrict the investigation to those elements that form a coherent set as measured by the structure of the language in question.

This book is a revised version of my 2001 doctoral dissertation with the same title, submitted to and approved by the humanities faculty of the University of Nijmegen, the Netherlands. Besides numerous corrections, some rephrasing, and a slight reordering, the present text has been enlarged with many examples and references. Most of the quantitative analyses that were in the thesis have been removed, as I feel now that they are in need of a more strictly stratified typological sample. Notwithstanding these changes, the main conclusions of the thesis remain.

The reception of the thesis has been very rewarding, and I thank various colleagues for comments and additions, most of which have in some form found their way into the present text. I have only very pleasurable memories of the defence of the thesis, apparently a horror to some, thanks to the detailed questions and comments of Hein Steinhauer, Ekkehard König, Grev Corbett, Pieter Muysken, Steve Levinson, Cees Versteegh, and Roeland van Hout. Later, Frits Kortlandt, George van Driem, Richard Rhodes, Wouter Kusters, Johannes Helmbrecht, D. N. S. Bhat, Claudia Gerstner-Link and Simon van Dreumel provided me with valuable additions or drew my attention to some problematic aspects of the thesis. As the thesis was almost finished, I first met Mixail Daniel and Elena Filimonova, who had recently completed their theses on typological aspects of person marking (unfortunately for me in Russian). Our exchange has been, and still is, opening up new directions of investigation. The committee of the ALT-junior award, consisting of Masha Koptjevskaja Tamm, Bill Croft, Edith Moravcsik, Miren Lourdes Onederra, and Vladimir Plungian had many useful comments and additions. I also thank the audiences at the Cognitive Typology conference in Antwerp, the DGfS meeting in Marburg, and various TIN meetings in Utrecht, who patiently listened to and cogently discussed my papers pertaining to the content of this book. Finally, the reviewers for Oxford University Press, Bill Croft, Ronnie Cann, and Christopher Culy, and the editorial commentary by OUP's John Davey and Jacqueline Smith, together with the copy editing of Sarah Barrett, greatly improved and streamlined the present book. Of course, the responsibility for the content of this book remains completely mine.

This book would never have materialized without the help of many people. Above all, my parents not only made it possible in an existential sense; they also surrounded me with an environment of intellectual openness. I will never forget that bulky birthday present which turned out to be Douglas Hofstadter's *Gödel, Escher, Bach*. This book has been a major stimulus for a scientific career. At university, the inspiring classes by Pieter Seuren persuaded me to switch from my initial love, mathematics, to reading linguistics. Subsequently, I became hooked on the world's linguistic variation through the fascinating classes of Leon Stassen. His detailed knowledge and careful scrutiny of the variability of linguistic structure has strongly influenced my perspective on language. In the last phase of writing the thesis, the pleasurable fieldwork classes with Hein Steinhauer confirmed my interest in those down-to-earth aspects of lesser-known languages that are always more intricate than one would have expected.

Daily life at the Institute for General Linguistics and Dialectology in Nijmegen (where the thesis was written) has been greatly enriched by the various meetings with fellow AiOs and other colleagues, be it in the context of ProZA, POEZie, at coffee breaks (with biscuits!), lunch, or dinner. In particular, I want to thank Dick Smakman, Marie-José Palmen, and Lisanne Teunissen for practical assistance in scientific matters. I also thank Ad Foolen and Henk van Jaarsveld for always having some time available to listen to my latest linguistic (or other) musing. As for the wider community of PhD students in the Netherlands, I thank everybody at the various LOT schools for making them so much fun, especially Dirk Janssen and Christine Erb, who both accompanied me to the former East Germany after we had all three finished our theses.

Moving to Berlin, I felt immediately at home at the Zentrum für Allgemeine Sprachwissenschaft (ZAS) and at the English Department of the Free University of Berlin. I am especially grateful to Ekkehard König and Paul Law for making this move possible. The deadline for this revision of my thesis coincided with the deadline for the new project proposals at the ZAS, and I thank Frans Plank,

Patrick Steinkrüger, Tom Güldemann, Laura Downing, and Sabine Zerbian for the collaboration in these stress-filled times. At the Free University, Daniel Hole and Volker Gast have been excellent colleagues, always available to read and comment upon any text that I came up with. Finally, I have found a true congenial spirit in the person of Horst Simon at the Humboldt University of Berlin.

In the meantime, life went on outside academia. In Nijmegen, I have had a wonderful home with wonderful roommates at the Annastraat over the years; thank you all very much for sharing these years with me. Sterre and Ceciel van Aalst gave a special twinkle to my life; thank you both for being so considerate and patient. And without all you tango dancers, acrobats, jugglers, figure skaters, game fanatics, puzzle designers, and other friends-in-action, I would have probably lost my mind in the word processor.

The greatest joy has been to share my life, both inside and outside academia, with Paula-Irene Villa. Here in Berlin, we have finally intertwined our lives also in practical matters, not least as a result of little joyful Leo Imre, who is crawling around my desk while I write these words of gratitude. Thank you both for your love, help, and inspiration.

MC

List of Abbreviations

1	speaker	IMP	imperative
2	addressee	IMPERF	imperfective
3	other	INCL	inclusive (=1+2 and
/	or		1+2+3 combined)
-	morpheme boundary	IRR	irrealis
?	morpheme with unidentified meaning/function	LOC	locative
		LOG	logophoric
+	combination of persons into a group	MASC	masculine
		NAME	personal name
→	agent/patient combination	PAST	past
ASSOC	associative	PERF	perfective
DEB	debitative	PLACE	geographical name
DECL	declarative	PLUR	plural
CLIT	clitic	POSS	possessive
COM	comitative	PRES	present
COND	conditional	PRON	independent pronoun
COP	copula	PURP	purposive
DEM	demonstrative	REPET	repetative
DL	dual	SG	singular
EMPH	emphatic	TAM	not further specified tense/aspect/mood marker
EXCL	exclusive (=1+3)		
FEM	feminine	WH	question word
FUT	future		

1 Introduction
Objective, Definitions, Method, and Some History

> Haiku, you ku, he
> She, or it kus, we ku, you
> Ku, they ku. Thang ku.
> Ted Hipple, *The Traditional Grammarian as Poet*

1.1 The feat of Domingo de Santo Tomás

The history of linguistic investigation is full of discoveries. One of those discoveries was made by a Spanish Dominican friar known by the name of Domingo de Santo Tomás. By way of introduction, the story of his insight will be told here to illustrate the theme and the approach of the present investigation.[1]

In 1540, Domingo de Santo Tomás set sail from Spain on his way to Peru. He belonged to a group of missionaries that were recruited by Francisco Martinéz Toscano to work in this newly discovered part of South America. At that moment, only seven years after the defeat of the Inca Empire by Francisco Pizarro, the journey to this new Spanish territory must have been full of perils and uncertainty. Yet, Domingo de Santo Tomás survived the trip and managed to do his missionary work among the native people of Peru. His catechistic work made him an expert in the 'lengua general', the general language spoken in the region, nowadays referred to as Quechua.

In 1555, after fifteen years of missionary work, Domingo de Santo Tomás returned to Spain, determined to carry out much work. Among many other things, he had taken on the task of informing the authorities in Spain about the miserable situation of the native people of Peru. Further, he wanted to take care in person of the printing of his grammar-cum-dictionary of the Quechua language. This resulted in the *Grammática o arte de la lengua general de los Índios de los Reynos del Peru*, which appeared in 1560, printed in Valladolid in an astonishingly large edition of 1,500 copies. The outline of this Quechua grammar follows the traditional descriptions of the grammar of Latin. However, there are numerous details where the Latin format does not suffice for the intricacies of the Quechua

---

[1] The (sparse) biographical materials on Domingo de Santo Tomás are from Rodolfo Cerron-Palomino, as added to the 1994 facsimile edition of the original text of de Santo Tomás (1560).

language. In many aspects this language is different from Latin, and the classical descriptive format had to be enhanced to explain the structure of Quechua.

One of the inventions that Domingo de Santo Tomás introduced in his grammar is an explanation of the difference between the two forms for 'we' that are found in Quechua. He explains that one of the two forms is used for 'we, including the person or persons that are spoken to', and the other form is used for 'we, excluding the person or persons with whom we are talking'. This difference can only be made explicit in English by adding extra linguistic material, like *we all here present* for the inclusive meaning, or *we, me and my friends* for the exclusive meaning:

The plural of this pronoun *ñóca* is *ñocánchic* or *ñocáyco*, which mean 'we'. It is to be noted that between *ñocánchic* and *ñocáyco* there are two differences, one intrinsic, due to their meaning, the other extrinsic, due to the verb that corresponds to them.... The first is that although *ñocánchic* and *ñocáyco* both mean 'we', *ñocánchic* means 'we', with the connotation of including the person as such with whom we are speaking; like when speaking with Indians, when we want to give to understand that they also take part, and that they are included in the meaning of what we say with this pronoun *we*; as when one would say: 'God created us', we will use that pronoun, *ñocánchic*, that is, 'we, including also the Indians'. But if we want to exclude them from the meaning or the speech ... in this language (to be more explicit) it is not necessary to add any clarification, except to use the pronoun *ñocáyco*, meaning 'we', with the connotation of excluding the person or persons with whom we are talking from the plurality. (de Santo Tomás 1560: 8–9; my translation)[2]

Today, almost 450 years after the publication of this explanation, the analysis is still considered accurate. Even the terminology has remained; this opposition is known today as a difference between an 'inclusive' and an 'exclusive' first person plural. The merits of this discovery are not to be underestimated. Domingo de Santo Tomás had to work out this aspect of the grammatical system of Quechua from scratch. The grammatical description of languages other than Latin or Greek was still in its infancy.[3] The difference between an inclusive and an exclusive variant of the word 'we' was unheard of, even inconceivable, in the

---

[2] 'El plural deste pronombre *ñóca* es *ñocánchic* o *ñocáyco*, que quiere dezir "nosotros". Y es de notar que entre *ñocánchic* y *ñocáyco* ay dos differencias, una intrínseca, de parte de la significación dellos, otra extrínseca, de parte del verbo que les corresponde... La primera es que, aunque *ñocánchic* y *ñocáyco* significan "nosotros", el *ñocánchic* significa "nosotros", connotando & incluyendo en sí la persona con quien hablamos: como hablando con indios, si quisiéssemos dar a entender que también entran ellos y se incluyen en la habla que hablamos con este pronombre *nosotros*, como diziende: a nosotros nos crió Dios, usaríamos de este pronombre *ñocánchic*, esto es "nosotros, incluyendo también los indios". Pero si los quisiéssemos excluir a ellos de la tal razón o plática... en este langua (por ser más abundante) no ay necessidad de añadir determinación alguna sino solamente usar de este pronombre *ñocáyco*, que quiere dezir "nosotros", connotando que se excluye de aquella pluralidad la persona o personas con quien hablamos.'

[3] The first printed grammar other than of Latin or Greek is the Spanish grammar by Lebrija from 1492. In total, Rowe (1974) counted only 10 languages other than Latin and Greek of which printed grammars appeared before the Quechua grammar by Domingo de Santo Tomás—who was probably unaware of any of these other descriptions, except for the Spanish grammar of Lebrija.

occidental tradition of grammatical analysis. None of the major languages in Europe and in the Near and Middle East shows such an opposition. The nearest languages (from a European perspective) which have an inclusive/exclusive difference are some remote Caucasian languages, some Nilo-Saharan languages in the sub-Saharan savannah of Africa, and most Dravidian languages in southern India.[4] As it turned out, the Quechua-speaking people in distant South America were the first to direct western attention to this peculiar possibility of human language.[5] Yet once the difference between the two forms of 'we' is explained, it appears to be a completely natural distinction. After some time, one even starts wondering how it is possible to do without this very practical device in linguistic interaction.

The story of de Santo Tomás illustrates the basic impetus for cross-linguistic research, which is the method that will be followed in the present work. Cross-linguistic research attempts to learn about the possibilities of human language by studying the various ways in which communities around the world put their linguistic competence to work. A comparison of the structure of very diverse languages presents an opportunity to escape the limitations of the (linguistic) imagination. The scientific lore about the extent of variation of human language is strongly biased by the structure of presently known languages. Certain possibilities of human language would never be conceived if it were not for the fact that they happen to exist. It was the existence of an overtly marked inclusive/exclusive opposition in Quechua that opened the eyes of the western linguistic tradition to the possibility of such categories. In contrast, other possibilities might be thought of as logically possible, but turn out to be unattested among the world's language.[6]

In this study, I will use the variety of the world's linguistic structures to sketch an outline of the possibilities of human language—within a restricted domain. The story of Domingo de Santo Tomás also illustrates the domain of the present study. In this study, I want to address the question of what possibilities human languages use to mark the participants in a speech act. Thus formulated, this is a rather extensive domain of inquiry. In all languages, there are many ways to refer

---

[4] The Dravidian linguistic tradition dates back to at least the *tolkappyam* from *c*.100 BC. In this linguistic analysis there is no mention of an inclusive/exclusive distinction, although the classical texts appear to be consistent with the presence of this distinction (Lehmann 1994: 57–8). It is difficult to reach any definitive conclusions, but it seems that the inclusive/exclusive distinction was present, but simply not observed as a fact to be described by the classical Dravidian linguists. The Dravidian linguistic tradition was strongly influenced by the classical Indian tradition, which did not describe an inclusive/exclusive distinction—with good reason, as there was no such distinction in Sanskrit.

[5] More details on the history of the discovery of the inclusive/exclusive opposition can be found in Haas (1969), Hardman (1972), Mannheim (1982), Suárez Roca (1992), and Adelaar (1993).

[6] If a particular logically possible structure is not attested among this world's languages, it is not necessary to categorize it as 'impossible'. The actual languages of this world do not necessarily exhaust the possibilities of linguistic structure. However, the more languages are taken into the comparison, the unlikelier it becomes for a non-attested structure to be an actual possibility for human language. Still, it might be better to talk about 'improbable' rather than 'impossible' when discussing non-attested structures in the world's linguistic diversity.

to 'me, myself and I'. One finds expressions like *the undersigned* or *the present author*; or simply *Michael* or *Mr Cysouw*; not to speak of the numerous other epithets that could be used to refer to this specific person. Once the full expressive power of any natural language is taken into account, the possibilities of marking participants in a speech act become innumerable.

Given the right context, almost every kind of word in a language can be used to refer to a speech-act participant. To remain within workable limits, this investigation will only deal with an analysis of the PARADIGMATIC STRUCTURE of SPECIALIZED person marking. This definition of the subject introduces two important restrictions on the domain of investigation. First, the person markers have to be grammaticalized as a specialized part of a language. The markers have to be specifically devoted to person marking. The variety of referential possibilities is restricted in this study to those linguistic elements that do nothing else besides person marking, as, for example, the English words *I* and *you*. Second, such specialized person markers are investigated from the structural context of the paradigm. Specialized person markers are normally found to be part of a closed set of person markers that are treated identically within the structure of a language. Such a set of equivalent markers is called a paradigm. The precise referential value of a person marker can only be specified in relation to the other person markers in the paradigm.

In this introductory chapter, miscellaneous definitional, methodological, and historical aspects are discussed. At the beginning of each chapter, the specific definitions, methodological issues, and results of earlier research pertaining to the topic of that particular chapter are discussed extensively. In this chapter, addressed to the more than casual reader, a survey of the approach taken in the present study is given. First, the definitions and delimitation of the domain are made explicit in Section 1.2. Some methodological issues will be dealt with in Section 1.3. In Section 1.4, previous cross-linguistic work on person marking is discussed. Finally, Section 1.5 offers a survey of the structure of the book and leads to the core of the present work: the cross-linguistic variation of the paradigmatic structure of person marking.

1.2 Definitions and delimitation

1.2.1 Preamble

Language is a communicational device. Reference to the participants in a communicational setting can be marked linguistically in various ways. A father who is talking to his baby might refer to himself by using the word *daddy* as in *daddy is busy now*. In English, such self-reference by using a full noun is a marked construction, mainly to be heard in motherese. However, in other languages, like Thai, this usage is much more widespread, to be found throughout the various registers of the language (Cooke 1968: 44–55). In all languages, many different words can be used for self-reference, although in some languages it will take more conversational preparation to make the self-referring usage of a word intelligible. The problem is that words with self-reference change their referential value depending on the person who is speaking. The understanding of such shifting reference is known to present major difficulties to the language-learning child. Jespersen (1922: 123) tells a delightful story of two children, one of whom does not get the shifting reference of the word *enemy*. We can envision the incredulous child shouting: *I am the enemy, not you!* Jespersen calls such linguistic elements SHIFTERS. All linguistic elements that are used in a deictic ('pointing') function are shifters. Locational deixis (*here, there*), time deixis (*now, tomorrow*), and participant deixis (*I, you*) all involve shifting reference of linguistic elements (Jespersen 1922: 123–4; Bühler 1934: 79–148; Jakobson 1971 [1957]; Hengeveld 1997).

Amidst all these shifters, this study will deal only with specialized shifters used for reference to speech act participants. To be included in the investigation, the shifters have to be specialized. This means that they have no other possible usage besides being a shifter. The words *here*, *now*, and *I* are such specialized shifters. In contrast, words like *daddy* or *enemy* can be used as shifters, but do not necessarily function as such. Second, this investigation will deal only with shifters used for reference to participants in the speech act. Basically, the speech act dyad of speaker and addressee will be the starting point for the present investigation. Summarizing, there are three criteria for linguistic elements to be included in the investigation: they have to be a shifter, specialized for that function, and used for reference to speech act participants. Henceforth, linguistic elements that adhere to these three criteria are called PERSON MARKERS (see further Section 1.2.2).

Person markers, as defined above, do not stand alone within a language. They are part of a closed set of person markers that have an identical place in the structure of a language. Such a set of elements is called a PARADIGM. This investigation addresses the question to what extent the structure of person-marking paradigms is found to vary cross-linguistically. This survey of the variability of the paradigmatic structure can be read as a prolegomenon to a theory of the 'richness' of a paradigm (see further Section 1.2.3). Diachronically, person markers do not behave differently from other linguistic elements. They grammaticalize from independent nouns into person markers. Also, independent pronouns grammaticalize into inflectional person markers. All specialized participant shifters will be included in this study, irrespective of whether they are morphologically independent or bound. Moreover, all person-marking 'agreement' is included. The inflation of the word 'agreement' and the often-assumed primacy of morphologically independent person markers over inflectional ones are countered (see Section 1.2.4). Finally, some borderline cases and some problems with the cross-linguistic delimitation of the domain will be discussed (see Section 1.2.5).

1.2.2 Person and number

This study is concerned with specialized shifters that are used for reference to speech act participants. The (extra-linguistic) setting of a speech act invokes a few salient cognitive categories. The principal categories of participant deixis are SPEAKER (the originator of the speech) and ADDRESSEE (the recipient of the speech). Or, following Wierzbicka (1976), one might simply say that these principal categories are I and YOU, respectively. All deixis that does not include either of these categories can be summarized negatively. The OTHER participant is everything (not necessarily human or animate) that is neither speaker nor addressee. These categories will form the basis of the present investigation. The specialized linguistic elements that code these categories are called person markers. Following the conventions of the occidental grammatical tradition, the speaker will be coded as FIRST PERSON; the addressee will be coded as SECOND PERSON; and any other participant will be coded as THIRD PERSON.[7] The linguistic coding of these three categories will be discussed extensively in Chapter 2.

There is more to a conversation than speaker and addressee. In an analysis of conversational practices, Goffman (1979) argues for a decomposition of the notions 'speaker' and 'addressee'. The traditional notion 'speaker', he argues, is a cluster of various communicational functions, like 'animator' (i.e. 'the sounding box'), 'author' (i.e. 'the agent who scripts the lines') and 'principal' (i.e. 'the party to whose position the words attest') (Goffman 1979: 16–17; cf. Levinson 1988: 169). Likewise, the traditional notion of 'addressee' is to be decomposed into, at least, the functions 'hearer', 'unaddressed', 'over-hearer', 'bystander', and 'eavesdropper' (Goffman 1979: 8–9). In a thorough reappraisal of Goffman's proposals, Levinson (1988: 170–80) further systematizes the decomposition of 'speaker' and 'addressee'. There are various reasons why one would want to have a more finely grained description of the possible functions of a participant. The most promising area of application is the ethnography of speaking, as Levinson shows (1988: 192–221; cf. Varenne 1984). However, for the analysis of grammatical structure, the merits of the decomposition of the traditional speech act roles are less obvious. The basic opposition between speaker and addressee is rather commonly grammaticalized among the world's languages. In contrast, none of the finer-grained role distinctions are attested as grammaticalized categories:

The classical analysis has held up remarkably well in the face of recent comparative analysis. The great majority of languages exhibit the three persons in a paradigm of pronouns, verb agreement, or elsewhere. (Levinson 1988: 182–3)

---

[7] I am tempted to use the abbreviations S, A, and O for speaker, addressee, and other. However, exactly the same letters are used to analyse ergative structures in the tradition of Dixon (1979). There, the letters S, A, and O stand for subject, agent, and object. To avoid confusion, I have decided to keep to the traditional numbers 1, 2, and 3 as abbreviations for speaker, hearer, and other, respectively. The use of numbers should not be interpreted as a sign of inherent ranking of the categories (cf. Greenberg 1993); they are only used as abbreviations for reference to the basic speech act participants.

The predominant grammaticalization of the traditional referential categories 'speaker' and 'addressee' is probably a result of functional pressures, Levinson argues. Prototypically, language is an interactional device with two speech act participants who organize their speech in a turn-taking sequence. The speaker/addressee roles in the turn-taking system are prototypically reflected in the structure of language:

Quite probably, the universal tendency in languages to distinguish, in pronominal categories or elsewhere, primarily and prototypically the two deictic categories of first and second person, is related closely to the superordinate categories of speaker and addressee/recipient that are the basis of the turn-taking system. (Levinson 1988: 176)

However, by proposing this explanation, Levinson counters Goffman's original motive for a finer-grained distribution of referential categories. Of course, Goffman argues, the prototypical speech act situation is a dyadic one, but many other configurations are attested, and are probably just as common in daily speech interaction:

The ratified hearer in two-person talk is necessarily also the *addressed* one, that is, the one to whom the speaker addresses his visual attention and to whom, incidentally, he expects to turn over the speaking role. But obviously two-person encounters, however common, are not the only kind; three or more official participants are often found. In such cases it will often be feasible for the current speaker to address his remarks to the circle as a whole, encompassing all his hearers in his glance, according them something like equal status. But, more likely, the speaker will, at least during periods of his talk, address his remarks to one listener, so that among official hearers one must distinguish the addressed recipient from *unaddressed* ones. (Goffman 1979: 9; italics original)

Goffman argues convincingly that much more is possible. However, it is an empirical question whether these possibilities are also used in the grammatical structure of language. As it appears now, this is not the case. Earlier research did not come up with any example, and during my investigations for the present work I have also not come across any new claims in this direction. Languages do not use more finely grained interactional categories in their grammatical structure. Still, it is important to keep open the possibility that grammatical markers have simply not been recognized as such. For the present investigation, I will disregard any of these more finely grained categories and restrict myself to the traditional gross categories 'speaker' and 'addressee'.

Based on these two principal categories, groups of participants can be formed. Groups of participants consist of more than one participant and are thus necessarily plural. For example, speaker and addressee can make up a group, or speaker and other, or addressee and other. All theoretically possible combinations will be discussed extensively in Chapter 3. In that chapter, it will also be argued that the notion 'plural' is not appropriate for these groups of participants. Groups of participants consist of more than one individual, so they are plural by definition.

8 Introduction

However, they are plural in a completely different sense from that in which normal nouns can be plural. As will be argued later in Chapter 6, the notion of number marking within the domain of person marking is better reserved for categories that are traditionally known as dual, trial, etc. Finally, there is a recurrent claim in the literature that there are some languages with a special set of person markers, variously called 'compound pronouns' or 'complex pronouns'. This phenomenon will be discussed in Chapter 5. It will be argued there that these are indeed a special kind of pronoun, and yet do not mark any new person categories.

1.2.3 Paradigmatic structure

Grammaticalized person markers do not occur in isolation within a language. They preferably appear in a PARADIGM of person markers. The structure of a person-marking paradigm is the central aspect of the present inquiry. I will investigate the structure of paradigms that show at least an opposition between speaker and addressee. Some elucidation of the notion of a paradigm in the present work will be given in this section.

First, a central assumption is that a person-marking paradigm is a closed class of linguistic elements that occur in complementary distribution. To put it another way, a paradigm is a set of linguistic elements that occur in the same syntagmatic place in the structure of a language. The syntagmatic/paradigmatic duality is used in the same way as it was originally proposed by de Saussure (1916: 170–80).[8] For example, the subject pronouns of English constitute a paradigm, as they occur in complementary distribution as subject of a predicate. The object forms of the pronouns belong to a different paradigm because these forms are used in a different syntagmatic place in the language (see Gvozdanović 1991 and Stump 2001: 43 for broader definitions of what constitutes a paradigm).

Second, there is no impossible reference in a paradigm. That is to say, the mutually exclusive elements in a person-marking paradigm fill out the complete referential array of possible participants. For example, singular reference is often divided into 'speaker', 'addressee', and a third class, the third class comprising all reference that is not either of the first two. This third 'non-person' (Benveniste 1966: 228) simply fills all possibilities that are not taken care of by the other elements in the paradigm. A similar tendency is attested for plural marking. If there is no specialized element for any plural reference, then the missing referential value is taken over by one of the other elements in the paradigm.

---

[8] The syntagmatic/paradigmatic duality is rightfully connected to de Saussure. However, de Saussure uses the term 'associatif' instead of the expected term 'paradigmatique'. He reserved the word 'paradigme' for the traditional notion of declension (cf. de Saussure 1916: 15).

Preferably, a person-marking paradigm is referentially complete.[9] It is not the language in which *tout se tient*, but the paradigm.

Third, I will interpret a paradigm as a closed space of alternative options. The individual person markers in a paradigm do not arrive at their referential value intrinsically, but in mutual delimitation vis-à-vis the other elements in the paradigm. The space of possible reference is subdivided into referential categories by the available elements in the paradigm. The referential space allotted to a specific element in a paradigm can only be defined in relation to the other elements. This perspective of the paradigm is reminiscent of the division of vowel space by the available phonemic vowels. A low open vowel /a/ is a rather different vowel when it is found in a three-vowel system as compared to when it is found in a seven-vowel system. Another analogous concept to the paradigm is the *Wortfeld* in lexicography, as proposed by Trier (1931), in which the meaning of a word is dependent on the meaning of other closely related words.

Fourth, the present study will be concerned with the internal structure of person paradigms. Given the phonological structure of a language, I will look at the kinds of opposition that are marked within the closed space of a paradigm. It does not matter whether these oppositions are marked by just one phoneme, or whether the pronouns are phonemically completely different. I will have nothing to say about the phonological (dis)similarity of individual person markers in a paradigm (*pace* Section 7.5.3). In a way, *he* is more similar to *she* than it is to *you*. But then, *he* is just as similar to *she* as it is to *we*. And, of course, it is tempting to analyse *your*, *her*, and *their* as showing a possessive marker *-r*. However, such similarities do not have to be meaningful. Given the restricted number of phonemes in a language, such similarities are bound to occur by pure chance (various approaches to the phonological similarity between pronouns are discussed by Mühlhäusler and Harré 1990: 50–2, Howe 1996: 32–42, Nichols and Peterson 1996, and Rhodes 1997).

Fifth, a paradigm is only a small part of a complete language. Normally, there are multiple person-marking paradigms within a single language. English has independent pronouns—both in a nominative and in an oblique form; then there are possessive pronouns; and finally there is a paradigm of person markers in the present inflection. All in all, there are at least four different paradigms that share the referential work. I have not attempted to formulate a criterion that would distinguish one of the various paradigms as the primary one. It is not the languages as wholes, but the individual paradigms within each language, that are the crux of the comparison. The cross-linguistic comparison in this investigation is on a sub-language level (cf. the 'item-based' approach from Nettle 1999).

---

[9] The word 'preferably' has been added because there are some exceptions, as there are always exceptions to a cross-linguistic generalization. Specifically, problems arise in the case of a paradigm with zero independent pronouns. In a few extreme cases, there are only two independent pronouns (one for speaker and one for addressee), and all other reference is zero (see Sections 2.5.3 and 4.3.5). It is probably better to consider these zeros as non-existing. Such paradigms with non-existing marking are not referentially complete.

Consequently, a particular language can appear multiple times in this investigation, each time with a different paradigm. The result of this approach is an insight into the paradigmatic structure of person marking. Only indirectly will this help us to understand the functioning of a whole language.

Combining this perspective of paradigmatic structure with the perspective of person marking as explained in the previous section, I have arrived at the following definition of the object of investigation. I will investigate the structure of paradigms that show at least an opposition between speaker and addressee in the marking of singular participants. There are two borderline issues concerning this definition. First, some paradigms do not show an opposition between singular speaker and addressee. Some such cases are included in the investigation as borderline examples of person marking. Second, there are cases that have an opposition between speaker and addressee, but that have a non-uniform paradigmatic structure. These cases are excluded from this investigation for reasons of cross-linguistic comparability.

The first of these issues is important for the classification of paradigms like the English or French inflection. Both kinds of inflection are included in this study as borderline cases of person marking. Following the definition of person marking as outlined in the previous section, the English inflection should not be included because there is no opposition between the form of (*I*) *speak* versus (*you*) *speak*. In both cases the inflection is zero. However, the English inflection still has an opposition between speaker/addressee and any other singular participant: (*I/you*) *speak* versus (*he/she/it*) *speaks*. There is still a faint notion of person marking (see Section 2.3.3 for comparable cases). In contrast, the (spoken) French inflection has no opposition in the singular: (*je*) *parl(e)* versus (*tu*) *parl(es)* versus (*il/elle/on*) *parl(e)*. In all three forms, the (phonological) inflection is zero. Speaker and addressee are not marked at all in the French singular inflection. Still, there is a person-like opposition in the plural *parlons* versus *parlez*. This situation is rather unusual cross-linguistically—the few attested examples are discussed in Section 2.3.4.

The second issue, concerning non-uniform paradigmatic structure, is important for the classification of a few troublesome cases in which the marking of the speaker and addressee is syntagmatically different, yet both markers belong to a single paradigm. The worst troublemakers are paradigms in which the first person is marked by a suffix and the second person is marked by a prefix, or vice versa. An example of such a paradigm is found in the Berber languages. The subject inflection in Berber is a suffix in the first person singular, but a prefix in the first person plural. Second person marking is a combination of prefixes and suffixes.[10] Another instance of such a combination of prefixes and suffixes is attested in the

---

[10] See e.g. the Berber language Tamazight (Willms 1972: 196). This structure of Berber is reminiscent of (and diachronically related to) the imperfect affixes of the Semitic languages, as e.g. described for Cairene colloquial Arabic by Gary and Gamal-Eldin (1982: 100). The Arabic imperfect is discontinuous. Most of the reference is marked by prefixes, but gender and part of the number reference are disambiguated by suffixes.

Muskogean languages of North America. The first person agent marking in the Muskogean languages is a suffix, but all other person markers are prefixes.[11] Finally, the object marking in the Tequistlatecan languages of Mexico shows different affixation for first and second person. A first person object is marked as a prefix while all other persons are marked as suffixes.[12] To conclude, paradigms with a mix of prefixes and suffixes for speaker and addressee reference occur among the world's languages, although they are not common from a worldwide perspective. The few examples just mentioned are disregarded in the present investigation.

The reason to disregard discontinuous paradigms is of methodological nature. It is often difficult to decide in a cross-linguistic investigation what counts as a person paradigm. Most prominently, this problem surfaces with inflectional paradigms. Often, very many different categories are marked somewhere in the inflection of a verb. If simply all inflectional marking is included that is somehow related to person marking, the results of a cross-linguistic comparison will be biased towards the person categories that one expects to find (see the criticism on Forchheimer in Section 1.4.2). For a pure comparison of paradigmatic structure, the extent of a paradigm is restricted to those elements that occur in the same inflectional 'slot'.

An example will illustrate this strict definition of the paradigm. An inflected verb from Upper Bal (a dialect of the South Caucasian language Svan) is shown in (1.1). The paradigm presented is the imperfect of the verb *ama:r*, a verb of Class A meaning 'to prepare' (Tuite 1997: 28). Aspects of person marking are attested both as prefixes and as suffixes. In the present investigation, the person inflection from Upper Bal is analysed as two different paradigms, one prefixal and one suffixal, as shown in (1.2). The prefixal paradigm is the most genuine person-marking device, distinguishing speaker from addressee, and even separating an inclusive, as shown in (1.2a). The suffixal paradigm is a borderline case of person marking. There is no opposition between speaker and addressee, but speaker/addressee is marked by a special morpheme different from the marking of other, and different from plural participants, as shown in (1.2b).

(1.1) Upper Bal inflection (combined version)

	Singular	Plural	
1	*xw-ama:r-äs*	*l-ama:r-ad*	Inclusive
		xw-ama:r-ad	Exclusive
2	*x-ama:r-äs*	*x-ama:r-ad*	
3	*ø-ama:r-a*	*ø-ama:r-a*	

---

[11] This structure is found throughout the Muskogean family. For data on Chickasaw, see Payne (1982: 359); for Alabama, see Lupardus (1982: 66–74); for Koasati, see Kimball (1985: 107); and for Choctaw, see Nicklas (1974: 31). Haas (1977) proposes an origin of this person marking by grammaticalization of auxiliaries.

[12] For data on Highland Chontal, see Turner (1966: 65, 68) and for data on Huameltultec Chontal, see Waterhouse (1967: 356).

(1.2) Upper Bal inflection (split version)

a. Prefixal paradigm

Inclusive	*l-...*
Exclusive	*xw-...*
2	*x-...*
3	*ø-...*

b. Suffixal paradigm

	Singular	Plural
1	*...-äs*	*...-ad*
2		
3	*...-a*	

1.2.4 Specialization and grammaticalization

Only person markers that are SPECIALIZED shifters are considered in this study. Independent pronouns like *I* or *you* in English are such specialized shifters: the reference of these words has to shift with the speaking participant. It is impossible for them not to shift.[13] In contrast, words like *daddy* can be used as a shifter, but are not necessarily used in that sense. Such words are excluded from the investigation. For languages like English, this restriction still leaves the specialized shifters to be investigated. In some languages, however, nothing remains when all non-specialized shifters have been removed. This situation is attested in many South-East Asian languages. For example, Cooke (1968) has made an extensive investigation of person marking in Thai, Burmese, and Vietnamese. The range of possibilities to mark person is overwhelming. Proper names, kin terms, and normal nouns are regularly used for speaker or addressee reference.[14] For Thai, Cooke mentions twenty-seven more or less specialized first person markers and twenty-two second person markers (1968: 11–18). Moreover, these are only a tiny portion of the possibilities: 'not even personal pronouns are listed in their entirety in each language, much less other pronominally used forms' (p. 2). It also turns out that most of these person markers are still interpretable in the original (non-shifting) meaning. They mean, for example, 'individual', 'crown of the head', or 'servant'. The least one can say is that 'real' person markers are a mystifying category in Thai. I would even say that 'real' person markers do not exist (but see Diller 1994: 167–9 for another opinion). Of course, it is perfectly possible to perform self-reference in Thai; it is even possible to do so in many more ways than in English. However, there is not one basic specialized ('grammaticalized') way to do so.

This problem is strongly related to the question whether there is a universal basic way to express reference to the speech roles. This question has been much

---

[13] The only possibility for the English pronoun *I* not to shift with the speaker is in a meta-linguistic use, as, when talking about a novel, one says: *It is the 'I' of the novel that is the murderer!*

[14] Somewhat less exotically, this was also found in Swedish, 'where until comparatively recently title and name were used in place, or in avoidance of pronominal address' (Howe 1996: 11, citing Mårtensson 1988).

disputed in the literature. A universal presence of concepts isomorphic to 'I' and 'you' has been forcefully defended by Wierzbicka (1976; 1996) and her followers within the framework of Natural Semantic Metalanguage (e.g. Goddard 1995; 2001: 8–10; Diller 1994: 167–9; Onishi 1994: 362–7). Also, Greenberg claims that 'there must always be distinct first and second singular independent pronouns' (Greenberg 1993: 21). In contrast, Harré (1993) and Mühlhäusler and Harré (1990) remain sceptical as to the universality of concepts like the English *I* and *you*. I follow their scepticism and so, in order not to confuse the present analysis more than is necessary, I have disregarded paradigms that are not clearly specialized for the marking of person.

Specialization of shifters can occur by grammaticalization from erstwhile nouns, as in Thai. Early proposals for such a nominal origin of pronouns have been made by von Humboldt (1830) and Blake (1934). However, it turns out to be rather difficult to find good examples of this grammaticalization. Once the person markers are specialized, the original nominal meaning is in most cases long gone. An exemplary case is the Classical Malay noun *sahaya*, meaning both 'servant' and 'I-humble/polite', which turned into modern Indonesian *saya*, meaning 'I-neutral/non familiar'. The word *sahaya* no longer exists in Indonesian and *saya* does not mean 'servant'. In this example, a semi-grammaticalized shifter, *sahaya*, turned into a completely grammaticalized shifter *saya* (H. Steinhauer, p.c.).

Another aspect of the grammaticalization of person markers leads from independent pronouns to inflectional person marking (often called 'agreement').[15] Givón (1976) argues explicitly for this continuum to be interpreted as showing that there is no structural difference between the two forms of person marking. Person can be marked independently or inflectionally. The reasons for a particular language to choose either of these possibilities remain unclear. However, from a cross-linguistic perspective, the two strategies are not a priori different:

...the tacit assumption [is] that agreement and pronominalization are two distinct processes. I will suggest below that they are fundamentally one and the same phenomenon, and that neither diachronically nor, most often, synchronically could one draw a demarcating line on any principled grounds. (Givón 1976: 151)

In most of the generative literature on pronominal marking, this continuum is not accepted. Independent pronouns and inflectional person marking are considered to be two completely different aspects of linguistic marking. The reason for the persistence is probably the high status of the PROJECTION PRINCIPLE

---

[15] There is an extensive literature on the notion of agreement which tries to cope with the large variation of agreement-like features among the world's languages (Corbett 1979; 1994; Lehmann 1982; 1983; Moravcsik 1978; 1988). The provisional conclusion is that agreement is about covariation between two linguistic elements. Whether one of the two is controlling the other differs from construction to construction, and from language to language. It is surely not true that there is a universal direction in the control structure between independent personal pronouns and inflectional person marking.

14   *Introduction*

as formulated by Chomsky (1981: 29). This principle proposes a strong constraint on syntactic analyses and the intermediate transformations. It implies that at every level of syntactic analysis, the arguments of each predicate are to be present (overt or covert). Independent pronouns are possible instantiations of arguments; inflectional person marking is seen as agreement of the predicate with these arguments. Thus, a regular noun or an independent pronoun has to be present at each level of syntactic analysis. There has been an attempt to lessen the power of this principle by allowing argument status to inflectional person marking (or clitics), and considering independent pronouns as optional adjuncts. This idea was originally proposed by Jelinek (1984) to explain non-configurationality:

I argue that the clitic pronouns do not constitute agreement (AGR) with a nominal... My claim will be that verbal argument arrays (argument positions) in LS are satisfied always and only in PS in Warlpiri by clitic pronouns, and that nominals are simply optional adjuncts, with non-argumental functions. (Jelinek 1984: 44)

Much has since been written on the argumental status of inflectional person markers. For example, Baker (1990; 1991) attempted to improve on the original proposals. Others, like Saxon (1986: 142) in a description of Dogrib, oppose these proposals. From a more descriptive point of view, the discussion has been fuelled by Mithun (1986; 1991). Finally, the debate seems to have ended after the publication of an article by Austin and Bresnan (1996) which shows that Jelinek's analysis of Warlpiri does not hold for close relatives of Warlpiri:

The clitic pronouns that Jelinek (1984) and others take to be the source of non-configurationality in Warlpiri are simply an areal feature of Australian languages that is independent of the characteristics of free word order, null anaphora, and split NP's. They do not provide the unifying explanation for non-configurationality of the Warlpiri type. (Austin and Bresnan 1996: 263)

Notwithstanding all the commotion, the idea that inflectional person markers could be more important for the structure of a language than its independent pronouns does not seem to have found its way into the generative canon. Generative textbooks like Webelhuth (1995) and Culicover (1997) do not mention any of the arguments, nor cite any of the literature dealing with this proposal. The independent pronouns are still considered to be the principal person-marking system, and the term 'agreement' remains to be used practically as a synonym of inflectional person marking in most of the syntactic literature.[16]

---

[16] Jelinek's (1984) proposal that inflection is for some languages better considered as the principal person-marking system had already been developed by the classical Arabian grammarians from the eighth century AD onward (Versteegh 1997: 77–81). They ran into trouble in the tenth century AD when they tried to reconcile Aristotelian logic (which was based on a strictly separable predicate/argument structure, apparently also a central principle of Chomsky's approach to linguistic structure) with their traditional grammatical analysis (Abed 1991).

In contrast, I will follow Givón's proposal, and treat independent pronouns and inflectional person marking as two different, though a priori equivalent, ways of person marking. Whether there is a difference between the two strategies is not at first sight clear. I will include both inflectional person markers and independent pronouns in my search for the variability of paradigmatic structure. I include (in principle) each and every person-marking paradigm of a language in the investigation, without restrictions as to the function of the paradigm within the language.[17] I will not choose one paradigm per language as representing the 'real' person marking system of the language (cf. the criticism of Forchheimer in Section 1.4.2).

1.2.5 Remaining delimitations

The object of the present investigation is the marking of person in the singular and the non-singular. The restriction to the combination person/number may sound natural to many readers, but from a cross-linguistic perspective the separation of these two dimensions from other dimensions is far from obvious. At the risk of raising unnecessary suspicion, I want to show in this section why it is not instantly clear how this domain can be delimited cross-linguistically, by presenting a few examples of paradigms that cross the boundary of person and number. The following selection of examples and references is intended to show the inherent variability of human language. Even the present seemingly clearly distinct domain of linguistic structure turns out to have fuzzy edges. For a more elaborate survey of possible categories in person systems, see Mühlhäusler and Harré (1990: 60–88).

The first and most far-ranging restriction is that I will disregard gender marking. I will not only disregard the gendered elements in the paradigms and retain the rest, but I will disregard most paradigms when they contain gendered forms. The reason for this rather crude decision is that I do not know which forms to leave out when there are various gender forms. In fact, a separate chapter on the interrelation between gender and person marking was planned, but did not

---

[17] In fact, there is one important restriction on the paradigms included. Only paradigms are considered that are used as argument in a clause. The other major grammatical construction with person markers, namely pronominal possession, is disregarded in this study. The reason for this restriction is a practical one. The original impetus for compiling the present collection of cross-linguistic data was to look for the differences in argument status of person markers. It was only after most of the data collection and much of the analysis had been done that I decided that it was impossible to analyse the argument status of a person marker without first analysing the structure of the paradigm. To control whether the omission of pronominal possession influences the conclusions of this investigation, I have looked at the structure of such paradigms. This has been more than just a cursory glance, although it has not been representative enough to be reported on here. My impression is that the omission does not influence the conclusions put forward in this work. The only place where a different conclusion might be reached concerns zero marking for speaker-reference (see Section 2.5.2).

materialize. For more information on the interrelation between gender and person, see Corbett (1991: 126–32) and Plank and Schellinger (1997). Only in a few exceptional cases have I retained paradigms that distinguish two gender forms in the third person singular, the most unmarked place for gender to be distinguished.

The complete variation of gender marking in the domain of person marking deserves more that just a cursory glance. To raise interest in this subject, I will present two examples of a more curious kind of interrelation between gender and person. The first example comes from Barasano, an eastern Tucanoan language spoken in Peru. The gender/person suffixes in Barasano mark gender and animacy in the third person. Curiously, the inanimate suffix is also used for speech act participants:

Agreement of person, number, gender and animacy between subject and verb is required, and is shown by subject agreement markers which occur in final position in the phrase. ... -*ha* is used for all inanimates, and for speech-act participants, i.e. first or second person, singular or plural. (Jones and Jones 1991: 73–4)

A comparable structure to the one from Barasano, though in a completely different part of the world, is the usage of zero gender marking in Archi, a Nakh-Dagestanian language from the Caucasus (Corbett 1991: 127–8, citing Kibrik et al.). The second unusual structure is found in the Afro-Asiatic stock, being widespread throughout the Semitic, Cushitic, and Berber languages. In these languages, the pronominal prefixes often have the same form for the second person and for the third person feminine. The morpheme for the third person masculine is different. In the Cushitic languages, however, this third person masculine is often identical with the first person singular; an 'interlocking' pattern, as it is called by Tucker and Bryan (1966: 15–16). The opposite kind of 'interlocking' is attested in Burmeso and Orya, two languages from New Guinea. In these languages, the first person singular prefix is identical to the third person singular feminine, and the second person singular prefix is identical to the third person singular masculine (Donohue 2000: 344–7). In all these cases, it is questionable whether the marking should be considered to be person marking. However, if the suffix *-s* in English marks person, then these systems are surely to be interpreted as person marking as well.

Another major omission of the present work is that I will disregard honorific usage of pronouns and specialized polite forms of pronouns (Head 1978; Mühlhäusler and Harré 1990: 131–67; Simon 1999). This is a tricky delimitation, as it is often difficult to distinguish the 'real' referential usage from the 'metaphorical' polite usage of a pronoun (see e.g. the analysis of the Malay pronouns by Gil 2001: 355). However, most descriptions are quite clear on the distinction between referential value and honorific usage. Also, it appears from conversational analysis that the referential and the metaphorical instances of pronoun use are distinguishable (Schegloff 1996: 441–9). I will only present a single—somewhat unusual—case of honorific usage of pronouns to exemplify the intricate complications that can arise in this dimension. This interesting metaphorical usage of person distinctions is found in Galela, a West Papuan language spoken on Halmahera in Indonesia. In this language, the difference between inclusive and exclusive first person plural is mixed with honorific usage. In specific contexts, the inclusive form is used as a polite variant of the first person exclusive:

...a situation as where a man asks members of another family to give money to his own family...His own family is referred to by *na-* [inclusive] which is interpreted to mean exclusive, polite. Sociolinguistically, what happens is that by including the addressee grammatically, the man relieves his embarrassment for having to ask for money. (Shelden 1991: 165–6)

A different kind of social intertwining of pronouns is attested in Australia. Some Australian languages have specialized person markers that have to be used when referring to kin (Dixon 1980: 247, 276). For example in the Mamu dialect of Dyirbal, a specialized pronoun is attested to refer to the combination 'self and spouse' (Dixon 1972: 50–1). Specialized kin-related person markers are most prolifically found in the Arandic family, for example in the languages Alywerre (Koch 1997) and Mparntwe Arrernte (Wilkins 1989: 126–8). In these languages, various sets of specialized pronouns exist in which reference depends on patrimoiety and generation.

Other traditional pronominal elements are disregarded, like indefinite pronouns (see Haspelmath 1997 for a typological survey), interrogative pronouns, reflexive pronouns, and reciprocal pronouns. In many languages, however, the reflexive and reciprocal markers belong structurally to the person-marking paradigm. For example, the object paradigm in the Athabascan languages includes specialized reflexive and reciprocal morphemes (on Slave, see Rice 1989: 431; on Navaho, see Young and Morgan 1987: 8). Another example of the fluid division between reflexive, reciprocal, and personal pronouns is found in Mundani, a Grassfields language from Cameroon. In Mundani, the object pronoun is used for person reference, but also for reflexive and reciprocal marking. Structurally, there is no difference between the three meanings of the Mundani sentence as presented in (1.3).

(1.3) Mundani (Parker 1986: 149)
bɔ́ɔ' n'tɨŋá áwɔ́b
3PL.PRON.SUBJ help 3PL.PRON.OBJ
'They are helping them.',
'They are helping themselves.', or
'They are helping each other.'

18 Introduction

In some person paradigms, the spatial configuration of the referents is specified in more detail. An example of spatial specification is attested in the paradigm of independent pronouns from Cuna, a Chibchan language from Panama. All independent pronouns are characterized by a suffix -*i*. However, this suffix is also added to the demonstrative roots, distinguishing four grades of locational specificity: 'this', 'the same', 'that', and 'yonder'. These demonstrative roots are morphophonetically included in the person-marking paradigm (Holmer 1946: 190). Another variant of spatial specification in the person-marking paradigm is attested in Ute, a Uto-Aztecan language of Oregon. In the third person, an opposition between visible and non-visible is grammaticalized (Givón 1984: 356–7). Finally, a combination of spatial specification and marking of visibility is found in Kwakiutl (Boas 1947: 252). More information on the interaction between personal pronouns and spatial configuration can be found in a thorough typological investigation of demonstrative pronouns by Diessel (1999).

A variant of the spatial specification is discourse specification. Instead of marking the place of the object in real space, the place of the referent in the space of the discourse can be specified by specialized pronominal forms. A specific way of grammaticalizing discourse specification is by so-called obviative third person markers. Obviative markers indicate that the intended referent is not the participant who is most prominent in the discourse; it is 'the other one' that is intended. Obviative marking is most famous as a characteristic of the Athabascan languages like Slave (Rice 1989: 431) and Navaho (Young and Morgan 1987: 8). It is, however, widespread throughout North American languages, as in the Algonquian languages, for example in Menomini (Bloomfield 1962: 44).

Some languages distinguish special logophoric pronouns. The precise extent of the usage of logophoric pronouns differs from language to language, but the general idea behind these pronouns is that they are used in quoting other people. For example, Babungo, a Grassfields language spoken in Cameroon, has such specialized logophoric pronouns. The pronoun *yì* is a logophoric third person pronoun that is generally used as a subject in embedded sentences (Schaub 1985: 111–13). The complex logophoric pronoun *vìŋyì* is used for 'semi-direct speech'. Semi-direct speech is direct speech of a participant in a story (Schaub 1985: 2). This is exemplified in example (1.4). Instead of the logophoric pronoun, also the inclusive first person plural pronoun *nsôo* or the third person plural pronoun *vǎŋ* could have been used here (Schaub 1985: 3).

(1.4) Babungo (Schaub 1985: 2)
fɔ̀káy   gí   lāa   síi   kà   vìŋyì   yɨ̀   kɔ́
tortoise say   that doubt can   **LOG**   do   what
'Tortoise said, "What can **we** do?"'

Yet another aspect of person marking that will be disregarded in the present investigation is specialized portmanteau forms for transitive constructions. In many languages around the world, sentences like 'I see you' are not formulated by using two separate pronouns or inflectional person markers, but by using one person marker that is specialized for this combination of subject and object. For example, such specialized person prefixes are attested for various transitive combinations in Diegueño, a Yuman language of California. The prefixes ʔ-, m-, and ø- are used for the first, second, and third person intransitive, respectively. Two other prefixes, n^j- and $ʔn^jm$-, belong to the same paradigm, but these prefixes are used for the transitive combinations of 1subject/2object and 2subject/1object, respectively (Langdon 1970: 139–40). The occurrence of transitive portmanteau forms in Australian languages is extensively discussed by Heath (1984; 1991). More recently, Heath (1998) gives a quick but thorough survey of such forms in American languages.

Finally, two apparently idiosyncratic person markers are found in New Guinea. In the Papuan language Salt-Yui, a special person suffix for 'speaker alone' is described. There are two suffixes for first person. First, there is a regular first person suffix -m(in). This suffix is ambiguous in its reference because it is used both for singular and plural reference. In some cases, another suffix -l is used to stress the fact that the speaker alone is intended. This special dimension apparently only exists in the first person (Irwin 1974: 14–15).[18] In Elema, an indigenous trade language in south-east New Guinea, a special pronoun for 'addressee questioned' is described. There are two pronouns for second person. The pronoun *eme* is used for the second person in statements and the pronoun *a* is used for second person in questions (Mühlhäusler 2001: 743; citing Dutton). This is faintly reminiscent of the so-called conjunct/disjunct pattern, in which the reference to first and second person is reversed in questions (Hale 1980; see also example (2.5) and the discussion there).

This list of the many facets of person marking among the world's languages is probably far from complete. The more languages are studied, the more strange and unexpected phenomena (from a Eurocentric perspective) will crop up. Every delimitation proposed for a cross-linguistic study is bound to encounter exceptions and problematic cases when confronted with the actual linguistic variation. Still, in this variation it is not chaos that rules: in the remainder of this work, I will show that there are still clear tendencies and near-universal generalizations to be made. However, the balance between generalizations and exceptions is a precarious one. Forgetting the exceptions might present a picture of the structure of human language that is over-simplistic. In contrast, disregarding the gross generalizations amidst the variation might suggest a massive variability of linguistic structure that is not representative of the actual situation. I will seek a balance between the extremes.

---

[18] Irwin (1974: 14) uses the word 'exclusive' for this specialized 'speaker alone' form, but it is clear from the description that this pronoun is rather different from what is in the present work (and normally in the literature) called an exclusive pronoun.

20 *Introduction*

1.3 Methodology

1.3.1 Preamble

The present investigation consists methodologically of three different kinds of study. Some parts use a cross-linguistic method, some use a typological method, and some use a crypto-diachronic method. In Section 1.3.2, I will discuss the difference between the cross-linguistic method and the typological method. Basically, the cross-linguistic method will be used to arrive at a firm basis for the typology. In Section 1.3.3, I will discuss a few special methodological aspects of the construction of the typology, specifically the question of sampling. Finally, in Section 1.3.4, I will present a hybrid method, a combination of cross-linguistic and diachronic ideas, which I call 'crypto-diachronic'. This method will be used to tap into the diachronic dynamics of the paradigmatic structure of person marking. The result of this crypto-diachronic study will be a cognitive map, which links paradigmatic structures that are conceptually (and probably also diachronically) close to each other.

Before I turn to these themes, I offer a few words of gratitude and caution. The words of gratitude are directed to the authors of the grammatical descriptions that provide the necessary data for my investigation. The method they use to identify phonemes and morphemes seems to be fairly accurate and stable. That is to say, the statement that there exists a certain morpheme in a language can normally be made with relative certainty. Also, the acknowledgement of a paradigm in a language is usually rather straightforward. However, the question of the function or meaning of the morphemes is a completely different problem. I see the most important task of descriptive linguistics as a search for the best-fitting and most compelling analysis of the meaning of specific morphemes (or combinations of morphemes). The present investigation builds on the large body of work compiled by the authors of such invaluable descriptions of specific languages. I am writing this book standing on the proverbial shoulders of giants.

The words of caution concern the information on individual languages quoted in this work. I have attempted to quote only original sources, tracking down all references to their roots. Only in a few cases have I been unable to get hold of the original source. In those cases, I have added the name of the author of the original source to the reference in which I found the data. The data as quoted in this book have been copied as accurately as possible from the original source. However, I cannot guarantee that I have in all cases represented the data in the intended format. I suggest that any reader who wants to quote data from this work consults the original sources to prevent any accumulation of misquotation.[19]

---

[19] I have to make a disclaimer as to the names of the various languages mentioned in this book. The names for many languages in the world are misnomers for various reasons. Over the last decades, many of these languages have been renamed to suit the wishes of the speakers of the language itself. I completely support this political movement. However, for reasons of scientific clarity, I have consistently referred to languages by the name used in the source that I have consulted—even if that

1.3.2 Typology versus cross-linguistic research

There is a methodological difference between constructing a typology and doing cross-linguistic research. Basically, the construction of a typology is only part of a cross-linguistic investigation. However, the non-typological side of cross-linguistic research is often taken for granted in methodological statements (*pace* Croft 1990: 1–18). For the present work, the cross-linguistic investigation has been of major importance for the subsequent typology. In fact, most of the research time has been spent on cross-linguistic work, while the typology was compiled relatively quickly once the parameters had been fixed.

A TYPOLOGY should be based on a definition which is independent of the linguistic structure of any particular language—a *tertium comparationis*. A typology is meaningless if it is not constrained by an explicitly stated and independently formulated subject to be compared in the world's linguistic variation. On the basis of a *tertium comparationis*, languages can be categorized on how they express that subject in their linguistic structure. However, a *tertium comparationis* is never theory-independent. It presupposes something to be universally expressible in language. This universal hypothesis originates in the theoretical background on which the typology is based. In this strict interpretation, typology is always a hypothesis-testing methodology. Given a view about the structure of human language, the world's linguistic variation can be used to test this view by making a typology. In the present study, the hypotheses to be tested will come from a CROSS-LINGUISTIC investigation. I see cross-linguistic research as the attempt to understand language by combining different viewpoints from different languages and different grammarians into a coherent picture.[20] The differences that are found in grammars are not necessarily caused by the language: they could just as well arise from the viewpoint of the grammarian. As a matter of principle, however, I assume that all descriptions are good reflections of the language.[21] Every grammar is probably incomplete; certain aspects are omitted, on other aspects extensive digressions are added. However, in many cases such a bias of a description is caused by a 'bias' in the structure of the language. A particular language may structurally stress certain functions of human

---

name is no longer used. My usage of such old-fashioned language names should in no way be interpreted as a political statement.

[20] The philosophical background to this interpretation of cross-linguistic research is the insight that the most difficult problem for scientific inquiry is to bypass the 'spectacles of tradition'. People cannot observe objectively; there is always some prior experience or knowledge that interferes with the observation, colouring it and making every observation always an interpretation. One way to bypass this obstacle to some extent is to combine different viewpoints. Different viewpoints are often caused by different 'spectacles'. On the presupposition that the alternative perspectives look in more or less the same direction, but from different points of view or with different magnitudes of resolution, the different results obtained from alternative perspectives can be used to understand the influences of the 'spectacles' on the resulting picture. By combining different views, a new level of understanding can hopefully be reached (cf. Feyerabend 1975).

[21] In some cases, I have been able to correct clear errors in the description by comparing the data of different sources of the same or of closely related languages. Such errors are checked with the original author (if possible), and are always explicitly noted in footnotes to the data presentation.

communication, prompting a grammarian to spend more time dealing in greater depth with this particular function. The differences between the descriptions of the world's languages are better seen as a possible opening to new insights than as a nuisance that complicates comparison.

Cross-linguistic research and typology depend on each other in an interpretational cycle. For the cross-linguistic part of the research, traditional linguistic notions, like 'pronoun', 'first person', or 'plural', are taken as a starting point. These traditional notions, and many others, are part of an ancient heritage of metalanguage, of talking about language, that have proved successful for that purpose. But being successful in the past does not mean that these terms transcend theory. These words are (part of) a theory about language, just as any other linguistic theory. Such traditional terms propose a format with which one can tackle the interpretation of linguistic structures. They are words that help to understand the structure of a language, but it should be realized that they do not necessarily have to be appropriate for all languages.[22] In some cases, I will propose a slight reformulation of the interpretation of traditional concepts to be able to deal with the attested cross-linguistic variation. Based on these revised concepts, a typology of the world's linguistic variation will be made. This typology tests the revised concepts, and the results of this test can be used as a starting point for the next round of cross-linguistic research. In the present work, Chapters 2, 3, and 6 employ a cross-linguistic method. Building on this basis, the second part of Chapters 2 and 3, and the Chapters 4, 5, and 7, describe the cross-linguistic diversity and present a typology.

1.3.3 Sampling in typology

The typological side of this investigation needs some more methodological explication. The typological work consists of two different parts. The first part is the compilation of the typology itself, and the second part is an analysis of this typology. Let me first explain how the typology itself has been compiled. In Chapters 4 and 8, the various paradigmatic structures of person marking are classified into different types. This compilation of different paradigmatic types was mainly driven by the urge to present the wide range of possibilities that is attested regarding person marking in the world's languages. The sample of languages for this compilation was not fixed beforehand. Of course, every part of the linguistic globe has been included in this typology, but this diversity constraint has only been taken as a baseline condition, not as a guarantee for empirical success. Every single example of a rare paradigmatic structure has been included in the sample to show the inherent variability of human language. The result is a

---

[22] With traditional terminology, I refer to the kind of theoretical assumptions that Dixon (1997: 128–35) refers to as his Basic Linguistic Theory: 'Over the past few hundred years work has been done on language from every part of the world, with many aspect of linguist theory being rethought, reformulated and refined as a result. The term Basic Linguistic Theory has recently come into use for the fundamental theoretical concepts that underlie all work in language description and change, and the postulation of general properties of human language' (Dixon 1997: 128).

broad typology that includes many cases that are only attested in one or two examples. On the other hand, not every case of the commonly occurring paradigmatic structures is included. After a representative group of a specific common paradigmatic structure had been described, I stopped the collection of more exemplars of such common patterns. In this part of the typology I have attempted to describe exhaustively the world's linguistic diversity at the expense of overestimating the frequency of the more unusual possibilities of human language.

In the analysis of this typology, I have classified the diversity into types that are common and types that are rare. There are two criteria for a pattern to be COMMON: the pattern should be attested widely dispersed over the world's languages (typically there are more than fifteen examples attested) and it should be a typical pattern in at least two genetic units. The first criterion assures that the pattern is found independently in different languages, beyond the influence of common genetic origin or areal contact. The second criterion assures that the pattern is relatively stable, as the attested examples are not all exceptional variants within their genetic group. In contrast, a structure is RARE if there are one or two unrelated examples, or eventually a few closely related examples. The distinction between common and rare is not rigorously clear cut. I also distinguish SEMI-COMMON paradigmatic structures that fall between common and rare. Typically, the semi-common patterns occur in more than five genetically and areally independent cases and there is one instance of a genetic family in which the patterns is commonly attested.

The boundary between rare patterns and non-attested patterns is equally troublesome.[23] Many different rare paradigmatic structures are attested, but still many more theoretically possible structures are not attested. I will not give any interpretation to the fact that some structures are attested, albeit rarely, and others are not attested at all. The circumstance in which a particular rare pattern occurs in the present sample, as opposed to other paradigmatic structures that do not occur, is probably incidental. If I had studied more languages, or if there had been more languages in the world, some more rare cases would probably have turned up. When confronted with the wide variety of linguistic structures in the world's languages, I do not see any reason why a certain pattern would be impossible for a language. There are clearly structures that are *improbable*, but nothing seems to be *impossible*. I will present all rare patterns that have been attested to show the inherent variability of linguistic structure. As a result, all generalizations that will be formulated will have some counterexamples. Typological generalizations are never to be interpreted as universals in the strict sense, but as statistically preferred patterns of linguistic structure (Comrie 1989: 19–20; Dryer 1997; Cysouw 2002).

A few (preliminary) quantitative analyses are performed in Chapter 10. These analyses use the set of examples that had been compiled in Chapter 4 to perform some quantitative calculations. The sample for these analyses is not constrained

---

[23] Sometimes, a further distinction is made between RARA and RARISSIMA (as proposed by F. Plank, p.c.). Rara are types that are rare, but attested in more than one case, independently of each other. Rarissima are types attested only in one isolated case.

24 *Introduction*

to be representative of the actual world's languages (as, for example, proposed by Rijkhoff and Bakker 1998). Still, I believe that the results of these quantitative analyses are valuable. The number of cases is high, and the diversity of the sample is large. Even more strongly, the sample covers each and every structure that I know of, including all quaint cases. A methodology more strongly constrained by statistical representativeness would probably find less diversity, not more. This means that any correlation that holds for the present diversity sample will surely also hold for a statistically constrained sample.

1.3.4 Crypto-diachrony

Chapters 8 and 9 use yet another method to reach yet another goal. I will call the method CRYPTO-DIACHRONIC, which is a combination of cross-linguistic and diachronic ideas. The main objective of this method is to get an inkling of the similarity between the various paradigmatic structures of person marking. The typological Chapters 4 and 7 result in a set of paradigmatic structures that are commonly encountered among the world's languages. These paradigmatic structures are not invariable instances of linguistic form, but perpetually changing configurations of morphemes. Structures that are similar will change more easily from one to the other. From the typological investigation, a hypothesis can be distilled on the similarity of paradigmatic structure in the form of a two-dimensional similarity space. In this similarity space, similar paradigmatic structures are placed near to each other. I will use the crypto-diachronic method to test the hypothetical similarity space of paradigmatic structure. In Chapters 8 and 9 I will look at groups of closely related languages that have slightly different paradigmatic structures, a method reminiscent of intragenetic comparison, as proposed by Greenberg (1969: 184–94). The morphemes in these paradigms are individually cognate. However, the paradigmatic configuration of the morphemes is slightly different. I assume that these paradigmatic differences are caused by a relatively recent change in one direction or the other. In most cases, I do not propose a direction of change: in this sense, I am not proposing any diachronic developments. However, I conclude from such examples that the paradigmatic structures involved are similar. By compiling a large set of such cognate paradigms, I will be able to build a similarity map of paradigmatic structures.

1.4 Previous cross-linguistic investigations

1.4.1 Preamble

There exists a massive literature on person marking, but the majority of these investigations deal with the analysis of the pronominal elements of a particular language or of a group of closely related languages. These studies mainly provide continuously improved analyses of the pronominal systems of these languages. In some studies, a theoretical hypothesis is confronted with the phenomena found in a particular language or language group. In others, idiosyncratic peculiarities of the language in question bring about new grammatical concepts to describe linguistic phenomena. Yet, in contrast to this plethora of individual studies, the amount of literature that takes a cross-linguistic perspective on person marking is rather limited. In such cross-linguistic work, the variety of structures used by languages for person marking is compared in an attempt to arrive at a better understanding of what is meant by the concept of 'person' marking. I will here discuss the few cross-linguistic investigations of person marking that were published in the second half of the twentieth century. I do not discuss specific claims about cross-linguistic variation made by the various authors. The history of typological claims will be discussed wherever appropriate throughout the present work. In this section, only the general approach and the methodological issues of the studies are discussed.

The first extensive cross-linguistic collection and comparison of person marking was compiled by Forchheimer (1953). I will discuss his work, together with some of the devastating critiques that were published at the time of publication, in Section 1.4.2. Some cross-linguistic claims about person marking are found in the typological work of Greenberg and his co-workers. I will review these works in Section 1.4.3. Mühlhäusler and Harré (1990) wrote a monograph predominantly dealing with the deictic aspects of person marking, using data from a wide variety of languages. I will discuss their work in Section 1.4.4. Finally, I will discuss a short article by Laycock (1977) in Section 1.4.5, which in spirit is much like the present investigation.[24]

1.4.2 Forchheimer and his critics

Over the last fifty years, the main reference for anybody who wanted to know anything about pronominal systems has been Forchheimer's *The Category of Person in Language* from 1953. The enduring reference to this work stands in strong contrast to the hostile reactions which appeared shortly after the book was published. Householder's (1955) review in *Language* was highly critical. He objects to the classification 'of language phenomena in terms of some

---

[24] In the generative literature, and particular in the wake of Government and Binding theory, there has been a great deal of attention paid to the anaphoric use of pronominal elements. I do not feel competent to review this extensive literature, which as a whole could be interpreted as being cross-linguistic because many different languages are discussed by many different authors. Unfortunately, it does not seem characteristic of the generative tradition to compile review articles in which a large body of publications is summarized for non-specialists. However, the main body of work in this tradition appears to be based on analyses of Germanic and Romance languages. There are relatively few attempts to reconcile the European-based analyses with phenomena found in other languages. To an outside observer of generative developments like me, the results do not look promising for a true cross-linguistic theory (cf. Huang 1995; Mühlhäusler and Harré 1990: 55–7).

pre-established pattern of Latin grammar or some triumph of logic' (Householder 1955: 94), and he argues for a more explicit way of selecting data. Householder even starts off referring to Forchheimer as an amateur, indicating that he does not intend to take the work seriously:

The linguistic amateur, like the amateur in other fields, has characteristic virtues and vices. He is usually enthusiastic, sanguine, and industrious, often learned. His goals and ideals, on the other hand, may appear strange, even futile, to his more conventional colleagues. (Householder 1955: 93)

Hymes's (1955) review in the *International Journal of American Linguistics* is equally trenchant. He objects to the inaccurate presentation of the data and the implicit diachronic argumentation: 'Perhaps so weak a book should not have been written; on the other hand, it is the only one in its field' (p. 300). There are indeed many points in Forchheimer's study that call for criticism. However, one can hardly expect such a ground-breaking investigation to be perfect. The work by Forchheimer is a first attempt at a cross-linguistic comparison of the structure of pronominal marking. Among the many problems, I believe there to be many stimulating aspects in Forchheimer's investigation, although the correct conclusions are only covertly stated in the work itself. The main error, I believe, is the title of the book, which puts the reader (and Forchheimer himself) on a wrong track.

Forchheimer's study is truly cross-linguistic in nature. He explains that he has 'examined a good five hundred grammars and word lists... general works and collections on almost all areas' (1953: 2), although only about seventy different languages are actually discussed in the book (Ingram 1978: 218). This wide array of linguistic diversity that is included in the comparison is typical of the German tradition of linguistic comparison and classification as it existed around the start of the twentieth century (cf. Müller 1876–87; Schmidt 1926; Royen 1929). Unfortunately, Forchheimer followed this tradition at a time when nobody was really interested in such work. The restricted number of languages discussed stems from Forchheimer's primary interest in the diversity of linguistic structure. He does not list all languages that he has investigated, but only those languages that exemplify a particular type of structure:

Wherever I have found or suspected unusual or new material I have changed from the extensive to an intensive study of that linguistic stock or area... after a certain stage had been reached, examination of more languages did no longer show new types. (Forchheimer 1953: 2–3)

The types that he was interested in are various 'person patterns' or 'person systems' (p. 2). However, his main interest lies not in the paradigmatic structure as I have defined it (see Section 1.2.3), but in the morphological patterns of the marking of number in the pronominal domain. This central occupation with the morphological structure can be inferred from the kinds of type that are distinguished in the typology. His classification consists of types like 'Languages with Morphological Plural of Pronouns' or 'Languages without Morphological but with Lexical Plural at least in the First Person'. The result is a typology of the morphological coding of the connection between person and number (pp. 11–19). This goal of Forchheimer's investigation can be directly connected to the influence of Wilhelm Schmidt (esp. 1926: 316–34), an influence explicitly mentioned by Forchheimer in the acknowledgements to his book.

A central problem with Forchheimer's study (criticized by both Householder 1955: 94 and Hymes 1955: 295) is that he does not define the criteria to select the person-marking data from the various descriptions. He takes the term 'person marking' to be a self-explanatory term, describing a certain universally applicable concept of linguistic structure. Forchheimer implicitly took the rough equivalents of West European pronouns as the data for his study. By definition, these elements will mark for person, but the unanswered question is whether these elements necessarily form a special category. He does not give any criteria on which to decide whether a particular set of person-marking morphemes form a category. It is surely true that every language can mark person in some way, but whether every language has a category of person remains unproven. This point leads to another problem with the implicit assumptions in Forchheimer's study. Not only does he assume a category of person in all languages, he also claims to be able to extract *the* system of person marking for all languages:

From any fairly reliable grammar, be it conservative or modern, prescriptive or descriptive, scholarly or written by an interested traveller, it is possible to work out *the* system of person peculiar to a language. (p. 1; italics added)

Many languages have an independent pronoun system alongside inflectional pronominal systems. It remains unclear how Forchheimer decides which one is *the* system. Sometimes, he takes an independent person-marking paradigm as *the* system. In other cases, he includes an inflectional paradigm in his sample as *the* pronominal system:

Personal pronominal elements are found in different forms. They may occur either as enclitics (affixes), or as so-called free, separate, independent, disjunctive, or absolute pronouns.... After studying hundreds of systems, I became convinced that the affix-pronouns often represent the pure pronominal elements. (p. 23)

It seems that Forchheimer finds *the* system of person marking in all languages not as an empirical result, but because of an a priori assumption that there has to be such a thing in all languages. In conclusion, it can be said that his reasoning can only be understood if the existence of a universal and unitary person system is taken for granted and not as the result of his investigation. From this discussion it should not be concluded that such an assumption is wrong altogether. It is only on the basis of assumptions that questions can be asked and results can be reported.

28 Introduction

Problems arise when the assumptions are confused with the research questions and the conclusions. This occurs, for example, when Forchheimer claims universal status for his assumed categories, as he occasionally does: 'The distinction of speaker, addressed, and neither speaker nor addressed is universally found' (p. 39). This conclusion is not correct, given the approach that Forchheimer uses. He *assumes* that the person categories exist; he does not *investigate* whether they actually do. One can regret the fact that he took this perspective. He could indeed have performed a different investigation, but, ultimately, he did what he did:

> ...he intends to concern himself mainly with the morphological and etymological relationships of the actual forms in each language. What a lost opportunity! When he could have actually studied the grammatical category of person, found out which languages do and which do not have such a category, determined the various systems in the different languages and compare them. (Householder 1955: 94)

In general, besides rather overt flaws in the presentation of the data (Householder 1955: 97–9; Hymes 1955: 294–5) and some confusion between assumptions and results, the work is an interesting effort to do cross-linguistic research at a time when linguistics was not very interested in such work. Maybe the major mistake Forchheimer made was the title of his study: *The Category of Person in Language*. He does not investigate this theme, but assumes that the category of person exists. It would have been better if he had called the book something like *Number Marking in Person Systems* (for a comparable evaluation of Forchheimer's work, and for many details concerning Forchheimer himself, see Plank 2002).

1.4.3 Greenberg and his co-workers

The reception of Joseph Greenberg's famous 1963 article on universals of grammar contrasts sharply with the hostile reaction to Forchheimer's study. In only ten years the scientific climate had changed drastically, as some of the same points of criticism that were raised against Forchheimer's study can also be raised against Greenberg's article. The most important point of criticism to be made is that Greenberg—just like Forchheimer—does not explicate on which grounds he selects his data. Greenberg even explicitly states that 'no attempt at definition of categories will be attempted' (Greenberg 1963: 92). He ignores this aspect because he wants to concentrate on other questions:

> To have concentrated on this task, important in itself, would have, because of its arduousness, prevented me from going forward to those specific hypotheses, based on such investigation, which have empirical import and are of primary interest to the nonlinguist. (p. 74)

In the 1963 article, besides the well-known universals on word order, there is also a section on morphology, where Greenberg makes some claims about pronominal elements. Here he claims universal status for three persons and two numbers in his Universal 42: 'All languages have pronominal categories involving at least three persons and two numbers' (p. 96). Forchheimer made an almost identical claim, but there is a slight difference in phrasing. Greenberg does not claim that there is something like *the* pronominal system. He instead argues that there are three persons and a number opposition somewhere in each language. He does not claim a single primary paradigm with these characteristics for each language. Yet the same criticism that was raised in the discussion of Forchheimer's approach applies here. If the selection criterion is to find elements comparable to the European pronominal elements in other languages, one will probably always find them. The remaining problem is whether those elements form a genuine category, as seen from the point of view of the structure of the language in question.

Following Greenberg's approach to language universals, the 'Project on Language Universals' took place in Stanford between 1967 and 1976, directed by Charles Ferguson and Joseph Greenberg. The results of this project were published in four impressive volumes in 1978. In the third volume, *Word Structure*, there is an article 'Typology and Universals of Personal Pronouns' by David Ingram. Here, even more strongly than in the case of Forchheimer's study, what is presented as results are assumptions in disguise. This is even more startling as Ingram is explicit about his assumptions and questions. Still, he does not seem to notice that his conclusions are implied in his assumptions. Ingram is explicit about the questions he will address: 'what are the roles or combinations of roles in the speech act that each language considers to be of sufficient importance to mark by a separate lexical form?' (Ingram 1978: 215–16). To investigate this question, Ingram chose to use the data as presented by Forchheimer in his book. Yet one should be very careful in using Forchheimer's data. In fact, Forchheimer's data can only be used for the particular goal for which they were compiled: to make a morphological typology of number marking in the pronominal domain. Ingram does not realize that it is unsafe to formulate cross-linguistic conclusions about the paradigmatic structure of person marking on the basis of the data presented by Forchheimer. He simply takes Forchheimer's data and computes the statistical frequencies of particular paradigmatic types. Forchheimer's sample, however, was designed to show the different morphological possibilities to code number in the pronominal domain. Forchheimer's data do not give an accurate statistical survey of the world's linguistic possibilities of paradigmatic structure. Ingram's conclusions thus stand on shaky ground (although they will turn out to be more or less correct): 'Four systems . . . are more frequent than others . . . The six person system [I, thou, he, we, you, they] is by far the most common system in languages' (Ingram 1978: 219).

More problematic still is Ingram's proposal of universal features to analyse the systems found. He offers the features 'speaker', 'hearer', and 'other' for person and 'singular', 'dual', 'trial', 'plural', and 'unmarked' for number. These features are not results of the cross-linguistic study, but are explicit statements of the assumptions. Householder comments as follows on these 'results':

He [referring to Forchheimer, but it also applies to Ingram, MC] chose to investigate the words which might conceivably translate *I, thou, we, you, he, she, it, they*. Could he possibly have taken any other step which would as surely guarantee in advance that he would discover nothing? (Householder 1955: 94)

In the mid-1980's Greenberg started a project entitled 'The Diachronic Typology of Pronominal Systems'. Despite the name, the articles that he published during this project (Greenberg 1985; 1988; 1993) deal with cross-linguistic variation, more than with typology or diachrony as such. He presents ample data showing the variability of linguistic structures to be found in the world's languages and hardly claims any restrictions on the possibilities of linguistic structures. Increasingly through the articles, he is taken by the problem of the traditional terminology, thus questioning as such the assumptions implied. The rhetorical structure in these articles is completely different from the investigations I have discussed so far. In these articles, Greenberg considers a particular traditional grammatical term to be a theoretical proposal for linguistic analysis. He no longer takes these terms for granted (as they have been for centuries), but discusses whether they might be improved upon. He shows different instantiations of the terms in different languages, and finally he asks whether the phenomena attested form a category.

Instead of assuming implicitly the correctness of the traditional terminology, he transforms the traditional terminology into a question. For example, in the article about the category 'first person inclusive dual' (Greenberg 1988), he notes that this category to indicate 'you and me' (if it exists in a particular language) is ambiguous cross-linguistically. It is either a special category of person, or a category of number. He concludes: 'we have sacrificed the notion of a uniform and universally valid set of typological categories by positing an ambiguous one' (Greenberg 1988: 12). In another article, he questions the traditional three-person analysis (Greenberg 1993). But although he shows that various linguistic phenomena do not fit in with the three-person analysis (such as zero third persons and inclusive persons), in the end he defends the three-person analysis because it seems to occur so often among the world's languages:

The traditional notion of a pronominal category of person with three members seems defensible. After all, the three-person pattern may be the result of historical accident, but it is a recurrent one. (Greenberg 1993: 20)

This approach taken by Greenberg in these later works will be followed in the present investigation. The traditional categories used to analyse person marking are not taken for granted, but tested on their accuracy against the available cross-linguistic variation.

1.4.4 Mühlhäusler and Harré

The starting point for Mühlhäusler and Harré in their seminal work *Pronouns and People* (1990) is diametrically opposed to that of the authors discussed so far. The implicit, or sometimes even explicit, goal of the preceding authors was to find universals of human language, or at least restrictions in the attested linguistic diversity. Mühlhäusler and Harré instead focus on the extent of linguistic relativity. They assume a tight interrelation between language and the social context and consequently stress the many ways in which linguistic structure can vary. A few theoretical assumptions of their work will be summarized here. First, they approach pronouns from their deictic side, leaving aside the anaphoric aspect of pronominal marking:

A number of significant questions one might wish to ask about pronouns either have never been asked or else have received only marginal attention. Instead, linguists have chosen to address an issue, anaphoricity, that may be insoluble and that to us appears to be of only minor interest. (Mühlhäusler and Harré 1990: 59)

To highlight this deictic approach, I would rather want to talk about 'person' instead of 'pronoun', but that is a minor terminological quibble. Second, Mühlhäusler and Harré assume that person markers are found in small closed sets, reminiscent of what I call a paradigm:

The term [pronoun] has been used in grammatical classifications of words to refer to a closed set of lexical items that, it is held, can substitute for a noun or a noun phrase... When we talk of a 'closed set', we imply that in human language only a small, definite repertoire of pronoun forms is found in each. (p. 9)

They seem to imply that each language has such a closed set, but I doubt that this is universally true (as, for example, argued for Thai, as discussed in Section 1.2.4). Still, the majority of the world's languages indeed seem to have such a closed set of person markers. Finally, Mühlhäusler and Harré stress the fact that the existing descriptive devices for the analysis of grammatical structure are in need of reconsideration and improvement, reminiscent of the approach of Greenberg in his later papers:

We thus need to have a descriptive apparatus sufficiently sensitive to describe all emic distinctions people actually make in all the world's cultures in relation to the subject matter for which the etic concepts are designed, in our case the functioning of... pronouns. As will be demonstrated eventually, the available etic tools may well be incomplete or even inadequate. (Mühlhäusler and Harré 1990: 61)[25]

Regrettably, Mühlhäusler and Harré observe the problem of traditional terminology, but do not really put forward a new proposal to improve the cross-linguistic analysis of pronouns. In general, the work by Mühlhäusler and Harré is

---

[25] See n. 4 in Ch. 6 on the etic/emic distinction.

32 *Introduction*

a valuable addition to the cross-linguistic knowledge about the variability of person marking among the world's languages. The main omission in their work, however, is the aspect opposite to variability: the restrictions on the variation. Mühlhäusler and Harré do not investigate which of the many phenomena they discuss are common and which are rare. Neither do they present a geographical or structural analysis of the variation. Yet they did not intend to cover these questions. Consequently, they leave those questions to be answered by others. I will attempt to do so to some extent in the present investigation.

1.4.5 Laycock on New Guinean pronouns

Laycock's (1977) article on pronoun systems in Papuan languages is restricted in extent and scope, but in spirit it is strongly related to the approach taken in this investigation. Laycock's article deals only with an areally restricted set of languages, although from an area that is generally seen as one of the most linguistically diverse regions of the world: New Guinea. Within this areal restriction, he only included independent pronouns in his comparison.[26] He acknowledges that most languages seem to have more than one pronominal system, all of which can have a different internal structure:

A language may—and usually does—have a number of pronoun systems. Pronouns may be free or bound, emphatic or non-emphatic, full or abbreviated; they may also appear with different case-endings. Each such set may form a different system in that different categories are distinguished. (Laycock 1977: 33)

In contrast to the authors discussed previously, Laycock does not assume that there is one central pronoun system without indicating how to select that system out of the multiple available paradigms. He instead takes a formal characteristic to select his data: he compares those sets of person markers that are morphologically independent. By using this methodology, Laycock cannot draw any conclusions about the structure of a complete language. It could very well be that a particular opposition is not attested in the independent pronouns, but that this opposition can be found somewhere else in the language (e.g. in inflectional person marking). Because of this method, Laycock cannot speak about the structure of language as a whole; but this drawback is compensated by the fact that he is immune to the criticism of Eurocentrism. If one searches for the presupposed categories known from Standard Average European languages, one will probably find them somewhere in any language. The real question should be whether the phenomena found form a category in the language. This was one of

---

[26] There are a few more investigations of person marking that explicitly restrict the scope of the data to independent pronouns, in particular Chlenova (1973), Sokolovskaya (1980), and Schwartz (1986).

Householder's criticisms of Forchheimer:

> It is nonsense to talk of a category wherever a language 'possesses the means for expressing a concept' ... since, by definition, any natural language possesses the means for expressing anything. It is not the ability to express, but the inability to leave unexpressed that usually shows the presence of a category. (Householder 1955: 94)

Laycock's main conclusion is that the pronominal systems of Papuan languages are not in conformity with Greenberg's Universal 42 ('all languages have pronominal categories involving at least three persons and two numbers': see Section 1.4.3). Most importantly, he finds pronominal systems consisting of only two or three members (Laycock 1977: 35). I will specifically discuss this criticism of Greenberg's Universal 42 in Section 3.6.2. Laycock's approach—to include only independent pronouns in the comparison—is a methodologically coherent method, although restricted in its scope. I will extend this approach by including each and every person-marking paradigm, whether independent or inflectionally marked (see Section 1.2.3). The same pros and cons arise. On the negative side, this method does not leave any room for conclusions about the structure of a language as a whole. On the positive side, however, it restricts the influence of Eurocentrism, which can otherwise be found in the form of implicit decisions to include the most familiar paradigm from a particular language in the investigation.

1.4.6 Conclusion

The focus and methodology of the present investigation have their clear precursors. First, the focus on person deixis is shared with Mühlhäusler and Harré (1990). Second, the interest for the paradigmatic structure is also found in the work of Laycock (1977) and Ingram (1978). The concern to find a suitable metalanguage for the cross-linguistic variability of person deixis is shared with Mühlhäusler and Harré (1990) and the later work by Greenberg (1988; 1993). The wish to lay out the cross-linguistic diversity attested among the world's languages is also the goal of Forchheimer (1953) and Mühlhäusler and Harré (1990). Finally, the attempt to formulate typological restrictions on this diversity is also found in the early work by Greenberg (1963) and in the work by Ingram (1978). In sum, these goals present an ambitious plan for the present work.

1.5 Outline of the book

This book is divided into four parts. The first part (Chapters 2 and 3) deals with person marking. The second part (Chapters 4 and 5) investigates the paradigmatic structure of person marking. These two parts form the core of the present study. The third part (Chapters 6 and 7) adds an analysis of number marking to this core.

The fourth part (Chapters 8 and 9) uses the typological results of the preceding chapters to investigate possible changes in paradigmatic structure by comparing small differences between close relatives. The results of these investigations are summarized in Chapter 10.

Part I, 'Person Marking', starts off with a cross-linguistic analysis of singular person marking (Chapter 2). The three singular categories, 'speaker', 'addressee' and 'other', which will be the basis for the investigation throughout this work, are introduced. A typology will be presented of paradigms that do not distinguish all three categories. Also, the status of zero marking of singular categories is investigated in detail. Building on this foundation, the marking of plural person marking will be investigated (Chapter 3). The concept of 'plural' for the analysis of person marking is discarded and the notion 'group' is proposed as a replacement. The various theoretically possible group categories are discussed against the background of the attested cross-linguistic variation. Also, a first advance towards a typology of the marking of these group categories is made. A typology will be presented of the 'first person complex', which is the set of groups that include at least the speaker.

Part II, 'Paradigmatic Structure', investigates the structure of the singular and the group categories combined. First, a complete typology of the attested paradigmatic structures is presented (Chapter 4). This compilation is a lengthy and maybe somewhat boring enumeration of case after case of paradigms of person marking. Along the way, a division into 'common' and 'rare' paradigmatic structures will be made. Some intermediate cases are classified as 'semi-common'. Two major hierarchies are the result: the Explicitness Hierarchy and the Horizontal Homophony Hierarchy. Second, a survey of the paradigmatic structure of compound pronouns is presented (Chapter 5). There is a recurrent claim in the literature that languages with such compound pronouns have special person categories. I investigate these pronouns, and argue that they are indeed a special class of pronouns, yet they do not present any new person categories.

Part III, 'Number Incorporated', extends the core of person categories as discussed so far with elements that explicitly mark number. Because I have replaced the traditional concept of 'plural' by the notion 'group' (in Chapter 3), the traditional notion of 'number' has to be redefined within the person marking domain (Chapter 6). On this basis, the typology of the core categories can be extended with these redefined number categories. In particular, the various forms of dual marking are extensively discussed (Chapter 7). This survey results again in a lengthy chapter listing the many attested possibilities of linguistic structure. As a result, a Dual Explicitness Hierarchy will be presented. A dual version of the Horizontal Homophony Hierarchy (from Chapter 4) is not corroborated by the data.

Part IV, 'Cognate Paradigms', reformulates the typological hierarchies from the previous chapters as a hypothesis for diachronic change (Chapter 8). Two paradigms that are close to each other on these typological hierarchies are hypothesized to be similar. Diachronic change is taken to follow roughly the similarity as described by the typological hierarchies. To test this hypothesis, cases of cognate paradigms are collected. It turns out that the hypothesis fares rather well. The paradigms with dual marking are then integrated in this crypto-diachronic analysis (Chapter 9). The outcome will be a network of interconnected paradigms, which maps the similarity of paradigmatic structure.

Finally, the main conclusions from all these chapters are summarized in Chapter 10. Also, some prospects for further research are discussed and a few post hoc analyses of the large body of data included in the present work are presented in this last chapter.

Part I
Person Marking

In those days his true self was still fighting with his assumed self, and winning. Person and persona, the man and his mask had separate identities then, he knew which was which.

Jeanette Winterson, *Gut Symmetries*

The term PERSON is as old as the Western tradition of grammatical analysis. The English grammatical usage of the word person is a loan translation from the Latin grammatical term *persona*. In turn, the Latin *persona* was adopted from Greek linguistics, in which the equivalent word *prósopon* was used. This word is already attested in the oldest linguistic text in the occidental tradition that is known today, the *Tékhne Grammatiké* by Dionysius Thrax (*c.*100 BC):

Prósopa tría, prôton, deúteron, tríton; prôton mèn af hoû ho lógos, deúteron dè pròs hòn ho lógos, tríton dè perì hoû ho lógos. (edition of Uhlig 1883: 51)

There are three persons, first, second and third. The first is the originator of the utterance, the second the person to whom it is addressed and the third the topic of the utterance. (translation by Kemp 1987: 181)

The word *prósopon* was introduced by Greek linguists, comparing language metaphorically to a play. Like the Latin *persona*, it is the word for 'mask' in the theatre, hence for 'dramatic character' or 'role' (Lyons 1977: 638). The language user can take different roles in the linguistic interplay, changing his mask from speaker to addressee and back.

Part I investigates the various grammatical ways of marking person. Chapter 2 deals with the three basic concepts: speaker, addressee, and other—a division almost identical to the classical analysis by Thrax. In that chapter, I will restrict myself to the singular usage of these concepts. Chapter 3 deals with the non-singular marking of person. The classical approach fares less well here. To be able to describe the cross-linguistic variation in non-singular marking, I will propose the concept GROUP as an alternative for plurality in the domain of person marking.

2 One Among the Crowd
The Marking of Singular Participants

2.1 Introduction

Pronominal paradigms vary widely among the world's languages. It will be a long journey to get this variation under control. I will proceed in small steps, limiting myself each time to a conveniently arranged subset of the variation. Inevitably, this will lead to some ad hoc decisions to include certain themes in one chapter or another, but everything that has to be said will come up eventually. This chapter deals with singular pronominal marking. In the introductory chapter, I have defined pronominal systems as paradigms that show at least an opposition between the marking for speaker and addressee. In this chapter, one category will be added to these two: the category 'any other singular participant'. There are maximally three different morphemes to be discussed here: one for speaker, one for addressee, and one for any other. The Latin inflectional pronominal paradigm is exemplary; there are three suffixes, *-o*, *-s*, and *-t*. Paradigms that have fewer than these three morphemes (like the English present with only two suffixes, *-ø* and *-s*) will be the crux of this chapter.

The principal objective of this chapter is to provide a typology of singular person marking (Section 2.2). Various kinds of homophony between the singular categories are attested. The major part of this chapter will consist of a description of examples of singular homophony. Almost everything that is theoretically possible will be shown to exist (Section 2.3). Next, I will argue that the examples attested do not corroborate the hypothesis that the 'richness' of singular marking is linked to the usage of independent pronouns (Section 2.4). Subsequently, some attention will be paid to the occurrence of zeros in singular pronominal marking. Among others, the question will be raised here whether these zeros should be considered as non-overt marking, or maybe better seen as non-existing marking (Section 2.5). Finally, a summary will be presented (Section 2.6).

2.2 Possible patterns

The three-morpheme paradigm, like the Latin singular suffixes, occurs frequently in the languages of the world. However, I have found examples of pronominal paradigms with fewer than three singular morphemes in many languages, spread

	(Sa)	(Sb)	(Sc)	(Sd)	(Se)
Speaker	A	A	A	A	A
Addressee	B	B	B		
Other	C		A	B	

FIG. 2.1. *Possible types of singular homophony*

out over the whole world. In these cases, some of the three categories are coded by the same morpheme. I will use the term HOMOPHONY as a theory-neutral term to refer to morphemes that mark for different categories. In the literature, various terms are used for this phenomenon—syncretism, homophony, homonymy, polysemy, and merger—with differing connotations (see Luraghi 2000 for a survey). The main point of controversy is whether a homophony is systematic or not. I do not want to decide a priori between accidental or systematic in the case of a homophony. In the present work, the term 'homophony' should be interpreted as meaning simply that two categories (that are distinguished for cross-linguistic reasons) are referred to by the same sounds—they are *homo-phonein*.

There are four theoretically possible kinds of homophony within the boundaries of the three singular persons. These four possibilities are shown in Figure 2.1, along with the basic case in which all three persons are distinct.[1] The five possibilities will be referred to as (Sa)–(Se); 'S' standing for singular. The Latin singular suffixes, with three different suffixes for the three categories, form an (Sa) type paradigm. Latin will be taken as a prototypical example of this type; I will regularly refer to this type as LATIN-TYPE. This structure is well known and will not be exemplified further. I will come back to the Latin-type paradigm in Section 2.5 to discuss the distribution of zeros in this kind of paradigm.

The homophonous types are less common and less well known. The first two possibilities in Figure 2.1, (Sb) and (Sc), have an opposition between speaker and addressee. Possibility (Sb) can be characterized as marking first versus non-first and (Sc) as marking second versus non-second. In contrast, possibilities (Sd) and (Se) do not mark the difference between speaker and addressee, and, consequently, (Sd) and (Se) do not mark person in the strict sense. However, both possibilities will be included as borderline cases of person marking. A structure of type (Sd) still has an opposition between the speech act dyad (speaker and addressee) and any other participant, so there is still a marginal presence of person marking. In contrast, possibility (Se) shows no person marking in the singular at all, but a few paradigms in which person marking is found only in the non-singular will be discussed below.

---

[1] The capital letters in the table are variables designating identical morphemes by the same letter and different morphemes by different letters. Other combinations of letters than the ones presented do not yield any new possibilities. Type (Sb), for example, could just as well have been indicated by the letters B for speaker and A for the combination of addressee and other. That would have amounted to the same paradigmatic structure.

In the next section I will discuss many examples of these forms of homophony. It takes some effort to find such examples, which indicates that they are indeed uncommon. However, the examples that will be discussed here are highly varied in their structure and widely dispersed among the languages of the world, which shows that singular homophony is not as unusual as often thought.[2]

2.3 Singular homophony

2.3.1 *Dutch-type homophony (Sb)*

A homophony of type (Sb), showing an opposition between speaker and the rest, is found in the Dutch pronominal inflection.[3] In the Dutch present, there is an opposition between a bare stem, which is used for the first person singular, shown in (2.1a), and a stem with a suffix *-t*, which is used for second and third person, shown in (2.1b, c). As a mnemonic device, I will use the label DUTCH-TYPE interchangeably for (Sb). Within the Germanic family, the Dutch-type homophony is also found in the present inflection of the Icelandic weak verbs. These verbs all have identical marking for second and third person. The morphemes used for the combined second/third person differ, though, according to the class of the verb (Thráinsson 1994: 158–61).

(2.1) Dutch (personal knowledge)
    a. *ik*   *loop-ø*
       1SG.PRON walk-1SG
      'I walk.'
    b. *jij*   *loop-t*
       2SG.PRON walk-2/3SG
      'You walk.'
    c. *hij/zij/het* *loop-t*
       3SG.PRON walk-2/3SG
      'S/he walks.'

---

[2] The occasional discussion of such homophonous structures in the literature is often severely restricted, leading to a wrong impression of the cross-linguistic possibilities. Noyer (1997: 112–13), for example, only discusses examples of the (Sd) homophony, and uses the existence of such cases to argue for a feature [±participant] in morphology. This argument becomes devoid of content in the light of the existence of the other kinds of homophony as presented in this chapter. Another example is Sasse (1993: 670), who only notices 'rare reports of neutralisation of 2nd and 3rd person', i.e. cases of (Sb).
[3] When I classify Dutch as (Sb), I refer to the inflection in Standard Dutch, with canonical word order subject–verb. The different Dutch dialects show a wide variety of homophony. All the different types distinguished in Figure 2.1 are found within the dialectal variation of the Netherlands (van den Berg 1949: 7). Besides the dialectal variation, there is also variation within the Standard variety. The inflection of Standard Dutch changes with the word order, a rather exotic phenomenon. In some contexts (like questions or when temporal adverbs are fronted for emphasis), the subject follows the finite verb. In these cases the pronominal inflection is of type (Sd), with a zero first and second person, and a suffix *-t* for the third person.

42 *Person Marking*

In Dutch it is necessary to use an independent pronoun along with the inflected verb. A sole inflected verb is not a complete utterance in Dutch. It is often argued that an independent pronoun is necessarily added because of the structurally 'impoverished' inflectional paradigm. However, this is not a necessary requirement for human language. There are also languages that have the same Dutch-type inflectional paradigm, but without obligatory use of independent pronouns. In Lengua, a Mascoian language from Paraguay, the pronominal prefixes show a homophony just like Dutch, exemplified in (2.2). Unlike Dutch, it is not necessary to add an independent pronoun in Lengua. It is left to pragmatic inference to identify the referent. Independent nouns (or independent pronouns) can, of course, be added, as shown in (2.2c).

(2.2) Lengua (Susnik 1977: 98–9)
    a. *ék-çlïngkyïk*
       1-go
       'I go.'
    b. *ab-lïngàé*
       2/3-hear/feel
       'You hear/feel.' or 'S/he hears/feels.'
    c. *ab-waaktêyïk   sēnçlït*
       2/3-return   man.DEM
       'That man returns.'

The pronominal suffixes in Chitimacha, an extinct language from southern USA, also show a structure of the Dutch-type, exemplified in (2.3). Just as in Lengua, it is not felt necessary to clarify the ambiguity of the non-first suffix in Chitimacha:

The [non-first] includes reference to either second or third person, and the actual reference in particular situations depends on the context. Ambiguity may be avoided by the use of the [independent] personal pronoun... but apparently the possibility of confusion is not as great as one might suppose, for sentences without independent pronouns are very common. (Swadesh 1946: 324)

(2.3) Chitimacha (Swadesh 1946: 317)
    a. *get-ik*
       beat-1SG
       'I beat.'
    b. *get-i*
       beat-2/3SG
       'You beat.' or 'S/he beats.'

The Dutch-type homophony is also attested among the Papuan languages from New Guinea (Haiman 1980: xl). In some of these languages, the morpheme for the non-first is zero. This is the opposite markedness situation as in the case of

Dutch, where the first person morpheme was found to be zero. Apparently, it is possible for either of the two elements in an (Sb)-paradigm to be zero. A zero non-first morpheme is found, for example, in the Papuan language Wambon, as shown in (2.4). In Wambon, just as in Lengua and Chitimacha, the use of independent pronouns is not obligatory. They can optionally be used to disambiguate the reference of the 'impoverished' pronominal paradigm (see Section 2.4). As well as in Wambon, a Dutch-type homophony is also found in the verbal suffixes of the closely related languages Kombai (de Vries 1989: 145) and Awju (Boelaars 1950: 70–1), all belonging to the Awyu-Dumut family. Further, this homophony is found in the subject suffixes of the Papuan languages Siroi, a Madang language (Wells 1979: 30–1), Magi, a Mailuan language (Thomson 1975: 631–2), and Moraori, a Trans-Fly language (Boelaars 1950: 46).[4]

(2.4) Wambon (de Vries 1989: 24)
   a. *andet-ep-mbo*
      eat-1SG-PAST
      'I ate.'
   b. *andet-ø-mbo*
      eat-2/3SG-PAST
      'You/he/she/it ate.'

A special kind of Dutch-type homophony is attested among various Tibeto-Burman languages. In the literature on these languages, the phenomenon is commonly referred to as a CONJUNCT/DISJUNCT system, following Hale (1980). Conjunct marking is used for first person and disjunct for both second and third person, as exemplified in (2.5). The special characteristic of these structures is that the marking of conjunct and disjunct is reversed in various sentence types, typically in complement clauses and questions. However, for the current discussion it suffices to note that there is a Dutch-type homophony in these languages. A homophony has been described for Tibetan, Monpa, Newari, Akha (DeLancey 1992), Dumi (van Driem 1993: 143–4), and Bunan (Sharma 1996: 93–5).

(2.5) Kathmandu Newari
   (DeLancey 1992: 40–1, citing Hargreaves)
   a. *ji*   *wan-ā*
      1SG.PRON   go-1PAST
      'I went.'
   b. *cha*   *wan-a*
      2SG.PRON   go-2/3PAST
      'You went.'

---

[4] Laycock (1977) mentions the independent pronouns of the Papuan languages Morwap and Amanab as examples of a Dutch-type homophony, although he does not include any data on these languages. These languages are cited without checking by Mühlhäusler (2001: 741). More recent information on Amanab does not substantiate Laycock's claim on this language (Minch 1991: 31–2). I have not been able to check the Morwap claim.

c. *wo*   *wan-a*
   3SG.PRON   go-2/3PAST
   'S/he went.'

A comparable system to the Tibeto-Burman conjunct/disjunct system is found in the Barbacoan languages from Ecuador. In Awa Pit, both statements and questions have a Dutch-type homophony (Curnow 1997: 189–202).[5] Curnow notes that the independent pronouns are not obligatorily used:

> Awa Pit recognises the 'usual' three persons lexically, in its pronouns.... Of course the common ellipsis in Awa Pit means that the personal pronouns are not often used, except to indicate emphasis or to disambiguate utterances. (p. 189)

In all cases discussed so far, the homophony is attested in bound morphology. However, it is also possible for independent pronouns to show this unusual structure, as illustrated in (2.6) by examples from Qawesqar, an Alcalufan language from Chile. The pronoun *ce* is used for first person and *caw* for second and third person. There is no person inflection in Qawesqar, so there is no automatic disambiguation of the homophony. I have been unable to find an example with a third person singular reference of *caw* in the grammar by Clairis (1985). However, the pronouns do not distinguish number, so I have given here an example with third person plural reference instead.

(2.6) Qawesqar (Clairis 1985: 463–4)
   a. *ce*   *as*   *seqwe*
     1PRON go   FUT
     'Voy a ir.' (I will go.)

   b. *qwa*   *caw*   *cefanas*   *seqwe*
     WH   2/3PRON   drink   FUT
     '¿Qué cosa vas a tomar?' (What do you want to drink?)

   c. *ce*   *caw*   *asa*   *qwaloq*
     1PRON   2/3PRON   go   know
     'Les voy a enseñar que me voy.' (I will tell them that I go.)

To conclude this survey of the Dutch-type (Sb) homophony, I quickly review the remaining few examples from around the globe.[6] First, the aorist and

---

[5] Curnow (1997: 189, citing Vásquez de Ruíz) mentions Guambino as another Barbacoan language with a first/non-first markedness structure. Tsafiki, a third Barbacoan language, shows a related structure, but Dickinson (1999: 31) argues that the marking 'is clearly not coding subject agreement. [...It] only occurs when the source of the information is also a primary participant in the state or event.' She shows that this primary participant can refer to any person, depending on the context and verb semantics.

[6] The pronominal prefixes from almost all Semitic, Cushitic, and Berber languages (all belonging to the Afro-Asiatic stock) have a regular homophony between second person singular and third person singular feminine, but a different prefix for third person singular masculine (Hetzron 1990: 660). These are not included here because there is no complete second/third homophony.

imperfect inflection from the Southern Slavonic languages show a homophony between second and third person singular, the homophonous persons being zero-marked. The homophony is already attested in Old Church Slavonic (de Bray 1951: 17–20) and in the modern Southern Slavonic languages Bulgarian, Macedonian, and Serbo-Croatian (de Bray 1951: 225, 287–9, 342–3). A Dutch-type homophony for the aorist and imperfect is even reconstructed for proto-Slavonic (Schenker 1993: 98–9), although it is not attested in any of the other extant Slavonic languages. Second, the pronominal prefixes for intransitive subject in the Siberian Chukotko-Kamchatkan languages (viz. Chukchee, Koryak, and Kamchadal) show this structure (Comrie 1980a). Third, a Dutch-type homophony is found in various Nakh-Dagestanian languages from the Caucasus. Helmbrecht (1996: 136–8) presents the languages Tsakhur, Zakatal', Akhvakh, and Megeb as showing an opposition between first and non-first. Both in the Chukotko-Kamchatkan and in the Nakh-Dagestanian case, the non-first categories are marked as zero. Finally, in Kenuzi-Dongola, a Sudanic language in Africa, there is a regular homophony between second and third person, through all tenses and aspects. The examples in (2.7) are from the Dongola dialect.[7]

(2.7) Kenuzi-Dongola (Reinisch 1879: 67)
    a. *ai*   *tóg-ri*
        1SG.PRON   beat-1SG
        'I beat.'
    b. *er*   *tóg-im*
        2SG.PRON   beat-2/3SG
        'You beat.'
    c. *ter*   *tóg-im*
        3SG.PRON   beat-2/3SG
        'S/he beats.'

2.3.2 Spanish-type homophony (Sc)

In paradigms of type (Sc), the marking of speaker and other is identical, as opposed to the marking of addressee. In other words, there is an opposition between the marking of second person and the marking of non-second person. Examples of type (Sc) are rare, but paradigms of type (Sc) do exist. Perhaps surprisingly, this type of homophony is found in the Spanish inflection, though

---

[7] Wiesemann (1986a: viii) claims that Bolante, a West Atlantic language from Guinée Bissau is an example of a Dutch-type homophony, although she does not mention her source. Sasse (1993: 670) repeats this claim without checking; alas, because it appears to be an error. N'diaye-Correard (1970: 108) shows that both the personal prefixes and the independent pronouns have a Latin-type paradigm distinguishing three persons in the singular. The prefixes *ha-* and *bɔ-* that are mentioned by Wiesemann as homophonous person markers are in fact class markers for the human singular and plural, respectively (N'diaye-Correard 1970: 20).

TABLE 2.1. *Spanish non-periphrastic paradigms*

All singular persons different	1st and 3rd person singular identical
Indicative present Indicative preterite Indicative future	Indicative imperfect Indicative conditional Subjunctive present Subjunctive imperfect Subjunctive future

not in all paradigms. It is exemplified in (2.8) with forms of the imperfect. This homophony is not only found in the imperfect but in many of the various tense-aspect-mood inflections. In Table 2.1, all non-periphrastic inflectional tense-aspect-mood categories are presented, showing that many of them have the non-second homophony (Butt and Benjamin 1988: 185–7). The frequent occurrence of this homophony in Spanish may be surprising, as this language is often quoted as a prototypical example of a language with 'rich agreement' (e.g. Harbert 1995: 221–2). Rich agreement in turn is presented as one of the preconditions for pro-drop. Spanish indeed has pro-drop, so logically a homophony between first and third person would qualify these paradigms as 'rich' (see Section 2.4). I will use the label SPANISH-TYPE as a mnemonic device for this homophony, interchangeably with the label (Sc). Also within the Romance family, a Spanish-type homophony is also found in the imperfect inflection from Siciliano (Bigalke 1997: 60–1).

(2.8) Spanish (personal knowledge)
    a. *habla-ba-ø*
       speak-PAST-1/3SG
       'I spoke.' or 'S/he spoke.'
    b. *habla-ba-s*
       speak-PAST-2SG
       'You spoke.'

Another example of a Spanish-type homophony is found in the Papuan language Koiari. In Koiari, the portmanteau suffixes for person-tense-mood display a typical Papuan realis/irrealis opposition. In all realis paradigms, the first person singular is equivalent to the third person singular (using the suffix *-nu* or *-ma*) but different from the second person singular (using a suffix *-nua* or *-a*). This is shown in (2.9) for the past suffixes. In the closely related language Ömie, a comparable non-second person homophony is attested, notably in the present tense (Austing and Upia 1975: 544).

(2.9) Koiari (Dutton 1996: 24)
    a. *da*   *ereva-nu*
        1SG.PRON   see-1/3 SG.PAST
        'I saw it.'

    b. *a*   *ereva-nua*
        2SG.PRON   see-2SG.PAST
        'You saw it'.

    c. *ahu*   *ereva-nu*
        3SG.PRON   see-1/3.PAST
        'S/he saw it'.

The 'defective' pronominal paradigm in Koiari is supplemented by independent pronouns. These pronouns in Koiari are probably obligatorily used, as all examples in the short grammatical sketch by Dutton (1996) have an overt subject, either an independent pronoun or a full noun phrase. Also, the use of an independent pronoun does not add emphasis. Instead, pronouns are fronted to add emphasis (including an emphatic suffix *-ike*). When such a fronted emphatic pronoun is used, the 'unmarked' independent pronoun still shows up in the sentence, as shown in (2.10). This indicates that the independent pronoun is obligatorily present.

(2.10) Koiari (Dutton 1996: 64)
    da-ike,   *kailaki-ge*   *da*   *guramarero*
    1SG.PRON-EMPH   PLACE-LOC   1SG.PRON   sit[8]
    'I live at Kailiki.' or 'I am the one who is living at Kailiki.'

A Spanish-type homophony is also found in Ika, a Chibchan language from Peru. Most morphology in Ika is suffixed, but the pronominal inflection is prefixed. For the marking of the subject there is only one prefix in the singular: a second person *nʌ-*. There is no overt marking for the other singular participants. This amounts to a homophony of type (Sc), with a zero for the non-second person marking. Just as in Koiari, Ika has a mechanism to disambiguate first person from third person. All ambiguity in Ika vanishes once the total marking in the sentence is taken into account. The independent pronouns are normally not used (Frank 1990: 26, 121–2). In Ika, however, ambiguity is not resolved by the use of independent pronouns, but by auxiliaries. There is ample use of auxiliaries in Ika, incorporating the marking of tense and evidentiality. Interestingly, time deixis interferes with person deixis in these auxiliaries. In Table 2.2, the singular forms of the various past tenses of the verb *tšua*, meaning 'to see', are shown (Frank 1985: 89). The same form of the auxiliary, *ukuin*, is used for immediate past in the second person, but also for unmarked past in the first person. The use of this

---

[8] This verb is in an irrealis tense, which is not inflected for person (Dutton 1996: 23).

48 Person Marking

TABLE 2.2. *Ika singular person marking*

	Immediate past	Past	Far past
Speaker	ø-tšua uwin	ø-tšua ukuin	ø-tšua-na-rua
Addressee	nʌ-tšua ukuin	nʌ-tšua užin	nʌ-tšua-na
Other	ø-tšua ʌwin	ø-tšua užin	ø-tšua-na

auxiliary thus implies some sort of person deixis. It is unclear whether these auxiliaries should be interpreted as tense markers or as person markers. They are something in between tense and person markers. Frank (1985: 90) concludes: 'Considered as markers of "degree of relevance" or "distance between verbs and reference point", the [auxiliaries] make more sense. Person, time and (un-) witness all enter into the relationship between an event and the speech situation.'

Finally, examples of the Spanish-type (Sc) homophony are also found in the Germanic family. Currently, it is found in the German past and in the indicative preterite and subjunctive inflection of weak verbs in modern Icelandic. The morphophonological form of these suffixes in Icelandic falls into six classes, but all show the same structural (Sc) homophony (Thráinsson 1994: 159). The Spanish-type homophony in the preterite is also found in older versions of Germanic languages, notably in Gothic, Middle Dutch (Schönfeld 1959: 144–6), and Old English (Robertson and Cassidy 1954: 141). Interestingly, in all early Germanic languages the independent pronouns were not as strictly obligatory as they are today, although they were regularly used (Howe 1996: 11–13). The Old English homophonous paradigm, for example, was not connected to the obligatory use of the subject pronoun. The pronoun could be dropped in Old English, although an overt subject reference had to be not too far away:

In PDE [Present Day English] it is obligatory for the subject position...to be filled...In early OE [Old English], the NP was facultative, as in Latin...However, in OE, 'subjectless' sentences were restricted to cases where the subject had been named in the preceding clause. (Görlach 1997: 91)

2.3.3 English-type homophony (Sd)

In paradigms of type (Sd), speaker and addressee are marked identically, as opposed to the marking of the category 'other'. This paradigm is a borderline case of person marking, as there is no opposition between speaker and addressee. English is one of the 'exotic' cases that show this homophony in the marking of singular participants. English has a homophony of type (Sd) in its inflectional marking: zero for first and second person, -s for third person. I will use the label ENGLISH-TYPE to indicate this paradigmatic structure of person marking, interchangeably with (Sd).

An English-type homophony, but with opposite markedness as in English, is found in the present tense of Hunzib, a Nakh-Dagestanian language from the Caucasus. The present tense suffix has two different forms: *-č(o)* for first or second person and zero for third person. Examples are shown in (2.11). The same homophony of speaker and addressee reference is found in the related Nakh-Dagestanian language Lak (Helmbrecht 1996: 131).

(2.11)   Hunzib (van den Berg 1995: 83)
    a. *də*   *hīyaa-č*   *ə̃cu*
       1SG.PRON open-1/2.PRES door
       'I (shall) open the door.'
    b. *mə*   *bok'o.l-čo*   *heƛe*
       2SG.PRON gather-1/2.PRES walnut
       'You will gather walnuts.'
    c. *oλul*   *hīyaa-ø*   *ə̃cu*
       DEM   open-3.PRES   door
       'S/he opens the door.'

This paradigmatic structure is also found in the imperfect tense of the South Caucasian language Svan, a neighbour of Hunzib, though unrelated to it (Tuite 1997: 23–9). It is questionable whether these Caucasian paradigms really should be considered pronominal marking. It is probably better to consider them as tense marking, with a slightly different status of the third person in the paradigm. Just as in Ika, in the previous section, different deictic categories (time and participant deixis) are intermingled, making it difficult to classify the paradigm as one or the other. The same can be argued for English, as the suffix *-s* is only used in the present tense—so it is in fact just as much a tense marker as it is a person marker.

A paradigm of the English-type, with both third and non-third overtly marked, is found in the Papuan language Waskia. Waskia has a typical Papuan realis/irrealis distinction in the verbal inflection. The realis marking consists of three tenses (present, past habitual, past simple). All three have an English-type homophony. The forms of the present tense are shown in (2.12). Examples (2.12a, b) show the suffix *-sam*, which is used both with first and with second person. Example (2.12c) shows the suffix *-so* that is used with third person. Independent pronouns are regularly used to clarify the subject, as in examples (2.12a, b):

In unmarked sentences ... the subject is *not* normally omitted from declaratives and questions, but it is often deleted from imperatives. It is also missing in all impersonal sentences. (Ross and Paol 1978: 8; emphasis added)

However, a different impression arises when all subject marking is counted in the short accompanying text (Ross and Paol 1978: 110–15). It turns out that, contrary to the above quotation, it is quite normal to omit the subject. For the forty-six inflected verbs in the text (counting all three persons, imperatives omitted), there are only twenty-six overt subjects (46 per cent). Slightly more than half of the subjects are omitted in this text. This indicates that the presence of a subject is not really obligatory, although it is common.

(2.12) Waskia (Ross and Paol 1978: 67, 112, 49)
    a. *ane   itakta   yu   na-sam*
       1SG.PRON   now   water   drink-1/2SG.PRES
       'I am drinking water now.'
    b. *'ai   ni   ait   omu   arigi-sam   i?*
       hey   2SG.PRON   bird   DEM   see-1/2SG.PRES   WH
       'Hey, do you see that bird?'
    c. *Gagi   kaemkasik   ko   nagu-so*
       NAME   evil spirit   about   fear-3SG.PRES
       'Gagi fears the evil spirit.'

An English-type homophony is also found in the perfective suffixes from the Semitic language Maltese (Aquilina 1965: 131) and in the subject prefixes of Krongo, a language spoken in Sudan (Reh 1985: 185). I know three examples of this type among American languages. The first case is the Oto-Manguean language Pame, which has a suffix *-p* for third person and a suffix *-k* for non-third (Manrique 1967: 344). The second example is the Sahaptin language Nez Perce. In intransitive constructions, as shown in (2.13), the third person is marked by a prefix *hi-* and the non-third by zero marking. The independent pronouns can be optionally added; they are shown in brackets in the example sentences.

(2.13) Nez Perce (Rude 1985: 31)
    a. *('íin)   páayna*
       1SG.PRON   arrive
       'I arrived.'
    b. *('íim)   páayna*
       2SG.PRON   arrive
       'You arrived.'
    c. *('ipí)   hi-páayna*
       3SG.PRON   3-arrive
       'He arrived.'

The final example of an English-type homophony is attested in the Siouan language Winnebago. In contrast to all previous cases, in Winnebago the homophonous person markers are morphologically independent particles, *e* for third person and *ne* for all other persons (Lipkind 1945: 29). For some unspecified reason, Lipkind refrains from calling them pronouns. However, there are no other

TABLE 2.3. *Waskia singular irrealis suffixes*

	Future	Imperative	Desiderative
Speaker	...-iki	...-iko	...-ako
Addressee	...-i	...-ko	...-ako
Other	...-uki	...-uko	...-ako

independent words that could be called pronouns except for these particles. So either these particles are pronouns or there are no pronouns in this language.

2.3.4 French-type homophony (Se)

In the paradigms of type (Se), all the singular persons are marked identically, so it is not clear whether such a paradigm really marks person, or rather something else. For example, consider the irrealis suffixes from Waskia, a Papuan language from New Guinea. The singular forms of these suffixes are shown in Table 2.3 as they are presented by Ross and Paol (1978: 68). The future and the imperative paradigms clearly mark person; they are of the Latin-type (Sa). In contrast, the desiderative paradigm does not mark person. The suffix *-ako* only marks the desiderative mood. A comparable phenomenon is found in the past inflection of Dutch. The Dutch past is marked by *-de* for all persons in the singular and by *-den* in the non-singular. Historically, this inflection distinguished various person categories (Schönfeld 1959: 144–6), but nowadays it marks only singular versus non-singular, not person.

For there to be person marking with a homophony of type (Se), there has to be an opposition in the non-singular person categories (which does not exist in the desiderative of Waskia nor in the past of Dutch). To my knowledge, such a situation is highly unusual among the world's languages. The inflectional person marking of French is a good example of a homophony of type (Se). There is no phonological person marking in the singular *chante/chantes/chante*. There is of course a difference in spelling but no difference in pronunciation. However, there is a difference in the plural between the first and second person: *chantons* versus *chantez*. A comparable case is the Italian present subjunctive, which has identical shape in all singular persons but different forms in the plural (Schwarze 1988: 79). Two other examples are the Icelandic middle verb inflection (Thráinsson 1994: 162) and the past verb inflection from the Papuan language Kapau (Oates and Oates 1969: 34–5).

It is often difficult to draw the line between a French-type (Se) homophony and number marking. One could argue that the endings of *chantons* and *chantez* are number markers that incidentally happen to have developed different forms for the two persons. This might sound awkward (and historically it is, of course, not true for French), but this is exactly the situation in the Algonquian languages.

In Southwestern Ojibwe, for example, number is marked by suffixes which have different forms for first person (*-min*), second person (*-m*), and third person (*-wak*) (Schwartz and Dunnigan 1986: 305). A comparable split of number marking is also observed in Huave, a language spoken in Mexico (Stairs and Hollenbach 1969: 48–53). A thorough diachronic investigation of such cases might reveal whether these splits in the number marking are historically diminished person paradigms, comparable to French, or whether they have another origin.

2.3.5 Summary

Homophony of singular pronominal marking is a rare phenomenon, but it is definitely a possibility for human language. The large number of examples in this section might suggest that it is relatively normal for a pronominal paradigm to have a homophony in the singular. However, it is not—for two reasons. First, only a restricted set of all the pronominal paradigms of each language shows the homophony. All languages that were mentioned have a homophony but the homophony is never a characteristic of all pronominal paradigms in the language. Second, to obtain this collection, I have explicitly looked for examples instead of using a strict typological sampling procedure. My impression is that singular homophony is too rare a phenomenon to reach a noticeable frequency in a strict typological sample. Because of the scarce occurrence, it is difficult to estimate the frequency of singular homophony among the world's languages. The present fifty-six cases amount to 0.8 per cent of the ±6,700 languages in the world (following the numbers from the Ethnologue). To be on the safe side, my informed guess is that singular homophony maximally occurs in about 2 per cent of the world's languages.

The cases presented in this survey are summarized in Table 2.4. In the table, the types are subdivided as to the occurrence of zeros in one of the categories. Only one of the theoretical possibilities is not attested in this survey: the Spanish-type homophony with a zero second. Perhaps this last possibility will appear when the search is continued (see Section 2.5.1 for a discussion of the distribution of the zeros).

Looking at the relative frequencies, the Dutch-type homophony is clearly more common than the others. Using terminology as proposed by Heath (forthcoming), the consciousness model of person marking (opposing first person to second/third) is more frequent than the speech role model (opposition first/second to third) or the pragmatic model (opposing second to first/third). This skewing does not indicate any universal law of linguistic structure, as all kinds of homophony are attested in high enough frequencies to establish them as possible structures of human language. However, the number of languages with an opposition between first and non-first indicates a preference for human language to single out the speaker from the other participants when marking person.

TABLE 2.4. *Typological summary of examples of singular homophony*

Occurrence of zeros	Examples
'Dutch-type' (Sb)	
No zeros	Papuan (Awyu, Moraori, Siroi), Tibeto-Burman (Akha, Newari, Tibetan, Monpa, Dumi, Bunan), Barbacoan (Awa-Pit, Guambino), Lengua, Qawesqar, Chitimacha, Kenuzi-Dongola
First is zero	Germanic (Dutch, Icelandic)
Non-first is zero	Papuan (Wambon, Kombai), South Slavonic (Old Church Slavonic, Bulgarian, Macedonian, Serbocroatian), Chukotko-Kamchatkan (Chukchee, Koryak, Kamchadal), Nakh Dagestanian (Tsakhur, Akhvakh, Zakatal', Megeb)
'Spanish-type' (Sc)	
No zeros	Papuan (Koiari, Ömie), Siciliano
Second is zero	—
Non-second is zero	Germanic (Icelandic, German, Gothic, Old English, Middle Dutch), Spanish, Ika
'English-type' (Sd)	
No zeros	Waskia, Lak, Maltese, Nez Perce, Winnebago, Krongo
Third is zero	Hunzib, Svan
Non-third is zero	English, Pame
'French-type' (Se)	
No zeros	Italian, Kapau
Singular is zero	French, Icelandic, Algonquian (?), Huave (?)

An important generalization from the examples presented in this section is that singular homophony is almost exclusively found in inflectional paradigms. Only two examples of singular homophony are attested in independent pronouns, namely in Qawesqar and Winnebago. This observation can be formulated as a statistical implication in (2.14). In the logically reversed version in (2.15), the implication states that independent pronouns preferably do not have a homophony in the singular. In other words, for independent pronouns it is necessary to distinguish clearly the three main singular categories.

(2.14) Homophony Implication

singular homophony → inflectional paradigm

(2.15) Homophony Implication (reversed formulation)

independent pronouns → speaker ≠ addressee ≠ other

It should not be concluded from this implication that all languages have at least three different overt independent pronouns—one for speaker, one for addressee, and one for other. This conclusion is not allowed for three reasons. First, there are

54 Person Marking

at least two counterexamples (Qawesqar and Winnebago). Second, there are languages that do not have 'real' independent pronouns (see Section 1.2.4), and for those languages the antecedent of the implication is not met. Third, the 'other' category is not as straightforward as the 'speaker' and 'addressee' categories. In many languages, the 'other' category is not marked by a specialized pronominal morpheme. All that is implied in the statement in (2.15) is that the marking for 'other' is not identical to the marking of 'speaker' or 'addressee'. The implication makes no claim for the specific linguistic form of the marking of the singular categories; they could also be zero. I will discuss a potential problem with zero marking in the third person in Section 2.5.3.

The fact that singular homophony is mainly attested in inflectional paradigms can easily be explained in the context of grammaticalization. Merger of person oppositions will only happen in the last phase of grammaticalization: the erosion of bound morphology. For the Germanic languages, the 'impoverished' singular marking arose because an original three-way distinction of the Latin type wore off through time. However, for most of the other examples that have been discussed in this section there are no historical records. Moreover, often not enough data are available for a comparative reconstruction. It is thus impossible to say anything definitive about the way these singular paradigms arose. In principle, it seems perfectly possible that homophonous paradigms can arise in other ways than through wear. Constructively, a morpheme for any of the person categories might arise alone, leaving the rest unmarked. Another path towards a homophonous paradigm might lead through mixed marking of different deictic categories, as in Ika and Svan. Future research has to decide whether such a constructive origin of inflectional person marking is indeed possible.

2.4 Singular homophony and pro-drop

In some languages, singular homophony is seen as a problem. The contemporary West Germanic languages, but also Koiari, Waskia, and Ika, show a tendency to disambiguate the homophonous singular persons in some way. In Germanic and in Koiari, the disambiguation is achieved by using independent pronouns that are co-referential with the homophonous inflection. In Ika, a more intricate combination of various linguistic devices does the same job without the use of the independent pronoun (see Section 2.3.2). For many languages, however, it is noted explicitly in the descriptions that the singular homophony in the pronominal paradigm does not lead to a surplus of other markings. In Wambon, Lengua, Chitimacha, Spanish, Awa Pit, and Nez Perce it is no problem that the singular homophony creates some ambiguity in the structure of the language. Most of the time, enough information is present in the discourse to fill the referential gaps left by a homophonous paradigm. The speakers of many languages do not find it necessary to disambiguate the three singular persons all the time. It seems perfectly possible for a human language to do without a morphological distinction between all three persons.

To exemplify the different impact of singular homophony, I will make a comparison of the person marking in Wambon and English. Wambon and English both are languages with a singular homophony. In the English inflection, the speaker and the addressee are marked identically. In the Wambon inflection, the addressee and the other are marked identically (see Section 2.3.1). Still, there is an important difference between these languages. English uses its independent pronouns obligatorily; Wambon does not. To show the differences and correspondences between person marking in Wambon and English, I have analysed the use of inflection and independent pronouns as they occur in the Wambon texts as included in the grammar by de Vries (1989). I will concentrate on the marking of first person subjects, and compare the Wambon structure with the structure of the English translation by de Vries. This kind of comparison is full of pitfalls, as the structure of Wambon differs strikingly from English. For example, Wambon makes ample use of switch-reference and serialization. Both phenomena strongly influence the structure of the sentence. Still, I think that a comparison of the Wambon texts with the English translation is possible. Remarkably enough, the English translation consists of syntactically correct sentences of English while the style is rather poor. This poor style probably reflects the intention of the grammarian to translate the Wambon text as closely as possible to the original. I interpret the translation as being the closest possible reflection of the original stories in syntactically correct English. From this assumption it is possible to compare the way pronominals are used in the structure of both languages.

The results of the counts are presented in Table 2.5.[9] For the original Wambon texts, as well as for the English translation, the number of independent pronouns in subject function has been counted. The independent pronouns of Wambon hardly occur (only nine cases). By contrast, independent pronouns are often used in the English translation (eighty cases). The number of finite verbs that are marked for first person subject is then counted for Wambon (seventy-four cases). For English, this count is not so straightforward, as there is no inflectional first person marking. In the English translation, I counted the number of finite verbs that have a first person subject (ninety-two cases).[10] The percentage of pronouns per finite verb gives a rough indication of the differences in use between the independent

---

[9] The counts are based on two texts from the grammar by de Vries (1989). The two texts ('the pig hunt', pp. 117–18, and 'sawing', pp. 120–8) are chosen because they have numerous first person subjects. I counted first persons singular and plural for these texts. In the plural, Wambon also has a homophony with an opposition between first and non-first person, so the markedness situation is comparable to the singular. If I had only counted the singular pronominal elements, the number of instances would have been much smaller, and the results less revealing.

[10] The number of English finite verbs (92 cases) is higher than the number of independent pronouns (80 cases) due to conjunction reduction. A sentence like 'I pursued it and saw it lying close' has only one first person subject pronoun ('I') while there are two finite verbs that have a first person subject ('pursued' and 'saw').

TABLE 2.5. *First person marking compared between Wambon and English*

	Wambon	English
Finite verbs in first person	74	92
Independent first person pronouns	9	80
Proportion pronouns per finite verb	12%	87%

pronouns of both languages. Wambon uses a pronoun for 12 per cent of the finite verbs, against 87 per cent for English. Also, the sparse use of the Wambon independent pronoun is not determined by a regular syntactic structure. The function of the independent pronoun of Wambon is to put emphasis on the subject.[11]

The Wambon inflection is the central person-marking device in the language, not the independent pronouns. Although this language has 'impoverished' person-marking inflection, it is not necessary to use the independent pronouns for disambiguation. English also has a homophonous inflection, but in this case it is necessary to use the independent pronouns. This shows that the often-heard argument that English obligatorily uses its independent pronouns *because* of the impaired inflectional system does not hold as a universal characteristic of human language. As can be seen from the Wambon case, it is possible for a human language to have an 'impaired' inflectional pronominal paradigm but still not to use the independent pronouns obligatorily.

This conclusion is at odds with the 'pro-drop' hypothesis or, at least, it restricts the space for its interpretation. Pro-drop, the hypothesis states, is licensed by 'rich agreement':

It has been long noted that *pro*-drop tends to occur in languages with rich subject-agreement morphology, such as Spanish and Italian, but not in languages such as French and English, which have relatively impoverished agreement morphology. (Harbert 1995: 222)

To my knowledge, it has never been made explicit what exactly it means for a personal agreement paradigm to be 'rich'. However, it can be concluded from the examples in this chapter that it is possible to conflate the reference between the three basic singular categories and still have pro-drop. Thus, singular homophony does not necessarily make the paradigms 'poor'.

---

[11] To make a better argument, the use of the independent pronouns should of course be investigated from the structure of the discourse. A full analysis of Wambon discourse is beyond the scope of the present work. Impressionistically, the independent pronouns in Wambon are used at turning points of the story. This indicates that the use of the independent pronouns is at least partially regulated by the structure of the discourse.

The difficulty in formulating cross-linguistically valid characteristics of the richness of a pronominal paradigm has also been noted by Jaeggli and Safir (1989: 27–8). They propose another property of inflectional person marking as the licensing condition for pro-drop: 'null subjects are permitted in all and only languages with morphologically uniform inflectional paradigm' (p. 29). With 'uniform' paradigms they mean, roughly, person marking that is either always zero or never zero. However, the correlation between a non-uniform inflectional paradigm and pro-drop also does not work for the case of Wambon. Nor does it for Spanish, Svan, and Pame, to name just a few languages where I have at least some preliminary indication of the usage of the pronouns. All these languages have non-uniform person marking and pro-drop.[12]

Summarizing, an equivalent singular structure that licenses pro-drop in Wambon (and other languages) prompts English (and other languages) to prevent pro-drop. So the 'richness' of a pronominal paradigm does not reside in the marking of singular participants. Paradigm uniformity does not appear to be the solution to the question because the occurrence of zeros does not correlate with pro-drop. My impression is that the pro-drop phenomenon does not correlate with any feature of inflectional person marking, once a large sample of the world's languages is considered.

2.5 The distribution of zeros

2.5.1 Zeros in homophonous paradigms

Zero marking is particularly common in paradigms with a homophony, as discussed in Section 2.3. The only theoretically possible case that I have not found is a second versus non-second paradigm (Spanish-type) with a zero second person marker (see Table 2.4). This one missing case precisely corresponds to a claim made by Uspensky (1972: 68):

If a zero expression occurs in the form of a certain person in the indicative mood, then, included in the meanings thus expressed (i.e. by a zero mark) we find the meaning of the 3rd person or that of the 1st person.

---

[12] The opposite combination (uniform person marking with non-pro-drop) is attested in German and Icelandic. To explain these problematic cases, Jaeggli and Safir propose that 'the correct approach to this issue is to require that the tense and AGR elements of inflection be represented in the same node' (1989: 33). This method is reminiscent of the proposal by Hawkins (1983) to reach exceptionless implicational universals by concatenating criteria in implicational chains. However, Dryer (1997: 141–2) shows that this method is not valid. The problem is that it is always possible to add an extra criterion to eliminate the last problematic cases, but there is no possibility of validating such a proposal because there are not enough languages to test whether it is an accidental or an essential criterion.

58   *Person Marking*

The data that led to this claim are not made explicit by Uspensky, but he seems to have formulated his claim in exactly these words to account for the various inflectional structures of the Germanic languages. There is no sign in the short article that he knew of all the different possibilities that I have sketched in this chapter. Still, the formulation appears to be a masterful generalization of the cases as described in Section 2.3. However, a few counterexamples to Uspensky's claim will be presented below in Section 2.5.2. These counterexamples are non-homophonous Latin-type paradigms with a zero second person. Another problem with Uspensky's claim is that I can see no reason why just this one case would be impossible for a human language. A much better proposal to explain the missing case has been put forward by Baerman (2001). Reformulated in my own words, his observation is that markedness can explain the distribution of zeros. In a Spanish-type paradigm, the second person is marked relative to non-second person and the marked category is less likely to be zero than the unmarked. This argumentation also holds for the Dutch-type paradigms; here, the paradigms with a zero first person are strongly under-represented. Probably, the missing case is not the result of a strict universal but the result of a tendency to avoid markedness reversals. Eventually, when more languages have been studied, I believe that this last type will also be attested somewhere.

2.5.2   *Zeros for speaker or addressee*

In the vast majority of pronominal paradigms in the world's languages, there is no singular homophony in the paradigm; all three singular persons are marked by different morphemes. In such paradigms, each of the three participants (speaker, addressee, and other) could, in principle, be zero. However, it turns out that not all participants are equally likely to be zero. Specifically, zero marking for speaker or addressee reference is only scantily found among the world's languages (Koch 1994: 31–7; Siewierska and Bakker 2000). Some of the examples that appear at first glance to have zero marking for speaker or addressee turn out to be fallacies.[13]

First person zero marking is extremely rare. The Rumanian present tense is an example (Mallinson 1986: 274). The only other examples that I know are the

---

[13] Some examples of fallacious zeros are found in descriptions of Wiyot, Maba, and Marghi. In the Algic language Wiyot, a zero is described for speaker reference by Reichard (1925: 74), but a later description only lists zero as a possible allomorph for a suffix *-a* (Teeter 1964: 71). For the Nilo-Saharan language Maba, Tucker and Bryan (1966: 202) presents paradigms with a zero second person, but it turns out on closer inspection that this zero is only one of the possible allomorphs (Tucker and Bryan 1966: 195). Finally, Burquest (1986: 77) lists a zero for the speaker reference in the aorist of the Chadic language Marghi. However, this is a misinterpretation of the data in the original source by Hoffmann (1963: 174). Hoffmann gives a paradigm in the aorist without a first person, but this is probably because the examples in the paradigm are questions. Questions to the speaker (i.e. yourself) are probably left out because they are pragmatically strange. There are other examples of aorists in the texts as presented by Hoffmann, and in these examples speaker reference is marked overtly.

pronominal inflections from Alagwa (Whiteley 1958: 32–3; Mous, in preparation: 54–5) and Burunge (Kießling 1994: 124), two Southern Cushitic languages from Tanzania.[14] However, zero-marked first persons occur more often in the marking of kin-term possession (Croft 1990: 145–6; Koch 1994: 51–4). In the context of kin-term possession, the first person seems to be the unmarked participant, and consequently it is sometimes found marked as zero. I cannot judge whether the preference for zero first person marking is cross-linguistically far-reaching in such constructions, because I have not included the marking of pronominal possession in the present investigation.

Pronominal paradigms with a zero addressee reference are slightly more frequent compared to paradigms with a first person zero, although the overall number of examples is so low that it is difficult to judge whether this difference is typologically valid. The first example with a zero addressee comes from Bongo, a Nilo-Saharan language from Sudan. In Bongo, the pronouns cliticize in front of the verb in the past tense, as in (2.16a), but remain independent when there is another word in between the pronoun and the verb, as in (2.16b). The first person singular pronoun *ma* cliticizes as *m-*, see (2.16c), but the second person singular pronoun *i* disappears altogether, leaving a zero, shown in (2.16d).[15]

(2.16) Bongo (Santandrea 1963: 62, 94)
    a. *b-ony*
       3SG-eat
       'He/she/it ate.'
    b. *'da   bu   dukpa amony 'bu kururi kpáu*
       then 3SG.PRON after eat   eggs python all
       'So he then ate all the eggs of the python.'
    c. *m-ony*
       1SG-eat
       'I ate.'
    d. *ø-ony*
       2SG-eat
       'You ate.'

Another example of a zero marked for addressee reference is found in Grebo, a Kru language from Liberia. In many Kru languages the first and second person independent pronouns can be omitted when they directly precede certain

---

[14] There does not appear to be a zero first person in the closely related language Iraqw (Elderkin 1988: 81–2). However, after some cumbersome morphophonological analyses, Elderkin (p. 87) concludes that 'verbs with obstruent stems seem to have ø marking first person'.

[15] A comparable phenomenon is found in the related language Bagirmi. For Bagirmi, a disappearing second person pronoun clitic is described in Gaden (1909: 10, 15). In a short description of another related language, Beli, it is noted that there are no clitic forms of the pronoun (Santandrea 1963: 110).

auxiliaries; in those cases person is marked by different tones on the auxiliary (Marchese 1978: 121). Grebo is a special case among the Kru languages, since the pronouns can be omitted with all indicative verbs, also without the presence of an auxiliary. In that case, the lexical verbs show tonal differences to mark person (Innes 1966: 62–3). However, when the pronouns are overtly present— with no person-marking tone—then there is no overt marking of the second person in the indicative mood (Innes 1966: 50, 61). The second person exists in other moods (and in the indicative of other Kru languages: Marchese 1978: 117–18) but not in the indicative of Grebo, as exemplified in (2.17).

(2.17) GREBO (Innes 1966: 61)
    a. *ne₁*   *du₁ nɛ₄ ne₃*
       1SG.PRON   pound
       'I have pounded it.'

    b. ø   *du₄ nɛ₄ ne₃*
       2SG.PRON   pound
       'You have pounded it.'

A different kind of zero addressee marking is linked to the imperative. Imperatives are prototypically directed to the addressee; addressee reference is the unmarked situation for an imperative. Consequently, imperatives are normally zero marked for addressee reference (Kurylowicz 1964: 241; Greenberg 1966: 44; Koch 1994: 57–9). Imperatives are a possible source for zero-marked addressees in other constructions. In most languages, the imperative is a special construction, not marked for person at all. In some languages, however, the imperative is generalized to include other manipulative speech acts (Givón 1990: 806–24). Such moods are often marked for person with a zero addressee. This is, for example, found in the Papuan language Daga. The imperative in Daga has a debitive meaning: 'the imperative suffixes cover the area of meaning of "must" and "should"' (Murane 1974: 56). This meaning is also relevant with first and third person subjects. The person marking of this debitive in Daga, presented in (2.18), shows a Latin-type paradigm with a zero addressee.

(2.18) Daga (Murane 1974: 56)
    a. *war-ap*
       get-1SG.DEB
       'I must get (it).'

    b. *wat-ø*
       get-2SG.DEB
       'You must get (it).' or 'Get (it)!'

    c. *war-ep*
       get-3SG.DEB
       'He must get (it).'

Singular Persons 61

A comparable case with zero addressee reference is found in the irrealis suffixes in the Papuan language Waskia. These suffixes were shown earlier in this chapter in Table 2.3. They can be analysed as showing a suffix *-i* for future and a suffix *-ko* for imperative. In both cases, the addressee marking is zero. Just as in Daga, this imperative in Waskia is better analysed as a debitive: 'the imperative ... denotes not only the imperative as in English ... but also concepts expressed in the English modal verbs "must", "should" and "ought to"' (Ross and Paol 1978: 69).

2.5.3 Zeros for third person

Zero marking for speaker or addressee is rare among the languages of the world. In contrast, a zero for the marking of the 'other' participant is found commonly, in all parts of the world. This predominance is easily explained by basic markedness. The third person is the unmarked person, and the unmarked person has the highest probability of being zero. However, to conclude that a language has a zero is in principle, a dangerous statement. A zero is not directly observable, and there should be good reasons to propose an empty category. This is a general problem in all morphological analysis, but it becomes particularly important in the case of a zero third person. In contrast to the first and second person, the third person is not a positively defined category: a third person is defined negatively as the category that is not first or second. A good argument is necessary to propose zero marking for this 'non-person' (Benveniste 1966: 228–31). A reasonable argument for the existence of a zero third can be made when the first and second person marking are overt inflections. When an uninflected stem occurs that is paradigmatically equivalent to first and second person, and that is functionally in complementary distribution with first and second person, then it is fairly safe to propose a zero third person. The Mongolian language Buriat is an example of a language with zero third person for subject reference, illustrated in (2.19). The first and second person are marked by overt suffixes, different from each other, but the third person does not have an overt suffix. The verbs without suffix have a strict reference: these verbs do not refer to speaker or addressee. This is enough reason to propose a zero third person suffix.

(2.19) Buriat (Poppe 1960: 57)
    a. *jaba-na-b*
       go-PRES-1SG
       'I go.'
    b. *jaba-na-š*
       go-PRES-2SG
       'You go.'
    c. *jaba-na-ø*
       go-PRES-3SG
       'He/she/it goes.'

62   Person Marking

This phenomenon is found regularly in the languages of the world. The following list presents a rough outline of the geographical distribution. This is not intended as an exhaustive listing of this phenomenon, but it should give an impression of the areas where inflectional third person zero forms are found. To start, it is rather unusual to find zero third persons in Africa: there are only some incidental cases in Nilo-Saharan.[16] Travelling through the Eurasian continent, zero third persons are rarely found within Indo-European. Only the languages of the Brythonic subgroup of the Celtic languages have a zero third person.[17] It is found more often in Uralic, both in the Ugric and in the Samoyedic languages.[18] Also, zero third persons seem to be widespread in Altaic.[19] In contrast, zero third persons are only rarely found in the Semitic family.[20] A zero third person has been reconstructed for proto-Sino-Tibetan, and still a large part of the contemporary Sino-Tibetan languages actually show a third person zero (DeLancey 1987: 806–9). Because there is hardly any bound pronominal marking among the languages from mainland South-East Asia, there is no chance of finding a zero third person in inflectional patterns. The same holds for many Austronesian languages, which have mainly independent pronominal marking. Zero third person forms appear to be rare among those Austronesian languages that have inflectional person marking. In contrast, third person zeros are common among the non-Austronesian languages in New Guinea in paradigms for inflectional undergoer marking.[21] In Australia, roughly half of the languages have pronominal clitics. These regularly show third person zeros.[22] In North America, third person zeros are common; in South America they seem to occur much less frequently.[23]

---

[16] e.g. Madi (Crazzolara 1960: 72–3, 83–4), Temein (Tucker and Bryan 1966: 258–9), Didinga (Odden 1983: 154–7, 166), and Tubu, a dialect of Teda (Lukas 1953: 111).

[17] e.g. Breton (Stephens 1993: 373–5) and Cornish (George 1993: 446–7).

[18] In the Ugric family, see e.g. Hungarian (Tompa 1968: 167), Mansi (Keresztes 1998: 399–400), and Khanti (Abondolo 1998a: 372–4). In the Samoyedic family, see e.g. Nganasan (Helimski 1998: 502–4) and Nenets (Salminen 1998: 533–4).

[19] e.g. Buriat, shown in example (2.19) and Turkish (Lewis 1967: 106).

[20] In roughly all Semitic languages/dialects the third person masculine of the perfect is zero. I do not include this as a case of third person zero in this list because there is generally an overt third person feminine suffix in the same paradigm. That is, I follow the general analysis of occidental linguists in putting the feminine suffix in the same paradigm as the other pronominal suffixes; consequently, the third person is not completely zero. Note though, that the classical Arabic linguistic tradition did not include the feminine suffix among the pronominal suffixes, for good reasons (Versteegh 1997: 80–1). In contrast, there is a real zero third person found in the enclitic personal pronouns of some of the modern Aramaic variants Mandaic (Macuch 1965: 155) and Neo-Aramaic Assyrian (Tsereteli 1978: 57, 60).

[21] e.g. Daga (Murane 1974: 44), Yagaria (Renck 1975: 21), and Siroi (Wells 1979: 28).

[22] Dixon (1980: 363–70) gives the Western Desert languages and Walmatjari as examples of zero third person clitics.

[23] In North America, zero third persons are found consistently in the Yuman languages (e.g. Maricopa: Gordon 1986: 15–21) and the Muskogean languages (e.g. Chickasaw: Payne 1982: 359). Other cases are Tonkawa (Hoijer 1933: 72–6) and Kwakiutl (Boas 1947: 252). In South America, examples are much more difficult to find. Incidental examples are the object affixes in Ika (Frank 1990: 52) and the object affixes in Huallaga Quechua (Weber 1986: 334).

The zeros in the inflectional morphology are fairly straightforward. However, some languages are said to have a zero third person marker in the paradigm of morphologically independent pronouns. These missing markers are much more prone to be misinterpreted when they are called zeros. Often, a third person independent pronoun simply does not exist. The function fulfilled by an overt third person pronoun as attested in West European languages is fulfilled by other linguistic means in such languages. There are numerous possibilities for a language to express the function of an independent third person pronoun. For example, a demonstrative ('this', 'that', etc.) can be used, or a full noun phrase ('the man'), or a proper name ('John'). As every language already has multiple means to express third person, it seems better to assume a priori that non-bound third person pronouns do not exist. Such an approach seems better than to generate needless zeros.[24]

A particularly fine example showing that zero third person independent pronouns are sometimes better interpreted as non-existing is the pronominal marking from Yidiɲ, a Pama-Nyungan language from Australia. Yidiɲ has independent first and second person pronouns and no pronominal inflection or clitics on the predicate, as is shown in (2.20a, b). The third person pronoun is 'zero'. Normally, no marking at all is present for a third person subject, as shown in (2.20c). Other linguistic means, like demonstratives or full noun phrases, can be used for clarification, but these are often not used because the reference is clear from the context. Moreover, there is positive evidence that the absence of pronominal marking does not imply the presence of a zero. In Yidiɲ, the meaning 'third person' cannot be inferred from the absence of any marking because it is also possible for first or second person subject to be zero, as shown in (2.20d). It has to be contextually determined who is the subject of sentences like (2.20c, d); there is no unambiguous linguistic clue (Dixon 1977: 165–94).

(2.20)   Yidiɲ (Dixon 1977: 516, 527, 528, 531)
  a. ɲayu   ḍuŋga:na
     1SG.PRON   run.PURP
     'I had to run.'

  b. ɲundu   gana   waŋga:ḍin
     2SG.PRON   try   get up.IMPERF
     'You try to wake up.'

  c. ḍuŋga:ɲ
     run.PAST
     'He ran away.'

---

[24] The same problem (whether non-overt independent pronouns are zero or simply do not exist) arises by the zero second person independent pronoun in Grebo from example (2.17). My impression is that the zero in Grebo is indeed better interpreted as non-existing. This also seems to be the way it is dealt with in the description by Innes (1966: 50, 61).

64   *Person Marking*

      d. *banḍi:ldaɲu   bama   ŋabi*
         find come   person   many
      'I came and found lots of people.'

The crucial argument for the existence of a zero is that the counterpart (here: speaker and addressee marking) is obligatorily marked in a certain 'slot' of the linguistic structure. The emptiness of this slot can then be interpreted as having a meaning:

[A zero] is therefore possible only under specific circumstances and in a specific context, namely one that allows, or even favours, the evocation of the (absent) paradigmatic counterpart. A hearer, however, can be expected to notice an absence 'automatically' only if the missing counterpart is itself 'automatic'—i.e. very probable—in the particular context. In short, a syntactic zero is possible only when the non-occurring (positive) alternative is so likely that it in fact constitutes the norm. (Garcia and van Putte 1989: 369–70)

In case of inflectional marking, this is obviously true. Inflectional paradigms have—by definition—a fixed linguistic 'slot', and the non-occurrence of any marking in this slot can be given a linguistic interpretation. In the case of independent pronouns, this is not necessarily the case. Often, independent pronouns are relatively free to occur in various places in the sentence, and the absence of a pronoun is not a linguistic sign. As illustrated by the example from Yidiɲ the absence of an independent pronoun cannot always be interpreted as a reference to third person. The concept 'zero' independent pronoun is at the very least a highly troublesome one. More daringly put: zero independent third person pronouns in languages without obligatorily present independent pronouns do not exist.

2.6 Conclusion

Much is possible in human language. There are numerous possibilities to mark participants, even when only the three singular categories—'speaker', 'addressee', and 'other'—are considered. A few general tendencies have been extracted from the diversity. First, it has been shown that homophony between any two of the three categories is possible, although such homophonous paradigms are not numerous among the languages of the world. Examples of almost all logical possibilities exist; only one of nine theoretical possibilities has not been attested. The missing case is a highly marked structure, which probably has not been attested because the number of languages investigated has not been high enough. One homophony is clearly more common than the others: the first/non-first opposition, with the option for the non-first to be zero. When a language marks person rudimentarily, explicit marking of the speaker is the favourite option. Second, examples of singular homophony exist almost exclusively in inflectional paradigms—or, in a reversed formulation, independent pronouns almost never show homophony. When person is marked using independent words, the reference to speaker, addressee, and others is preferably not mixed. Third, in the case of homophonous inflectional paradigms, it is often argued that it is necessary to add independent pronouns for clarification because these 'impoverished' paradigms have lost some of their disambiguating power. As I have argued, this is not necessarily the case. In many cases, languages with singular homophony are still 'pro-drop'. Finally, when all three singular categories are marked differently, it is highly unusual to use a zero for the marking of speaker or addressee. More commonly, the 'other' category is marked zero. However, in the case of an unmarked 'other' it is difficult to argue for the existence of the zero form. Only in inflectional marking can good arguments be made for the existence of a zero 'other'. In the case of independent pronouns, a zero 'other' is often better interpreted as the non-existence of a third person pronoun.

Now the groundwork has been done, it is time to proceed and expand the investigation of person marking on these foundations. The three singular categories that have been the subject of this chapter ('speaker', 'addressee', and 'other') will now be used to approach the marking of what has traditionally been called 'plural' person marking.

3 Group Marking
Redefining Plurality in the Pronominal Domain

3.1 Introduction

After singular comes non-singular. In this chapter, the first—cautious—steps are taken into the domain of non-singular pronominal reference. The diversity of non-singular pronominal marking is so extensive that all the following chapters will deal with some aspect of this theme. In this chapter, the basic framework for the analysis of non-singular marking will be developed. The main objective of this chapter is to redefine the notion of plurality in the pronominal domain. The notion GROUP is proposed to replace plurality. This perspective is not completely different from the traditional one. The difference between 'plural' and 'group' only amounts to a small change, but the new perspective allows for a cross-linguistically more sensible typology. A few consequences of the new definition are discussed in this chapter, but the full typology on the basis of this perspective is postponed to the next chapter.

This chapter starts with a discussion of the definition of the phenomena to be reviewed. These definitional aspects of non-singular marking will be discussed in Section 3.2. Next, the terminology needed to talk about non-singular marking will be discussed in Section 3.3. In this section, the problems with the traditional notion of plurality in the pronominal domain are summarized. The notion GROUP is proposed to improve on the deficiencies of plural. Equipped with a proper definition and terminology of group marking, I will review the theoretically possible categories within these definitional boundaries in Section 3.4. A complete typology on the basis of the possible categories turns out to be rather laborious. Therefore, only part of the complete typology will be taken up in this chapter. In Section 3.5, the typology of the FIRST PERSON COMPLEX is discussed. The first person complex consists of the categories that are subsumed under the meaning of the English pronoun *we*. The typology of the other group categories is postponed till the following chapter. The various patterns of the first person complex that are attested in the world's languages are discussed in Section 3.6. Some generalizations are drawn from this partial typology in Section 3.7. Finally, the content of this chapter is summarized in Section 3.8.

3.2 Definition

The subject of the present chapter is the marking of pronominal elements with non-singular reference. The basic definitional property for a pronominal morpheme to be included in the present discussion is that it has to refer to more than one person or object. Three extra criteria will be added to this basic definition. First, the multiple persons or objects have to be in the same predicative role. Second, the morpheme has to be unmarked as to the specific amount of elements. Finally, the morpheme should not include the regular reference for any singular person or object.

The first extra criterion is that the multiple persons or objects have to be in the same predicative role. Note that it is not necessary to act together to be in the same predicative role. A sentence like 'The students lifted the heavy table' refers to a situation where the students act together (the subject of the sentence has collective reference). However, a sentence like 'The students passed the exam' normally means that all students individually passed the exam (it has distributive reference). Still, the students in the second sentence are all in the same predicative role. This condition is important because there are languages that have pronominal elements that refer to more than one person, but these persons are not in the same predicative role. An example is presented in (3.1), from the Yuman language Mojave. The pronominal prefix n^y- refers to two persons. In one possible meaning, the two persons are first person subject and second person object (glossed as '1 → 2'). In another possible meaning of the prefix n^y-, the two persons are third person subject and first person object (glossed as '3 → 1'). No other meaning is possible for this prefix. Concluding, the pronominal prefix n^y- refers to more than one person or object, so it fits in with the basic property of the definition. However, the persons or objects referred to by n^y- are not in the same predicative role, so this prefix is excluded from the present study by the first extra criterion of the definition (see Heath 1991; 1998 for a survey of this phenomenon in Australia and America).

(3.1) Mojave (Munro 1976: 12)
n^y-*masde:k*
1→2/3→1–afraid
'I'm afraid of you.' or 'He's afraid of me.'

The next two extra criteria concern the specification of the number of participants. The basic definition states that reference should be made to more than one person or object. However, the specific number of persons or objects should not be specified. Specialized pronominal elements for reference to a specific number of persons, like duals, trials, or paucals, are excluded here; they will be taken up in Part III. In this chapter, only those elements are included which are unmarked for the number of participants. Finally, elements that can refer to singular participants are also excluded. This is an important restriction. Often, there are no grammaticalized plural forms in a pronominal paradigm. The singular forms are used for the plural as well. Taking Mojave as example again, its intransitive pronominal prefixes distinguish first, second, and third person singular. However, there are no special prefixes that mark a group of more than one person. The same singular prefixes are used for plural marking. As shown in (3.2), there is often no number marking at all in a Mojave sentence. The subject of this sentence can be either singular 'I' or plural 'we'. The meaning has to be recovered from the discourse. It is possible in the Yuman languages to specify plurality, but it is never marked by a pronominal element.[1]

(3.2)   Mojave (Munro 1976: 15)
        ʔ-aherk
        1-put in jail
        'I put him in jail.' or 'We put him in jail.'

Elements like the prefix ʔ- of Mojave, that mark for both singular and plural, are not included in this chapter. Only pronominal elements that are specialized for plural marking are included. A consequence of this strict definition is that there are paradigms, like the pronominal prefixes from Mojave, that have no (specialized) morphemes for plural marking.[2]

3.3 Terminology

Now that the definition is clarified, it is time to take a look at the terminology. Over the last century, there has been an ongoing but rather covert discussion about a suitable metalanguage to approach the marking of person in human language. Many deficits of the traditional approach have been noted. However,

---

[1] The marking of plurality in the Yuman languages is quite complex, using affixes, stem changes, or even completely different verbal stems for singular and plural subjects. All in all, there are about 25 different ways to mark plurality (e.g. on Mojave, see Munro 1976: 224–32), the distribution of which is still a puzzle to the specialists: 'Some efforts have been made in previous descriptions of Yuman languages to class certain plural markers as indicating collective as opposed to distributive plural... or to refer to semantic similarities among the verbs which take a given plural marker.... However, I do not feel that any of these typologies adequately explains the puzzling distribution of plural markers' (Munro 1976: 227).

[2] This definition of the notion 'specialization' should not be interpreted diachronically. In the case of the English independent pronouns, for example, one could argue that the pronoun *you* was originally a specialized plural pronoun, which is nowadays also used for singular marking. Still, in the present usage of the term 'specialization' the pronoun *you* is a singular pronoun and there is no specialized plural counterpart. By this usage, I disregard historical developments, but also synchronically different directional possibilities of syncretisms (cf. Stump 2001: 212–18). The reason for this rather strong reduction is solely practical: I needed a strict and simple classification scheme to be able to compare a large number of pronominal paradigms without entangling myself in a web of fine-grained typological distinctions.

there is still no widely accepted replacement for the traditional term 'plural', which turns out, on closer inspection, to be a rather awkward concept for the description of non-singular pronominal categories. I will make an attempt at the long overdue reformulation by replacing 'plural' with the notion GROUP.[3] The reasons for this reformulation will be laid out in this section. All that follows in the present work can be read as a prolonged argument for the validity of this new terminology.

Person marking that refers to a non-singular set of persons or objects, as defined in the previous section, is normally called 'plural'. However, there is a problem with this term. The meaning of plurality within the domain of pronominal marking is rather different from the standard notion of plural. Normally, a singular morpheme, like the English word *chair*, refers to a single object that falls into the class of chairs. A plural, like *chairs*, refers to a group of objects, each of which belongs to the class of chairs. Transferred to the pronominal domain, this analysis states that the first person singular refers to a single person that belongs to the class of speakers. No problem so far. However, the consequent next step would be that a first person plural refers to a group of persons that all individually belong to the class of speakers. In other words, the first person plural is literally a group of speakers. The English pronoun *we* would, in this analysis, mean something like 'the group of persons currently speaking in unison'. This is clearly not what *we* prototypically means; *we* normally refers to a group of people, only one of whom is currently speaking (Jespersen 1924: 192; Benveniste 1966: 233; Lyons 1968: 277; Moravcsik 1978: 354, n. 12). The most common meaning of 'we' strongly resembles the meaning of a nominal case marker that is known as the ASSOCIATIVE. An associative case marker is, for example, found in Hungarian. Hungarian has a nominal plural suffix *-ok*, as in (3.3a). This phrase is used to refer to a group of people that all have the name John. There is a different associative suffix *-ék*, as in (3.3b). With this suffix, the phrase means something like 'John and his group'.

(3.3) Hungarian (Corbett and Mithun 1996: 5)
    a. *János-ok*
       NAME-PLUR
       'more than one John'
    b. *János-ék*
       NAME-ASSOC
       'John and associates', 'John and his group'

The prototypical meaning of 'we' is associative. 'We' means something like 'I and my associates', in which the associates could be either addressees or others. A real 'plural I' is possible, but rather odd (see the next section for an extensive

---

[3] Howe (1996: 9) also uses the term 'group' instead of the term 'plural'.

discussion). For the 'second person plural', the situation is different. Here, both the plural reference 'you all, present audience' and the associative reference 'you and your associates' make sense. The prototypical meaning of the 'second person plural' is probably associative (see the next section for an extensive discussion). For the 'third person plural', both the plural and the associative meaning are completely normal, but the prototypical meaning is probably plural (Moravcsik 1994). Summarizing, the meaning of the so-called 'plural' pronominal elements contain both plural and associative notions. This makes the term 'plural' in the domain of pronominal marking semantically awkward and somewhat confusing. It is better to avoid this term.

This theoretical argument can be supplemented with an empirical observation. It is uncommon to find pronominal paradigms that use nominal strategies to mark plurality. Normally, the 'plural' in the pronominal domain is marked differently from the plural of regular nouns in the language. Benveniste (1966) has already made this observation: 'In the great majority of languages, the pronominal plural does not coincide with the nominal plural' (Benveniste 1966: 233; my translation).[4] Examples of nominal plural marking in pronouns exist, but they are generally hard to find. There are some pronouns with morphologically transparent plural forms: plural pronouns that are built by regular derivation from the singular forms. Yet the pronominal marking for plurality is in most of these cases (synchronically) different from the nominal marking for plurality.[5] In those few cases where a nominal plurality marker is found in the pronominal paradigm, it is either found in part of the paradigm only, or it is functionally superfluous (because the singular and plural forms would still be different if the plural marker were removed), or it is only optionally used. It is really uncommon for a pronominal paradigm to use a nominal plural marker as the *only* identification of plurality. An example of such a rarity is found in Trumai, to be discussed shortly. After the case from Trumai, I discuss two other cases (Korean and Canela-Kraho) in which the pronominal plural marking is to some extend a extension of nominal number marking (for a few more examples, see Corbett 2000: 76–7, 134–5).

An instance of a complete overlap between pronominal and nominal number marking is attested in Trumai, a genetically isolated language from Brazil (Monod-Becquelin 1975: 175). The person markers *ha* and *hi* (meaning 'I' and 'you', respectively) are combined with the plural postposition *uan* to form 'we' and 'you-plural'. The same pluralizer is also used with nouns. From the description and the accompanying texts (Monod-Becquelin 1975: 226–47), it

---

[4] 'Dans la grande majorité des langues, le pluriel pronominal ne coïncide pas avec le pluriel nominal.'

[5] Regular pronominal marking for plurality is commonly related to nouns like 'fellow' or 'people'. The marking 'I-fellow' or 'I-people' should probably be read as marking an associative case: 'I and my fellows' or 'I and my people' (cf. Section 4.3.5).

appears that this pluralizer is used obligatorily with pronouns and human nouns, but it is not consistently used with non-human nouns:

It is clear that the two person markers *ha* and *hi* can be combined with the pluraliser *ha uan* = 1st person+plural = we; just as *kiki* = a man, *kiki uan* = the men. (Monod-Becquelin 1975: 175; my translation)[6]

In Korean, the plural marking is used obligatorily in polite levels of address in all but the first person plural:

In non-deferential levels of address, there is a separate stem for 1st plural. However, the other persons use the same stem [as the singular], but are obligatorily marked by a number suffix. (Sohn 1994: 284)

For example, in the 'level II' pronouns in Korean (used when the addressee of third person referent is generally equal to or lower than the speaker, yet he or she is an adult) the second person singular pronoun is *tangsin* and the second person plural pronoun is *tangsin-tul* (Sohn 1994: 287). The suffix *-tul* is the regular number marker for nouns, used obligatorily when the noun is definite (Sohn 1994: 268–9). However, the first person plural is *wuli*—rather different from the first person singular *ha*. *Wuli* is only optionally extended with the nominal suffix *-tul*. It can be concluded that there is some nominal plural marking in pronouns, but only in a restricted part of the paradigm.

Another example where pronominal elements use the same plural marking as regular nouns is found in Canela-Kraho, a Gé language from Brazil. The plural particle *me* is found with pronominal arguments, as in (3.4b), as well as with nominal arguments, as in (3.4c). However, this particle is not obligatorily used in the language, and even when it is used, the context has to make clear whether it is the subject or the object that is meant to be plural:

Number is sometimes expressed by the particle *me*, 'plural', usually where the referent is human and more specifically, Indian.... The context alone indicates whether the subject or the object is being pluralized. (Popjes and Popjes 1986: 185)

(3.4) Canela-Kraho (Popjes and Popjes 1986: 175, 186)
    a. *Capi   te   i-pupun*
       NAME   PAST   1-see
      'Capi saw me.'
    b. *Capi   te   me   i-pupun*
       NAME   PAST   PLUR   1-see
      'Capi saw us (exclusive).'

---

[6] 'Il est clair que les deux personnels <ha> et <hi> se combinent avec le pluralisateur <ha uan> = 1re personne+pluriel = nous; comme <kiki> = <un homme>, <kiki uan> = <les hommes>.'

c. *hũmre te   me   rop   cahhyr*
    man   PAST   PLUR   dog   beat
   'The men beat the dog.'

To sum up, the marking of non-singular pronominal elements is neither semantically nor morphologically similar to nominal plural marking. A much better approach for the analysis of pronominal paradigms is to talk about group marking instead of plural marking. This may seem like a terminological quibble, but this slight change in perspective leads to a rather different typology—one that is better suited to tackle the cross-linguistic variation of non-singular pronominal marking. Basically, the change in perspective from plural marking to group marking is a change in emphasis from NUMBER to KIND. In other words, a change will be proposed from a QUANTITATIVE to a QUALITATIVE criterion. The traditional notion highlights the number of participants: there are singular (one) and plural (more than one) pronouns. The difference between the two is one of quantity. From this perspective, there are three basic singular participants (speaker, addressee, and other), and likewise there are also three basic plural participants (speaker-plural, addressee-plural, and other-plural)—in total six different pronominal elements. This traditional classification is not only semantically and morphologically awkward, as set out above; it also gets tangled up when it has to incorporate the difference between an inclusive and an exclusive first person plural. A new dimension has to be introduced to take care of this opposition because this distinction has no place in the basic six-way typology. However, the inclusive/exclusive opposition is not at all independent of the six-way typology. The inclusive/exclusive opposition is only found in the first person plural (the purported inclusive/exclusive distinction in the second person will be discussed—and dismissed—in the next section). A complete new dimension to account for a single extra form is rather a waste of apparatus.

The perspective that will be taken here is a different one. In this view, there are groups of participants, as opposed to singular participants. These groups are analysed according to the kind of participants of which they are composed. A group, for example, can consist of the speaker and the addressee, or of the addressee and some other participant, etc. The number is not important, only the kind of participants involved. The group perspective is a qualitative approach to non-singular marking. This perspective will be shown to be semantically and morphologically less awkward, and to incorporate the inclusive/exclusive distinction automatically.

3.4 Towards a typology of groups

Based on the threefold division of singular participants (1: speaker, 2: addressee, 3: other), there are seven logical possibilities to form groups. The seven possibilities are shown in Table 3.1.[7] The numbers in the table refer to the kind of participants, the amount of each kind is not important.[8]

Of the seven possible groups, four include the speaker: 1+1, 1+2, 1+3, and 1+2+3. These are all subsumed under the meaning of English *we* (Quirk et al. 1985: 340). Franz Boas was the first to distinguish these four possible meanings of the English pronoun *we*. He also concludes that a 'true first person plural' (i.e. 1+1) is impossible:

When, therefore, we speak of a first person plural, we mean logically either self and person addressed [1+2], or self and person or persons spoken of [1+3], or finally, self, person or persons addressed, and person or persons spoken of [1+2+3]. *A true first person plural* [1+1] *is impossible, because there can never be more than one self.*' (Boas 1911b: 39; number notation and italics added)

On a slightly different interpretation, however, the 'true first person plural' exists as a conceptual category. Boas interpreted the first person as reference to the SELF, and of course, only one self can speak at a time.[9] When first person is interpreted as reference to the SPEAKER, as is done here, then a 'true first person plural' (1+1) can be interpreted as a group of speakers, speaking together in unison. Mühlhäusler and Harré (1990: 201–5) observe that the use of 'we' in the meaning of a 'group of persons speaking in unison' is found in the phenomenon of MASS SPEAKING:

[Examples are] football chanting, ritual mass speaking, as in a church service, the mass speaking of children at play and finally the reactions of a concert audience. There are many

---

[7] See Sokolovskaya (1980: 90), Zwicky (1977), Plank (1985: 130–52), Henderson (1985) and Greenberg (1988: 13–15) for comparable approaches using slightly different notations. See Goddard (1995) for a reformulation of such an approach within the context of Natural Semantic Metalanguage. A different line of thought uses feature combinations (Buchler and Freeze 1966; Buchler 1967: 42; Ingram 1978: 222–7) or the fancier, though logically equivalent, idea of intersecting sets (Hollenbach 1970; Noyer 1992: 147–8; Dalrymple and Kaplan 2000: 780–7). The main difference between the present approach and the feature/set approach is the inclusion (and subsequent empirical dismissal) of the categories 1+1 and 2+2 in the present work. Most recently, inspired by phonology, a hierarchical ordering of features is used to analyse person marking (Harley 1994; Harley and Ritter, forthcoming). The current version of this proposal is obviously much too restricted to cope with the linguistic diversity of person marking.

[8] It is an old practice to abbreviate inclusive and exclusive with the numbers 1 & 2 and 1 & 3, respectively. Jespersen (1924: 213) remarks that the notations '1/2' and '1/3' have been used in 'some works dealing with Amerindian languages'. I have been unable to track down an instance of this notation. The first complete analysis of plural pronouns as combinations of singular participants is probably by Hollenbach (1970), although she does not use the plus sign. An early usage of the plus sign for inclusive and exclusive first person plurals can be found in Lounsbury (1953). The plus sign is for the first time consistently used by Hale (1973) and Zwicky (1977). There is some variation in the literature, as sometimes 1+1 is found for the first person plural exclusive, where I use 1+3, e.g. various articles in Wiesemann (1986a) and also in Hale (1973: 315).

[9] The self is a much-debated concept in philosophy and ethnology. For a summary of the relevant aspects of this debate for linguistics, see Mühlhäusler and Harré (1990: 104–22) and Foley (1997: 261 ff.). For the analysis of linguistic structure, the concept of the self is a theoretical burden, rather than a blessing. The concept 'speaker' is more appropriate for the present purpose. Alternatively, for the analysis of language use, the concept 'self' is indispensable.

TABLE 3.1. *Possible groups of participants*

Group	Description
1+1	'we', mass speaking
1+2	'we', including addressee, excluding other
1+3	'we', including other, excluding addressee
2+2	'you-all', only present audience
2+3	'you-all', addressee(s) and others
3+3	'they'
1+2+3	'we', complete

other forms of mass speaking, such as what occurs at political rallies.... In order for there to be mass speakings at all, the members of the speaking group or groups must achieve a high degree of co-ordination of their actions. (Mühlhäusler and Harré 1990: 201–2)

An example is *We are the champions*, sung by a soccer audience after their team has won, or *We want more*, shouted by a concert audience. This is a marked usage of the English pronoun *we*, but the pronoun can be used that way. Still, this does not make 1+1 a linguistic category. For it to be a linguistic category, the notion of mass speaking should exist as a grammaticalized category at least in some languages in the world. As far as I know, however, there is no language in the world that distinguishes a separate morpheme for mass speaking. It seems that Boas was on the right track when he proclaimed that 1+1 was an impossible category. His rationale does not hold, but his intuition was right. Semantically, 1+1 is a feasible category, but it is not linguistically salient. For the rest of the discussion here, I will disregard this category altogether (cf. Zwicky 1977: 731, n. 1).

Just like 1+1, the category 2+2 is not widely recognized as a viable linguistic category—at least in principle. When addressing a group of people, there is a difference between whether 'you (more than one person)' addresses only the present audience and no one else, or whether other people, not directly addressed, are included. The reference only to the present audience is indicated here by 2+2; the general group address is indicated by 2+3. Lyons describes this difference as follows:

A distinction might also be made between an 'inclusive' and 'exclusive' use of the 'second person plural' (in a slightly different sense of 'inclusive' versus 'exclusive'). The English pronoun *you* may of course be either singular or plural.... As a plural form, it may be either 'inclusive' (referring only to the hearers present—in which case it is the plural of the singular *you*, in the same sense as *cows* is the plural of *cow*) or 'exclusive' (referring to some other person, or persons, in addition to the hearer, or hearers). (Lyons 1968: 277)

Many situations in which in English 'you (more than one person)' is used are instances of 2+2. One could think of a situation like a school class address. A teacher asking *Should I tell you more about this?* is referring only to the present audience (2+2), not to all the students in his course, some of which might be absent. However great the semantic plausibility, the category 2+2 is not found grammaticalized in the languages of the world (Moravcsik 1978: 356; Greenberg 1988: 14; McGregor 1989: 450, n. 8). I know of one clear source in which a morphological difference between 2+2 and 2+3 is claimed. Hewitt (1979) notes that in the Caucasian language Abkhaz, a difference is made between an exclusive and an inclusive second person plural.[10] The exclusive form *šʲart* indicates 'you excluding them', which ends up identical in meaning to what I have called 2+2. The inclusive form *šʲa(rà)* indicates 'you including them'; what I have called 2+3 (note that Hewitt's usage of the terms inclusive and exclusive in this context is exactly the reverse of the usage by Lyons as quoted above). This opposition is not very strong within the language: the exclusive forms are hardly used; the 'inclusive forms may and usually do appear where one would expect the exclusives' (Hewitt 1979: 156–7). Also, this opposition remains a special characteristic of Abkhaz; it is not found in any of the other north-west Caucasian languages (cf. the descriptions in Hewitt 1989: 101, 176–7, 298, 378).

Another claim that approaches a grammaticalized opposition between 2+2 and 2+3 is made for Mao Naga, a Tibeto-Burman language from India. Giridhar (1994) describes an opposition between two second person plural pronouns that appears to be an inclusive/exclusive opposition: '*nikhrumüi* ... would mean all its referents are present; it does not refer to anyone not present whereas *nitamüi* ... could' (p. 141). However, there are two reasons to discard this as a true opposition between 2+2 and 2+3. First and foremost, this opposition, as marked by the affixes *-khru* versus *-ta*, is a special kind of number marking that can be used with all nouns and all non-singular pronouns; it even transects a regular inclusive/exclusive distinction that is present in the first person (Giridhar 1994: 139–40). The opposition between *-khru* and *-ta* marks a difference between homogeneity and heterogeneity, and thereby can be used to differentiate between a homogeneous 2+2 group and a heterogeneous 2+3 group:

Plurality is expressed in two ways: [a] *ta* signals a plurality which is an exclusive part of an [unidentified] inclusive whole, a homogeneous subset of a heterogeneous set and [b] *-khru* signals a plurality which is an inclusive whole. In the case of substantives, the inclusive whole that *-khru* marks is homogeneous while in the case of pronouns, it is heterogeneous. (Giridhar 1994: 114)

---

[10] Hewitt's analysis of an inclusive/exclusive opposition in the second person plural probably goes back to Š. K. Aristeva et al. (1968) *Grammatika abxazskogo jazyka; fonetika i morfologija* [*Grammar of the Abkhaz language; phonetics and morphology*] (Suxumi: Alašara, 1968). On p. 35, they say that *hara* is inclusive first person plural and *hart* is exclusive first person plural. Then they comment: 'the second person plural is formed analogously: *shvara*, "you-plural" and *shvart*, "you-plural".' Thanks to R. Smeets (p.c.) for pointing out the original reference to me. He also explains that the effect of the suffix *-t* is probably comparable to the function of the French postposition *autres* in *nous autres* en *vous autres*. The same suffix *-t* is found in the demonstrative elements of Abkhaz, but then in the function of a pluralizer.

76   Person Marking

The two different second person plural pronouns thus do not mark a difference between 2+2 and 2+3. They are better interpreted as part of a separate number dimension that is found in all nouns and pronouns. The regular inclusive root *i-* and exclusive root *a-* can both be marked with either affix *-ta* or *-khru*, leading to a four-way distinction in the first person plural:

Thus, *ata iniu-li* 'in our ... village' refers necessarily to a single village to the exclusion of other villages whereas *akhrumüi inui-li* 'in our ... villages' necessarily means a plurality of village identities, a melange, for instance, of the villages of Punanamai, Pudunamai, Shong shong and Kalinamai.... *ita*, on the other hand, denotes inclusiveness on the listener exclusion/inclusion axis and exclusiveness on the exclusive part—inclusive whole axis so that *itanui* 'our village(s)' is ambiguous as to number. If what is meant is a single village, then the identity is village. If, on the other hand, it means 'our village' then the group is bound by an identity other than village which it cuts across. The essential point is that *ta* indicates a singularity of identity, and a plurality of number which is homogeneous at some level of identity unlike *-khru* which signals plurality both of identity and number, a plurality which is heterogeneous at some level of identity. (Giridhar 1994: 140)

The second reason to discard the opposition between *nikhrumüi* and *nitamüi* as a true example of the difference between the person categories 2+2 and 2+3 is that there also exists a pronoun *nitakhrumüi*, which combines the affixes *-ta* and *-khru* into one pronoun, marking respect: 'plural pronouns marked by *ta*, typically, carry a signification of disrespect, disgust or frivolity.... The dignified counterparts of such pronouns ... are those marked by *ta* followed by *-khru*' (Giridhar 1994: 141). Summarizing, the apparent opposition between 2+2 and 2+3 in Mao Naga is not part of the pronominal paradigm. The marking by *-ta* and *-khru* is a general possibility for marking homogeneity/heterogeneity in plural expression, to be found in nouns and all non-singular pronouns.[11] Overall, it seems implausible, if not impossible, for a language to have a grammaticalized category 2+2 in the pronominal paradigm.[12] Simon (2001) presents an extensive documentation and investigation of all claims from the literature and their empirical support. He also concludes that the evidence is meagre at best. I will disregard this category from now on.

The categories 1+1 and 2+2 are thus possible linguistic categories, but they are not grammaticalized in human language. This absence can be explained by noting that the conversational settings in which the semantic categories 1+1 and 2+2 are attested are extremely marked. In the case of multiple speakers (mass

---

[11] I thank D. N. S. Bhat for pointing out this case to me.

[12] Comrie (1980b: 837) mentions South-East Ambrym as an example of a language with the same peculiarity as Abkhaz, but gives no reference to substantiate this claim. Plank (1985: 147) takes the claim at face value. The claim probably goes back to Parker (1970: ix, 43) who lists two different forms for 'you-plural' in his dictionary of South-East Ambrym: *xami*, which is glossed as 'you plural inclusive', and *xamim*, which is glossed as 'you plural exclusive'. However, I have not been able to find any description of this phenomenon in the literature on other variants of Ambrym (cf. Paton 1971: 13–18, 119–24). Simon (2001) makes a plausible claim that *xami* and *xamim* are dialectal variants. The village in which Parker did his fieldwork lies exactly on the border of the two dialects.

speaking) and of multiple addressees (present audience), the group has to act as if it were a single entity. The multiple speakers have to 'speak as one', and the multiple addressees have to 'be conceived as one'. The (practical) problem is that speech in unison must be carefully planned and eye contact with more than one person is only achieved in specific situations, like class address (McGregor 1989: 440). Yet if such a situation arises, it is not necessary to consider combinations like 1+1 or 2+2 as separate categories; they can readily be conceived as metaphorical extensions of the corresponding singular categories. In this way, a remarkable reduction of the metalanguages as proposed by Plank (1985: 130–52) or Greenberg (1988: 13–15) can be achieved. They both distinguish all cases with multiple occurrence of the number 1, 2, and 3 as feasible linguistic categories. However, if 1+1 is unnecessary, so is 1+1+3, 1+1+1+3, etc. Following from the exclusion of 2+2, the same argument can be made for the exclusion of 2+2+3, 2+2+2+3, etc. And combinations like 1+1+2+3 or 1+2+2+3 are unnecessary, for the same reason.[13]

When these two categories are dismissed, five categories remain from the seven logical possibilities as outlined in Table 3.1. Three of the remaining categories include the speaker: 1+2, 1+3, and 1+2+3. These categories all exist as grammaticalized categories in the world's languages. However, in English they are not distinguished morphologically. All three have to be translated into English by the pronoun *we*. The categories 1+2 and 1+2+3 include reference to the addressee. They are both known as an 'inclusive first person plural', or INCLUSIVE for short. To express their content in English, a paraphrase like *we, I and you* has to be used. Some pronominal paradigms in the world's languages distinguish between the two categories 1+2+3 and 1+2. In such paradigms, the category 1+2+3 refers to a group that includes the speaker, the addressee, and at least one other. This is known in the literature as an AUGMENTED INCLUSIVE. On the other hand, the category 1+2 is known in the literature as the MINIMAL INCLUSIVE. In this case, only the present audience is included, prototypically one singular addressee. More discussion of these categories will be presented in

---

[13] In a reply to a comparable argument by McGregor (1989), Greenberg (1989) raises the important issue of the function of a typological classification. He argues that a classification is not only a description of attested possibilities, but should also point towards distinctions which might exist, but have not been noted until now because the linguistic metalanguage did not allow them to be described (Greenberg 1989: 454). I agree that we should be alert to yet unknown hypothetical distinctions; but in this case it seems to me rather a waste of apparatus to include all the encumbering multiple combinations of 1 and 2 in the metalanguage only because of some non-attested possibilities. Besides this theoretical argument, Greenberg presents a few languages to argue for the necessity of multiple addressees in the metalanguage. However, these examples do not convince me. The cases of Palaung and Sierra Popoluca are interesting, but they do not argue for multiple addressees (see below, Ch. 7, n. 21, and Section 4.5.6, respectively, for a discussion of these cases). A third case presented by Greenberg concerns the Philippine pronouns. The Pampangan pronoun *tamu* is built from the parts *ta* (1+2) and *mu* (2), but its meaning is clearly 1+2+3, not 1+2+2 as Greenberg would have it (Gonzales 1981: 172). Also, the equivalent pronoun *tayo* in the related language Ilocano is built from the parts *ta* (1+2) and *yo* (2+3); see also Reid (1979: 270) and Section 3.6.5.

78 Person Marking

Section 3.6.5. The category 1+3 refers to a group excluding the addressee. This is generally known as the 'exclusive first person plural', or EXCLUSIVE for short. In English, it has to be paraphrased as something like *we, I and the ones I was talking about, not including you*. The final two categories from Table 3.1 are well known and do not need explanation. The categories 2+3 and 3+3 are equivalent to the traditional second person plural and third person plural, respectively. As far as these categories are concerned, the group perspective is not much different from the plural perspective.

3.5 A partial typology: the first person complex

The five different group categories (1+2, 1+3, 1+2+3, 2+3, and 3+3) can be marked linguistically in numerous different ways. At one side of the spectrum, they can all five be marked with a specialized morpheme. That would amount to a maximally differentiated paradigm. At the other extreme, none of the categories could have a specialized morpheme: all group reference could be marked using singular pronominal elements. That would amount to a minimally differentiated paradigm. In between these two extremes there are all kinds of different ways to combine the categories. Counting all the possible combinations, there turn out to be 203 theoretically possible patterns.[14] To find a way through the bewildering amount of 203 feasible patterns, I will start off with a subset of the five categories. The point of departure will be the FIRST PERSON COMPLEX, i.e. the set of categories that include the speaker. There are three categories that include the speaker: 1+2, 1+3, and 1+2+3. With only three categories and the possibility of non-existence there are fifteen possible patterns (see below for a list). In this section I will show which of these fifteen patterns are attested among the world's languages. In Section 3.6 I will give a description of the attested patterns. I will draw some generalizations on the basis of the attested patterns in Section 3.7. The distribution of the other two categories—2+3 and 3+3—relative to the patterns of the first person complex is a long story, to be taken up in the next chapter.

All patterns that are theoretically possible with the three categories from the first person complex are shown in Figure 3.1. A capital letter in this table indicates that there is a specialized morpheme for this category—or combination of categories. A dash indicates that this category is linguistically coded for by a morpheme that also marks a singular category. The possibilities are ordered according to the number of specialized morphemes that are present. The first pattern distinguishes three different morphemes for the three different categories.

---

[14] The total of 203 possible combinations is calculated by taking the sixth so-called Bell number. A Bell number B_n represents the total number of possible dissections of a set of n different elements. In this case there are five different categories (1+2, 1+3, 1+2+3, 2+3, and 3+3) and the possibility of non-existence. The number of possible dissections of these elements is $B_6 = 203$.

Redefining Plurality 79

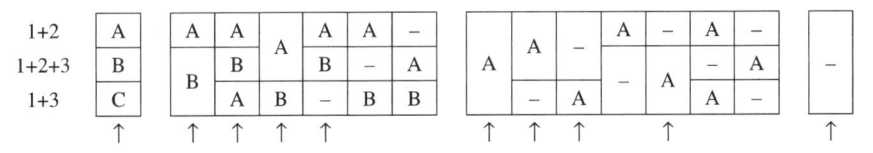

FIG. 3.1. *Possible patterns of first person complex*

Next follow the six possible patterns with two specialized morphemes. Then the seven possibilities with only one specialized non-singular morpheme are shown. Finally, the only possible pattern with no specialised morpheme for either of the three non-singular categories closes the list of possible patterns. In total, this makes fifteen different patterns. I have found ten of these fifteen patterns in the world's linguistic variation—they are marked with an arrow in Figure 3.1.

The ten attested patterns are repeated in Figure 3.2, separated into three groups. The first five patterns are common among the world's languages. They are designated for ease of reference as (Pa)–(Pe). The other five patterns are rare. The first two of these rare patterns, (Pf) and (Pg), appear slightly more common than the other rare ones. The distinction between common and rare is fairly clear-cut. There are dozens of examples of the common patterns, but only very few examples of the rare patterns. This indicates that the five common patterns are a rather different sort; they are the preferred structures for a pronominal paradigm.

The common patterns ask for more attention than can be covered in this chapter because these five common patterns show many different combinations with the remaining two categories, 2+3 and 3+3. Full discussion of the structural variability and the geographical distribution of these five common types is postponed till the next chapter. The (extensive) list of examples of the common patterns, as presented in the next chapter, should be a reasonable argument for their commonness. In this chapter, only a basic outline of the structure of the common patterns will be presented in Sections 3.6.1–5. The remaining five types are found only in incidental cases. All paradigms attested of these rare types will be described in Section 3.6.6.

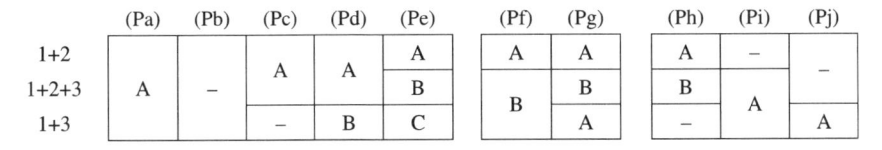

FIG. 3.2. *Attested patterns of the first person complex*

80 *Person Marking*

3.6 Different kinds of 'we'

3.6.1 Type (Pa): unified-we

The structure of type (Pa) is well known. This is the structure found in the English independent pronouns in which there is a single undifferentiated form, *we*. The meaning of a morpheme like the English *we* is best characterized as a group of more than one person, including the present speaker, but unmarked as to the other persons in the group. It unifies the referential categories 1+2, 1+3, and 1+2+3 into the marking of one morpheme. I will use the name UNIFIED-WE for this type of paradigm. Two examples of the unified-we type will be given special attention here, because they are classified differently in the literature. These two paradigms, from Assiniboine and Nyulnyul, are presented as special paradigmatic structures by Greenberg (1988: 9) and McGregor (1996a: 40–1) respectively. However, following the definitions as used in the present work, these paradigms are cases of the unified-we type.

Greenberg (1988: 9) presented the active prefixes from the Siouan language Assiniboine as an example of a special paradigmatic structure, which he called the 'Assiniboine-type' paradigm. There are indeed paradigms of this Assiniboine-type attested among the world's languages (they will be discussed here as type (Pf) in Section 3.6.6), but Assiniboine itself is not one of them. The problem is that the special opposition Greenberg reported for Assiniboine is not marked inside the person paradigm itself, but by a combination of person prefixes and number suffixes. The special characteristic of Assiniboine is the difference between category 1+2 (speaker and addressee, no others) and all other categories in the first person complex. There is thus a difference between 'we: I and you' and all other forms of 'we'. These other forms of 'we' consist of both inclusive and exclusive reference. This is indeed a very special division of the first person complex. Two example sentences from Assiniboine are presented in (3.5). Sentence (3.5a) shows an example with 1+2 reference; sentence (3.5b) shows an example with the other 'we' reference. However, the crucial difference between the two sentences is not found in the form of the person prefix. The prefix *u̧k-* is identical in both cases. The difference between the two kinds of reference is marked by the presence or absence of the plurality suffix *-pi*. Without this suffix, the reference is 1+2; with the suffix *-pi*, the reference is 1+2+3 or 1+3. This is a very interesting referential division, but it is morphologically not part of the person marking, which has only one form *u̧k-* for all referential possibilities of 'we'. These prefixes from Assiniboine are thus of the unified-we type.

(3.5) Assiniboine (Levin 1964: 31–2, 93)
    a. *u̧k-áksa*
       1PL-chop off
       'I and you chop off something.'

b. **uk̲-ákipta-pi**
1PL-argue-PL
'We argued with him.'

Following Greenberg's analysis, McGregor (1996a: 40–1) argues that the prefixes from the Australian language Nyulnyul are also of the Assiniboine-type. He argued rightly that Nyulnyul resembles Assiniboine strongly, but the consequence is that Nyulnyul does not have special person marking, for the same reason as Assiniboine did not have it. There is only one prefix for 'we' in Nyulnyul, the prefix *ya-*. McGregor explains that this prefix is sometimes attested without number marking, in which case the reference is to 1+2:

[*ya*] occasionally occurs without the number marking prefix when it refers to the speaker-hearer dyad: that is, when reference is made to the 1&2 minimal category. (McGregor 1996a: 40)

However, the prefix itself is identical in all referential variations. It is the number suffix *-rr-* that marks the special referential properties of 'we' in Nyulnyul. In this case, the problems are even stronger than in Assiniboine, because the opposition between presence and absence of the number suffix is not completely regular, judging from the examples given by McGregor (1996a). The example presented in (3.6) has 1+2 reference, but there is still a plural suffix on the verb.

(3.6) Nyulnyul (McGregor 1996a: 42)
ngay   a   juy   ya-li-rr-jid   Derby-ung
I   and   you   1PL-IRR-PL-go   PLACE-all
'You and I might go to Derby.'

The person prefixes from Assiniboine and Nyulnyul are of the unified-we type, following my definitions. The kind of paradigm that Greenberg originally intended to describe as the Assiniboine-type exists, but the Assiniboine and Nyulnyul cases are not part of that type. Examples of 'real' Assiniboine-type paradigms will be discussed in Section 3.6.6.

3.6.2 Type (Pb): no-we

Paradigms of type (Pb) are the diametrical opposite of the previous type. Instead of one overarching form for all 'we' categories, (Pb) paradigms have no specialized pronominal element for 'we' at all. Most examples of pronominal paradigms without any form for 'we' have no specialized group marking at all. This is, for example, found in the English inflectional marking, where all the plural forms are identical to the first and second person singular: they are all zero. The English person inflection is a pronominal paradigm of type (Pb). I will use the name NO-WE for this type of paradigmatic structure.

Pronominal paradigms of type (Pb), with no specialized marking for 'we', are less well known than the other common types of paradigms. It has even been claimed that 'we' is a universally grammaticalized category for human languages. This claim implies that the no-we type should not exist. The most explicit formulation of this claim is found in Ingram's Universal 1: 'there are at least four persons in every language: I, thou, he, we' (Ingram 1978: 227).[15] In this universal, Ingram talks about whole languages. He claims every LANGUAGE has a form for 'we'. In contrast, I look at the structure of individual PARADIGMS in a language. These different perspectives imply that there are two different versions of the universal claim: a strong and a weak version. The strong version claims that every pronominal paradigm has at least four persons:

(3.7) Universal 'we' (strong version)
There are at least four persons in every PARADIGM: I, thou, s/he, and we.

As the English inflection shows, it is easily possible for an individual paradigm to have no form for 'we'. Such paradigms are even relatively common among the world's languages. The complete distribution of this paradigmatic type is discussed in Section 4.3.5. The strong version of the universal 'we' is clearly not true. Accordingly, the claim by Ingram must be interpreted as a weaker version of this universal. A particular person paradigm may have no form for 'we', but then there will still be another paradigm somewhere in the language that fills this gap. The English inflection may have a 'no-we' structure, but English also has independent pronouns with an overt form for 'we'. This weak version of Ingram's universal in (3.8) would hold when all languages that have a no-we paradigm also have another pronominal paradigm that includes at least an element for 'we'.

---

[15] The claim for the universal existence of the first person plural has been around for a long time. An early hint, and implicit explanation, of this claim is made by Schmidt (1926): 'Denn gerade bei der Erfassung der Person, besonders der ersten Person, tritt der Begriff der individuellen Einheit am stärksten hervor. Gerade die scharfe Erfassung der Einheit ist aber auch die notwendige psychologische Vorbedingung für die Herausarbeitung der Mehrheitsformen' ('The notion of individual unity arises most prominently with the conception of person, especially of the first person. It is the precise conception of unity that is the necessary psychological precondition for the expression of plural forms': Schmidt 1926: 316). Forchheimer (1953), who builds on the work of Schmidt, transforms this into a true claim of a universal first person plural: 'My research has borne out Schmidt's statement for the plural without exception... I have found several languages where the word for "I" can also serve to express "we", they all possess, besides that, a word for "we". The only exception is Chinese Pidgin English.... I found no record of a language distinguishing "thou" and "you", but not "I" and "we", whereas the opposite is frequent' (Forchheimer 1953: 12). A comparable claim, though less strong, returns as Greenberg's Universal 42: 'All languages have pronominal categories involving at least three persons and two numbers' (Greenberg 1963: 96). Moravcsik (1978) remarks on Greenberg's universal that it should be interpreted as meaning that the first person universally shows a plural: 'Although... in all languages there will be some context where number distinctions in all three persons will be significant, this does not mean that the personal pronominal paradigm consisting of free forms will have number distinctions manifested in all three persons. The generalization concerning the number distinctions in free personal pronominal forms seems to be this: it is universally present in the first person but not in the second and third' (Moravcsik 1978: 352).

(3.8) Universal 'we' (weak version)
There are at least four persons in every LANGUAGE: I, thou, s/he, and we.

However, even in this weaker version, this universal is not absolute. There are counterexamples, although they appear to be rare. The clearest case of a language that contradicts the weak version of the universal is the Brazilian language Mura Pirahã. Mura Pirahã has singular pronouns and clitics, which are derived from the pronouns. The pronouns and clitics can optionally be used co-referentially, as shown for the second person in (3.9).

(3.9) Mura Pirahã (Everett 1987: 249)
 ti gíxai gí xibáobá
 1   2PRON 2CLIT hit
 'I hit you.'

Besides the pronouns and the related clitics, no other pronominal paradigms exist. The special property of the pronouns (and the clitics) is that they do not have any group-marking elements. They have only elements with singular reference:

The three basic Pirahã pronouns are worthy of attention because they comprise one of the simplest pronoun systems known. They are often optional in discourse, meaning that their functional load is not as great as that for pronouns in many languages (especially given the fact that Pirahã has no form of agreement marked on the verb aside from clitics and cliticized pronouns). (Thomason and Everett forthcoming)

There are no markers of number anywhere in the language. There is simply no way to refer overtly to a group of more persons in a grammaticalized form. Other constructions have to be used:

Pirahã not only has no plural pronouns, it has no number anywhere in its grammatical system—no number agreement, no singular-plural distinctions in nominals, and no numerals at all. Moreover, there is no direct evidence of plural forms in any surviving Mura or Pirahã data of any period. (Thomason and Everett forthcoming)

The only way to mark groups of participants is by conjunction of pronouns (Everett 1986: 281). This conjunction is zero marked, as shown in (3.10).

(3.10) Mura Pirahã (Everett 1986: 281)
 ti gíxai pío ahápií
 1   2PRON also go
 'You and I will go (i.e. we will go).'

Other languages that contradict the weak version of the universal 'we' are Classical Chinese, Kawi (Old Javanese), and the Yuman language Maricopa. In Classical Chinese, as in Mura Pirahã, there probably was no number marking at all. In any case, nouns and pronouns made no distinction between singular and plural forms (Norman 1988: 89). Likewise in Kawi, where plurality does not appear to be grammaticalized (Becker and Oka 1995 [1974]: 112–13). In Maricopa, numerous ways to mark number exist, but number is never marked in a pronominal paradigm (Gordon 1986: 21–3, 58, 90–101).

3.6.3 Type (Pc): only-inclusive

The next two pronominal paradigms, type (Pc) and (Pd), both distinguish between an inclusive 'we' and an exclusive 'we'. In the case of paradigms of type (Pc), the exclusive 'we' does not have a specialized morpheme. In almost all cases, the exclusive 'we' is marked by the same morpheme that is used for the first person singular. I will use the label ONLY-INCLUSIVE for this pattern of non-singular marking. The complete list of examples of this type of marking will be presented in Section 4.5.6. This pattern is exemplified here with a few sentences from Maká, a Mataco-Guaicuruan language from Paraguay. Maká has pronominal prefixes that show a large range of allophonic variation (Gerzenstein 1994: 98). In the examples presented here, the allophone *hoy-* is used both for the first person singular, as in (3.11a), and for the exclusive first person 1+3, as in (3.11b). The two meanings are distinguished by a plural suffix *-ił*. The important point is that there is no specialized morpheme for the marking of the category 1+3 within the person prefixes. The category 1+3 is marked with the same prefix as is used for the first person singular.

(3.11) Maká (Gerzenstein 1994: 106, 103)
    a. ***hoy**-otoy*
       1-dance
       'Yo bailo.' (I am dancing)
    b. ***hoy**-otoy-ił*   *tse-kheen*
       1-dance-PLUR   FEM-DEM
       'Yo y ella bailamos.' (We, she and I, are dancing)

By way of contrast, the inclusive 'we' is marked by a specialized prefix. The prefix *xi(t)-* is used for the reference to the speech-act dyad 'I and you', as shown in (3.12a). The same prefix can also by used together with a plural suffix, as shown in (3.12b).[16] With this plural suffix, the reference is to a group of type 1+2+3: speaker, hearer and others also. The categories 1+2 and 1+2+3 are combined into one inclusive prefix, only to be distinguished by a plural suffix.

(3.12) Maká (Gerzenstein 1994: 103, 176)
    a. *akha'*   ***xit**-otoy*
       2PRON   INCL-dance
       'Tú y yo bailamos.' (We, you and I, are dancing)

---

[16] The referents of *xi(t)-* in example (3.12b) are in an object role. For participants in an object role a plural suffix *-xu'* is used, different from the plural suffix *-ił* as used for participants in a subject role (Gerzenstein 1994: 138).

b. *inekhewel* ***xi**-yi-lan-xu'*   *na'*   *qametenaX*
   1+2+3PRON   INCL-3-kill-PLUR   DEM   tiger
   'A nosotros, el tigre nos mata.' (The tiger killed us)

3.6.4 Type (Pd): inclusive/exclusive

Paradigms of type (Pd) distinguish inclusive 'we' from exclusive 'we' just like the previous 'only-inclusive' (Pc) pattern. However, in the case of (Pd) both categories are marked by specialized morphemes. This pattern will be referred to as INCLUSIVE/EXCLUSIVE. It is an extremely common pattern, with much variation. This pattern is demonstrated here with some examples from Apalai, a Carib language spoken in Brazil. A specialized inclusive pronominal prefix *s(yt)-* is found in the subject prefixes of Apalai. The two example sentences in (3.13) show that this prefix can be used for the dyad of speaker and addressee, as in (3.13a), and for reference to a general inclusive, as in (3.13b).

(3.13)   Apalai (Koehn and Koehn 1986: 69, 59)
     a. ***s**-ytỹ-tase*   *kokoro*   *j-epe*   *tykase*
        INCL-poison fish-IMP   tomorrow   1-friend.POSS   say
        ' "Let us poison fish tomorrow, my friend", he said.'

     b. *otoko xixi a-htao*   *eramaṽko ropa*   ***syt**-a-tose*
        where sun COP-when   turn back   again   INCL-COP-PRES.PLUR
        'When will we all turn back?'

The inclusive prefix *s(yt)-* is different from the exclusive prefix *ynan(y)-*, as shown in (3.14a). The exclusive prefix is also a specialized non-singular prefix, which is the essential difference between these prefixes from Apalai and the prefixes from Maká in the previous section. The reference to a speaker in Apalai is marked by a prefix *y-*, which might historically be related to *ynan(y)-*, but synchronically they are clearly different prefixes.

(3.14)   Apalai (Koehn and Koehn 1986: 78, 108)
     a. *mame*   *more*   ***ynan**-urumekane*   *ropa*   *maikuato-hpe*   *exiryke*
        then   that   EXCL-leave   again   ant-infested   place
        'Then we abandoned that place again because of its being infested with ants.'

     b. *y-pipohno*
        1-hit
        'I hit it.'

3.6.5 Type (Pe): minimal/augmented

The last common type, (Pe), distinguishes three different forms for 'we'. The inclusive 'we' is further divided into two different forms, called a MINIMAL

INCLUSIVE and an AUGMENTED INCLUSIVE. The minimal inclusive refers only to the speech act dyad of speaker and addressee (1+2). The augmented inclusive refers to any group of participants that at least includes the present speaker and addressee, but possibly also others (1+2+3). This opposition is additional to the opposition between an inclusive and an exclusive 'we', as in the previous type (Pd). A paradigm with such a threefold distinction will be called a MINIMAL/AUGMENTED paradigm.

Many different approaches to describing the three forms can be found in the literature. Notwithstanding the plethora of descriptive terminology, I have decided to take all these paradigms together and consider them as one and the same type. There are two main criteria for paradigms to be included within this type. First, they should have three different forms for 'we' (which distinguishes this type from the other types discussed in this chapter); second, they should not have any dual forms for the second or third person (which distinguishes this type from paradigms with duals as discussed in Section 7.4). It then turns out that this seemingly exotic paradigmatic structure is found relatively frequently among the world's languages. A full description of the known cases of such paradigms will be presented in Section 4.5.2. In the rest of this section, I will discuss the scientific developments that have led to the present analysis of this kind of paradigm.

Franz Boas (1911b: 39)—as quoted in Section 3.4 above—first acknowledged the possibility of these three different forms for 'we', but he knew of no language that actually has all three as different morphemes. The meanings of 1+2 and 1+2+3, Boas says, may differ in reference but are not expressed by separate morphemes in any language:

> I do not know of any language expressing in a separate form the combination of the three persons [1+2+3], probably because this idea readily coalesces with the idea of self and person spoken to [1+2]. (Boas 1911b: 39; number notation added)

If this were true, this would mean that the minimal/augmented type (Pe) does not exist as a distinct type of pronominal paradigm. However, the distinction between 1+2 and 1+2+3 is found among the world's languages. The oldest description where this distinction is explicitly noted is by Foster and Foster (1948) of the Mixe-Zoque language Sierra Popoluca in Mexico:[17]

> The exclusive plural [1+3] excludes the person or persons addressed. The limited inclusive plural [1+2] includes the speaker and the person or persons addressed, and excludes any other who may be present or referred to. The generalized inclusive plural [1+2+3] includes the speaker, person, or persons addressed, and any other person or person present, or absent and referred to. (Foster and Foster 1948: 19; number notation added)

---

[17] Although this quotation from the grammar of Sierra Popoluca describes exactly a division of type (Pe), I will not classify this language as belonging to this type. The reason is that the pronominal elements of Sierra Popoluca consist of pronominal prefixes and number suffixes. Following the definitions that I use, the pronominal prefixes are classified as only-inclusive (Pc), with separate number marking. See Section 4.5.6 for a discussion.

Redefining Plurality 87

	Singular	Dual	Plural
1 inclusive	co	ta	tayo
1 exclusive			mi
2	mo	yo	
3	na	da	

FIG. 3.3. *Traditional analysis of Ilocano pronouns*

The importance of this observation was first noted by Forchheimer (1953: 93). However, the idea of 'limited' and 'generalized' inclusives only caught on in the scientific literature in the wake of a short article by Thomas (1955) on the pronouns in the Philippine language Ilocano. He argued that the traditional description of the Ilocano pronouns is not satisfactory. The traditional description of Ilocano, shown in Figure 3.3, distinguishes between an inclusive and an exclusive plural, but also adds a special form for the dual (Bloomfield 1942: 194). The default description of such a language with three different forms for 'we' is a division by the terms 'inclusive', 'exclusive', and 'dual'. Thomas formulates two points of criticism on this traditional analysis. First, the referential properties of the dual in these paradigms are more restricted than the name implies; second, there is no other dual around somewhere else in the language:

The 1st dual label is not completely accurate, as the use is restricted to cooperative action by one speaker and one hearer; no one else may be included.... There is no substantiation from the structure of the rest of the language for the existence of a dual number in Ilocano. (Thomas 1955: 205)

To clarify the first of these problems, I discuss the account of a comparable pronominal paradigm from a recently published grammar of Limbum, a Grassfields language from Cameroon. In the grammar the following description is found of the three forms for 'we':

Limbum differentiates between exclusive, inclusive and dual 'we'. The form *wìr* is used when the speaker wants to exclude the hearer(s) and *sìì* when the speaker wants to include the hearer(s). When there are only two people involved, i.e. the speaker and the addressee, the dual form *sò* is used. (Fransen 1995: 179)

In the quote, an 'inclusive', an 'exclusive', and a 'dual' form are mentioned. Intuitively, a dual form refers to a group of two persons, but in the quoted description it can be read that this dual necessarily includes the addressee. This form is better called an inclusive dual (see Figure 3.4).

The second, and more important, argument against the traditional terminological trinity dual-inclusive-exclusive is that paradigms that distinguish these three forms of 'we' normally do not have any other dual forms in other parts of

88 Person Marking

	Intuitive division	Actual division
1+3, more than two	exclusive	exclusive
1+3, exactly two	dual	
1+2, exactly two		dual
1+2+3, more than two	inclusive	inclusive

FIG. 3.4. *Different interpretations of the terminological trinity dual-inclusive-exclusive*

the language.[18] These paradigms all look like the example paradigm from Ilocano. There are no other duals, except for the inclusive dual. For Ilocano and Limbum, and many others, the inclusive dual pronoun is the only dual form in the language.[19] To invoke a completely new category—the dual—for the analysis of this one morpheme is a waste of apparatus. In the wake of Thomas's groundbreaking analysis for Ilocano, Conklin comments that the traditional analysis is 'hardly elegant, economical, or convincing' (1962: 134).[20] A better approach to paradigms with three different forms for 'we' is to focus on the KIND of participants, instead of the NUMBER of participants. Going back to the Ilocano pronouns, the opposition between the dual *ta* and the inclusive *tayo* is better labelled using the terminology as developed in Section 3.4. The opposition can be expressed as a difference between including only the addressee in the case of *ta* (1+2) and including the addressee and others in the case of *tayo* (1+2+3).

In the original article, Thomas (1955) generalized the opposition between 1+2 and 1+2+3 to the whole paradigm, as shown in Figure 3.5. He aligned 1+2 with the singular persons and analysed 1+2+3 as the 'plural' of 1+2. As the terms 'singular' and 'plural' are obviously inadequate, he used the terms 'simple' versus 'more':

A third analysis... would present the oppositions of Speaker : Hearer : Speaker-Hearer persons and simple: 'more' or 'plus' numbers. This 'more' component indicates that there is more than just the primary person. (Thomas 1955: 208)

Conklin (1962: 135) introduced the terms 'minimal membership' versus 'non-minimal membership' instead of 'simple' versus 'more'. Today, this phenomenon

---

[18] This claim is substantiated by the data as presented by Plank (1996: 131, table 11). In the large database on various forms of dual marking compiled by Plank and his co-workers, there is only one language that combines the marking of a 'first person inclusive dual only' with nominal dual marking. The special status of the first person pronominal marking for the occurrence of dual forms had already been noted by von Humboldt (1994 [1827]: 156) and later reinforced by Plank (1989: 305, 311–12; 1996: 130–1). Humboldt also presents an explanation for the preference of a dual in the first person: the combination of speaker and addressee form a natural pair.

[19] There are a few pronominal paradigms among the world's languages that distinguish three 'we'-categories and also have a dual for the second and third person. These paradigms are, consequently, interpreted as a different kind. They will be discussed in the chapter on dual marking, in Section 7.4.

[20] However unconvincing, there are still theoretical analyses in which the dual analysis is preferred (e.g. Noyer 1992: 196; Dalrymple and Kaplan 2000: 784–5).

	Minimal	Augmented		
1+2	ta	tayo	1+2	+3
1	co	mi	1	+3
2	mo	yo	2	+3
3	na	da	3	+3

FIG. 3.5. *Minimal/augmented analysis of Ilocano pronouns*

is normally referred to as an opposition 'minimal' versus 'augmented', following McKay (1978). Taken at face value, this analysis as shown in Figure 3.5 presents a nice coherent picture of the paradigmatic structure. Surely, when compared to the traditional analysis, as shown in Figure 3.4, the minimal/augmented analysis presents an impressive improvement. Still, there are two problems with this analysis. Both problems concern the generalization of the opposition between 1+2 and 1+2+3 to the whole paradigm, not the opposition between 1+2 and 1+2+3 as such.

The first problem is that the MORPHOLOGICAL structure of these paradigms does not confirm the minimal/augmented analysis. If the minimal/augmented opposition were valid for the whole paradigm, then one would expect to find some pronominal paradigms with morphologically transparent marking of the four augmented categories. In such a paradigm, the four augmented categories would be derived morphologically from the four minimal categories by way of a regular 'augmented' morpheme. However, there are hardly any examples of such a morphologically transparent minimal/augmented paradigm among the world's languages (see Section 8.5.2).[21]

The second problem concerns the DIACHRONIC DEVELOPMENT of the minimal/augmented paradigm. The generalized analysis as shown in Figure 3.5 seems to argue for a development from the only-inclusive type (Pc). The only-inclusive paradigm looks like the minimal set of a minimal/augmented paradigm, and a historical development from the only-inclusive to the minimal/augmented paradigm seems a reasonable guess. However, it turns out to be impossible to find any good evidence for this transition. There is much better evidence for the transition from the inclusive/exclusive type (Pd) to the minimal/augmented paradigm (Greenberg 1988: 6). The full evidence for this transition will be presented in Section 8.5.2. Anticipating that discussion, the connection to inclusive/exclusive (Pd) paradigms can be made plausible by taking another look at the Ilocano

---

[21] There are many examples of only-inclusive (Pc) paradigms that can be pluralized. In these cases, the plural forms have the same referential values as an augmented set. However, these plurals are never marked directly in the pronominal system. In all cases I have seen, the plural marker for a (Pc) paradigm is marked independently from the pronominal elements; e.g. the plural marker is a suffix, while the pronominal elements are prefixes.

	Singular	Group	
		ta	1+2
		tayo	1+2+3
1	co	mi	1+3
2	mo	yo	2+3
3	na	da	3+3

FIG. 3.6. *Singular/group analysis of Ilocano pronouns*

paradigm. The pronoun *tayo* in Ilocano is the odd one out as it is the only one, which is bisyllabic. It looks as though *tayo* is a later addition, made up from the 1+2 pronoun *ta* and the 2+3 pronouns *yo*. Interestingly, in the closely related language Pampangan, the equivalent pronoun *tami* is also the only disyllabic pronoun, but in this case it is made up from the 1+2 pronoun *ta* and the 2 singular pronoun *mi* (Gonzales 1981: 172–3). The two different structures of this pronoun argues for a late addition (see also the various origins of 1+2+3 as discussed by Reid 1979: 270). Also, there are many Philippine languages that have an inclusive/exclusive (Pd) or a minimal/augmented (Pe) pattern (Reid 1971), but I know of none that has an only-inclusive pattern (Pc).

For these reasons, paradigms like the Ilocano pronouns will be presented in yet another type of analysis in the present work. The paradigms will be displayed with two columns, distinguishing the singular and the group morphemes, as shown in Figure 3.6.[22]

3.6.6 Rare types

Finally, five other patterns of the first person complex are attested among the world's languages, but these patterns are rare. The examples of these patterns are incidental cases, probably only to be explained separately for each case with its own peculiar history. I will only synchronically describe all these rare cases in this section, and disregard them in later chapters. The rare patterns of the first person complex are repeated in Figure 3.7.

These five structures seem to fall in two classes. The first two patterns, (Pf) and (Pg), have no overlap between singular and non-singular categories, and are both attested in more than one case. In the other three patterns, an overlap between singular and non-singular is found, and these three patterns are each represented by

---

[22] Forchheimer (1953) seems to hint at a distinction between the minimal/augmented analysis (cf. Figure 3.5) and the singular/group analysis (cf. Figure 3.6) on the basis of the morphological structure of the forms for 'we'. His type IV-A4 can be compared to the singular/group analysis, and his IV-A2 to the minimal/augmented analysis (Forchheimer 1953: 83–4). However, I see no crucial difference in this respect between the presented paradigms from Winnebago (p. 88) and Sierra Popoluca (p. 93).

	(Pf)	(Pg)	(Ph)	(Pi)	(Pj)
1+2	A	A	A	–	
1+2+3	B	B	B	A	–
1+3		A	–		A

FIG. 3.7. *Rare patterns of the first person complex*

only one case. However, the number of examples is so small that it is difficult to judge whether this distinction in frequency is typologically salient. Future research has to discover whether the first two patterns have a different status compared to the others. The unusual structures of the pronominal paradigms that will figure in this section will be described by using the scheme as developed in Figure 3.6. The first column shows the singular forms, the second column shows the non-singular forms.

Type (Pf) has two different forms for 'we'. At first glance this might resemble an inclusive/exclusive type (Pd) paradigm, but actually the referential values of the two morphemes are different. In the case of (Pf), there is a specialized morpheme for the speech act dyad and another specialized morpheme for all other references of 'we'. This second morpheme has exclusive reference, but also augmented inclusive reference.[23] I know of three cases of this kind of paradigm, the first two of which are inflectional. In both these inflectional cases, the referential values of the inflectional morphemes can be exactly established because the independent pronouns in both languages distinguish augmented inclusive (1+2+3) from exclusive (1+3) and both pronouns are cross-referenced by the same homophonous affix on the verb. Shown in (3.15) is the first example of this unusual paradigmatic structure. This is the paradigm of the pronominal prefixes from the Australian language Bardi (Metcalfe 1975: 123).[24] Shown in (3.16) is the second inflectional example: the paradigm of the imperfect suffixes from the Papuan language Kunimaipa. In the case of Kunimaipa, other inflectional paradigms in the language are attested with different structures, one of which will follow shortly. The contrast between the various paradigmatic structures ensures that the strange-looking structures are genuine (Geary 1977: 26; Pence 1968: 110).[25] The final example of this type is the paradigm of the independent pronouns of Tiwi, a non-Pama-Nyungan language from Australia (Lee 1987: 101). In the description of Tiwi by Osborne (1974: 54),

---

[23] Greenberg (1988: 9) uses the name 'Assiniboine-type' for this paradigmatic structure, after the Siouan language Assiniboine. By my definition, however, Assiniboine is not part of this type. See Section 3.6.1 for an extensive discussion of the Assiniboine prefixes. The independent pronouns from Assiniboine (Greenberg 1989: 457) and also from the closely related Siouan language Lakhota (Van Valin 1977: 74–5) are also claimed to be of this type. However, Rood (1996: 454) does not corroborate this analysis in a recent description of Lakhota. The disagreement centres around the question whether the verbal suffix *-pi* can be used with independent pronouns or not.

[24] The independent pronouns from Bardi make up a minimal/augmented paradigm. They can be found in Metcalfe (1975: 49–50, 129).

[25] The independent pronouns from Kunimaipa have a unusual structure involving also dual forms. See Section 7.6 for a discussion of the independent pronouns from Kunimaipa.

92 Person Marking

a pronoun *ngagha* is observed for augmented inclusive. The difference between the two descriptions might be accounted for by dialectal differences, or it could be the result of recent changes. Note that in young people's speech, the minimal inclusive *muwa* has been lost as well, which results in a complete loss of the inclusive/exclusive opposition in the independent pronouns (Lee 1987: 101–3).[26]

(3.15) Bardi subject prefixes

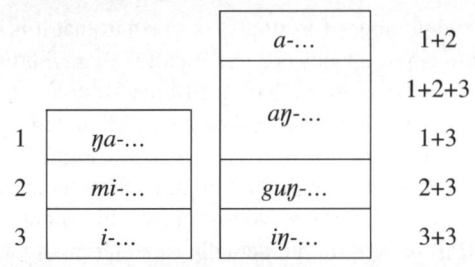

		a-...	1+2
		aŋ-...	1+2+3
1	ŋa-...		1+3
2	mi-...	guŋ-...	2+3
3	i-...	iŋ-...	3+3

(3.16) Kunimaipa imperfect suffixes

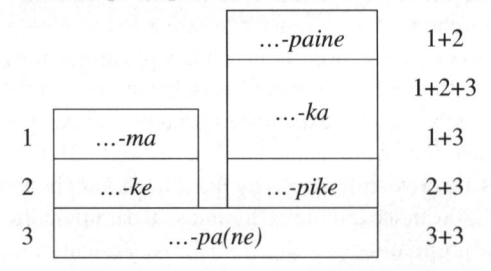

		...-paine	1+2
		...-ka	1+2+3
1	...-ma		1+3
2	...-ke	...-pike	2+3
3	...-pa(ne)		3+3

(3.17) Tiwi pronouns

		muwa	1+2
		ngawa	1+2+3
1	ngiya		1+3
2	nginja	nuwa	2+3
3	ngarra/nyirra	wuta	3+3

Paradigms of type (Pg) distinguish a separate form for 1+2+3, but unite the references to 1+2 and 1+3. This paradigmatic structure is found in the subject

---

[26] A related case is found in Guató, a Macro-Gé language from Brazil. The pronominal inflection is a complicated mix of pre- and suffixes, among them a prefix *ga-* for minimal inclusive and a prefix *dʒa-* for the remaining combination of augmented inclusive and exclusive reference (Palácio 1986: 368–9).

pronouns from Yaouré, a Mande language from Ivory Coast, as shown in (3.18). There are two different forms of 'we' in Yaouré:

kàà, which has an inclusive reference (the speaker and a group of listeners) and *kū*, which has either a dual reference (you and I) or an exclusive reference (the others and I).... The *kàà* form of the first person plural frequently reacts differently from the other pronouns. (Hopkins 1986: 192)

The morpheme *kàà* for augmented inclusive is the odd one out, as its morphophonological behaviour is different from the other pronouns. Possibly, this 1+2+3 pronoun is a recent addition to the pronominal paradigm.[27]

(3.18) Yaouré pronouns

		kū	1+2
		kàà	1+2+3
1	ā̄	kū	1+3
2	ī	kā	2+3
3	ē	ō	3+3

Other languages with (Pg) type paradigms are the Australian languages Gooniyandi and Bunaba. The independent pronouns from Gooniyandi are shown in (3.19). The difference between the two possible meanings of *ngidi* can be disambiguated by number suffixes. However, these number suffixes are only optionally used (McGregor 1989: 438–9; 1990: 167–9; 1996b). The same structure is found in the independent pronouns of the closely related language Bunaba (Rumsey 1996; 2000: 70–2). In both Gooniyandi and Bunaba, the verbal inflection shows the same structure (McGregor 1990; Rumsey 2000: 80–8).

(3.19) Gooniyandi pronouns

		ngidi	1+2
		yaadi	1+2+3
1	nganyi	ngidi	1+3
2	nginyi	gidi	2+3
3	niyi	bidi	3+3

---

[27] In Dan, another Mande language from Ivory Coast, there is a full 8-way pronominal system, with distinct elements for the categories 1+2, 1+3 and 1+2+3 (Doneux 1968: 45–7). However, most Mande languages do not show any sign of a minimal/augmented opposition. The Yaouré structure is an exceptional structure, not only worldwide, but also within its own family (Valentine Vydrine, p.c.).

94 Person Marking

A paradigm of type (Ph) separates the two different forms of the inclusive 'we' (1+2 and 1+2+3), but fails to grammaticalize the exclusive 'we' 1+3. The only example of a paradigm of type (Ph) that I am aware of comes from the Australian language Tiwi. The subject prefixes from Tiwi come in different variants. The version of interest here is the paradigm used when there is a masculine third person object, and the tense is non-past. This paradigm is shown in (3.20). Other prefixal paradigms from Tiwi do not show this structure. Even within the language itself, this seems to be a marked paradigmatic structure (Osborne 1974: 38; Lee 1987: 173).

(3.20) Tiwi non-past subject prefixes (masculine object)

			mu-...	1+2
			ŋa-...	1+2+3
1		ŋə-...		1+3
2		ṉə-...		2+3
3	a-...		wu-...	3+3

The perfective suffixes from Kunimaipa have a different structure compared to the imperfective suffixes shown in (3.16). The perfective suffixes, shown in (3.21), are the only example of a paradigm of type (Pi) that I am aware of. In this paradigm, the 1+2 reference is made by the same morpheme as is used to refer to the speaker alone. The other referential possibilities of 'we' are taken together with the second person plural (Pence 1968: 110).

(3.21) Kunimaipa perfective suffixes

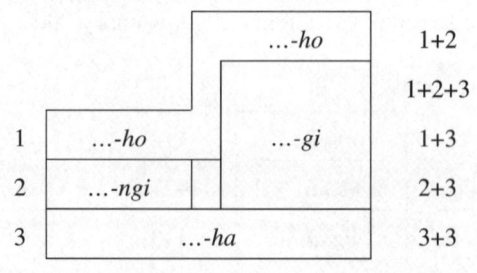

			...-ho	1+2
				1+2+3
1	...-ho		...-gi	1+3
2	...-ngi			2+3
3		...-ha		3+3

Finally, in a pronominal paradigm of type (Pj) there is a special morpheme for 'we', which refers to a group of category 1+3. One of the singular forms is used for the reference of 1+2 and 1+2+3. I know of only one example of this type (Pj), found in the inflection of the Papuan language Binandere. Shown in (3.22) are the 'past II stative' suffixes, but all other suffixal paradigms have the same structure (Capell 1969b: 16–31).

(3.22) Binandere past II stative suffixes

		...-ana	1+2
			1+2+3
1	...-ana	...-ara	1+3
2	...-ata	...-awa	2+3
3	...-evira	...-ara	3+3

The number of examples of these rare paradigms is so small and the structures are so heterogeneous, that it is difficult to draw any conclusive generalizations about this group. The main point that can be made is that these structures are unusual for human language.

3.7 Generalizations

Five patterns out of the fifteen theoretical possibilities for the first person complex are common among the world's languages. These five are summarized in Table 3.2. Only a few incidental paradigmatic structures are attested that do not belong to one of these five types. These five common patterns will be discussed extensively in the next chapter. In this section, I will formulate some generalizations on the structure of the common patterns. These generalizations will separate the five common patterns from the rare or unattested patterns.

In the majority of the world's languages, there is no separation between 1+2 and 1+2+3. Together these form the inclusive category, as opposed to the

TABLE 3.2. *Common marking types of the first person complex*

Name of type	Description of pattern
No-we	None of the three categories (1+2, 1+2+3, 1+3) is marked by a specialized morpheme.
Unified-we	All three categories (1+2, 1+2+3, 1+3) are marked by the same specialized morpheme.
Only-inclusive	The categories 1+2 and 1+2+3 are together marked by a specialized morpheme; the category 1+3 is not marked by a specialized morpheme.
Inclusive/exclusive	The categories 1+2 and 1+2+3 are marked by the same specialized morpheme; the category 1+3 is marked by a separate specialized morpheme.
Minimal/augmented	All three categories (1+2, 1+2+3, 1+3) are marked by separate specialized morphemes.

96   Person Marking

		Specialized inclusive	
		Yes	No
Specialized exclusive	Yes	Inclusive/exclusive, minimal/augmented	–
	No	Only-inclusive	Unified-we, no-we

FIG. 3.8. *Implication: exclusive → inclusive*

exclusive 1+3. An interesting generalization arises, with the structure of Binandere in (3.22) being the only exception: a specialized inclusive can exist without a specialized exclusive, but a specialized exclusive cannot exist without a specialized inclusive. This generalization can also be formulated as an implication (3.23). The logic behind this implication is illustrated by the cross-tabulation in Figure 3.8. If there is specialized marking for the exclusive in a pronominal paradigm, then there is specialized marking for the inclusive (cf. Universal 43 from Sokolovskaya 1980: 95). Or formulated in reverse order: there can only be a specialized exclusive when there is already a specialized inclusive.

(3.23)   Addressee inclusion implication I

Exclusive → Inclusive

In some languages, the inclusive is divided into two categories: a minimal inclusive (1+2) and an augmented inclusive (1+2+3). The split between the categories 1+2 and 1+2+3 is almost exclusively found in the form of a paradigm of the minimal/augmented type (Pe). There are only a few incidental cases of differently structured paradigms with a split between 1+2 and 1+2+3 (see types (Pf) and (Pg) in Section 3.6.6). Disregarding those incidental cases, the generalization that can be made is that in case of a split inclusive, there is always a specialized exclusive. This implication is shown in (3.24). The rationale behind this implication is illustrated by the occurrences as shown in Figure 3.9. If there is a split inclusive in a pronominal paradigm, then there is specialized marking for the exclusive 1+3. Or, formulated in reverse order: there can only be a split inclusive when there is already a specialized exclusive.

		Split inclusive	
		Yes	No
Specialized exclusive	Yes	Minimal/augmented	Inclusive/exclusive
	No	–	Unified-we, no-we, only-inclusive

FIG. 3.9. *Implication: split inclusive → exclusive*

(3.24) Addressee inclusion implication II
        Split Inclusive → Exclusive

These two implications can be combined into a hierarchy, but some care has to be taken in the formulation of this hierarchy. It might be tempting to concatenate the two implications to something like 'split inclusive → exclusive → inclusive', but that is logically not a valid generalization. The implications can be combined into a hierarchy when they are read as conditions. This becomes clear when both reversed formulations, as I have called them above, are taken together. These reversed implications are repeated here as (3.25). Combined, they state that there has to be an inclusive for there to be an exclusive, and there has to be an exclusive for there to be a split inclusive.

(3.25) There can only be an exclusive when there is also an inclusive;
        There can only be a split inclusive when there is also an exclusive.

This hierarchy of conditions is set out as a hierarchy of questions in Figure 3.10. The first choice in the hierarchy is whether there is any specialized marking at all for the first person complex. If there is, then the next question is whether there is specialized marking for the inclusive. If that is available, the next decision is whether the exclusive is overtly marked by a specialized morpheme. Finally, if all of this is true, then the inclusive can be split into a minimal inclusive and an augmented inclusive. The result is an implicational hierarchy of paradigmatic types. The hierarchy consists of a series of conceptual choices

\multicolumn{6}{c}{Is there any specialized form for 'we'?}
No	\multicolumn{5}{c}{Yes}
	\multicolumn{5}{c}{Is the inclusive specialized?}
	No	\multicolumn{4}{c}{Yes}
		\multicolumn{4}{c}{Is the exclusive specialized?}
		No	\multicolumn{3}{c}{Yes}
			\multicolumn{2}{c}{Is the inclusive split?}
↓				No	Yes
	↓				
			↓		
				↓	↓
No-we	Unified-we	Only-inclusive		Inclusive/ exclusive	Minimal/ augmented
(Pb)	(Pa)	(Pc)		(Pd)	(Pe)

FIG. 3.10. *Hierarchy of common structures of the first person complex*

98   *Person Marking*

that have to be made. These choices are interdependent: after each choice, only one of the possible decisions leads to a new choice. These choices form a hierarchy, and consequently the resulting types form a hierarchy as well. This hierarchy of types is summarized in (3.26).

(3.26)   First Person Hierarchy

no-we > unified-we > only-inclusive > inclusive/exclusive > minimal/augmented

3.8   Conclusion

This chapter started with some criticism of the concept 'plural' within the pronominal domain. Plurality is semantically a rather awkward concept for pronominal elements. 'Plural' pronouns are not always plural; more often their meaning is associative. Instead of plurality, the perspective of group marking was introduced, and followed throughout the chapter. The group perspective is not only semantically better equipped for the analysis of pronominal elements; it also naturally includes the widespread distinction between inclusive and exclusive 'we'.

There are seven theoretically possible groups. Five of these seven categories are actually attested in the world's linguistic variation. The five categories in the group perspective are: 1+3 (exclusive 'we'), 1+2 (minimal inclusive 'we'), 1+2+3 (augmented inclusive 'we'), 2+3 (plural 'you'), and 3+3 ('they'). As a start, only the marking of the first person complex was taken up in this chapter. The first person complex comprises the categories that include reference to the speaker: 1+3, 1+2, and 1+2+3. These three categories are all subsumed under the English pronoun *we*. The three categories of the first person complex can be combined theoretically into fifteen different marking patterns. Of these fifteen theoretical patterns, ten are attested in the world's languages. Five out of these ten are common, the other five are only found in incidental cases. The five common patterns form the First Person Hierarchy.

However, this is only a preliminary version of the definitive model of paradigmatic variation that will be developed in the next chapters. In general outline it is accurate, but some refinements and additions will be necessary once more categories and historical considerations are taken into account. First, I will now turn to a complete description of the paradigmatic variability of singular and group marking combined.

PART II
Paradigmatic Structure

> By focusing attention upon a small range of relatively esoteric problems, the paradigm forces scientists to investigate some part of nature in a detail and depth that would otherwise be unimaginable.
>
> Thomas S. Kuhn, *The Structure of Scientific Revolutions*

The grammatical term PARADIGM comes from the Greek *parádeigma*, which simply means 'example'. In the course of the first centuries BC, this word acquired the specific meaning of a prototypical example for grammatical declension or inflection, as in the famous series *amo, amas, amat* or *rosa, rosae, rosae, rosam, rosâ*. In the modern usage, the meaning of the term 'paradigm' refers to a set of grammatically conditioned forms that are all derived from a single root or stem. This sense of the term is attributed to Ferdinand de Saussure. In essence, this attribution is right, yet de Saussure used *rapport associatif* for what is today called a paradigm, and reserved the word *paradigme* for the classical meaning of declension and inflection (de Saussure 1916: 15, 170–80). Much later, Thomas Kuhn, in *The Structure of Scientific Revolutions*, adopted the term paradigm in imitation of the traditional grammatical usage of the word: 'In its established usage, a paradigm is an accepted model or pattern, and that aspect of its meaning has enabled me, lacking a better word, to appropriate "paradigm" here' (Kuhn 1962: 23).

In Part II I will investigate the structure of paradigms (in the modern sense of the word) that are used for person marking. In Chapter 4, an extensive typology of the paradigmatic structures attested among the world's languages will be presented. The first goal of this chapter is to present the wide variety of possibilities attested among the world's languages, and to classify this variation into a typology. Second, and most importantly, I will categorize the various types on a scale between common and rare, so as to add some relief to the monotone listing of possibilities. This typology will result in two hierarchies of person marking: the Explicitness Hierarchy and the Horizontal Homophony Hierarchy. In Chapter 5, the claim for even larger paradigms of person marking is investigated. These paradigms include so-called compound or complex pronouns besides the regular person markers. By a comparative investigation of various languages with such compound pronouns, I will show that there is indeed a special kind of pronoun attested. However, in the present state of description, these pronouns do not appear to add any new referential person categories to the paradigm.

4 The Diversity of the Core
A Survey of Patterns of Singular and Group Marking

4.1 Introduction

In the classical analysis of the *pronomen*, various *accidentia* ('attributes') of the pronoun were distinguished. For example, in the *Tékhne Grammatiké* by Dionysius Thrax, 'persons, genders, numbers, cases, shapes, species' are mentioned as possible attributes of pronouns (Uhlig 1883: 64; Kemp 1987: 182). Somewhat differently, the *Ars Minor* by Donatus lists the attributes 'quality, gender, number, form, person, case' (Chase 1926: 33). Many slightly different version of the list of attributes can be found in the classical literature, but all agree on one basic point: there is an unordered list of characteristics that are equally relevant to the analysis of pronouns. This classical analysis is rather different from what is found in more recent grammatical work. Today, the PERSONAL pronouns have been put at the top as the prototypical kind of pronoun, and the attributes person and number have become the central pivot for their description. However, there has never been a clear decision to change the perspective. Over the ages, the special status of the combination person/number has diffused slowly and largely unnoticed into grammatical practice. It dates back at least to *De Emendata Structura* (1524) by Thomas Linacre. He gives these two attributes a special place among the others because they occur with all declinable word classes (Luhrman 1984: 185, 205).[1] Over the following centuries, the combination person/number virtually becomes the basic framework to describe pronouns. Today, the special status of the person/number combination can be found in almost all grammars of particular languages, but also in more general works on personal pronouns such as Forchheimer (1953) and Kurylowicz (1964: 148–57), to name just two. The general acceptance of the primacy of the person/number combination indicates that there is a sense in which these two belong together, although a justification is never made explicit; the assumption has always been tacit.[2]

---

[1] The same special treatment of the combination person/number is also found in *De Causis* (1540) by Julius Scaliger (Luhrman 1984: 243). The first prolegomena to the prominence of the person/number combination can also be found in early descriptions of English (Vorlat 1975: 199–218) and Dutch (Dibbets 1995: 204–6).

[2] Not everybody, however, agrees on the special status of the combination person/number. In particular, many of the more theoretically oriented works on grammatical structure still treat person as

In this chapter, the complete variability of person/number marking among the world's languages will be described and classified according to their ubiquity. This chapter is structured as follows. In Section 4.2 the metalanguage for the description of the various paradigms is explained. This metalanguage will be used throughout the chapter, casting all examples in the same mould. The result of this unification is that the various structures can easily be compared. Also in Section 4.2, the criterion for distinguishing between common and rare paradigmatic structures is defined. Sections 4.3–6 will consist of a survey and discussion of the paradigmatic variation. The presentation in these sections will be rather lengthy, listing example after example of many different paradigmatic structures and their distribution among the world's languages. In total, fifty-six different paradigmatic structures will be described, of which eight will be classified as common and five as semi-common. The remaining forty-three patterns are rare. Finally, a summary and an analysis of the attested variation is presented in Section 4.7 and a conclusion in Section 4.8.

4.2 Method of classification

From the short historical survey in the introduction, it can be inferred that there is a sense in which the combination of person and number is at the core of pronominal marking. At the same time, however, the categories of person and number are two different dimensions. In this chapter, I will present a position in between these two approaches. For a proper cross-linguistic comparison of person marking, it is most promising to approach the analysis of number from a slightly different angle. In this perspective, the number dimension is split into two parts: 'general' non-singular reference (unmarked plural) and 'restricted' non-singular reference (dual, paucal, etc.). GENERAL NON-SINGULAR REFERENCE is defined as the marking that makes no difference as to the cardinality of the included referents, as long as the number is greater than a language-specific minimum, but at least greater than one. In contrast, for RESTRICTED NON-SINGULAR REFERENCE the cardinality of the set of referents is of crucial importance. In this chapter, general non-singular marking is surveyed together with singular marking. The unity of singular and general non-singular becomes obvious when the notion of 'plural' is replaced by the notion of 'group', as argued for in the previous chapter. In contrast to the quantitative nature of the concept number, groups have been defined qualitatively based on various combinations of the three singular participants. Both singular and group marking are considered to be unmarked for number in the present work (see Figure 4.1). The marking of restricted non-singular person reference will be pursued in Part III.

---

an individual attribute, separate from number (Jespersen 1924: 212–15; Lyons 1968: 276–81; 1977: 636–46; Croft 1990: 149–50).

Survey of Paradigmatic Structure 103

	Unmarked for number	Marked for number	
Traditional division:	SINGULAR	GENERAL NON-SINGULAR (PLURAL)	RESTRICTED NON-SINGULAR (DUAL, TRIAL ETC.)
Perspective of the present work:	Unmarked for number		Marked for number

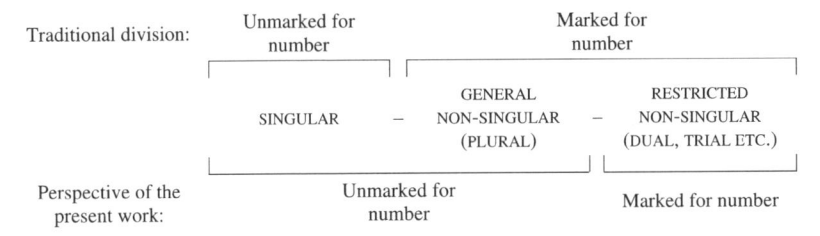

FIG. 4.1. *Different approaches to number marking in the pronominal domain*

In the preceding chapter, five kinds of group turned out to be salient linguistic categories. The three singular persons and the five groups of persons make up a core of eight categories for person reference. Not all pronominal paradigms grammaticalize all eight referential categories: some paradigms mark them all, others distinguish only a few different morphemes. In this chapter I will present the attested diversity of paradigmatic structures, ranging from paradigms with only two different morphemes up to paradigms that maximally distinguish all eight categories by different morphemes. Much is possible, but not everything is equally likely to be found. The main goal of this chapter is to decide which paradigmatic patterns are common and which are rare.

The presentation of the various paradigmatic structures in this chapter is streamlined by using a consistent metalanguage for all paradigms. In this way, the different structures can be easily compared. This metalanguage consists of the eight core categories: the three singular categories (1, 2, and 3) and the five different groups distinguished in the previous chapter (1+2, 1+2+3, 1+3, 2+3, and 3+3). This eight-way division is an improvement compared to the traditional six-way division, as argued extensively in the preceding chapter. First, it avoids the semantically troublesome notion of 'plural' in the pronominal domain. Second, it takes care of the inclusive/exclusive distinction in an integrated way. This eight-way division will be used instead of the traditional six-way division as a reference structure for the discussion of pronominal paradigms. The paradigms will be shown in a fixed graphic format, with the singular categories in the leftmost column and the group categories in the rightmost column, as presented in Figure 4.2. The various labels used for the different categories are added to the figure.

Different categories that are marked by one morpheme in a particular paradigm are shown as contiguous blocks without lines in between the categories. The term HOMOPHONY is used in a theory-neutral sense to talk about different kinds of combination of the various categories into the reference of one morpheme (see Section 2.2). I distinguish between three different kinds of homophony. A SINGULAR HOMOPHONY is a combination of different singular categories into the reference of one morpheme. The possible variants of singular homophony were

104   Paradigmatic Structure

			NON-SINGULAR		
		1+2	Minimal inclusive	Inclusive	First
SINGULAR		1+2+3	Augmented inclusive		person
Speaker	1	1+3	Exclusive		complex
Addressee	2	2+3	Second person plural		
Other	3	3+3	Third person plural		

FIG. 4.2. *Outline for presentation of paradigmatic structures*

extensively discussed in Chapter 2. A VERTICAL HOMOPHONY is a combination of different non-singular categories into the reference of one morpheme. Finally, a HORIZONTAL HOMOPHONY is a combination of a singular with a non-singular category into the reference of one morpheme. These three kinds of homophony are exemplified in Figure 4.3. In this figure, only homophony is shown between categories that happen to be contiguous blocks in the graphic format used. This is not necessarily so. Sometimes, non-contiguous categories are homophonous. In such cases, the blocks are connected with small corridors, as can, for example, be seen in examples (4.29) and (4.31).

In the previous chapter, I investigated the first person complex as the central classificatory device for the typology of paradigmatic structure. The first person complex is the set of group morphemes that include at least the first person, viz. the categories 1+2, 1+2+3, and 1+3 (see also Figure 4.2). Five of the fifteen possible patterns of the first person complex account for the great majority of the attested paradigmatic variation. These five major patterns of the first person complex are repeated here in Figure 4.4. Other structures of the first person complex were also attested, but these turned out to be only incidental cases that will not be considered in this chapter (see Section 3.6.6). The five major patterns are divided into two classes depending on whether or not there is an inclusive/exclusive opposition. This difference will turn out to be of major importance in explaining the cross-linguistic variation.

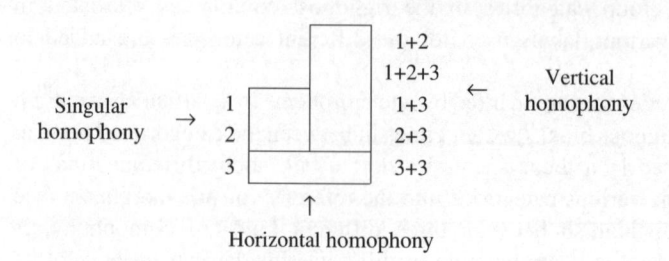

		1+2	
		1+2+3	← Vertical
Singular	1	1+3	homophony
homophony →	2	2+3	
	3	3+3	
		↑	
	Horizontal homophony

FIG. 4.3. *Different kinds of homophony*

	No-we	Unified-we	Only-inclusive	Inclusive/exclusive	Minimal/augmented
1+2			A	A	A
1+2+3	–	A	A	A	B
1+3			–	B	C

FIG. 4.4. *Major patterns of first person complex*

The five major patterns of the first person complex can be combined in various ways with the remaining group categories (2+3 and 3+3) and the singular categories (1, 2, and 3). In this chapter, fifty-eight different patterns are described in which languages order these eight categories. These fifty-eight different paradigmatic structures are not equally distributed over the world's linguistic variation. I will make a threefold distinction between COMMON, SEMI-COMMON, and RARE depending on the frequency and distribution of a pattern. The judgements that I present in this chapter are to be interpreted as a proposal to bring some order to the bewildering number of possibilities. The three classes are part of a continuum, which is only divided into these discrete classes to make it more accessible. The continuous nature of the variability makes the boundaries at times troublesome, and future research might indicate a different categorization.

There are two criteria for a pattern to be common: the pattern should be attested as widely dispersed throughout the world's languages (typically there are more than fifteen examples attested) and it should be a typical pattern in at least two genetic units. The first criterion assures that the pattern is found independently in different languages, beyond the influence of common genetic origin or areal contact. The second criterion assures that the pattern is relatively stable, as the attested examples are not all exceptional variants within their genetic group. Of the fifty-eight different paradigmatic structures that will be discussed in this chapter, eight will be classified as common. In contrast, a structure is rare if there are one or two unrelated examples, or eventually a few closely related examples. There are forty-five rare patterns described in this chapter, which all appear to be incidental examples of linguistic variation. I also distinguish five few semi-common paradigmatic structures, which fall between common and rare. Typically, the semi-common patterns occur in more than five genetically and areally independent cases and there is one instance of a genetic family in which the patterns is commonly attested.

The presentation of all cases will be divided into four sections. The pattern of the non-singular marking will be the principal guideline for the classification of the various paradigmatic structures. The basic division is between paradigms without an inclusive/exclusive opposition (Sections 4.3 and 4.4) and the paradigms with an inclusive/exclusive opposition (Sections 4.5 and 4.6). Within this basic division, the kind of vertical homophony will be used for a next level of classification. First, the SPLIT PATTERNS will be discussed. Split patterns are

106   *Paradigmatic Structure*

those structures that do not have any vertical homophony. Then the paradigmatic structures with a vertical homophony will be presented. The paradigmatic structures that are classified as common all turn out to belong to the class of split patterns. Separate subsections are devoted to showing that each of these common paradigmatic structures is indeed frequent among the world's languages, and to presenting a rough outline of their areal and genetic distribution. Given more time and energy, the lists of the common paradigmatic structures could easily be expanded. However, at present the main goal is to argue that these patterns are common, not to establish the precise fraction of the world's languages that have such common paradigmatic structures.

4.3 No inclusive/exclusive: split non-singular

4.3.1 Preamble

Paradigms without an inclusive/exclusive opposition are characterized by combined marking of all referential values for 'we'. The three different kinds of 'we' (1+2, 1+2+3, and 1+3) are all marked with the same morpheme. The English pronoun *we* is an example of such a unified form. In this section, only the SPLIT paradigms will be discussed. This means that there are three different non-singular morphemes in all cases that will be presented; one for the combined 'we', one for 2+3 and one for 3+3. Within this restriction, there are various paradigmatic structures attested, depending on the kind of homophony between these three non-singular categories and the singular categories. All in all, fifteen different paradigmatic structures will be presented in this section. Among these paradigms, four paradigmatic structures are common. These common variants will be referred to as the LATIN-TYPE paradigm (Section 4.3.2), the SINHALESE-TYPE paradigm (Section 4.3.3), the BERIK-TYPE paradigm (Section 4.3.4), and the MARICOPA-TYPE paradigm (Section 4.3.5). In the discussion of these structures, a rough outline of the geographical and genetic stratification will be presented. Besides these four common patterns, eleven rare split paradigmatic structures are attested (Section 4.3.6).

4.3.2 Latin-type paradigm

The Latin-type paradigm is well known as a structure of pronominal paradigms. In such a paradigm, there is a threefold distinction between the non-singular categories 'we', 'you-all', and 'they'. These categories are distinct from each other and they are also distinct from the singular marking. A prototypical example of this pattern is the Latin inflection. In (4.1), the suffixes of the Latin present indicative are shown. The same inflectional paradigmatic structure can still be found in the inflection of the south-western Romance languages Portuguese,

Catalan, and Italian (Posner 1996: 39–43). The Latin-type paradigmatic structure is often considered the prototypical pattern of all pronominal marking. As I will show in the rest of this chapter, it is in fact only one of the patterns that can be found regularly among the languages of the world. Other patterns can also be regarded as typical for the structure of human language. The Latin-type paradigm is indeed a common pattern, but it is not the only common one.

(4.1) Latin present indicative

		...-mus	1+2
			1+2+3
1	...-o		1+3
2	...-s	...-tis	2+3
3	...-t	...-unt	3+3

Paradigms of the Latin type are widespread among the Indo-European inflections, although they are not as widespread as is often assumed.[3] The Indo-European independent pronouns often have gender distinctions, or use demonstrative elements in the third person. Such paradigms are close to the Latin-type, but they are not prototypical examples of this type. Still on the Eurasian continent, paradigms of the exact Latin-type are commonly attested in the Uralic inflection.[4] It is also found in the Turkish inflection (Lewis 1967: 106–7).

Most African languages have gender distinctions (or class marking) in the third person. Cases of 'pure' Latin-type paradigms without gender or class marking can be found among the independent pronouns of the Mande languages and the Nilotic languages.[5] Many South-East Asian languages do not have grammaticalized morphemes for non-singular marking, and consequently these do not have a Latin-type paradigm. Modern Chinese developed a Latin-type independent pronoun system, and in some variants there is even an inclusive/exclusive distinction (Norman 1988: 117–21, 157–8).

---

[3] The Latin-type paradigm is found among the Iranian languages (Sims-Williams 1998: 144–9), the Slavic languages (Andersen 1998: 445–6), and the Brythonic languages Breton (Stephens 1993: 373–5) and Early Cornish (George 1993: 446–7). Many paradigms of independent pronouns in European language have roughly a Latin-type paradigm. However, there are almost always gender distinctions in the third person singular and sometimes even in other categories, like the gender distinctions in the Spanish first and second person plural (Plank and Schellinger 1997: 70).

[4] Short descriptions of Uralic languages can be found in Abondolo (1998b). Most Uralic languages have a Latin type inflection. See e.g. Estonian (pp. 140–1), Finnish (pp. 171–4), Mordva (pp. 197–201), Mari (pp. 229–31), and Udmurt (pp. 289–91).

[5] For Mande, see e.g. Vai (Welmers 1976: 43), Mauka (Ebermann 1986: 74), Koranko (Kastenholz 1987: 1720), and Kpelle (Westermann 1924: 14–15). For Nilotic, see e.g. Maasai (Tucker and Mpaayei 1953: 200), Lotuho (Muratori 1938: 72), Southern Nilotic (Rottland 1982: 137–9, 151, 194, 229, 248–9), and Dinka (Nebel 1948: 15).

Further south, into the Pacific, there are only exceptional examples of a Latin-type paradigm among the Austronesian languages, because most pronominal paradigms have an inclusive/exclusive opposition.[6] In contrast, paradigms of the Latin-type are widespread among the Papuan languages from New Guinea.[7] Finally, Latin-type paradigms are found throughout the American languages, but they are not as common here as elsewhere in the world.[8]

4.3.3 Sinhalese-type paradigm

The next common type of paradigmatic structure is only slightly different from the Latin-type paradigm. The defining characteristic of the present paradigm is that it does not have a specialized element for the category 3+3, the third person plural. The paradigms in this section mark the third person plural together with the third person singular. In the case of independent pronouns, it is possible (but not necessary) for the categories 3 and 3+3 to be marked outside the pronominal system. Both categories can be marked by demonstratives or other linguistic material which strictly speaking does not belong to the pronominal domain. Such paradigms with zero (or non-existing, see Section 2.5.3) third person marking are also included here. An example of this type of paradigm is shown in (4.2). These are the independent pronouns from Sinhalese, an Indo-Aryan language from Sri Lanka (Gair 1970: 32–3).

(4.2) Sinhalese pronouns

		api	1+2
			1+2+3
1	mamə		1+3
2	ohee	oheela	2+3
3	(demonstratives)		3+3

The Sinhalese-type paradigm is found in Eurasia, albeit scarcely. Apart from Sinhalese, more cases are attested among Indo-Aryan languages where third persons are often demonstratives (Masica 1991: 251). It is also found in some other languages on the Eurasian continent that do not have third person marking

---

[6] Lynch (1998: 101) mentions the independent pronouns of the Siau family in the West Sepik Province of Papua New Guinea (e.g. Sera, Sissano, Ali, Tumleo, and Ulau-Suain), Kiribati, and possibly one or two varieties of Fijian.

[7] A few random examples of Latin-type paradigms from new Guinea are the Daga inflection and independent pronouns (Murane 1974: 34, 42–4, 63–9), the Waskia future inflection (Ross and Paol 1978: 68), and the Asmat subject suffix (Voorhoeve 1965: 85). This type of pronominal paradigm seems to be widespread, as can be seen from the surveys of Papuan languages by Voorhoeve (1975) and Wurm (1975b).

[8] e.g. the West Greenlandic intransitive inflection (Fortescue 1984: 288), the Ika independent pronouns (Frank 1990: 26), and the Epena Pedee independent pronouns (Harms 1994: 186, 58).

Survey of Paradigmatic Structure 109

within the pronominal domain, for example, the independent pronouns from Kannada, a Dravidian language from India (Sridhar 1990: 203), Buriat, an Altaic language from Siberia (Poppe 1960: 49–52), and Lezgian, a Nakh-Dagestanian from the Caucasus (Haspelmath 1993: 184).

Sinhalese-type paradigms are uncommon in Africa, but this pattern is a general characteristic of the Southern Nilotic subject prefixes. The structure with five different prefixes is found throughout the Southern Nilotic languages. The third person is always overtly marked in Datooga and Omotik, but only occasionally in the Kalenjin languages; in the latter it is often zero. The forms for Proto-Southern Nilotic as reconstructed by Rottland (1982: 243–4) are shown in (4.3).

(4.3) Proto-Southern Nilotic subject prefixes

			1+2
		*kɪ/kɛ-...	1+2+3
1	*a-...		1+3
2	*ɪ-...		*ɔ-...	2+3
3		*kɔ/ø-...	3+3

Paradigms of the Sinhalese-type are common among North American languages. It is, for example, generally found in the Salish pronominal systems (Newman 1980: 156; Davis 2000: 500, 513) and in the Muskogean pronominal affixes. It is exemplified here in (4.4) with the patient prefixes from the Muskogean languages Chickasaw (Payne 1982: 359).[9] A Sinhalese-type paradigm is also found in the Nootka indicative suffixes (Swadesh 1936: 82), shown here in (4.5). It was probably also found in the extinct South American language Muisca (Gonzáles de Pérez 1987: 74).

Finally, there are also languages from New Guinea with a pronominal paradigm of the Sinhalese-type. This pattern is, for example, found in the independent pronouns from Sentani (Cowan 1965: 16) and Asmat (Voorhoeve 1965: 143). The Asmat independent pronouns are shown in (4.6).

(4.4) Chickasaw patient prefixes

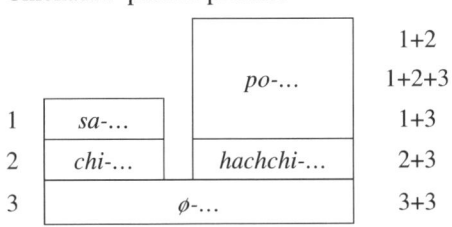

			1+2
		po-...	1+2+3
1	sa-...		1+3
2	chi-...		hachchi-...	2+3
3		ø-...	3+3

---

[9] The same structure is also found in other Muskogean languages, e.g. Alabama (Lupardus 1982: 66–74), Koasati (Kimball 1985: 107), and Choctaw (Nicklas 1974: 31).

110   *Paradigmatic Structure*

(4.5)   Nootka indicative suffixes

		...-(m)in	1+2
			1+2+3
1	...-(m)ah		1+3
2	...-(m)eʔic	...-(m)eʔico	2+3
3	...-ma	3+3

(4.6)   Asmat pronouns

		me	1+2
			1+2+3
1	da		1+3
2	wa	ma	2+3
3	na	3+3

4.3.4 Berik-type paradigm

The third common paradigmatic structure has even more horizontal homophony. In this type of paradigm, only one non-singular morpheme is grammaticalized. A morpheme exists for the complete first person complex, nothing else. In contrast, the other two group categories (2+3 and 3+3) are marked by the corresponding singular morphemes. This means that the morpheme for 2 also marks the category 2+3 and the morpheme for 3 also marks the category 3+3. This paradigmatic structure will be called a Berik-type paradigm, as it is exemplified here by the independent pronouns from Berik, a Tor language spoken on New Guinea. Shown in (4.7) is the paradigm referred to as 'Subject$_1$' in the description. There are many more formally and functionally different forms of the independent pronouns, but they all show this same paradigmatic structure (Westrum and Wiesemann 1986: 38–9).

(4.7)   Berik pronouns

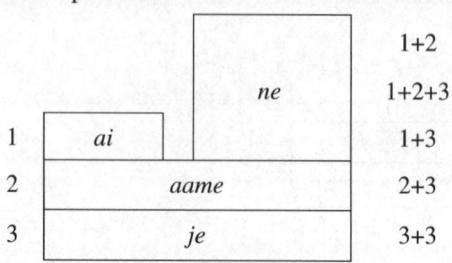

		ne	1+2
			1+2+3
1	ai		1+3
2	aame	2+3
3	je	3+3

Survey of Paradigmatic Structure   111

```
        Berik-type                           Sierra Popoluca-type

                  |      | 1+2                         |      | 1+2
           'we'  |      | 1+2+3              'we'    |      | 1+2+3
    1    |_____|      | 1+3         1     |_____|      | 1+3
    2    |_____| 2+3         2     |_____| 2+3
    3    |_____| 3+3         3     |_____| 3+3
```

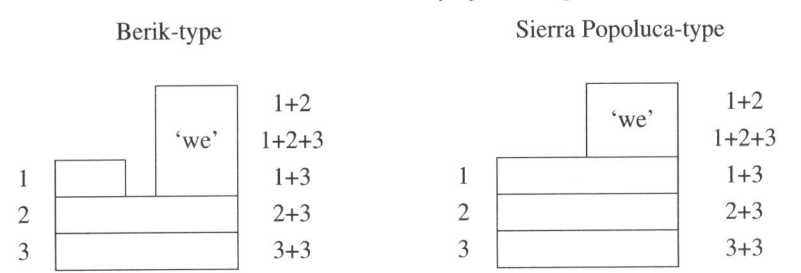

FIG. 4.5. *The difference between the Berik-type and the Sierra Popoluca-type*

Before I proceed with the other examples of the Berik-type paradigm, a word of caution is in order. The Berik-type paradigm is very similar to another paradigm that will be discussed later in this chapter, the Sierra Popoluca-type. Some extra care has to be taken to ensure that a paradigm is indeed an example of the Berik-type. The two similar paradigms are shown schematically in Figure 4.5. They might appear rather different, but in practice they are easily mistaken for each other. The significant correspondence between the two paradigms is that they have only one non-singular morpheme, and in both cases this morpheme is to be translated into English with the pronoun *we*. Taken at face value, both paradigms seem to consist of four different elements: 'I', 'you', 'he/she/it', and 'we'. However, the two variants of 'we' are rather different. In the case of the Berik-type, this morpheme has both the inclusive and the exclusive reading. In the Sierra Popoluca-type, the morpheme marking 'we' has only an inclusive reading. The main argument to classify a paradigm as a case of the Berik-type, and not as a case of the Sierra Popoluca-type, is by transitive uses of this 'we', as in sentences like 'We see you'. An important presupposition of this sentence is that the object 'you' is not part of the subject 'we'. The sentence 'We see you' can normally only be interpreted if the 'we' has exclusive reading. This fact can be used to distinguish the two paradigms. If the specialized form of 'we' can be used in sentences like 'We see you', then the 'we' can also be used to mark the exclusive. In this case, the paradigm is of the Berik-type.

Besides in Berik, this pattern is also found in Kuman, another Papuan language from New Guinea. The independent pronouns from Kuman are shown in (4.8), as presented by Foley (1986: 70, citing Piau).[10] The pronouns from Kuman resemble the ones from Berik, but they are at most distantly related and spoken in completely different regions of the Island. A third example of this paradigmatic structure among the Papuan languages is found in Jéi (Boelaars 1950: 49).

---

[10] This language is referred to as Kamanagu by Capell (1940: 54) and Forchheimer (1953: 65–6).

(4.8) Kuman pronouns

		no	1+2
			1+2+3
1	na		1+3
2		ene	2+3
3		ye	3+3

Paradigms of the Berik-type are found in the Siouan language family from North America. It is exemplified in (4.9) with the active prefixes from Mandan (Mixco 1997: 17). As can be seen from the transitive sentence (4.10), the meaning of the prefix *rų-* can also be exclusive. The addressee is the object of the verb 'to tell', so this addressee is probably not part of the subject 'we'. This structure is also found in another Siouan language, Assiniboine (Levin 1964: 31–2). The prefix *u(k)-* can have both inclusive and exclusive reading, as shown in (4.11). Example (4.11a) is explicitly described as an inclusive. Example (4.11b) is a transitive sentence with an addressee as object. Because the addressee is in object function here, it is not part of the subject. This means that the 'we' subject does not include the addressee; the 'we' subject is exclusive in reference. The same structure as in Assiniboine is also described for Lakhota by Van Valin (1977: 5, 10–13).

(4.9) Mandan active prefixes

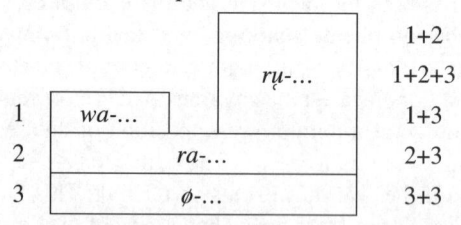

			1+2
		rų-...	1+2+3
1	wa-...		1+3
2		ra-...	2+3
3		ø-...	3+3

(4.10) Mandan (Mixco 1997: 17)
 rų-rį-kirąktoʔš
 EXCL-2-tell
 'We will tell you.'

(4.11) Assiniboine (Levin 1964: 31, 64)
 a. ųk-áksa
  1+2-chop
  'I and you chop off something.'
 b. cazé-ų-ni-yata-pi
  ?-EXCL-2-call-PLUR
  'We call you.'

Other examples in America will only be listed here. First, the pronominal prefixes from Coahuilteco, a language isolate from Texas, are of the Berik type (Troike 1996: 655). Switching to South America, a Berik-type paradigm is attested in the pronominal prefixes from Chulupi, a Mataco-Guiacuruan language from Paraguay (Susnik 1968: 66–8). Finally, Berik-type paradigms are found in the Gé family from Brazil, specifically in the pronominal prefixes from the closely related languages Xerente (Wiesemann 1986b: 365), Xavante (Lachnitt 1988: 33), and in the person markers from Xokleng (Urban 1985: 167), shown in (4.12).[11]

(4.12) Xokleng person markers

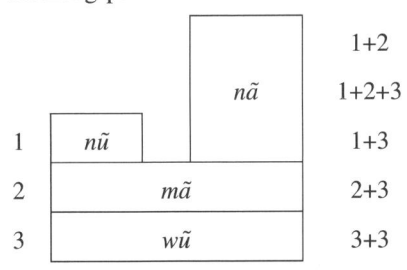

			1+2
		nã	1+2+3
1	nũ		1+3
2		mã	2+3
3		wũ	3+3

Another group of languages with a pronominal paradigm of the Berik-type is the Eastern Nilotic family, a subgroup from the Nilo-Saharan stock in Africa. The structure of the subject prefixes from these languages is exemplified here with the prefixes from Turkana (Dimmendaal 1982: 120), shown in (4.13). From the example sentences in (4.14), it can be seen that the prefix kì- can have both an inclusive and an exclusive reading. There is an inclusive/exclusive difference in the independent pronouns, and kì- can be used co-referentially with both.[12]

(4.13) Turkana subject prefixes

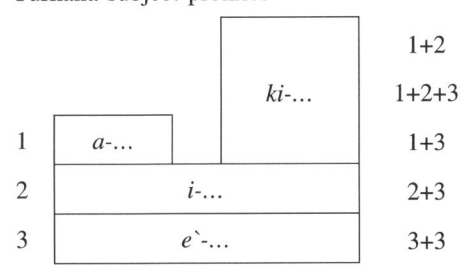

			1+2
		ki-...	1+2+3
1	a-...		1+3
2		i-...	2+3
3		e`-...	3+3

---

[11] The forms shown in (4.12) are probably the same forms as the 'nominative' forms as described by Wiesemann (1986b: 363). However, the paradigm as presented by Wiesemann also distinguishes number in the second and third person, so it might be that Xokleng is not a good example of a Berik-type paradigm.

[12] For other Eastern Nilotic languages, the same structure is found in Teso (Tucker and Bryan 1966: 470), Maasai (Tucker and Mpaayei 1953: 53), and Lotuho (Tucker and Bryan 1966: 470). For a general discussion of the form of the prefixes, see Dimmendaal (1983: 279).

(4.14) Turkana (Dimmendaal 1982: 122)
    a. *kì-losì   sʊà*
       1PL-go   EXCL
       'We (exclusive) will go.'

    b. *kì-losì   ŋwɔ̀nį̀*
       1PL-go   INCL
       'We (inclusive) will go.'

In the Nilo-Saharan stock, I know of two other Berik-type paradigms: the prefixes from Mbay, a central Sudanic language from Chad (Keegan 1997: 24), and the prefixes from Lango, a Western Nilotic language from Tanzania (Noonan 1992: 91–3). In Lango, the second person plural is disambiguated from the second person singular by a suffix *-wùnú*. A final example of the Berik-type is the paradigm of the object prefixes from Georgian, a South Caucasian language (Cherchi 1999: 30–1).

It appears less easy to find examples of the Berik-type, compared to the abundance of examples of the previously discussed Latin-type and Sinhalese-type. Still, there are a few families in which the Berik-type is found throughout the family, and there is a good geographical spread of examples.[13] This is enough to grant this type the status of common, although it should be kept in mind that it is less common than the two previous types.[14]

4.3.5 Maricopa-type paradigm

The fourth common paradigmatic structure without an inclusive/exclusive opposition fits nicely with the preceding ones. Again, there is more horizontal homophony, this time to the point that there is no specialized non-singular category anymore. This paradigmatic structure is exemplified in (4.15) with the intransitive prefixes from Maricopa, a Yuman language from the USA (Gordon 1986: 15–21). All three singular categories are also used for non-singular marking. The categories 1+2, 1+2+3, and 1+3 are taken together with 1; the category 2+3 is taken together with 2 and the category 3+3 is taken together with 3. Foley

---

[13] The Semitic imperfect prefixes have to be mentioned in this context, although they are strictly speaking not of the Berik-type. In almost all Semitic languages, second and third person imperfect are marked by prefixes and number is marked by suffixes. The complicating factor is that third person singular feminine uses the same prefix as the second person (Hetzron 1990: 660).

[14] Forchheimer (1953: 65–6) also mentions the Korean independent pronouns as an example of the Berik-type paradigmatic structure. More recent descriptions suggest that the independent pronouns from Korean are not a good example of a Berik-type paradigm, although they might historically be derived from such a structure. Synchronically, the independent pronouns have a separate stem for the first person plural in non-deferential contexts. The other non-singular forms do not have a separate stem. However, these non-singulars are obligatorily marked by a number suffix (Sohn 1994: 284–7). I interpret this number suffix as part of the pronominal paradigm. Consequently, the paradigm is not an example of the Berik-type, but of the Latin-type (see also Section 3.3).

(1986) remarks that such a paradigmatic structure is rare: 'such a system seems unusual among the languages of the world, in which person and number are commonly expressed together in a single morpheme' (p. 132). Contrary to this position, I will show in this section that this system is fairly widespread among the world's languages. This structure can occur both in inflectional paradigms and in morphologically independent paradigms. I will discuss these two possibilities separately because there are special considerations for both kinds of marking.

In most languages that have such a pattern in their inflection, these person markers are prefixes, and there are affixes somewhere in the language (often suffixes) that mark number. This inflectional pattern, as described for Maricopa, can be found in all Yuman languages.[15] In general, it is widespread among the languages of America.[16] Other than these, there are hardly any inflectional examples from other parts of the world.[17]

(4.15) Maricopa intransitive subject prefixes

		1+2
		1+2+3
1	ʔ-...	1+3
2	m-...	2+3
3	∅-...	3+3

A Maricopa-type paradigm is also frequently attested among independent pronouns. However, it is often difficult to say whether the marking of the group categories is taken over by the singular pronouns, or whether there is no marking at all for the group categories (cf. the discussion in Section 2.5.3 on zero marking). Both options seem to occur, although a clear dividing line cannot be

---

[15] e.g. Mojave (Munro 1976: 10–14), Diegueño (Langdon 1970: 139–40), Yavapai (Kendall 1976: 5–8), and Yuma (Halpern 1946: 281–2).

[16] Travelling north to south through America, let me just mention a few other fairly randomly chosen examples of this pattern. All these examples consist of pronominal prefixes and number suffixes. Pronominal prefixes of the Maricopa-type are found in the Siouan languages Hidatsa (Matthews 1965: 55, 71; Robinett 1955: 177) and Crow (Lowie 1941: 31–6). The pronominal prefixes of the isolated languages Kutenai (Garvin 1948: 171–87), Washo (Jacobsen 1964), and Acoma Keresan (Maring 1967: 77–9, 83–5) are of this type. Pronominal prefixes with number suffixes are also found in the Otopamean languages Pame (Manrique 1967: 343–4), Chichimeco Jonaz (Lastra de Suárez 1984: 29–30), and Ixtenco Otomí (Lastra 1998: 12). The same structure is attested in Coatlán Mixe, a Mixe-Zoque language from Mexico (Hoogshagen 1984: 8). In South America, the inflectional prefixes from Ayoreo, a Zamucoan language from Paraguay, are of this type (Susnik 1973: 52–7), and the Mataco-Guaicuruan languages Abipon (Najlis 1966: 30–4; Susnik 1986/7: 91–3) and Mataco (Hunt 1940: 40–4) as well.

[17] Some incidental cases are the Central Sudanic languages Logbara (Crazzolara 1960: 73) and Mamvu (Vorbichler 1971: 227–8) and the East Papuan language Nasioi (Hurd and Hurd 1970: 47–55).

drawn. The independent pronouns of the American language Acoma Keresan are a case where the extension into the non-singular pronouns does not seem possible. The Acoma pronouns only distinguish two forms: *hínumˤé* and *hišumˤé*. These two words are strictly used to mark speaker and addressee. They can not be used for 'we' or 'you-plural' respectively. This pronominal paradigm only consists of two elements; the rest of the categories are non-existent (Maring 1967: 43–4, 113–14). A different and more common situation is found in Salt-Yui, a non-Austronesian language from Papua New Guinea. Just as in Acoma, there are only two independent pronouns. In Salt-Yui, the two pronouns are *na* and *ni*. These pronouns are used for speaker and addressee reference. There is no third person pronoun; other linguistic material is used to mark this function. Also, there is no number distinction in this pronominal paradigm (Irwin 1974: 32). In the case of Salt-Yui, however, the independent pronouns can also be used for plural reference. As shown in (4.16a), the first person pronoun can also be used for 'we'. In (4.16b), a second person pronoun is used for 'you-plural'. A plural noun *yasu*, meaning 'two people', is added for clarification. In other examples (not shown here) the noun *yalhobi*, meaning 'fellows' is used to clarify the plurality of *ni* (Irwin 1974: 74). The paradigmatic structure of the independent pronouns of Salt-Yui as shown in (4.17) is probably identical to the Maricopa structure as shown in (4.15). Some caution has to be exercised, as there is no clear example of an inclusive use of the pronoun *na* in the grammar.

(4.16) Salt-Yui (Irwin 1974: 135, 61)
    a. na   ama   ha   holo   wamga...
       1   girls talk collecting walk
       'When we court the girls...'

    b. ni   yasu   ala   mol   dibilge
       2   two people inside COP say
       'You are both inside!'

(4.17) Salt-Yui pronouns

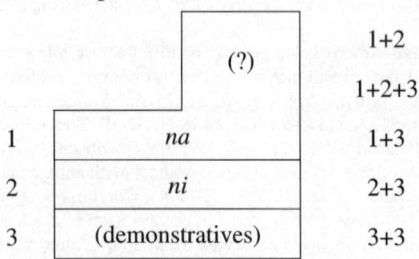

		(?)
		1+2
		1+2+3
1	na	1+3
2	ni	2+3
3	(demonstratives)	3+3

In many languages, number is not marked inside the pronominal paradigm. Often plurality is only marked as an overt addendum to pronouns. In Salt-Yui, words like 'people' and 'fellows' are used to mark plurality. In Golin, a language from New Guinea related to Salt-Yui, the word *kobe*, meaning 'people' is used (Foley 1986: 70, citing Bunn).[18] In many South-East Asian languages there are so-called associative markers that can be used to produce group-marking reference from singular referential elements (see Section 3.6.2). Such associative markers turn a pronoun 'I' into something like 'I and my fellows', which can be translated as 'we', although only in the exclusive meaning. In modern Cantonese a suffix *-dei* is used, as exemplified in (4.18). This suffix is found not only with independent pronouns but also with proper names, like *Ling*. The same situation is found in Japanese, using a suffix *-tachi*.[19]

(4.18) Cantonese
ngo — I
ngo-dei — I and associates, 'we'
lei — you
lei-dei — you and associates, 'you-all'
ah Ling dei — Ling and his associates, Ling and that crowd

In Vietnamese, nominal elements like *chúng* (a word from Chinese origin meaning 'many, the people'), *bon* (meaning 'gang'), or *tui* (meaning 'clique') are used to mark plurality (Nguyen 1996: 10–11). This addition seems obligatory to mark plural. In this case the associative marking is grammaticalized as part of the pronominal paradigm. Consequently, it is no longer a case of a Maricopa-type paradigm, but an example of a Latin-type paradigm. In other languages, however, the addition to disambiguate nouns is only needed when the context requires it. The optional use of associative marking is also found in Classical Chinese, where a word meaning 'group' or 'associates' could be used to overtly mark plurality (Norman 1988: 89–90).

A Maricopa-type paradigm in independent pronouns is a fairly widespread phenomenon. South-East Asian and New Guinean examples have already been discussed extensively. Let me add two examples from South America to extend the geographical distribution of this kind of pronominal paradigm. The independent pronouns from Xerente, a Gé language from Brazil, is probably of the Salt-Yui type, although the description is not completely clear on this point (Wiesemann 1986b: 361, 364–8). The independent pronouns from Paez, a language from Colombia, are clearly described as a paradigm of this type, although there are different forms for gender (Rojas Curieux 1991: 52–3).

---

[18] Separate marking for plurality of pronouns is also found in Manem, another non-Austronesian language from Papua New Guinea, not directly related to Salt-Yui and Golin (Voorhoeve 1975: 416). The short grammatical notes in the source do not mention the precise function of this pluralizer.

[19] These data on associative marking come from a data file compiled by E. Moravcsik, collected through a query on the Linguistlist (Moravcsik 1994). On Cantonese, see also Norman (1988: 219–20). On Japanese, see also Shibatani (1990: 371–2).

118   *Paradigmatic Structure*

4.3.6   Rare variants

There are a few examples of paradigms with a split non-singular that do not belong to one of the four common paradigmatic structures that have just been discussed. First, I will present those cases that have aberrant combinations of horizontal homophony. Then I will discuss the cases with a special 'diagonal' overlap between singular and non-singular marking. Finally, there are some paradigms with a singular homophony. All these cross-linguistically unusual structures, as presented in this section, have a split non-singular: they all have three different morphemes for the traditional categories first–second–third plural.

Probably the most famous case of horizontal homophony is the paradigm of the English pronouns shown in (4.19). The formerly plural element *ye/you* has taken over the reference of the singular *thou/thee* (Howe 1996: 170–75). Exactly the same structure is attested in various variants of South American Spanish pronouns, where the formerly plural pronoun *vos* has taken over the reference of the singular *tu*. The same change took place in Dutch, but the distinction between a singular and plural second person has been restored by the addition of a new plural pronoun *jullie* (Howe 1996: 220–7). Because all these well-known and extensively described languages underwent this change, it is sometimes thought of as a common change. It might be a common change, but its end state is not common at all. The paradigmatic structure of the English pronoun, as shown in (4.19), is not attested frequently among the world's languages. Even for English, the overarching *you* is mainly found in the standard language. In a thorough study of present-day English, Wales (1996) observes: 'many dialects and varieties of English seem to find a formal distinction extremely useful between a single addressee and more than one, at least for statements and questions' (pp. 16–17, 73). A final case of the same paradigmatic structure as in English is the pronoun paradigm from Xokleng, a Gé language from Brazil, shown in (4.20). Just as in English, there is a gender distinction in the third person singular (Urban 1985: 167).[20]

(4.19)   English pronouns

		we	1+2
			1+2+3
1	*I*		1+3
2	*you*		2+3
3	*he/she/it*	*they*	3+3

---

[20] Wiesemann (1986b: 363) describes these pronouns as 'non-nominative'. It may seem that there is a separate 2+3 form in this description, but that form is made by adding the plural marker *mẽ*. This plural morpheme is an independent element in most Gé languages, and is strictly speaking not part of the pronominal paradigm (Popjes and Popjes 1986: 185; Wiesemann 1986b: 361).

(4.20) Xokleng pronouns

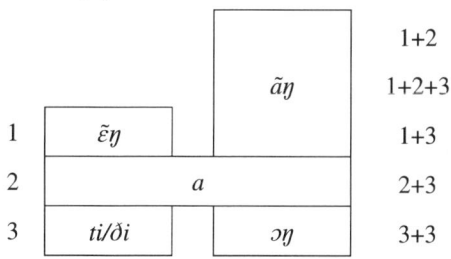

		ãŋ	1+2
			1+2+3
1	ẽŋ		1+3
2	a		2+3
3	ti/ði	ɔŋ	3+3

A few cases distinguish singular from non-singular only in the second person, precisely the opposite distribution of horizontal homophony as in English. The first example comes from Classical Ainu, shown in (4.21). The prefixes shown are used for transitive subject marking (Shibatani 1990: 25). Exactly the same paradigmatic structure is found in the independent pronouns of Tairora, a highland language from New Guinea, shown in (4.22). These pronouns are related to the pronouns from Usarufa, as shown later in (4.44). The data on Tairora are from Foley (1986: 255). Still another example with the same structure is the paradigm of the affixes from Gubden, a dialectal variant of Dargi, shown in (4.23). Dargi is a Nakh-Dagestanian language spoken in Dagestan. This paradigm is related to the suffixes of literary Dargi, as shown later in (4.45). The data on Gubden are from Helmbrecht (1996: 138).

(4.21) Classical Ainu transitive subject prefixes

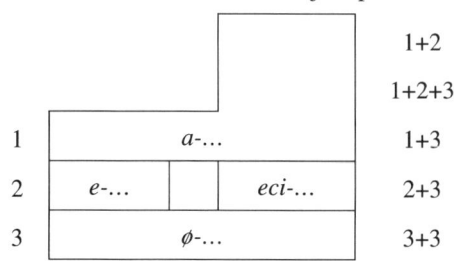

		a-...		1+2
				1+2+3
1				1+3
2	e-...		eci-...	2+3
3		ø-...		3+3

(4.22) Tairora pronouns

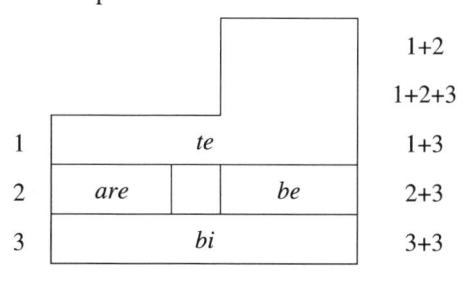

		te		1+2
				1+2+3
1				1+3
2	are		be	2+3
3		bi		3+3

120 *Paradigmatic Structure*

(4.23) Gubden subject suffixes

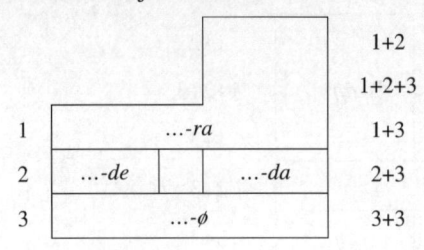

			1+2
			1+2+3
1	...-ra		1+3
2	...-de	...-da	2+3
3	...-∅		3+3

The final two possibilities of horizontal homophony are even rarer. I know one language with a horizontal homophony in the first and second person, but not in the third. Shown in (4.24) are the person prefixes from Big Nambas, a language spoken on the island of Malekula, part of Vanuatu, in the Pacific. There are other affixes in the language that indicate number, so the difference between the singular and the plural is marked regularly, though not in the pronominal paradigm as such (Fox 1976: 52–61).

Horizontal homophony in the first person only is shown in (4.25) as attested in the independent pronouns of the Papuan language Marind (Drabbe 1955: 28). A suffix -*ke* can be used to mark plurality in the first person, but the description explicitly notes that this suffix is an associative marker (Drabbe 1955: 138).

(4.24) Big Nambas subject prefixes

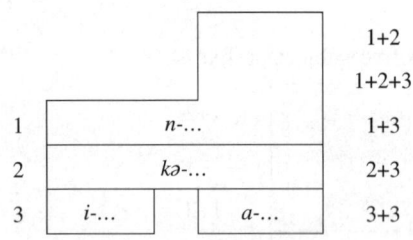

			1+2
			1+2+3
1	n-...		1+3
2	kə-...		2+3
3	i-...	a-...	3+3

(4.25) Marind pronouns

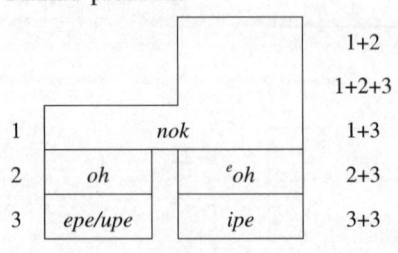

			1+2
			1+2+3
1	nok		1+3
2	oh	ᵉoh	2+3
3	epe/upe	ipe	3+3

There are also examples of an overlap between singular and non-singular in which the person reference differs. This special kind of horizontal homophony is

Survey of Paradigmatic Structure 121

iconically called DIAGONAL homophony. The first example of diagonal homophony is the paradigms of the actor prefixes from Vanimo, a Sko language from Papua New Guinea, as shown in (4.26). In this case, there is a homophony between the first person singular and the second person non-singular (Foley 1986: 134, citing Ross).

The exact opposite kind of homophony is attested in the paradigm of the independent pronouns form the Papuan language Suki, shown in (4.27); the second person singular is identical to the first person non-singular (Foley 1986: 72, citing Voorhoeve). The same structure is attested in the subject affixes of the Papuan language Ekagi, distantly related to Suki (Drabbe 1952: 48).[21] Almost the same structure as in Suki is shown in (4.28); these are the pronominal prefixes from Classical Nahuatl, an Aztec language from Mexico. The same diagonal homophony as in Suki is found here, but there is also a horizontal homophony in the third person. A plural suffix -*ʔ* disambiguates the homophonous prefixes (Newman 1967: 193). This structure is commonly found in the contemporary Aztecan languages.[22] Diagonal homophony involving a third person appears to be very rare, although incidental examples are attested in combination with vertical homophony; see (4.63) in Section 4.4.4.

(4.26)   Vanimo actor prefixes

			1+2
		n-...	1+2+3
1	ø-...		1+3
2	m-...	ø-...	2+3
3	h/b-...	d-...	3+3

(4.27)   Suki pronouns

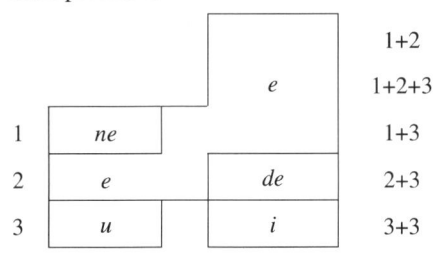

			1+2
		e	1+2+3
1	ne		1+3
2	e	de	2+3
3	u	i	3+3

---

[21] There might be some more examples in the Eastern Highlands of New Guinea, depending on whether the markers are interpretated as person markers or not (cf. Hua, Gahuku, and Benabena as discussed in Foley 1986: 134–6; cf. Stump 2001: 216–17).

[22] cf. Milpa Alta Nahuatl (Whorf 1946: 384), North Puebla Nahuatl (Brockway 1979: 170), Huasteca Nahuatl (Beller 1979: 269), and Pipil (Campbell 1985: 54).

(4.28) Classical Nahuatl agent prefixes

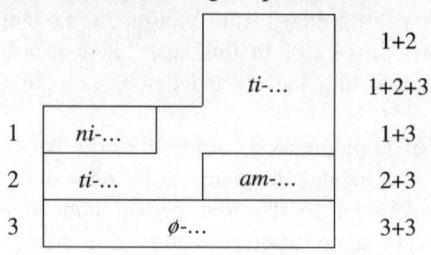

			ti-...	1+2
				1+2+3
1	ni-...			1+3
2	ti-...	am-...		2+3
3		∅-...		3+3

Finally, a few examples have a singular homophony together with a split non-singular. This type of paradigm is found in the Spanish imperfect suffixes, presented in (4.29). Roughly half the different suffixal paradigms in Spanish have this structure (Butt and Benjamin 1988: 185–7). Exactly the same paradigmatic structure is found in the Icelandic weak past (Thráinsson 1994: 159). Another kind of singular homophony is found in the Icelandic weak present, as shown in (4.30). In this case there is a homophony between second and third person singular (Thráinsson 1994: 159). The presented paradigm is found with verbs of class 1; the forms for other verb classes differ slightly, but all classes have the same paradigmatic structure. Exactly the same paradigmatic structure is also attested in the aorist and imperfect suffixes of the Southern Slavonic languages Bulgarian, Macedonian, and Serbo-Croatian (de Bray 1951: 225, 287–9, 342–3). A further variant is the paradigm of the imperfect suffixes from Siciliano, the San Fratello dialect, as shown in (4.31). This case shows a combination of a singular homophony and a horizontal homophony (Bigalke 1997: 60). Finally, (4.32) shows a complete homophony of all singular persons, as attested in the Italian present subjunctive (Schwarze 1988: 79). The same structure is found in the middle present indicative of Icelandic (Thráinsson 1994: 162) and in the French present inflection.

As these are all well-known European languages, it might appear that it is common for homophony to be found in the singular but not in the plural. From a worldwide perspective, however, this is a marginal phenomenon restricted to Europe. These paradigmatic structures with only singular homophony are rather unusual cross-linguistically. In general, if there are three different specialized forms for the non-singular, then it is very likely that there are also three different forms in the singular.

(4.29) Spanish imperfect suffixes

				1+2
			...-mos	1+2+3
1	...-∅			1+3
2	...-s	...-is		2+3
3	...-∅	...-n		3+3

(4.30) Icelandic weak present suffixes (class 1)

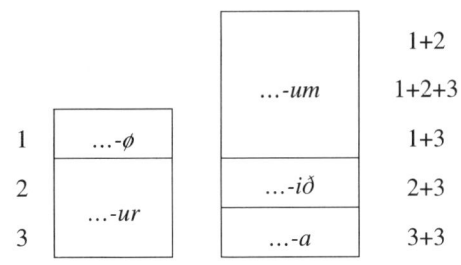

		...-um	1+2
			1+2+3
1	...-ø		1+3
2		...-ið	2+3
3	...-ur	...-a	3+3

(4.31) Siciliano imperfect suffixes

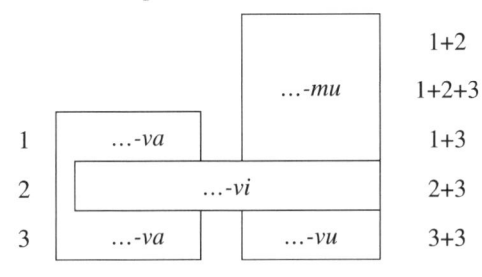

			1+2
		...-mu	1+2+3
1	...-va		1+3
2	...-vi		2+3
3	...-va	...-vu	3+3

(4.32) Italian present subjunctive suffixes

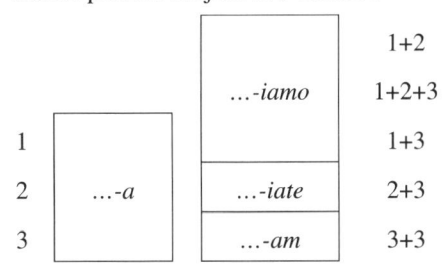

			1+2
		...-iamo	1+2+3
1			1+3
2	...-a	...-iate	2+3
3		...-am	3+3

4.4 No inclusive/exclusive: homophonous non-singular

4.4.1 Preamble

After the discussion of paradigms with a split non-singular, I will now turn to the paradigms with vertical homophony. The four different possibilities of vertical homophony without an inclusive/exclusive opposition are shown in Figure 4.6. All four possibilities exist and will be discussed in turn in Sections 4.4.2–5. Within each vertical homophony, various paradigmatic structures are attested, depending on the interaction between the singular and non-singular. In total, twenty-four different paradigmatic structures are attested, of which four will be classified as semi-common.

124   *Paradigmatic Structure*

| | Split | Homophonous patterns ||||
		1/2	2/3	1/3	Unified
1+2					
1+2+3	A		A	A	
1+3		A			A
2+3	B			B	
3+3	C	B	B	A	

FIG. 4.6. *Possible kinds of vertical homophony without an inclusive/exclusive opposition*

4.4.2   1/2-homophony

The first kind of homophony to be discussed is characterized by identity of the marking of first person plural and the second person plural. The paradigms with a 1/2-homophony show a large amount of variation. The most widely occurring structure is exemplified by the independent pronouns of the Athabascan languages. The pronouns from the Slavey variant of the Athabascan language Slave are presented in (4.33). This SLAVE-TYPE paradigmatic structure can be found in many Athabascan languages.[23] The prefixal object marking in all Athabascan languages shows the same structure, throughout the family (e.g. Rice 1989: 253, 431).

(4.33)   Slave pronouns

1	sį		1+2
2	nį	naxį	1+2+3
			1+3
			2+3
3	ʔedį	ʔegedį	3+3

I know of various examples outside the Athabascan family where exactly the same Slave-type paradigmatic structure is found. The first is shown in (4.34). These are the independent pronouns from Awa, a highland language from Papua New Guinea (Loving 1973: 85). Another Papuan example with this structure is the paradigm of the subject prefixes from Mombum, a language of the Central

---

[23] Other examples of the Slave-type among the Athabascan languages are found in the independent pronouns of Chiricahua Apache (Hoijer 1946: 76, 78, 83), Navaho (Young and Morgan 1987: 7–8), Kato (Goddard 1912: 33), and Hupa (Goddard 1905: 29).

and South New Guinea family (Boelaars 1950: 30–1). Unrelated to these two Papuan cases, the same structure is attested in the subject prefixes of the Fehan dialect of Tetun, an Austronesian language from Timor (van Klinken 1999: 173), as shown in (4.35).

(4.34) Awa pronouns

		ite	
			1+2
			1+2+3
1	ne		1+3
2	ade		2+3
3	we	se	3+3

(4.35) Fehan subject prefixes

		∅-...	
			1+2
			1+2+3
1	k-...		1+3
2	m-...		2+3
3	n-...	r/n-...	3+3

Two examples of the Slave-type are found in Africa. The first is the person inflection from the Tommo-so variant of Dogon, a Volta-Congo language from Mali, as shown in (4.36). There are many different portmanteau forms for the category 3+3, fused with aspect and an eventual negation. The presented form -eŋ is the 'positive stative' morpheme (Plungian 1995: 30). The other example from Africa is noted by Lefebvre (1998: 142, citing Brousseau), who describes a Slave-type paradigm for the Kwa language Fongbe, spoken in Benin. The first and second person plural are identically marked by mí. Lefebvre argues that the division as found in traditional descriptions of Fongbe between a low-high tone for first person plural and a mid tone for second person plural is phonemically irrelevant. The traditional description of Höftmann (1993: 51, 93) clearly distinguishes phonemically between a high-tone mí for first person plural and a low-tone mì for the second person plural.

Lefebvre uses the purported homophony in Fongbe to argue for relexification in the Haitian Creole pronouns in (4.37), which have a Slave-type homophony

126   *Paradigmatic Structure*

(Lefebvre 1998: 141; cf. Holm 1988: 201, who notes that this paradigm is only found in southern Haitian Creole). The same structure is also found in other creoles, notably in Sranan and Ndyuka (Holm 1988: 204). In contrast, Huttar and Huttar (1994: 461) describe two different pronouns *wi* and *u* for the Ndyuka first and second person plural, respectively. However, they point out that there are various phonological rules which have the result that 'in most environments pronoun forms ambiguous between 1st and 2nd plural can occur' (p. 462).

(4.36)   Dogon positive stative suffixes

		…-y	1+2
			1+2+3
1	…-m		1+3
2	…-w		2+3
3	…-ø	…-eŋ	3+3

(4.37)   Southern Haitian Creole pronouns

			1+2
		nou	1+2+3
1	mwen		1+3
2	ou		2+3
3	li	yo	3+3

There are also various paradigmatic structures with other kinds of homophony added to the 1/2-homophony. These are all incidental cases, classified here as rare. In the first of these rare paradigmatic structures, a singular homophony is attested, which is a mirror image of the non-singular homophony. This structure is exemplified with the imperfect suffixes from the South Caucasian language Svan, shown in (4.38). There are also pronominal prefixes in Svan that co-occur with these suffixes. These prefixes are of a completely different paradigmatic type, to be discussed in Section 4.5.6 (Tuite 1997: 28). Another example of the same structure is attested in the Papuan language Waskia, shown in (4.39). The suffixes presented are the past simple suffixes (Ross and Paol 1978: 67–8).

Survey of Paradigmatic Structure   127

(4.38)   Svan imperfect suffixes

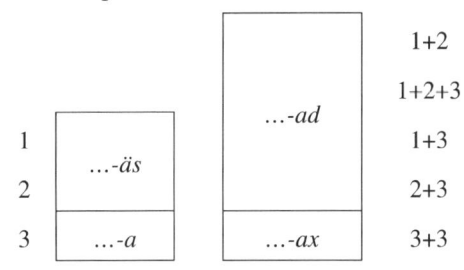

1	...-äs	...-ad	1+2
			1+2+3
			1+3
2			2+3
3	...-a	...-ax	3+3

(4.39)   Waskia past simple suffixes

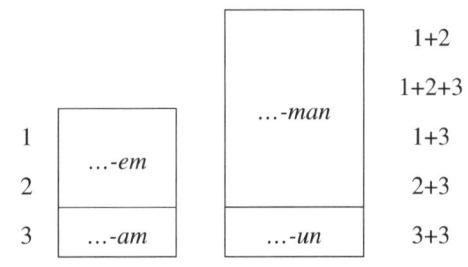

1	...-em	...-man	1+2
			1+2+3
			1+3
2			2+3
3	...-am	...-un	3+3

Slight variations on the Svan-type are found in Lak, a Nakh-Dagestanian language from the Caucasus. The non-past suffixes from Lak are shown in (4.40). A horizontal homophony is added in the third person. In the past suffixes from Lak, two forms for the first and second person are also homophonous (Helmbrecht 1996: 131). This structure is exemplified in (4.41) by the prefixes for progressive and habitual from Nez Perce, a Sahaptin language from North America. Number can be marked by suffixes. In other aspects, notably the perfective and irrealis, a number prefix *pe-* is found together with the pronominal prefix *hi-* (Rude 1985: 30–9).

(4.40)   Lak non-past suffixes

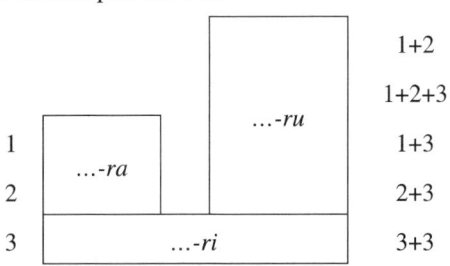

1	...-ra	...-ru	1+2
			1+2+3
			1+3
2			2+3
3	...-ri		3+3

128   *Paradigmatic Structure*

(4.41)   Nez Perce progressive/habitual prefixes

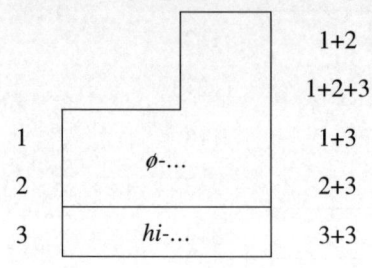

		1+2
		1+2+3
1	∅-...	1+3
2		2+3
3	hi-...	3+3

Not all paradigms with a 1/2-homophony show a mirror relationship between singular and non-singular. The first of these asymmetric patterns is found in Kenuzi-Dongola, a Nilo-Saharan language from Sudan. The suffixes shown in (4.42) mark the present of the Dongola dialect. This paradigm has a singular homophony between second and third person (Reinisch 1879: 65). The subject prefixes from Ika, a Chibchan language from Peru, are shown in (4.43). In this case, there is a homophony between first and third person singular (Frank 1990: 50–1).

(4.42)   Dongola present suffixes

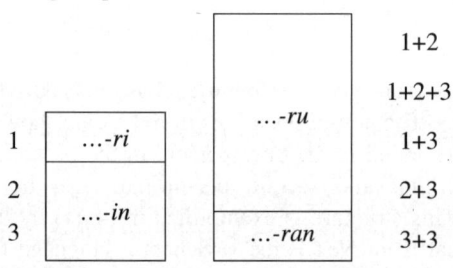

			1+2
		...-ru	1+2+3
1	...-ri		1+3
2			2+3
3	...-in	...-ran	3+3

(4.43)   Ika subject prefixes

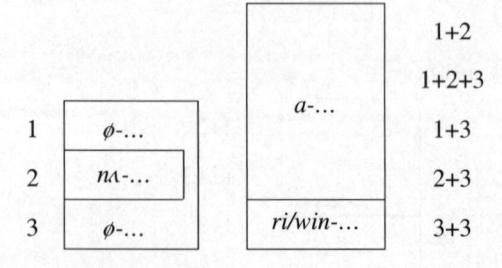

			1+2
		a-...	1+2+3
1	∅-...		1+3
2	nʌ-...		2+3
3	∅-...	ri/win-...	3+3

There are also a few cases that have a horizontal homophony together with a vertical homophony. Such a paradigmatic structure is attested in the independent pronouns from Usarufa, a highland language from New Guinea (Foley

1986: 255), shown in (4.44). This paradigm is related to the independent pronoun from Awa, presented in (4.34). A slightly different pattern is found in literary Dargi. In this case, the third person non-singular is marked together with the third person singular. It is possible to disambiguate the second person plural by using a suffix -*ya*, but this suffix is not obligatorily used (van den Berg 1999: 155–6). Some dialectal variants of Dargi have a separate morpheme for the second person plural; for example Gubden, as shown in (4.23).

(4.44) Usarufa pronouns

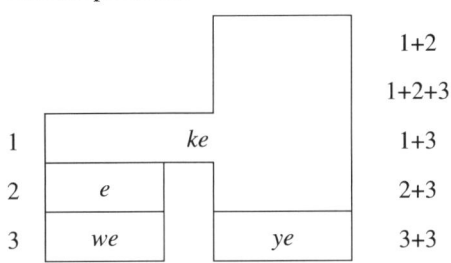

		ke	1+2
			1+2+3
1			1+3
2	*e*		2+3
3	*we*	*ye*	3+3

(4.45) Dargi subject suffixes

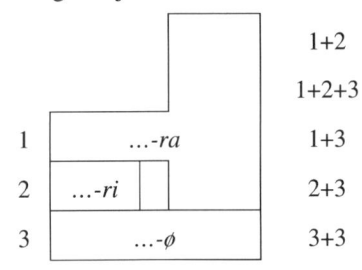

		…-*ra*	1+2
			1+2+3
1			1+3
2	…-*ri*		2+3
3		…-∅	3+3

4.4.3 2/3-homophony

Characteristic of the 2/3-homophony is the conflation of the categories 2+3 and 3+3, resulting in an opposition between 'we' and 'non-we'. This homophony is exemplified by the unmarked form of the Nez Perce independent pronouns, shown in (4.46). There are other paradigms of independent pronouns in Nez Perce besides the one presented here, but all have exactly the same paradigmatic structure (Rude 1985: 123). A fair number of cases of exactly this NEZ PERCE-TYPE paradigmatic structure are attested. In South America, it is found in Warekena, an Arawakan language from Venezuela. The independent pronouns from Warekena are shown in (4.47), but the same structure is also found in the inflectional marking. This pronominal pattern is probably an innovation of Warekena, as it is not found in any other Arawakan language (Aikhenvald 1998: 293, 322). Also in South America, the same homophony is attested in the pronominal affixes from

130 Paradigmatic Structure

Warao, an isolate from Venezuela (Romero-Figeroa 1997: 64–6). In this case, the homophonous second and third plural are zero-marked.

(4.46) Nez Perce pronouns

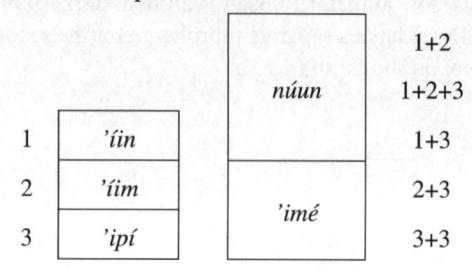

		núun	1+2
			1+2+3
1	'íin		1+3
2	'íim	'imé	2+3
3	'ipí		3+3

(4.47) Warekena pronouns

		waya	1+2
			1+2+3
1	nuya		1+3
2	piya	niya	2+3
3	(demonstr.)		3+3

In Africa, an example of this structure is the paradigm of the object pronouns in (4.48) from Wolof, an Atlantic language from Senegal (Sauvageot 1965: 91–2). Further, it is particularly common among French-based creoles. It is found in the pronouns of Mauritius Creole, shown in (4.49), Seychellois Creole, Réunion Creole (Stein 1984: 66), and northern Haitian Creole (Holm 1988: 201).

(4.48) Wolof object pronouns

		nu	1+2
			1+2+3
1	ma		1+3
2	la	lɛn	2+3
3	kɔ		3+3

(4.49) Mauritius creole pronouns

			1+2
		nou	1+2+3
1	mo		1+3
2	to		2+3
		zot	
3	li		3+3

It has been claimed in the literature that this pattern is typical for languages from the highlands of New Guinea. For example, Foley (1986: 72) calls it 'the typical highlands conflation of second and third persons in the nonsingular'. He even reconstructs a paradigm of independent pronouns for Proto-Gorokan with a Nez Perce-type paradigm, although it should be noted that, purely synchronically, none of the Gorokan languages has this kind of independent pronoun system (Foley 1986: 248–9). Indeed, in the verbal inflections of the highland languages of New Guinea a 2/3-homophony is often found, but almost always in combination with a dual with the same homophony (to be discussed in Section 7.3.3). The only 'pure' example of a Nez Perce-type paradigm among the Papuan languages that I know of is the paradigm of the subject suffixes in (4.50) from Kati, a Central and Southern New Guinean language (Boelaars 1950: 80–1).

(4.50) Kati subject suffixes

			1+2
		...-up	1+2+3
1	...-an		1+3
2	...-ep		2+3
		...-ip	
3	...-on/un		3+3

The suffixal paradigm from Kombai, shown in (4.51), is different from the Nez Perce-type paradigm in (4.46) because there is a homophony in the singular, mirroring the non-singular. This type of paradigm is also relatively regularly attested—it will be referred to as the KOMBAI-TYPE paradigm. The paradigm from Kombai can probably be analysed as a first person marker -*f* and a plural marker -*o* (de Vries 1989: 145). A Kombai-type paradigmatic structure is attested in Wambon (de Vries 1989: 145) and Awju (Boelaars 1950: 70–1), both closely related to Kombai. Another Papuan example of the Kombai-type is the paradigm of the subject suffixes from Moraori, a Trans-Fly language (Boelaars 1950: 46).

132 Paradigmatic Structure

(4.51) Kombai subject suffixes

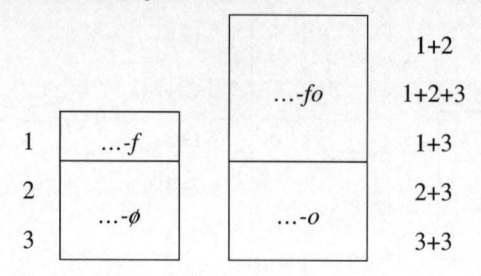

			1+2
		...-fo	1+2+3
1	...-f		1+3
2			2+3
3	...-ø	...-o	3+3

The Kombai-type paradigm is also found in the pronominal inflection of Chitimacha, an extinct language from the USA, shown in (4.52). Just as with the suffixes from Kombai, the suffixes from Chitimacha may be analysed as consisting of a separate number -nV- and person morpheme -Vk (Swadesh 1946: 317–18). In South America, the same pattern is attested in the pronominal prefixes shown in (4.53) from Lengua, a Mascoian language from Paraguay. There is considerable morphophonological variation; the presented prefixes are only one of a series of forms that all have the same paradigmatic structure. It does not seem possible to separate person from number marking in this case (Susnik 1977: 98). Among the Tibeto-Burman languages, an example of the Kombai-type is attested in Bunan, a language spoken in India. Shown in (4.54) are the present suffixes, but other tenses have the same paradigmatic structure (Sharma 1996: 94–5).

(4.52) Chitimacha subject suffixes

			1+2
		...-nuk	1+2+3
1	...-ik		1+3
2			2+3
3	...-i	...-na	3+3

(4.53) Lengua subject prefixes

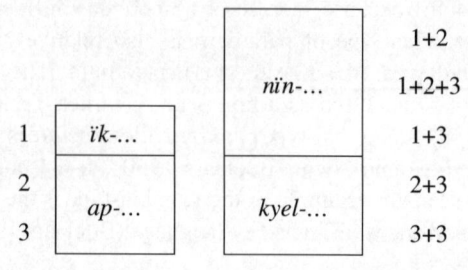

			1+2
		nïn-...	1+2+3
1	ïk-...		1+3
2			2+3
3	ap-...	kyel-...	3+3

Survey of Paradigmatic Structure 133

(4.54) Bunan present suffixes

			1+2
		...-khe?	1+2+3
1	...-gye?		1+3
2	...-gani	...-kha:	2+3
3			3+3

Finally, there are some slight variations of the Kombai-type. These paradigmatic structures appear to be incidental cases. In the Chukotko-Kamchatkan languages Chukchee, Koryak and Kamchadal, here exemplified in (4.55) by the indicative intransitive prefixes from Koryak (Comrie 1980a: 64, 67), the singular and non-singular forms with a 2/3-homophony are both marked identically by zero. The same paradigmatic structure is found in the future suffixes of the Tibeto-Burman language Rongpo (Sharma 1996: 102). Another slight variant of the Kombai-type paradigm is the suffixal paradigm in (4.56) from the Caucasian language Megeb (Helmbrecht 1996: 138). In this case, there is also a horizontal homophony in the first person. Exactly this same paradigmatic structure is found in Kiwai, a Trans-Fly language from New Guinea (Foley 1986: 132, citing Ray) and in the indicative of Awa-Pit, a Barbacoan language from Ecuador (Curnow 1997: 189–203). An important case of this paradigmatic structure is found in Qawesqar, an Alcalufan language from Chile. The importance lies in the fact that these are morphologically independent pronouns (Clairis 1985: 463–4).

(4.55) Koryak intransitive prefixes

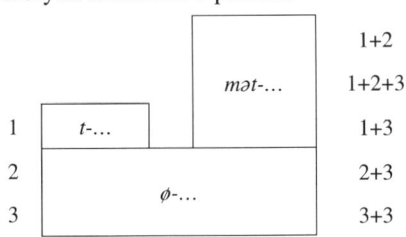

			1+2
		mət-...	1+2+3
1	t-...		1+3
2		∅-...	2+3
3			3+3

(4.56) Megeb subject suffixes

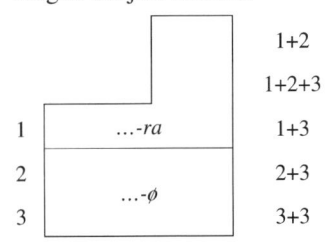

		1+2
		1+2+3
1	...-ra	1+3
2	...-∅	2+3
3		3+3

134 Paradigmatic Structure

To conclude the examples of 2/3-homophony in the non-singular, two aberrant paradigms are shown in (4.57) and (4.58). The first are subject suffixes from Gadsup, a highland language from New Guinea (Frantz and McKaughan 1973: 440) and the second are the middle suffixes from Icelandic (other than the present indicative: Thráinsson 1994: 162).

(4.57) Gadsup subject suffixes

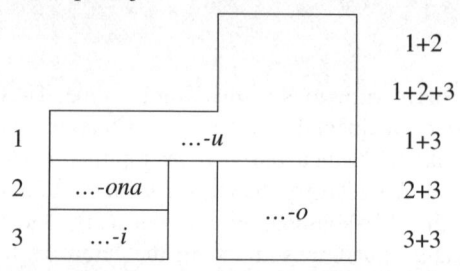

		...-u	1+2
			1+2+3
1			1+3
2	...-ona		2+3
		...-o	
3	...-i		3+3

(4.58) Icelandic middle preterite indicative suffixes

		...-um	1+2
			1+2+3
1			1+3
2	...-i		2+3
		...-u	
3			3+3

4.4.4 1/3-homophony

Characteristic of the 1/3-homophony is the identity between the first person and the third person non-singular. This is not really a common pattern; it is only regularly found in a group of languages on the south-eastern tip of Papua New Guinea. Outside that area, I know only of incidental languages that show this homophony. The main paradigmatic structure with a 1/3-homophony is exemplified in (4.59) with the past suffixes from Omië, a Papuan language from the south-eastern tip of Papuan New Guinea (Austing and Upia 1975: 544). Such an OMIË-TYPE paradigm is also found in the pronominal inflection of the neighbouring language Orokaiva. The Orokaiva marking is exemplified here with the so-called 'indicative Mid Past B' paradigm, shown in (4.60). Other suffixal paradigms in Orokaiva have exactly the same paradigmatic structure (Healey et al. 1969: 62). This paradigmatic structure is also found in the related language Korafe (Farr and Farr 1975: 747–9). Orokaiva and Korafe belong to the Binanderean family, which is only distantly related to the Koiarian family to which Omië belongs. However, the resemblance between the paradigms points at least to a strong areal influence.

(4.59) Omië past suffixes

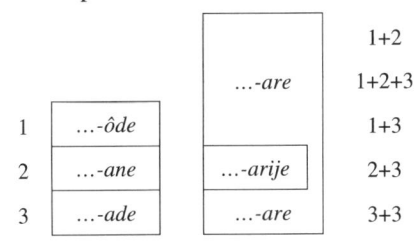

			1+2
		...-are	1+2+3
1	...-ôde		1+3
2	...-ane	...-arije	2+3
3	...-ade	...-are	3+3

(4.60) Orokaiva indicative mid past b suffixes

			1+2
		...-ara	1+2+3
1	...-ana		1+3
2	...-a	...-awa	2+3
3	...aja	...ara	3+3

In Africa, an Omië-type paradigm is found in Bagirmi, a Nilo-Saharan language from Chad. The forms presented in (4.61) are the independent pronouns as found in isolation (Gaden 1909: 10). The same structure exists in the inflection of the Toro variant of Dogon, a Niger-Congo language from Mali (Calame-Griaule 1968: xxxv). This pattern is also described by Mangold (1977: 49 ff.) for the pronominal suffixes from Wolof, an Atlantic language from Senegal. Both first and third suffixes are -ńu (with a palatal nasal). However, Sauvageot (1965: 88–9) differentiates between a suffix -nu (with an apical nasal) for the first person plural and a suffix -ɲu (with a palatal nasal) for the second person plural.

(4.61) Bagirmi pronouns

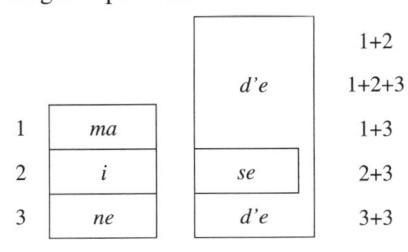

			1+2
		d'e	1+2+3
1	ma		1+3
2	i	se	2+3
3	ne	d'e	3+3

In some cases, the homophony between first and third person is mirrored in the singular. This is, for example, found in the inflection of Middle Dutch. Shown in (4.62) are the past suffixes of Middle Dutch (Schönfeld 1959: 144–5). The same paradigm is attested in the past inflection of contemporary German (Eisenberg 1994: 367–71). Another example of a Middle Dutch-type structure is the Omië suffixes for the present (Austing and Upia 1975: 544).

136   *Paradigmatic Structure*

(4.62)   Middle Dutch past suffixes

			1+2
		...-en	1+2+3
1	...-ø		1+3
2	...-es	...-et	2+3
3	...-ø	...-en	3+3

Finally, an aberrant paradigmatic structure is attested in German. The present suffixes from German are shown in (4.63). There is a cross-linguistically unusual homophony between third person singular and second person plural in this paradigm (Eisenberg 1994: 367–71). The suffixes indicating completed action in the Sudanic language Midob show exactly the same structure as the German suffixes (Thelwall 1983: 107).

(4.63)   German present suffixes

			1+2
		...-en	1+2+3
1	...-e		1+3
2	...-st	...-t	2+3
3	...-t	...-en	3+3

4.4.5 Unified homophony

Paradigms with a unified homophony have the same marking for all non-singular categories. The six paradigmatic structures with this homophony are rare and highly varied. All patterns with this homophony are classified as rare. A first variant is exemplified here in (4.64) with the undergoer suffixes from Una, a Papuan language from Irian Jaya (Louwerse 1988: 31–2). The same paradigmatic structure is found in the present suffixes of the Tibeto-Burman language Rongpo (Sharma 1996: 101).

(4.64)   Una undergoer suffixes

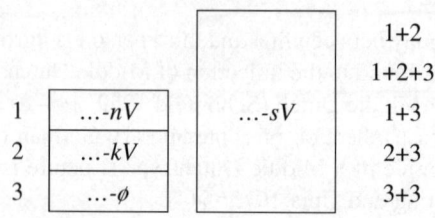

			1+2
			1+2+3
1	...-nV	...-sV	1+3
2	...-kV		2+3
3	...-ø		3+3

Survey of Paradigmatic Structure 137

The other cases of a unified homophony additionally show homophony in the singular. A paradigm with a second/third person singular homophony is attested in the inflection of Standard Dutch. The suffixes for the present, without inversion, are shown in (4.65). The usage of a second person non-singular suffix *-t* (just like in German, as shown in (4.63) above) can still be found, but is considered to be rather old-fashioned. Almost the same structure is found in the present suffixes of the Papuan language Waskia, shown in (4.66), but this time with a first/second singular homophony (Ross and Paol 1978: 67–8). The Old English past suffixes in (4.67) had a unified homophony with a first/third singular homophony (Robertson and Cassidy 1954: 141).

(4.65) Dutch present suffixes

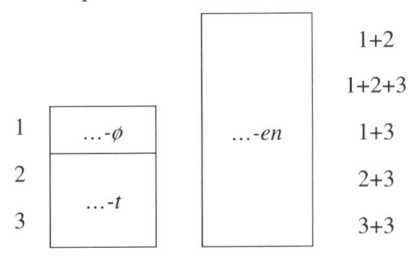

1	...-ø	...-en	1+2
			1+2+3
			1+3
2	...-t		2+3
3			3+3

(4.66) Waskia present suffixes

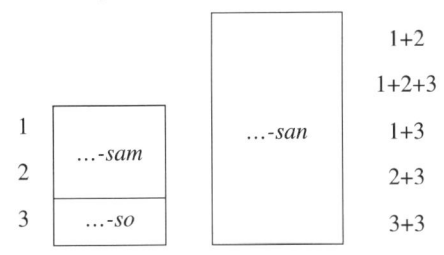

			1+2
			1+2+3
1	...-sam	...-san	1+3
2			2+3
3	...-so		3+3

(4.67) Old English past suffixes

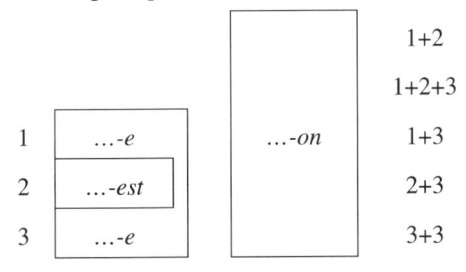

			1+2
			1+2+3
1	...-e	...-on	1+3
2	...-est		2+3
3	...-e		3+3

Finally, I know of two cases of a unified non-singular combined with horizontal homophony. The most famous of these cases with a unified homophony is found in Modern English. The present inflection of English verbs is shown in (4.68). All group categories are marked identically, by zero, and this same zero is found in the singular. The other example is found in the Papuan language Koiari. The present/imperfect suffixes from Koiari are shown in (4.69). Just as in English, all group categories are marked identically, and this same suffix is used for the second person singular. Unlike English, this suffix is not used for the first person singular. The same paradigmatic structure is also found in the past/perfect of Koiari (Dutton 1996: 23).

(4.68)   English present suffixes

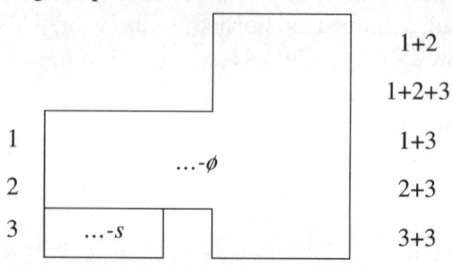

		1+2
		1+2+3
1		1+3
2	...-∅	2+3
3	...-s	3+3

(4.69)   Koiari present/imperfect suffixes

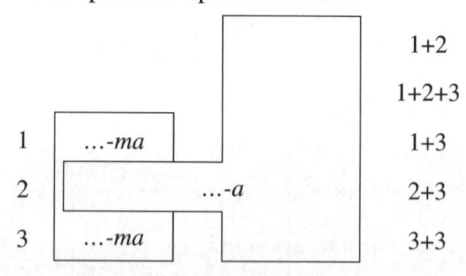

			1+2
			1+2+3
1	...-ma		1+3
2		...-a	2+3
3	...-ma		3+3

4.5   Inclusive/exclusive: split non-singular

4.5.1   Preamble

Now I will turn to the paradigmatic structures that distinguish between inclusive and exclusive. The presence of this distinction will turn out to be a good predictor for various aspects of the variability of paradigmatic structure. In this section, only the split patterns will be considered. Split patterns are those paradigmatic structures that do not have a vertical homophony between the inclusive or exclusive categories on the one hand and the categories 2+3 and 3+3 on the other hand. All in all, seven different paradigmatic structures will be presented in this section. Among these paradigms, four paradigmatic structures are common and one is semi-common. The common variants will be called the MARANAO-TYPE paradigm (Section 4.5.2), the MANDARA-TYPE paradigm (Section 4.5.3), the TUPÍ GUARANÍ-TYPE paradigm (Section 4.5.4), and the SIERRA POPOLUCA-TYPE paradigm (Section 4.5.6). The KWAKIUTL-TYPE paradigm (Section 4.5.5) is classified as semi-common. There are almost no other examples of split paradigmatic structures. The few cases attested have aberrant combinations of horizontal homophony. Singular homophony is not attested among the paradigms with an inclusive/exclusive oppostion (Section 4.5.7).

4.5.2 Maranao-type paradigm

The independent pronouns from Maranao, an Austronesian language from the Philippines, are presented in (4.70). The paradigm differentiates all eight person categories (McKaughan 1959). It turns out that this seemingly exotic paradigmatic structure is found relatively frequently among the world's languages.

(4.70)   Maranao pronouns

		ta	1+2
		tano	1+2+3
1	ako	kami	1+3
2	ka	kano	2+3
3	sekanian	siran	3+3

Paradigms of the Maranao-type are abundantly found on the Philippines. Well-known cases, besides Maranao, are Ilocano (Thomas 1955) and Hanunóo (Conklin 1962: 134–5). A large number of examples of this paradigmatic structure are included in a collection edited by Reid (1971: 1–43). This work presents short descriptions of the phonology and pronominal categories of forty-three minor Philippine languages. Of these, thirty-one are described as having a Maranao-type paradigm. The other twelve languages do not have the opposition between minimal and augmented inclusive. The Maranao-type is found all over the Philippines, and it can at least be reconstructed for proto-Cordilleran (Reid 1979).

Examples of the Maranao-type paradigm are attested frequently among the non-Pama-Nyungan languages from Australia.[24] It is found among inflection and independent pronouns of the Daly river languages.[25] Some more examples are found among the Gunwingguan languages and among the independent pronouns of the Nyulnyulan languages.[26] An incidental example from the Pama-Nyungan

---

[24] Dixon (1980: 351–6) speculates whether a Maranao-type paradigm might be reconstructed for Proto-Australian, but this seems implausible. A more fruitful proposal is to reconstruct a Maranao-type paradigm only for the non-Pama-Nyungan languages (Blake 1988: 7; 1991: 222).
[25] e.g. Maranungku (Tryon 1970: 17–42) and Malakmalak (Birk 1976: 30–1, 47–81). For a wider view on the Daly river auxiliary verbs and their person suffixes, see Tryon (1976: 679).
[26] For Gunwingguan, e.g. Wardaman (Merlan 1994: 108, 125). For Nyunyulan, e.g. Bardi (Metcalfe 1975: 48–50) and Nyulnyul (McGregor 1996a: 23).

languages is found in the independent pronouns from Uradhi (Crowley 1983: 352–6).[27]

A few incidental cases of the Maranao-type paradigm are attested among Papuan languages. The independent pronouns from Mountain Koiali in southeastern New Guinea show this paradigmatic structure. Other related Koiarian languages do not have such a paradigm (Garland and Garland 1975: 429, 434–5). On the other side of the island, the independent pronouns of Kemtuik also have a Maranao-type structure (Donohue and Smith 1998: 72, n. 4). Final examples in this area are the East Papuan languages Santa Cruz and Nanggu, spoken in the Solomon Islands (Wurm 1969: 77–83).

Unexpectedly, the Maranao-type paradigm shows up quite frequently in Africa. Most examples are found around the 'elbow' of Africa, centred on Cameroon and Nigeria. The Maranao-type occurs in various families of the Niger-Congo stock and in the Chadic family of the Afro-Asiatic stock.[28] In North America, the Maranao-type paradigm is found in a few languages from western USA (California and Oregon).[29] In South America, the only example that I am aware of is found in Chayahuita, a Cahuapanan language from Peru (Hart 1988: 262). Finally, this paradigmatic structure is attested in the isolated language Nivkh from Siberia (Gruzdeva 1998: 25–6).

---

[27] In the description of Uradhi (Crowley 1983), the labels for the forms *ampu(la)* and *ana(βa)* are mixed up. They are glossed 'exclusive non-singular' and 'inclusive plural' respectively (Crowley 1983: 354–5). This is an error, as can clearly be seen from the example sentences 1–10 of text III (Crowley 1983: 397–8). In these sentences, the pronoun *ana-* is used in what is clearly an exclusive sense (excluding the addressee to whom the story is told). Terry Crowley adduces his 'sloppy proofreading' (Crowley, p.c.) as an excuse. He clearly knew better, as the labels are correct in his description of the related language Anguthimri (Crowley 1981: 169–71).

[28] Among the Niger-Congo languages, the Maranao-type paradigm is attested in the basic pronouns of the Grassfields languages in Cameroon, e.g. Limbum (Fransen 1995: 179–80), Bamileke (Anderson 1985: 63, 68), and Babungo (Schaub 1985: 193–4). It is also found in Dii, an Adamawa language from Cameroon (Bohnhoff 1986: 126–7) and in the Mande languages Dan (Doneux 1968: 45–7) and Northern Looma (Valentine Vydrine, p.c.). Distantly related to the Niger-Congo stock, it is also found in the Kordofanian languages Ebang and Moro (Schadeberg 1981: 67, 92). Among the Chadic languages, the Maranao-type paradigm is found in Margi (Hoffmann 1963: 73–4; Burquest 1986: 77, 82), Gude (Hoskison 1983: 48), Lele (Frajzyngier 2001: 109–11), Lamang (Wolff 1983: 82–7), Hdi (Frajzyngier and Shay 2002: 83–4, 123–6), and in the Ron languages (Jungraithmayr 1970: 371).

[29] A Maranao-type paradigm is attested in the independent pronouns and in the enclitics of the Southern Numic branch of the Uto-Aztecan family. It is described extensively for Ute-Southern Paiute (Sapir 1992 [1930]: 176–8; Press 1979: 44–6; Givón 1980: 50; 1984: 356) and Kawaiisu (Zigmond et al. 1990: 45–6). The same paradigmatic structure is also found in Tübatulabal, another Northern Uto-Aztecan language. In the description of Tübatulabal by Voegelin (1937a: 135), the exclusive form *-(g)ila'aŋ* is glossed as 'dual exclusive'. However, this appears to be a mistake: this morpheme can also have plural reference. This can be inferred from the usage of this morpheme in text 27, especially in a scene where a group of 5 or 6 boys are playing (Voegelin 1937b: 225, sentences 116–34). The narrator, who was one of the boys, tells the audience, 'We were playing during the day', using the exclusive form. This form clearly does not have dual reference in this context. Outside the Uto-Aztecan family, but areally in close contact, a Maranao-type paradigm is found in the independent pronouns and in the intransitive pronominal prefixes of Southern Sierra Miwok (Broadbent 1964: 43, 93).

4.5.3 Mandara-type paradigm

The next common paradigmatic structure is exemplified in (4.71) with the non-completive pronouns from Mandara, a Chadic language from Cameroon (Burquest 1986: 78). The paradigmatic structure of the Mandara-type was characterized by Ingram (1978: 219) as one of four structures that is 'more frequent than the others'. Indeed, this paradigmatic structure is widespread among the world's languages. The following list is far from complete, but it will give an impression of the areal distribution of this particular paradigmatic structure.

(4.71)　Mandara non-completive pronouns

		má		1+2
				1+2+3
1	yá		ŋá	1+3
2	ká		kwá	2+3
3	á		tá	3+3

Patterns of the Mandara-type are numerous and easy to find. In Africa, cases are attested mainly south of the Sahara. In the Afro-Asiatic stock, it is found among the Chadic and the Cushitic languages.[30] In the Nilo-Saharan stock, it is described for all languages from the Teso-Turkana subgroup.[31] Finally, in the Niger-Congo stock, this type of paradigm is encountered in the basic pronouns of some of the Grassfields languages and in the subject pronouns of some of the Atlantic languages.[32] An inclusive/exclusive opposition might not be a prototypical characteristic of African languages, but still it is quite commonly found, contrary to claims that it is a rare phenomenon in Africa (e.g. Nichols 1992: 123–4).

On the Eurasian continent, paradigms of the Mandara-type are uncommon, but attested in widely dispersed languages. It is found, for example, in the Caucasus and in Siberia.[33] In Chinese, the Mandara-type is encountered in most modern northern varieties, but it was not present in the classical language (Norman 1988: 89, 157–8). It is possible that an inclusive developed through

---

[30] For Chadic, e.g. the independent pronouns from Podoko and Mandara (Burquest 1986: 78, 83). For Cushitic, e.g. the enclitics from Somali (Kirk 1905: 29–30, 103–4).

[31] e.g. the independent pronouns from Turkana (Dimmendaal 1982: 207) and Karamojong (Novelli 1985: 107).

[32] For the Grassfields languages, e.g. Aghem (Hyman 1979: 47, 49). This structure is also found in the Beboid language Noni (Hyman 1981: 15). The Mandara-type structure is only found in the basic pronouns of these languages. In both languages, there are also compound pronouns with a rather different structure (see Section 5.3.4). For the Atlantic languages, e.g. Adamawa Fulfulde (McIntosh 1984: 116–22) and Palor (D'Alton 1983: 201–3).

[33] For the Caucasus, e.g. the independent pronouns from Chechen (Nichols 1994: 32). For Siberia, e.g. the Tungusic languages Even (Malchukov 1995: 12, 16) and Evenki (Bulatova and Grenoble 1999: 33).

areal influence from the Siberian or Mongolian languages. However, the opposite development—loss of the inclusive/exclusive distinction—has occurred in Mongolian (Sanzheyev 1973: 74). The Mandara-type paradigm is not encountered in the Indo-European stock except for independent pronouns in the Indo-Aryan languages Gujarati (Tisdall 1892: 18) and Marathi (Pandharipande 1997: 376, 381). Probably, both languages borrowed the inclusive/exclusive opposition from the neighbouring Dravidian languages (Masica 1991: 251). The inclusive/exclusive opposition is not found in the Dravidian language Kannada, probably under the influence of the neighbouring Indo-Aryan languages (Sridhar 1990: 205). The contact situation between Dravidian and Indo-Aryan shows again (just as in the Chinese-Mongolian situation) that the influence can go both ways. An inclusive/exclusive opposition is common among the Dravidian languages, but the Mandara-type paradigm is not so often found.[34] Most pronominal paradigms of Dravidian languages are of the Tupí-Guaraní-type that will be discussed in the next section.

Travelling into the Pacific, the Mandara-type paradigm is described regularly for Austronesian languages.[35] In contrast to the abundance of cases among the Austronesian languages, it is sometimes assumed in the literature that an inclusive/exclusive distinction is exceptional among the non-Austronesian languages of New Guinea and the surrounding islands (e.g. Lynch 1998: 167). However, independent pronouns with a Mandara-type paradigm are attested regularly among the non-Austronesian languages in the Bird's Head (Vogelkop) of New Guinea, leading over the 'neck' of the Bird's Head towards the mainland, and in non-Austronesian languages on the islands west of New Guinea.[36] This can probably be explained by Austronesian influence. However, influence in the opposite direction is also attested. The Siao family, a group of Austronesian languages spoken on the eastern mainland of New Guinea, have lost the inclusive/exclusive distinction, probably under influence of the non-Austronesian

---

[34] e.g. the pronominal inflection in Koya (Tyler 1969: 92) and in Tamil (Asher 1982: 173–4).

[35] Among the Oceanic branch of Austronesian, the Mandara-type paradigm is, for example, found in the independent pronouns from Motu, Mono-Alu, Nakanamanga, Pulawat (Lynch 1998: 100–1), and Big Nambas (Fox 1976: 30). Examples of independent pronouns of this type from Austronesian languages outside the Oceanic branch are Toba Batak (Nababan 1981: 77) and Chamorro (Topping 1973: 107). There are also some Austronesian languages that have an inflectional Mandara-type paradigm e.g. Uma (Esser 1964: 36), Trukese (Lynch 1998: 103–4), Tondano (Sneddon 1975: 104, 113), and Toba Batak (Nababan 1981: 77).

[36] Voorhoeve (1975) lists many examples of independent pronouns of the Mandara-type. A large part of these data are from preliminary field reports. However inconclusive, these descriptions indicate that this paradigmatic structure is fairly common in Irian Jaya. Voorhoeve mentions as examples the Mairasi-Tanah Merah stock (pp. 424–5), the West Bomberai stock (pp. 433–4), the South Bird's Head family (pp. 438–9), and the Inanwatan family (p. 440). The Mandara-type is also found among the Island non-Austronesian languages, west of Irian Jaya (Capell 1975: 693–6). Neither of these rather preliminary descriptive surveys presents any information on inflectional paradigms. I know of two non-Austronesian languages in this area with an inflectional Mandara-type paradigm: the isolate Warembori (Donohue 1999: 28–30) and the North Halmahera language Galela (Shelden 1991: 162). There are probably more inflectional cases, but it is difficult to find good data.

languages (Lynch 1998: 101). The Mandara-type paradigm is only incidentally found in Australia, as most pronominal paradigms with an inclusive/exclusive distinction also distinguish dual forms.[37] These paradigms with duals will be discussed in Section 7.5.2.

Finally, the Mandara-type paradigm is described for geographically widely dispersed American languages, although it is not attested very frequently.[38] In general, an inclusive/exclusive opposition in any of its various forms is frequently attested among American languages; it is just this particular Mandara-type paradigmatic structure which turns out to be rather uncommon.

4.5.4 Tupí-Guaraní-type paradigm

The next common paradigmatic structure differs only slightly from the previous Mandara-type. The only difference is a homophony in the third person. The categories 3 and 3+3 are marked identically. This structure is not found as frequently as the previously discussed Mandara-type. Still, there are enough cases to grant this TUPÍ-GUARANÍ-TYPE the status of common. Paradigms of this type are the general structure of the intransitive prefixes of the Tupí-Guaraní family in South America.[39] The paradigms are so strongly alike that the paradigmatic structure can even confidently be reconstructed for proto-Tupí-Guaraní (Jensen 1990: 120). The reconstructed active prefixes are shown in (4.72).

(4.72) Proto-Tupí-Guaraní intransitive active prefixes

		*ya-...		1+2
				1+2+3
1	*a-...		*oro-...	1+3
2	*ere-...		*pe-...	2+3
3		*o-...		3+3

The independent pronouns of Dravidian languages are regularly of the Tupí-Guaraní-type. Shown in (4.73) are the pronouns from Toda (Emeneau 1984: 95, 98). The third person pronouns are not specialized person markers, but general

---

[37] An incidental case without a dual is the paradigm of the pronominal inflection from Gunin (McGregor 1993: 44–6).
[38] e.g. the independent pronouns from Shuswap, a Salish language from Canada (Kuipers 1974: 59), the pronouns from Ojibwe, an Algonquian language from the USA (Schwartz and Dunnigan 1986: 296), and the pronouns from Retuarã, a Tucanoan language from Colombia (Strom 1992: 34–5).
[39] e.g. Guajajara (Bendor-Samuel 1972: 86–92), Guarani (Adelaar and Silva Lôpez 1988: 31–5), Aché (Susnik 1961: 98), Asurini (Harrison 1971: 30), and Mundurukú (Crofts 1973: 69–70, 88–91).

144 *Paradigmatic Structure*

referential elements that are also used as demonstratives. This paradigmatic structure is a general characteristic of Dravidian languages, although it is not found in all Dravidian languages.[40] The same situation as in Dravidian is found in the Tucanoan languages, spoken around the border of Colombia, Brazil, and Ecuador in South America. In some Tucanoan languages, the third person pronouns are identical to the demonstrative pronouns, as in Macuna shown in (4.74).[41] In other Tucanoan languages, the third person pronouns and the demonstratives are alike, but not identical (Malone 1988: 126).

(4.73) Toda pronouns

		om	1+2
			1+2+3
1	*o.n*	*em*	1+3
2	*ni.*	*nïm*	2+3
3	(demonstratives)		3+3

(4.74) Macuna pronouns

		bādi	1+2
			1+2+3
1	*jɨ*	*gɨa*	1+3
2	*bĩ*	*bĩa*	2+3
3	(demonstratives)		3+3

Finally, I will present a few incidental cases of the Tupí-Guaraní-type paradigm. First, the imperfective pronouns from Ngizim, a Chadic language from Nigeria, are shown in (4.75). This case is interesting because, unlike the previous examples, the Ngizim independent third person pronoun is not a demonstrative item (Burquest 1986: 76). Next, the transitive subject prefixes from Colloquial Ainu (Shibatani 1990: 28) are shown in (4.76). Two final cases of this paradigmatic structure are attested in Ticuna, a language isolate spoken mainly in Brazil (Anderson 1966: 6–10), and in Sinaugoro, a Papuan Tip language from New Guinea (Tauberschmidt 1999: 16–17).

---

[40] e.g. Malayalam (Asher and Kumari 1997: 258, 266), Tamil (Asher 1982: 143–4, 148–9), and Koya (Tyler 1969: 59–60). For a general account of Dravidian pronominal structure, see Caldwell (1913 [1856]: 414–15, 420).

[41] See also Siona (Malone 1988: 126) and Koreguaje (Gralow 1993: 15).

(4.75) Ngizim imperfective pronouns

		wàa	1+2
			1+2+3
1	naa	jàa	1+3
2	kaa	kwaa	2+3
3	aa	3+3

(4.76) Colloquial Ainu transitive subject prefixes

		a-...	1+2
			1+2+3
1	ku-...	ci-...	1+3
2	e-...	eci-...	2+3
3	∅-...	3+3

4.5.5 Kwakiutl-type paradigm

The next paradigmatic structure has both a horizontal homophony between 3 and 3+3 and between 2 and 2+3. This type is exemplified in (4.77) by the subject suffixes from Kwakiutl, a Wakashan language from Canada (Boas 1947: 252).[42] This KWAKIUTL-TYPE paradigm is found well distributed over the world's diversity, but is never attested as a widespread characteristic within a linguistic family. As a result, this paradigm is not common—following the criteria formulated in Section 4.2. However, this kind of paradigm occurs far more often than the rare paradigms. Therefore, it is classified as 'semi-common'.

(4.77) Kwakiutl subject suffixes

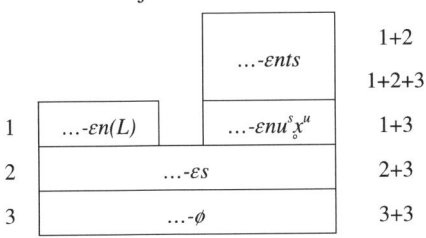

		...-ɛnts	1+2
			1+2+3
1	...-ɛn(L)	...-ɛnu̥ˢxᵘ	1+3
2	...-ɛs	2+3
3	...-∅	3+3

In South America, this pattern is manifested in the intransitive prefixes from Apalai, a Carib language from Brazil, as shown in (4.78). The (non-collective animate) independent pronouns have the same paradigmatic structure (Koehn and Koehn 1986: 95, 108). The intransitive suffixes from Huallaga, a Quechua

---

[42] The system for spatial deixis is disregarded here. I interpret this spatial system as a separate system, although it cross-cuts the pronominal system. The same structure as in Kwakiutl is found in the related language Heiltsuk (Rath 1981: 77).

146 *Paradigmatic Structure*

language from Peru show the same structure (Weber 1986: 334). Finally, the intransitive subject pronouns from Maxakali, a Gé language from Brazil, are shown in (4.79). Other pronominal paradigms in Maxakali have an identical structure (Popovich 1986: 352–3, 356).

(4.78) Apalai intransitive prefixes

		s(y)-...		1+2
				1+2+3
1	*ø/y-...*	*ynan(y)-...*		1+3
2		*o/m-...*		2+3
3		*n(y)-...*		3+3

(4.79) Maxakali intransitive subject pronouns

		yũmũg		1+2
				1+2+3
1	*'ũg*	*'ũgmũg*		1+3
2		*'ã*		2+3
3		*'ũ*		3+3

Another source of this paradigmatic type is the Austronesian stock. The independent pronouns from Acehnese are presented in (4.80). In Acehnese, different honorific versions of these pronouns exist; the presented morphemes are the familiar forms (Durie 1985: 117). The pronouns from Karo Batak are structured identically (Woollams 1996: 108). Somewhat further away, the hypothetical prefixes from the Micronesian language spoken on Palau (Josephs 1975: 103 ff.) and the independent pronouns of the Papuan Tip language Mekeo (Jones 1998: 147) show the same Kwatiutl-type pattern. Finally, unrelated to Austronesian, this pattern is attested in the object prefixes from the South Caucasian language Svan, as shown in (4.81). The separate exclusive is probably an innovation in Proto-Svan (Tuite 1997: 23).

(4.80) Acehnese pronouns

		geutanyoe		1+2
				1+2+3
1	*kee*	*kamoe*		1+3
2		*kah*		2+3
3		*jih*		3+3

(4.81) Svan object prefixes

		gw-...		1+2
				1+2+3
1	m-...		n-...	1+3
2		ž-...		2+3
3		x-...		3+3

4.5.6 Sierra Popoluca-type paradigm

The final common pattern with an inclusive/exclusive position again has more horizontal homophony. Besides an inclusive 'we', there are no other non-singular morphemes. In this common pattern, the category 1+3 aligns with 1, 2+3 with 2, and 3+3 with 3. This is exemplified in (4.82) with the prefixes from Sierra Popoluca, a Mixe-Zoque language from Mexico (Foster and Foster 1948: 17–19; Elson 1960: 207). By using a plural suffix *-tá?m*, the difference between the singular reference and the group reference is disambiguated. This is shown in (4.83a, b). It is also possible to use the plural suffix with the inclusive prefix *ta-*. By using this combination, it is possible to distinguish between 1+2 and 1+2+3, as is shown in (4.83c, d).[43]

(4.82) Sierra Popoluca subject prefixes

		ta-...	1+2
			1+2+3
1	ʔa-...		1+3
2	mi-...		2+3
3	ø-...		3+3

(4.83) Sierra Popoluca (Foster and Foster 1948: 19)
    a. *ʔa-moŋ-tá?m-pa*
       1-sleep-PL-IMPERF
       'We (exclusive) are sleeping.'

---

[43] The pronominal system of Sierra Popoluca is described by Foster and Foster (1948: 17–19) as being of the minimal/augmented type. In fact, this description is the first known description of a minimal/augmented pronominal system (see Section 3.6.5). I do not follow the Fosters in this analysis. By the classification as used in the present work, the pronominal prefixes of Sierra Popoluca are separated from the other affixes (cf. Elson 1960: 207). Notably, the separate number suffix is not included in the discussion of the pronominal prefixes. Only when the pronominal prefixes were considered together with this number suffix could eight different referential values be distinguished (comparable to the 8 different forms of a minimal/augmented paradigm).

b. *mi-móŋ-tá?m-pa*
2-sleep-PL-IMPERF
'You (plural) sleep.'

c. *ta-moŋ-pa*
1+2-sleep-IMPERF
'We (inclusive) will sleep.'

d. *ta-moŋ-tá?m-pa*
1+2-sleep-PL-IMPERF
'We (inclusive plural) will sleep.'

Example sentences like (4.83a) are crucial in classifying a pronominal paradigm as a special type. This SIERRA POPOLUCA-TYPE paradigm is strongly similar to the pattern of the Berik-type, as discussed in Section 4.3.4. Both patterns have only one non-singular morpheme, which is in both cases to be translated as 'we'. However, the possible referents for this 'we'-morpheme in Sierra Popoluca is different from Berik, as shown in Figure 4.7. The difference between the two patterns is the marking for the category 1+3. In the Berik-type, the category 1+3 is marked identical to the categories 1+2 and 1+2+3, adding up to a general form like the English 'we'. In the Sierra Popoluca-type, the category 1+3 is marked identical to the speaker, leaving 1+2 and 1+2+3 as sole meanings of the form 'we'. Taken at face value, the two types might look alike, as both only have one non-singular form to be translated into English using the pronoun 'we'. However, the structures are significantly different, and should be clearly distinguished (see also Section 4.3.4).

The Sierra-Popoluca paradigm is often analysed as a 'four-person' system. Analysed as such, the paradigm from Sierra Popoluca would look as shown in (4.84). This four-person analysis is entirely analogous to my analysis, as presented in (4.82), but stripped down to the essentials.[44] I will stick to the more laborious

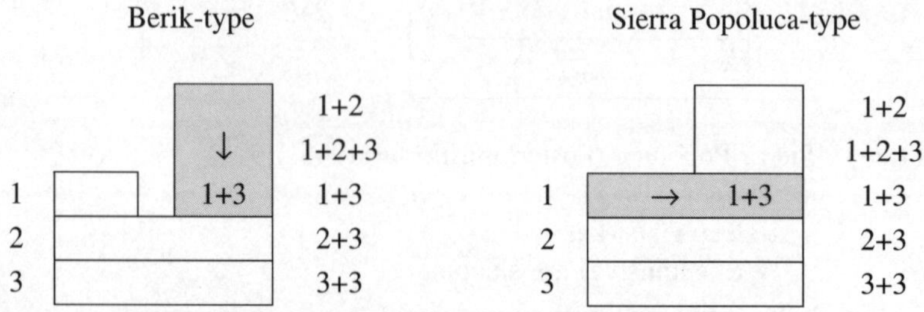

FIG. 4.7. *The Sierra Popoluca-type compared to the Berik-type*

---

[44] There is a small tendency in the descriptive literature to call this inclusive a 'fourth' person, because this inclusive goes along with the other 'singular' marking (e.g. Hardman 1966: 56; Osborne 1974: 38; Gerzenstein 1994: 83). This usage of 'fourth' person is semantically awkward and conceptually confusing, and should be avoided (cf. Hymes 1972: 105). Veerman-Leichsenring (2000: 322) analyses this inclusive as a person form with 'general or collective meaning'. It is unclear to me

analysis as in (4.82) so that these paradigms can more easily be compared with the other patterns discussed in this chapter. However, for the description of individual languages that have a pronominal paradigm of this sort, an analysis like that in (4.84) is to be preferred.

(4.84) Sierra Popoluca '4-person' analysis

1+2	ta-...
1	ʔa-...
2	mi-...
3	ø-...

The examples attested of the Sierra Popoluca-type, to be discussed shortly, show that this paradigmatic structure is common. This is different from what has been claimed in the literature, where this type is often depicted as rather exotic and exceptional. For example, Plank (1985) claims that 'these paradigms are rather untypical as far as the relation between person and number is concerned' (p. 143; my translation).[45]

However, this paradigmatic structure is a typical pattern of American languages. As well as in Sierra Popoluca, it is attested in various languages in North and Middle America. Shown in (4.85) is the prefix paradigm from Winnebago, a Siouan language (Lipkind 1945: 22–8). It is also attested in the Caddoan languages Wichita (Rood 1996: 600), Caddo (Chafe 1976: 65–70), and Pawnee (Parks 1976: 164–75). In Middle America, it is attested in the Mixtecan languages Chalcatongo Mixtec (Macaulay 1996: 138–43) and Ocotepec Mixtec (Alexander 1988: 263–4). In these two Mixtecan languages, the original existing non-singular pronouns were reanalysed as honorific pronouns, leaving a paradigm of the Sierra Popoluca-type.

In South America, the pronominal inflection of Maká, a Guaicuruan language from Paraguay, shows this structure (Gerzenstein 1994: 83–97). One of the various allophonic variants of this paradigm is shown in (4.86). Next, the independent pronouns and the pronominal inflection from Jaqaru, an Aymaran language from Peru, both have a Sierra Popoluca-type paradigm (Hardman 1966: 79). Other examples are the pronominal prefixes from Canela-Kraho, a Gé language from Brazil (Popjes and Popjes 1986: 175) and the subject suffixes from Tarma, a Quechua language from Peru (Adelaar 1977: 89–93, 127–8). Finally, the pronominal

---

whether this is just a question of terminology, or whether there are different kinds of category involved.

[45] '... diese Paradigmen in einer Hinsicht, das Verhältnis von Person und Numerus betreffend, eher untypisch sind.'

150   *Paradigmatic Structure*

affixes and the independent pronouns from the Campa languages (a subgroup of Arawakan) have this paradigmatic structure (Wise 1971: 67; Payne 1981: 34; Reed and Payne 1986: 324–7).

(4.85)   Winnebago active prefixes

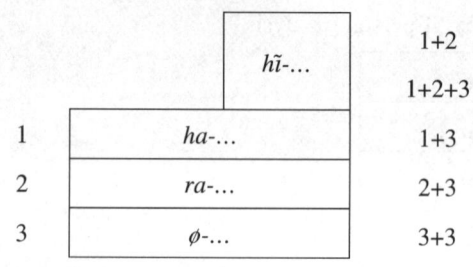

		hĩ-...	1+2
			1+2+3
1	ha-...		1+3
2	ra-...		2+3
3	∅-...		3+3

(4.86)   Maká subject prefixes

		xitV-...	1+2
			1+2+3
1	hVy-...		1+3
2	ɬ(V)-...		2+3
3	t(V)-...		3+3

Paradigms of the Sierra-Popoluca type are also found among the Papuan languages of New Guinea. Shown in (4.87) are the pronominal roots from Nimboran (Anceaux 1965: 167). Other examples of this paradigmatic structure in New Guinea are found in the Border family. Both the independent pronouns of Imonda (Seiler 1985: 44) and the short form of the pronouns in Amanab (Minch 1991: 31–2) have a Sierra Popoluca-type structure. A final example of this pattern among Papuan languages, shown in (4.88), is the paradigm of the subject suffixes from Salt-Yui, a language from the East New Guinea Highlands family (Irwin 1974: 14–15).

(4.87)   Nimboran pronominal roots

		io-...	1+2
			1+2+3
1	na-...		1+3
2	ko-...		2+3
3	no-...		3+3

Survey of Paradigmatic Structure 151

(4.88) Salt-Yui subject suffixes

	...-bil	1+2
		1+2+3
1	...-m(in)	1+3
2	...-n	2+3
3	...-m/ng	3+3

Finally, I know of a few isolated examples of this paradigmatic type. The first is the paradigm of the subject prefixes from the South Caucasian language Svan, shown in (4.89). Just as in Sierra Popoluca, there are suffixes in Svan to disambiguate the number reference of these prefixes. These suffixes form an interesting paradigm in themselves; they have been discussed in Section 4.4.2 (Tuite 1997: 23). Other isolated examples are the subject prefixes from the Nilo-Saharan language Ngiti (Kutsch Lojenga 1994: 190–3, 220) and the independent pronouns from Chrau, a Mon-Khmer language from Vietnam. In Chrau, these pronouns 'may be used as plural without modification...but plurality is often indicated by preposing *kha* or *khay*' (Thomas 1971: 138).

(4.89) Svan subject prefixes

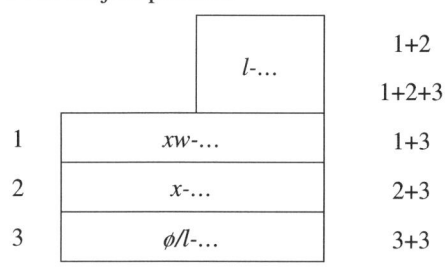

	l-...	1+2
		1+2+3
1	*xw-...*	1+3
2	*x-...*	2+3
3	*∅/l-...*	3+3

(4.90) Chrau pronouns

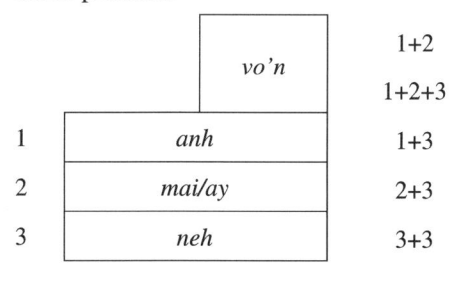

	vo'n	1+2
		1+2+3
1	*anh*	1+3
2	*mai/ay*	2+3
3	*neh*	3+3

4.5.7 Rare variants

All previously discussed (semi-)common paradigmatic structures are characterized by various kinds of HORIZONTAL HOMOPHONY. Other combinations of horizontal homophony are virtually unattested in split paradigms with an inclusive/exclusive opposition. Two different kinds of horizontal homophony are attested in the actor prefixes of the Australian language Warrwa. Horizontal homophony in the first person only, as shown in (4.91a), is found in the future. Horizontal homophony of first and second but not third person, as shown in (4.91b), is found in the non-future (McGregor 1994: 41). Horizontal homophony in first and second person only is also attested in Tiwi, though with a minimal/augmented opposition in the inclusive, as shown in the previous chapter in example (3.20).

(4.91) Warrwa actor prefixes
    a. Future   b. Non-future

	ya-...	1+2	
		1+2+3	
1	nga-...	1+3
2	mi-...	ku-...	2+3
3	ø-...	ngi-...	3+3

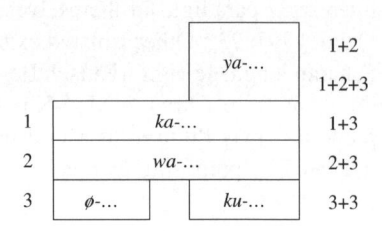

	ya-...	1+2	
		1+2+3	
1	ka-...	1+3
2	wa-...	2+3
3	ø-...	ku-...	3+3

There are a few more exceptional combinations of horizontal homophony, but they all show additional vertical homophony, and they are therefore discussed elsewhere in the present work. Horizontal homophony in the first person only is attested in Binandere, as shown in (3.22). Horizontal homophony in the second person only is attested in Kisar, as shown in (4.98). Horizontal homophony in the first and second person only is attested in Lenakel, as shown in (4.97). Horizontal homophony in the first and third person only is attested in Kunimaipa, as shown in (3.21).

4.6 Inclusive/exclusive: homophonous non-singular

4.6.1 Preamble

This section presents a survey of paradigms that have an inclusive/exclusive opposition; but not all non-singular categories are marked separately. A homophony in the non-singular is called VERTICAL HOMOPHONY in the present work. There appear to be various restrictions on the occurrence of vertical homophony in a paradigm with an inclusive/exclusive opposition. Among the five different

Survey of Paradigmatic Structure 153

	Split	Homophonous patterns			
		Inclusive/2	Inclusive/3	Exclusive/2	Exclusive/3
1+2 1+2+3	A	A	A	A	A
1+3	B	B	B	B	B
2+3	C		C		C
3+3	D	C		C	

FIG. 4.8. *Possible kinds of vertical homophony with an inclusive/exclusive opposition*

non-singular categories (1+2, 1+2+3, 1+3, 2+3, and 3+3) many kinds of vertical homophony are theoretically possible; however, only a very small set of these possibilities is attested.

The first restriction is a matter of definition: the marking for inclusive and exclusive cannot be homophonous, because in that case the pattern would not belong in this section. The other restrictions are empirical findings. First, morphemes that mark minimal inclusive (1+2) versus augmented inclusive (1+2+3) are never homophonous with any other category (despite some exceptional patterns discussed in Section 3.6.6). Second, no more than two non-singular categories are homophonous, ignoring the minimal/augmented inclusive opposition for a moment. With these restrictions, there remain five possible kinds of homophony as shown in Figure 4.8. These five kinds of homophony are all attested, but the details of the paradigmatic structures differ widely. Many of the paradigms additionally show some kind of horizontal homophony. Depending on the specific combination of vertical and horizontal homophony, twelve different paradigmatic structures are attested distributed over the five different kinds of vertical homophony. Singular homophony is completely unattested among these paradigms.

4.6.2 Inclusive/2-homophony

The most famous examples of the inclusive/2-homophony are attested in the Algonquian family. The (intransitive) pronominal prefixes from the Algonquian languages are exemplified in (4.92a) with data from South-Western Ojibwe (Schwartz and Dunnigan 1986: 305).[46] In this language, the inclusive marking is identical to the marking of the second person plural, which is in turn identical to

---

[46] cf. Eastern Ojibwa (Bloomfield 1956: 44), Menomini (Bloomfield 1962: 36–40), Cree (Wolfart 1996: 399–400), and Passamaquoddy-Maliseet (Leavitt 1996: 9–10). The pronominal prefixes can be reconstructed for proto-Algonquian (Bloomfield 1946: 97–9; Goddard 1990: 108) and probably the homophonous usage of *ki-* as well (Richard Rhodes, p.c.). In contrast, *ki-* is only used for second person and not for inclusive reference in Blackfoot (Frantz 1991: 22).

154   Paradigmatic Structure

the singular addressee; they are all marked by the prefix *kit-*. It should be added that the Algonquian languages use obligatory suffixes to mark number. In combination with the prefixes, these affixes disambiguate seven categories. The combined prefixes and suffixes are shown in (4.92b).

(4.92)   South-western Ojibwe intransitive affixes

a. Prefixes only   b. Prefixes and suffixes

	a.				b.	
	kit-...	1+2			kit-...-min	1+2
		1+2+3				1+2+3
1	int-...	1+3	1	int-...	int-...-min	1+3
2	kit-...	2+3	2	kit-...	kit-... m	2+3
3	ø-...	3+3	3	ø-...	ø-...-wak	3+3

Other examples of the inclusive/2-homophony have different kinds of paradigmatic structures. The first case is the object marking of the Australian language Tiwi (Osborne 1974: 39; cf. Lee 1987: 180), shown in (4.93). The final case of an inclusive/2-homophony is found in Sanuma, a Yanomam language from Venezuela/Brazil. Shown in (4.94) is the paradigm of the non-emphatic independent pronouns (Borgman 1990: 149). The unusual vertical homophony between 'we' and 'you' of the pronoun *makö* is illustrated in sentence (4.95a). There is a special exclusive 'we' morpheme *samakö*. This exclusive form is exemplified in sentence (4.95b). In this sentence, the speaker is discussing a group of non-present co-workers, using an exclusive 'we'. With the use of an exclusive, he indicates that the addressee (probably the author of the grammar, listening to the story) was not part of that group.[47]

---

[47] The possible case of an inclusive/2-homophony is found in the Khoisan language Nama, but this case is not convincing. The Nama pronominal root *saa* is used for both inclusive and second person reference (Hagman 1977: 44). However, the central problem is that *saa* only has the inclusive interpretation when a first person clitic is attached to it. In this combination, the inclusive meaning can be constructed componentially from the constituting parts 'you' and 'we', just as e.g. Tok Pisin inclusive *yumi* consists of the parts *yu* 'you' and *mi* 'I'. For this argument, it is important to understand the structure of Nama person marking. The main device for subject person marking in Nama are pronominal clitics (called person-gender-number markers by Hagman 1977, but nominal designants by Haacke 1977). These clitics occur obligatorily in each sentence on second position, but they do not have an inclusive/exclusive opposition. In contrast, the pronominal roots (among them *saa*) only occur sparingly, and are almost always followed by a pronominal clitic. In the incidental constructions in which the roots are not followed by a clitic, the only possible reference of *saa* is second person singular (Hagman 1977: 36; Haacke 1977: 47–8). The meaning of *saa* is 'you', and the apparent homophony with the inclusive is a result of the combination with a first person non-singular clitic.

(4.93) Tiwi object prefixes

		mani-...	1+2
			1+2+3
1	məni-...	məwəni-...	1+3
2	məṇi-...	mani-...	2+3
3	ø-...	wəni-...	3+3

(4.94) Sanuma non-emphatic pronouns

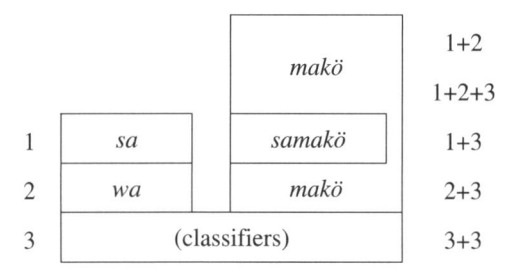

		makö	1+2
			1+2+3
1	sa	samakö	1+3
2	wa	makö	2+3
3	(classifiers)		3+3

(4.95) Sanuma (Borgman 1990: 150, 153)
    a. *makö   kali-palo   mai   kite*
       1+2/2+3 work-REPET NEG FUT
       'We/you (Plur) are not going to work.'

    b. *Poa Pisita ha   ĩ   samakö pewö kali-palo*
       PLACE   LOC REL 1+3   all   work-REPET
       'In Boa Vista we all work.'

4.6.3 Inclusive/3-homophony

An inclusive/3-homophony is attested in the pronominal prefixes of Huave, shown in (4.96a). There is massive allomorphy in these pronominal affixes, though all variants have the same paradigmatic structure. Just as in the Algonquian languages, number suffixes disambiguate this homophony. Once these number suffixes are taken into account, as shown in (4.96b), all eight categories are distinguished (Stairs and Hollenbach 1969: 48–53).

156   *Paradigmatic Structure*

(4.96)   Huave subject affixes

a. Prefixes only

	a-...	1+2
		1+2+3
1	sa-...	1+3
2	i-...	2+3
3	a-...	3+3

b. Prefixes and suffixes

		a-...-ar	1+2
		a-...-a:c	1+2+3
1	sa-...	sa-...-an	1+3
2	i-...	i-...-an	2+3
3	a-...	a-...-ïw	3+3

An inclusive/3-homophony, but without horizontal homophony in the third person, is found in Lenakel, an Austronesian language from Vanuatu, shown in (4.97). In this case, the homophony does not cause other marking (specifically the independent pronouns) to be used for disambiguation (Lynch 1978: 45). Comparable patterns are found in the other languages of the Tanna family to which Lenakel belongs (Lynch 1967: 46–8; 1986: 274). See also the paradigm from the Tanna language Kwamera that is discussed in Section 7.5.4.

(4.97)   Lenakel subject prefixes

		k-...	1+2
			1+2+3
1		i-...	1+3
2		n-...	2+3
3	r-...	k-...	3+3

4.6.4   Exclusive/2-homophony

The exclusive/2-homophony is attested among Austronesian languages on and around the island of Timor. This pattern is illustrated in (4.98) with the subject prefixes from Kisar (Blood 1992: 3). This homophony is probably an accidental merger of the proto-Central Malayo-Polynesian prefixes *ma-* for exclusive, *mi-* for second person plural and *mu-* for second person singular (A. van Engelenhoven, p.c.). It is found in various languages of the Timor subgroup of Central Malayo-Polynesian (Austronesian).[48]

---

[48] cf. Lamalera (Keraf 1978: 74–6), Dawanese (Steinhauer 1993: 133), Sika (Lewis and Grimes 1995: 605), and Roti (Fox and Grimes 1995: 615).

(4.98) Kisar subject prefixes

		k-...	1+2
			1+2+3
1	u-...		1+3
		m-...	
2			2+3
3	n-...	r-...	3+3

The same homophony, though without horizontal homophony, is found in the subject suffixes as shown in (4.99) from the Tungusic language Udihe (Nikolaeva and Tolskaya 2001: 212). The case of Udihe appears to be a singularity among the Tungusic languages.[49] A final variant of this homophony is attested in the Australian language Tiwi. The intransitive subject prefixes in the non-past are presented in (4.100). Note the presence of an opposition between minimal and augmented inclusive (Osborne 1974: 38; Lee 1987: 173). See also the prefixes from the Australian language Burarra, as discussed in Section 7.6.

(4.99) Udihe subject suffixes

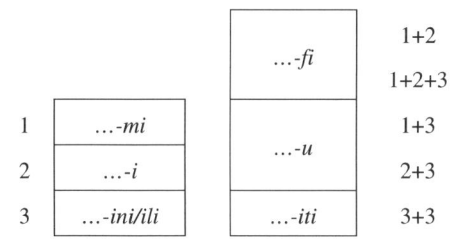

		...-fi	1+2
			1+2+3
1	...-mi		1+3
		...-u	
2	...-i		2+3
3	...-ini/ili	...-iti	3+3

(4.100) Tiwi intransitive non-past prefixes

		mu-...	1+2
		ŋa-...	1+2+3
1	ŋə-...		1+3
		ŋə-pə-...	
2	ṇə-pə-...		2+3
3	a(pə)-...	wu-...	3+3

---

[49] In an older survey of the Tungusic languages, Benzing (1955) does not find this homophony in any Tungusic language. He differentiates for Udihe between a suffix -u for exclusive and a suffix -hu

4.6.5 Exclusive/3-homophony

The exclusive/3-homophony is attested in the intransitive suffixes of Shuswap, a Salish language from Canada. In Shuswap, the exclusive is marked identical to the third person singular and non-singular, shown in (4.101). An independent pronoun *k̓ax°* is used to disambiguate the exclusive 'we' from the third person (Kuipers 1974: 45, 59).

Another case of an exclusive/3-homophony is the paradigm of the intransitive pronominal prefixes from Waiwai, a Carib language from Brazil, shown in (4.102). Just as in Shuswap, this homophonous pattern of Waiwai needs disambiguation. The difference between the category 1+3 and the third person has to be clarified by the use of an independent pronoun *amna* for the exclusive 'we'. A pair of examples demonstrating the Waiwai marking of the exclusive and inclusive is shown in (4.103). Different from Shuswap, the Waiwai pronominal prefixes also show a horizontal homophony in the second person (Hawkins 1998: 178–9). In a survey of the Cariban family, Derbyshire (1999) notes that a homophony between exclusive and third person appears to be the rule in the Cariban family: 'except for Makushi and Kuikúro, the [exclusive] prefix is identical in form and function with third person, and a free pronoun *ana* (or cognate) is always present' (p. 32). For another example of this homophony, see the suffixes from the Papuan language Binandere, as discussed in Section 3.6.6.

(4.101) Shuswap intransitive suffixes

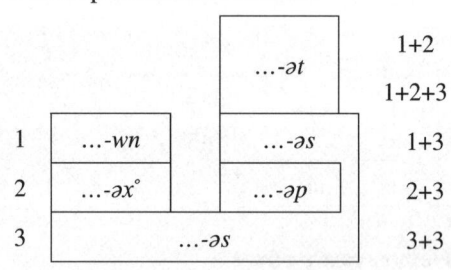

		...-ət	1+2
			1+2+3
1	...-wn	...-əs	1+3
2	...-əx°	...-əp	2+3
3	...-əs	3+3

(4.102) Waiwai intransitive prefixes

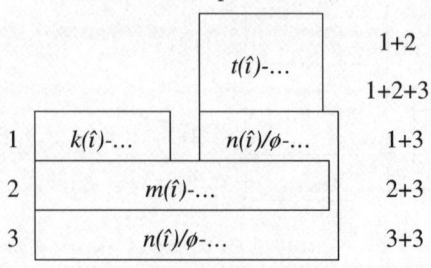

		t(î)-...	1+2
			1+2+3
1	k(î)-...	n(î)/ø-...	1+3
2	m(î)-...	2+3
3	n(î)/ø-...	3+3

for second person plural (Benzing 1955: 1078). However, according to Nikolaeva and Tolskaya (2001: 51), there is no phonemic /h/ any more in Udihe.

(4.103) Waiwai (Hawkins 1998: 179)
    a. *amna*   *nu-puru*
       1+3.PRON   3-roast
       'We (exclusive) roasted it.'
    b. *tî-htînoyasî*   *amñe*
       1+2-know   later
       'We (inclusive) will know it later.'

4.6.6 2/3-homophony

Finally, the 2/3-homophony is found in Kunama, a Nilo-Saharan language from Eritrea, shown in (4.104). The presented suffixes are used with verbs of type I/type S (Reinisch 1881: 53; Bender 1996: 19). A second example of this homophony, shown in (4.105), is attested in the Uto-Aztecan language Northern Paiute (Snapp et al. 1982: 61). When these two incidental cases are compared with the abundance of examples of a 2/3-homophony without an inclusive/exclusive opposition (see Section 4.4.3), it already appears that the presence of an inclusive/exclusive opposition has strong repercussion on the rest of the paradigm. This observation will be generalized in Section 4.7.

(4.104) Kunama subject suffixes

		...-di	1+2
			1+2+3
1	...-na	...-ma	1+3
2	...-nu	...-mu	2+3
3	...-su		3+3

(4.105) Northern Paiute object pronouns

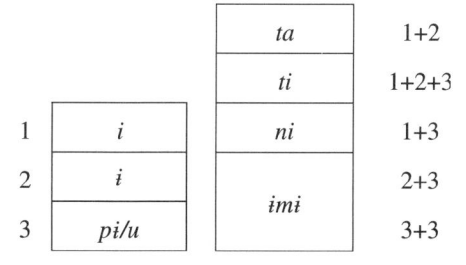

		ta	1+2
		ti	1+2+3
1	i	ni	1+3
2	i	imi	2+3
3	pi/u		3+3

TABLE 4.1. *Number of different paradigmatic structures attested*

	No inclusive/ exclusive		With inclusive/ exclusive			Total
	4.3	4.4	4.5	4.6	3.6.6	
Common patterns	4	—	4	—	—	8
Semi-common patterns	—	4	1	—	—	5
Rare patterns	11	20	2	12	5	50
Total	15	24	7	12	5	63

4.7 Generalizations

In this chapter, fifty-eight different paradigmatic structures have been described and classified as being either common, semi-common, or rare. The frequencies are summarized in Table 4.1, together with the five rare paradigmatic structures presented in Section 3.6.6. In these numbers, a difference can be observed between paradigms with and without an inclusive/exclusive opposition. There are thirty-nine (15+24) different paradigmatic structures without an inclusive/exclusive opposition and twenty-four (7+12+5) with such an opposition. This difference becomes even more significant when it is considered that paradigms with an inclusive/exclusive opposition have theoretically a far greater potential to form different kinds of homophony because there are more categories distinguished. In this section, I will argue that this quantitative observation is part of a broad generalization about the paradigmatic structure of person marking: the more categories are distinguished in a paradigm, the less paradigmatic variation exists. Or, formulated from a slightly different perspective, the more explicit the person marking, the less acceptable it is for a paradigm to confound various categories. The arguments for this generalization will be presented while summarizing the paradigmatic variation, starting from the most explicit paradigmatic structures. In the course of this summary, the precise predictions of this broad generalization will be made explicit.

Paradigms that distinguish a minimal from an augmented inclusive show hardly any variation. I found one common pattern, the Maranao-type (Section 4.5.2), and only very few variants. In this chapter, rare patterns with a minimal/augmented inclusive were presented in (4.100) from Tiwi and in (4.105) from Northern Paiute. In Section 3.6.6 a few more rare paradigmatic variants were presented. I interpret this strong homogeneity as an indication that the opposition between a minimal and an augmented inclusive is a late addition to the paradigmatic structure. Only if all other categories are distinguished can a minimal/augmented distinction in the inclusive eventually be added. This hypothesis has to be tested by investigating diachronic evidence, a topic that will be pursued in Section 8.5.2.

Survey of Paradigmatic Structure 161

Mandara-type	Tupí Guaraní-type	Kwakiutl-type	Sierra Popoluca-type

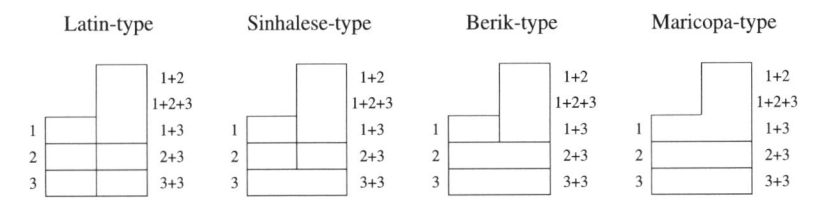

(schematic paradigm diagrams, each with cells: 1+2, 1+2+3, 1+3, 2+3, 3+3 for rows 1, 2, 3)

FIG. 4.9. *(Semi-)common paradigmatic structures with an inclusive/exclusive opposition*

Paradigms that distinguish inclusive from exclusive (but without a minimal/augmented inclusive opposition) are much more common and much more varied in their structure. I found three common and one semi-common paradigmatic structures (Sections 4.5.3–6), schematically represented in Figure 4.9. These four patterns are characterized by various kinds of horizontal homophony along the lines of a person hierarchy as shown in (4.106). I will call this hierarchy the HORIZONTAL HOMOPHONY HIERARCHY. Other combinations of horizontal homophony are almost unattested in paradigms with an inclusive/exclusive opposition (Section 4.5.7).

(4.106) Horizontal Homophony Hierarchy I (with inclusive/exclusive)
no homophony < third < second < exclusive

Vertical homophony is attested in paradigms with an inclusive/exclusive opposition, although it is rare (Section 4.6). The 2/3-homophony is especially rare, being almost unattested (Section 4.6.6), which is noteworthy because this homophony is semi-common in paradigms without an inclusive/exclusive opposition (Section 4.4.3). Almost all these case of vertical homophony also have some kind of horizontal homophony. Finally, singular homophony is completely unattested in paradigms with an inclusive/exclusive opposition.

Paradigms without an inclusive/exclusive opposition are much more varied in their structure. I found four common paradigmatic structures (Section 4.3.2–5), schematically presented in Figure 4.10. These four patterns are characterized by various kinds of horizontal homophony along the lines of a person hierarchy as

Latin-type	Sinhalese-type	Berik-type	Maricopa-type

(schematic paradigm diagrams, each with cells: 1+2, 1+2+3, 1+3, 2+3, 3+3 for rows 1, 2, 3)

FIG. 4.10. *Common paradigmatic structures without an inclusive/exclusive opposition*

162   *Paradigmatic Structure*

shown in (4.107). This hierarchy is strongly reminiscent of the hierarchy with an inclusive/exclusive distinction just mentioned in (4.106). There are a few exceptions to this hierarchy, including some cases with 'diagonal' homophony, but they are rare (Section 4.3.6).

(4.107)   Horizontal homophony hierarchy II (no inclusive/exclusive)
no homophony < third < second < first

Four semi-common paradigmatic structures with vertical and/or singular homophony are attested in paradigms without an inclusive/exclusive opposition (Sections 4.4.2–4). These four semi-common patterns are schematically presented in Figure 4.11. First, the Slave-type paradigm (with 1/2-homophony) is the most common of the patterns with vertical and/or singular homophony. This homophony makes referential sense, as it combines all non-singular references which includes speaker or addressee or both (viz. 1+2, 1+2+3, 1+3, and 2+3, but not 3+3) into the reference of one morpheme. The Nez Perce-type paradigm (with a 2/3-homophony) combines the categories 2+3 and 3+3 in contrast to the categories 1+2, 1+2+3, and 1+3. This homophony can be analysed as a speaker-centred opposition between all categories that include at least the speaker and all categories that do not include the speaker. This opposition between speaker and non-speaker is directly transferable to the singular (see Section 2.3.1). This explains the relative ubiquity of the Kombai-type, which exhibits a speaker/non-speaker opposition both in the singular and in the non-singular. There are some more examples of this mirror structure with additional horizontal homophony (see the paradigms (4.55) and (4.56) and the references there).[50] The fourth and least frequent of the semi-common patterns,

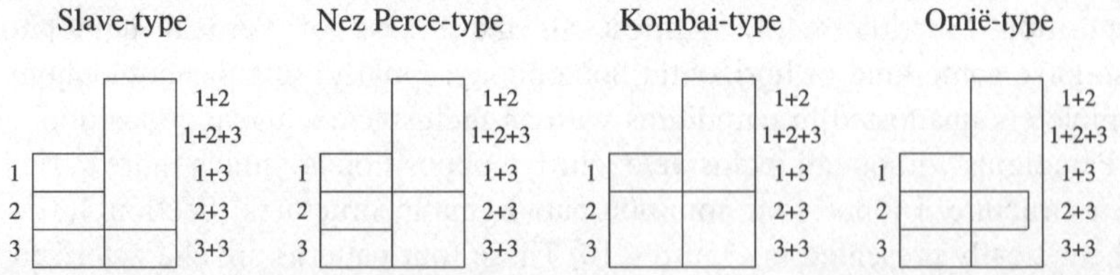

Fig. 4.11. *Semi-common paradigmatic structures without an inclusive/exclusive opposition*

---

[50] An example of a addressee versus non-addressee opposition in both singular and non-singular is the prefixal paradigm of the Algonquian languages in (4.92). However, this pattern appears to be rare cross-linguistically. It is remarkable that the third option—speaker/addressee versus non-speaker/ addressee in both singular and non-singular—is only incidentally attested. This opposition is semi-common in the non-singular only (i.e. the Slave-type paradigm, Section 4.4.2) and also attested in the singular only (i.e. the English-type singular homophony, Section 2.3.3), but only exceptionally attested in both at the same time. I had expected this pattern to be more widespread, but I have been unable to find more cases than the few mentioned in paradigms (4.38)–(4.41).

TABLE 4.2. *Variability related to the marking of 'we'*

	Marking of 'we'		
	Minimal/ augmented	Inclusive/ exclusive	No inclusive/ exclusive
Horizontal homophony	Rarissima	Common	Common
Vertical homophony	Rarissima	Rare	Semi-common
Singular homophony	Nonesuch	Nonesuch	Semi-common
Exceptions to horizontal homophony hierarchy	Nonesuch	Rarissima	Rare

the Ömie-type paradigm (with the 1/3-homophony), combines the categories 1+2, 1+2+3, 1+3, and 3+3, in contrast to 2+3. This homophony does not make sense referentially. I consider this paradigmatic structure to be a by-product of linguistic variability.

Table 4.2 presents a summary of the variability of paradigmatic structure depending on the marking of 'we'. The terms RARISSIMA and NONESUCH have been proposed by Frans Plank (p.c.) to deal with variants of linguistic structure that are singularities or not attested at all, respectively. As can be read from the table, the paradigmatic variability expands as the explicitness of the marking of 'we' reduces from left to right in the table. These qualitative observations corroborate the quantitative observations in Table 4.1.

The fact that vertical and singular homophony hardly occur in paradigms with an inclusive/exclusive distinction is interpreted by another generalization. I will capture these dependencies by the notion PURE PERSON, a gradual notion describing how explicit the speaker and addressee are distinguished in a paradigm. A combined first person non-singular, like the English *we*, is a mix of these categories. It includes reference to speaker and addressee (1+2, 1+2+3) as well as reference to speaker without addressee (1+3). The status of the addressee is not consistently made clear. The reference to the various person categories is not kept 'pure'. A paradigm that distinguishes inclusive from exclusive marks Pure Person, as this paradigm prefers not to mix the marking to speaker and addressee. Horizontal homophony between 1 and 1+3 or between 2 and 2+3 is fine, but homophony between, for example, 2+3 and 1+3 is disfavoured because it would mix reference to speaker and addressee. In contrast, if the inclusive and exclusive are combined, as in English *we*, then the person marking is not 'pure' anymore. The paradigm is open to other mixes of person categories, resulting in various kinds of singular and vertical homophony.

Thus, vertical and singular homophony are found almost exclusively in paradigms without an inclusive/exclusive opposition. The rare counterexamples are discussed in Section 4.6. An even stronger fact is that singular homophony occurs almost exclusively in paradigms that also have vertical homophony.

164   Paradigmatic Structure

Singular homophony without vertical homophony is only attested incidentally in a few European languages (Section 4.3.6). Abstracting away from various rare patterns, these structural dependencies are summarized by the EXPLICITNESS HIERARCHY as presented in (4.108). This hierarchy describes the order in which the various person categories in a paradigm are explicated. The hierarchy can be used in future research as a tool to evaluate the 'power' of a person-marking paradigm: the more to the right, the more explicit the category person is marked.

(4.108) Explicitness Hierarchy

$$\frac{\text{singular}}{\text{homophony}} > \frac{\text{vertical}}{\text{homophony}} > \text{unified-we} > \frac{\text{inclusive/}}{\text{exclusive}} > \frac{\text{minimal/augmented}}{\text{inclusive}}$$

This Explicitness Hierarchy can be straightforwardly combined with the two horizontal hierarchies that were discussed above. The result is an interconnected model of the paradigmatic structure of person marking, as shown in Figure 4.12.[51]

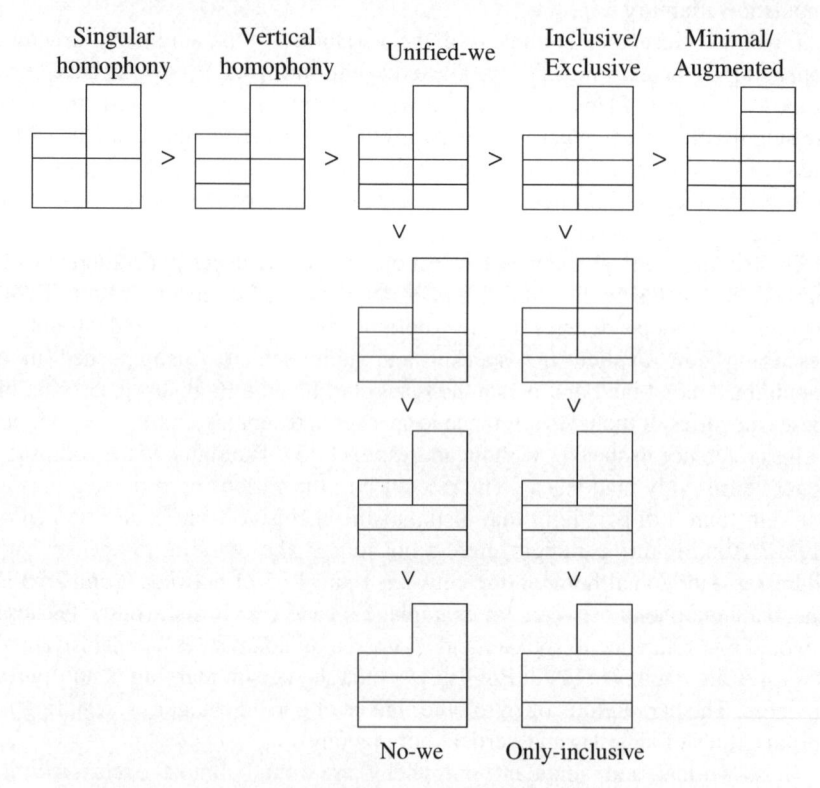

FIG. 4.12. *Model of the paradigmatic structure of person marking*

[51] Note that the paradigmatic structures that are shown for singular and vertical homophony are not the only possibilities—these depicted patterns are only an illustration of this part of the model.

This model is a refinement of the first person hierarchy in (3.26). It shows the most frequent paradigmatic structures ordered in a two-dimensional space according to the structural dependencies between the patterns. This model can be interpreted as showing the paths of least effort for the diachronic development of paradigmatic structure. This interpretation will be extensively discussed and tested in Part IV.

4.8 Conclusion

In this chapter, a wide variety of paradigmatic structures has been presented: in total, fifty-eight different structures have been described. Together with the five rare structures from the previous chapter, a total of sixty-three paradigmatic structures have been found. From this impressive variation, it can already be inferred that the traditional six-way paradigm is not the only and probably not the basic paradigmatic structure for a pronominal paradigm. It seems rather far-fetched to proclaim all other kinds of paradigm to be either extended or corrupted versions of the six-way paradigm. Accordingly, one of the major goals of this chapter has been to establish which other paradigmatic structures are commonly found among the world's languages and which ones are the 'real' exceptions amidst the massive variation. The distinction between the common and rare has been made on partly qualitative grounds. The common paradigmatic structures are attested often, widely dispersed over the world's languages, and they are a general characteristic of at least a few genetically close-knit groups. In contrast, the rare paradigmatic structures are only found in incidental cases; even within their close family the same paradigmatic structure is normally not found. Eight patterns were classified as common, five as semi-common, and the remaining as rare. The structural properties of the (semi-)common paradigmatic structures were analysed and the result is a model of the paradigmatic structure of person marking. This two-dimensional model combines the Explicitness Hierarchy and the Horizontal Homophony Hierarchy into a web of interconnected paradigmatic structures according to the structural similarities between the patterns. This model will return in Part IV, where it will be tested as to its diachronic interpretation. But first, in the next chapter, the claim is investigated that there are languages which have even more person categories than the eight categories that were the basis for the survey of the present chapter.

5 Compound Pronouns
Other Person Categories Disqualified

5.1 Introduction

There is a recurrent claim in the literature that even more person categories are attested in the form of so-called COMPOUND PRONOUNS (Forchheimer 1953: 132–5; Hagège 1982: 112; Wiesemann 1986a: viii; Noyer 1997: 148–54). Compound pronouns are a special kind of compound made up from two personal pronominal elements. In some languages such pronominal compounds are (semi-)grammaticalized, which leads to very large pronominal paradigms. Some authors propose to interpret these compound pronouns on a par with the singular and plural pronouns:

> It seems as if there are three contrastive levels in the pronominal system: singular simple pronouns contrasting to plural simple pronouns; and plural simple pronouns contrasting to complex [compound] pronouns. (Voorhoeve 1967: 428)

When these compound pronouns are included as part of person domain, this leads to extremely large paradigms of person. For example, when simple and compound pronouns are taken together, then there are up to nineteen different person markers in Ghomala', a Grassfields language in Cameroon. This paradigm made Wiesemann claim that Ghomala' has 'the most complex pronoun system as far as person categories are concerned' (Wiesemann 1986a: viii). However, I doubt whether these compound pronouns are really special person markers. In this chapter, I will review the available descriptions of such compound pronouns, only to conclude that they are indeed a special kind of pronoun (and not normal compounds) but that the claim for special person categories is rather weak. Until more specific descriptions of these compound pronouns become available, it seems best not to consider them as specific person markers.

These pronominal compounds are constructed in a very special way. The first part of the compound is a plural pronoun that incorporates the reference of the second pronoun. At a cursory glance, the second pronoun might appear redundant. However, the second part of the compound is a specification of the group referred to by the first pronoun. This special way of forming pronominal compounds is explained in Section 5.2. It will be argued there that these compounds are sometimes (semi-)grammaticalized, and can then reasonably be seen as pronouns, not as compounds. Due to their special characteristics, I will refer to them as COMPOUND PRONOUNS.[1] However interesting these compound pronouns may be, they are found only in a very restricted region of the world: all examples that I know of come from central-western Cameroon.[2] These examples are discussed in Section 5.3. Although all these languages are closely related, both areally and genetically, variation is attested in the construction of the compound pronouns. Some generalizations concerning the structure of the compound pronouns are presented in Section 5.4. The question remains whether these compound pronouns are really a viable cross-linguistic phenomenon, as they are only found in such a restricted region. However, there is an indication that they could have been more widespread, given a different linguistic world. Compound pronouns are constructed on the basis of an INCORPORATIVE reading of the first part of the compound (Hyman 1979: 53), a phenomenon widely attested among the world's languages (as discussed in Section 5.5).

5.2 From compound to pronoun

The basic characteristics of compound pronouns are exemplified here by the pronouns from Aghem, a Grassfields language from Cameroon. Aghem has seven monosyllabic simplex pronouns, a paradigm of the Mandara-type. The forms that are presented in (5.1) are the object forms, which are only slightly different from the subject forms (Hyman 1979: 47, 49). The object forms are shown because they are used for the formation of the compound pronouns, to be discussed shortly.

---

[1] The oldest reference to these compounds as special pronouns is by Meinhof (1906: 54), but he does not use a special name for them. Forchheimer (1953: 132–5) follows up on the examples given by Meinhof, calling the elements 'compound pronouns'. They are also known as 'complex pronouns'. The first to use the term 'complex' was Voorhoeve (1967: 427). In the recent descriptive literature, these pronouns are alternatively called 'compound pronouns' (e.g. Hyman 1981: 17; Fransen 1995: 183) or 'complex pronouns' (e.g. Hyman 1979: 53; Anderson 1985: 63; Parker 1986: 134). I will use the term 'compound pronoun', as this name highlights the dual nature of these elements: partly specialized pronoun, partly compound of two pronouns.

[2] There are many more pronouns in the world's languages that are historically related to a compound of two pronouns. An obvious case is the inclusive, e.g. the pronoun *yumi* from Tok Pisin, which is composed of the second singular *yu* and the first singular *mi* (Foley 1986: 67). I will not discuss this kind of compound here. A compound like *yumi* does not add any new categories to the ones already discussed, and there is no incorporative reading. The opposite is claimed for the compound pronouns discussed in this chapter. They are said to form a new kind pronoun, different from the possibilities that were discussed in the previous chapters.

(5.1)   Aghem simplex pronouns

		`sè´	1+2
			1+2+3
1	mùɔ´	ghà?´	1+3
2	wò`	ghè´	2+3
3	`wín	´ghé	3+3

Two of these simplex pronouns can be combined into a complex noun phrases, like *them and me* in (5.2a). In English, a noun phrase like *them and me*, although syntactically possible, sounds pragmatically rather marked. A sentence like *The photo shows them and me* can only be interpreted with a clear distance between the group of others, 'them', and the speaker, 'me'. A pragmatically unmarked choice would be to use an exclusive pronoun, as in *The photo shows us*. Another possibility in English, with a slightly different meaning, is the sentence *The photo shows them with me*. However, in many languages, including Aghem, there is no special 'and' conjunction. These languages use the comitative preposition 'with' as a conjunctor between all noun phrases (Stassen 2000). Consequently, there is only the possibility as shown in (5.2a), meaning something in between 'them and me' and 'them with me'.

(5.2)   Aghem (Hyman 1979: 53)
    a. *ghé*   *à*   *mùɔ*
       3+3   COM   1
       'them and me'
    b. *ghà?-à*   *ghé*
       1+3-COM   3+3
       'us and them' or 'me and them' or 'us and him'

At first sight, the phrase shown in (5.2b) is not much different: it shows a noun phrase meaning something like 'us and them'. However, this phrase can also mean 'me and them' or 'us and him'. Hyman explains:

> ... all this [phrase] says is that there are at least three people and at least one of them has to be first person and another one has to be third person. It says nothing about the internal composition of the group.... The two parts are welded together in an *incorporative* bond. (Hyman 1979: 53; italics added)

The term 'incorporative' refers to the fact that the reference of the second part of the compound is incorporated in the first part. In (5.2b), the group 3+3, 'them', is a fraction of the group 1+3, 'us'. This is different from both the English *us and them* (where the groups are separate) and the English *us with them* (where the groups are joined into one group, but there is still no overlap between the referents of 'us' and 'them'). These compounds seem to be most naturally translated into English by the first part only. Example (5.2b) means 'us', although the reference to these persons is specified in more detail in Aghem. Compounds such as (5.2b), with an incorporative reading of the first pronoun, are considered to be a special structure, called COMPOUND PRONOUNS.

There are nine such compound pronouns in Aghem, and they are presented in (5.3). All compound pronouns consist of two simple (object) pronouns, with the linker *à* incorporated morphophonetically into the first part. The compound pronouns are ordered according to the form of the constituting parts: the forms with identical first parts are put in the same rows, the forms with identical second parts are put in the same columns. The first element of a compound pronoun is always plural. This is easily explained, as only plural pronouns can have an incorporative reading.

(5.3) Aghem compound pronouns

	2	2+3	3	3+3
1+3	ghàʔà-wò	ghàʔà-ghɛ̀	ghàʔà-wìn°	ghàʔà-ghé
1+2				sàà-ghé
2+3			ghàà-wìn°	ghàà-ghé
3+3			ghèè-wìn°	ghèè-ghé

Only a selected set of pronoun combinations is used as compound pronouns. Combinations of pronouns in Aghem are either a regular compound, as in (5.2a), or a compound pronoun. The regular compounds of two pronouns are called CUMULATIVE by Hyman (1979: 52). All cumulative compounds are shown in Figure 5.1. In this figure, the dark grey areas are those combinations that yield reciprocal or reflexive meanings—if they are interpretable at all. Reflexives and reciprocals are not included in this study, and consequently, these compounds are disregarded here.[3] The light grey area shows the combinations that form compound pronouns. Only in these combinations does the incorporative reading of the first pronoun take place. Note that there is no overlap between the incorporative compound pronouns and the cumulative combinations of pronouns. There remain a few combinations that are not used. Their meanings are taken care of by alternatively possible reference of the compound pronouns.

In the interpretation of compound pronouns, two new referential functions can arise: dual and inclusive reference. When the second part of a compound is a

---

[3] For Aghem there are indeed no compound pronouns for reflexive and reciprocal contexts (Hyman 1979: 54), but this is not necessarily so for other languages. For another Grassfields language from Cameroon, Bamileke, reciprocal compound pronouns are described by Voorhoeve (1967: 427).

Paradigmatic Structure

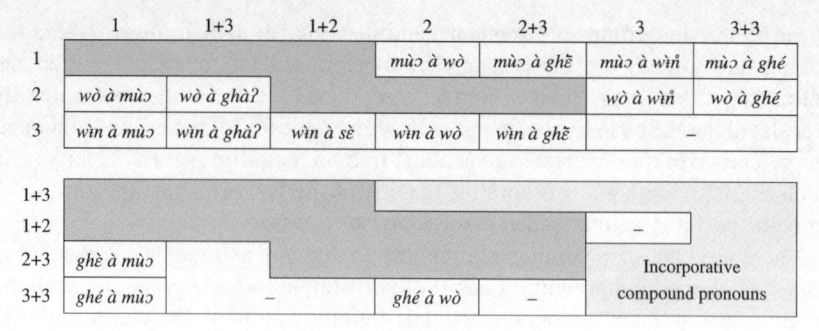

	1	1+3	1+2	2	2+3	3	3+3
1				mùɔ à wò	mùɔ à ghɛ̃	mùɔ à wɨ̀n	mùɔ à ghé
2	wò à mùɔ	wò à ghà?				wò à wɨ̀n	wò à ghé
3	wɨ̀n à mùɔ	wɨ̀n à ghà?	wɨ̀n à sè	wɨ̀n à wò	wɨ̀n à ghɛ̃		–
1+3							
1+2							–
2+3	ghɛ̀ à mùɔ					Incorporative compound pronouns	
3+3	ghé à mùɔ	–		ghé à wò	–		

FIG. 5.1. *Cumulative compound pronouns from Aghem*

singular, then the compound pronoun has dual meaning. The pronoun *ghàʔà-wò*, literally 'we-exclusive with you-singular', means 'we including you', or better simply 'I and you'. Compound pronouns can become dual pronouns, a category that did not exist in any of the languages known to exhibit compound pronouns. Also, for many of the languages to be discussed in Section 5.3, the compound pronouns are the only way to express a difference between inclusive and exclusive. In some of these languages, the compound pronouns with inclusive reference even grammaticalize into simplex inclusive pronouns.

Besides the dual and inclusive functions of compound pronouns, it is unclear what differentiates the simplex plural pronouns from the compound pronouns. When the second part of a compound pronoun is plural, then either or both of the constituting persons can have plural meaning. For example, the compound pronoun *ghàà-ghé*, literally 'you (plural)-they', can mean either 'you (singular) and they', 'you (plural) and he', or 'you (plural) and they'. These referential possibilities are also covered by the simplex *ghɛ̀*.[4] The difference between these pronouns is not one of reference. I suspect that there is a difference regarding the internal organization of the participants. Probably, a compound pronoun is used when there are two different groups set up in the discourse, that are now acting together for a short moment. The two groups are not put together into one new group, as they will remain separate later on. Parker (1986: 136–7) hints at such an analysis for Mundani. However, none of the descriptions gives a clear analysis of the use of the compound pronouns. The most direct analysis is found in a description by Voorhoeve (1967) for Bamileke. He states that the compound pronouns relate to the plural pronouns just as the plural pronouns relate to the singular ones:

The meaning of complex [compound] pronouns cannot be clearly distinguished from that of simple plural ones. . . . However, the composition of the group of participants is much clearer defined, if complex [compound] pronouns are used. It seems as if there are three contrastive

---

[4] Theoretically, there might be a difference here between the meanings 2+2 and 2+3 (see Section 3.4), but there is no clear indication in that direction in any of the descriptions of compound pronouns that I have consulted.

levels in the pronominal system: singular simple pronouns contrasting to plural simple pronouns; and plural simple pronouns contrasting to complex [compound] pronouns. (p. 428)

In a sense, this makes a nice analysis: different singular participants can be combined into a group to form 'plural' pronouns. Then, different groups (whether singular or plural) can be combined into a compound pronoun to form yet another kind of person marker. Still, the fact remains that the reference of plural pronouns and compound pronouns overlap. A detailed analysis is needed to decide whether compound pronouns are indeed a further level of group formation, or whether they are just a pragmatical side-effect of compounding pronouns. For now, their status as a new kind of pronoun remains doubtful, although promising.

To summarize, there are three characteristics of compound pronouns. The first characteristic is closest to a definitional property: the reference of this first plural pronoun INCORPORATES the reference of the second part. The individual parts of the compound pronoun are not to be added together; the second part is only a clarification of the referential properties of the first part. Consequently, different meaning are often possible. A compound pronoun with the parts 'we' and 'they' can mean 'we and he', 'we and they', or 'I and they'. Second, any available linker is FUSED morphophonetically into the first part, or both parts of the compound are fused together. This indicates grammaticalization of the compound. Third, the first part of the compound is always a PLURAL pronoun—this characteristic in fact follows from the first. For an incorporative reading to be possible, a non-singular pronoun is necessary. The first two characteristics—incorporative meaning and fusion—are strong indications that there is indeed a special phenomenon here.

The only explicit descriptions of compound pronouns come from languages that are spoken in a very restricted part of Cameroon, to be discussed in the next section. It is difficult to judge whether compound pronouns really are found only in Cameroon, or whether this strong areal restriction is a result of descriptive practice. Maybe the existence of compound pronouns is a phenomenon only known to specialists in the languages in and around Cameroon, and stays unnoticed in the description of other languages.

5.3 The Bantoid compound pronouns

5.3.1 Preamble

There are numerous descriptions of compound pronouns found in grammars of Bantoid languages from Cameroon. I will discuss the structure of the compound pronouns from the languages mentioned in (5.4), all member of the Bantoid subgroup of the Niger-Congo family. Most examples of compound pronouns are found among the Grassfields subgroup of the Bantoid languages. It is a clearly areal phenomenon, as all languages in (5.4) are spoken in Western Cameroon, on the border with Nigeria (see the map in Grimes 1996: 188).

172   *Paradigmatic Structure*

(5.4)   Genetic classification of the Bantoid languages discussed
        Beboid: Noni
        Narrow Bantu: Akɔɔse
        Grassfields: Momo: Mundani
                        Ring: Babungo, Aghem
                        Mbam-Nkan: Bamileke, Ghomala', Limbum,
                                    Mbili, Ngiembɔɔn

In discussing these languages I will rephrase the descriptions of the compound pronouns following a unifying format. To ensure comparability, I will analyse all compound pronouns formally, according to their constituent parts. In almost all cases, the compound pronouns are transparent combinations of simplex pronouns. When the compound pronouns are ordered according to the constituting parts, then the compound systems of the various languages are structured highly alike, something which is not directly obvious from the individual descriptions.[5] In Section 5.3.2 I will present what appears to be the basic paradigm of compound pronouns. Starting from a Latin-type six-way simplex pronoun paradigm, eight compound pronouns are formed. In Section 5.3.3 I will present a common development, in which two of the compound pronouns fuse to form simplex pronouns, a minimal and an augmented inclusive. In Section 5.3.4 I will present another development, in which only one of the compound pronouns is grammaticalized into a general inclusive. Finally, in Section 5.3.5, I will discuss the strange case of Ghomala'.

5.3.2   The basic compound paradigm

The pronominal systems of Mundani and Mbili are posited here to have basic paradigms of compound pronouns. The reason for this proposal is that they do not have an inclusive/exclusive distinction in their simplex pronouns. In the Bantoid languages, there is normally no inclusive/exclusive opposition, but many of the languages with compound pronouns do have such an opposition. As will be shown below, these inclusive pronouns can often be related to (erstwhile) compound pronouns. In Mundani and Mbili, a reanalysis of compound into an inclusive simplex pronoun has not (yet) taken place.

Mundani has a Latin-type six-way monosyllabic pronoun system as shown in (5.5a). Besides these simplex pronouns, there are eight compound pronouns as shown in (5.5b). The first part of the Mundani compound pronouns is identical to the simplex plural pronouns, but the second part needs elucidation. The forms *nè* and *nì*, in the first two columns, are second person forms that are normally only found after the preposition *ne*, 'with'. In the second and fourth column (the second part of the compound is plural here) a pluraliser *bá* is added (Parker 1986: 132, 135).

---

[5] I will disregard all forms that have logophoric reference. Special logophoric third person forms are found regularly in this part of Africa, and in some languages they also take part in the formation of compound pronouns, e.g. Noni (Hyman 1981: 15–18) and Babungo (Schaub 1985: 198).

(5.5) Mundani pronouns
a. Simplex pronouns

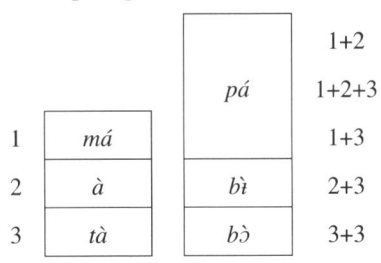

			1+2
		pá	1+2+3
1	má		1+3
2	à	bì	2+3
3	tà	bɔ̀	3+3

b. Compound pronouns

	2	2+3+Plur	3	3+Plur
1+3	bá nè	bá nì bá	bá tò	bá tò bá
2+3			bí tò	bí tò bá
3+3			bɔ́ tò	bɔ́ tò bá

Almost the same paradigmatic structure as in Mundani is found in Mbili. The Latin-type simplex pronoun paradigm is shown in (5.6a). The paradigm of the compound pronouns of Mbili in (5.6b) is smaller as in Mundani—the compounds with a third person first part are missing—but the general outline is highly similar (Ayuninjam 1998: 236–7). Most parts of the compound pronouns are transparently related to the simplex pronouns. The pronoun *yi* in the third column is probably related to the non-human third person pronoun *i*. The origin of *ben* in the second row is not explained in the description.

(5.6) Mbili pronouns
a. Simplex pronouns

			1+2
		bɛɛ	1+2+3
1	mi		1+3
2	u	ni	2+3
3	á	búgú	3+3

b. Compound pronouns

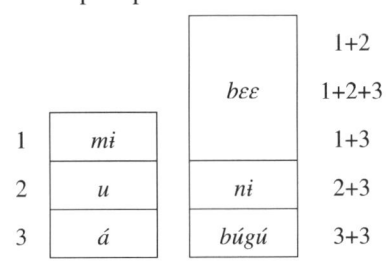

	2	2+3	3	3+3
1+3	bɛɛ-gu	bɛɛ-ni	bɛɛ-yi	bɛɛ-búgú
2+3 (?)			ben-yi	ben-búgú

5.3.3 Two inclusives innovated

Ngiembɔɔn shows a transition between compound and simplex pronouns. At first sight it looks as if there is a Maranao-type eight-way simplex pronoun paradigm, as shown in (5.7a), but the inclusive forms 1+2 and 1+2+3 are of recent origin. The two polysyllabic pronouns *pɔ́gɔ̀* and *pégè* are fused compound pronouns (Anderson 1985: 63). When they are still taken as compound pronouns in origin, the Ngiembɔɔn system of compound pronouns, shown in (5.7b), is identical to the Mundani system of compound pronouns. A compound meaning 'we and you' can apparently grammaticalize into an inclusive pronoun.

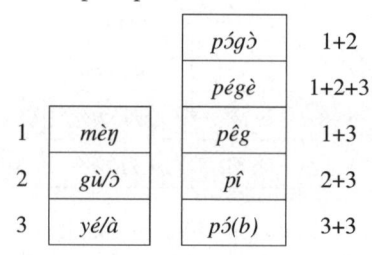

(5.7) Ngiembɔɔn pronouns
  a. Simplex pronouns

		pɔ́gɔ̀	1+2
		pégè	1+2+3
1	*mèŋ*	*pêg*	1+3
2	*gù/ɔ̀*	*pî*	2+3
3	*yé/à*	*pɔ́(b)*	3+3

  b. Compound pronouns

	2	2+3	3	3+3
1+3	*pêg+ɔ > pɔ́gɔ̀*	*pêg+a+pi > pégè*	*pèg yè*	*pég-à pɔ̀*
2+3			*pì yè*	*pî-a pɔ̀*
3+3			*pɔ̀ yè*	*pɔ́b-à pɔ̌*

Almost the same situation as in Ngiembɔɔn is found in Akɔɔse. There are eight monosyllabic pronouns, shown in (5.18a). However, the two inclusive pronouns are of compound origin as shown in the paradigm of the compound pronouns in (5.8b). The monosyllabicity of the two inclusive compound pronouns is an indication of their strongly grammaticalized nature (Hedlinger 1981; Dorsch 1911: 249–50).

(5.8) Akɔɔse pronouns
  a. Simplex pronouns

		sóò	1+2
		syá	1+2+3
1	*mè*	*sé*	1+3
2	*wè*	*nyí*	2+3
3	*mɔ́*	*bɔ́*	3+3

b. Compound pronouns

	2	2+3	3	3+3
1+3	sé+wè > sóò	sé+à+nyí > syá('né)	sú'mɔ́	sya'bɔ̂
2+3			nyú'mɔ́	nyá'bɔ̂
3+3			bú'mɔ́	bɔ́'bɔ̂

The simplex pronouns from Babungo are shown in (5.9a). In the description, Babungo is noted to have a Maranao-type paradigm with eight monosyllabic pronouns and the simplest set of compound pronouns of all languages discussed here (Schaub 1985: 193–8). There are only four compound pronouns, as shown in (5.9b).[6] However, in the light of the systems from Ngiembɔɔn and Akɔɔse, the two simplex inclusives probably have a compound origin. It might even be possible to reconstruct their origin from the same composition as in Ngiembɔɔn and Akɔɔse, although the first part of these compounds in Babungo remains enigmatic $ns(?)+ghɔ̂ > nsôo$ and $ns(?)+vìŋ > nsíŋ$. Such a reconstruction has to be investigated with more knowledge about the phonological and diachronic processes of the language than I can offer.

(5.9) Babungo pronouns
   a. Simplex pronouns

	nsôo	1+2
	nsíŋ	1+2+3
1	mɔ́	yìa	1+3
2	ghɔ̂	vìŋ	2+3
3	ŋwé	vɔ̌ŋ	3+3

b. Compound pronouns

	2	2+3	3	3+3
1+3	(nsôo)	(nsíŋ)	yía-ŋwé	yía-vɔ̌ŋ
2+3			víŋ-ŋwé	víŋ-vɔ̌ŋ

---

[6] The compound pronouns with an incorporative reading shown here are called 'selective' by Schaub (1985: 196). There are a few more compound pronouns mentioned in the grammar, but they all have obligatory plural reference of the first part. This is comparable to the cumulative compound pronouns as described in Section 5.2; they are called 'additive' by Schaub (1985: 198). These cumulative compound pronouns, as they are called here, are made with a linker vɨ, an indefinite pronoun. There are only three different cumulative compounds: yía vɨ vɔ̌ŋ, nsíŋ vɨ vɔ̌ŋ, and víŋ vɨ vɔ̌ŋ (Schaub 1985: 196, 198).

Limbum is also described as having a Maranao-type eight-way simplex pronoun system (Fransen 1995: 179–80). The two inclusive forms in this paradigm, as shown in (5.10a), present an even greater challenge for a compound reconstruction in the manner of the previously discussed cases. Only the fact that *sìì* and *wìì* end identically in *ìì* could indicate a historical relation between those forms. The compound pronouns, as shown in (5.10b), are unusual for various reasons (Fransen 1995: 183–5). First, the concord marker *ó-* is used instead of the third person plural pronoun (Fransen 1995: 193). However, the most interesting aspect of these compounds concerns the first two columns of (5.10b). The two compound pronouns in these columns are composed of a second person plural with the two simplex inclusives. This kind of compound is not found in any other language with compound pronouns. These compounds have the same meaning as the combination first person plural/second person, as in Ngiembɔɔn and in most other languages discussed here. If the simplex inclusives are indeed erstwhile compound pronouns, then these compounds with *wìì* represent a second cycle of forming compound pronouns. The meaning of the third column of the compound pronouns (with *-yī* as second part) is slightly different in Limbum, when compared to the other languages cited here. In all other languages these forms are strictly dual. The plural first part of the compound can only have the incorporative reading. In Limbum, however, the compounds shown here in the third column can also be used with reference to more than two persons, meaning respectively 'we and he/she', 'you (plural) and he/she', and 'they and he/she' (Fransen 1995: 184). It is unclear why Limbum deviates from the other languages in this aspect; it might be simply a difference in descriptive practice.

(5.10) Limbum pronouns
a. Simplex pronouns

		sò̀	1+2
		sìì	1+2+3
1	mè̀	wìr	1+3
2	wè̀	wìì	2+3
3	(y)í	wōwìì	3+3

b. Compound pronouns

	1+2	1+2+3	3	3+3
1+3			wìr-yī	wìr-wōwìì
2+3	wìì-sò̀	wìì-sìì	wìì-yī	wìì-wōwìì
concord			ó-yī	ó-wōwìì

5.3.4 One inclusive innovated

The simplex pronouns from Noni are shown in (5.11a). It is a Mandara-type seven-way system with only one specialized inclusive. Hyman analyses the simplex inclusive pronoun *beènè* as a compound pronoun, historically derived from a combination of the two pronouns *beè+bèn*. The resulting pronoun *beènè*, however, is grammaticalized as a simplex form. It is used in turn as the first part of the compound *beènè-bɔ́*, as shown in (5.11b). Note that the 1+3 part of the compound pronouns, *beè*, is different from the simplex 1+3, *bèsèn*. Historically, they are based on the same element (Hyman 1981: 15, 17).

(5.11) Noni pronouns
a. Simplex pronouns

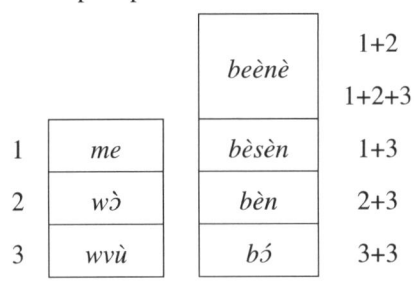

		beènè	1+2
			1+2+3
1	me	bèsèn	1+3
2	wɔ̀	bèn	2+3
3	wvù	bɔ́	3+3

b. Compound pronouns

	2	2+3	3	3+3
1+3	beè-wɔ̀	beè+bèn > beènè	beè-wvù	beè-bɔ́
1+2				beènè-bɔ́
2+3			bènɛ̄-wvù	bènè-bɔ́
3+3			bɔ́-wvù	bɔ́-bɔ́

For comparison with the other languages, I repeat the data from Aghem from Section 5.2. There is a seven-way simplex pronoun system, shown in (5.12a), identical to the Noni simplex paradigm (Hyman 1979: 49). Shown here are the simplex object pronouns, because these are used for the construction of the compound pronouns, as shown in (5.12b). The compound pronouns also strongly resemble the structure found in Noni. The main difference is that the simplex inclusive `sè´ is not related (anymore?) to the compound 1+3 with 2+3.

(5.12) Aghem pronouns
a. Simplex pronouns

		`sè´	1+2
			1+2+3
1	mùɔ´	ghàʔ´	1+3
2	wò`	ghè´	2+3
3	`wín	´ghé	3+3

b. Compound pronouns

	2	2+3	3	3+3
1+3	ghàʔà-wò	ghàʔà-ghè	ghàʔà-wìn°	ghàʔà-ghé
1+2				sàà-ghé
2+3			ghàà-wìn°	ghàà-ghé
3+3			ghèè-wìn°	ghèè-ghé

A variation on the last examples can be found in Bamileke. Again, there are seven monosyllabic pronouns, as shown in (5.13a). Shown here are the simplex object pronouns because they are used to form the compound pronouns, also when the compound is a subject. The inclusive bɜ̀n is not clearly related to a compound. However, it shows slightly different tone behaviour compared with the other pronouns, which points towards a different origin from the other simplex pronouns, perhaps a compound (Voorhoeve 1967: 422). The inclusive is not used in the compound pronouns, as shown in (5.13b).

(5.13) Bamileke pronouns
a. Simplex pronouns

		bɜ̀n	1+2
			1+2+3
1	mə	°bag´	1+3
2	uɨ	°bin´	2+3
3	jé	bó	3+3

b. Compound pronouns

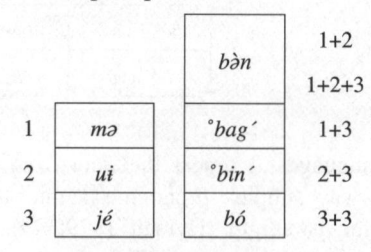

	2	2+3	3	3+3
1+3	bâg-uɨ̀	bág-à-bìn`	bâg-jé	băg-à-bo
2+3			bîn-jé	bín-à-bo
3+3			bô-jé	bó-à-bo

5.3.5 The strange case of Ghomala'

Finally, there is Ghomala', which is claimed to have the largest inventory of compound pronouns of the cases discussed here. The extensive set of pronouns made Wiesemann (1986a: viii) claim that Ghomala' has the world's most extensive pronoun system. Unfortunately, there is not much information available on the pronouns in this language. I will analyse these data within the framework developed in this chapter. Still, numerous questions will have to be answered by future research on this language.

The monosyllabic pronouns from the short note by Wiesemann (1986a: viii, citing Fossouo) form a Maranao-type eight-way person system, as shown in (5.14a). The compound pronouns as shown in (5.14b) are also from Wiesemann. They are organized so as to show the strong similarity to the previously discussed cases, especially to the compound pronouns of Noni in (5.11b) and Aghem in (5.12b). In comparison to Noni and Aghem, two compound pronouns are missing in Ghomala' (indicated by a star in the paradigm), but there is a complete extra series, build with the compound part *yɨ*, which is an emphatic third person singular pronoun (Ntage and Sop 1972: 37). It is unclear what this extra series means.[7]

(5.14) Ghomala' pronouns
a. Simplex pronouns

		pu	1+2
		pə	1+2+3
1	gó	pyə	1+3
2	o	po	2+3
3	e	wap	3+3

b. Compound pronouns (Wiesemann 1986a)

	2	2+3	3	3+3	3
1+3	pyawu	*	pyəé	pyəapu	pyayɨ
1+2				pəapu	pəayɨ
2+3			poé	poapu	poayɨ
3+3 (?)			pué	*	

---

[7] Noyer (1997: 150) is amazingly definitive in his interpretation of the rather uninformative presentation by Wiesemann (1986a: viii) on Ghomala'. Noyer interprets the difference between the -é series and the -ayɨ series as being a 'difference between set-inclusive and set-union'. If his interpretation is right, then the -ayɨ series are not compound pronouns, as they do not have the incorporative reading of the first part of the compound.

180   *Paradigmatic Structure*

From the scanty notes on Ghomala' by Ntage and Sop (1972: 36–40), a different set of compound pronouns can be distilled, as shown in (5.15).[8] This paradigm is completely in line with the sets as described for Noni and Aghem. In the description by Ntage and Sop (1972: 36–40), the inclusives *pu* and *pə* take the same position as the other compound pronouns, although they are written as enclitic to the previous word (Ntage and Sop use the grapheme '*a*' for the Schwa 'ə'). This is a clear indication that they are erstwhile compounds. Also, the three simplex forms for 'we'—*pu, pə,* and *pyə*—show a strong phonological similarity. This also makes it probable that both inclusive forms have a compound origin, as in Ngiemboon and in some other languages discussed. Following the history of the Ngiemboon inclusives, the minimal inclusive *pu* in Ghomala' might originate from the complex *pyawu*, as mentioned by Wiesemann (the compound part *-wu* or *-bu* is a variant of the second person singular object pronoun: Ntage and Sop (1972: 37, 41).[9] A compound development for the augmented inclusive *py-a-po > pə* seems unlikely. Whatever its origin, *pə* is now a constituent part of the compound pronouns, just as in Noni and Aghem, which shows that this pronoun is completely grammaticalized as a simplex pronoun. In this interpretation of the data from Ntage and Sop, the apparently strange case of Ghomala appears to be similar to the better described cases of Noni and Aghem.

(5.15)   Ghomala' compound pronouns (Ntage and Sop 1972)

	2 (?)	2+3 (?)	3	3+3
1+3	(pû)	(pa)	pyə é	pyəapú
1+2				paapú
2+3			po é	poapú
3+3 (?)			pú é	puâpú

---

[8] The description by Ntage and Sop (1972) was brought to my attention through the work of Noyer (1992; 1997). However, there are some infelicities in Noyer's presentation of the data. He simply unites the compound pronouns from Wiesemann (1986a) and Ntage and Sop (1972) into one (even bigger) paradigm, as if each had missed those pronouns not mentioned by the other. However, the different description are much more likely to reflect different variants of the language, either by space, time, or speaker. Also, Noyer (1997: 151) cites glosses from Wiesemann (1986) that the latter did not give. Although Noyer's interpretation seems to be the one intended by Wiesemann, one has to read between her lines to reach this interpretation. Also, somewhat unluckily, in the table of the Ghomala' pronouns in Noyer (1997: 150), the second row has been misprinted: all pronouns should have been placed one position to the left (cf. Noyer 1992: 183). Finally, in citing Voorhoeve (1967) on Bamileke, Noyer (1997: 152) misses the simplex inclusive *bə̀n*.

[9] The morpheme *pu* is found both as a simplex minimal inclusive and as a constitutive part of the complex pronouns. However, the meaning of the compound pronouns indicates that this *pu* is not an inclusive but a third person plural here, maybe related to the simplex pronoun *wap*.

5.4 Generalizations

The paradigmatic structure of the compound pronouns is very similar in the various languages discussed. However, there are strong indications that compound pronouns are an individually acquired phenomenon, and not a genetic feature. In all languages, the compound pronouns are transparently constructed out of the simplex pronouns of the same language. Although the simplex pronouns are historically related between the languages, the compound pronouns are clearly made up from the 'own' simplex pronouns of a language. The compound pronouns themselves are not directly related to the compound pronouns of other languages. The same principles for making compound pronouns are found in all languages, but each language uses its own inventory to make them. The idea of making compound pronouns is borrowed (or developed in parallel), not the compound pronouns themselves.

There are some differences between the languages as to which compound pronoun are used, and as to how many different compounds are distinguished. The basic paradigm appears to comprise eight compound pronouns, like the paradigm from Mundani in (5.5b). A few descriptions mention less compound pronouns (Mbili and Babungo) and a few mention more (Noni, Aghem, and Ghomala'). Whether these differences are artefacts of the descriptional practice or real differences between the languages has to be decided by more detailed research into these languages.

Another structural characteristic is the linker -*a*-. In many languages that were discussed, this linker is used between the parts of the compound. In central Africa, -*a*- is a widespread morpheme to link linguistic elements. Interestingly in this context, -*a*- is mainly found with compound pronouns that have a plural second part. The only exception to this generalization is found in Aghem.

The meaning of the compound pronouns also turns out to be strongly similar. When the second part of the compound is originally a singular pronoun, then the compound has dual meaning. A compound of the form 'we and he' means 'I and he'. The only exception to this generalization is found in Limbum, where the compound with the form 'we and he' can both mean 'I and he' and 'we and he'. When the second part is plural, then both parts of the compound can have a plural reference. A compound with the form 'we and they' can either mean 'I and they', 'we and he', or 'we and they'.

Finally, there is a strong referential connection between compound pronouns meaning 'I and you' and inclusive pronouns. In some of the languages, compound pronouns with the meaning 'I and you' have been grammaticalized into simplex inclusive pronouns. Once they are completely grammaticalized, these simplex inclusive pronouns can again be used as building part for complex pronouns (Noni, Aghem, and Limbum). Different stages in this grammaticalization are documented by the structures as found in the languages discussed in the previous section.

5.5 The incorporative reading revisited

The central property of compound pronouns as found in the Bantoid languages is the INCORPORATIVE reading of the first pronoun. The first part of a compound pronoun is taken as a reference to the whole, incorporating the reference of the second part. A phrase that literally says 'we and you' means rather something like 'I and you'. Although compound pronouns are only found in a restricted area in Cameroon, the incorporative use of a plural pronoun is widespread in the languages of the world (see Schwartz 1988 for a typological survey, and Lichtenberk 2000: 3–8 for a recent discussion of the available literature). I will discuss here a few fairly randomly chosen examples to show various forms of the incorporative reading among the world's languages, without any intention of presenting an exhaustive survey.

Some languages use a plural pronoun in conjunctions where one would expect a singular one. For example in Bari, a Nilotic language from Sudan, when pronouns are conjoined, the first pronoun always has to be plural, also when only a single participant is meant. This is exemplified in (5.16). However, there are no complex pronouns in Bari—at least, they have never been described as such (Spagnolo 1933: 212–13).

(5.16) Bari (Spagnolo 1933: 212)
a. *yi   ko   dɔ*
   1+3   with   2
   'I and you' (lit. 'we with you')
b. *ta   ko   nan*
   2+3   with   1
   'You and I' (lit. 'you all with me')

Other examples of an incorporative reading, outside Africa, can be found in Mundari, a Munda language from India, and in Tagalog, an Austronesian language from the Philippines. Both examples show a conjunction of a pronoun with a proper name, not of two pronouns. Still, the pronoun in both cases has the incorporative reading. The Mundari example in (5.17) can only mean 'I and Paku', because the pronoun is dual. The incorporative reading of this dual pronoun implies that the total group consists of two persons, one of whom is Paku, and consequently the other has to be the speaker. The Tagalog example in (5.18), using a plural pronoun, can mean both 'them and Juan' and 'him and Juan'.

(5.17) Mundari (Hoffmann 1903: 24–5)
   aling   Paku-lo
   1+3DL   Paku-COM
   'I and Paku' (lit. 'we with Paku')

(5.18) Tagalog (Schachter and Otanes 1972: 116)
sila   ni   Juan
3+3   CONJ   Juan
'them/him and Juan'

A last example of an incorporative reading of plural pronominal marking comes from West Greenlandic Inuktitut, an Eskimo-Aleut language. In this language, the inflectional pronominal marking can have an incorporative reading, as shown in (5.18). The literal translation 'We will leave with you' may sound like fine English, but there is an interesting difference between the Inuktitut and the English meaning of this sentence. In the Inuktitut sentence, only two persons will leave, so the best translation is 'You and I will leave'. The literal translation in English implies that there will be more than two participants, as the 'you' is normally not interpreted as part of the 'we'. The Inuktitut 'we' inflection has an incorporative reading, incorporating the 'you'.

(5.19) Inuktitut (Fortescue 1984: 257)
illil-lu   aalla-ssa-aqut
2-COM   leave-FUT-1+3
'You and I will leave.' (lit. 'We will leave with you.')

These examples can only indicate that the incorporative use of the plural pronouns is widespread among the languages of the world. The examples in this section are from all over the world (Bari in Africa, Mundari in Asia, Tagalog in the Pacific, and Inuktitut in America) and they are genetically diverse. Compound pronouns can best be seen as (semi-)grammaticalized use of the incorporative use of plural pronouns. Perhaps if compound pronouns were a more widely known phenomenon, they might be described for other languages as well.

5.6 Conclusion

Pronoun or compound, that is the question. I have argued in this chapter that the compound pronouns of the Bantoid languages in Cameroon are indeed to be interpreted as a special kind of pronoun. The compound pronouns show a rather different structure from normal compounds: they are clearly grammaticalized in comparison to normal compounds, and the semantic interpretation is different from other compounds. This semantic interpretation is the most salient characteristic of these pronouns. The first part of the compound pronouns is to be interpreted incorporative: it includes the reference of the second part of the pronoun. This incorporative reading of a pronoun is widespread among the world's languages, indicating that the restricted occurrence of compound pronouns—which are only found in Cameroon—is probably accidental.

184 Paradigmatic Structure

A different question is whether these compound pronouns are new person categories, leading to the largest inventory of person categories among pronominal systems, as claimed by Wiesemann (1986a: viii). I doubt this. The referential value of the compound pronouns either builds categories that are well known, like duals or inclusives, or has identical reference as to the non-singular simplex pronouns. However, more in-depth research is needed on the use of the compound pronouns as opposed to the group pronouns. If there are contexts which require a compound pronoun, and which do not allow for the simplex pronouns to be used, that would be an argument for a special referential status, although restricted contextually. From the available sources, it appears that the compound pronouns are freely interchangeable with simplex group pronouns, yielding a different pragmatic value, not a different referential value. Consequently, until further notice, the compound pronouns are not included as special person categories.

PART III
Number Incorporated

'I never ask advice about growing,' Alice said indignantly.
'Too proud?' the other enquired.
Alice felt even more indignant at this suggestion. 'I mean,' she said, 'that one can't help growing older.'
'*One* can't, perhaps,' said Humpty Dumpty; 'but *two* can. With proper assistance, you might have left off at seven.'

Lewis Carroll, *Through the Looking-Glass and What Alice Found There*

Number marking in language is not like counting. In contrast to the infinite nature of counting, there is only a small set of number categories attested in the world's languages. The most widely known linguistic numbers are the singular and the plural. Then there is also the dual, marking a pair. Other claimed possibilities for marking quantity in human language are the trial, the quadral, and the paucal. The paucal is a number category that roughly 'leaves off at seven'.

In Part III I will deal with the subject of number in the domain of person marking. In Chapter 6, I argue that singular and plural are both unmarked for number when it comes to person marking. Number in person marking only starts off with the dual. On this basis, the cross-linguistic possibilities of number marking are investigated. In Chapter 7 a typology of the dual is presented, which is the most widespread number category in the domain of person marking. Many different paradigmatic structures are presented that have dual marking. At the end of this chapter, this variation is summarized and the Dual Explicitness Hierarchy is proposed as a major generalization.

6 Cardinality
Redefining Number in the Pronominal Domain

6.1 Introduction

The marking of quantity—more traditionally called 'number'—in human language is a complex and multifaceted subject. In *The Philosophy of Grammar*, Otto Jespersen introduces the discussion of number with the warning that grammatical number is more complex than basic counting:

> Number might appear to be one of the simplest natural categories, as simple as 'two and two are four'. Yet on closer inspection it presents a great many difficulties, both logical and linguistic. (Jespersen 1924: 188)

Jespersen continues with an extensive discussion of various aspects of number marking in the grammars of human languages. Among many other things, he notes the problematic status of the plural in the pronominal domain, characterizing the pronoun 'we' as being 'essentially vague' (p. 192). Still, he does not conclude that the analysis of 'we' as a plural should be reconsidered. Yet this is exactly what is being proposed in the present work. The traditional use of plurality in the pronominal domain implies that the number of participants is important. However, as has been argued before (see especially Chapter 3), the categories traditionally called 'plural' are better interpreted as unmarked for number. The difference between the traditional approach and the perspective taken here is illustrated in Figure 6.1. A GROUP of participants has been defined as a specific combination of various singular participants (see Section 3.3). A group is unmarked for number because the number of participants is not important. Of course, a group necessarily refers to more than one person. Yet the definition of a group is based purely on qualitative characteristics of the constituting parts. The KIND of participants that form the group is important, not the NUMBER of the included participants.

In the previous chapters, the discussion was restricted to pronominal marking that is unmarked for number; in particular the marking of singular participants and groups of participants. In this chapter I will turn to the marking of number in the pronominal domain.[1] The main concept that will be used to describe the

---

[1] In line with the objective of the present work, I will restrict myself to the marking of number within the pronominal domain, and ignore the marking of number on nouns. There is a powerful universal saying that 'the differentiation of number with nouns implies that with pronouns'

188   Number Incorporated

```
Traditional division:    Unmarked for              Marked for
                         number                    number
                    ┌─────────────────────┐  ┌──────────────────────────┐
                                      GROUP        RESTRICTED GROUP
                    SINGULAR    –               –
                                     (PLURAL)        (DUAL, TRIAL, ETC.)
                    └─────────────────────────────┘  └──────────────────────┘
Perspective of the       Unmarked for              Marked for
present work:            number                    number
```

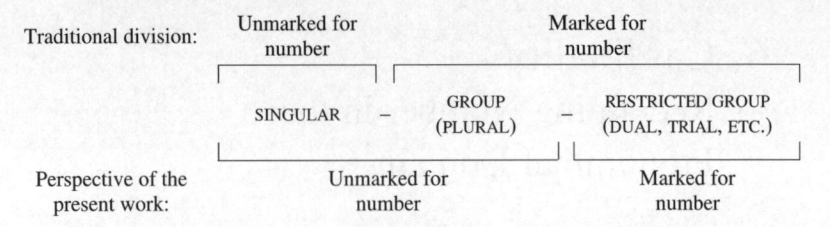

FIG. 6.1. *Different perspectives on number marking in the pronominal domain*

marking of number will be RESTRICTION. Groups, I will argue, can be restricted to the MINIMUM number of participants or, eventually, to a SMALL number. The concepts 'minimal' and 'small' are proposed as specifically pronominal categories for marking cardinality. In most cases, the concepts 'minimal' and 'small' can be freely translated as 'dual' and 'paucal', respectively.

In this chapter, I will first address the method that will be used to describe the different forms of number in pronominal paradigms. An important aspect of cross-linguistic research is a metalanguage on the basis of which the variable forms of human language can be compared. The metalanguage for the marking of number will be presented in Section 6.2. The next section deals with the claim that a minimally restricted group is more marked than an unrestricted group. Roughly speaking, this is true for pronominal paradigms. Still, there are some counterexamples and problematic cases, which will be discussed in Section 6.3. The complete typology of the various forms of minimally restricted group marking in pronominal paradigms is too extensive to be dealt with in the context of this chapter, and will be presented separately in the following chapter. The cross-linguistic variety of small number marking—trial, quadral, and paucal as they are traditionally called—is much more restricted compared to the wide variation in marking minimal number. These kinds of number marking will be discussed in Section 6.4. This chapter will be concluded in Section 6.5.

6.2   A metalanguage for number marking

This and the following chapter deal with the marking of pronominal number in its various appearances. In this section, the typological scheme for the analysis of the number in pronominal paradigms will be presented. I have chosen to use a scheme that distinguishes one category more than is needed, but this surplus power

(Plank 1989: 298). More recent research still substantiates this claim, although more counterexamples have been found (Plank 1996: 124). This claim was first formulated by von Humboldt (1994 [1827]: 156–7), later repeated by Schmidt (1926: 316) and by Forchheimer (1953: 12). This observation implies that the present investigation of number within the pronominal domain encompasses also a large part of the variability of number marking on nouns (see Corbett 2000 for a recent typological survey).

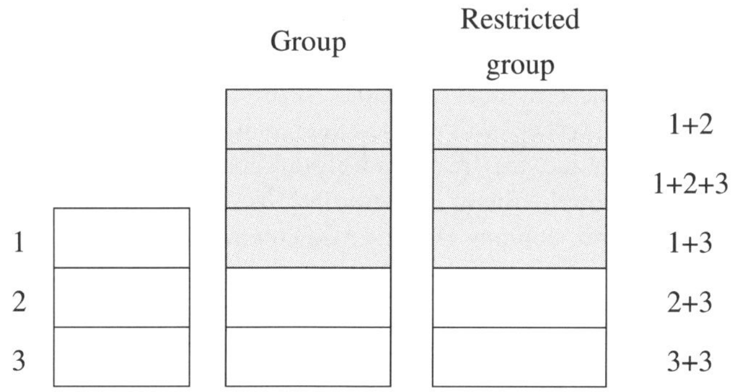

Redefining Number 189

```
                Restricted
      Group      group
                               1+2
                               1+2+3
   1                           1+3
   2                           2+3
   3                           3+3
```

FIG. 6.2. *Paradigmatic scheme for number marking*

will become of use later on. The scheme is shown in Figure 6.2. The first two columns consist of the categories as discussed in the previous chapters. The new column to the right is simply a copy of the group categories, labelled RESTRICTED GROUP. The idea behind the label 'restricted' is that it restricts the number of participants in the group to what is minimally needed.[2] For example, to form an exclusive group 1+3, at least the speaker and an unspecified set of others is needed. Restricted to its minimum, two persons are needed: the speaker and a single other participant. In other words, the category 'restricted 1+3' is a dual.

The restricted forms are mostly dual in nature, but not in all cases. A special case is the category 'restricted 1+2+3'. This category can never be a dual, as there are at least three persons involved in the category 1+2+3. Traditionally, the category 'restricted 1+2+3' is analysed as a trial. Glasgow (1964: 109–10) was the first to notice that for some languages the designation trial is referentially correct, but the morphological structure of some languages puts this trial on a par with the duals. Glasgow used the name 'dual honored' for this phenomenon. McKay (1978) later introduced the name 'unit augmented'. I opted for the name 'restricted group', as this label is referentially accurate and captures both the traditional dual and this special trial 1+2+3 form (see Section 7.6).[3] The labels

---

[2] The word 'restricted' is also used by McGregor in the context of pronominal marking, but in a rather different sense. He uses it to describe the unusual structure of pronominal reference in Gooniyandi, which was discussed in Section 3.6.6 (McGregor 1989: 439; 1990: 167–9). Corbett (2000: 22, n. 18) comments that the term 'restricted plural' is sometimes used in the literature instead of 'paucal'. He does not say where this usage can be found.

[3] There is an important difference between the labels 'restricted group' and 'unit augmented'. The label 'restricted group' is an etical label (cf. n. 4 below on the etic/emic distinction). This label is independent of the structure of a particular language. Such language-independent labels are necessary for a cross-linguistic comparison of different structures from different languages. In contrast, the label 'unit augmented' is an emic label, intended to capture the categorization that is made by a specific language. The benefits of the label 'unit augmented' for the description of a particular paradigmatic structure has been convincingly illustrated for some Australian languages by McKay (1978; 1979; 1984; 1990), but this does not necessarily make this analysis useful as the basis for a cross-linguistics comparison (cf. Section 7.6).

'group' and 'restricted group' are proposed to replace the traditional labels 'plural' and 'dual', respectively, in the pronominal domain. However, for purposes of readability, I will often use the term 'dual' instead of 'restricted group'. In the same sense, the terms 'plural' and 'group' will be used interchangeably in this chapter.

Contrary to common practice, the 'restricted group' column is placed to the right of the unrestricted 'group' column in Figure 6.2. Traditionally, the dual is placed to the left of the plural column. However, to emphasize the fact that the restricted column marks an extra dimension relative to the group column (namely the quantity of persons in the group), the restricted forms are added sequentially to the right onto the existing framework. This follows the general consensus that the dual is more marked than the plural (see also Section 6.3).

As was said before, this framework distinguishes one category more than is needed. In the scheme in Figure 6.2, six different categories would be translated into English as 'we' (shaded grey in the figure). However, all six different forms for 'we' are never distinguished morphologically in a paradigm. Five boxes would suffice to represent the variability of the world's languages. A better representation for the possible categories would be the structure as shown in Figure 6.3. The two different boxes for 1+2 are joined to one category because the group 1+2 and the restricted group 1+2 have the same reference: the pair of speaker and addressee. The scheme from Figure 6.3 is referentially sufficient for describing the various forms of the restricted group marking. However, there are numerous pronominal paradigms that emphasize the dual character of their first person pronouns, and in those cases the representation in Figure 6.3 is problematic.

The crux of the problem is the double nature of the category 1+2. This category, traditionally called 'inclusive dual', has been aptly named an 'ambiguous category' by Greenberg (1988). The label 'inclusive dual' refers to a group of two people (dual), including the speaker and the addressee (inclusive). Some pronominal paradigms with such an inclusive dual mark the linguistic form overtly as dual. In such a paradigm, the inclusive dual is surrounded by other dual forms.

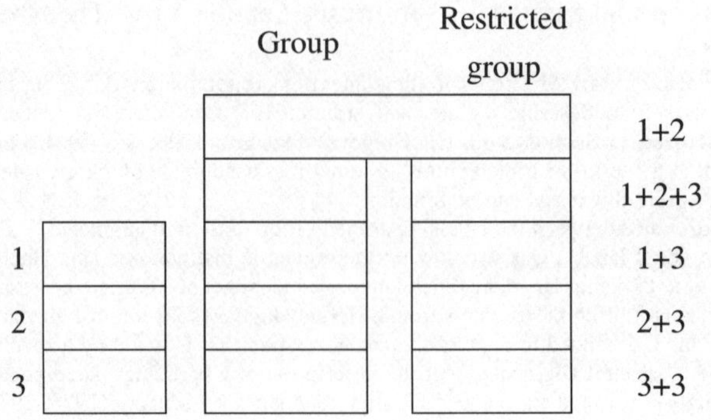

FIG. 6.3. *Alternative scheme for paradigms with number marking*

Redefining Number 191

An example of this marking pattern is found in the independent pronouns from Maori, as shown in (6.1). The dual forms are specifically marked by a suffix *-ua* (Harlow 1996: 6). Other paradigms take a different perspective. The independent pronouns from Umpila, a Pama-Nyungan language from Australia, are structured rather differently, as shown in (6.2). The inclusive dual *ŋali* from Umpila does not follow the pattern of the other dual forms that are marked by a suffix *-baʔamu* (Dixon 1980: 355–6).

(6.1) Maori pronouns

		Group	Restricted group	
		tā-tou	tā-ua	1+2(+3)
1	au	mā-tou	mā-ua	1+3
2	koe	kou-tou	kōr-ua	2+3
3	ia	rā-tou	rā-ua	3+3

(6.2) Umpila pronouns

		Group	Restricted group	
		ŋali		1+2
		ŋambula		1+2+3
1	ŋayu	ŋana	ŋana-baʔamu	1+3
2	ŋanu	ŋuʔula	ŋuʔula-baʔamu	2+3
3	nhulu	bula	bula-baʔamu	3+3

For languages such as Maori, the inclusive dual is explicitly a dual form (that is also inclusive), but for other languages, like Umpila, it is basically an inclusive form (that is also dual). The referential value is identical in both cases, but the paradigmatic structure that surrounds the ambiguous inclusive dual is different in each case. Both variants of the inclusive dual are shown in Figure 6.4 in the arrangement in which they will be represented in the present work. A horizontal combination of categories represents an inclusive dual with emphasis on the inclusivity. In such paradigms, the two inclusives are not distinguished by

192   *Number Incorporated*

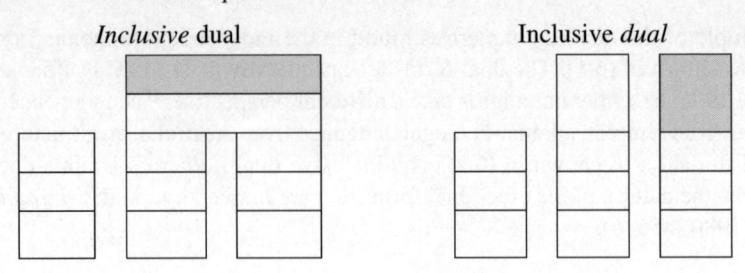

FIG. 6.4. *The ambiguous nature of the inclusive dual*

number, but by a difference between the two groups 1+2 and 1+2+3. A vertical combination of categories represents the inclusive dual with focus on the duality. In such paradigms, the two inclusives are distinguished by number, and the labels on the vertical axis will be combined into one inclusive category, 1+2(+3). In the alternative scheme as shown in Figure 6.3, it is not possible to highlight this ambiguous character of the inclusive dual. Only one of the two natures of the ambiguous inclusive dual can be shown there.

A special situation occurs when the emphasis of the inclusive dual is on the inclusivity (as in the leftmost paradigm in Figure 6.4). In these cases, the inclusive dual is best analysed along with the singular forms, as shown in Figure 6.5. Of course, referentially, the inclusive dual is never a singular form, but some languages align this category structurally with the singulars. In other words, in such languages, the inclusive dual is etically non-singular, but emically singular.[4] In the transition as shown in Figure 6.5, the labels of the columns change. In the etical presentation (the leftmost version) the labels are 'singular', 'group', and 'restricted group', respectively. In the emical presentation (the rightmost version), these labels cannot be used because they are referentially incorrect. In the rightmost version, the labels 'minimal', 'augmented', and 'unit-augmented' are more appropriate (McKay 1978). Only for reasons of cross-linguistics comparison have I retained paradigms with an *inclusive* dual category in its etically justified position (the leftmost version). However, in all cases where the inclusive dual is depicted as a horizontal bar, this should be interpreted as signifying that this category is emically singular.

---

[4] Pike's (1954: 8–26) ETIC approach to language is strongly reminiscent of what in typology has come to be called the *tertium comparationis*: the (language-independent) reference structure on which a cross-linguistic comparison is based. Pike puts it thus: 'one of the component goals [of the etic approach] may be said to be nonstructural or classificatory in the sense that the linguist, in using this approach, devises logical categories of systems, classes, and units therein without attempting to make them reflect the structuring discoverable in particular individual languages' (Pike 1954: 8). A typology can be seen as a catalogue and interpretation of the various EMIC instances of the etic categories. '[The emic approach] is an attempt to discover and to describe the pattern of that particular language or culture in reference to the way in which the various elements of that culture are related to each other' (Pike 1954: 8).

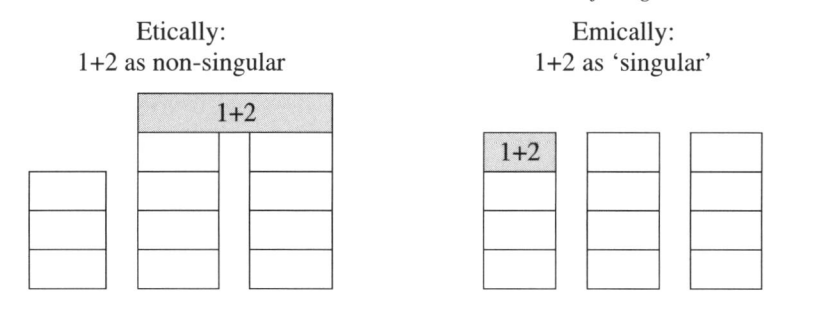

Etically: Emically:
1+2 as non-singular   1+2 as 'singular'

FIG. 6.5. *The singular-like status of the* inclusive *dual*

6.3 Markedness reversals

The present analysis of number marking in pronominal paradigms is based on an important assumption. It assumes that restriction to the number of participants in a group is linguistically marked relative to reference to an unrestricted amount. Put more clearly, the analysis starts from the typology of group marking (as established in the previous chapters) and develops an analysis of the marking of number from there. With this method, I suggest that everything there is to say about number marking can be formulated as an addendum to group marking. In this section, I will raise some doubts as to this assumption, only to conclude in the end that it is still safe to proceed this way.

There is a general claim in the literature that the dual is marked relative to general non-singular marking (Corbett 2000: 38–50). The basic claim was formulated by Greenberg in one of his well-known universals. In Universal 34, he claims: 'No language has a trial number unless it has a dual. No language has a dual unless it has a plural' (Greenberg 1963: 94). Roughly speaking, this is also true within the pronominal domain. Still, there are some counterexamples and problematic cases in which the markedness is reversed (cf. Plank 1989: 318). These examples once again highlight the fact that general tendencies among the world's languages should never be interpreted too rigorously as universal characteristics.

The cases in which the markedness is reversed can be subdivided into three groups. First, there are pronominal paradigms that show REFERENTIAL markedness reversal. Such paradigms have non-singular forms, but the unmarked value of these non-singular forms is dual. Second, there are pronominal paradigms that show MORPHOLOGICAL markedness reversal. Such paradigms have both dual and plural forms, but the plural is morphologically derived from the dual. Finally, there are pronominal paradigms that show STRUCTURAL markedness reversal. Such paradigms have both dual and plural forms, but there are more categorial distinctions in the dual than in the plural.

194 Number Incorporated

The first set of counterexamples consists of paradigms that show referential markedness reversal. In these cases, the unmarked non-singular prototypically refers to a group of two persons. Reference to more than two persons can, if necessary, be explicitly marked with an extra morpheme. More specifically, such paradigms have only one non-singular column. These non-singular forms encompass both dual and 'more-than-dual' reference. Unexpectedly, in those contexts where a distinction is needed, it is the reference to 'more-than-dual' that is in need of extra marking. An example of referential markedness reversal is found in the pronouns from the Athabascan language Navaho (Reichard 1951: 80–9). The form *nxíh* can be used meaning 'we' with plural and dual reference. At first glance, this strongly resembles a normal plural, just as the English pronoun *we* can be used for both plural and dual reference. Interestingly, though, in Navaho, when it has to be made explicit that there is a difference between two or more than two persons, then the bare form *nxíh* is used for the meaning 'we two'. A prefix *da-* is used to form the pronoun *da-nxíh*, meaning 'we, more than two'. In the description by Reichard, it is put as follows:

Speakers often fail to distinguish dual and plural, using the same forms for both, unless a distinction is needed, when *da-* is prefixed to the dual forms [to produce plural forms]. (Reichard 1951: 80)

The same situation can be found in the Californian language Achumawi. In the indicative mood, Achumawi uses a suffix *-má* to disambiguate the plural from the dual. This suffix is not part of the pronominal paradigm, because the pronominal elements are prefixes. The unmarked meaning of the non-singular pronominal prefixes is dual; reference to more than two has to be made explicitly by adding *-má* (de Angulo and Freeland 1931: 91). Both descriptions that are quoted here are rather old. Either this phenomenon has escaped the attention of more recent linguists (it is, for example, not discussed by Corbett 2000), or it was mistakenly reported in the older sources.

The second set of counterexamples consists of paradigms that show morphological markedness reversal. In these cases, the paradigms have different forms for dual and 'more-than-dual' reference. However, when the morphophonological structure of these forms is scrutinized, it turns out that the forms with 'more-than-dual' reference are morphologically marked relative to the dual forms. An example of morphological markedness reversal is found in the independent pronouns from the Uralic language Nganasan, shown in (6.3). The 'more-than-dual' pronouns are derived fully regularly from the dual by a suffix *-ŋ* (Helimski 1998: 501–2). Note that the morphology reverses the markedness, while the structural markedness is unimpaired: all specialized dual forms have a specialized plural counterpart. There are at least as many group morphemes as there are restricted group morphemes.

(6.3) Nganasan pronouns

		Group	Restricted group	
		mï-ŋ	mi	1+2(+3)
1	mənə			1+3
2	tənə	tï-ŋ	ti	2+3
3	sïtï	sïtï-ŋ	sïtï	3+3

Another example of morphological markedness reversal is found in Damana, a Chibchan language from Colombia. The independent pronouns from Damana are shown in (6.4). The plural pronouns are clearly derived from the dual pronouns by using a suffix *-nyina* (Amaya 1999: 76). For comparison, the independent pronouns of Ika, a language closely related to Damana, are shown in (6.5). The dual morphemes in Damana are identical to the plural forms in Ika. The forms with the suffix *-nyina* are not attested in Ika (Frank 1990: 26). Probably, Damana has reanalysed the plural pronouns into dual pronouns, and added a new set of plural pronouns with the suffix *-nyina*. There are some more examples of the Damana-Ika case, in which the duals of a particular language are identical to the plural forms of a close cognate. An example is the inflectional paradigm from Kwamera, an Oceanic language from Vanuatu shown in (7.38), and the closely related paradigm of Lenakel, as shown in (4.97). The dual morpheme *k-* from Kwamera is found as a general non-singular in Lenakel. The general non-singular from Kwamera is not found in Lenakel. Another example is the independent pronouns from two other Oceanic languages, Maori in (7.28) and Rapanui in (7.35). The dual morphemes of the second and third person (as still found in Rapanui) have taken over the reference of the plural in Maori.

(6.4) Damana pronouns

		Group	Restricted group	
		nabi-nyina	nabi	1+2(+3)
1	ra			1+3
2	ma	mabi-nyina	mabi	2+3
3	na	ijkuna-nyina	ijkuna	3+3

196 *Number Incorporated*

(6.5) Ika pronouns

		niwi	1+2
			1+2+3
1	nʌn		1+3
2	ma	miwi	2+3
3	a	ikʌŋa?	3+3

The third kind of counterexamples contradicts the markedness structure as proposed by Greenberg's universal. The universal can be interpreted as a markedness cline in which the plural is less marked than dual. In markedness theory, the occurrence of more oppositions is generally interpreted as a sign of low markedness (Greenberg 1966: 27). Accordingly, paradigms that have categorial oppositions in the dual that are not attested in the plural do not follow this markedness cline. I will call this phenomenon structural markedness reversal, because the structure of the paradigm does not follow the direction of markedness as proposed by Greenberg's universal. I have found a few examples of such paradigmatic counterexamples. All these cases have an inclusive/exclusive opposition in the dual but not in the plural. In all these cases, however, the descriptions are not exhaustive and doubt can be raised as to the analysis. Still, as it stands now, these descriptions exist and have to be reckoned with. The independent pronouns of the Papuan language Samo, shown in (6.6), are a case in point (Voorhoeve 1975: 391–2). Another example comes from the extinct American language Coos as presented later in (7.22).

(6.6) Samo pronouns

		Group	Restricted group	
			ala	1+2(+3)
		ɔi		
1	ã		oli	1+3
2	nɔ̃	nĩ	nĩli	2+3
3	yɔ̃	yã / diyɔ̃	ili	3+3

It appears that reversals of the markedness of number exist. The examples discussed indicate that not all pronominal paradigms in the world's languages consider the dual to be a marked category relative to the general non-singular. These cases highlight the fact that general tendencies in the structure of human language are never simply universal laws. However, the number of examples with markedness reversal is low and it is generally hard to find examples of the kind discussed in this section. I will disregard these counterexamples in the subsequent chapters, and discuss number marking as a specialized variation of group marking.

6.4 Other numbers

The previous sections have laid the foundation for the discussion of the different ways in which number is marked in pronominal paradigms. The most prolific number category in the pronominal domain is the dual. However, the variability of dual marking is too extensive to be dealt with here. The next, rather lengthy chapter is devoted to the description and analysis of the complete variation of dual marking. I will now turn to other number categories reported in the literature. Analogously to the dual, categories such as the 'trial' (referring to a group of three), 'paucal' (referring to a few), and even an incidental case of a 'quadral' (referring to a group of four) have been described in the literature. In this section, I will present a review of the distribution and the structural diversity of the pronominal paradigms with trial, quadral, or paucal marking. Although these categories exist, they are not as widespread as the dual.

A major observation on the areal/genetic distribution is that these number categories are only found in the Pacific. I have never come across a pronominal paradigm with a trial, a quadral, or a paucal other than among the Austronesian languages or among the non-Austronesian languages from New Guinea and the surrounding islands. Put differently, number marking (other than the dual) seems to be a Melanesian characteristic (Lynch 1998: 102).[5] Of course, the linguistic variation in the Melanesian region is immense. Still, this clear geographical restriction gives the impression that these categories are highly marked. The main origin of these categories seems to be the large family of Austronesian languages. These languages are known to have strongly influenced other languages in the Pacific.[6] The trial, quadral, and paucal appear to be common because they happen to be found in one of the most extended and widespread linguistic genealogies of the world (the Austronesian stock). Typologically speaking, these number categories are not common. Also, the structural diversity of these kinds of number marking is restricted. Most examples of trials, quadrals, or paucals simply add a complete set of morphologically slightly changed dual forms to the paradigm. Only two incidental

---

[5] I know of one, albeit poorly described, exception. In the Gé language Apinayé, the pronominal prefix *vamẽ-* is translated as 'they four' (Callow 1962: 115, n. 4).

[6] Schmidt (1926: 318–20) proposes an influence in the other direction. In his view, extensive number marking originated among the Papuan languages and was subsequently borrowed by the Austronesian languages. This scenario seems less likely once the immense diversity of the Papuan languages is taken into account. Only very few languages out of the many different Papuan languages have a trial or paucal. In contrast, trials are relatively common among the surrounding Austronesian languages. Maybe Schmidt underestimated the diversity of the Papuan languages, wrongly taking the trial of Kiwai, shown here in (6.7), as representative for all Papuan languages. Even so, Schmidt's description of the variety of Papuan languages is impressively detailed for his time (Schmidt 1926: 148–54). This indicates that he should have known about the exceptional structure of Kiwai among the Papuan languages.

cases do not follow this typical structure. This regularity confirms the impression that the marking of higher number categories is a highly constrained phenomenon.

The various forms of higher number marking are all morphophonologically related to the dual forms in the paradigm. Consequently, trials, paucals, and quadrals will all be interpreted as specialized versions of restricted group marking. To incorporate these categories in the present framework, the dual will be analysed as a minimally restricted group. Extending this proposal, other number categories will be analysed as groups restricted to a specific amount; restricted to either three, four, or a few participants. The paradigms of the various number categories will be depicted with extra columns in between the already present dual and group columns; all the columns that mark number are gathered under the heading of 'restricted group'.[7]

A paradigm with a trial is attested in the independent pronouns in (6.7) from the Papuan language Kiwai (Foley 1986: 72, citing Ray). This is the only example of a complete set of trial forms in a paradigm without an inclusive/exclusive opposition. Examples of a trial are numerous among the Austronesian languages, but these paradigms always differentiate between an inclusive and an exclusive trial, as exemplified in (6.8) with the subject pronouns from the Oceanic language Lonwolwol Ambrym.

(6.7)   Kiwai pronouns

	Group	Restricted group — Trial	Dual	
	nimo	nimoibi	nimoto	1+2(+3)
1	mo			1+3
2	ro	nigo	nigoibi	nigoto	2+3
3	nou	nei	neibi	neito	3+3

(6.8)   Lonwolwol Ambrym pronouns

	Group	Restricted group — Trial	Dual	
	εr	ensUl	entaro	1+2(+3)
1	ni	genεm	genεmsUl	genεmro	1+3
2	nεk	gami	gamsUl	gamro	2+3
3	ŋae	ŋe	ŋerUl	ŋero	3+3

[7] The division between a minimal inclusive (1+2) and an augmented inclusive (1+2+3) is not attested with higher number marking. Still, I have decided to retain the allotted space in the diagrams to enhance the visual comparison with other paradigms presented in the present work.

Redefining Number 199

The dual is often diachronically related to the plural plus a suffix meaning 'two', and the trial is related to the plural with a suffix meaning 'three'. In Ambrym, the dual is formed with the numeral *-ro*, meaning 'second' and the third with a suffixed numeral *-sUl*, meaning 'three' (Paton 1971: 16, 45, 47).[8] Notwithstanding this origin, not all duals and trials are used for precisely two and three persons, respectively. The exact referential possibilities for the dual and trial are taken for granted in most grammars. Only in a few descriptions is the usage of these categories extensively described. In most cases, it turns out that it is possible to deviate from the exact number of participants. A good example is found in the description of another Oceanic language, Paamese, shown in (6.9). The structure of the pronominal paradigm resembles the paradigm from Lonwolwol Ambrym in (6.8). This time, the suffigated numerals are *-lue* and *-telu*, meaning 'two' and 'three' respectively (Crowley 1982: 80–1). Yet Crowley prefers to call the 'trial' by the name 'paucal'. The following quotation describes extensively how intricately the reference of the trial/paucal is construed.[9]

The conditions governing the use of the paucal and the plural are rather more complex. The basic factor that is involved is the absolute size of the group being referred to. Intersecting with this parameter however is the question of relative size, i.e. whether the group being referred to is contrasted with some larger group within which it is subsumed. When the absolute number is low (say between three and about half a dozen), the paucal is generally used, whether or not there is any contrast with a larger group. (However, the plural will still very occasionally be used even with these low numbers when there is no such contrast.) When the absolute number is in the middle range (say between about half a dozen and a dozen or so), the most significant parameter is that of relative number. For example, one's own patrilineage will be referred to paucally when it is contrasted with the village as a whole, which will be plural. On the other hand, the patrilineage will be expressed in the plural when contrasted with the nuclear family, which will be in the paucal. As the absolute number increases over the middle range, relative number again becomes less significant, and the plural is generally used for all numbers over a dozen. (However, even with very large numbers, the paucal is occasionally used when the contrast in number is expressed. So while the entire population of Paama will normally be expressed in the plural, even when contrasted with the country as a whole, it has been heard referred to paucally.) (Crowley 1982: 80–1)

---

[8] It is fairly easy to find examples of this type among the Oceanic languages. The independent pronouns of Tolai also have a dual and a trial inclusive and exclusive (Mosel 1984: 93). Lynch (1998: 102) mentions Anejom̃ as another example of the same structure.

[9] The independent pronouns of Kwaio are also described using the label 'paucal', although the suffix that marks these forms *-oru* is the numeral three (Keesing 1985: 27–34). Lynch (1998: 102) mentions the Nadrau dialect of Fijian as another example of this structure.

(6.9) Paamese pronouns

	Group	Restricted group			
		Group	Paucal	Dual	
		iire	iatelu	ialue	1+2(+3)
1	inau	komai	komaitelu	komalu	1+3
2	kaiko	kamii	kamiitelu	kamilu	2+3
3	kaie	kaile	kaitelu	kailue	3+3

Taken at face value, it seems that there are two different types of pronominal system in the descriptions of Austronesian languages: one with a trial category and one with a paucal (as distinguished e.g. by Lynch 1998: 102–3). However, it is unclear whether there really is a difference in linguistic structure between these languages, or whether there is only a difference in descriptive practice. The case for a true trial in a pronominal paradigm has, to my knowledge, only been made for Larike, an Austronesian language spoken on Ambon:

> It should be stated explicitly that Larike trials are true trial forms. In other words, they represent the quantity three, and are not used to refer to the more vague notion of several, as is a paucal or limited plural. (Laidig and Laidig 1990: 92)

In all other cases, when the precise referential possibilities of the trial/paucal are discussed in a grammar, then the vote goes to paucal reference. Often, reference will be made to the origin of the trial as a grammaticalized numeral 'three'. In the process of grammaticalization, however, the meaning of the numeral 'three' generally changes to 'few'. This is, for example, argued for the history of the pronouns from the Malaita family of the Solomon Islands. The numeral 'three' is grammaticalized into the pronominal paradigm, but in the majority of cases the meaning changes in this grammaticalization process from 'trial' to 'paucal':[10]

> Only one language, 'Are'are, has retained the original four number system with a true trial number. Other southern languages, including Kwaio, Sa'a, Langalanga, and Lau, have retained the four number system, but the original trial forms have changed their meaning to 'few' or a restricted plural. That the original meaning was 'trial' is evident from the fact that the trial pronouns were a compound with the number 'three'. (Simons 1986: 33)

And what about the quadral? A quadral is said to occur in the pronominal paradigm of the Oceanic language Sursurunga, shown in (6.10). Although Hutchisson (1986: 5) uses the label 'quadral', his description does not restrict this form to referential usage with groups of four participants only. The 'quadral' can

---

[10] Another possible grammaticalization path of the trial is found in Mokilese, as described by Corbett (2000: 34, citing Harrison). Here, the trial becomes the plural and the original plural becomes a 'greater' plural. See Corbett (2000: 30–5) for an extensive discussion of this 'greater plural'.

also be used for more participants, reminiscent of the use of the trial as a paucal. The use of the 'quadral' is rather clearly described in the following quote from Hutchisson as being paucal in nature. Corbett (2000: 26–30) labels this quadral more suitably a 'greater paucal'.[11]

Since plural pronouns are never used with relationship terms, the use of these terms skews number reference for both trial and quadral forms (although not for dual) that trial comes to mean a minimum of 3, and quadral a minimum of 4. Either can stand for plural, although quadral is probably more frequently used. (Hutchisson 1986: 10)

(6.10) Sursurunga pronouns

		Group	Greater paucal	Paucal	Dual	
		git	gitat	gittul	gitar	1+2(+3)
1	iau	gim	gimat	gimtul	giur	1+3
2	iəu	gam	gamat	gamtul	gaur	2+3
3	on / əi	di	diat	ditul	diar	3+3

(Restricted group spans Greater paucal, Paucal, Dual)

Finally, there are a few paradigms where a trial/paucal is not consistently marked throughout the paradigm. I will list the two examples attested as an illustration of yet more possible structures for pronominal paradigms. A paucal without an inclusive/exclusive distinction is found in the independent pronouns from the Papuan language Yimas, shown in (6.11). Foley describes the referential properties of the paucal as referring to 'a few, from three up to seven, but variable depending on context' (Foley 1991: 111–14). The special characteristic of Yimas is a vertical homophony in the paucal. Besides the paradigm from Yimas, I have come across one other special paradigm with number marking higher than dual. In the independent pronouns from the Austronesian language Biak, as shown in (6.12), a trial is found only in the third person (Steinhauer 1985: 470, 479–80).[12]

---

[11] Schmidt (1926: 319) mentions Marina from Vanuatu, as well as Gao from the Solomon Islands, as other examples showing a quadral. I was unable to track down the original sources describing these languages. Corbett (2000: 29) mentions Sursurunga's close relative Tangga as a candidate for a 'greater paucal'. Corbett (2000: 25, 29) also discusses Lihir and Marshallese as languages with a 'fifth' number set, which in all cases is of paucal nature.

[12] Hein Steinhauer (p.c.) suggest that the pronouns with the ending -*ʔo* are historically related to the numeral three. The referential value of this numeral has been extended to encompass all group reference (cf. morphological markedness reversal as discussed in Section 6.3). This proposal fits with the observation by Schmidt (1926: 319) that many unrestricted plurals in the Austronesian languages are related to former specific number markers.

(6.11) Yimas pronouns

| | | Group | Restricted group || |
			Paucal	Dual	
		ipa	paŋkt	kapa	1+2(+3)
1	ama				1+3
2	mi	ipwa		kapwa	2+3
3		(locative deixis)			3+3

(6.12) Biak pronouns

| | | Group | Restricted group || |
			Trial	Dual	
		ʔo		ʔu	1+2(+3)
1	ai'a	nʔo		nu	1+3
2	'au	mʔo		mu	2+3
3	i	si/na	sʔo	su	3+3

To summarize, number marking higher than dual is neither areally nor structurally very diverse. Areally, the examples are only found in Melanesia. Structurally, almost all patterns are completely regular extensions of one of the standard dual patterns. The only structural exceptions are the patterns from Yimas and Biak. In most cases, true trials and quadrals do not exist. Historically, these morphemes clearly mean 'three' or 'four', but once they become grammaticalized into the pronominal paradigm, the meaning almost always changes to paucal and greater paucal, respectively.

6.5 Conclusion

In this chapter, the marking of number in the pronominal domain has been redefined around the concept 'restricted group'. Previously (in Chapter 3) a GROUP of participants had been defined on a qualitative basis: the kind of participants that form a group is important, not the number. Expanding on this basis, a RESTRICTED GROUP of participants has been defined in this chapter as a group that is marked for the minimally needed number of participants. For example, the group 1+3 minimally needs two participants (one speaker and one other) for it to retain its characteristic constitution. In most cases, the minimally restricted group is identical to what traditionally has been called a dual. However, this terminology also includes the paradigms that have a minimally restricted 1+2+3 group. This minimally restricted 1+2+3 group consists of three participants (one speaker, one addressee and one other) and has been referred to, traditionally, as a trial.

In most cases, the restricted group is marked relative to the unrestricted group. However, there are a few counterexamples to this markedness cline. Three different kinds of markedness reversal have been discussed. First, there are cases that show referential markedness reversal. In such cases, the default referential value of an unmarked group morpheme is dual. Second, there are cases that show morphological markedness reversal. In these cases, the unrestricted group morphemes are derived morphologically from the restricted forms. Finally, there are cases that show structural markedness reversal. In these cases, the set of restricted group morphemes has more oppositions than the set of unrestricted group morphemes. There appear only to be very few of those counterexamples to the markedness cline.

Besides that dual, there are various other categories that mark quantity in the pronominal domain. Other categories that have been described in the literature are trials (referring to three participants), quadrals (referring to four participants), and paucals (referring to a few participants). The areal and genetic dispersion of these categories in pronominal paradigms is strongly restricted: they have been attested exclusively in the Pacific. Moreover, the structural diversity of these paradigms is low. Most cases are simply regular extensions of the paradigms with duals, adding a morphologically slightly changed copy of the dual forms to the paradigm. Another point is that, judging from the existing descriptions, true trials are extremely rare and true quadrals do not exist. Trials are mostly 'paucals' and quadrals 'greater paucals'. The labels 'trial' and 'quadral' are mostly attested in sources that do not expand on the referential possibilities of these forms. The diachronic source of these categories has indeed a clear numeral value (trials and quadrals derive regularly from numerals meaning 'three' and 'four', respectively) but once they grammaticalize, they form paucals. In the present framework, a paucal will be reformulated as a SMALL restricted group.

7 The Diversity of Restricted Groups
A Survey of Dual Person Marking

7.1 Introduction

It has often been claimed that duals are most prominent in the marking of 'we'. The oldest of these observations was made by Wilhelm von Humboldt in his paper on the dual:

Some of these languages take the perspective of duality from the speaking and the addressed person, the I and YOU. In these languages, the dual is part of the pronoun and only extends into the rest of the language as far as the influence of the pronoun reaches; it is restricted sometimes to the pronoun of the first person plural only, to the concept of WE (von Humboldt 1994 [1827]: 156; my translation).[1]

Whether this is true or not (I will come back to Humboldt's claim in Section 7.3.4), there is much more variation in the paradigmatic structure of dual marking in the pronominal domain, a variability for greater than Humboldt could acknowledge—given the available grammatical descriptions of his time. This chapter will mainly present a survey of this variability of linguistic structure, the facts that every theory of linguistic structure will have to deal with.

This chapter starts off in Section 7.2 with a short note on terminology and on the method that is used to make a typology of the variation. Subsequently, the various forms of dual marking will be discussed. First, I will deal with paradigms that do not distinguish inclusive from exclusive in Section 7.3. Then I will discuss the various possibilities of combining dual marking with an inclusive/exclusive opposition. These possibilities will be ordered according to the number of different forms in the paradigm that are to be translated into English as 'we', starting with paradigms with three forms for 'we' in Section 7.4 and leading up to paradigms with five different forms for 'we' in Section 7.6. In Section 7.7, some careful generalizations are formulated based on the attested diversity. Finally, Section 7.8 summarizes this chapter.

---

[1] 'Einigen dieser Sprachen nehmen die Ansicht des Dualis von der redenden und angeredeten Person, dem ICH und dem DU her. In diesen haftet derselbe am Pronomen, geht nur so weit in die übrige Sprache mit über, als sich der Einfluss des Pronomen erstreckt, ja beschränkt sich bisweilen allein auf das Pronomen der ersten Person in der Mehrheit, auf den Begriff des WIR.'

Survey of Restricted Groups 205

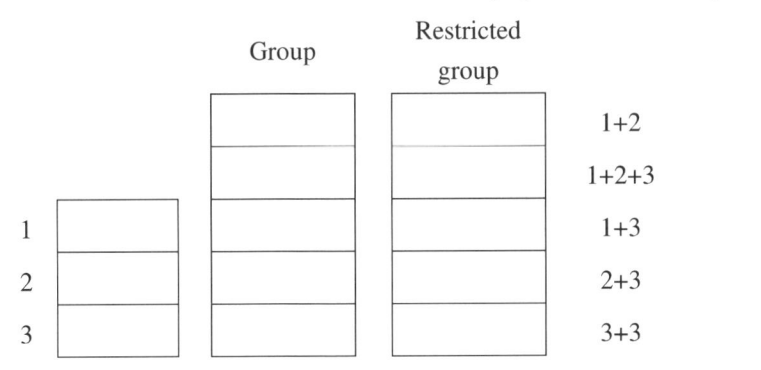

FIG. 7.1. *Scheme for the presentation of paradigms with restricted group ('dual') forms*

7.2 Method and terminology

In this chapter, the diversity of pronominal paradigms with specialised dual forms will be organized into a typology. For this typology, a fixed scheme will be used for all examples. This scheme was introduced in the previous chapter; it is repeated here in Figure 7.1. In this scheme, the column marked GROUP is roughly equivalent to what traditionally is called plural. As discussed extensively in Chapter 3, a group has been defined qualitatively as a set of participants; for example, 1+3 is a group that includes the speaker and some others, but no addressee. The column marked RESTRICTED GROUP is roughly equivalent to what traditionally is called dual. As outlined in the preceding chapter, a restricted group is defined as the set of participants that is minimally needed to form this group, which are two participants in the case of 1+3, a group for which at least one speaker and one other participant are needed. The restricted groups are in most cases duals, except for the restricted 1+2+3, in which case three participants are minimally needed. In other words, the restricted 1+2+3 has trial reference. Practically, the labels 'group' and 'restricted group' are new and therefore somewhat cumbersome. In the running text, the traditional terms 'plural' and 'dual' will be used regularly, but they should always be interpreted as meaning 'group' and 'restricted group' respectively.

7.3 Duals without inclusive/exclusive

7.3.1 Preamble

The major pattern with dual marking, but without an inclusive/exclusive opposition, has a full series of dual morphemes, one for each person. This pattern is discussed in Section 7.3.2 under the name of DUAL-UNIFIED-WE. In the next three sections, examples are presented of paradigms that have specialized dual forms but do not have a full series of dual categories. A division will be made between VERTICAL homophony (different persons of the same number are marked by the same morpheme, discussed in Section 7.3.3) and HORIZONTAL homophony (different numbers of the same person are marked by the same morpheme, discussed in Section 7.3.4). In Section 7.3.5, the incidental cases that combine vertical and horizontal homophony in the same paradigm are presented. Finally, Section 7.3.6 will summarize the variation.

7.3.2 The dual-unified-we paradigm

The major paradigmatic structure with dual marking but without an inclusive/exclusive opposition is called the dual-unified-we paradigm. In total, this paradigm consists of nine morphemes: three singular morphemes (1, 2, and 3), three group morphemes (the 'plural' forms of the singular categories), and three restricted group ('dual') variants of these non-singular morphemes. This is a common structure for a pronominal paradigm. In his typological analysis of personal pronouns, Ingram (1978: 219) classified this paradigm as one of the 'four systems that are more frequent than the others'. In this section, I will present a survey of the worldwide distribution of this paradigmatic type. This survey does not attempt to be exhaustive: more examples may rather easily be found in the areas or families to be discussed. The present goal is to show that this pattern is common, and present a rough outline of its geographical distribution.

Starting in Europe, a pronominal inflection with dual marking can be reconstructed (partly) for proto-Indo-European (Szemerényi 1990: 235), but there are only traces of a dual to be found in the pronominal inflection of contemporary Indo-European languages. A full dual set is only found in the inflection of Lithuanian (Schmalstieg 1998: 470), and some partial dual paradigms are found in the inflection of some Slavonic languages (see Section 7.3.3). A complete dual-unified-we paradigm, as shown in (7.1), is found in the independent pronouns of the Slavonic language Lower Sorbian (Stone 1993: 622).

(7.1) Lower Sorbian pronouns

		Group	Restricted group	
		my	*mej*	1+2(+3)
1	*ja*			1+3
2	*ty*	*wy*	*wej*	2+3
3	*wono / wona*	*woni*	*wonej*	3+3

Travelling east through Eurasia, this paradigmatic type is common in Siberian languages of the Uralic family.[2] A complete dual-unified-we pronoun system can also be found in South-East Asia.[3] Crossing the Bering Strait to America, duals of this type are attested in Eskimo-Aleut.[4] However, the dual-unified-we paradigm is not very widespread in other American languages, as most pronominal paradigms with duals also distinguish inclusive from exclusive.[5] The dual-unified-we paradigm is commonly found among the non-Austronesian languages of Papua New Guinea.[6] Finally, the dual-unified-we paradigm is common in Australia (Dixon and Blake 1979: 11).[7]

7.3.3 Vertical homophony

Homophony in a dual-unified-we paradigm comes in two guises. First, different persons within the same number can be coded by one and the same morpheme. I will call this vertical homophony, as two categories in the same (vertical) column are combined into the marking of one morpheme. The examples of this kind of homophony will be discussed in this section. The other kind of homophony, which I will call horizontal homophony, marks the same person in different numbers by one and the same morpheme. Examples of this kind of homophony will be discussed in the next section. These two kinds of homophony appear to be mostly mutual exclusive: I have only found two paradigms in which both kinds of homophony co-occur. These will be discussed in Section 7.3.5.

The most commonly occurring kind of vertical homophony is a homophony between second and third person. The independent pronouns from Kalam, as shown in (7.2), illustrate a first variant, with a 2/3-homophony in the restricted group ('dual') but not in the unrestricted group ('plural') marking (Foley 1986: 71, citing Pawley). This paradigmatic structure is regularly attested among the non-Austronesian languages of New Guinea.[8] The same pattern is also found in the person inflection of the Slavonic languages Slovene (de Bray 1951: 415–16;

---

[2] e.g. Khanti (Abondolo 1998a: 373–5) and Mansi (Keresztes 1998: 398–9).

[3] In Tibeto-Burman, e.g. the independent pronouns from Meithei (Chelliah 1997: 79), Chepang, and Kham (Bauman 1975: 273, 282); in Miao Yao, e.g. the Hmong Njua independent pronouns (Harriehausen 1990: 124); in Mon-Khmer, e.g. the independent pronouns from Khmu (Premsrirat 1987: 32–3).

[4] e.g. the North Slope Iñupiaq suffixes (MacLean 1986: 62–3) and the Central Yup'ic independent pronouns (Woodbury 1981: 231–3).

[5] Examples of a pure dual-unified-we system can be found, e.g. the paradigm of the independent pronouns from Lake and Bodega Miwok (Freeland 1947: 35; Callaghan 1974).

[6] Numerous examples can be found in Wurm (1975b) and in Voorhoeve (1975), e.g. the Bosavi family (Voorhoeve 1975: 393–4) and the Duna-Bogaya family (p. 396).

[7] Dixon (1980: 329) mentions Warrgamay and Pitjantjatjara as examples of this paradigmatic type, and reconstructs a dual-unified-we paradigm for Proto-Pama-Nyungan (cf. Blake 1988: 6).

[8] The same structure as in Kalam is also found in the Papuan languages Baruya (Wurm 1975b: 499, citing Lloyd 1973) and Fore (Foley 1986: 74, citing Scott). There are different claims about the independent pronouns of Wiru. Wurm (1975b: 489, citing Kerr) describes the Wiru paradigm as identical to the structure as found in Kalam in (7.2) but Foley (1986: 72, citing Kerr) describes a paradigm identical to the structure as found in Yagaria in (7.3).

208 *Number Incorporated*

Priestly 1993: 418) and Upper Sorbian (de Bray 1951: 743; Schuster-Sewc 1996: 161–2).

In New Guinea, a homophony between second and third person is also found both in the dual and in the plural (Foley 1986: 71–2; Wurm 1975b: 487). This is, for example, attested in the past/future suffixes from Yagaria (Renck 1975: 90–6), as shown in (7.3).[9] The opposite situation (homophony in the group marking, but not in the restricted group) is not attested. This asymmetry substantiates the claim that the dual is more marked than the plural. Any opposition that is distinguished in the dual is also found in the plural; to put it differently, the dual will normally not show a distinction unless the plural has it (see Section 6.3 for some examples of markedness reversal). Finally, the conflation of second and third person is incidentally extended into the singular as well. This is, for example, attested in the past suffixes from Siroi (Wells 1979: 30–1), as shown in (7.4).[10]

(7.2)   Kalam pronouns

		Group	Restricted group	
		cn	*ct*	1+2(+3)
1	yad			1+3
2	nad	*nb*		2+3
			nt	
3	nwk	*ky*		3+3

(7.3)   Yagaria past/future suffixes

		Group	Restricted group	
		...-un	...-u?	1+2(+3)
1	...-u			1+3
2	...-an			2+3
		...-a	...-a?	
3	...-i			3+3

---

[9] The same paradigmatic structure as in Yagaria is also found in Amele, both in the independent pronouns and in the verbal inflection (Roberts 1987: 208), in the inflection of Kewa (Franklin 1971: 57–8), and in the inflection of Kuman (Foley 1986: 70, citing Piau).

[10] Exactly the same paradigmatic structure as in Siroi can be found in the suffixes from Magi (Thomson 1975: 631–2).

Survey of Restricted Groups 209

(7.4) Siroi past suffixes

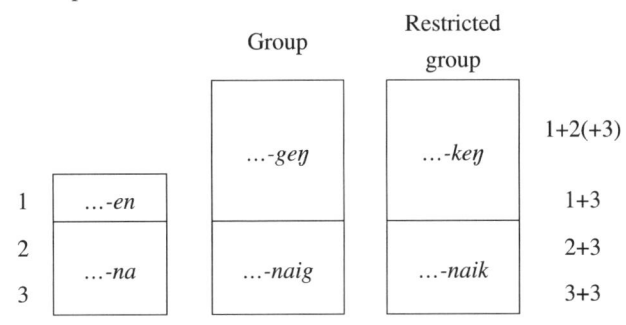

	Group		Restricted group	
		...-geŋ	...-keŋ	1+2(+3)
1	...-en			1+3
2	...-na	...-naig	...-naik	2+3
3				3+3

The two other theoretically possible kinds of vertical homophony are only found in incidental examples. A 1/2-homophony (homophonous first and second person dual and plural) is attested in verb inflection of the close relatives Tinan and Manchad, two Tibeto-Burman languages (Sharma 1996: 86–91). These suffixes are illustrated by the present suffixes from Tinan in (7.5). A 1/3-homophony (homophonous first and third person dual and plural) is found in the Aleut inflection (Geoghegan 1944: 51). There are various morphophonological different forms of this paradigm, but the homophony between the first and the third person in the dual and the plural is attested in all variants; one of them is shown in (7.6).

(7.5) Tinan present subject suffixes

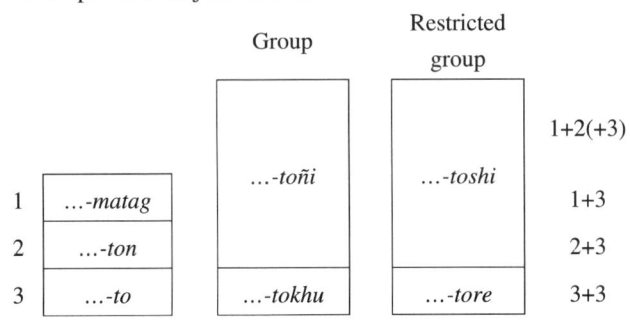

	Group		Restricted group	
		...-toñi	...-toshi	1+2(+3)
1	...-matag			1+3
2	...-ton			2+3
3	...-to	...-tokhu	...-tore	3+3

(7.6) Aleut subject suffixes

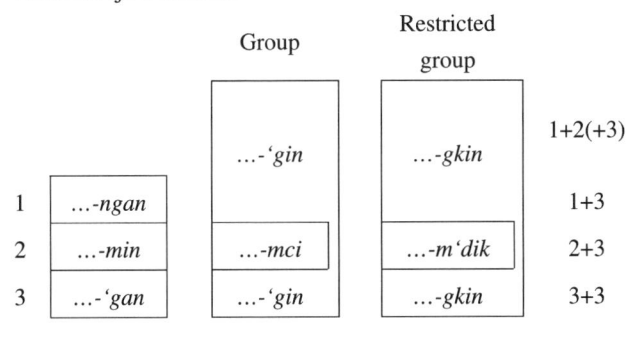

	Group		Restricted group	
		...-'gin	...-gkin	1+2(+3)
1	...-ngan			1+3
2	...-min	...-mci	...-m'dik	2+3
3	...-'gan	...-'gin	...-gkin	3+3

7.3.4 Horizontal homophony

In a paradigm with horizontal homophony, morphemes are used for different numbers of the same person. Horizontal homophony thus neutralizes the number opposition in a particular person. In almost all examples that will be discussed in this section, there is horizontal homophony between plural and dual categories.[11] This observation is in concord with the idea that the dual is marked relative to the plural, and the plural relative to the singular (see Section 6.3). A homophony between dual and plural simply neutralizes number in the upper range of this markedness cline.

The main interest of this section is the question of which persons show horizontal homophony. In Chapter 4, it turned out that the possibilities of homophony in paradigms without dual marking were strongly governed by a person hierarchy $1>2>3$: if first person has horizontal homophony, then also second, and if second person has horizontal homophony, then also third (see Section 4.7). In a thorough reappraisal of von Humboldt's work on the dual, Plank (1989) formulates a cautious version of this person hierarchy when it comes to dual marking. He summarizes his findings in two implicational universals:[12]

If only one person differentiates a dual, it will very likely be the 1st rather than the 2nd or 3rd. If only two persons differentiate a dual, the 1st is much likelier to be one of them than the 3rd. (Plank 1989: 305)

Although Plank's implications are formulated carefully enough to be true, I will suggest a slightly different generalization. When there are grammaticalized dual forms in a pronominal paradigm, then it is extremely rare for there to be no dual involving all persons. Dual forms show up across the paradigm, or not at all. There are only very few examples that have a dual only in a part of the pronominal paradigm. Among these few examples, a dual in the first person is indeed slightly more frequent then other duals, but the total amount of cases is too low to allow for any significant generalizations.[13]

I will start the survey of horizontal homophony with those paradigms that are in concord with the $1>2>3$ person hierarchy. First, the examples with horizontal homophony in the second and third person are discussed. These pronominal paradigms only have a dual in the first person. A potential problem with these cases is that a dual 'we' is often very close to an inclusive 'we'.

---

[11] The only exceptions to this generalization are the paradigms from Kewa in (7.9) and Nganasan in (6.3); see also Kwamera in (7.38).

[12] cf. Universal 46 from Sokolovskaya (1980: 97).

[13] I have to point out that there is a difference in interpretation between Plank's typology and mine regarding the first person inclusive dual. As argued in Sections 3.6.5 and 4.5.2, an inclusive dual without any other pronominal duals is not interpreted here as a dual, but as a special form of group marking (viz. minimal inclusive), which only happens to be dual as well. The predominance of duals in the first person as observed by Plank (and von Humboldt, as quoted at the start of this chapter) is probably due to these sole inclusive duals. Due to the different interpretation in the present work, the special status of the first person when it comes to dual marking is strongly diminished.

However, the descriptions of the following languages explicitly mention that different forms for 'we' are to be distinguished on the basis of number. The dual 'we' often has a preference for an inclusive reading (referring to the speech act dyad), but it can be shown to have possible exclusive reference as well. The first of these languages is Yidiɲ, a Pama-Nyungan language from Australia (Dixon 1977). A specialized dual form is only found in the first person, as shown in (7.7). Dixon explicitly mentions the dual (and not inclusive) meaning of ŋali:[14]

The main point to note is that ŋali forms are seldom used. In fact, ŋaɲḍi is frequently used to refer to two people (one of whom is the speaker). . . . ŋali is used particularly when it is desired to emphasise TWO people (as opposed to three, etc.). . . . [ŋali] is most frequent used in an 'inclusive' sense, for referring to speaker and addressee . . . but it is clear that it can have 'exclusive' reference, to speaker and a third party. (Dixon 1977: 165–6, 179)

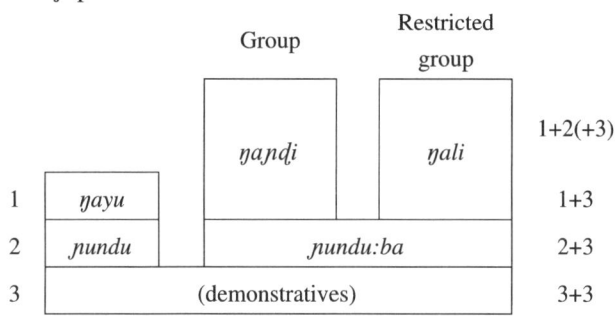

(7.7)   Yidiɲ pronouns

		Group	Restricted group	
		ŋaɲḍi	ŋali	1+2(+3)
1	ŋayu			1+3
2	ɲundu	ɲundu:ba		2+3
3		(demonstratives)		3+3

The same paradigmatic structure as in Yidiɲ is found in the Papuan language Arapesh, a language from the Toricelli family (Fortune 1942: 45–9). In the description, it is noted explicitly that the distinction between the two forms for 'we' is one of number, not a difference between inclusive and exclusive: 'there is no distinction between first person exclusive and first person inclusive, such as obtains widely in the languages of the sea peoples of the adjoining Melanesian area' (Fortune 1942: 45).[15] This paradigmatic structure is also attested in the pronouns from Hatam, a West Papuan language from the Bird's Head of New Guinea (Reesink 1999: 40–1) and in Kadiwéu, a Mataco-Guiacuruan language from Brazil (Griffiths and Griffiths 1976: 98–9).

Another variant of horizontal homophony in concord with the person hierarchy is described for Gothic, where specialized dual forms exist for the first and second

---

[14] The dual form ŋali is hardly used. If it disappeared, then the dual would be completely lost in Yidiɲ. The complete loss of the dual has already happened in Tjapukai, a language closely related to Yidiɲ. In the short sketch of Tjapukai by Hale (1976a: 237) no mention at all is made of the existence of any dual pronouns.

[15] In Bukiyip, a language closely related to Arapesh, the independent pronouns do not show any horizontal homophony. However, the subject prefixes in Bukiyip have exactly the same paradigmatic structure as shown here for Arapesh (Conrad and Wogiga 1991: 13–15).

person, but not in the third. The dual forms are not very often found in the Gothic corpus (Streitberg 1920: 140). Shown in (7.8) are the suffixes for the present of the strong verb *nim-*, meaning 'to take'. This pattern is found throughout the inflection classes of Gothic (Streitberg 1920: 139 ff.). A special variant of horizontal homophony in the third person only is found in the independent pronouns of Kewa, a non-Austronesian language from Papua New Guinea, shown in (7.9). This paradigm has a horizontal homophony between third singular and dual, but a separate third person plural (Franklin 1971: 34). This structure contradicts the generalization that horizontal homophony always neutralizes the distinction between dual and plural. The same structure is also found in the Uralic language Nganasan, as shown earlier in (6.3).

(7.8) Gothic present suffixes

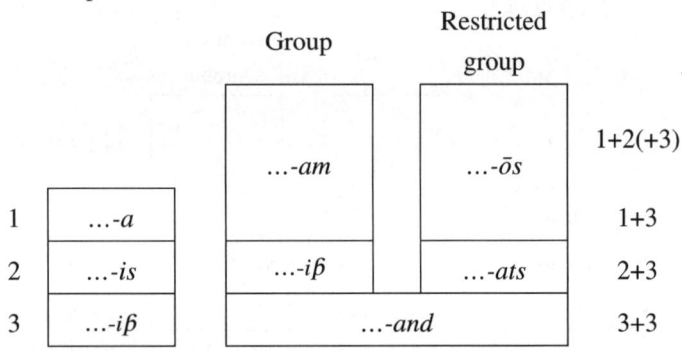

	Group	Group	Restricted group	
		...-am	...-ōs	1+2(+3)
1	...-a			1+3
2	...-is	...-iþ	...-ats	2+3
3	...-iþ	...-and		3+3

(7.9) Kewa pronouns

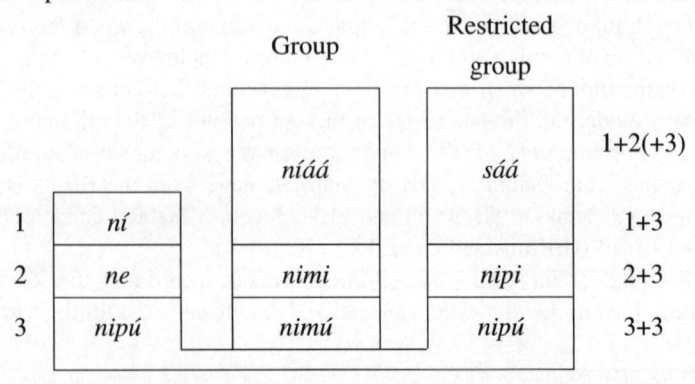

		Group	Restricted group	
		níáá	sáá	1+2(+3)
1	ní			1+3
2	ne	nimi	nipi	2+3
3	nipú	nimú	nipú	3+3

There are four different paradigmatic structures that contradict the person hierarchy: horizontal homophony only in the second person; only in the first person; both in the first and third but not in the second person; and finally, both in the first and second, but not in the third person. There are examples of all kinds described in the literature, although they are not numerous. Still, these examples show that such patterns are a possibility for the structure of human language.

The first kind of pattern is attested in all inflectional person marking in the Uralic language Mansi (Keresztes 1998: 398–407). It is illustrated in (7.10) with the past suffixes, which show horizontal homophony in the second person only. Another paradigm with horizontal homophony in the second person only is found in Yareba, as presented later in this chapter in (7.14). However, there is much more homophony in this paradigm, which makes it difficult to classify strictly as a case of horizontal homophony. Next, a horizontal homophony in the first person only is found in Aleut. Shown in (7.11) are the independent pronouns in the nominative (Geoghegan 1944: 32). For another example of horizontal homophony in the first person only, see the paradigm from Kapau as discussed later in (7.15).[16] Third, I know of one clear example with horizontal homophony in the first and third, but not in the second person. The subject pronouns from the Omotic language Dizi, shown in (7.12), only have a separate dual for the second person (Allen 1976: 383). Earlier descriptions of this language did not mention this dual (Allen 1976: 392, n. 6). Finally, there are a few languages with horizontal homophony in the first and second but not in the third person. First, Tunica, an extinct language from North America, had a separate third person dual in the independent pronouns and in the prefixal pronominal paradigm (Haas 1946: 347–63). The independent pronouns are shown in (7.13), although these are only the masculine forms. On the other side of the world, this phenomenon is described for the independent pronouns of the Papuan language Buin (Wurm 1975a: 794, citing Laycock).[17]

(7.10) Mansi past suffixes

	Group		Restricted group	
		...-uw	...-əmen	1+2(+3)
1	...-əm			1+3
2	...-ən	...-en		2+3
3	...-∅	...-ət	...-iy	3+3

---

[16] Plank (1989: 303) mentions ancient Greek (which lost the dual, starting in the first person) and Classical Arabic as examples like the Aleut pronouns with a dual in the second and third person, but not in the first. From the list of forms presented by McElhanon (1975: 548), it appears that the independent pronouns from the Papuan language Rawa are of the same paradigmatic structure as the pronouns from Aleut in (7.11). However, the presented first person plural form *nâre* is probably a mistake. The comparison with the possessive suffixes (McElhanon 1975: 550) suggest that it should be *nâne*.

[17] Plank (1989: 304) also mentions southern Arabic varieties as examples of languages that only have a dual in the third person. An example with an inclusive/exclusive distinction is Achumawi, as discussed later in this chapter in (7.36).

214   *Number Incorporated*

(7.11)   Aleut nominative pronouns

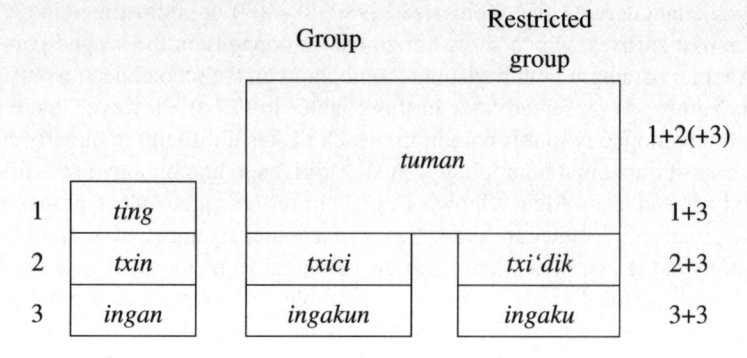

	Singular	Group	Restricted group	
		tuman		1+2(+3)
1	*ting*			1+3
2	*txin*	*txici*	*txi'dik*	2+3
3	*ingan*	*ingakun*	*ingaku*	3+3

(7.12)   Dizi pronouns

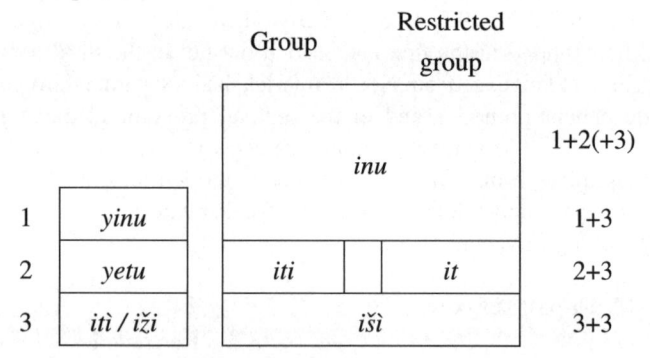

	Singular	Group	Restricted group	
		inu		1+2(+3)
1	*yinu*			1+3
2	*yetu*	*iti*	*it*	2+3
3	*iti / iži*	*iši*		3+3

(7.13)   Tunica masculine pronouns

	Singular	Group	Restricted group	
		ʔinima		1+2(+3)
1	*ʔima*			1+3
2	*ma*	*winima*		2+3
3	*ʔuwi*	*sema*	*ʔunima*	3+3

Summarizing the examples discussed, there does not appear to be great empirical support for a person hierarchy for dual marking. There are only very few examples in concord with it, and roughly just as many counterexamples. However, every generalization based on this small set of cases suffers from lack of significance.

Survey of Restricted Groups 215

7.3.5 Vertical and horizontal homophony

A few paradigmatic structures mix various forms of homophony. They are all found among Papuan languages, which are a hotbed for special structures of dual marking. A combination of a vertical 2/3-homophony and a second person horizontal homophony is attested in the independent pronouns from the Papuan language Yareba (Weimer and Weimer 1975: 675–90), as shown in (7.14). Mention should be made in this context of the inflectional suffixes from the Papuan language Kapau. Kapau has various pronominal paradigms in the indicative mood. The suffixes for the immediate future distinguish seven different morphemes, which form a typical Papuan paradigm such as the one from Yagaria in (7.3). Other tenses have reduced this paradigm to rather strange patterns, involving dual in non-first person only. The most extreme reduction is found in the distant past, as shown in (7.15). It combines singular homophony with a horizontal homophony in the first person and vertical homophony between second and third person (Oates and Oates 1969: 26–35).

(7.14) Yareba pronouns

		Group	Restricted group	
			wa	1+2(+3)
1	na	ya		1+3
2	a		ya	2+3
3	dawa	ema		3+3

(7.15) Kapau distant past suffixes

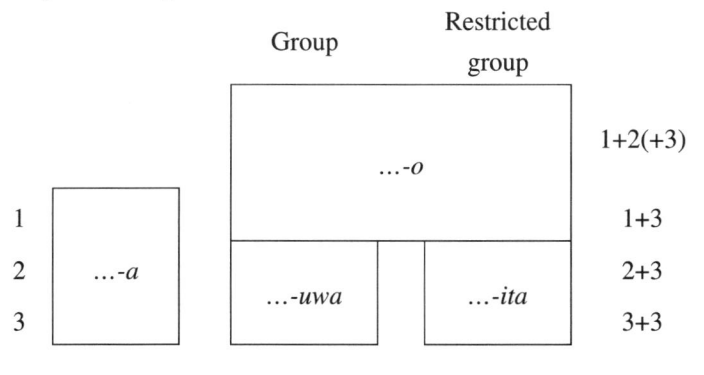

		Group	Restricted group	
		…-o		1+2(+3)
1				1+3
2	…-a	…-uwa	…-ita	2+3
3				3+3

7.3.6 Summary

The 'complete' dual-unified-we paradigm is widespread through the world's languages. This paradigmatic type is attested in many cases, independently of areal or genetic bonds. Besides this common paradigmatic structure, a large variety of patterns with horizontal homophony and/or vertical homophony is found, although only rarely are both kinds of homophony attested in the same paradigm. In total, fourteen different paradigmatic structures with some kind of homophony have been described in this section.

Almost all cases with vertical homophony have a 2/3 homophony between second and third person. Other kinds of vertical homophony are only attested incidentally. This is rather different from what has been found for paradigms without a dual. Among paradigms without a dual, all possible variants of vertical homophony are attested and the 1/2 homophony is the most frequent (see Section 4.4). Also, vertical homophony without duals is attested throughout the world. In contrast, the examples of vertical homophony with a dual as discussed in this section are almost all found among the Papuan languages of New Guinea.

The cases with horizontal homophony are more varied than the cases with vertical homophony, both in their structure and in their areal/genetic distribution. All kinds of combinations of horizontal homophony occur in scattered examples throughout the world's languages. There is a slight preference for duals to be at least present in the first person, but the number of homophonous examples is too low to allow any significant generalization.

For a few of the homophonous examples, the duals are characterized as 'hardly attested' or 'disappearing' (in particular in Aleut, Gothic, and Yidiɲ). At least for these cases, it seems correct to characterize the homophony as a form of deterioration of the paradigm. In the other cases, however, and notably in many Papuan examples, there is no sign indicating that the lack of explicitness in reference is felt as poverty of the system.

7.4 Duals with inclusive/exclusive: three times 'we'

7.4.1 Preamble

The following three sections will all deal with paradigms that have both dual marking and an inclusive/exclusive opposition. Substantial variation is attested in the interaction of duality and the inclusive/exclusive opposition, resulting in various numbers of morphemes that are to be translated into English as 'we'. In this section, the paradigms that have three different forms for 'we' are discussed.

The paradigms with three different forms for 'we' are a hybrid group. They look alike, but there are important differences between the various examples. The two defining characteristics of these paradigms (the presence of dual marking and three different forms for 'we') prompted the name DUAL-3WE as a cover term for them. Among the dual-3we patterns there are six different paradigmatic structures attested, and among these there are four different distributions of the three forms for 'we'. The examples of dual-3we paradigms are almost all incidental exemplars within their close family. Still there are many of these 'incidents', indicating that dual-3we patterns are a clear possibility for the structure of human language.

Before the various examples of dual-3we paradigms are discussed, a clarification of the defining features is needed. Earlier, another paradigmatic type was introduced, which also has three different forms for 'we': the Maranao-type paradigm with a minimal/augmented opposition in the inclusive (see Section 4.5.2). The three forms for 'we' in that paradigmatic structure are minimal inclusive (1+2), augmented inclusive (1+2+3), and exclusive (1+3). The paradigms to be discussed in this section are rather different. The main difference is the marking of the dual. The Maranao-type paradigms do not have dual forms for second or third person. In general, the category 'dual' is of no importance to those paradigms. In contrast, the dual-3we pronominal paradigms in this section clearly have dual forms in the second and third person. The difference between these two structures is schematically shown in Figure 7.2.

In the dual-3we paradigms, the three different forms for 'we' also distinguish dual forms, but it is in this part of the paradigm that the hybrid character of these paradigmatic structures prevails. One possibility is that the dual is only attested in the exclusive (Section 7.4.4) or only in the inclusive (Section 7.4.5). It is also possible to have an inclusive/exclusive opposition in the dual, but not in the plural (Section 7.4.3). Conversely, it is possible to have an inclusive/exclusive opposition in the plural, but not in the dual (Section 7.4.2). This last option appears to be slightly more common than the others.

It might be the case that the slight differences between the referential values of the three forms for 'we' are due to different descriptional practices, but it is also possible that there are real linguistic differences at stake here. My estimate is that both factors play a role. An argument for the variable descriptions is the case of the Wik-Munkan pronouns, shown in (7.27). The same grammarian presents different analyses of this paradigm on different occasions. In contrast, an

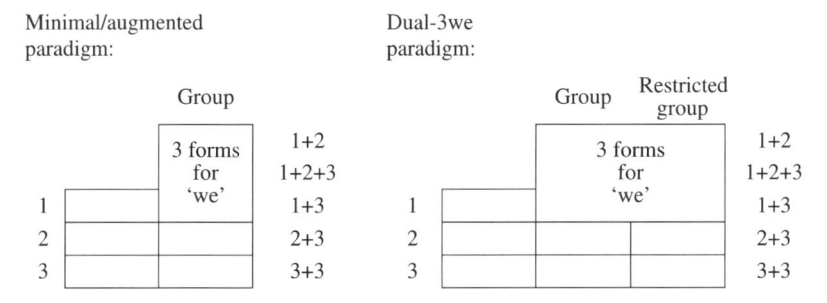

FIG. 7.2. *The difference between the minimal/augmented and the dual-3we paradigms*

218 Number Incorporated

important argument for the inherent variability of this kind of paradigm will be presented in Section 9.5. It will be argued there that the various dual-3we paradigms have cognates showing many different paradigmatic structures. This indicates that the variability of the dual-3we paradigm may be caused by different historical pathways leading to this kind of paradigm. By this argument, the hybrid character of this paradigmatic type has linguistic saliency.

7.4.2 Inclusive/exclusive in plural only

In the first variant of a dual-3we pattern, there is a single dual form and an inclusive/exclusive opposition in the plural. This kind of dual-3we structure appears to be the most widespread variant of the various dual-3we structures to be discussed. The first example, shown in (7.16), is from the Australian language Kuku-Yalanji (Oates and Oates 1964: 7). The second example, shown in (7.17), is the paradigm of the independent pronouns from the Tibeto-Burman language Jiarong (Bauman 1975: 131–2, 276).

(7.16) Kuku-Yalanji pronouns

	Group	Group	Restricted group	
		ŋana	ŋali(n)	1+2(+3)
1	ŋayu	ŋanjin		1+3
2	yuudu	yurra	yubal	2+3
3	ñulu	jana	bula	3+3

(7.17) Jiarong pronouns

	Group	Group	Restricted group	
		yo	ndžo	1+2(+3)
1	ŋa	ŋəñiɛ		1+3
2	no	ño	ŋəndžA	2+3
3	mə	məñiɛ	məndžAs	3+3

The third example, shown in (7.18), is the paradigm of the independent pronouns from the Papuan language Tuaripi, part of the Eleman family on the south-eastern tip of Papua New Guinea (Wurm 1975b: 515). Two further Papuan examples of this pattern come from the Binanderean family. This family is also found in the south-eastern tip of Papua New Guinea, but the Binanderean languages are spoken on the opposite coast as the Eleman languages. Shown in (7.19) is the paradigm of the independent pronouns from Guhu-Samane (Richard 1975: 781). The other example, shown in (7.20), is from Korafe, a language closely related to Guhu-Samane. This paradigm has a typical Papuan vertical homophony between the second and third person. Morphologically, it appears that the exclusive pronoun *namane* is a later addition. The suffix *-mane* is consistently glossed as 'plural' in the short sketch by Farr and Farr (1975: 734–5), although it is never presented as a plural marker on nouns.[18]

(7.18)   Tuaripi pronouns

		Group	Restricted group	
		ereita	elaka	1+2(+3)
1	ara(o)	ela(o)		1+3
2	a(o)	e(o)	euka	2+3
3	are(o)	ere(o)	ereuka	3+3

(7.19)   Guhu-Samane pronouns

		Group	Restricted group	
		napa	naka	1+2(+3)
1	(a)na	nana		1+3
2	nii	nike	nipe	2+3
3	no	noko	nopo	3+3

---

[18] In Korafe, the difference between inclusive and exclusive can also be marked in the dual, by preposing either the second person singular pronoun, to make *ni nangae* for inclusive reference, or the third person singular pronoun, to make *nu nangae* for exclusive reference. These forms rarely occur (Farr and Farr 1975: 734).

(7.20) Korafe pronouns

		Group	Restricted group	
		namonde	nangae	1+2(+3)
1	na	namane		1+3
2	ni	ne(monde)	nengae	2+3
3	nu			3+3

7.4.3 Inclusive/exclusive in dual only

The next kind of paradigm with three different forms for 'we' is much rarer than the preceding pattern. In the following cases, the three forms for 'we' are described as 'inclusive dual', 'exclusive dual', and 'plural'. There is an inclusive/exclusive distinction in the dual, but not in the plural (a case of structural markedness reversal, see Section 6.3). The first example, shown in (7.21), is the paradigm of the independent pronouns from the Papuan language Samo (Voorhoeve 1975: 391–2). The second example, shown in (7.22), is the paradigm of the pronominal prefixes from Coos, an extinct language from Oregon (Frachtenberg 1922a: 321).

(7.21) Samo pronouns

		Group	Restricted group	
		ɔi	ala	1+2(+3)
1	ã		oli	1+3
2	nɔ̃	nĩ	nĩli	2+3
3	yɔ̃	yã/diyɔ̃	ili	2+3

(7.22) Coos subject prefixes

		Group	Restricted group	
		ɬîn-...	îs-...	1+2(+3)
1	n̥-...		xwîn-...	1+3
2	eᵉ-...	cîn-...	îc-...	2+3
3	ø-...	îɬ-...	úx-...	2+3

7.4.4 Dual in exclusive only

Yet another kind of dual-3we paradigm is shown in (7.23). It is the paradigm of the independent pronouns from Yagua, a genetically isolated language from Peru. The three different forms for 'we' are described as 'exclusive dual', 'exclusive plural', and 'inclusive' (Payne 1993: 20). This is a rather unusual distribution that has not been observed before in any typological survey of pronominal systems, as can be inferred from the following claim by Moravcsik: 'no language has been encountered which distinguishes a dual and a plural in the exclusive but not in the inclusive' (Moravcsik 1978: 352, n. 11). Moreover, this unusual paradigmatic structure is not only attested in Yagua. The independent pronouns from the Australian language Ngankikurungkurr are another example, shown in (7.24). In the description of this language, a plural form of the inclusive is added to the paradigm, using a postposition, *nime*, meaning 'all' (Hoddinott and Kofod 1988: 94). Strictly speaking, this postposition does not belong to the pronominal paradigm. To bring home the point that this pattern is indeed attested, a third example is shown in (7.25), from the Papuan language Savosavo (Todd 1975: 813).[19]

(7.23) Yagua pronouns

		Group	Restricted group	
		vúúy		1+2(+3)
1	ráy	núúy	nááy	1+3
2	jíy	jiryéy	sa̧a̧dá	2+3
3	níí	ríy	naadá	3+3

(7.24) Ngankikurungkurr pronouns

		Group	Restricted group	
		nayin		1+2(+3)
1	ngayi	ngagurr	ngagarri	1+3
2	nyinyi	nagurr	nagarri	2+3
3	nem / ngayim	wirrim	wirrike	3+3

---

[19] In the short note on Savosavo by Capell (1969a: 9–14), the dual forms of the inclusive and exclusive appear to be reversed. Also, a special form *edo mai* is presented for the inclusive dual. However, the word *edo* is the numeral 'two' (Todd 1975: 839). Strictly speaking, this word does not belong in the pronominal paradigm.

(7.25) Savosavo pronouns

	Group	\multicolumn{2}{c}{Restricted group}	
		\multicolumn{2}{c}{*mai*}	1+2(+3)
1	*añi*	*ave*	*age*	1+3
2	*no*	*me*	*pe*	2+3
3	*lo / ko*	*ze(po)*	*to*	3+3

A slight variant on this pattern is the paradigm of the independent pronouns from the Australian language Burarra, as first described by Glasgow (1964). She approaches the description of the pronouns of Burarra in a special way, anticipating what later will be called a 'unit-augmented' analysis (see Section 7.6). However, two pairs of pronouns in her scheme are identical, leaving only three different forms of 'we' (Glasgow 1964: 110–11; 1984: 15). Interpreting her description in the framework as used here, the nominative pronouns divide the referential person space as shown in (7.26). The most interesting part is the morpheme *ngatippa*. This pronoun combines the references that are traditionally called 'inclusive trial' and 'exclusive dual', a highly remarkable combination in traditional terminology and extremely unusual cross-linguistically.

(7.26) Burarra pronouns

		Group	Restricted group	
		\multicolumn{2}{c}{*ngarripa*}	1+2
		ngayburrpa	*ngatippa*	1+2+3
1	*ngaypa*			1+3
2	*nginyipa*	*anagoyburrpa*	*anagotippa*	2+3
3	*nipa*	*birripa*	*bitipa*	3+3

7.4.5 Dual in inclusive only

Finally, one paradigm in this hybrid dual-3we type shows yet another distribution of the three forms for 'we' over the various referential possibilities. This special case is attested in the Australian language Wik-Munkan. This example highlights the problematic status of the description of these paradigms, as the same author describes slightly different paradigmatic structures on different occasions. The paradigm shown in (7.27a) comes from Godfrey and Kerr (1964: 76) and the paradigm shown in (7.27b) from Godfrey (1964: 14). Apart from some slight phonemic changes, and the general drop of the final vowel in (7.27b), the pronominal elements in these paradigms are identical. However, the analysis of the three forms for 'we' are different. Comparative evidence can shed some more light on this situation. Wik-Munkan is part of the Middle Paman sub-family, and in a comparative study of Middle Paman, Hale (1976b: 56–7) confirms the analysis from (7.27b). This structure is related to the minimal/augmented paradigm (see Section 9.5.3). Probably, the analysis as shown in (7.27a) was a mistake.[20] Whatever the 'real' structure of the Wik-Munkan pronouns is, these two paradigms show that it is sometimes difficult for a grammarian to decide what the precise function of the various forms for 'we' is.

(7.27) Wik-Munkan pronouns

a. Following Godfrey and Kerr (1964)

		Group	Restricted group	
		nampi	ngaali	1+2(+3)
1	ngaya		ngana	1+3
2	ninta	niya	nipa	2+3
3	nila	tana	pula	3+3

b. Following Godfrey (1964)

		Group	Restricted group	
		ngamp	ngal	1+2(+3)
1	ngay	ngan		1+3
2	nint	niiy	nip	2+3
3	nil	tan	pul	3+3

---

[20] The description of the Tübatulabal pronouns by Voegelin (1937a: 135) present another case of a comparable mistake (cf. n. 29 in Chapter 4 above).

7.4.6 Summary

Four different possibilities of marking the three forms of 'we' have been discussed in this section. The impression that arises from all these examples is one of disorder. There may simply be many possibilities for the paradigmatic structure, but another option is that some of the descriptions are sloppy with regard to the precise referential properties of the various forms for 'we'. For most of the examples in this section, the pronominal elements are not extensively documented. Normally, only the paradigm is presented, without further arguments for the division of reference. It might well be that the division of the reference between the three forms for 'we', once they are studied in more detail, is less variable than appears from these examples. It also might not. A clue that points in the direction of a real inherent variability of the dual-3we paradigms is that the examples are almost all incidental cases within their narrow family. Close relatives of these languages are of various paradigmatic structures, as will be discussed extensively in Section 9.5. Finally, nine out of the twelve examples presented are from south-eastern New Guinea and north-western Australia, which indicates that the distribution of this type of paradigm is strongly areally restricted.

7.5 Duals with inclusive/exclusive: four times 'we'

7.5.1 Preamble

The next patterns to be discussed distinguish four different forms for 'we'. In almost all examples to be discussed, the four forms for 'we' arise through a cross-section of the oppositions dual/plural and inclusive/exclusive. The most common structure also has a dual/plural opposition for the second and third person. The examples with such a full set of dual forms are discussed in Section 7.5.2 under the heading of DUAL-INCLUSIVE/EXCLUSIVE. In Section 7.5.3, a special paradigmatic structure with four forms for 'we' is discussed. Referentially, this pattern is identical to the dual-inclusive/exclusive paradigm. However, the morphological structure is rather different—different enough to deserve separate mention and a separate name: PARTIAL-UNIT-AUGMENTED. Next, in Section 7.5.4, the paradigms that do not have a full set of dual forms are discussed. The few examples mostly show horizontal homophony. Vertical homophony is only attested in two incidental cases. Finally, Section 7.5.5 will summarize the discussion of paradigms with four forms for 'we'.

7.5.2 The dual-inclusive/exclusive paradigm

The first kind of pattern to be discussed with four different forms for 'we' is the dual-inclusive/exclusive paradigm. This paradigm consists of eleven different morphemes: three singular morphemes (1, 2, and 3), four group morphemes (inclusive, exclusive, second plural, and third plural), and dual versions of these four group morphemes.[21] This is a common type of paradigmatic structure, characterized by Ingram (1978: 219-20) as one of the 'four systems that are more frequent than the others'; but it is not so easy to find examples of this type outside the Pacific. In this section, I will present a survey of the distribution of this type of paradigm over the languages of the world.

A complete dual-inclusive/exclusive paradigm is regularly found in Oceanic (Austronesian) languages. Lynch (1998: 102) gives examples from Yapese, Nakanai, A'jië, and Samoan. The pattern is here exemplified in (7.28) by the pronouns from another Oceanic language, Maori (Harlow 1996: 6). Such paradigms are also commonly found among the independent pronouns in Australian languages.[22] Outside the Pacific, there are only a few examples, and they often do not have a completely regular eleven-morpheme system. Often, the third person morphemes are borderline cases to demonstratives. Some true cases are attested among the Tibeto-Burman languages.[23] In North America, the dual-inclusive/exclusive paradigm is relatively frequent.[24] Finally, an incidental case of a dual-inclusive/exclusive paradigm is found in Kunama, a Nilo-Saharan language from Eritrea (Bender 1996: 18). As far as I know, this is a unique pattern for an African language. Although it might be an unusual case, it is exceptionally stable. Over a century ago, Reinisch (1881: 17) described exactly the same paradigm for the independent pronouns.

---

[21] A possible example with a different referential division of the four forms for 'we' is described for the Mon-Khmer language Palaung by Milne (1921: 17-18). The paradigm of independent pronouns looks like a normal pattern with a dual/plural and an inclusive/exclusive opposition. However, Milne emphasizes that there is no inclusive/exclusive opposition. He describes an opposition between 'present' versus 'absent' instead. Of course, the present/absent opposition is rather close to the inclusive/exclusive opposition. An addressee is always present at the speech act situation, so an inclusive dual is always 'present'. However, a third person can be either present or absent. Consequently, exclusive marking is crucial to decide between an inclusive/exclusive opposition and a present/absent opposition. On this point, Milne's description is quite clear. It is present/absent that is marked by the different morphemes, not inclusive/exclusive. However, in the short note on the Palaung pronouns by Burling (1970: 14-17), no mention is made of a present/absent opposition. Instead, he presents a normal inclusive/exclusive opposition. I did not find any other sources on Palaung that could shed more light on the question of which analysis is the right one.

[22] Dixon (1980: 329, 335-6) mentions Dhalandji, Gupapuyŋu, Gumbaynggir, Nyanwaygi, and Thargari. Warlbiri also belongs in this list (Hale 1973: 315-16).

[23] In the Tibeto-Burman languages, third person pronouns are often diachronically related to demonstrative elements (Bauman 1975: 107). Yet Bauman (1975: 265-304) lists Bahing, Bunan, Kanauri, and Manchati as examples of full dual-inclusive/exclusive paradigms with 'real' third person forms.

[24] On the west coast, e.g. Siuslaw (Frachtenberg 1922b: 468) and Chinook (Boas 1911a: 580-1, 626). Dual-inclusive/exclusive paradigms are also found among the Iroquoian languages, e.g. the intransitive prefixes from Oneida (Lounsbury 1953: 60-1), Cherokee (Cook 1979: 22), and Tuscarora (Williams 1976: 156). The same structure is found in the pronouns in the Oto-Manguean language Mazahua (Suárez 1983: 81-2).

(7.28) Maori pronouns

		Group	Restricted group	
		tātou	tāua	1+2(+3)
1	au	mātou	māua	1+3
2	koe	koutou	kōrua	2+3
3	ia	rātou	rāua	3+3

7.5.3 The partial-unit-augmented paradigm

A different kind of paradigm with four different forms for 'we' is a paradigm that I will call PARTIAL-UNIT-AUGMENTED. At first glance, such paradigms are identical to the dual-inclusive/exclusive paradigms. However, once their morphophonological structure is scrutinized, a slight but important difference can be observed. As an example of this pattern, the independent pronouns from the Australian language Umpila are shown in (7.29). The dual forms are marked by a special dual suffix -baʔamu. The only dual form that does not use this suffix is the inclusive dual ŋali (Dixon 1980: 355–6).

(7.29) Umpila pronouns (version I)

		Group	Restricted group	
		ŋambula	ŋali	1+2(+3)
1	ŋayu	ŋana	ŋana-baʔamu	1+3
2	ŋanu	ŋuʔula	ŋuʔula-baʔamu	2+3
3	nhulu	bula	bula-baʔamu	3+3

Because of this difference in the morphophonological structure of the dual forms, I propose to represent the Umpila pronouns as shown in (7.30). In this representation, the difference between the two inclusive pronouns ŋali and ŋambula is not one of number, but one of person. The opposition dual/plural inclusive is replaced by the roughly equivalent opposition minimal/augmented inclusive. In this way, the connection between these paradigms and other paradigms with a minimal/augmented opposition is emphasized (see also Section 9.5.3). If the dual forms as marked by -baʔamu are disregarded, then the paradigmatic structure is of the Maranao-type (see Section 4.5.2). In contrast, if the category 1+2+3 also distinguishes a separate restricted group morpheme, then the resulting structure is of the unit-augmented type, which will be discussed in Section 7.6. Because of the similarity to the unit-augmented type, I call the paradigm of Umpila a PARTIAL-UNIT-AUGMENTED paradigm.

(7.30) Umpila pronouns (version II)

		Group	Restricted group	
		ŋali		1+2
		ŋambula		1+2+3
1	ŋayu	ŋana	ŋana-baʔamu	1+3
2	ŋanu	ŋuʔula	ŋuʔula-baʔamu	2+3
3	nhulu	bula	bula-baʔamu	3+3

This kind of paradigm is found in various linguistic families from Australia. Most examples are found among the non-Pama-Nyungan languages in the northwestern part of Australia, except for Umpila, which is part of Pama-Nyungan. The partial-unit-augmented paradigm seems to be a typical Australian phenomenon.[25] A somewhat covert example of this pattern is found in direct pronouns from the Australian language Alawa, as shown in (7.31). In this case, there is no overt suffix marking the dual, but a regular alternation between -l- and -ř- (Sharpe 1972: 57).

(7.31) Alawa pronouns

		Group	Restricted group	
		ñanu		1+2
		ñalu		1+2+3
1	ŋina	ŋalu	ŋaŕu	1+3
2	ñagana	wulu	wuŕu	2+3
3	nul̥a / ŋadul̥a	yilul̥a	yiŕul̥a	3+3

---

[25] Examples are attested in Warrwa of the Nyulnyulan family (McGregor 1994: 20–1), in Ngalakan of the Gunwingguan family (Merlan 1983: 71), in Maranungku of the Daly family (Tryon 1970: 16), and in Jaminjung of the Djamindjungan family (Schulze-Berndt 2000: 64). A possible case of a partial-unit-augmented paradigm outside Australia is attested in the Gé language Apinayé. However, the description is not particularly explicit in this respect (see Section 9.4.3).

7.5.4 Homophonous paradigms

There are only a few examples of paradigms with an inclusive/exclusive distinction that show horizontal or vertical homophony. I have predominantly found cases of HORIZONTAL homophony. Such examples combine different numbers of the same person into the marking of one morpheme. The alternative VERTICAL type of homophony—homophony of different person with the same number—is not attested (despite the obligatory exception to the cross-linguistic rule). In one case, vertical and horizontal homophony are combined.

Horizontal homophony in the third person only is found in Tibeto-Burman. Shown in (7.32) are the independent pronouns of Limbu (van Driem 1987: 25–8). The same structure is described for the independent pronouns from Camling, a language closely related to Limbu (Ebert 1997: 43). Horizontal homophony in the second person only is found in the Australian language Dhuwal. Shown in (7.33) are the nominative pronouns from the Djapu dialect (Morphy 1983: 51–5). The same structure is described for the independent pronouns of Sedang, a Mon-Khmer language from Vietnam (Smith 1979: 80). Horizontal homophony in second and third person is attested in Rapanui, an Oceanic language from Easter Island (Du Feu 1996: 140).[26] Another example is the independent pronoun paradigm from Kilivila, an Oceanic language spoken on the Trobriand Islands (Senft 1986: 46–7).[27] Finally, horizontal homophony in all but the third person is attested in the North American language Achumawi. The verb prefixes in the indicative mood from Achumawi are shown in (7.36). In Achumawi, a verb suffix *-má* is used to disambiguate plural from dual, but for the third person there is a separate dual prefix, and the suffix *-má* is not used (de Angulo and Freeland 1931: 91).[28]

(7.32) Limbu pronouns

	Group	Group	Restricted group	
		ani	anchi	1+2(+3)
1	aŋga	anige	anchige	1+3
2	khɛnɛʔ	kheni	khenchi	2+3
3	khunɛʔ / khɛy	khunchi / khɛŋkaʔ	khunchi / khɛŋkaʔ	3+3

---

[26] The pronouns are almost identical to the pronouns from Maori in (7.28), except for the horizontal homophony in the second and third person. Note that the dual forms for the second and third person have persisted in Rapanui; they have taken over the plural reference (cf. Section 6.3).

[27] The markedness of the four different forms of 'we' in Kilivila is here different from the Limbu case. In Limbu there is an EXCLUSIVE suffix *-ge*, but in Kilivila there is a PLURAL suffix *-si* (Senft 1986: 31). The Kilivila first person marking is an example of morphological markedness reversal (cf. Section 6.3).

[28] The suffix *-má* is used to mark the plural. The unmarked form of the non-singular prefixes have dual reference. This is a case of referential markedness reversal (cf. Section 6.3). Also note that this

Survey of Restricted Groups 229

(7.33) Dhuwal pronouns

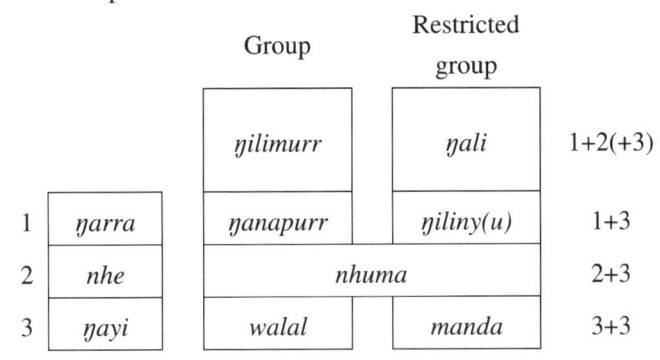

		Group	Restricted group	
		ŋilimurr	ŋali	1+2(+3)
1	ŋarra	ŋanapurr	ŋiliny(u)	1+3
2	nhe	nhuma	nhuma	2+3
3	ŋayi	walal	manda	3+3

(7.34) Kilivila pronouns

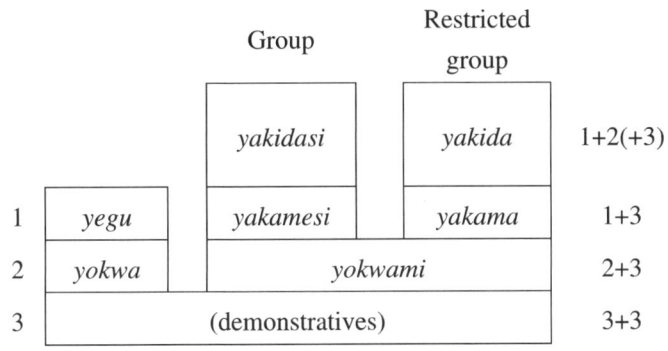

		Group	Restricted group	
		yakidasi	yakida	1+2(+3)
1	yegu	yakamesi	yakama	1+3
2	yokwa	yokwami	yokwami	2+3
3		(demonstratives)		3+3

(7.35) Rapanui pronouns

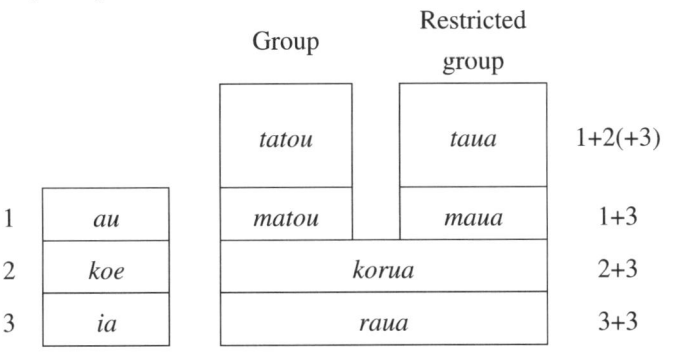

		Group	Restricted group	
		tatou	taua	1+2(+3)
1	au	matou	maua	1+3
2	koe	korua	korua	2+3
3	ia	raua	raua	3+3

paradigm does not have four different forms of 'we' and does not, strictly speaking, belong in this section. However, this appeared to be the most logical place to discuss this aberrant paradigmatic structure.

(7.36) Achumawi subject prefixes

	Group	Restricted group	
		h-...	1+2(+3)
1	s-...	s.h-...	1+3
2	k-...	gìdz-...	2+3
3	y-...	eiy-...	3+3

From the previous examples, it is clear that horizontal homophony is a possibility for paradigms with a dual and an inclusive/exclusive opposition, although it is not particularly widespread. Even stronger, VERTICAL HOMOPHONY is completely exceptional, being attested only in two incidental examples. The first zof these examples is the Papuan language Suena. However, vertical homophony in this language is only found in the inflection of the indicative mood in the remote tense, as shown in (7.37). Other pronominal paradigms in this language do not show this unusual pattern (Wilson 1969: 97). Second, a special paradigmatic structure is found in Kwamera, an Oceanic language from Vanuatu. Kwamera has pronominal subject prefixes on the verb. The subject prefixes are normally followed by a number prefix to disambiguate the reference, but the subject and number paradigms can be separated morphologically (Lindstrom and Lynch 1994: 12). The subject paradigm is shown in (7.38). The exclusive reference is taken care of by the singular form *iak-* that is used for reference to the speaker. This general use of *iak-* can be seen as an extended case of horizontal homophony. In the same paradigm, the dual form *k-* shows a vertical homophony between the inclusive dual and the third person dual reference. This paradigm from Kwamera is the only example I am aware of that combines a separate horizontal and vertical homophony with an inclusive/exclusive opposition; a very unusual structure indeed. Some example sentences have been added to exemplify the referential possibilities of these prefixes. In (7.39a, b) the two different inclusive forms for 'we' are shown. However, (7.39a) can also refer to a third person dual. The prefix for 'I' and the exclusive 'we' (1+3) are identical, as can be seen in (7.39c, d).[29]

---

[29] Compare the Kwamera prefixes with the prefixal paradigm of the closely related language Lenakel, which has been discussed in (4.97). In Lenakel, the prefix *k-* has general plural reference. No dual prefixes are attested in Lenakel.

(7.37)   Suena indicative remote past suffixes

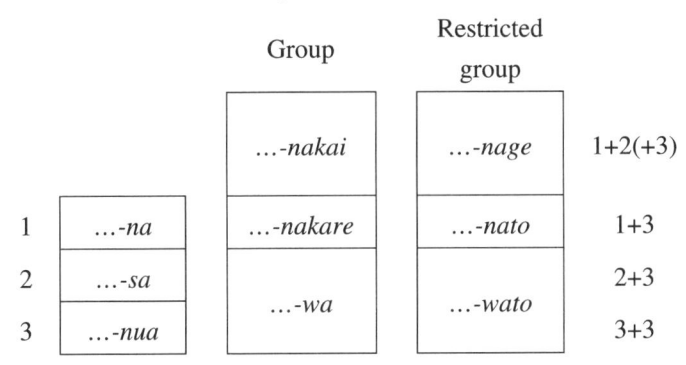

	Group	Group	Restricted group	
		...-nakai	...-nage	1+2(+3)
1	...-na	...-nakare	...-nato	1+3
2	...-sa	...-wa	...-wato	2+3
3	...-nua			3+3

(7.38)   Kwamera subject prefixes

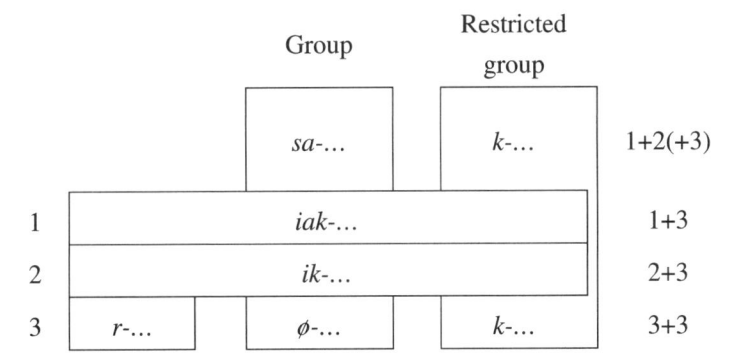

	Group	Group	Restricted group	
		sa-...	k-...	1+2(+3)
1	iak-...	iak-...	iak-...	1+3
2	ik-...	ik-...	ik-...	2+3
3	r-...	ø-...	k-...	3+3

(7.39)   Kwamera (Lindstrom and Lynch 1994: 11, 14)
   a. *k-rou-ánumwi*
      1+2+3/3+3-DUAL-drink
      'We two (inclusive) drink.' or 'They two drink.'
   b. *sa-ha-iputa*
      1+2+3-PLUR-climb
      'We (inclusive) climb.'
   c. *ia-pkata-mha*
      1-see-NEG
      'I didn't see it.'
   d. *ia-ha-vehe*
      1-PLUR-come
      'We (exclusive plural) come.'

7.5.5 Summary

The major group of paradigms with four different forms for 'we' is the set of dual-inclusive/exclusive paradigms. These paradigms have a dual/plural opposition both in the inclusive and in the exclusive. In total there are eleven morphemes in such a paradigm. Examples of the dual-inclusive/exclusive paradigm are commonly found among the world's languages. Roughly speaking, the main areas/families where this paradigm is found are the Oceanic family, the Pama-Nyungan family, the Tibeto-Burman family, and the languages from North America. A special variant of the eleven-morpheme paradigm is the PARTIAL-UNIT-AUGMENTED paradigm. The referential structure of this paradigm is identical to the dual-inclusive/exclusive paradigm, but the morphological structure is significantly different. This paradigm is almost exclusively found in Australia. Besides these 'complete' patterns, there are seven different homophonous paradigmatic structures attested. The majority of these few cases attested show horizontal homophony; vertical homophony is only exceptionally attested.

7.6 Duals with inclusive/exclusive: five times 'we'

The last phenomenon that will be tackled in this chapter is referentially a trial, but it is better analysed as a twisted kind of dual. This paradigmatic structure, known as a 'unit-augmented' pattern in the literature, has been one of the major reasons to replace the term 'dual' in the pronominal domain by the term 'restricted' (see Section 6.2).

This special pattern has five different forms for 'we', exemplified here with its paradigm case: the independent pronouns from the Australian language Rembarrnga, as shown in (7.40) and (7.41). The crucial element is the independent pronoun *ngakorrbbarrah*. This pronoun is traditionally analysed as an inclusive trial, meaning 'I, you and one other person'. A dual-like analysis for this pronoun was first proposed by McKay (1978).[30] Following the analysis of McKay, it is better to interpret the pronouns of Rembarrnga as an extended version of the Maranao-type (or 'minimal/augmented') paradigm.

The Maranao-type paradigm (see Section 4.5.2) has an opposition between a minimal and an augmented inclusive. The MINIMAL INCLUSIVE is used to refer to the combination of the two principal speech act participants—speaker and addressee. Because this pair is categorized as a singular morpheme, it can be 'pluralized'. This 'pluralized' form is called the AUGMENTED INCLUSIVE. Now, in Rembarrnga, this 'singular' pair is not only 'pluralized' but also 'dualized'. The pronoun *ngakorrbbarrah* refers to the speech act dyad plus one extra person. This

---

[30] Glasgow (1964) should be mentioned as a clear precursor of this analysis. Her terminology is a little awkward, but she already had the same ideas as McKay (1978). Compare the Burarra independent pronouns, presented in (7.26).

group consists of three persons, and therefore, in the referential sense, it is a trial. However, paradigmatically, this form aligns with the other duals, using the 'dual' suffix *-bbarrah*. Extending the minimal/augmented terminology, McKay dubbed this phenomenon 'unit augmented'. His analysis of Rembarrnga is shown in (7.40).

(7.40)   Rembarrnga pronouns (version I)

	Minimal	Augmented	Unit augmented	
1+2	*yɨkkɨ*	*ngakorrɨ*	*ngakorr-bbarrah*	1+2+3
1	*ngɨnɨ*	*yarrɨ*	*yarr-bbarrah*	1+3
2	*kɨ*	*nakorrɨ*	*nakorr-bbarrah*	2+3
3	*nawɨ / ngadɨ*	*barrɨ*	*barr-bbarrah*	3+3

For purposes of comparison and unification, I choose to represent this paradigm slightly differently, as shown in (7.41). I use this graphic representation to highlight the connection with the other paradigms discussed in this work; I do not intend this representation to have different implications compared to the representation in (7.40). As described in Section 6.2, the label 'unit augmented' in the paradigm is replaced here with the label 'restricted group'. The term UNIT-AUGMENTED is used for the paradigmatic structure as a whole. This paradigmatic structure is typically found among the non-Pama-Nyungan language from Australia, but there are also a few cases outside this area. In the following survey, two rare variants of the unit-augmented pattern will also be discussed.

(7.41)   Rembarrnga pronouns (version II)

		Group	Restricted group	
		yɨkkɨ		1+2
		ngakorrɨ	*ngakorr-bbarrah*	1+2+3
1	*ngɨnɨ*	*yarrɨ*	*yarr-bbarrah*	1+3
2	*kɨ*	*nakorrɨ*	*nakorr-bbarrah*	2+3
3	*nawɨ / ngadɨ*	*barrɨ*	*barr-bbarrah*	3+3

In Australia, this pattern is mainly found in the Gunwingguan family. Rembarrnga is part of the Gunwingguan family; other Gunwingguan languages with the same paradigmatic structure are Ngandi (Heath 1978: 54), Mangarayi (Merlan 1982: 102), and Nunggubuyu (Heath 1984: 241–8). A unit-augmented paradigm is also found in the independent pronouns of the Australian language Nyikina of the Nyulnyulan family (McGregor 1989: 446, citing Stokes). A special case is the Burarran family. In (7.42) the intransitive prefixes from Ndjébbana (McKay 1978: 32; 2000: 209) are shown. These prefixes form a complete

234   *Number Incorporated*

unit-augmented paradigm. The intransitive prefixes from the related language Burarra are shown in (7.43). These prefixes from Burarra distinguish five different forms for 'we', in a unit-augmented-like division (Glasgow 1984). However, the exclusive non-singular forms are identical to the second person non-singular forms.[31]

(7.42)   Ndjébbana intransitive prefixes

		Group	Restricted group	
		(karr)ka-...		1+2
		ngabarra-...	ngirri-...	1+2+3
1	nga-...	njarra-...	njirri-...	1+3
2	dja-...	narra-...	nirri-...	2+3
3	ka / nja-...	barra-...	birri-...	3+3

(7.43)   Burarra intransitive prefixes

		Group	Restricted group	
		arr-...		1+2
		nguburr-...	arri-...	1+2+3
1	ngu-...	nyiburr-...	nyirri-...	1+3
2	nyi-...	nyiburr-...	nyirri-...	2+3
3	{a}-...	aburr-...	{a}birri-...	3+3

Outside Australia, this paradigmatic type is almost unattested. There might be unit-augmented systems among the Gé languages in South America, but the cases that I know of are only poorly described.[32] The only clear examples of a unit-augmented paradigm outside Australia are found in two Papuan languages. The first example is Weri, a language of the Goilalan family in southeastern New

---

[31] This vertical homophony in the inflectional paradigm of Burarra can be disambiguated by adding an independent pronoun. However, the independent pronouns are of another atypical paradigmatic structure, with homophony between 1+2+3 and 1+3, presented in (7.26) above. The independent pronouns as well as the pronominal inflection allow some representational ambiguity, but together they function as a full unit-augmented system.

[32] Maybe Kayapo has a unit-augmented paradigm (Wiesemann 1986b: 368–9). See Section 9.4.3 for a discussion of this pronominal marking in the Gé languages.

Guinea. The independent pronouns from Weri are shown in (7.44). In this case, the restricted forms are regularly derived from the group morphemes, by using a suffix -*ip* (Boxwell 1967: 36). The independent pronouns from Kunimaipa, a close relative of Weri, are shown in (7.45). This paradigmatic structure turns out to be rather unusual. There are only four different forms for 'we' in Kunimaipa (*rei*, *rei-pi*, *rari*, and *rari-pi*). However, the referential values of these four forms can only be understood if the paradigm is analysed as a variant of the unit-augmented paradigm of Weri. The form *rei-pi* is a general dual form, used for both inclusive and exclusive dual. The form *rari-pi* is the odd one out: it used only for restricted 1+2+3 (Geary 1977: 17–18; Pence 1968).[33] The other example outside Australia is described for the East Papuan language Reefs, spoken in the Solomon Islands in (7.46). There is a clearly separable suffix -*le* for the restricted group forms (Wurm 1969: 83).

(7.44) Weri pronouns

		Group	Restricted group	
		tepir		1+2
		tëar	tëar-ip	1+2+3
1	ne	ten	ten-ip	1+3
2	në	ar	ar-ip	2+3
3	pä	pët / pëar	pëar-ip	3+3

(7.45) Kunimaipa pronouns

		Group	Restricted group	
		rei-pi		1+2
		rari	rari-pi	1+2+3
1	ne	rei	rei-pi	1+3
2	ni	ari	ari-pi	2+3
3	pi	paru	paru-pi	3+3

[33] The use of the suffix -*pi* in Kunimaipa is said to be 'optional' (Geary 1977: 17). It is added here to show the resemblance with the Weri paradigm. Without the suffix -*pi*, the structure of the independent pronouns in Kunimaipa would be of the same type as the exceptional structure that is also found in the independent pronouns from Gooniyandi and Yaouré, as described in Section 3.6.6.

(7.46) Reefs subject suffixes

	Group		Restricted group	
		...-d^yi		1+2
		...-de	...-dele	1+2+3
1	...-nɔ	...-ŋo	...-ŋole	1+3
2	...-mu	...-mi	...-mile	2+3
3	...-gu	...-gui	...-guile	3+3

To summarize, the unit-augmented paradigm is a typical Australian phenomenon. There are only a few cases outside Australia, and those are found in the area closely surrounding Australia. The same geographical bias is also found in the partial-unit-augmented patterns, discussed previously in Section 7.5.3. As that name indicates, not only the geographical distribution but also the paradigmatic structure of the partial-unit-augmented paradigm is reminiscent of the unit-augmented paradigms discussed here. The relation between these two patterns is further investigated in Section 9.4.

7.7 Generalizations

In the survey as described in this chapter, thirty-three different kinds of paradigms are presented (see Table 7.1). Some of these paradigmatic structures are only attested in one isolated case; others are found widespread through the world's linguistic variation. A distinction between common, semi-common, and rare patterns is made in the table. Common patterns are widespread and are a commonly attested structure in at least a few genetic families. In contrast, rare patterns are only attested in a few incidental cases. Those patterns that have

TABLE 7.1. *Paradigmatic variation with restricted ('dual') marking*

	No inclusive/exclusive	With inclusive/exclusive			Total
		3 'we'	4 'we'	5 'we'	
Common patterns	1	–	1	–	2
Semi-common patterns	4	1	1	1	7
Rare patterns	10	5	7	2	24
Total	15	6	9	3	33

Survey of Restricted Groups 237

Dual-unified-we   Dual-inclusive/exclusive

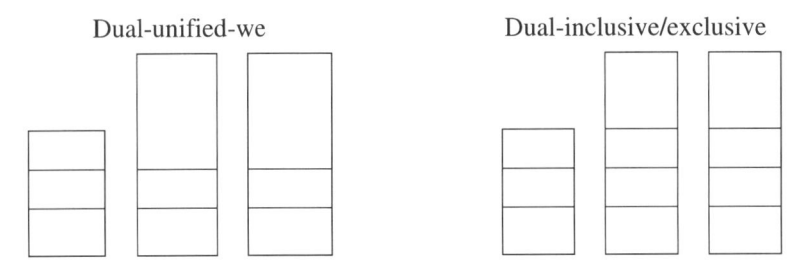

FIG. 7.3. *Common paradigmatic structures with dual marking*

been attested in more than three genetically independent cases are classified here as semi-common. These semi-common patterns are still rather rare; maybe 'semi-rare' would have been a better name. However, I have kept to the name 'semi-common' that has already been used in Chapter 4. The common and semi-common patterns will be summarized below.

The two most frequent and most widespread paradigmatic structures, classified as common, are the DUAL-UNIFIED-WE paradigm (see Section 7.3.2) and the DUAL-INCLUSIVE/EXCLUSIVE paradigm (see Section 7.5.2). These patterns are graphically represented in Figure 7.3. Both these patterns are attested throughout the world's languages, but they are most often found in a few specific areas or linguistic families. Both patterns are found regularly among the Pama-Nyungan languages, among the Tibeto-Burman languages, and among the languages from North America. Besides these shared preferences, the dual-unified-we pattern is also attested in Eurasia and among the Papuan languages from New Guinea. In contrast, the dual-inclusive/exclusive pattern is also common among the Oceanic languages.

The first two of the seven semi-common patterns are shown in Figure 7.4. Structurally, both patterns have a distinction between minimal and augmented inclusive. Areally, both patterns are almost exclusively found in northern Australia. The best-known of these patterns is the UNIT-AUGMENTED paradigm (see Section 7.6). A variant of the unit-augmented paradigm is the PARTIAL-UNIT-AUGMENTED paradigm (see Section 7.5.3). The only difference between the two is

Partial-unit-augmented   Unit-augmented

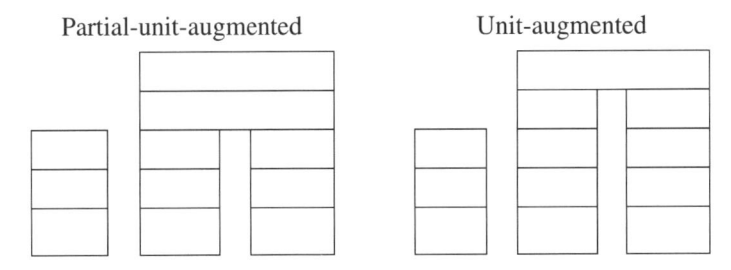

FIG. 7.4. *Semi-common patterns with a dual and a minimal/augmented opposition*

238 *Number Incorporated*

Inclusive/exclusive
in plural only

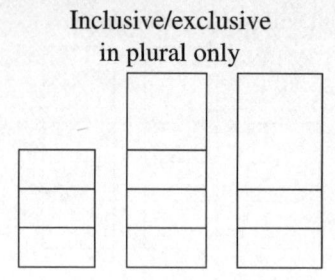

FIG. 7.5. *Semi-common pattern with a dual-3we structure*

the presence or absence of restricted 1+2+3 ('inclusive trial'). The partial-unit-augmented paradigm is functionally equivalent to the dual-inclusive/exclusive type (as shown in Figure 7.3). However, the morphological structure and areal distribution of the partial-unit-augmented paradigms indicate a connection to the unit-augmented paradigm.

There are many paradigmatic variants attested with three forms for 'we'. All these paradigmatic possibilities have been combined under the heading of DUAL-3WE (see Section 7.4). The referential values of these three different forms for 'we' are highly variable. In Section 9.5, it will be argued that the dual-3we patterns are an intermediate stage in between various other paradigmatic structures, which explains their highly variable nature. The great majority of dual-3we paradigms are found in northern Australia and in south-eastern New Guinea. All these patterns are idiosyncrasies within their close family. The paradigmatic structure that appears to be slightly more widespread than the others is shown in Figure 7.5. This semi-common pattern behaves according to the claim that the dual is more marked than the plural as it has an inclusive/exclusive opposition the plural, but not in the dual.

Two kinds of homophony have been distinguished: vertical homophony (between various persons in the same column) and horizontal homophony (between the same persons in various columns). A generalization that has already been observed before (in Section 4.7) can also be formulated for the paradigms as reviewed in this chapter: vertical homophony is fairly frequently attested in paradigms without an inclusive/exclusive distinction (see Section 7.3.3), but only incidentally in paradigms with an inclusive/exclusive distinction (see Section 7.5.4). The explanation proposed in Chapter 4 can also be used here. Namely, paradigms with an inclusive/exclusive opposition mark Pure Person: the person markers have to identify reference to speaker and addressee in all cases. The inclusive/exclusive distinction is a sign of Pure Person, as the combination speaker+addressee is structurally disentangled from the combination speaker+other. Once this opposition is present, other mixes of person (in the form of vertical homophony) are strongly disfavoured. In paradigms without an inclusive/exclusive opposition, in contrast, vertical homophony is a possibility of person

Survey of Restricted Groups 239

Kalam-type paradigm

Yagaria-type paradigm

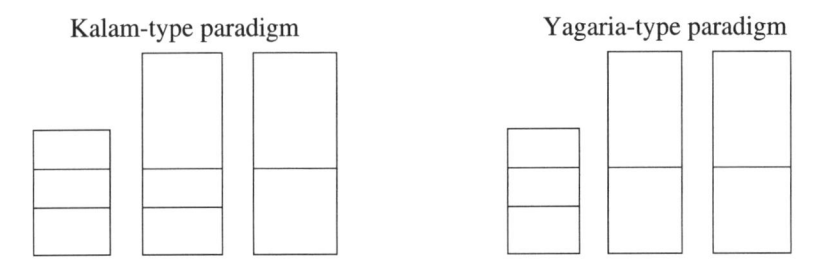

FIG. 7.6. *Semi-common patterns with a dual and vertical homophony*

marking. Only when the marking of inclusive and exclusive is combined is it possible for the reference to different persons to be homophonous.

The two semi-common paradigmatic structures with vertical homophony (and no inclusive/exclusive opposition) are shown in Figure 7.6. These patterns both have vertical homophony between the second and the third person. The KALAM-TYPE shows a vertical homophony in the dual only; the YAGARIA-TYPE shows the same vertical homophony both in the dual and in the plural. Vertical homophony between second and third person is quite frequent in paradigms with dual marking, although mainly attested in Papuan languages. Almost all examples of the two paradigmatic structures, as shown in Figure 7.6, are from the south-eastern part of New Guinea, with a strong emphasis on the East New Guinea Highlands (see Section 7.3.3). The other possible kinds of vertical homophony (between first and second person or between first and third person) are extremely rare in dual marking.

In paradigms without dual marking, as discussed earlier, horizontal homophony is particularly common (see Section 4.7). In contrast, horizontal homophony in paradigms with dual marking is rare (see Sections 7.3.4 and 7.5.4). One pattern, as shown in Figure 7.7, barely offers more than three examples, which gives it credit as semi-common here—roughly in line with Humboldt's claim as quoted at the start of this chapter. However, the number of cases is low and the variety of horizontal homophony is large; no predominance or hierarchy can be

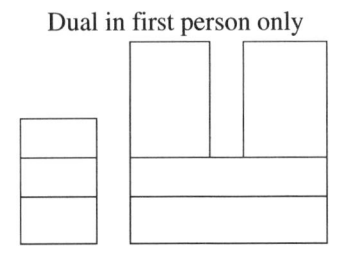

Dual in first person only

FIG. 7.7. *Semi-common pattern with a dual and horizontal homophony*

240   *Number Incorporated*

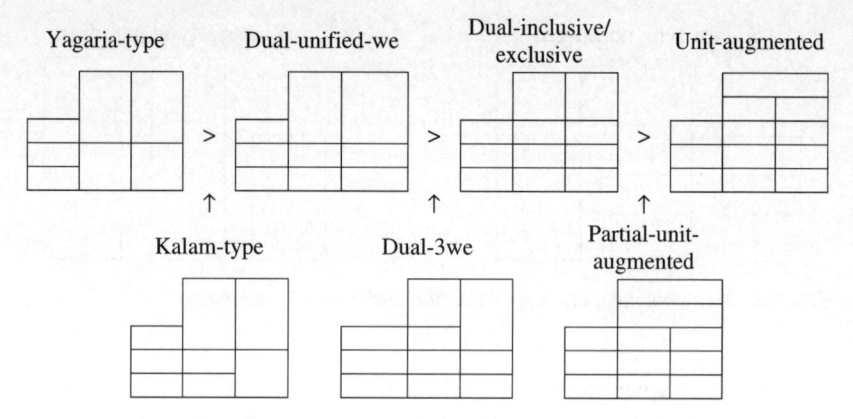

FIG. 7.8. *The Dual Explicitness Hierarchy and some intermediate forms*

confidently based upon such a set of cases. I will disregard this pattern in formulating any generalizations later on. A strong generalization concerning horizontal homophony is that horizontal homophony is almost exclusively attested between the restricted ('dual') and group ('plural') columns, in concord with markedness considerations.

Discounting the pattern with horizontal homophony, the remaining seven (semi-)common pattern are combined into the DUAL EXPLICITNESS HIERARCHY, in parallel to the Explicitness Hierarchy from Section 4.7. This hierarchy describes the tendency for dual marking to be more or less explicit along a line of four stages, illustrated in the upper row of Figure 7.8. The least explicit form of dual marking only distinguishes a dual 'we' from a dual 'non-we' (the Yagaria-type paradigm). In the next stage, the dual 'non-we' is split into a dual second person and a dual third person (the dual-unified-we paradigm). In the third stage, the marking of dual 'we' is split into an exclusive and an inclusive form (the dual-inclusive/exclusive paradigm). Finally, an opposition between the two inclusives is added to the paradigm (the unit-augmented paradigm).

The paradigms in the upper row of Figure 7.8 all show symmetry between the dual and the plural column. The other (semi-)common paradigmatic structures are shown in the second row of the figure. They can be interpreted as intermediate forms between the major stages of the Dual Explicitness Hierarchy.

The central part of this hierarchy is formed by the two most frequently attested and geographically most widespread paradigmatic structures (the dual-unified-we and the dual-inclusive/exclusive paradigm). The various paradigms around these two central patterns are less common. Moreover, these patterns are only found in a very restricted geographical area. All paradigms on the fringes of Figure 7.8 are almost exclusively found in north-western Australia and south-eastern New Guinea.

7.8 Conclusion

In this chapter, the large variety of possible ways of marking the dual in pronominal paradigms among the world's languages has been described. In total, thirty-three different paradigmatic structures have been attested, some more commonly than others. The higher frequencies of various paradigmatic structures are not accidental phenomena: the fact that some patterns are attested more often than others is the result of a multi-faceted force field that shapes linguistic structure. As a first impetus towards unravelling the complex of factors governing the structure of pronominal paradigms, a typological constraint on the organization of the dual marking in pronominal paradigms has been formulated in the form of the Dual Explicitness Hierarchy.

In the next chapters, I will investigate how this hierarchy of paradigmatic structures fares when the variation between closely related languages is considered. Miscellaneous cases of cognate paradigms will show not only that this hierarchy is a structural characteristic of human language, but also that it has chronic consequences.

Part IV
Cognate Paradigms

> The principle of imperfection is a general argument for history. In reverse, then, perfection becomes an argument against history—a denial, at least, of its importance, sometimes of its very existence.
>
> Stephen Jay Gould, *Time's Arrow, Time's Cycle*

Typology, by its very nature a synchronic kind of investigation, focuses on the major patterns of linguistic structure. Unfortunately, the little details that do not fit into the larger plan are much too easily dismissed as imperfections. Yet such imperfections can be fruitfully used to investigate the dynamics of linguistic structure—possibly leading to diachronic conclusions.

In the preceding chapters, various typological hierarchies have been established. In the following chapters, these hierarchies will be put to the diachronic test. If the typological hierarchies make any sense, then diachronic changes are expected to follow roughly along the lines of the hierarchies. This interpretation of the hierarcies is tested by a collection of cognate paradigms, a method that can best be described as being crypto-diachronic. It is still a typological investigation, yet it glances towards the historical-comparative method. In Chapter 8, the Explicitness Hierarchy and the Horizontal Homophony Hierarchy are investigated. In Chapter 9, the paradigms with dual marking are incorporated into the emerging web of similarity, a network of connections describing which paradigmatic structures are structurally—and diachronically—close to each other.

8 Connecting Paradigms
Person Paradigms through Time and Space

8.1 Introduction

Pronominal elements are among the most popular linguistic items for comparative research into the history and prehistory of language. The famous *Analytical Comparison of the Sanskrit, Greek, Latin and Teutonic Languages* by Bopp (1974 [1816/20]), one of the major early landmarks of the historical-comparative method, is a comparison of pronominal elements in different Indo-European languages. Pronominal elements have remained an important source of information in the historical-comparative line of research until the present day. In this extensive body of work, the locus of investigation has always been the individual pronominal elements. Although it is widely acknowledged that pronominal elements are bound into a paradigm, the paradigmatic structure as a whole has never been consistently included in a diachronic investigation. Such an investigation would ideally lead to a history of the structure of the paradigm, which is a different level of analysis altogether. In this and the following chapter, an attempt will be made to formulate a first outline of a theory on change of pronominal paradigms as a whole. This outline will be based on the typological investigations from the previous chapters.

In this chapter, the typological results from Chapter 4 will be used to investigate changes in paradigmatic structure. In that chapter, the major paradigmatic structures unmarked for specific numbers were summarized in two hierarchies: the Explicitness Hierarchy and the Horizontal Homophony Hierarchy. In this chapter, these synchronic hierarchies will be taken as hypotheses for the pathways of change of paradigmatic structure, to be tested by a collection of cognate paradigms. In the next chapter, the same method will be used to investigate the Dual Explicitness Hierarchy, as developed in Chapter 7.

In Section 8.2, I present the method that will be used to test whether the typological restrictions as formulated in the previous chapters can also be interpreted diachronically. The basic principle is to compile a sample of cognate paradigms, which are pronominal paradigms from closely related languages that show only small differences. Such small differences present a window on possible historical changes. The hypotheses to be tested by the collection of cognate paradigms are presented in Section 8.3. In the next two sections, the two hierarchies formulated in Chapter 4 are evaluated on the basis of cognate paradigms.

246   Cognate Paradigms

First, in Section 8.4, the Horizontal Homophony Hierarchy is scrutinized. This hierarchy turns out to be only partly interpretable in diachronic terms; paradigms seem able to move with big strides through this hierarchy. It is not necessary for a paradigmatic change to follow all separate stages of this hierarchy. However, it is not all chaos: there remain some barriers that paradigms do not seem to cross directly when moving through time and space. Second, in Section 8.5, the Explicitness Hierarchy is tested on the diachronic interpretation. This hierarchy appears to stand the test rather well. At least, it remains a good candidate for further diachronic investigation. Finally, in Section 8.6, the diachronically interpretable parts of the two hierarchies will be combined into a cognitive map of interconnected paradigmatic structures.

8.2   Cognate paradigms

The method that will be used to approach the diachronic dimension is to compile examples of COGNATE PARADIGMS and then interpret such exemplars as a window on the interrelations among different paradigmatic structures. The basic idea behind a set of cognate paradigms is that the paradigms are highly similar, but have a slightly different paradigmatic structure. Such cognate paradigms will be interpreted as showing a small (and perhaps even the smallest possible) paradigmatic change. In most cases that will be discussed, no stance will be taken as to the direction of the change. It would entail much more in-depth analysis of individual cases to establish a direction, and this would require too much analytic work to be able to retain the worldwide (and thus somewhat coarse-grained) perspective that is taken in the present work. Only a first step towards unravelling the diachronic dynamics of paradigmatic structure is taken here.

A few criteria have to be met for two pronominal paradigms to be branded as cognate. First, the two paradigms have to be found in two closely related languages. This criterion ensures that the similarity between the various paradigms is not a chance phenomenon. The relatedness between the languages has to be established on independent grounds, not on the basis of the form of the pronominal elements alone. For example, the Trans-New Guinea Phylum (a well-known problematic case for genetic classification in itself) is to a large extent established on the basis of resemblance between pronominal elements. This basis is far too small to compare the form of the pronominal paradigms. In general, the cognate paradigms presented in this chapter are found in very closely related languages, often on the verge of being dialectal variants. In most cases, the close relatives that will be taken into the comparison are both extant languages that are geographically not too distant from each other. However, in some of the cases that will be discussed in this chapter, the cognate paradigms come from 'diachronic' close relatives, i.e. from variants of the same language from different points in time. It is of lesser importance to the current aim whether the earlier variant is a

Paradigms through Time and Space 247

direct precursor of the later variant or whether it is a separate though extinct branch. For example, Gothic and present-day German are such diachronic close relatives, although Gothic is not a direct precursor of present-day German. The method used here is not a historical comparison, but a typological comparison that starts from the broad typological generalization and tunes into the fine-grained differences within a genetic group. The method is reminiscent of Greenberg's (1969: 184–94) intra-genetic comparison, and is in fact a combination of a typological and a historical-comparative approach. As this is still a rather unconventional method of which the specific problems and pitfalls have not yet been elucidated by a scientific history of trial and error, I will cautiously refer to it as a CRYPTO-DIACHRONIC method.

For a set of paradigms to be called cognate, it is necessary, but not sufficient, for the languages from which the paradigms are taken to be cognate. A second criterion for pronominal paradigms to be called cognate is that the paradigms at hand have to be cognate themselves. This means that the individual elements in the paradigm are related both in form and in function, and that the syntagmatic role of the paradigm is roughly identical within the structure of both languages. Consider as an example the present tense suffixes from Standard German and Standard Dutch (without inversion), as shown in (8.1). There is no doubt about the close relationship between the two languages within the West Germanic branch of the Indo-European stock. More importantly, the suffixes themselves show a strong resemblance, seen most strongly in the suffixes -*t* and -*en*, which are related both in form and function. Also, both paradigms play a roughly comparable role in the structure of the language, as both are used to mark present tense by suffixation to a verb.

(8.1) Continental Germanic present subject suffixes

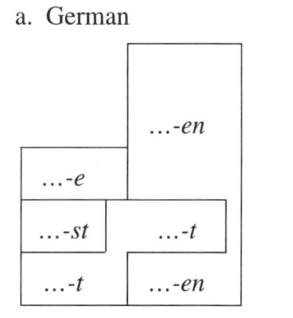

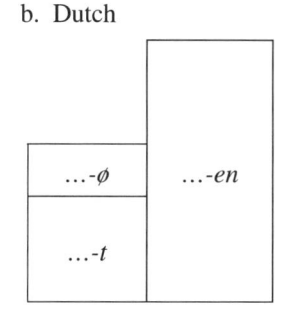

a. German

	...-*en*
...-*e*	
...-*st*	...-*t*
...-*t*	...-*en*

b. Dutch

	...-*en*
...-∅	
...-*t*	

The final criterion for two paradigms to be included here is that the paradigms have to show a small paradigmatic difference. These paradigmatic differences are the crux of the present chapter, as they present a window on the dynamics of paradigmatic structure. The preceding criteria ensure that the compared paradigms are almost identical. The attested differences in paradigmatic structure are thus small (perhaps the smallest possible) differences in paradigmatic structure. The cognate paradigms presented in this chapter differ only in one morpheme—or in very few semantically related morphemes. I have searched for examples that are extremely closely related, so any intermediate steps seem unwarranted for a connection between the cognate paradigms. For example, the singular homophony in the Dutch suffixes (addressee and other are marked identical by -*t*) is not found in German.

In this example, it is known that the singular homophony is a later development. However, in most of the cases to be discussed there is hardly anything known about the history of the languages. The comparison of cognate paradigms comes close to a historical investigation, but it should not be considered identical to it. A true diachronic investigation into paradigmatic structure would need to look much more closely into the minutiae of variation. In the present context, I will mainly survey cases where history has led to small differences in the paradigmatic structure. It is often difficult to establish a concise historical development that has led to the present situation only on the basis of the limited information that I consider. Only in some cases, I will claim that there has been a change from an extant paradigmatic structure in a particular language into a cognate paradigm of a close relative. Of course, all cases of cognate paradigms go back to a third, unattested, paradigmatic structure: the enigmatic proto-structure. Each of the two extant paradigms—now called 'cognate'—is the result of different changes from this historical predecessor. Literally speaking, the change is never from one cognate to another, but for both languages from the proto-structure to the extant structures. When I talk of a change from one extant structure to another, this should be taken as shorthand for a situation where one of the two structures is probably much closer to the paradigmatic structure of the proto-language than the other. An apparent change from one paradigm to the other could be due either to an addition or to a loss of morphemes. In most cases, I will not take a decision as to loss or addition. Consequently, I will propose that the different structures are related without proposing a direction of change. A true historical reconstruction of paradigmatic structure is left for another occasion.

To summarize, four criteria have to be met. Cognate paradigms have to be found in cognate languages, and the great majority of the individual morphemes in the paradigms have to be cognates themselves. Also, the paradigms have to have a functionally and formally comparable status within the language as a whole. Finally, the paradigms have to show some differences in their paradigmatic structure. This whole set of criteria is designed to leave only those cases that unambiguously show differences in paradigmatic structure that are small. Such examples of cognate paradigms are used here to argue that certain paradigmatic structures are similar. Paradigmatic structures can be shown to be closely connected by the existence of a set of cognate paradigms. All the examples of cognate paradigms that will be discussed in this chapter result in a web of interrelated paradigmatic structures, some more closely related than others.

8.3 Towards a theory of paradigmatic change

The present goal is to sketch a rough outline of the paths along which pronominal paradigms are connected, and to suggest that these connections can be interpreted as restrictions on the possible diachronic modifications of paradigmatic structure.[1] At present, reconstructions of a proto-paradigmatic structure are not informed by typological judgements of what is to be expected and what is unexpected (and so are to be taken with great caution), because there has been no typological investigation of the dynamics of paradigmatic structure. The present investigation is a first step towards that goal. This first step is to lay out the general lines of variation in the form of a cognitive map of interrelated paradigmatic structures. I hypothesize that paradigmatic change will proceed along the lines of this cognitive map. Examples of cognate paradigms form a window on a small part of the cognitive map, and a large set of such windows will hopefully give a better view on the outline of the whole landscape of paradigmatic variation.

The hypothesis to be tested in this chapter is that pronominal paradigms change along the lines of the two hierarchies formulated in Chapter 4: the Explicitness Hierarchy and the Horizontal Homophony Hierarchy. These hierarchies are interrelated as shown in Figure 8.1. The Explicitness Hierarchy is shown from left to right and the Horizontal Homophony Hierarchy is shown from top to bottom. The arrows between the paradigmatic structures represent the hypothesis about the expected cognitive map of paradigmatic structure. If paradigmatic change is to conform to the lines of the hierarchies, then examples of cognate paradigms are expected to turn up as links between adjacent paradigmatic structures in the cognitive map. Such examples only indicate that the hypothesis is feasible; they should not be read as an argumentation for a universal theory of paradigmatic change. Far from that: the possibilities for change are numerous, and the examples that will follow are only the first step to an encyclopedic collection of attested cases, which may lead in future to a fully-fledged theory of possible changes of a pronominal paradigm. The search for cognate paradigms has been restricted to the kinds of paradigm shown in Figure 8.1. These paradigmatic structures represent the common and semi-common patterns, as summarized in Section 4.7. The remaining rare paradigmatic structures do not fit into either of the two hierarchies that will be tested in this chapter, and will be disregarded here. This restriction to the more widely occurring paradigmatic structures has been made in order to have a chance to find multiple cases of a

---

[1] Laycock's (1977) description of the interrelation between various pronominal patterns in Papuan languages is an earlier investigation of the dynamics of paradigmatic structure. However, this short article is only an impressionistic sketch, without much data or an explication of the method of comparison. See also Mühlhäusler (1986: 168–71), who proposes a history of paradigmatic structure of pronouns in Creoles.

250 *Cognate Paradigms*

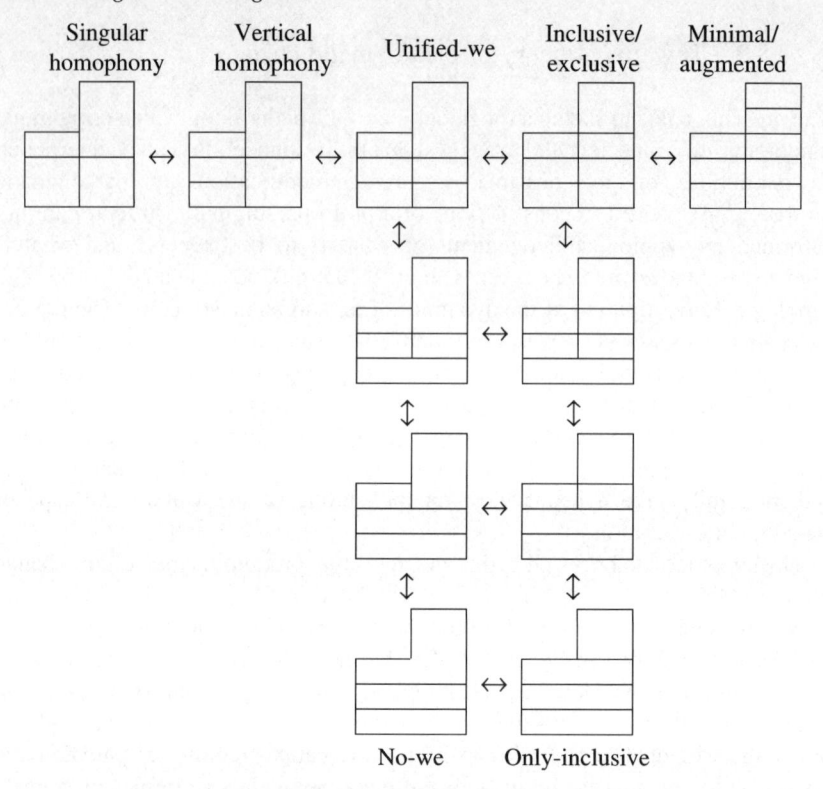

FIG. 8.1. *Hypothesized cognitive map, based on the Explicitness Hierarchy and the Horizontal Homophony Hierarchy*

particular connection between two paradigmatic structures. Good examples of cognate paradigms are not easy to find, which makes it necessary to claim some flexibility if a sufficient number of cases is to be produced.

A major problem with this method is that it is difficult to deal with connections that are not attested as a set of cognate paradigms. It is quite possible that, given a more extensive search, other examples would turn up eventually. In incidental cases, it is possible to construct an argument for the implausibility of an unattested connection by analysing the areal distribution of the various patterns. If two different paradigmatic structures are never found in the same geographical area, this is taken as an indication that the two structures are not closely connected (see especially Section 8.5.2). In most cases, however, the method of cognate paradigms can only be used as a way to test the validity of an independently formulated claim of paradigmatic connections. Given a hypothesis about how pronominal paradigms might be interrelated, examples of cognate paradigms can substantiate such a claim. It is in this sense that the examples in the present chapter should be interpreted.

8.4 Up and down the Horizontal Homophony Hierarchy

8.4.1 Preamble

The various paradigmatic structures on the Horizontal Homophony Hierarchy are repeated in Figure 8.2. The labels added to the paradigms in the figure refer to the marking of the first person complex, as discussed in Section 3.6:

- NO-WE refers to paradigmatic structures in which the marking for 'we' is identical to the marking for 'I'.
- UNIFIED-WE refers to paradigmatic structures in which there is one specialized morpheme for all meanings of 'we', comparable to the English pronoun *we*.
- ONLY-INCLUSIVE refers to paradigmatic structures in which there is only a specialized morpheme for the inclusive 'we' and the exclusive 'we' is identical to 'I'.
- INCLUSIVE/EXCLUSIVE refers to paradigmatic structures in which there is specialized marking for both the inclusive and the exclusive 'we'.

As a hypothesis, I propose that the paradigmatic structure is linked along the lines of the hierarchy, which would give rise to diachronic changes as indicated in Figure 8.2. If this hypothesis is any good, it is to be expected that there are pronominal paradigms in closely related languages that differ in only one step on this hierarchy. In this section, I will review a large set of examples to test this hypothesis. The connections attested will be described in two parts. First, in Section 8.4.2, the connections between the small paradigms in the upper left corner of Figure 8.2 are presented. These paradigms ('small', as they have only few oppositions) seem to be tightly interwoven, as numerous examples of cognate paradigms are attested

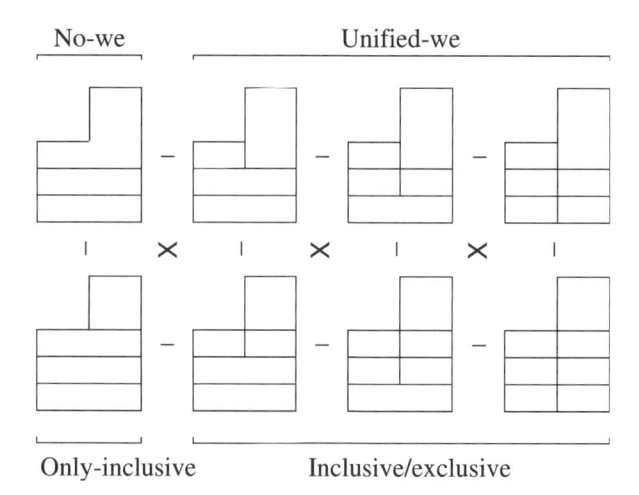

FIG. 8.2. *The Horizontal Homophony Hierarchy*

between the various paradigms. Second, in Section 8.4.3, the connections between these small paradigms and the larger paradigms, up the Horizontal Homophony Hierarchy, are presented. The picture becomes somewhat blurred here, indicating that the hypothesis can only approximate the diachronic dynamics of paradigmatic structure. An improved hypothesis is proposed in the summarizing Section 8.4.4.

8.4.2 Interconnecting the small paradigms

The small pronominal paradigms are found at the far end of the Horizontal Homophony Hierarchy. These paradigms have horizontal homophony in (almost) all persons; the only specialized non-singular forms are found in the first person complex. In this section, examples of connections between the three smallest paradigms (as highlighted in Figure 8.3) will be discussed.

Connections between these three paradigms are relatively easy to find. Examples from the Siouan, Chimbu, and Waris families are presented to illustrate the connection between these three paradigmatic structures. Some more examples will be shown *en passant* in the next section. In that section, the examples from Arawakan and Macro-Gé are of special interest, as they show that the diagonal connection in the triplet as highlighted in Figure 8.3 is also attested.

The first set of cognate paradigms to be reviewed here is found among the Siouan languages, spoken in northern USA. The agent prefixes of the different Siouan languages show only slightly different paradigmatic structures. This set of cognate paradigms presents an example of the connection between the three small paradigms. The agent prefixes from Hidatsa are shown in (8.2a). There are no specialized non-singular morphemes in this paradigm, although number can be marked by suffixes (Matthews 1965: 55, 71; Robinett 1955: 177). A specialized morpheme for unified-we is found in the agent prefixes from Mandan, shown in (8.2b). Otherwise, this paradigm from Mandan is identical to the paradigm from Hidatsa (Mixco 1997: 8). Finally, the agent prefixes from Winnebago are shown in (8.2c). This time, there is a specialized morpheme for the inclusive only (Lipkind 1945: 22; Greenberg 1988: 4–5, citing Susman).

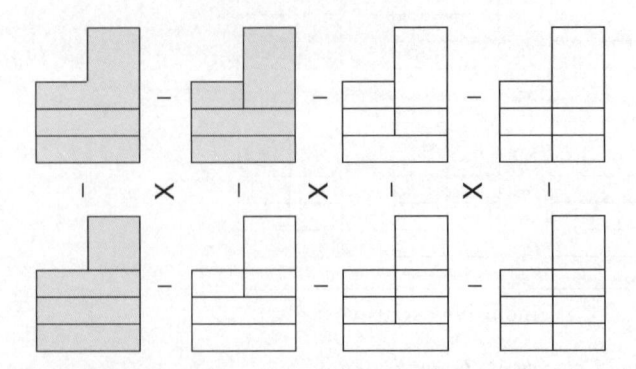

FIG. 8.3. *The small paradigms of the Horizontal Homophony Hierarchy*

(8.2) Siouan agent prefixes
    a. Hidatsa   b. Mandan   c. Winnebago

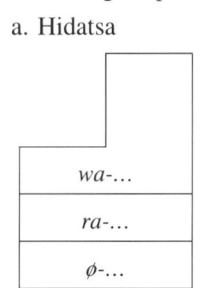

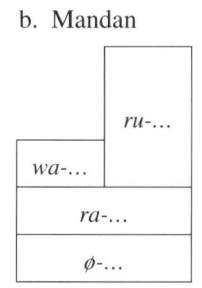

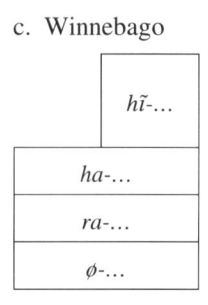

	Hidatsa	Mandan	Winnebago
		ru-...	hĩ-...
	wa-...	wa-...	ha-...
	ra-...	ra-...	ra-...
	∅-...	∅-...	∅-...

The Chimbu family is part of the East New Guinea Highlands stock, one of the parts that constitute the Trans-New Guinea Phylum in Papua New Guinea. The pronouns from the Chimbu family present an example of the smallest kind of paradigm that exists among the world's independent pronouns. These paradigms further illustrate the link between two different small paradigms. The independent pronouns from Golin (Foley 1986: 70, citing Bunn) and from Salt-Yui (Irwin 1974: 74) are identical. Both paradigms shown in (8.3a, b) fail to distinguish any specialized non-singular forms. The independent pronouns from Kuman are slightly different, as can be seen in (8.3c). Most salient for the present discussion is the existence of a specialized form for unified-we (Foley 1986: 70, citing Piau).

(8.3) Chimbu pronouns
    a. Golin   b. Salt-Yui   c. Kuman

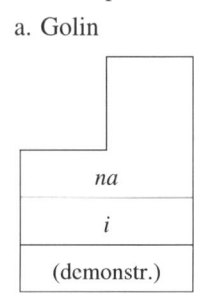

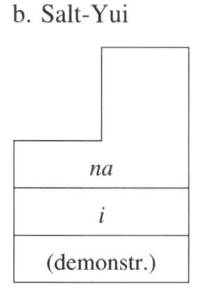

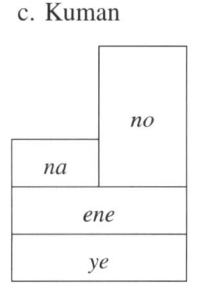

	Golin	Salt-Yui	Kuman
			no
	na	na	na
	i	i	ene
	(demonstr.)	(demonstr.)	ye

The Waris family belongs to the Border stock, which is also a part of the Trans-New Guinea Phylum in Papua New Guinea. The paradigms presented in (8.4) are the short forms of the independent pronouns, and are normally used in fluent speech. The long versions (with more oppositions) are used only when it is necessary to be referentially more explicit. In these paradigms, the phonological correspondences between Manem, shown in (8.4a), and the other two languages are rather opaque; only the first person singular is a clear cognate. On the (precarious) assumption that these paradigms are cognate paradigms, another connection between the various small paradigmatic structures is attested here. The Manem paradigm does not have any non-singular forms, although the plural marker *kiŋ* can be used to pluralize the reference (Foley 1986: 71; Voorhoeve 1975: 416).

254 Cognate Paradigms

A specialized inclusive pronoun is attested in the related Waris languages Amanab (Minch 1991: 31) and Imonda (Seiler 1985: 44), as shown in (8.4b, c).

(8.4) Waris short pronouns

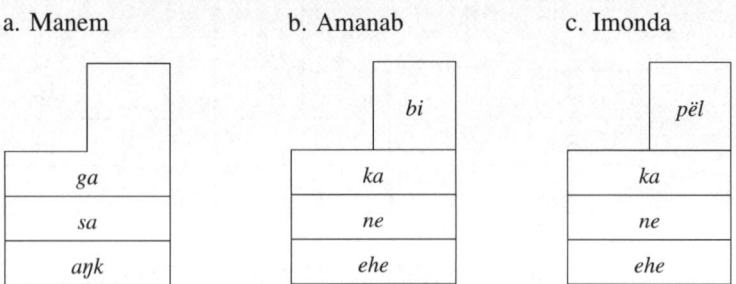

    a. Manem   b. Amanab   c. Imonda

ga
sa
aŋk

bi
ka
ne
ehe

pël
ka
ne
ehe

8.4.3 Up the hierarchy

The paradigmatic structure can be extended up the Horizontal Homophony Hierarchy. From the examples that will be presented in this section, it seems possible to take big strides through the hierarchy without passing through each stage separately. Once the first-person hurdle has been taken, the other non-singular forms can follow more easily. The structures that will be considered in this section are shown in Figure 8.4. Examples from Quechua, Arawakan, Macro-Gé, and Chinese will be discussed. All these families show pronominal paradigms that vary along the Horizontal Homophony Hierarchy, linking the smaller paradigms to the larger paradigms.

The first case comes from the Quechua languages in western South America. These paradigms show a connection between the small paradigms, discussed previously, and the larger paradigms with more specialized non-singular forms. The paradigms presented all mark the intransitive subject in the various Quechua languages. The paradigmatic structure with the smallest number of oppositions is found in Tarma Quechua, a Quechua variety spoken in Peru, and is shown in (8.5a). Plural marking exists, but is not part of the pronominal paradigm (Adelaar 1977: 89–93, 127–8). A slight departure from this paradigmatic structure is found

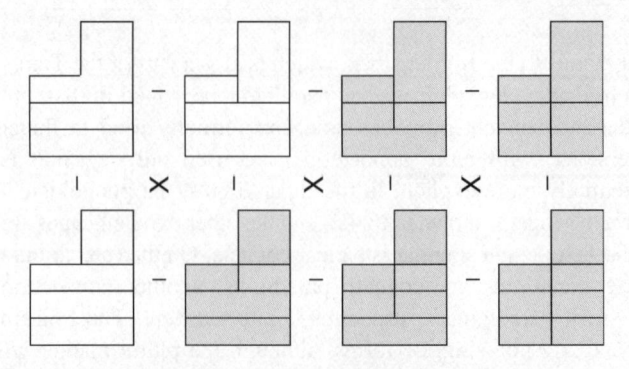

FIG. 8.4. *The larger paradigms that will be linked to the small paradigms*

Paradigms through Time and Space 255

in Huallaga Quechua. In Huallaga Quechua, the nominal plural marker *-kuna* is found in the pronominal suffixes with the first person singular only. The resulting paradigm is shown in (8.5b). The first person plural is an integral part of the pronominal paradigm, as it is an aberrant case among the pluralization strategies of Huallaga Quechua (Weber 1989: 95–6, 143–4). Both Huallaga and Tarma Quechua are central Quechua languages (subgroup I). The corresponding paradigm in the southern Quechua variants (subgroup IIc) is slightly different from these two central Quechua variants. Specialized marking of non-singular is found in all persons in southern Quechua. The suffixes from Bolivian Quechua are shown in (8.5c). This is the most extensive paradigm of the various Quechua subject paradigms (van de Kerke 1996: 120–5).

The cases reviewed until now mark an inclusive/exclusive opposition in the paradigm. However, in the northern variants of Quechua (subgroup IIb), the inclusive form *-nchi(k)* encompasses the same referential possibilities as the English pronoun *we*. This is rather different from the other varieties, where the morpheme *-nchi(k)* has only inclusive reference. The suffixes from Ecuadorian Quechua are shown in (8.5d), as described by Muysken (1977: 43–5; cf. Cole 1982: 143–5). It is possible to differentiate between singular and plural in the third person using a reciprocal suffix (W. Kusters, p.c.). The suffixes from Inga Quechua, a variant spoken in Columbia (also from subgroup IIb), is slightly different. As can be seen in (8.5e), an opposition between singular and non-singular in the third person is also grammaticalized here. The pluralizer *-cuna* is used to mark this opposition (Schwartz 1986: 423). The same morpheme is used in a different function in the paradigm from Huallaga.

It will be left to the specialist to propose the precise diachronic development that led to this variable situation (cf. Campbell 1997: 188–9). For the present purpose, it is sufficient to notice that these five paradigmatic structures are closely related, and that the similarities are roughly in line with the proposed connections as presented above. The two small paradigms (Tarma Quechua and Huallaga Quechua) are connected to larger paradigms (as in Bolivian Quechua and, in a different development, as in Ecuadorian and Inga Quechua). However, these connections do not follow the Horizontal Homophony Hierarchy step by step. Some stages appear to be taken at the same time. Apparently, these paradigmatic differences can arise in a relatively short time; the morphological changes that led to the variation presented have been quicker than the phonological changes that would lead to large differences in the morphemes themselves.

(8.5) Quechua intransitive subject suffixes

    a. Tarma Quechua   b. Huallaga Quechua   c. Bolivian Quechua

...-ñčik
...-:
...-ñ̊ki
...-ñ̊

...-nchi:	
...-:	...-:kuna
...-nki	
...-n	

...-nchik	
...-ni	...-yku
...-nki	...-nkichik
...-n	...-nku

256   *Cognate Paradigms*

d. Ecuadorian Quechua

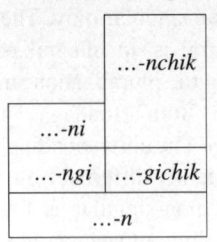

	...-nchik
...-ni	
...-ngi	...-gichik
...-n	

e. Inga Quechua

	...-nchi
...-ni	
...-ngui	...-nguishi
...-ø	...-cuna

The next set of examples of paradigmatic cognates is formed by the pronominal prefixes from various Macro-Gé languages, spoken in Brazil. These languages have been described showing variously organized strains of ergativity, which makes it difficult to compare functionally identical paradigms. The following paradigms are chosen because they show unmistakable similarity. The first case is the paradigm of the absolutive object prefixes from Xerente, shown in (8.6a). The prefix *wa-* has unified-we reference (Wiesemann 1986b: 365). The other two cases are paradigms of subject prefixes. The subject paradigm from Canela-Kraho is shown in (8.6b). In this case, the morpheme *pa-* has only-inclusive reference (Popjes and Popjes 1986: 175). The final case is the paradigm from Bororo, as presented in (8.6c). This paradigm has specialized morphemes for almost all non-singular categories (Crowell 1979: 206). The similarity between the Bororo and the Canela-Kraho paradigm is much stronger when compared to the Xerente paradigm. This indicates that the extra morphemes in the Bororo paradigm are probably added compared to the Canela-Kraho paradigm.[2]

(8.6)   Macro-Gé subject prefixes

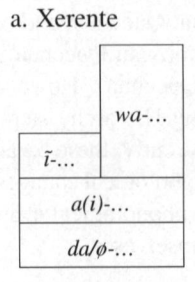

a. Xerente

	wa-...
ĩ-...	
a(i)-...	
da/ø-...	

b. Canela-Kraho

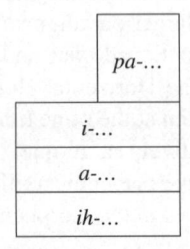

	pa-...
i-...	
a-...	
ih-...	

c. Bororo

	pa-...
i-...	xe-...
a-...	ta-...
u/ø-	e-...

---

[2] This proposed close link between the paradigmatic structures from Bororo and Canela-Kraho as opposed to Xerente does not coincide with the genetic classification (Campbell 1997: 195–6), or with the areal distribution (Grimes 1996: 22–3). Impressionistically, this situation seems to be widespread. The comparison of the paradigmatic structure often indicates a slightly different classification from the grouping based on mainly phonological characteristics.

Paradigms through Time and Space 257

Another group of cognate paradigms is found among the Arawakan languages. These languages are spread out over a large part of South America; Still, the subject prefixes as shown in (8.7) present a strong similarity between them. Unlike the Macro-Gé case above, the Arawakan examples present a link to a large paradigm without an inclusive/exclusive distinction. Exactly how these differences are to be explained by a diachronic change is a question that must be left to the specialists. The first paradigm is the subject paradigm from Campa, an Arawakan language spoken in Peru, shown in (8.7a). The central property for now is that the prefix *a-* has only inclusive reference (Payne 1981: 34; Reed and Payne 1986: 325). The next case is the subject paradigm from Ipuriná, an Arawakan language spoken in Brazil. The subject prefixes from Ipuriná are shown in (8.7b). This paradigm uses the prefix *á-* for all first person plural reference (Polak 1894: 7). In a recent description of this language, now called Apurinã, Facundes (2000: 384) describes a slightly different paradigm, shown in (8.7c), with a second person plural added. I do not know whether Polak missed this prefix or whether there was a linguistic chance. Finally, the subject prefixes from Bare, an Arawakan language spoken in Venezuela, are shown in (8.7d). These prefixes are rather different from the other two, although the similarity is strong in the singular forms. The most important difference is the set of overt non-singular forms for the second and third person (Aikhenvald 1995: 27).

(8.7) Arawakan subject prefixes
 a. Campa b. Ipuriná (Polak 1894)

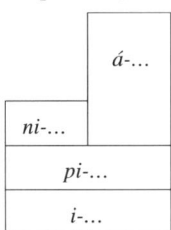

	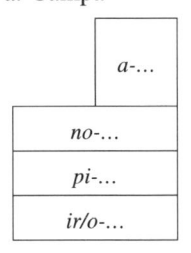 *a-*...
no-...	
pi-...	
ir/o-...	

	á-...
ni-...	
pi-...	
i-...	

 c. Apurinã (Facundes 2000) 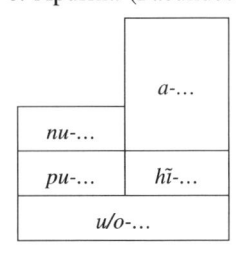 d. Bare

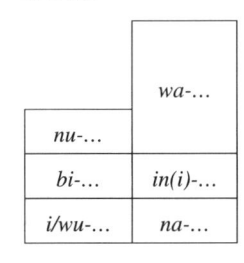

	a-...	
nu-...		
pu-...	*hĩ-*...	
u/o-...		

	wa-...	
nu-...		
bi-...	*in(i)-*...	
i/wu-...	*na-*...	

The final case rigorously cuts through the whole Horizontal Homophony Hierarchy. In Chinese, diachronic data show that a pronominal paradigm without any specialized non-singular forms developed a complete set of non-singular forms in one move, and in some variants added an inclusive/exclusive distinction on top of that. The classical Chinese language did not have specialized non-singular pronouns. The classical pronouns, as shown in (8.8a), show many different forms, probably distinguished by case. The history that led to the modern singular pronouns as shown in (8.8b) is rather complex, but the forms are undeniably related (Norman 1988: 89–90, 117–18). The modern Chinese varieties have specialized non-singular forms of the pronouns derived with a suffix *-men*. This suffix probably goes back to a compound nominal, meaning 'every person' (Norman 1988: 121). In most modern varieties of Chinese, there is a pronominal paradigm with a grammaticalized singular/non-singular opposition, as shown in (8.8b). In some northern variants, including the standard language, an inclusive pronoun, *zìjiā*, developed from the words for 'self-family'. This development led to the modern inclusive form *zánmen*, as shown in the (8.8c) paradigm (Norman 1988: 120–1, 157–8).

(8.8) Chinese pronouns
 a. Classical Chinese   b. Modern Chinese   c. Northern modern Chinese

| wŏ / wú / yú |
| rŭ / ěr |
| qí / zhi / yan |

	wŏmen
wŏ	
nĭ	nĭmen
tā	tāmen

	zánmen
wŏ	wŏmen
nĭ	nĭmen
tā	tāmen

8.4.4 Summary

The Horizontal Homophony Hierarchy is a strong typological generalization over the paradigmatic structures of pronominal paradigms among the world's languages. However, it is too strong when interpreted as a hypothesis for diachronic change. Most clearly, the connections on the upper side of the hierarchy are not followed strictly by the cases that were discussed. Paradigms move through the hierarchy quite easily.

Generalizing over the examples presented, a few tendencies for possible cognate paradigms can be formulated. First, the connections between the smaller paradigms are fairly strong. Many cases are attested showing a connection of these paradigmatic structures (see Section 8.4.2). In contrast, the connections to the larger paradigmatic structures are much messier than the hierarchy specifies. Various steps of the hierarchy can be skipped; paradigms can quite easily add (or lose) many of the non-singular morphemes. The different paradigms with

No-we   Unified-we

Only-inclusive   Inclusive/exclusive

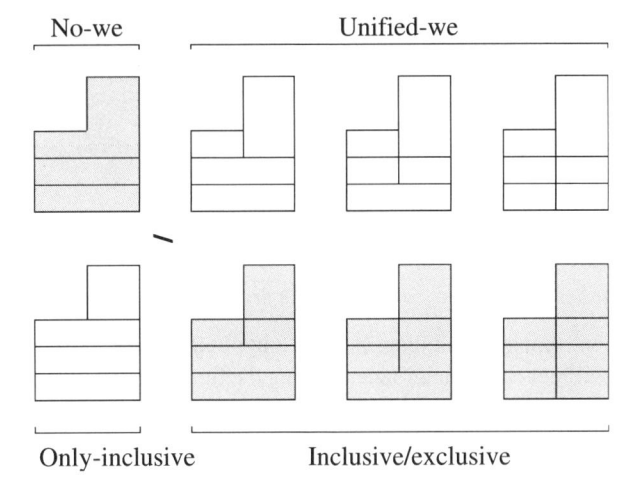

FIG. 8.5. *Unattested (diagonal) connection between no-we and inclusive/exclusive*

unified-we and inclusive/exclusive marking do not seem to be strictly ordered along the lines of the Horizontal Homophony Hierarchy (see Section 8.4.3). Finally, the diagonal connections are not very prominent among the examples attested, although some diagonal connections are found. The examples indicate that there is a possible connection between the unified-we and the only-inclusive paradigms (Siouan, Quechua, Macro-Gé, and Arawakan). However, the other diagonal is unattested. I found no connection between the no-we paradigm and the paradigms with an overtly marked inclusive/exclusive opposition (both paradigms are highlighted in Figure 8.5). These two paradigms are too distinct to be connected easily by a diachronic change. Both an inclusive 'we' and an exclusive 'we' are not added (or lost) at once. The route over one side or the other occurs more easily, adding one morpheme for 'we' at a time.

A more accurate picture of the possible connections between the various paradigms is obtained when only the structure of the first person complex is taken into account. From this perspective, the fine-grained connections from Figure 8.5 are collapsed into more broadly defined associations between paradigmatic structures. The resulting graph is shown in Figure 8.6. The only connection that is claimed here not to occur is the connection between no-we and inclusive/exclusive.

8.5 Up and down the Explicitness Hierarchy

8.5.1 Preamble

The Explicitness Hierarchy fares better than the Horizontal Homophony Hierarchy when reinterpreted as a hypothesis for diachronic change. The five stages of the

260   *Cognate Paradigms*

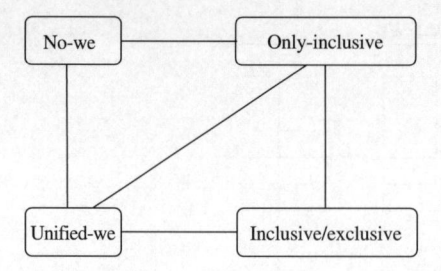

FIG. 8.6. *Connections attested between various types of the first person complex*

Explicitness Hierarchy are repeated in Figure 8.7. As a hypothesis, I propose that pronominal paradigms will develop diachronically along the lines of the hierarchy. If this hypothesis is any good, it is to be expected that there are pronominal paradigms in closely related languages that only differ in one stage on this hierarchy. In this section, I will review the examples that substantiate this hypothesis.

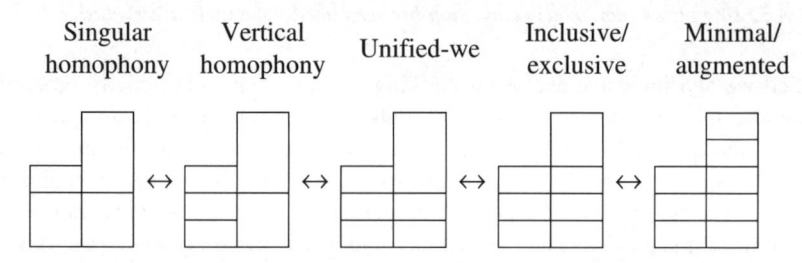

FIG. 8.7. *The Explicitness Hierarchy*

The presentation of the examples will follow the hierarchy from right to left; from more explicit to less explicit. First, in Section 8.5.2, the arguments for a connection between the minimal/augmented and the inclusive/exclusive paradigms will be discussed. In Section 8.5.3, the link between the inclusive/exclusive and the unified-we paradigms is taken up. Finally, in Section 8.5.4, the connection between the unified-we paradigm and the paradigms with singular and/or vertical homophony is discussed.

8.5.2 *Minimal/augmented inclusive (or not)*

The first step down the Explicitness Hierarchy is the connection between the minimal/augmented paradigm and the inclusive/exclusive paradigm. This connection is rather strong. A minimal/augmented opposition in the inclusive is only added when all other referential categories have already been grammaticalized. Two examples of this connection will be presented, one from the Philippines and one from the Chadic languages. Finally, some areal and structural considerations will be brought forward to show that the minimal/augmented paradigm is not connected to the only-inclusive paradigm.

The first case of a set of cognate paradigms on the Explicitness Hierarchy comes from the Philippines. These paradigms present a connection between a completely explicit paradigm (with eight different morphemes) and an almost completely explicit paradigm (with seven different morphemes). The independent pronouns from Cebuano are shown in (8.9a). Only the two kinds of inclusive reference are not distinguished (Wolff 1966: 14). The additional opposition between the minimal and the augmented inclusive is found in the closely related language Tagalog, as shown in (8.9b). The pronouns of Cebuano and Tagalog are almost identical. Only the Tagalog morpheme *tayo* is not found in Cebuano.

(8.9) Philippine pronouns
   a. Cebuano   b. Tagalog

	kitá
akú	*kamí*
ikáw	*kamú*
siyá	*silá*

	kata
	tayo
ako	*kami*
ikaw	*kayo*
siya	*sila*

The Chadic pronouns present another example of cognate paradigms at the high end of the Explicitness Hierarchy. The Ngizim perfective pronouns are shown in (8.10a). The third person plural forms are given as zero in the source, but zero independent third person pronouns are highly suspect (see Section 2.5.3). Yet, all other tense/aspect variations of the pronouns also show a homophony between third person singular and plural (Burquest 1986: 76). The paradigmatic structure of the Mandara completive pronouns, shown in (8.10b), is identical to that of Ngizim except for the opposition in the third person (Burquest 1986: 78). Most interestingly for the present purpose, Margi adds a minimal/augmented opposition (Hoffmann 1963: 73–4; Burquest 1986: 82), as shown in (8.10c). The dashes indicate that the Margi pronouns are clitics, which are added to a root *nà* to form independent pronouns.

(8.10) Chadic pronouns
   a. Ngizim perfective   b. Mandara completive   c. Margi roots

	wà
ná	*jà*
kà	*kwà*
	∅

	mà
yà	*ŋà*
kà	*kwà*
à	*tà*

	-mà
	-mər
-yù	*-'yà*
-gù	*-nyì*
-jà	*-ndà*

262   Cognate Paradigms

These examples from the Philippines and from Chadic show that there is a close connection between the minimal/augmented paradigm and the inclusive/exclusive paradigm. Greenberg (1988: 3–5) proposes another connection: between the minimal/augmented paradigm and the only-inclusive paradigm. Because of certain referential correspondences, this might seem a tempting proposal, but the areal distribution of the paradigmatic structures does not support this idea.

The reasoning by Greenberg (1988) goes as follows. The minimal/augmented paradigm (8.11a) is normally analysed with the inclusive dual 1+2 on a par with the singular persons, as shown in (8.11b). The second column is now formed by the 'augmented' versions of the first column. A natural connection for such a paradigm seems to be a connection to the same paradigms without the augmented forms (8.11c). Such a paradigm, with only the minimal categories, is identical to what has been called only-inclusive in the present work, as shown in (8.11d). Concluding, the minimal/augmented paradigm and the only-inclusive paradigm seem naturally connected.

(8.11)   a. Minimal/augmented   b. Minimal/augmented
            in present layout   in traditional layout

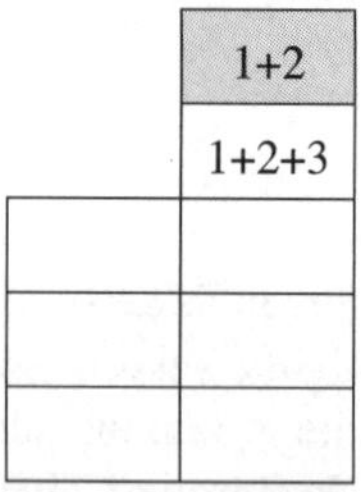

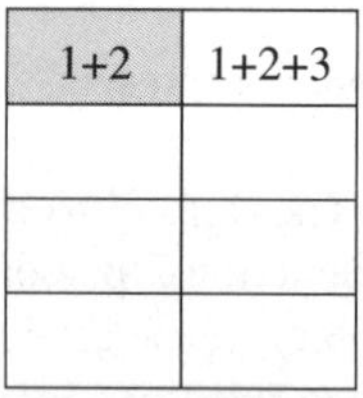

         c. Only minimal forms   d. Only minimal forms in the
            of minimal/augmented   present layout

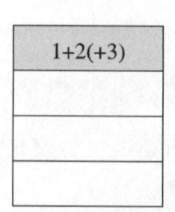

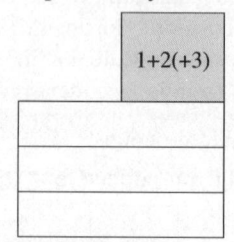

However, the areal distribution of these two paradigms brings a clear end to this strain of thought. The two paradigmatic structures never even come close geographically, nor are examples of both structures found within one and the same genetic family. In the worldwide survey, as described in Section 4.5.2, I found five regions where almost all minimal/augmented paradigms are attested. These areas typically include languages with large pronominal systems rather than small ones. The typical minimal/augmented regions are the Philippines, central Africa, south-western USA, northern Australia (especially non-Pama-Nyungan), and eastern New Guinea.[3] The only-inclusive paradigm is not found in these regions. The only-inclusive type is typically found in rather different areas: Irian Jaya, north-central USA, southern Mexico, and South America.[4] This geographical *dis*connection substantiates the typological picture that has been developed above, in which the only-inclusive type is far removed from the minimal/augmented type (cf. Figure 8.1).

Another argument against a direct connection between the minimal/augmented and the only-inclusive paradigm is the different morphological structure. If there were a set of 'minimal' and a set of 'augmented' morphemes, one would expect at least some of these paradigms to show a regular morphological derivation of the augmented set. In such examples, the augmented set should look like a regularly derived 'plural' of the minimal set. However, this is extremely rare, if it exists at all.[5] A morphologically regular derivation of the augmented inclusive and the exclusive (but not second and third person) is attested in Northern Paiute subject pronouns (Snapp et al. 1982: 61). The only completely regular derivation of an augmented set that I know of is mentioned in a footnote by Donohue and Smith (1998: 72, n. 4) for the Papuan language Kemtuik. I have been unable to find any other information on this language.

In some cases of a minimal/augmented paradigm, the augmented categories are morphologically marked. For example, Blake (1988; 1991) reconstructs a minimal/augmented paradigm for proto-non-Pama-Nyungan, shown here as (8.12). This paradigm turns out to have a regularly derived augmented set by the plural suffix *-rrV*. However, the roots of the minimal and the augmented set are already different. The plural marking is not necessary for the distinction. The 'augmented' number marking is probably a reinforcement, added only after the complete eight-way minimal/augmented paradigm arose.

---

[3] See Section 4.5.2 for the complete references; I will here only summarize the attested cases for the main areas. For the Philippines, see e.g. Tagalog, Maranao, and Hanunóo among many others. For central Africa, I mentioned Limbum, Bamileke, Babungo, Dii, Dan, Northern Looma, Ebang, Moro, Margi, Gude, Lele, Lamang, Hdi, and the Ron languages. For California, I mentioned Ute-Southern Paiute, Kawaiisu, and Southern Sierra Miwok; see also Northern Paiute as discussed in Section 4.6.6. For northern Australia, I mentioned Maranunku, Malakmalak, Wardaman, Bardi, Nyulnyul, Tiwi, and Uradhi. Finally, as Eastern New Guinea examples I mentioned Mountain Koiali, Santa Cruz, and Nanngu.

[4] See Section 4.5.2 for the complete references; I will here just summarize the attested cases for the main areas. For Irian Jaya, I mentioned Nimboran, Imonda, Amanab, and Salt-Yui. For north-central USA, I mentioned Winnebago, Pawneeî Wichita, and Caddo. For southern Mexico, I mentioned Sierra Popoluca, Chalcatongo Mixtec, and Ocotepec Mixtec. Finally, for South America, I mentioned Jaqaru, Campa, Maka, Canela-Krahô, and Tarma Quechua; see also the Carib paradigms discussed in Section 4.6.5.

[5] Greenberg (1988) already notes that the morphological structure of the minimal/augmented paradigms does not support his diachronic proposal. He tries to get around this problem by including morphological elements from outside the pronominal system in the analysis (in particular separate number marking). This strategy is not followed in the present work.

(8.12)   Proto-non-Pama-Nyungan pronouns

	Minimal	Augmented	
1+2	*nya	*nga -rrV	1+2+3
1	*ngay	*nyi -rrV	1+3
2	*nginy	*nu/ku -rrV	2+3
3	*nu/ngaya	*pu -rrV	3+3

8.5.3 Inclusive/exclusive (or not)

The next step of the Explicitness Hierarchy connects paradigms with an inclusive/exclusive opposition to paradigms without such an opposition. These two kinds of paradigm include all the major variants with some kind of horizontal homophony that were discussed in Section 8.4 above. In that section, various cases were presented that linked paradigms with an inclusive/exclusive opposition to paradigms without such an opposition. For the sake of completeness, I add two cases of cognate paradigms here, found among the Western Nilotic and among the Dravidian pronouns.

An example of this connection can be found in the independent pronouns of the Luo subgroup of Western Nilotic, spoken in Sudan. In (8.13a), the pronouns from Lango are shown (Bavin 1981: 90; Noonan 1992: 108). Shown in (8.13b) are the pronouns from Päri (Andersen 1988: 297). The only paradigmatic difference is the exclusive form in Päri that is not found in Lango.[6]

(8.13)   Western Nilotic pronouns
   a. Lango   b. Päri

	wán
án	
yín	wún
én	gín

	wání	
ʔáaní	ʔɔɔní
ʔíiní	ʔúunú
yíní	gíní

Another example is found in the independent pronouns of the Dravidian languages. The Dravidian independent pronouns usually do not have specialized third person forms, using demonstratives instead. The general structure of Dravidian pronouns is exemplified in (8.14b) with pronouns from Malayalam (Asher and Kumari 1997: 226–7, 255–8). In Kannada, the exclusive/inclusive

---

[6] These two languages are only taken to exemplify the pronouns in the Luo languages. Other languages from this family have strongly resembling paradigms. The pronouns from Anywa (Lusted 1976: 499; Reh 1996: 164) are almost identical to the pronouns from Päri. The pronouns from Shilluk (Westermann 1911: 13) and Acholi (Kitching 1907: 9; Crazzolara 1955: 64) are almost identical to the pronouns from Lango.

Paradigms through Time and Space 265

distinction that is found in most Dravidian languages has been lost. The pronouns from Kannada in (8.14a) probably have lost the inclusive/exclusive opposition under influence of the neighbouring Indo-Aryan languages (Sridhar 1990: 203).

(8.14) Dravidian pronouns

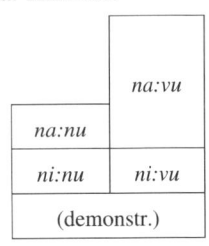

a. Kannada

	na:vu
na:nu	
ni:nu	ni:vu
(demonstr.)	

b. Malayalam

	nammaḷ
ɲaan	ɲaŋŋaḷ
nii	niŋŋaḷ
(demonstr.)	

8.5.4 Vertical and singular homophony (or not)

The final step on the Explicitness Hierarchy links the 'complete' unified-we paradigm to the paradigms with various kinds of vertical and/or singular homophony. It turns out to be much harder to find examples that illustrate this connection than it has been for the other connections that have been discussed. The reason is probably that there are many fewer paradigms with singular and/or vertical homophony when compared to the abundance of examples of the other paradigmatic structures. Also, the variation is large within the group of paradigms with singular and/or vertical homophony. Still, a few cases of cognate paradigms have been attested, in the Arawakan family, in the Germanic family, and possibly in the Gorokan family.

A connection between a unified-we paradigm and a vertical homophony is attested in the Arawakan languages in South America. Some other Arawakan structures have already been discussed in Section 8.4.3. For the present purpose, the agent prefixes from Bare (Aikhenvald 1995: 27) and Warekena (Aikhenvald 1998: 293) are of interest; they are presented in (8.15). The prefixes from Bare show a complete unified-we paradigm, distinguishing second from third person non-singular. In the cognate paradigm from Warekena, these two forms are identical, possibly a historical merger.

(8.15) Arawakan agent prefixes

a. Bare

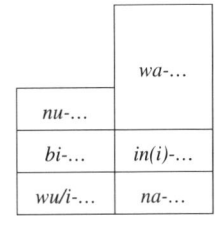

	wa-...	
nu-...		
bi-...	in(i)-...	
wu/i-...	na-...	

b. Warekena

	wa-...
nu-...	
pi-...	ni-...
yu/i/ø-...	

Cognate Paradigms

A well-known case connecting various forms of homophony is found in the Germanic languages. The suffixes shown in (8.16) are the present indicative inflections (dual forms are disregarded) from a few Germanic languages. The Latin suffixes are added in (8.16a) to represent the Proto-Indo-European structure, distinguishing six different morphemes. The Gothic equivalents to the Latin suffixes in (8.16b) still do not show any vertical or singular homophony, although a curious 'diagonal' homophony between the third person singular and the second person plural is found here. This 'diagonal' homophony is also attested in German (and in Middle Dutch), but in German also a vertical homophony is found. The suffix -*en* marks both the first and third person plural. Finally, in (8.16d), the Standard Dutch inflection (without inversion) has extended the vertical homophony of the suffix -*en* to all non-singular referential categories, and has added a singular homophony for addressee and other reference.

(8.16) Germanic and Latin present subject suffixes

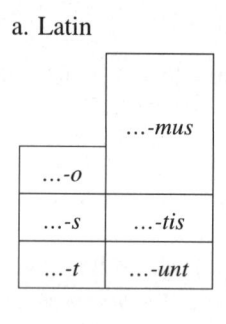

a. Latin

	...-*mus*
...-*o*	
...-*s*	...-*tis*
...-*t*	...-*unt*

b. Gothic

	...-*am*
...-*a*	
...-*is*	...-*iþ*
...-*iþ*	...-*and*

c. German

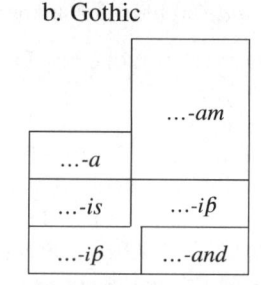

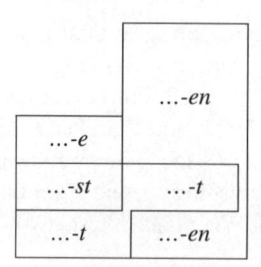

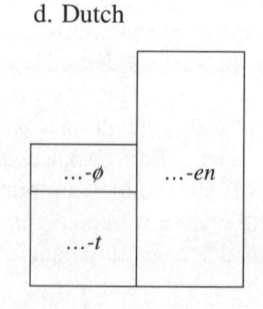

	...-*en*
...-*e*	
...-*st*	...-*t*
...-*t*	...-*en*

d. Dutch

	...-*en*
...-*ø*	...-*en*
...-*t*	

A final example is found in the Gorokan family, part of the East New Guinea Highlands stock in Papua New Guinea. Foley (1986: 248–9) reconstructs the independent pronouns from Proto-Gorokan as shown in (8.17). The non-singular shows a vertical homophony. However, none of the Gorokan languages (Foley discusses paradigms from Gende, Siane, Benabena, Kamano, and Fore) synchronically displays such a vertical homophony. All languages distinguish second from third person non-singular. So, if this reconstruction is valid, all these Gorokan languages lost the vertical homophony at some time in the past. Foley's argument for this peculiar reconstruction is that the second person plural can only be reconstructed as a compound of first and third plural. When it is taken into consideration that this kind of homophony is rather frequently attested among the non-Austronesian languages in New Guinea, this surprising paradigmatic structure for a reconstruction seems to make sense.

(8.17) Proto-Gorokan pronouns

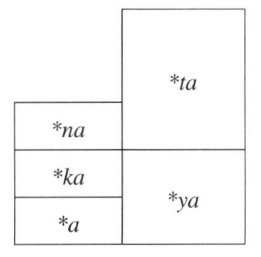

	*ta
*na	
*ka	*ya
*a	

8.5.5 Summary

The examples presented indicate that the Explicitness Hierarchy fares rather well in the diachronic interpretation. The different stages of the hierarchy are all attested by some examples of cognate paradigms. Examples that jump over different stages of the hierarchy are not attested. Of course, different kinds of cognate paradigm might turn up in further research, which would indicate that more possibilities for the diversification of pronominal paradigms exist through time and space. However, from the present data it can be concluded that the Explicitness Hierarchy is a good model to describe some aspect of the diachronic dynamics of pronominal paradigms.

8.6 Conclusion

In this chapter, the hypothesis was tested whether the synchronic restrictions on the structure of pronominal paradigms (as formulated in the form of hierarchies) can be reinterpreted diachronically. If this turns out to be feasible, then (part of) the explanation of the synchronic restrictions could be attributed to diachronic reasons (cf. Plank and Schellinger 2000). If the structure of human language tends to change in specific directions (for whatever reason), the results of these changes will be shown as a skewed distribution of the possible types in a sample of the world's linguistic diversity.

The method used to test the diachronic validity of the synchronic restrictions was to search for cognate paradigms. Cases of such cognate paradigms are pronominal paradigms from genetically closely related languages that are

268   Cognate Paradigms

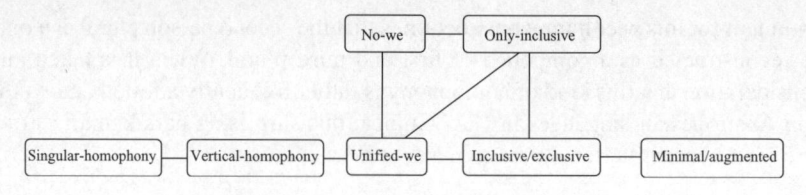

```
                    ┌───────┐    ┌──────────────┐
                    │ No-we │────│ Only-inclusive│
                    └───────┘    └──────────────┘
                        │     ╲       │
┌──────────────────┐ ┌──────────────────┐ ┌───────────┐ ┌──────────────────┐ ┌──────────────────┐
│Singular-homophony│─│Vertical-homophony│─│Unified-we │─│Inclusive/exclusive│─│Minimal/augmented │
└──────────────────┘ └──────────────────┘ └───────────┘ └──────────────────┘ └──────────────────┘
```

FIG. 8.8. *Cognitive map of interconnected paradigmatic structures*

functionally identical and phonologically closely related. Under these conditions, any differences that might occur in the paradigmatic structure is probably the result of a very shallow change. Examples of such shallow changes present a window on the diachronic connections between the various paradigmatic structures.

Only the major paradigmatic types from Chapter 4 were included in the present search for cognate paradigms. These major types are ordered by two interrelated typological hierarchies, the Explicitness Hierarchy and the Horizontal Homophony Hierarchy. The Horizontal Homophony Hierarchy did not prove to be a good hypothesis for diachronic change, although some aspects of it could be retained. It turned out that the fine-grained stages of the hierarchy could easily be passed by diachronically. However, a coherent picture emerged when the hierarchy was condensed to the structure of the first person complex only. The Explicitness Hierarchy fares much better as a hypothesis for the diachronic change.

Finally, the confirmed connections from the two individual hierarchies can be brought together in one cognitive map of interconnected paradigms, as shown in Figure 8.8. This map is put forward as an informed hypothesis about the lines along which paradigmatic change will happen. More research in detail is needed before the diachronic dimension can be said to be anywhere near being understood. However, the upshot of the present chapter is that a first outline of a theory of paradigmatic change is presented; one that is not based on stories of change from incidental examples, but based on the general patterns of pronominal paradigms as attested among the world's languages. In the next chapter, this cognitive map will be enlarged by paradigms with number marking.

9 Cognate Paradigms Revisited
Connecting the Dual

9.1 Introduction

A pronominal paradigm is not an isolated, unchangeable structure. Quite the contrary: the structure of a pronominal paradigm is highly variable through time and space, and the variation in paradigmatic structure, even between closely related languages, is remarkable. Individually, pronominal elements are relatively stable, but the structure of pronominal paradigms appears to change rather easily. The resulting variability of paradigmatic structure might make one wary of any typological generalization or diachronic analysis of the paradigmatic structure because both types of investigation need an object with some stability to yield results. However, each of these analyses can be combined to compensate for the other's deficiencies. Typology abstracts away from the small variations and focuses on the major transitions in the synchronic structure of human language. In contrast, historical-comparative study starts from small variations between close relatives to develop generalizations about diachrony. Typology can inform a comparative investigation about the chances with which a particular structure occurs. In return, comparative investigation can enhance a typology by adding transitions between the types distinguished.

In this chapter, I will use a crypto-diachronic method to incorporate the typology of dual marking from Chapter 7 into the cognitive map as established in the previous chapter. The typology of dual marking resulted in the Dual Explicitness Hierarchy. As a hypothesis, this typological hierarchy is interpreted as a pathway for diachronic change. I will use examples of cognate paradigms to test this hypothesis. If the hierarchy allows for a diachronic interpretation, I expect to find examples of cognate paradigms linking two paradigms that are adjacent on the hierarchy, approximating the dynamics of paradigmatic structure through time and space.

In Section 9.2, the typological hypothesis for the crypto-diachronic analysis is presented. Then, the attested connection between the various patterns will be discussed in three sections. First, the examples involving the typical DUAL patterns are discussed (the dual-unified-we paradigm, the dual-inclusive/exclusive paradigms, and dual paradigms with vertical homophony). These paradigms will be linked to each other and to the corresponding non-dual patterns in Section 9.3. Second, the MINIMAL/AUGMENTED opposition in all its variations (the minimal/augmented, the partial-unit-augmented, and the unit-augmented paradigms) will be shown to be connected in Section 9.4. Finally, the DUAL-3WE pattern and its multiple connections are discussed in Section 9.5. Abstracting somewhat from the quirky ways of language, the resulting web of interrelated paradigmatic structures will be reduced to a more conveniently arranged cognitive map in Section 9.6. This cognitive map will be extended with some more connections established in the previous chapter. The results of this investigation will be summarized in Section 9.7.

9.2 The typological hypothesis

It is highly instructive to analyse the variation between close relatives. Closely related languages normally show small differences in the paradigmatic structure of their pronominal elements. Sometimes, these small differences are typologically salient divisions between major paradigmatic structures. Pairs of paradigms, which consist of different paradigmatic structures, yet built from clearly cognate morphemes, are called cognate paradigms (see Section 8.2 for a more precise definition of the notion of cognate paradigms). In this chapter, a large collection of cognate paradigms is investigated to show the interrelations between the major paradigmatic structures with dual marking, as established in Chapter 7. These major patterns are repeated schematically in Figure 9.1. This figure is an abstraction from the large variety of paradigmatic structures that were attested, as only the major patterns are presented here (see Section 7.4).

The patterns from Figure 9.1 will not only be linked to each other, they will also be linked to the major paradigmatic structures without a dual. The patterns without a dual that will be considered in this chapter are presented in the upper row of Figure 9.2. These paradigmatic structures are ordered along the Explicitness Hierarchy, which runs parallel to the Dual Explicitness Hierarchy. As a diachronic interpretation, I hypothesize that the two hierarchies are connected to each other. This means that paradigms are expected to change along the lines as shown in Figure 9.2. If this hypothesis is any good, then cognate paradigms are expected to turn up linking adjacent paradigmatic structures in the figure.

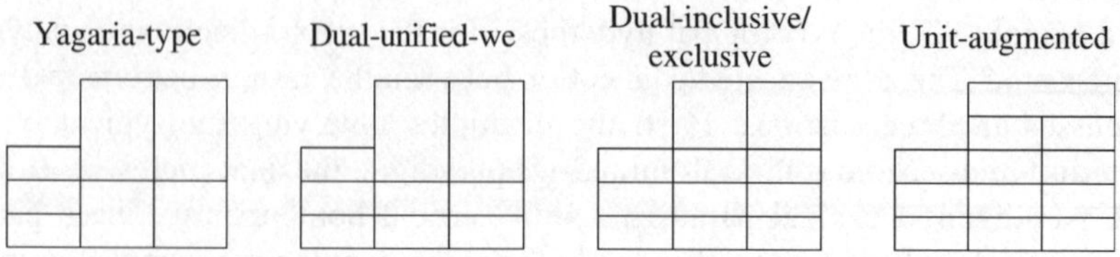

FIG. 9.1. *The Dual Explicitness Hierarchy*

```
                    ← Explicitness Hierarchy →
Vertical-                              Inclusive/        Minimal/
homophony       Unified-we             exclusive         augmented

   [paradigm    [paradigm              [paradigm         [paradigm
    box]    ×    box]      ×            box]      ×       box]
    |             |                      |                 |
   [paradigm    [paradigm              [paradigm         [paradigm
    box]    —    box]      —            box]      —       box]

Dual-vertical-                         Dual-inclusive/
homophony       Dual-unified-we        exclusive         Unit-augmented
                  ← Dual Explicitness Hierarchy →
```

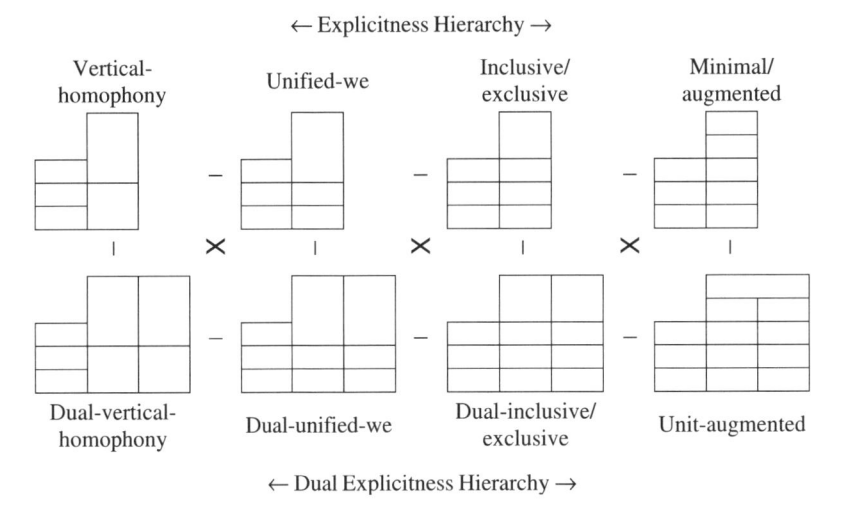

FIG. 9.2. *Hypothesized cognitive map, based on the Explicitness Hierarchy and the Dual Explicitness Hierarchy*

In what follows, I will present numerous cases of cognate paradigms, which will approximately confirm the hypothesized connections from Figure 9.2. After each set of examples, I will give some arguments why specific links are not attested. These arguments are not final, and could be falsified by a good example showing unambiguously that a particular connection exists. However, as long as I do not know of any clear example that shows such a direct connection, I assume that these links do not exist.

9.3 Linking the major dual paradigms

9.3.1 Preamble

In this first part of the discussion of the cognate paradigms, I will present examples of cognate paradigms involving the typical dual paradigms. They will be linked to each other and to the corresponding paradigms without a dual. Examples will be discussed from Finisterre-Huon, Pama-Nyungan, Uralic, Kiranti, and Miwok; a typologically, genetically, and areally highly diverse set of examples.

The first two cases, presented in Section 9.3.2, are from languages spoken in the Pacific. The Finisterre-Huon family is a group of Papuan languages from New Guinea and the Pama-Nyungan family is a large group of Australian languages. These cases show the interrelation between the major dual patterns. The next two cases, presented in Section 9.3.3, come from Eurasia. The Uralic

272   *Cognate Paradigms*

family is a group of far-flung languages spoken throughout Russia, and the Kiranti family is a sub-group of the Tibeto-Burman stock, spoken in Nepal. These examples link the major dual patterns to the corresponding patterns without a dual. Finally, the Miwok languages from California are discussed in Section 9.3.4. The various Miwok pronoun paradigms add some more connections between paradigms with or without a dual.

9.3.2   Different duals connected

The first two cases of cognate paradigms show connections between three major paradigmatic structures on the Dual Explicitness Hierarchy: the dual-inclusive/exclusive, the dual-unified-we, and the dual paradigms with vertical homophony. The independent pronouns from the Finisterre-Huon language Wantoat are shown in (9.1a). These pronouns have the typical New Guinea Highlands structure, showing a vertical homophony between the second and the third person non-singular (McElhanon 1975: 548). Wantoat is a language from the Finisterre range. In the independent pronouns from Kewieng, another language from the Finisterre range, the same structure is found. The somewhat loosely related languages from the Finisterre range belong quite probably to the same stock as the closely knit Huon family (Foley 1986: 244). The subject pronouns from the Huon language Nabak are shown in (9.1b). These pronouns are almost identical to the Wantoat pronouns, except for the extra opposition between the second and the third person in the non-singular (Fabian et al. 1998: 25). The third person pronouns in Nabak show signs of recent addition. The singular morpheme *ek* is compounded with the second person non-singular morphemes to form third person non-singular forms. The Nabak structure is probably diachronically later than the Wantoat structure. The same paradigmatic structure found in Nabak is also found in other Huon languages, such as Selepet, Ono, Kube, Kâte, and Kovai (McElhanon 1975: 548).

(9.1)   Finisterre-Huon pronouns
      a. Wantoat

		Group	Restricted group	
		nin	nit	1+2(+3)
1	nâ			1+3
2	gâ	gin	git	2+3
3	an			3+3

b. Nabak

	Group		Restricted group	
		nin	nit	1+2(+3)
1	neŋ			1+3
2	geŋ	in	it	2+3
3	ek	ekŋen	eget	3+3

Another link between various dual patterns is the connection between the dual-unified-we paradigm and the dual-inclusive/exclusive paradigm. Starting from the dual-unified-we paradigm, only an inclusive/exclusive distinction has to be added (both in the group and in the restricted group morphemes) to arrive at a dual-inclusive/exclusive pattern. In (9.2a), the independent pronouns from the Pama-Nyungan language Warrgamay are shown (Dixon 1981: 40). This is a typical paradigm among the Pama-Nyungan languages. In (9.2b), the independent pronouns from the neighbouring Pama-Nyungan language Nyawaygi are shown (Dixon 1983: 463–7). Almost the same pronouns are attested; the only difference is the appearance of separate exclusive forms. These exclusive forms are derived from the inclusive forms by a suffix, -liŋu. The inclusive forms in Nyawaygi are the same as the unified-we morphemes from Warrgamay in (9.2a). The dual-inclusive/exclusive paradigm from Nyawaygi is derived from a dual-unified paradigm as found in Warrgamay. This development is commonly attested among Australian languages:

> More than half the languages with a singular/dual/plural pronominal system show an inclusive/exclusive distinction, but there is no regularity to the distribution—languages of both types are found in every quarter of the continent. And whereas the four forms we reconstructed for 1 dual, 1 plural, 2 dual and 2 plural cannot be further analysed, it is nearly always possible to provide some analysis of inclusive/exclusive forms.... This suggest most strongly that an inclusive/exclusive distinction should not be attributed to pA [proto-Australian] but has evolved rather recently in a number of scattered groups of modern languages. (Dixon 1980: 335–6)

(9.2) Pama-Nyungan pronouns

a. Warrgamay

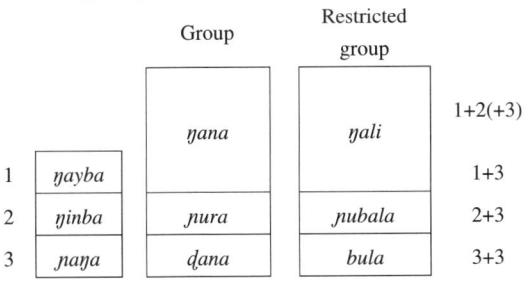

	Group		Restricted group	
		ŋana	ŋali	1+2(+3)
1	ŋayba			1+3
2	ŋinba	ɲura	ɲubala	2+3
3	ɲaŋa	ḍana	bula	3+3

b. Nyawaygi

		Group	Restricted group	
		ŋana	ŋali	1+2(+3)
1	ŋayba	ŋanaliɲu	ɲaliliɲu	1+3
2	ɲinba	ɲura	ɲubula	2+3
3	ɲaŋga	ḍana	bula	3+3

9.3.3 Duals lost and found

The next two cases of cognate paradigms will highlight the connections between the paradigms with a dual and the paradigms without a dual. A straightforward link is the connection between the unified-we and the dual-unified-we pattern. The only difference between these two patterns is a set of dual markers that is added to the set of group markers. This link is exemplified with independent pronouns from two Uralic languages: Udmurt (Csúcs 1998: 287) and Nganasan (Helimski 1998: 501) in (9.3a, b). The Nganasan paradigm has added dual pronouns by inserting a new set of group pronouns and reanalysing the old group pronouns as duals. This is a case of morphological markedness reversal as discussed in Section 6.3.

(9.3) Uralic pronouns

a. Udmurt

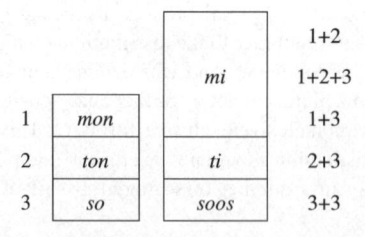

			1+2
		mi	1+2+3
1	mon		1+3
2	ton	ti	2+3
3	so	soos	3+3

b. Nganasan

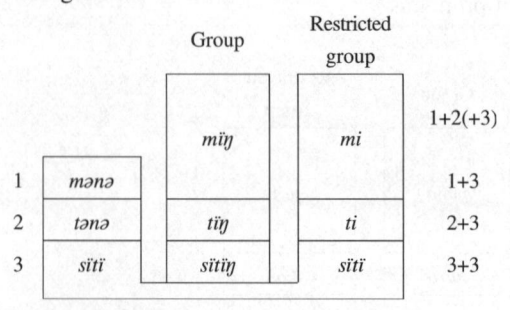

		Group	Restricted group	
		mïŋ	mi	1+2(+3)
1	mənə			1+3
2	tənə	tïŋ	ti	2+3
3	sïtï	sïtïŋ	sïtï	3+3

Connecting the Dual 275

The next set of cognate paradigms is found among the independent pronouns of the Kiranti languages (part of Sino-Tibetan), spoken in Nepal. The following languages have been selected out of the large variety of Kiranti languages because the pronominal forms are almost identical.[1] First, the pronouns from Thulung are shown in (9.4a). This paradigm has an inclusive/exclusive opposition, but no dual forms (Bauman 1975: 126–7). Second, the pronouns from Bahing are shown in (9.4b). These pronouns have a dual column, which results in a dual-inclusive/exclusive paradigm (Bauman 1975: 267). The dual column is clearly marked relative to the group column by a suffix, *-si*. However, it is not unequivocally clear that this represents a diachronically later addition because the suffix *-si* appears infixed in the 1+3 form *go:su:ku*. These paradigms from Thulung and Bahing are clearly cognate, but the historical direction of the changes leading to the present variety remains to be investigated by specialists. For the present purpose, it suffices to note that the dual-inclusive/exclusive paradigm is closely related to the inclusive/exclusive pattern.

(9.4) Kiranti pronouns
    a. Thulung

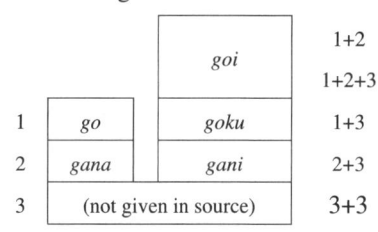

		goi	
			1+2
			1+2+3
1	*go*	*goku*	1+3
2	*gana*	*gani*	2+3
3	(not given in source)	3+3

    b. Bahing

		Group	Restricted group	
		go:i	*go:si*	1+2(+3)
1	*go*	*go:ku*	*go:su:ku*	1+3
2	*ga*	*gani*	*gasi*	2+3
3	*harem*	*haremdau*	*haremdausi*	3+3

9.3.4 Paradigmatic variation in Miwok

A striking case of cognate paradigmatic variation is found among the Miwok languages, spoken in California. This case was already observed by Freeland

---

[1] In contrast to the cases presented, the pronouns from other Kiranti languages are in need of extensive historical-comparative backing before it can be maintained that they are related; cf. Bauman (1975: 123–42), van Driem (1987: 25–8), and Ebert (1997: 43) for independent pronouns from some other Kiranti languages that are not immediately recognized as being cognate.

(1947: 35), Callaghan (1974: 384–5), and Greenberg (1988: 9–11). The differences between the independent pronouns of the various Miwok languages are small, and it seems to be within reach to reconstruct the complete history of the paradigmatic changes in the Miwok pronoun paradigm, though this task falls outside the scope of the present study. Clearly, a direct change from an extant paradigm of one of the Miwok languages into another, as proposed by Greenberg (1988: 9–11), does not do justice to the intricacies of the variation attested. Still, there are clear cognate paradigms with different paradigmatic structures among the Miwok languages. These indicate that there is a link between the inclusive/exclusive, the minimal/augmented, and the dual-unified-we paradigms. The orthography of the Miwok pronouns used here is taken from Callaghan (1974).

The differences in paradigmatic structures between the various Miwok languages centre around two linguistic elements, reconstructed as *ʔič·y- and *ʔoti··. The morpheme *ʔoti·· is a numeral 'two'; the history of *ʔič·y- is unknown (Callaghan 1974: 386). The reflexes of these proto-morphemes will be found in various functions in the different Miwok languages. The first variant is the paradigm of the independent pronouns from Southern Sierra Miwok, shown in (9.5a). This paradigm has an opposition between 1+2 and 1+2+3, forming a minimal/augmented paradigm. Both inclusive forms are made on the basis of the proto-Miwok *ʔoti··. The second part of these inclusive pronouns is, on the one hand, the first person plural suffix -me for 1+2 and, on the other hand, the first person inclusive plural possessive suffix -c·i for 1+2+3 (Callaghan 1974: 384; Broadbent 1964: 93). This possessive suffix -c·i is possibly historically related to the proto-Miwok *ʔič·y-. A different pattern is found in Bodega Miwok, shown in (9.5c). In this paradigm, the pronoun ʔóc·i is a reflex of the proto Miwok numeral *ʔoti·· by a regular sound change (Callaghan 1974: 385). In this case, the numeral 'two' has been reinterpreted as a first person dual and duals for the other persons are added analogously. In this way, a dual-unified paradigm has been formed.[2]

(9.5) Miwok pronouns

a. Southern Sierra Miwok

		ʔoti.me-	1+2
		ʔoti-c.i-	1+2+3
1	kan.i-	mah.i-	1+3
2	mi.ni-	mi-ko-	2+3
3	ʔis.ak-	ʔi-k.o-	3+3

---

[2] In Lake Miwok (which has the same paradigm structure as Bogeda Miwok) the pronoun ʔici is used by one of the informants as an idiosyncratic variant of ʔoci (Callaghan 1965: 283). This can be interpreted in different ways. Maybe an erstwhile opposition between ʔici and ʔoci has merged, or the pronoun ʔoci has replaced an older ʔici.

b. Plains Miwok

		ʔic.y-	1+2
			1+2+3
1	kan.i-	mas.i-	1+3
2	mi-	mok.o-	2+3
3	ʔis.y-	ʔi-k.o-	3+3

c. Bodega Miwok

		Group	Restricted group	
		má.-ko	ʔóc.i	1+2(+3)
1	kán.i			1+3
2	mí.	mí-k.o	mí-k.o̧s	2+3
3	ʔíti̧	ʔi-k.o	ʔí-k.o̧s	3+3

A direct link between the minimal/augmented pattern in (9.5a) and the dual-unified-we pattern in (9.5c) seems unlikely. Too many conceptual and morphological changes have to take place for a direct transition. An inclusive/exclusive pattern, as found in Plains Miwok and in Northern Sierra Miwok, seems a natural intermediate pattern. The independent pronouns from Plains Miwok are shown in (9.5b). The reconstructed form *ʔič·y- is attested as the inclusive first person plural ʔic·y-.[3] The pronoun paradigm thus forms an inclusive/exclusive pattern. This paradigmatic structure is an intermediate pattern between the clearly dual form in Bodega Miwok and the clearly inclusive forms from Southern Sierra Miwok. Geographically also, they represent a mediating

---

[3] There are some doubts about ʔic·y- as a general inclusive. Callaghan (1974: 386) analysed the reference of this morpheme as being minimal inclusive only (1+2), but she did not explain in which way the reference to the augmented inclusive (1+2+3) is made. In a later work, she glossed the meaning of ʔic·y- as 'we inclusive?/you & I' (Callaghan 1984: 296–7). She described a comparable restriction of the inclusive ʔic·y- to minimal reference (1+2) for the independent pronouns of Northern Sierra Miwok, a neighbouring Miwok language, which shows the same paradigmatic structure as Plains Miwok. Callaghan (1987: 397–8) glosses the morpheme ʔic·i- in Northern Sierra Miwok as 'thou & I'. However, much earlier, Freeland (1951: 30) analyses the morpheme ʔč·iʔ from Northern Sierra Miwok as a general inclusive, encompassing both the minimal (1+2) and the augmented (1+2+3) reference. In any case, the exclusive mas·i- cannot be used for the augmented inclusive, so a structure like Bardi in (3.15) is not a possibility (Catherine Callaghan, p.c.). This indicates that the morpheme ʔic·y is a general inclusive, which is probably only prototypically used for the speaker–addressee dyad 1+2.

278   *Cognate Paradigms*

position. Plains Miwok and Northern Sierra Miwok are spoken in between Southern Sierra Miwok and Bodega Miwok. However, the pronoun *ʔič·y-* is not indisputable as an intermediate between the other two languages. The major problem is that it cannot be reconstructed as an innovation of the numeral *ʔoti·-*. Still, the Miwok examples suggest two different links: between (9.5a) and (9.5b)—linking minimal/augmented to inclusive/exclusive—and between (9.5b) and (9.5c)—linking inclusive/exclusive to dual-unified-we. In other words, the inclusive/exclusive structure mediates between the other two. Whether the inclusive/exclusive structure as found in Plains Miwok can be identified with the proto-Miwok pronoun paradigm, from which the other two variants are derived, remains an open question.

9.3.5 Summary

The five examples of cognate paradigms discussed in this section show different connections between paradigmatic structures. These connections are summarized in Figure 9.3. The links on the upper row were established in Chapter 8. Several hypothetically possible connections remain open in the figure. First, connections to the paradigms with vertical homophony (on the far left side of Figure 9.3) are only sparsely attested. This is probably a result of the low frequency of occurrence of these patterns, which makes it less probable that a connection to these paradigms will be found among the world's languages. Second, connections to the paradigms with a minimal/augmented opposition (on the far right side of Figure 9.3) are not shown here, but they do exist. Cases of cognate paradigms involving these patterns will be discussed in the next section.

The most important missing link among the presented connections is a direct transition between the unified-we paradigm and the dual-inclusive/exclusive paradigm (see Figure 9.4). This direct connection is not attested. I hypothesize that too many paradigmatic changes have to happen at once for this transition to be instantiated by one change. This transition probably has to be made in several steps, for example, by taking a route over the dual-unified-we pattern, or over the inclusive/exclusive pattern. Of course, there might exist cases unknown to me that argue for this direct change, which I argue here not to be possible. However, I rest my case as a falsifiable hypothesis.

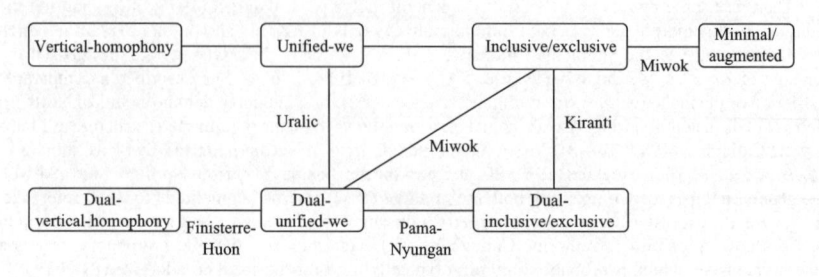

FIG. 9.3. *First approximation of paradigmatic interconnectivity*

Connecting the Dual 279

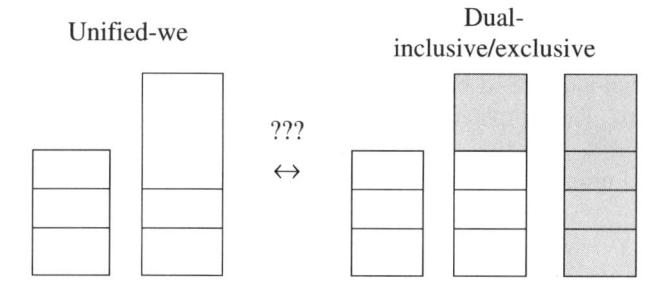

FIG. 9.4. *Unattested direct link between unified-we and dual-inclusive/exclusive*

9.4 Minimal/augmented and its variants

9.4.1 Preamble

In this section, I will present examples of cognate paradigms that link various paradigmatic structures that have an opposition between a minimal and an augmented inclusive. Three major paradigmatic structures with this opposition have been distinguished. They are schematically shown in Figure 9.5. These three paradigmatic structures are conceptually highly similar, and diachronically they seem to be closely related as well. Examples are presented from Nyulnyulan, Gunwingguan, and Gé. The examples in this section are somewhat biased towards Australia, because the unit-augmented paradigm and the partial-unit-augmented paradigm are typical Australian paradigms, only rarely to be found elsewhere. The Nyulnyulan and the Gunwingguan languages are both non-Pama-Nyungan families from Australia, to be discussed in Section 9.4.2. The case of the Gé languages from Brazil in Section 9.4.3, show that it is possible—though unusual—to find examples outside Australia.

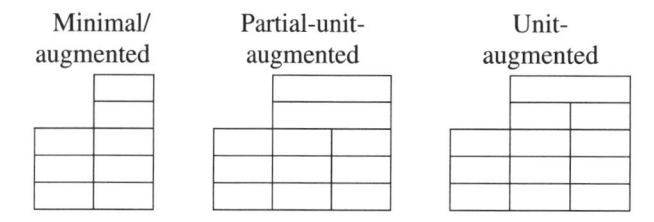

FIG. 9.5. *Major paradigmatic structures with a minimal/augmented opposition*

9.4.2 The Australian hotbed

The independent pronouns from the Nyulnyulan languages in Australia nicely illustrate the connection between the different variants of the minimal/augmented opposition. A case in point are the Nyunyulan independent pronouns from the languages Nyulnyul (McGregor 1996a: 23), Warrwa (McGregor 1994: 20–1),

280   Cognate Paradigms

and Nyikina (McGregor 1989: 446, citing Stokes). The Nyulnyul pronouns in (9.6a) form a minimal/augmented paradigm, the Warrwa pronouns in (9.6b) make up a partial-unit-augmented paradigm, and Nyikina in (9.6c) has a unit-augmented paradigm.[4] The morphemes are all clearly cognate.

(9.6) Nyulnyulan pronouns
   a. Nyulnyul

		yay	1+2
		yadir	1+2+3
1	ngay	yarrad	1+3
2	juy	kurr	2+3
3	kinyingk	(y)irr	3+3

   b. Warrwa

		Group	Restricted group	
		yawu		1+2
		yadirr		1+2+3
1	ngayu	yaarra	yaarra-wili	1+3
2	juwa	kurra	kurra-wili	2+3
3	kinya	yirra	jirra-wili	3+3

   c. Nyikina

		Group	Restricted group	
		yayoo		1+2
		yarrjoo	yarrjoo-mirri	1+2+3
1	ngayoo	yarrga	yarrga-mirri	1+3
2	joowa	goorrga	goorrga-mirri	2+3
3	ginya	yirrga	yirrga-mirri	3+3

[4] Nyulnyul is a dying language. The independent pronouns as shown in (9.6a) are dying with the rest of the language. Presently, the inclusive forms (1+2, 1+2+3) are hardly used by the last speakers of Nyulnyul. From older sources, the conclusion seems warranted that the paradigm as shown in (9.6a) existed until a few decades ago. McGregor explains: 'The 1&2 augmented forms [yadir] are absent from my corpus. The speakers who I worked with all employed the 1 augmented forms [yarrad] as general first non-singular pronouns, irrespective of whether or not the hearer was included. The full speaker very occasionally used the 1&2 minimal form [yay] for the speaker-hearer dyad. However, I was never able to elicit it systematically, and recorded it only a few times when it was uttered spontaneously' (McGregor 1996a: 22).

Another example linking different variations on the minimal/augmented theme is found in the Gunwingguan family in Australia. The independent pronouns from Ngalakan (Merlan 1983: 71) and Rembarrnga (McKay 1978: 28) are presented in (9.7a, b). The Ngalakan pronouns form a partial-unit-augmented paradigm; the Rembarrnga pronouns form a complete unit-augmented paradigm. There are various differences between these paradigms. There are different suffixes to mark these forms as independent pronouns (*-ka?* in Ngalakan and *-ʉ* in Rembarrnga) and the pronominal roots show quite some phonological differences. However, for the present purpose, the crucial correspondence between Ngalakan and Rembarrnga is the use of the cognate suffixes *-bira?* and *-bbarrah*, respectively. In Ngalakan, the use of this suffix leads to a partial-unit-augmented paradigm. In Rembarrnga, the addition of this suffix results in a complete unit-augmented paradigm.

(9.7) Gunwingguan pronouns

a. Ngalakan

		Group	Restricted group	
		yika?		1+2
		ŋurka?		1+2+3
1	*ŋayka?*	*yirka?*	*yirka?-bira?*	1+3
2	*ŋiñja?*	*ṇurka?*	*nurka?-bira?*	2+3
3	*niñja? / jiñja?*	*burka?*	*burka?-bira?*	3+3

b. Rembarrnga

		Group	Restricted group	
		yukkʉ		1+2
		ngakorrʉ	*ngakorr-bbarrah*	1+2+3
1	*ngʉnʉ*	*yarrʉ*	*yarr-bbarrah*	1+3
2	*kʉ*	*nakorrʉ*	*nakorr-bbarrah*	2+3
3	*nawʉ / ngadʉ*	*barrʉ*	*barr-bbarrah*	3+3

9.4.3 Paradigmatic variation in Gé

A final example showing a connection between the partial-unit-augmented paradigm and full unit-augmented paradigm is found among the prefixes of the Gé languages in Brazil. This is an interesting case, as it is the only example outside Australia that shows unit-augmented characteristics. However, it is not completely clear whether the non-singular marking is really grammaticalized. The sources are not explicit on this point. The Apinayé pronominal prefixes in

(9.8a) are described as a partial-unit-augmented structure (Callow 1962: 115).[5] A cognate paradigm is found in the absolutive prefixes from Kayapo, shown in (9.8b). This paradigm is described as a complete unit-augmented pattern, although the morphological status of morphemes in the paradigm is unclear. It might be the case that the number markers are morphologically independent.[6]

(9.8) Gé pronominal prefixes

a. Apinayé

		Group	Restricted group	
		paʔ-...		1+2
		mẽpaʔ-...		1+2+3
1	ič-...	mẽič-...	vaič-...	1+3
2	a-...	mẽa-...	vara-...	2+3
3	iʔ-...	mẽʔ-...	vaʔ-...	3+3

b. Kayapo

		Group	Restricted group	
		(gu) ba-...		1+2
		(gu) mẽ ba-...	(gwaj) ba-...	1+2+3
1	i-...	mẽ i-...	ar i-...	1+3
2	a-...	mẽ a-...	ar a-...	2+3
3	ø-...	mẽ ø-...	ar ø-...	3+3

Possibly, the Kayapo paradigm is better interpreted as an only-inclusive paradigm with separate number marking. The non-singular markers *mẽ* and *ar* are written as independent prefixes, indicating that these markers are not a full part of the pronominal paradigm (Wiesemann 1986b: 368–9). The same prefix *me* is also found in the closely related language Canela-Kraho, but in this case it is clearly described as an independent non-obligatory particle: 'Number is sometimes

---

[5] Note that the names for the inclusive and exclusive are reversed in the grammar. Callow (1962: 115, n. 1) uses the name 'inclusive' for what is normally called 'exclusive' and 'exclusive' for what is normally called 'inclusive'.

[6] Actually, the dual forms from Kayapo are designated as 'paucal' by Wiesemann (1986b). She does not present any further argumentation why these forms should have paucal rather than dual reference. It is possible that she uses the name 'paucal' in an idiosyncratic way to unify the referentially dual forms with the form *(gwaj) ba-*, which is strictly speaking a trial. Interpreted as such, Wiesemann's label 'paucal' refers to the same category that I have called 'restricted group', and which is normally called 'unit augmented' in the literature.

expressed by the particle *me* "plural", usually where the referent is human and, more specifically, Indian' (Popjes and Popjes 1986: 185). Another problem is the difference between the various forms of the inclusive. In Kayapo, the difference between the minimal inclusive (1+2) and the unit-augmented inclusive (restricted 1+2+3) is marked by the independent pronouns *gu* and *gwaj*. Strictly speaking, this difference is not part of the prefixal paradigm, as it is marked by independent elements. It is only because *gwaj* is possibly a contraction of *gu* with the dual marker *ar* that I have included this opposition in this paradigmatic structure.[7] If the number marking is not part of the pronominal paradigm at all (like in Canela-Kraho), then the paradigmatic structure of Kayapo is of a rather different type as shown here. More information on these languages is needed to decide on this issue.[8]

9.4.4 Summary

The three paradigms that were considered in this section are strongly connected. The minimal/augmented paradigm, the unit-augmented paradigm, and the partial-unit-augmented paradigm are conceptually closely related, as they all have an opposition between minimal and augmented inclusive. From the examples discussed in this section, it turns out that there are also close diachronic bonds between the paradigms. The various connections between the different variants of the minimal/augmented paradigm are summarized in Figure 9.6. They are added to the connections already established in

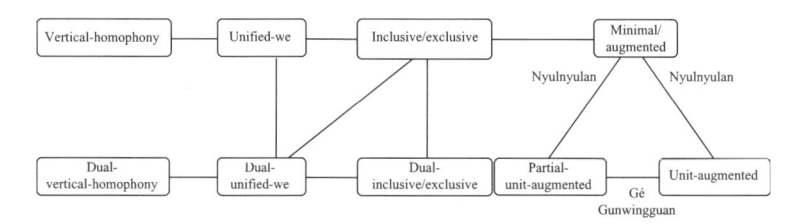

FIG. 9.6. *Second approximation of paradigmatic interconnectivity*

---

[7] The independent pronouns are 'almost obligatory' in case of the inclusive prefixes: 'In intransitive nominative clauses, the nominative [independent pronoun] is optional in the first, second and third persons, but almost obligatory (can be deleted in sloppy speech) in 1+2 person' (Wiesemann 1986b: 369). These obligatorily used pronouns have been added between brackets to the paradigmatic structure.

[8] A case that might shed some light on this situation is found in the Papuan language Amanab (Minch 1991: 31–2). In some crucial respects, the situation in the Amanab pronominal reference resembles the structure as described for the Gé languages. In Amanab, the normal form of the pronouns are proclitics with an identical 4-way paradigm as found in the prefixes from Canela-Kraho (see Section 4.5.6). The emphatic pronouns in Amanab add plural and dual marking to these proclitics. The paradigmatic structure of these emphatic pronouns in Amanab is a dual-inclusive/exclusive paradigm, roughly comparable to the Apinayé paradigm in (9.8a).

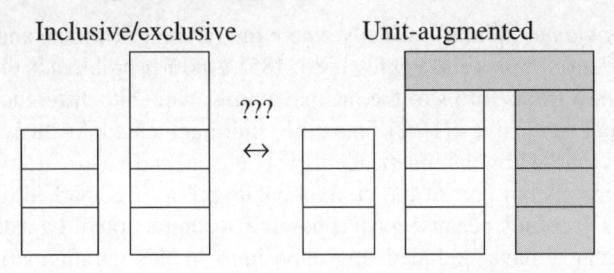

FIG. 9.7. *Unattested direct link between inclusive/exclusive and unit-augmented*

the previous section. Note that the dual-inclusive/exclusive and the partial-unit-augmented are referentially identical paradigms (see Section 7.5.3 for the reason to consider them separately).

Other direct connections probably do not exist. Specifically, one hypothesized link is left unattested. This missing link would connect the unit-augmented paradigm to the inclusive/exclusive paradigm. This hypothetical link is shown in Figure 9.7. I do not see how these paradigms could be directly connected. There are too many forms to be lost or added at once. The large number of forms would not be a problem if it were not for the diversity of the referential values of these forms. For this transition, no unifying feature is suitable to account for all forms at once. It is far more probable that this transition is mediated by other paradigmatic structures. I expect that developments as sketched in Figure 9.7 will only happen in a few separate steps. However, this hypothesis is open to falsification.

9.5 Dual-3we as an intermediate

9.5.1 Preamble

In this section, the dual-3we patterns are connected to the other paradigmatic types. The dual-3we paradigms do not form a homogenous group. Various different paradigmatic structures were distinguished in Section 7.4, which were discussed together because of two shared characteristics. First, these paradigms have three different forms for 'we' (hence the name '3we') and, second, these paradigms have a second and third person dual. Dual forms are also present amongst the three forms for 'we', but it is in this part of the paradigm that the variability of the dual-3we pattern prevails. This group of similar, but not completely identical, patterns turns out to be an intermediate structure, showing many different links to various other patterns. This diversity of connections confirms that the structural variability of the dual-3we paradigms is genuine and not an artefact of descriptive practices.

Examples are presented from Yalandyic, Oregon, Daly, Burarran, and Paman. Once again, these examples are biased towards languages from Australia. Only the case from the languages from Oregon is not from Australia. I expect this Australian bias to be a skewing caused by the areal distribution of the dual-3we paradigms themselves. The majority of the examples of dual-3we paradigms are found in north-western Australia and in south-eastern New Guinea.

The cases form Yalandyic and Oregon, presented in Section 9.5.2, show that dual-3we structures are connected to the major dual patterns. The cases from Daly, Burannan, and Paman, presented in Section 9.5.3, show that dual-3we structures are connected to the minimal/augmented pattern and its variants.

9.5.2 Links to regular dual patterns

The first case connecting the dual-3we paradigm to the other paradigms is found in the Yalandyic family (part of Pama-Nyungan) in Australia. The independent pronouns in Kuku-Yalanji show a dual-3we paradigm (Oates and Oates 1964: 7). The neighbouring close relative Guguyimidjir has a dual-unified-we paradigm (de Zwaan 1969: 135). As can be seen from the paradigms in (9.9a, b), almost all morphemes are identical. The main difference between the two paradigms is the presence (in Kuku-Yalanji) or absence (in Guguyimidjir) of a distinction between *ŋana* and *ŋanjin*. Only one of these—*ŋandan*, which is historically related to *ŋanjin*—is attested in Guguyimidjir, as described by de Zwaan (1969). However, Haviland (1979) notes that there is a geographical difference between the use of the two forms in Guguyimidjir. The form *ŋandan* is used in the inland; resulting in the paradigm from de Zwaan (1969) as shown in (9.9b). In the coastal dialect, the pronoun *ŋana* is used instead: 'most people at the Hopevale Mission now use *nganhdhaan* in preference to the coastal form *ngana*' (Haviland 1979: 65).[9]

(9.9) Yalandyic (Pama-Nyungan) pronouns
   a. Kuku-Yalanji

	Group	Restricted group	
1	ŋayu	ŋanjin	ŋana / ŋali(n) — 1+2(+3) / 1+3
2	yuudu	yurra	yubal — 2+3
3	ñulu	jana	bula — 2+3

---

[9] Haviland (1979) also reports the existence of an exclusive dual *ngalliinh*, although this form is not in common use anymore: 'most modern speakers do not make a distinction between inclusive ("you and I") and exclusive ("another person and I") in the first person dual, instead using *ngali* for an unspecified 1st person dual ("we two")' (Haviland 1979: 65).

b. Guguyimidjir

		Group	Restricted group	
		ŋandan	ŋali	1+2(+3)
1	ŋayu			1+3
2	nundu	yura	yubal	2+3
3	nulu	dana	bula	2+3

The two neighbouring languages Coos and Siuslaw in Oregon are probably, as far as is known today, not genetically related (Campbell 1997: 119, 309–22). However, the pronominal inflection of these languages presents a clear case of cognate paradigms linking the dual-3we pattern to the dual-inclusive/exclusive pattern. The Coos prefixes, presented in (9.10a), have a dual-3we structure (Frachtenberg 1922a: 321). The Siuslaw suffixes, presented in (9.10b), form a dual-inclusive/exclusive paradigm (Frachtenberg 1922b: 468). It is interesting to note that the cognate paradigms are prefixes in the one language but suffixes in the other. Probably, both paradigms are historically derived from an independent set of pronominal elements that were prefigated in Coos and suffigated in Siuslaw (Siuslaw shows an overall preference for suffixes). These 'proto-' independent pronouns are lost in the mists of time.[10]

(9.10) Coos/Siuslaw subject affixes

a. Coos prefixes

		Group	Restricted group	
		łin-...	îs-...	1+2(+3)
1	n̥-...		xwîn-...	1+3
2	eᵉ-...	cîn-...	îc-...	2+3
3	ø-...	îł-...	úx-...	2+3

---

[10] The independent pronouns that lead to the affixal paradigms are not the extant pronouns of either language. The extant independent pronouns in both Coos and Siuslaw are derived from the affix paradigms. In Coos, the independent pronouns are made by adding the prefixes in (9.10a) to a root -xka(n) (Frachtenberg 1922a: 395). In Siuslaw, the independent pronouns consist of the suffixes in (9.10b) added to the root nà- or nix(ts)- (Frachtenberg 1922b: 576).

b. Siuslaw suffixes

	Group		Restricted group	
		...-nł	...-ns	1+2(+3)
1	...-n	...-nxan	...-a^{u}xûn	1+3
2	...-nx	...-tcî	...-ts	2+3
3	...-∅	...-nx	...-a^{u}x	2+3

9.5.3 Links to minimal/augmented patterns

For the next case I return to Australia. The Daly family presents a case for a link between the dual-3we pattern and the partial-unit-augmented pattern. The subject pronouns of Ngankikurungkurr are presented in (9.11a). They form a dual-3we pattern with a gender distinction in the third person singular (Hoddinott and Kofod 1988: 94). The pronouns of the related Daly language Maranungku are shown in (9.11b). These pronouns form a partial-unit-augmented pattern (Tryon 1970: 16). These two paradigms are not as intuitively related as the earlier examples. On closer inspection, however, the differences are restricted to a few secondary aspects of the morphemes. First, the paradigms have different suffixes to mark number (*-gurr/rrim* and *-garri/rrike* in Ngankikurungkurr versus *-tya* and *-tamata* in Maranungku). When these differences are disregarded, the roots of the pronouns are almost identical. Of central importance for the present discussion is the difference between the inclusive forms in the two paradigms (*nayin* in Ngankikurungkurr versus *ngangku* and *kitya* in Maranungku). This difference makes these two paradigms a clear example of a cognate pair linking the dual-3we pattern to the partial-unit-augmented pattern.

(9.11) Daly pronouns

a. Ngankikurrungkurr

	Group		Restricted group	
		nayin		1+2(+3)
1	ngayi	ngagurr	ngagarri	1+3
2	nyinyi	nagurr	nagarri	2+3
3	nem/ngayim	wirrim	wirrike	3+3

b. Maranungku

		Group	Restricted group	
		ngangku		1+2(+3)
		kitya		
1	*ngany*	*ngatya*	*ngatamata*	1+3
2	*nina*	*nitya*	*nitamata*	2+3
3	*n(g)ankuny*	*witya*	*witamata*	3+3

Also in Australia, the Burarran family shows a link between the dual-3we paradigm and the unit-augmented pattern. The examples presented are the independent pronouns from Burarra (Glasgow 1984: 15), shown in (9.12a), and the independent pronouns from Ndjébbana (McKay 1990: 430; 2000: 203), shown in (9.12b). Only the masculine forms are shown here. The specialized feminine forms for the third singular and—quite unusually—for the dual forms are disregarded.

(9.12) Burarran pronouns

a. Burarra

		Group	Restricted group	
		ngarripa		1+2
		ngayburrpa	*ngatippa*	1+2+3
1	*ngaypa*			1+3
2	*nginyipa*	*anagoyburrpa*	*anagotippa*	2+3
3	*nipa*	*birripa*	*bitipa*	3+3

b. Ndjébbana

		Group	Restricted group	
		ngárrabba		1+2
		ngúrrabba	*ngirrikébba*	1+2+3
1	*ngáyabba*	*njírrabba*	*njirrikébba*	1+3
2	*njínjdabba*	*núrrabba*	*nirrikébba*	2+3
3	*nakébba*	*barrayabba*	*birrikébba*	3+3

A final case of cognate paradigms, again from Australian languages, connects the dual-3we paradigm to the minimal/augmented paradigm. This time, the examples are from the Paman family, a subgroup of Pama-Nyungan. A dual-3we paradigm is found in Wik-Munkan (Godfrey and Kerr 1964: 14). The conventional analysis of the three forms for 'we' is shown in (9.13a). However, in this case, a different layout seems more appropriate. This paradigm is shown in (9.13b), using an unconventional layout that suggests the possibility for a transition to the minimal/augmented paradigm.

The related minimal/augmented paradigm is found in Uradhi (Crowley 1983: 352–6). The Uradhi pronouns, as shown in (9.13c), may seem rather different, but they are closely related to those from Wik-Munkan. The difference is of a general phonotactic nature: Uradhi is one of the initial-consonant dropping languages of northern Australia. If the initial consonants from Wik-Munkan are removed, the Uradhi pronouns appear. Structurally, the pronouns *niya* (2+3) and *tana* (3+3) are lost in Uradhi. The former dual pronouns have taken over the complete non-singular marking.

Finally, the minimal/augmented paradigm can be extended with dual marking, leading back almost full circle to the paradigmatic starting point from Wik-Munkan. The newly added dual forms are found in Umpila, yet another Paman language (Dixon 1980: 355–6). As shown in (9.13d), Umpila has a partial-unit-augmented pattern, based on the same forms as Uradhi in (9.13c)—although in Umpila the initial consonants are preserved.[11]

(9.13)   Paman (Pama-Nyungan) pronouns

a. Wik-Munkan (version I)

	Group	Restricted group	
	nampi	*ngaali*	1+2(+3)
1	*ngaya*	*ngana*	1+3
2	*ninta*	*niya*	*nipa*	2+3
3	*nila*	*tana*	*pula*	2+3

---

[11] There is a strong affiliation between the pronouns from various Pama-Nyungan languages discussed in this chapter. All Pama-Nyungan examples are geographically located on or near the Cape York Peninsula, but show rather different paradigmatic structures. The pronouns from Kuku-Yalanji in (9.9a) and Wik-Munkan in (9.13a, b) are examples of the dual-3we type. Warrgamay in (9.2a) and Guguyimidjir in (9.9b) are examples of the dual-unified-we type. Nyawaygi in (9.2b) is an example of the dual-inclusive/exclusive type. Uradhi in (9.13c) is an example of the minimal/augmented type. Finally, Umpila in (9.13d) is an example of the partial-unit-augmented type. These paradigms are all clearly related to each other. The proto-Pama-Nyungan pronouns were probably of the dual-unified-we type (Dixon 1980: ch. 11; Blake 1988: 6). The development from there can probably be reconstructed as starting at the dual-unified-we, changing through the dual-3we pattern (with a possible side

b. Wik-Munkan (version II)

		Group	Restricted group	
		ngaali		1+2
		nampi		1+2+3
1	ngaya	ngana		1+3
2	ninta	niya	nipa	2+3
3	nila	tana	pula	2+3

c. Uradhi

		ali(βa)	1+2
		ampu(la)	1+2+3
1	ayu(βa)	ana(βa)	1+3
2	antu(βa)	ipu(la)	2+3
3	ulu(βa)	ula(βa)	3+3

d. Umpila

		Group	Restricted group	
		ŋali		1+2
		ŋambula		1+2+3
1	ŋayu	ŋana	ŋana-baʔamu	1+3
2	ŋanu	ŋuʔula	ŋuʔula-baʔamu	2+3
3	nhulu	bula	bula-baʔamu	3+3

9.5.4 Summary

The dual-3we type turns out to be an intermediate case between various paradigms with a dual. The various connections presented in this section are

route over the dual-inclusive/exclusive), to the minimal/augmented pattern, and eventually ending in the partial-unit-augmented pattern. Dixon (1980: 353–6) speculates about a reconstruction of a minimal/augmented paradigm for proto-Australian, partly on the basis of this paradigm from Umpila. The development outlined here seems to be a much better proposal to explain the structure of the Umpila pronominal paradigm. There seems no need to reconstruct a minimal/augmented pattern for all Australian languages (cf. Blake 1988).

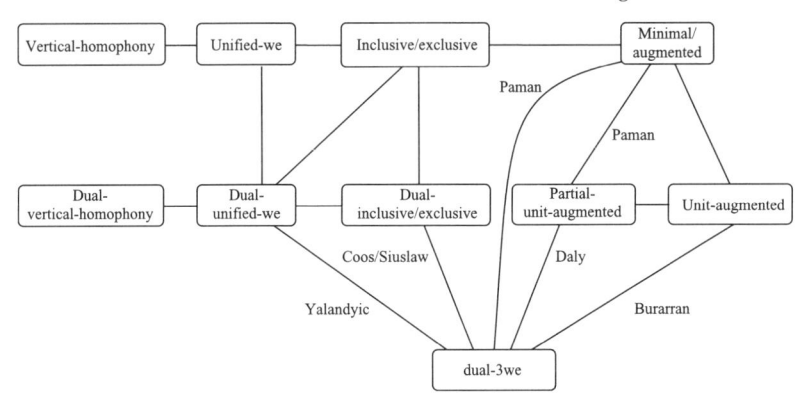

FIG. 9.8. *Complete version of paradigmatic interconnectivity*

summarized in Figure 9.8. I know of no direct connection between the dual-3we type and any other pattern. Perhaps some example will turn up in the future, but I do not expect this to happen. The overall impression is that the dual-3we pattern is clearly a dual pattern, mediating between other dual patterns. It is not related to the non-dual patterns such as the inclusive/exclusive or the unified-we patterns. There is a link to the minimal/augmented pattern because this pattern is conceptually an intermediate structure between the paradigms with a dual and the paradigms without a dual. The many different connections of the dual-3we paradigms give an impression of inherent variability. Consequently, the large variety of dual-3we structures (cf. Section 7.4) is genuine, and not an artefact of inaccurate descriptions.

9.6 Number marking incorporated

Two reductions of the complete set of paradigmatic connection will be made. As a result, the bewildering number of connections between the different paradigmatic types from Figure 9.8 will be reduced to a format that presents some promising typological generalizations. This reduced paradigmatic interconnectivity will be brought together with the analyses from the previous chapter. The result will be a cognitive map that shows the pathways through the similarity space of paradigmatic structure, directly linking paradigms that are cognitively near to each other.

The first reduction to be made is that the dual-3we pattern is left out. This pattern is never a typical pattern for a whole group of genetically related languages: all examples are incidental cases within their close family. Moreover, the dual-3we pattern turns out to be a mediating structure between the other paradigmatic structure with a dual. The general impression is that the dual-3we

292 Cognate Paradigms

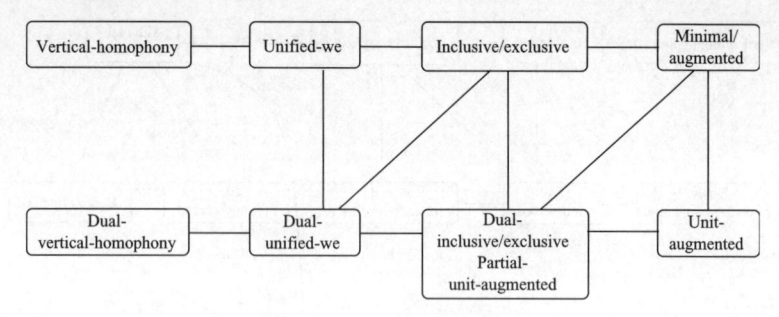

```
[Vertical-homophony] — [Unified-we] — [Inclusive/exclusive] — [Minimal/augmented]


[Dual-            ] — [Dual-      ] — [Dual-               ] — [Unit-
 vertical-homophony]   [unified-we ]   [inclusive/exclusive ]   augmented]
                                       Partial-
                                       unit-augmented
```

FIG. 9.9. *Reduced version of paradigmatic interconnectivity*

pattern is an incidental 'in-between' pattern, not a typical stable pattern for a human language (see Section 9.5). Second, the partial-unit-augmented pattern will be combined with the dual-inclusive/exclusive pattern. Both patterns distinguish exactly the same referential categories. The main difference (and the reason to keep them apart in the first place) was the morphological structure. The remaining set of paradigmatic connections is shown in Figure 9.9. This figure shows that many, though not all, of the connections from the typological hypothesis in Figure 9.2 (see Section 9.2) are attested.

However, not all hypothesized connections have been found. Notably, the diagonals from top left to bottom right do not show up. These connections both involve multiple category changes, and I have speculated that these changes happen in at least two separate steps. First, the path between the unified-we paradigm and the dual-inclusive/exclusive paradigm needs both an addition of a dual and an addition of an inclusive/exclusive opposition. These will not be added to the paradigm in one process. More likely, the changes will follow a slight detour through other, less divergent patterns. The other non-attested diagonal connects the inclusive/exclusive paradigm to the unit-augmented paradigm. This path needs both the addition of a dual and a separation of the two different inclusives. These changes will also not occur at once. In contrast, the two diagonals that are attested involve changes that can be accounted for by a single reanalysis. An inclusive can be reanalysed as a dual, trading, as it were, one category for the other. This reanalysis can only take place at the diagonals from upper right to lower left.

In Figure 9.10, the cognitive map is extended with some other patterns as discussed in previous chapters. In particular, the no-we and the only-inclusive patterns are shown on top of Figure 9.10. These connections (see Section 8.4) fit in perfectly with the others. In the top part of the figure, the same diagonal is found as in the dual part, linking two paradigmatic types through reanalysis. Both the only-inclusive and the unified-we paradigms have only one specialized element for 'we'. This element has a different referential value in both paradigms, but these two values are diachronically related. The other diagonal,

Connecting the Dual 293

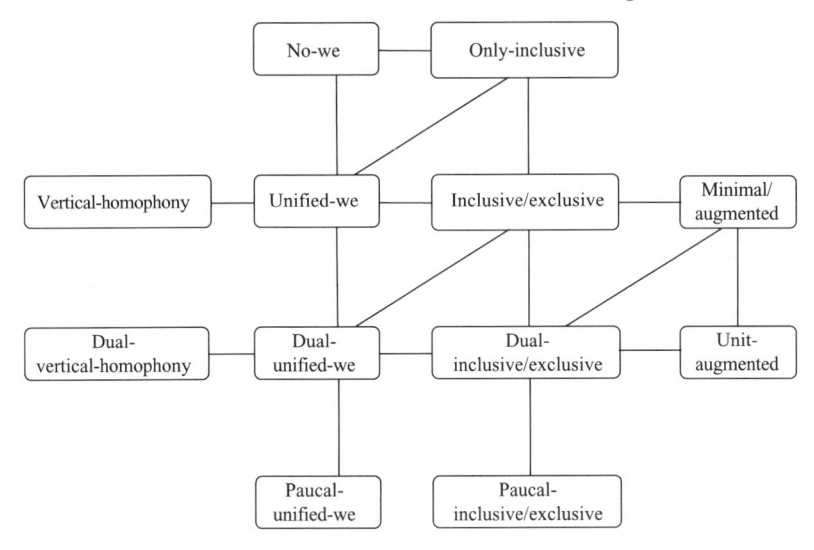

FIG. 9.10. *Cognitive map of paradigmatic structure*

hypothetically linking no-we to inclusive/exclusive, need two forms to arise or be lost in one change. This connection is not attested. Probably, a more gradual path is taken, intermediated by one or the other types.

On the lower side of the figure, the two main paradigms with paucal marking are added. An example of cognate paradigms linking the dual-unified-we to the paucal-unified-we is found in the Lower Sepik family from New Guinea. The languages Murik, Yimas, and Chambri from this family have a paucal-unified-we paradigm, but the language Karawari has only a dual-unified-we paradigm. Foley (1986: 219–21) argues that the proto-Lower Sepik pronominal paradigm had a paucal-unified-we paradigm. An example of cognate paradigms linking the dual-inclusive/exclusive to the paucal-inclusive/exclusive can be found in the Malaita family (a subgroup of the Oceanic languages) from the Solomon Islands. The southern languages Kwaio, Sa'a, Langalanga, and Lau have a paucal-inclusive/exclusive paradigm, but the northern language To'abaita has a dual-inclusive/exclusive paradigm. Simons (1986: 33–4) argues that the proto-Malaita pronominal paradigm had a paucal-inclusive/exclusive paradigm.

These paradigms with a paucal are not really common; the only examples of such paradigms are found in the area traditionally referred to as Melanesia: New Guinea and the surrounding smaller islands. The two patterns with a paucal are attested in south-east New Guinea and in north-west Australia, respectively. In general, the four lower outmost paradigmatic structures in Figure 9.10 (dual-vertical-homophony, unit-augmented, paucal-unified-we, and paucal-inclusive/exclusive) are all found in a strongly restricted region: south-eastern New Guinea, north-western Australia, and the nearby Oceanic languages.

Cognate Paradigms

The result is a cognitive map of paradigmatic structure. This map gives an impression of the similarity of the various patterns. The structures connected by a line are cognitively similar. Diachronic change of the paradigmatic structure will tend to proceed along the lines of this cognitive map.

9.7 Conclusion

In this chapter, a collection of cognate paradigms has been presented to test the hypothesis that pronominal paradigms change through time and space along the lines of previously established typological hierarchies. In previous chapters, the structure of pronominal paradigms has been shown to be ordered along the lines of two hierarchies: the Explicitness Hierarchy and the Dual Explicitness Hierarchy. These hierarchies were taken as a hypothesis for the possible changes of paradigmatic structure. To test this hypothesis, examples of cognate paradigms have been collected. Numerous cases have been presented, which show that many of the neighbouring paradigms on the hierarchies are closely related. The hypothesized connections are almost all attested. On the basis of the attested connections as discussed in this chapter, combined with the results from the previous chapter, a cognitive map has been constructed that shows how the various major paradigmatic structures are related to each other. The resulting similarity space can be interpreted as showing paths of 'least resistance' for diachronic change. It is surely not necessary for linguistic change to follow along the lines as shown in the cognitive map, yet it is likely. The connections between the various paradigmatic structures as shown in the map are the expected kinds of change. If another change is claimed to have happened, this requires additional explanation.

10 Finale
Summary and Prospects

> Très luisant
> Questionnez
> Du bout de la pensée
> Postulez en vous-même
> Pas à Pas
> Sur la langue
>
> Erik Satie, *Gnossienne No. 1*.

10.1 Summary of results

10.1.1 Preliminaries

The structural variation among the world's languages is overwhelming. Yet this variability should not be considered a nuisance to linguistic inquiry, but a potential source of insight into the possibilities of human language. Looking for a balance between gross generalizations and extreme relativism, I have attempted, in the present investigation, to catalogue the existing variability of the paradigmatic structure of person marking and to highlight structures that turned out to be more common than others. The existing variation shows a continuum from commonly attested paradigmatic structures, through a set of ever less common structures, up to structures that are not attested among the world's languages at all. Nothing seems to be impossible, although certain structures are clearly less probable.

In this study, the reference to speech act participants has been the subject of cross-linguistic investigation. Such reference is performed by words like the English *I* and *you*, but also by inflectional elements like the English suffix *-s*, which marks for 'not speaker nor addressee'. More specifically, only reference by specialized shifters has been included in this study. Specialized shifters used for speech act reference are called PERSON MARKERS (see Sections 1.2.2 and 1.2.4). Person markers are bound into a paradigm. A paradigm of person markers consists of a set of elements that are syntagmatically equivalent in the structure of a language. Functionally, each paradigm of person markers should at least have an opposition between (singular) speaker and addressee. Structurally, the elements in the paradigm have to be either all independent or all inflectional; and if they are inflectional, then they have to be all prefixes or all suffixes, filling the same inflectional 'slot' on a predicate. All person markers that belong to the same paradigm form the PARADIGMATIC STRUCTURE. Gender and honorifics, among the many other pronominal dimensions, are disregarded (see Section 1.2.3). This work specifically addresses the paradigmatic structure of the category person (see Section 1.2.5).

10.1.2 Person and number

The paradigmatic structure of person marking is traditionally analysed in two orthogonal dimensions: person and number. In this tradition, the dimension 'person' consists of three persons: first, second, and third. The dimension 'number' consists of the categories singular, plural, dual, trial, paucal, and possibly a quadral. I have argued that this analysis is not ideal to approach the cross-linguistic variation in person marking. Semantically, the notion 'plural' is not suitable for words like *we* because *we* is not the plural of *I*. Morphologically, the 'plural' person markers are, in the great majority of cases, not derived from the singular categories by regular plural marking. Moreover, the inclusive/exclusive opposition is only relevant in the first person plural, which indicates that 'person' and 'number' are not really orthogonal dimensions (see Section 3.3).

I have proposed a different analysis of person marking. The categories traditionally called 'plural' have been reanalysed as GROUPS of participants. These groups are inherently plural as they consist of more than one participant. Yet it is the KIND of participants in a group that is important, not the NUMBER. Seven different combinations of participants are theoretically possible. Of these, five different groups turned out to be cross-linguistically viable categories (see Table 10.1). Specifically, there are two groups that are not attested as a grammaticalized category in any of the world's languages, although they are theoretically possible and also functionally sensible: the choral-we and the plural-you addressing present audience only. The five remaining group categories form the basic grid for the typology of the paradigmatic structure of person marking together with the three singular categories. Graphically, these eight categories are depicted in a two-dimensional paradigm as shown in Figure 10.1. This graphical

TABLE 10.1. *The group categories*

	Group	Description
Attested	1+2	'we', including addressee, excluding other
	1+3	'we', including other, excluding addressee
	1+2+3	'we', complete
	2+3	'you-all', addressee(s) and others
	3+3	'they'
Not attested	1+1	'we', mass speaking
	2+2	'you-all', only present audience

Summary and Prospects 297

	Singular	Non-singular		
		1+2	Minimal inclusive	Inclusive — First person complex
		1+2+3	Augmented inclusive	
Speaker	1	1+3	Exclusive	
Addressee	2	2+3	Second person plural	
Other	3	3+3	Third person plural	

FIG. 10.1. *The paradigmatic scheme for the typological classification*

representation is used throughout the present study to allow for an easy comparison between the various paradigmatic structures (see Sections 3.4 and 3.5).

As a result of the recategorization from plural to group, the singular and the group categories are considered now as unmarked for number. In contrast, the dual, trial, and other traditional number categories are marked for number. A few cases show signs of a markedness reversal; in these cases, the dual is unmarked relative to the group marking. However, such reversals are only found in a small set of exceptional cases (see Section 6.3). Among the number categories, the dual is clearly the most prolific cross-linguistically. Other categories, mainly trial and paucal, occur only sparingly and in a restricted area (roughly the area that is known as Melanesia). Moreover, it is questionable whether trials really exist as a grammaticalized person category. On the basis of the published accounts, trials appear at the most very exceptionally in pronominal paradigms—most grammaticalized categories that are called trials are in fact paucals (see Section 6.4).

There is a claim in the literature that there are even more categories of person in the form of so-called COMPOUND PRONOUNS. This phenomenon was investigated in detail in Chapter 5. The special effect of these pronouns is reached through an incorporative reading of the first part of the compound, incorporating the reference to the second part of the compound. Such compounding of pronouns is quite widespread among the world's languages (see Section 5.5). However, in some Niger-Congo languages in Cameroon, these compounds are strongly grammaticalized (see Section 5.3). In some of these languages, the simplex inclusive pronouns can be shown to originate from erstwhile compound pronouns. These compound pronouns do indeed appear to be a special kind of pronoun, but I argued that they do not mark any new categories of person (see Section 5.2).

10.1.3 *Paradigmatic structure*

The typological variation in the markedness structure of these categories is large. In total, 102 different paradigmatic structures have been described in this investigation (see Table 10.2), not counting the various paradigms of compound pronouns as described in Chapter 5. If even more languages had been included in this investigation, this number would surely rise. This large variety of attested structures shows that the often-assumed basic six-way paradigm (three persons in two numbers) is only one among many possibilities.

This paradigmatic variation has been discussed throughout the book, divided into digestible chunks. First, the markedness structure of the three singular categories (speaker, addressee, and other) was investigated in Chapter 2. All theoretically possible kinds of homophony between these three categories were attested. Second, the markedness structure of the first person complex (i.e. all group categories that include at least the first person or, in other words, all categories that are to be translated into English as *we*) was investigated in Sections 3.5 and 3.6. Here, strong restrictions on the typological possibilities of human language are observed. Only ten out of fifteen possible structures are attested, and five of these ten are found in only one or two instances. The remaining five common structures of the first person complex are shown in Table 10.3. Third, a survey of the paradigmatic variability of singular and group marking was presented in Chapter 4. A summary of this variation was given in Section 4.7. Finally, a survey of the paradigmatic variation of the dual was presented in Chapter 7. A summary of this variation is given in Section 7.8.

There is a continuum of ubiquity attested, ranging from commonly attested structures, through semi-common and rare structures, to non-attested structures. Everything seems possible, yet some structures are clearly more probable than others. The main question is why certain paradigmatic structures are attested more commonly than others. As a prelude to this difficult question, some typological generalizations were formulated about the preferred paradigmatic structures of person among the world's languages. These generalizations are never universally true. They describe strong tendencies among the world's languages, but there are always some languages that do it differently. From the experience compiling the present typology of person marking, I am convinced that there are exceptions to every typological generalization. The structure of human language is more variable than sometimes assumed.

TABLE 10.2. *Summary of the number of different paradigmatic structures attested*

	Discussed in Section no.									Total
	3.6.6	4.3	4.4	4.5	4.6	6.4	7.3	7.4	7.5	7.6
Common patterns	–	4	–	4	–	–	1	–	1	–	10
Semi-common patterns	–	–	4	1	–	2	4	1	1	1	14
Rare patterns	5	11	20	2	12	4	10	5	7	2	78
Total	5	15	24	7	12	6	15	6	9	3	102

TABLE 10.3. *Common patterns of the marking of 'we'*

Name of type	Description of pattern
No-we	There is no specialized form for 'we' in the paradigm. The same morpheme that is used for the singular speaker 'I' is also used for 'we'.
Unified-we	There is one morpheme in the paradigm that translates as 'we', but only in the inclusive sense. The exclusive 'we' is marked by the same morpheme that is also used for reference to the singular speaker.
Only-inclusive	There is one morpheme in the paradigm that encompasses all reference of the first person complex, like the English pronoun *we*.
Inclusive/exclusive	There are two morphemes for 'we': one for inclusive reference and one for exclusive reference.
Minimal/augmented	There are three morphemes for 'we': one for minimal inclusive 'we' (only speaker and addressee), one for augmented inclusive 'we' (speaker addressee and other), and one for exclusive 'we'.

The generalizations are formulated as restrictions on the distribution of a few specific characteristics of paradigmatic structure. Three different characteristics of paradigmatic structure were distinguished, called HOMOPHONY. The usage of the term homophony is meant to reflect a rather theory-neutral approach to morphemes that are used with variable reference. The various typological generalizations concerning the distribution of these kinds of homophony will be discussed in turn. The different kinds of homophony that have been distinguished are:

- HORIZONTAL homophony between the singular and the non-singular;
- SINGULAR homophony within the three singular categories;
- VERTICAL homophony within the five non-singular categories.

10.1.4 Horizontal homophony

Horizontal homophony is characterized by a homophony between two categories, one of which is singular and one of which is non-singular. With three singular and five non-singular categories, there are fifteen theoretically possible kinds of horizontal homophony. However, four kinds of horizontal homophony account for the great majority of cases (other kinds of horizontal homophony, called 'diagonal homophony', are only attested in a few exceptional examples):

- The 3rd person singular is homophonous with the 3rd person non-singular.
- The 2nd person singular is homophonous with the 2nd person non-singular.
- The 1st person singular is homophonous with both exclusive and inclusive.
- The 1st person singular is homophonous with the exclusive only.

300   *Finale*

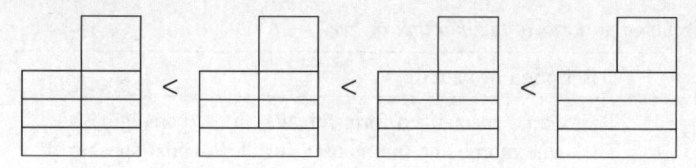

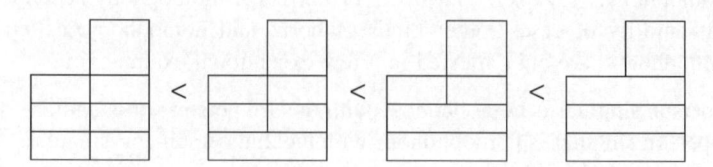

FIG. 10.2. *The Horizontal Homophony Hierarchy with an inclusive/exclusive opposition*

Moreover, the various kinds of homophony are connected by the Horizontal Homophony Hierarchy (see Section 4.7). There are two versions of this hierarchy, one for paradigms with an inclusive/exclusive opposition in (10.1), and one for paradigms without this opposition in (10.2). Both version of the hierarchy run parallel along the person hierarchy. Either there is no horizontal homophony or, if there is homophony, then it is first attested in the third person, and only subsequently in the second person. Only if both second and third persons already show homophony is homophony also attested in the first person. Cross-linguistically, there is a strong preference for this person hierarchy, ranking speaker above addressee above others. In some languages in some specific instances, this hierarchy might be ordered differently, but generalizing over the attested diversity among the world's languages, the 1 > 2 > 3 hierarchy is strongly substantiated by the occurrence of horizontal homophony. Both Horizontal Homophony Hierarchies are graphically represented by the paradigmatic structures in Figure 10.2 and Figure 10.3, respectively. The paradigmatic structures shown here follow the grid as presented in Figure 10.1.

(10.1)   Horizontal Homophony Hierarchy I (with inclusive/exclusive)
         no homophony < third < second < exclusive

(10.2)   Horizontal Homophony Hierarchy II (no inclusive/exclusive)
         no homophony < third < second < first

Horizontal homophony is also attested in paradigms with duals (see Section 7.3.4). If there is horizontal homophony in a paradigm with duals, then it is almost exclusively attested between a dual and general non-singular ('plural')

FIG. 10.3. *Horizontal Homophony Hierarchy without an inclusive/exclusive opposition*

category, thereby locally neutralizing the number opposition. This generalization is formulated as an implication in (10.3). Examples with only partial dual marking in the paradigm are infrequent. In general, either there is a dual for all persons, or there is no dual at all. In particular, no hierarchy of horizontal homophony is attested in paradigms with dual marking.

(10.3) Dual Homophony Implication

dual horizontal homophony → homophony between dual and plural

10.1.5 Singular homophony

Singular homophony is characterized by a homophony between two categories, both of which are singular. All theoretically possible kinds of homophony between the three singular categories were attested. However, a homophony between second and third person, resulting in a structure opposing 'I' to 'non-I', was clearly the most frequent (see Section 2.3). Almost all examples of singular homophony were attested in inflectional person marking—only two cases of homophony in independent pronouns were found (see Section 2.3.5). Generalizing, there is a strong cross-linguistic implication between singular homophony and inflectional marking, as formulated in (10.4). However, it should not be concluded from this implication that singular homophony is only possible in so-called 'non-pro-drop' languages. In many languages with a homophonous singular inflection, this inflection is functionally similar to the independent pronouns in English (see Section 2.4).

(10.4) Homophony Implication

singular homophony → inflectional paradigm

Singular categories are sometimes marked by zeros. If there is singular homophony and zero marking, then it is almost always the homophonous categories that are marked zero. This observation is formulated as an implication in (10.5). This implication can be explained by basic markedness considerations: the homophonous categories are structurally unmarked in relation to the non-homophonous category, and consequently it is the unmarked category that can be marked zero (see Section 2.5.1). If there is no singular homophony, then it is almost always the third person that is marked zero, as formulated in implication (10.6). Again, this is as expected according to basic markedness considerations, which state that third person is the most unmarked of the three singular persons (see Section 2.5.2). However, independent pronouns with a zero third persons are problematic. It might be better in some cases to speak of non-existing instead of zero third person pronouns (see Section 2.5.3).

302   *Finale*

(10.5)   Zero Homophony Implication

singular homophony *and* zero marking → zero homophony

(10.6)   Zero Singular Implication

no singular homophony *and* zero marking → zero third person

The occurrence of singular homophony is strongly restricted by various other paradigmatic characteristics. The large majority of paradigms with singular homophony does not have an inclusive/exclusive distinction, nor dual or any other higher number marking. Also, the large majority of singular homophony is attested in paradigms that also have vertical homophony.

10.1.6   Vertical homophony

Vertical homophony is characterized by a homophony between two categories, both of which are non-singular. However, the various kinds of homophony between the categories of the first person complex are not included under this heading (see Section 3.6). The ubiquity of vertical homophony differs according to the presence of an inclusive/exclusive distinction and according to the presence of dual marking. These two factors give rise to four different situations.

First, vertical homophony is most commonly attested in paradigms without an inclusive/exclusive opposition and without dual marking. All four different kinds of vertical homophony that are theoretically possible are attested (see Section 4.4). The homophony between first and second person non-singular is the most common. This combination is referentially a coherent cluster, as it includes all non-singular reference to speaker and addressee. It means something like 'a set of persons, which includes at least you or I'. One could think of this as a generalized form of 'we', in a sense 'The two of us talking here are involved somehow, without further specifying exactly who of us'. This homophony is in most cases attested without a singular homophony, which indicates that it is not felt as a mix of incompatible person categories (see Section 4.4.2). Also quite frequent is vertical homophony between second and third person non-singular. This homophony might be thought of as marking 'non-we'. Referentially, this is not a pure opposition, as reference to the addressee is found in both clusters. This homophony can only be interpreted as a plural variant of the 'I' versus 'non-I' structure in the singular. This interpretation is confirmed by the fact that this vertical homophony is regularly accompanied by the equivalent singular homophony between second and third person singular (see Section 4.4.3). The other two theoretical possibilities are attested in incidental examples only (see Sections 4.4.4–5).

Second, vertical homophony is attested in paradigms without an inclusive/exclusive distinction, but with dual marking. There is a clear predominance of a homophony between second and third person dual in this configuration. Most examples of this homophony are found in Papuan languages, which also regularly have the same homophony in the plural and also incidentally in the singular (see Section 7.5.4). In contrast to the paradigms without a dual, the combination of first and second person dual is only incidentally found. Probably the best explanation for this situation is to proclaim all vertical homophony with dual marking to be rare. It is only by historical coincidence that the Papuan languages have diversified to an extreme extent, spreading their particular second/third homophony in the dual.

Third, vertical homophony is only incidentally attested in paradigms with an inclusive/exclusive opposition. Without dual marking, all theoretically possible kinds of homophony are attested, yet all are equally rare (see Section 4.6). Most important, the combination inclusive with second person non-singular, which can be thought of as an addressee-centred cluster, is not more common that any of the other combinations of categories (see Section 4.6.2). Finally, paradigms with vertical homophony, an inclusive/exclusive opposition, and dual marking are rarissima. There are a few examples attested, to be interpreted as a sign of the inherent variability of linguistic structure (see Section 7.5.4).

To summarize, the paradigms with an inclusive/exclusive opposition show much less occurrence of vertical homophony than paradigms without such an opposition. This also holds for paradigms with a dual, though it might be better to say that paradigms with a dual are in general low on examples of vertical homophony. The most common kind of vertical homophony is between first and second person, including referentially all marking that includes at least the speaker *or* the addressee. Vertical homophony between second and third person is also common. This homophony is probably best seen as an extension of a singular homophony between second and third person singular.

10.1.7 Pure person and the Explicitness Hierarchy

A central cut-off point for variation of the paradigmatic structure of person marking is the inclusive/exclusive opposition. The paradigms without an inclusive/exclusive opposition allow for much greater liberty in combining different referential categories into the marking of one morpheme. Once there is an inclusive/exclusive opposition in the paradigm, the possible variation is strongly constrained. This observation can be subsumed under a theoretical concept that I call PURE PERSON. Paradigms of person can be more or less 'pure' in their conceptualization of the dimension person. The marking of person is directed to the role in the speech act, most importantly to the roles speaker and addressee. By definition, the paradigms included in this investigation mark at least some person oppositions. However, the extent of the marking of person varies between paradigms. The purer a paradigm of person, the more this paradigm is devoted to the marking of person.

304   Finale

The difference between inclusive and exclusive is a major breaking point of purity. This opposition overtly marks a difference between the combination speaker/addressee (inclusive) and speaker/others (exclusive) in the paradigm. In almost all paradigms, once this opposition is marked, all reference to the different persons is distinguished. No confusion of person in the form of singular or vertical homophony is allowed. Only in the case of total absence of any homophony (even horizontal homophony) is it possible for a paradigm to add an even more stringent person opposition between minimal inclusive and augmented inclusive. This opposition is the summit of the marking of pure person.

The concept of Pure Person gave rise to a hierarchy of paradigmatic structure called the EXPLICITNESS HIERARCHY (see Section 4.7). The Explicitness Hierarchy describes the order in which a particular set of oppositions in a paradigm is grammaticalized. The more of these oppositions are grammaticalized, the more explicit (or 'pure') is the reference to the various referential person categories. At the highest level, all eight person categories are differentiated by separate morphemes. On the way to a less explicit paradigmatic structure, there is a typological order in which the various categories are combined into the reference of one morpheme.

The various stages on this hierarchy are described in (10.7). The first oppositions to give way are the oppositions in the first person complex. Minimal inclusive (1+2) and augmented inclusive (1+2+3) are combined first, and next this cluster is combined with the exclusive (1+3) to yield a unified 'we' (like the English pronoun *we*). Only after the first person complex has been united can other non-singular categories be combined into clusters of referential categories (vertical homophony). Finally, only if the non-singular reference is thus strongly reduced in its referential explicitness can some of the singular categories be combined into the marking of one morpheme. Such a singular homophony (e.g. the zero marking in the English inflection, which marks for singular speaker and addressee) is the lowest rung of explicitness for a paradigm of person. Sometimes it is even questionable whether it is really person that is marked on this lowest rung. A comparable hierarchy was established for paradigms with a dual: the Dual Explicitness Hierarchy (see Section 7.7), as shown in (10.8). Both explicitness hierarchies are graphically represented by a few selected paradigmatic structures in Figures 10.4 and 10.5.

(10.7)   Explicitness Hierarchy

singular homophony > vertical homophony > unified-we > inclusive/exclusive > minimal/augmented

(10.8)   Dual Explicitness Hierarchy

dual-vertical homophony > dual-unified-we > dual-inclusive/exclusive > unit-augmented

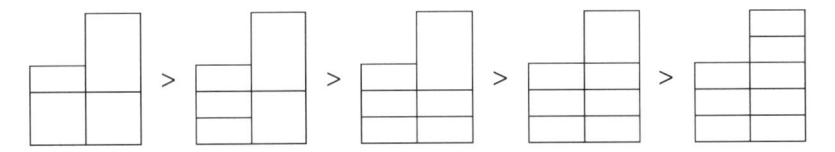

FIG. 10.4. *Explicitness Hierarchy*

Both these hierarchies describe a cross-linguistically salient conceptualization of the notion RICHNESS of a paradigm. The notion richness has been invoked in the generative literature to explain why certain languages allow pro-drop and others do not. Languages that have a rich inflectional subject paradigm, so the reasoning goes, do not need to add the independent pronoun. However, this reasoning does not work with the Explicitness Hierarchy. Even paradigms with a singular homophony, which are on the lowest rung of the Explicitness Hierarchy, are still found to allow pro-drop in many of the world's languages (see Section 2.4).

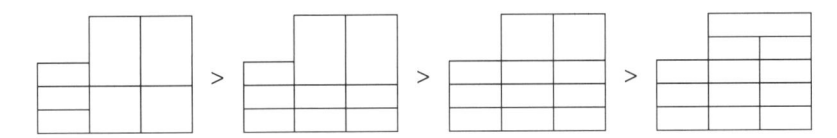

FIG. 10.5. *Dual Explicitness Hierarchy*

10.1.8 *Diachronic interpretation*

Typological hierarchies might be connected to the possible directions of language change. The hierarchies from the present investigation could, for example, be the result of certain restrictions on possible changes. To test whether the typological hierarchies may serve as hypotheses for language change, examples of cognate paradigms are collected in Chapters 8 and 9. The idea behind such cognate paradigms is that changes in paradigmatic structure may perhaps be visible through the small differences between closely related languages. Examples of such cognate paradigms present a window on the dynamics of language change. By compiling a large collection of such examples, an impression can be obtained of which paradigmatic structures are closely related (for methodological considerations, see Section 8.2).

It turned out that the Horizontal Homophony Hierarchy does not present a good hypothesis of diachronic change. Closely related paradigms appear to jump up and down this hierarchy in great strides (see Section 8.4). In contrast, the Explicitness Hierarchy presents a good format for diachronic change. Both for paradigms without a dual (see Section 8.5) and for paradigms with a dual (see

306   *Finale*

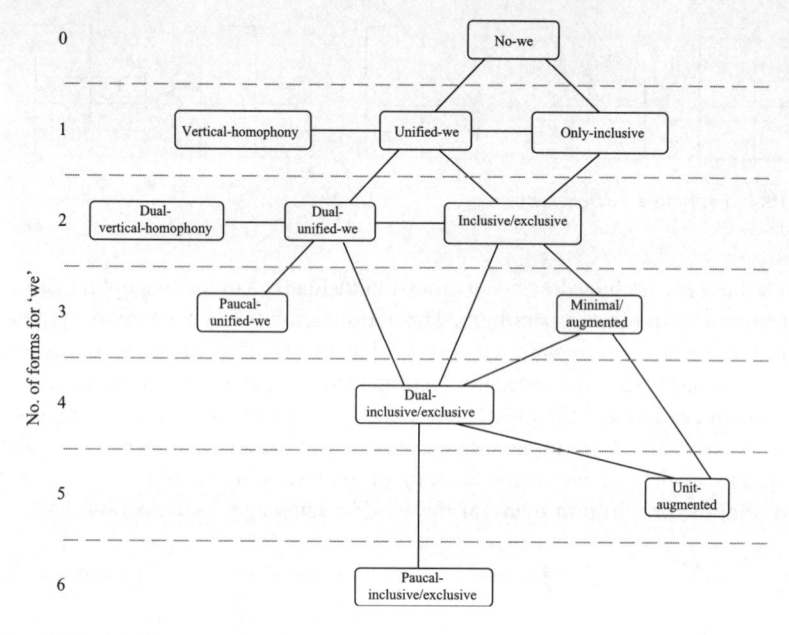

FIG. 10.6. *Similarity space of paradigmatic structure, ordered to the number of forms for 'we'*

Sections 9.3 and 9.4), this hierarchy is corroborated by various examples of cognate paradigms. In general, the diachronic dynamics of person paradigms are most clearly seen in the structure of the first person complex. The complete set of connections attested between the various types of marking for the first person complex is summarized in Figure 10.6, ordered to the number of forms in the paradigm that are to be translated into English as *we*. This map is a first outline of the similarity space of paradigmatic structure. The types directly connected by a line in the figure are strongly similar, as shown by the existence of cognate paradigms linking these types (see Sections 8.6 and 9.6).

10.2 Towards a theory of person marking

This investigation is a prolonged argument for the usefulness of the present framework to scrutinize the variability of person marking among the world's languages. The two main characteristics of this framework are its particular definitions of number and person. First, what is traditionally called singular and unmarked plural in the pronominal domain has been reanalysed as person categories that are unmarked for number. Second, these person categories that are unmarked for number are analysed according to the kind of participants that are referred to, leading to eight different person categories. The various possibilities of paradigmatic structure are consistently described within this framework, leading to a large number of generalizations as summarized in the preceding section.

In this section, I will propose an analysis of the structures that appear to be the core of the large paradigmatic variation, as summarized by the similarity space in Figure 10.6. This similarity space can be interpreted as the basic frame of a cognitive map of paradigmatic structure. The labels in the map refer to the structure of the first person complex. These labels describe the kind of marking in the paradigm that is used for the same reference as the English pronoun *we*. This is an abstraction from the rather large variability of paradigmatic structure— many structures did not find their way into the map because they occur only rarely. The structures belonging to this map are shown in Figure 10.7, illustrating the pattern for each of the labels in Figure 10.6. The central four paradigms are the structures described as 'the four systems that more frequent than the others' by Ingram (1978: 219; cf. Hagège 1982: 112). These patterns are indeed the most frequent ones, but the other paradigmatic structures are also commonly found and should not be put aside too easily.

The vertical dimension of Figure 10.7 can be described as a hierarchical tree of number oppositions.[1] The four rows will be discussed in turn from top to bottom. The paradigms that do not distinguish number are located in the upper row (stage N_1). The inclusive that is grammaticalized in the only-inclusive paradigm is not a special kind of number marking (an impression that might arise from the old name 'first person plural inclusive'), but a kind of person marking. The second row (stage N_2) is characterized by a consistently marked opposition between singular and group marking. There are many paradigms that fall between stages N_1 and N_2. The opposition between singular and group is not marked consistently throughout the paradigm when horizontal homophony is present. All paradigms on intermediate stages of the horizontal homophony hierarchy (see Section 10.1.4) fall between stages N_1 and N_2. The third row (stage N_3) consists of the paradigms with differentiated restricted group marking. Most of these paradigms have dual forms, but the unit-augmented paradigm (on the far right of the third row) also has a trial inclusive that behaves in parallel to the dual forms in the other paradigms. The label 'restricted group' has been proposed to cover both the dual and the inclusive trial reference. The fourth and final row (stage N_4) consists of the paradigms with paucal marking, called 'small group' in the present framework. This hierarchical tree of oppositions is shown in Figure 10.8.

The horizontal dimension of Figure 10.7 can be described as a hierarchical tree of person oppositions. Person is explicated in various stages from left to right

---

[1] The usage of trees here is reminiscent of the usage in Corbett (2000: ch. 2) or Gvozdanović (1985: 116–28; 1991: 153–8).

308   *Finale*

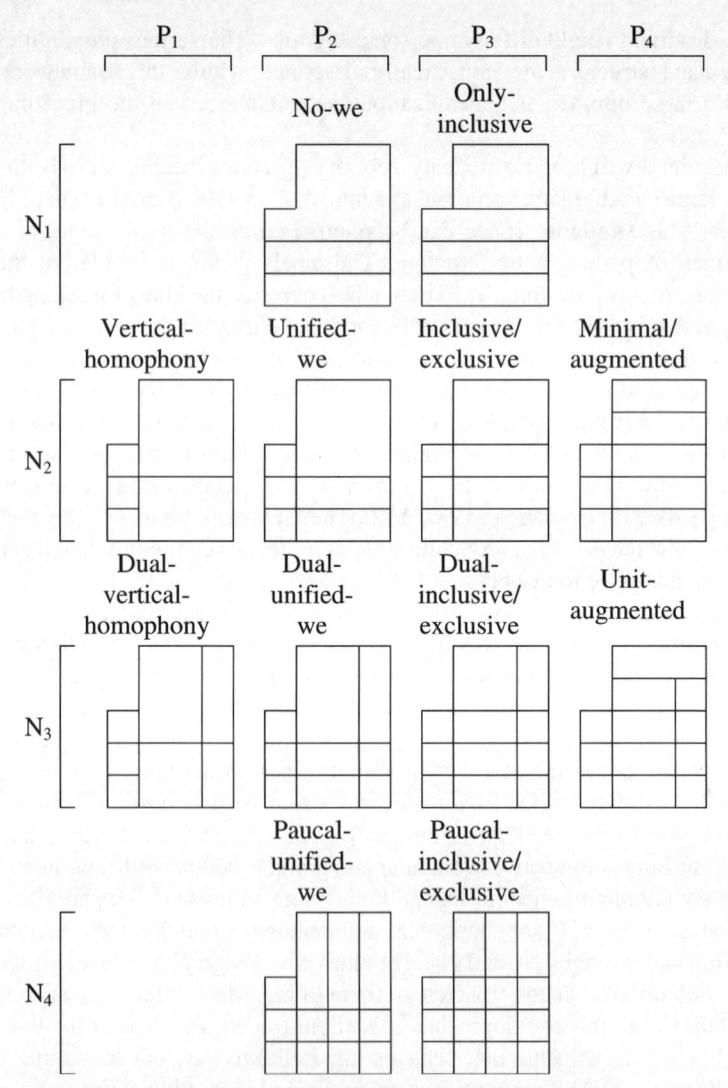

FIG. 10.7. *Examples of the paradigmatic structures in the cognitive map*

along the Explicitness Hierarchy (see Section 10.1.7). Not shown in the figure is the first stage of person explicitness (P_0), in which there is only a slight trace of person marking available. The first column in the figure (stage P_1) consists of paradigms that differentiate the three singular persons, but person marking is still intermingled in the non-singular. The paradigms presented in the second column (stage P_2) differentiate between first, second, and third person in the non-singular

```
N₁           Undifferentiated
             number marking
            ╱              ╲
N₂    Singular              Group
                           ╱      ╲
N₃              Restricted        Unrestricted
                  group              group
                                  ╱         ╲
N₄                           Small          Unrestricted
                             group             group
```

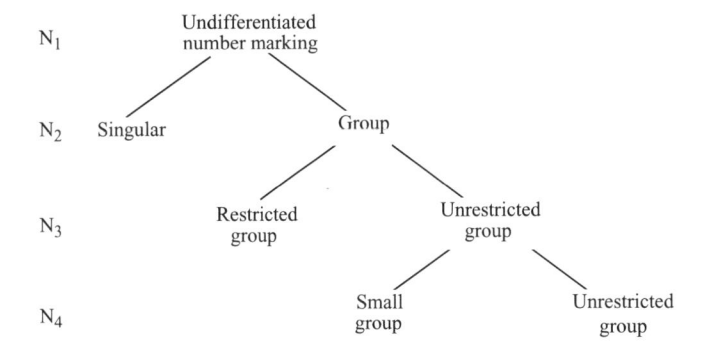

FIG. 10.8. *Hierarchical tree of number oppositions*

as well (though the difference between the singular and non-singular does not have to be marked, as shown by the case of the no-we paradigm). However, the first person non-singular is a mix of various referential person categories that can be further differentiated. The third column (stage P_3) is characterized by an opposition between exclusive (excluding the addressee) and inclusive (including the addressee) in the first person non-singular. The final column (stage P_4) differentiates a minimal inclusive from an augmented inclusive. The resulting hierarchy of person differentiation is summarized in Figure 10.9.

The linguistic variation and the generalizations put forward in the present work can guide the formulation of a theoretical framework of person marking that is informed by the diversity attested in the world's languages. The hierarchical analysis just presented, or the usage of features (as in Ingram 1978), eventually enhanced with set analysis (as in Noyer 1997 or Dalrymple and Kaplan 2000) or with a different kind of tree geometry (as in Harley 1994 or Harley and Ritter 2002) are attempts to capture the regularities of person marking in the world's languages. Although nothing is wrong with such an attempt, the problem is that any paradigmatic constellation that does not fit into any of these frameworks will be categorized as an accidental exception. However, it is still an open question whether there is really a distinction between accidental patterns and cases of structural homophony, 'which cannot be ascribed to paradigm inconsistency, and which are not attributable to phonological factors either' (Carstairs-McCarthy 1998: 330). From the present investigation, it appears that the division between what counts as an accidental exception and what counts as a structural homophony is not clear-cut. I leave it as a desideratum for future research to propose a framework in which gradual typological regularities can be accounted for. The central aim of this work is to make a plea for more attention to the (very large) actual diversity of the world's languages when developing a theoretical framework. A framework uninformed by the disparate linguistic structures

310   *Finale*

```
P₀                    Undifferentiated
                      person marking
                     /              \
P₁   Differerentiated              Undifferentiated
     singular persons              non-singular persons
                                  /              \
P₂                  Differentiated              Undifferentiated
                    non-first persons           first person non-singular
                    non-singular
                                               /              \
P₃                              Differentiated              Undifferentiated
                                exclusive                   inclusive
                                                           /              \
P₄                                              Minimal                Augmented
                                                inclusive              inclusive
```

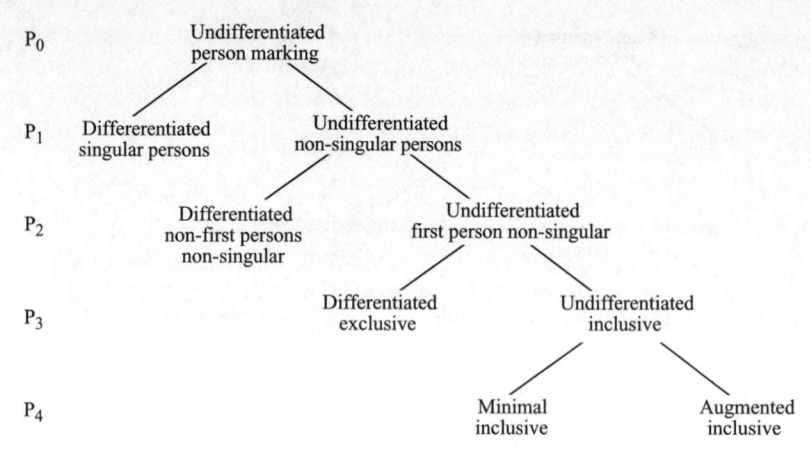

FIG. 10.9. *Hierarchical tree of person oppositions*

attested may sound plausible initially, but is easily falsified by the more 'exotic' examples.

10.3   Prospects

10.3.1   *Syntagmatic questions*

Even within the rather strong restrictions on the domain in the present investigation, the paradigmatic structure of person marking has turned out to be highly variable. I believe I have achieved a step in the direction of a better understanding of the marking of person in language. Yet much work remains to be done. Most importantly, this investigation only addressed the PARADIGMATIC structure of person markers. The logical next step is now to compare the SYNTAGMATIC structure of these paradigms in a cross-linguistic investigation.

One aspect of the syntagmatic structure is the function of each paradigm. The paradigms discussed in this study perform many different functions within the overall structure of a language. They mark, for example, the subject or the object of a predicate. Also, they can be more or less obligatorily required to form intelligible utterances in a language. These dimensions have not been separated in this investigation (cf. de Groot and Limburg 1986; Siewierska and Bakker 1996). Also, there might be large differences (or maybe interesting correspondences) between predicative uses of person markers (*I walk*) and other linguistic contexts, like isolated use (*it's me*) or pronominal possession (*my book*, cf. Siewierska 1998). Such questions can now be investigated with the present analysis of the paradigmatic structure as a possibly significant variable. The analysis of paradigmatic structure gives a proper basis for the investigation of the syntagmatic function.

Another syntagmatic aspect is the question of the importance of a particular paradigmatic structure within the whole of a language. This question addresses a possible difference between structural and accidental homophony—a difference that I have not made in this investigation. Using the present catalogue of structures, an attempt can now be made to investigate whether there is a cross-linguistically salient difference between structural and accidental homophony in person paradigms. For inflectional paradigms, at least four different stages of importance of a particular paradigmatic structure can be distinguished:

- only attested in one particular verb class;
- attested throughout all verb classes, but only in one particular tense/aspect;
- attested throughout all inflectional paradigms, but only for one particular predicative argument;
- attested throughout all inflectional paradigms.

If a particular pattern belongs to the first stage, then it is accidental within the structure of a whole language, but if it belongs to the fourth stage, it is a central property of the language. A question to be investigated in future research is whether the hierarchies of paradigmatic structure as formulated in the present work correlate with these stages.

Finally, a syntagmatic theme to be further investigated is the morphological status of the paradigm. Two examples of the kinds of question that can be asked will be discussed in the next two sections. The first question concerns the difference between inflectional or independent marking of a pronominal paradigm. The second addresses a possible difference between prefixal and suffixal person marking. Both these themes deserve in-depth study. Here, I will present some preliminary quantitative analyses to show that there is good reason to believe that there are correlations between the morphological status of a paradigm and the paradigmatic generalization from this investigation.

10.3.2 Independent versus inflectional marking

In the present investigation, the morphological status of the person marking was not a priori considered to have an influence on the structure of a pronominal paradigm. The present study encompasses the structure of both morphologically independent and inflectionally marked pronominal paradigms.[2] It is only now,

---

[2] The difference between independent and inflectionally marked paradigms is not a clear dichotomy, but more of a continuum. I have not bothered too much with the intermediate 'clitic' forms. At face value, these are not very frequently described as such in the grammars, and it would be a study in its own right to develop a useful cross-linguistic definition for clitics. The paradigms that could be classified as clitics were taken as being inflectional here.

after the structural analysis of the paradigms is completed, that a difference between the two can possibly be shown to exist. Previously, it was discovered that singular homophony occurs almost exclusively in inflectionally marked paradigms (see Section 2.3.5). In this section, this correlation will be shown to be part of a general correlation between the morphological status of a paradigm and the two structural hierarchies that were developed. I will show that both the Explicitness Hierarchy and the Horizontal Homophony Hierarchy are correlated with morphological status. In both cases, the correlation points in the same direction: the more oppositions in a paradigm, the larger the proportion of morphologically independent paradigms in the sample. Towards the other side of both hierarchies (for paradigms with less oppositions marked), the proportion of inflectional paradigms rises.

The data for these analyses are formed by the collection of pronominal paradigms as described in Chapter 4, in which fifty-eight different paradigmatic structures were presented. Counting all examples mentioned, a sample is constructed of 309 paradigms. This collection has been guided by the wish to include the complete variation known and thus to show the inherent variability of linguistic structure. All examples described in the chapter are included in the sample. This means that all fifty-eight different paradigmatic structures, including all quaint cases, are represented in the sample. The only constraint on the construction of the collection of 309 cases is that genetic families never count for more than three cases. This restriction has been introduced to avoid over-representation of paradigmatic structures that are commonly found in large and widespread families. Because of this approach, this 'diversity sample' is not strictly balanced over the world's linguistic diversity as measured by quantity and genetic distance (cf. Rijkhoff and Bakker 1998). However, it is not at all clear a priori whether genetic diversity is an important factor for paradigmatic diversity. Of course, a cross-linguistic sample should draw data from the known linguistic diversity of the world's languages. In other words, genetic diversity should be taken as a basis for the construction of a cross-linguistic sample. However, a tight method of genetic sampling only reduces the possibility of highlighting interesting cases. In the collection presented in Chapter 4, the number of cases and the distribution of these cases of the world's languages is wide enough to allow a cross-linguistic interpretation.[3]

The Explicitness Hierarchy is shown in Table 10.4. The percentages of inflectionally marked cases for each stage of the hierarchy have been added. There is a clear correlation between the explicitness of a paradigm and the morphological status, as is shown in Figure 10.10. The Horizontal Homophony Hierarchy is also analysed for the proportion of inflectionally marked paradigms.

---

[3] Throughout the following analyses, it should be kept in mind that the chances for a paradigm to be inflectional in the present sample of 309 cases is a little higher than 50 per cent. The mean percentage of inflectional cases is 55 per cent (169 inflectional versus 140 independent paradigms).

Summary and Prospects 313

TABLE 10.4. *Percentage of inflectional paradigms in the Explicitness Hierarchy*

	Minimal/ augmented	Inclusive/ exclusive	Unified-we	Vertical homophony	Singular homophony	Not fitting in hierarchy	Total
Independent	32	47	42	16	1	2	140
Inflectional	7	32	63	19	24	24	169
Total	39	79	105	35	25	26	309
% Inflectional	16%	41%	60%	54%	96%	92%	55%

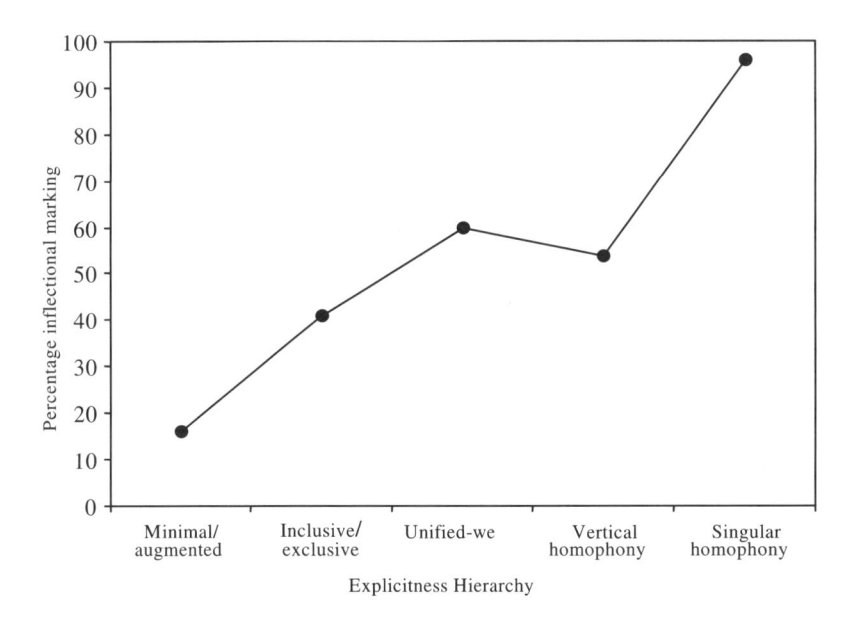

FIG. 10.10. *Correlation between the Explicitness Hierarchy and the proportion of inflectional marking*

The results are shown in Table 10.5, and the percentages are plotted in Figure 10.11. Again, the graph shows a correlation between less explicitness in the paradigm (meaning more horizontal homophony) and more inflectionally marked pronominal paradigms in the sample. The correlation is less strong than that found with the Explicitness Hierarchy, but a trend is visible.

These correlations are in need of an explanation. Both correlations point in the same direction: the more oppositions, the higher the proportion of independently marked pronominal paradigms and vice versa. In general, the correlation between low explicitness and inflectional marking is exactly as one would expect from the perspective of grammaticalization. A reduction in the explicitness of marking is paralleled by a reduction in morphological independence. However, there is no

TABLE 10.5. *Percentage of inflectional paradigms in the Horizontal Homophony Hierarchy*

	Independent	Inflectional	Total	% Inflectional
No horizontal homophony				26%
Latin-type (Sect. 4.3.2)	16	13	29	
Maranao-type (Sect. 4.5.2)	32	7	39	
Mandara-type (Sect. 4.5.3)	25	6	31	
Only 3rd person horizontal homophony				52%
Sinhalese-type (Sect. 4.3.3)	7	10	17	
Tupí-Guaraní-type (Sect. 4.5.4)	8	6	14	
2nd and 3rd person horizontal homophony				68%
Berik-type (Sect. 4.3.4)	3	13	16	
Kwakiutl-type (Sect. 4.5.5)	6	6	12	
1st, 2nd, and 3rd person horizontal homophony				61%
Maricopa-type (Sect. 4.3.5)	10	18	28	
Sierra-Popoluca-type (Sect. 4.5.6)	8	13	21	

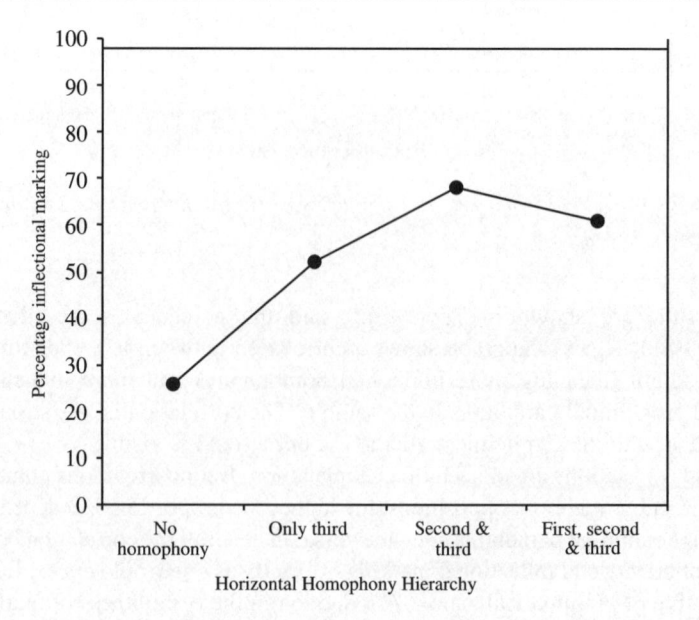

FIG. 10.11. *Correlation between the Horizontal Homophony Hierarchy and the proportion of inflectional marking*

indication that the hierarchy describes stages in a unidirectional change, as would be predicted by grammaticalization (see Chapters 8 and 9). Yet if a paradigm cliticizes, then it is more likely that this paradigm will subsequently be reduced than that it will be enlarged. This directional priority explains, at least partly, the skewing found, namely it can explain why there are more inflectional paradigms on the lower side of the hierarchy.

However, grammaticalization cannot explain why there are more independent paradigms on the higher side of the hierarchy. Speculatively, I propose the varying level of awareness that speakers have of linguistic elements as a subsidiary explanation. Independent pronouns (like all independent words) are real things to a linguistically naive speaker of a particular language. As speakers are consciously aware of the referential properties of independent words, unusual mixtures of referential categories are disfavoured. Highly explicit paradigms are therefore predominantly found as independent pronouns. At the other end of the spectrum, there is a lesser degree of awareness of inflectional morphemes, which opens up the possibility for unusual combinations of referential value for such elements, possibly as the result of historical merger. Consequently, paradigmatic structures that fall outside the Explicitness Hierarchy (labelled 'others' in Table 10.4) show a large proportion of inflectionally marked cases.

Pending tests of the validity of these explanations, it has to be noted that the current sample cuts through the different possible functional roles of the paradigmatic structure, subject, object, ergative, etc. I would expect the effect of any functional difference between the various cases to be evenly distributed over the present sample. However, future research must show whether this intuition is correct or not.

10.3.3 Asymmetry of affixation

Generalizing over the world's linguistic variation, there appears to be a strong preference for suffixation over prefixation. Grammaticalized elements are predominantly found after the root which they modify. In a typological study, Bybee et al. (1990: 4) found 426 grammatical prefixes (26 per cent) against 1236 grammatical suffixes (74 per cent). After a thorough investigation of the possible reasons for this predominance, the authors conclude that the preference for suffixation is due to the predominance of V-final languages:

Our proposal for explaining the suffixing predominance, then, is that grams at clause boundaries tend to affix at a very high rate, while the rate of affixation for clause-internal grams is determined by their meaning and relevance to the verb. The large number of suffixes in our sample, then, is due primarily to the fact that there are many more V-final language than V-initial, and the additional fact that the V-final languages are highly consistent in postposing verbal grams. (Bybee et al. 1990: 34)

316   *Finale*

In person markers, the predominance of suffixation is less clear. Reanalysing the data from Bybee et al. (1990: 9, 13, 15), there are 240 prefixed person grams (40 per cent) against 354 suffixed person grams (60 per cent) in their sample. There still is a preference for suffixation, although less strong than the overall preference. Moreover, Bybee et al. have counted each person-marking morpheme individually. They do not correct for the fact that person markers in a language are found together in a paradigm. The person markers in a paradigm are normally either all prefixes or all suffixes. So it might be interesting to count paradigms instead of individual person markers.

In the data described in Chapter 4, there are 169 inflectional person-marking paradigms mentioned. Of these, eighty-nine cases are prefixal paradigms (53 per cent) against eighty cases of suffixal paradigms (47 per cent). The difference between suffixation and prefixation has disappeared—there even appears to be a slight preference for prefixation. Counting all person markers separately, the slight preference is reversed (in line with the results from Bybee et al. 1990): there are 373 prefixal person markers (48 per cent) and 408 suffixal person markers (52 per cent).[4] These differences between the paradigm count and the person marker count are compatible. It turns out that there is a correlation between the size of the paradigm and the affixal status. As shown in Table 10.6, the smaller paradigms are more often prefixes and the larger paradigms are more often suffixes.

More specifically, there appears to be a strong correlation between the prefixal/suffixal status and the Horizontal Homophony Hierarchy. In Table 10.7, the number of inflectional paradigms with only horizontal homophony is listed. The major paradigmatic structures are all mentioned separately, along the line of the Horizontal Homophony Hierarchy. There is a strong correlation between horizontal homophony and prefixation (see Figure 10.12). Paradigms without horizontal homophony are predominantly suffixing, while paradigms with

TABLE 10.6. *Correlation between prefixation/suffixation and size of inflectional paradigms*

	No. of person markers					Total
	2–3	4	5	6	7–8	
Prefixal	24	36	21	5	3	89
Suffixal	11	18	23	17	11	80
Total	35	54	44	22	14	169
% Prefixal	69	67	48	23	21	53

---

[4] For these numbers, I have only counted person markers in the strict sense as defined in the present work. The person grams as counted by Bybee et al. (1990) also include other categories, like gender marking.

Summary and Prospects 317

TABLE 10.7. *Percentage/suffixation along the Horizontal Homophony Hierarchy*

	Independent	Inflectional	Total	% Inflectional
No horizontal homophony				8%
Latin-type (Sect. 4.3.2)	0	13	13	
Maranao-type (Sect. 4.5.2)	1	6	7	
Mandara-type (Sect. 4.5.3)	1	5	6	
Only 3rd person horizontal homophony				44%
Sinhalese-type (Sect. 4.3.3)	3	7	10	
Tupí-Guaraní-type (Sect. 4.5.4)	4	2	6	
2nd and 3rd person horizontal homophony				95%
Berik-type (Sect. 4.3.4)	13	0	13	
Kwakiutl-type (Sect. 4.5.5)	5	1	6	
1st, 2nd and 3rd person horizontal homophony				87%
Maricopa-type (Sect. 4.3.5)	17	1	18	
Sierra-Popoluca-type (Sect. 4.5.6)	10	3	13	

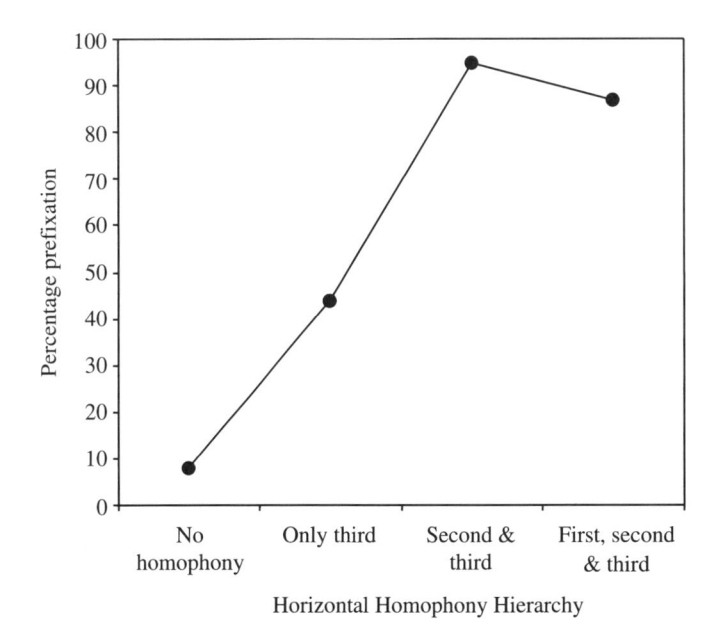

FIG. 10.12. *Correlation between prefixation and Horizontal Homophony Hierarchy*

318   *Finale*

horizontal homophony are predominantly prefixing. There seems to be something specifically relevant in the phenomenon of horizontal homophony, supporting the occurrence of prefixation. For example, it can be observed that very many of the prefixal paradigms with much horizontal homophony have separate suffixal number marking. However, future research will have to investigate this correlation with more care and consideration than has been possible here.

The prefixal/suffixal difference does not show the same correlation with the Explicitness Hierarchy (see Table 10.8). As shown in Figure 10.13, the Explicitness Hierarchy is (almost) inversely correlated with prefixal marking, despite the low percentage of prefixation for the minimal/augmented paradigms (the first point of the graph). However, there are only a few cases of this type (viz. seven), which reduces the significance of this point. This correlation might be

TABLE 10.8. *Prefixation/suffixation along the Explicitness Hierarchy*

	Minimal/ augmented	Inclusive/ exclusive	Unified-we	Vertical homophony	Singular homophony	Not fitting in hierarchy	Total
Independent	1	21	40	8	4	15	89
Inflectional	6	11	23	11	20	9	80
Total	7	32	63	19	24	24	169
% Inflectional	14%	66%	63%	42%	17%	63%	53%

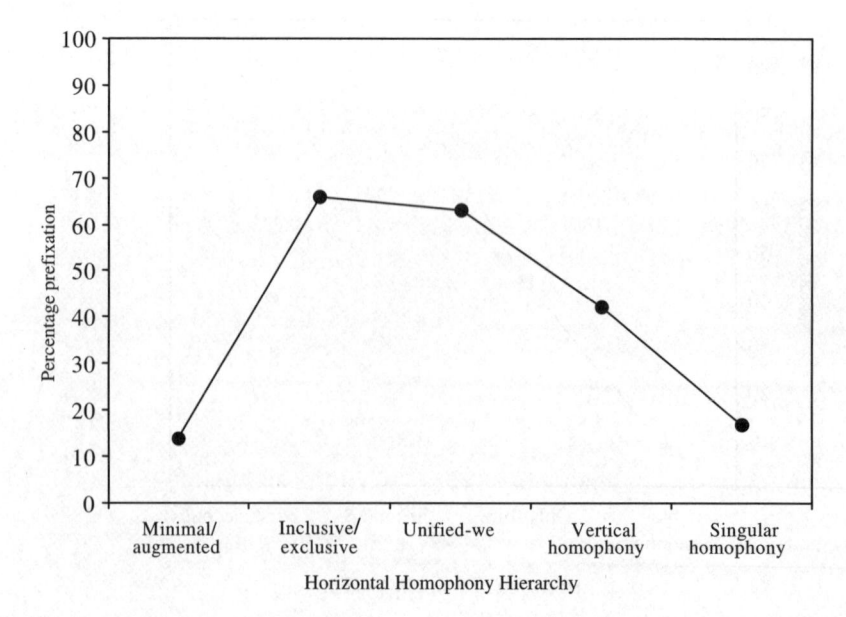

FIG. 10.13. *(Almost) inverse correlation between prefixation and Explicitness Hierarchy*

explained by noting that vertical and singular homophony are often signs of wear, which can be argued to be more frequent at the end of a word (although this explanation is discounted by Bybee et al. 1990). The precise details of these tendencies and the reasons for them have to be further investigated.

10.3.4 Gender in person paradigms

As one of the main delimitations for the present study, I have discarded the marking of gender (see Section 1.2.5). I have taken a more than incidental look at paradigms that mark gender, but this part of the investigation has not been sufficiently thorough to be reported on in the present study. Yet there is one observation on the marking of gender in person paradigms that seems promising as a hypothesis for further research. Quickly formulated, gender marking is not found in paradigms that have an inclusive/exclusive opposition. However, gender marking has to be more specifically defined for this hypothesis to make sense.

When studying gender marking in the domain of person marking, two cases have to be distinguished. First, gender marking in the third person is a separate question altogether. Many semantic and formal classifications can be found here (Corbett 1991). In the first or second person, natural gender (an opposition between male and female) is the only attested markedness strategy. Speaker and addressee are always human participants (or at least anthropomorphic non-humans). Apparently, the distinction between male and female is sufficiently dominant in the classification of human beings to appear time and again in the structure of human language. Gender marking in the reference to speaker or addressee can take many different forms. It is fairly uncommon for reference to the speaker to distinguish gender. Still, an example of this curious linguistic phenomenon is found in the South American language Paez, where the pronouns distinguish gender in both first and second person singular (Rojas Curieux 1991: 52). Gender is somewhat more commonly observed, cross-linguistically speaking, in person markers like 'you' or 'we' (Plank and Schellinger 1997). It is, for example, attested in Spanish, where two different forms for 'we' are found, *nosotros* for a group of males or mixed and *nosotras* for a group of females. The most prominent examples of gender in the second person are found among the languages in the Afro-Asiatic stock (see also Section 1.2.5 for a few more curious cases of gender marking in the first and second person).

Now, the hypothesis can be precisely formulated. If there is gender marking in the reference to any person marker, which includes reference to at least speaker or addressee, then such a paradigm will not make a distinction between inclusive

---

[5] The few cases that contradict the hypothesis are the Khoisan language !Xu, the Papuan languages Baniata and Vanimo, and the Australian language Ndjébbana (Plank and Schellinger 1997: 74–7). Note that these cases, except for !Xu, have a combination of gender and inclusive/exclusive marking in the dual forms only.

and exclusive. In traditional terminology, if there is gender marking in the first or second person (singular or plural), then there is no inclusive/exclusive opposition in the first person plural. From the data as reported by Plank and Schellinger (1997), it can be inferred that the hypothesis fares rather well cross-linguistically. Counter-examples are almost unattested.[5] However, it should be pointed out that gender marking in the first and second person is not frequent enough cross-linguistically to allow for any significant conclusion at this stage of investigation.

If this hypothesis turns out to hold after further investigation, a possible explanation can be found in the concept of Pure Person. Paradigms that mark an opposition between inclusive and exclusive have restricted themselves to mark person, and nothing else. Only if the marking of person is not completely explicit (so that there is no inclusive/exclusive opposition) is there a possibility for marking gender oppositions. One can look upon this as two different routes for the development of fine-grained referential categories for participant reference. On the one hand, a paradigm can specialize for the specific role the participants fulfil in the speech act. In this case the paradigm marks person, and gender is not attested in the paradigm. Otherwise, a paradigm can specialize for the marking of intrinsic characteristics of the participant. In that case, the paradigm can mark gender.

10.4 Wider application of results

Cross-linguistic investigation and linguistic typology, the kinds of research strategy used in the presented investigation, do not stand in isolation from other fields of linguistic investigation. As has been argued throughout this work, these investigations build on a long linguistic tradition of analysis, description, and classification. At the end now of my inquiries, the results of this study can hopefully be related to these domains of investigation and inspire future research.

An important result of this investigation is that the six-way paradigm—with three persons in the singular and three in the plural—is in no way to be seen as the basic paradigmatic structure of person marking. It is indeed a rather commonly attested structure, but it is not the only common one. There are many other common paradigmatic structures. This insight can enrich both descriptive practice and historical reconstruction. The wide variation of paradigmatic structures laid out in the preceding pages can guide the analysis of yet undescribed or only poorly described languages. Also, the typology of paradigmatic structure can be used in the context of a historical investigation to test whether a proposed reconstruction for a paradigm is in line with the attested distribution of diversity among the world's languages. Of course, it is not necessary for a reconstructed paradigm to belong to one of the commonly found paradigmatic structures. However, the argumentation for the reconstruction of a typologically rare paradigmatic structure has to be much more stringent than the argumentation for a reconstruction of a paradigmatic structure that is commonly attested among the world's languages. In this sense, the synchronic typology as presented in the present work can be used to evaluate historical reconstruction:

It has been proposed, as a basic contribution of synchronic typology to historical linguistics, that synchronic universals serve as touchstone for the validity or reconstructed systems. (Greenberg 1969: 174)

Finally, some insights have been presented that can inspire the development of the theory of linguistic structure. The regularity of the internal structure of paradigms of person, and especially the central place of the inclusive/exclusive opposition within this structure, are promising theoretical results. A more widely ranging prospect can be found in the notions of variability and specialization, as summarized in the concept of Pure Person. From the analyses presented of the paradigmatic structure of person marking, there appear to be clines between more and less explicit specialization of a subsystem within the overall structure of a language. The more specialized a subsystem, the less variability is possible. This process can be interpreted as a kind of meta-grammaticalization. Not only individual elements within a language, but also sets of interconnected elements as a whole can grammaticalize. In such a process of paradigmatic grammaticalization, changes in form and in function develop in an iconic relationship. Functionally, subsystems of a language grammaticalize by streamlining the function of the morphemes included within the confines of a specific overall function and, formally, regularize the paradigmatic structure. However, at least in the case of the paradigmatic structure of person marking, it is doubtful whether this meta-grammaticalization process is unidirectional. Developments in both directions seem possible.

References

Abed, S. B. (1991). *Aristotelian Logic and the Arabic Language in Alfarabi*. Albany, NY: State University of New York.
Abondolo, D. (1998a). 'Khanti'. In D. Abondolo (ed.), *The Uralic Languages*. London: Routledge, 358–86.
——(ed.) (1998b). *The Uralic Languages*. London: Routledge.
Adelaar, W. F. H. (1977). 'Tarma Quechua: Grammar, Texts, Dictionary'. Ph.D. thesis, University of Amsterdam.
——(1993). 'La Categoría del plural inclusivo en las lenguas americanas: Interpretación y realidad'. In M. P. A. M. Kerkhof, H. de Schepper, and O. Zwartjes (eds.), *España: ¿Ruptura 1492?* (Diálogos Hispánicos II). Amsterdam: Rodopi, 207–16.
——and L. Silva Lôpez (1988). 'Grammaticaal Overzicht van het Guarani'. *Wampum* 7: 11–60.
Aikhenvald, A. A. Y. (1995). *Bare* (Languages of the World/Materials 100). Munich: Lincom Europa.
——(1998). 'Warekena'. In D. C. Derbyshire and G. K. Pullum (eds.), *Handbook of Amazonian Languages*, vol. iv. Berlin: Mouton de Gruyter, 225–440.
Alexander, R. M. (1988). 'A Syntactic Sketch of Ocotepec Mixtec'. In C. H. Bradley and B. E. Hollenbach (eds.), *Studies in the Syntax of Mixtecan Languages*, vol. i (Summer Institute of Linguistics Publications in Linguistics 83). Arlington, Va.: Summer Institute of Linguistics, 151–304.
Allen, E. J. (1976). 'Dizi'. In M. L. Bender (ed.), *The Non-Semitic Languages of Ethiopia*. East Lansing, Mich.: African Studies Center, 377–92.
Amaya, M. T. (1999). *Damana* (Languages of the World/Materials 207). Munich: Lincom Europa.
Anceaux, J. C. (1965). *The Nimboran Language: Phonology and Morphology* (Verhandeligen van het Koninklijk Instituut voor Taal-, Land- en Volken-kunde 44). The Hague: Martinus Nijhoff.
Andersen, H. (1998). 'Slavic'. In A. G. Ramat and P. Ramat (eds.), *The Indo-European Languages*. London: Routledge, 415–53.
Andersen, T. (1988). 'Ergativity in Päri, a Nilotic OVS Language'. *Lingua* 75: 289–324.
Anderson, L. (1966). 'The Structure and Distribution of Ticuna Independent Clauses'. *Linguistics* 20: 5–30.
Anderson, S. C. (1985). 'Animate and Inanimate Pronominal Systems in Ngyembɔɔn-Bamileke'. *Journal of West African Languages* 15/2: 61–74.
de Angulo, J., and L. S. Freeland (1931). 'The Achumawi Language'. *International Journal of American Linguistics* 6: 77–120.
Aquilina, J. (1965). *Maltese*. London: English Universities Press.
Asher, R. E. (1982). *Tamil* (Lingua Descriptive Studies 7). Amsterdam: North-Holland.
——and T. C. Kumari (1997). *Malayalam* (Routledge Descriptive Grammars). London: Routledge.

Austin, P., and J. Bresnan (1996). 'Non-Configurationality in Australian Aboriginal Languages'. *Natural Language and Linguistic Theory* 14: 215–68.

Austing, J., and R. Upia (1975). 'Highlights of Ömie Morphology'. In T. E. Dutton (ed.), *Studies in Languages of Central and South-East Papua* (Pacific Linguistics C 29). Canberra: Australian National University, 513–98.

Ayuninjam, F. F. (1998). *A Reference Grammar of Mbili*. Lanham, Md.: University Press of America.

Baerman, M. (2001). 'The Interpretation of Person Syncretisms'. Paper presented at the 4th meeting of the Association for Linguistic Typology, Santa Barbara, Calif., 20 July 2001.

Baker, M. (1990). 'Pronominal Inflection and the Morphology–Syntax Interface'. *Chicago Linguistic Society* 26/1: 25–48.

——(1991). 'On Some Subject/Object Non-Asymmetries in Mohawk'. *Natural Language and Linguistic Theory* 9: 537–76.

Bauman, J. J. (1975). 'Pronouns and Pronominal Morphology in Tibeto-Burman'. Ph.D. thesis, University of California at Berkeley.

Bavin, E. L. (1981). 'Lango: Some Morphological Changes in Verb Paradigm'. In T. C. Schadeberg and M. L. Bender (eds.), *Nilo-Saharan: Proceedings of the First Nilo-Saharan Linguistic Colloquium*. Dordrecht: Foris, 89–100.

Becker, A. L., and I. G. N. Oka (1995 [1974]). 'Person in Kawi: Exploration of an Elementary Semantic Dimension'. In A. L. Becker, *Beyond Translation: Essays Towards a Modern Philology*. Ann Arbor, Mich.: Michigan University Press, 109–36.

Beller, R., and P. Beller (1979). 'Huasteca Nahuatl'. In R. W. Langacker (ed.), *Studies in Uto-Aztecan Grammar*, vol. ii: *Modern Aztec Grammatical Sketches* (Summer Institute of Linguistics Publications in Linguistics 56: 2). Arlington, Va.: Summer Institute of Linguistics, 199–306.

Bender, M. L. (1996). *Kunama* (Languages of the World/Materials 59). Munich: Lincom Europa.

Bendor-Samuel, D. (1972). *Hierarchical Structures in Guajajara* (Summer Institute of Linguistics Publications in Linguistics 37). Oklahoma: University of Oklahoma.

Benveniste, E. (1966). *Problèmes de linguistique générale* (Bibliothèque des Sciences Humaines). Paris: Gallimard.

Benzing, J. (1955). 'Die tungusische Sprachen: Versuch einer vergleichenden Grammatik'. *Akademie der Wissenschaften und der Literatur. Abhandlungen der Geistes- und Sozialwissenschaftliche Klasse* 11: 955–1049.

van den Berg, B. (1949). 'De Conjugatie van het Praesens in de Noordnederlandse Dialecten'. *Taal en Tongval* 1: 6–13.

van den Berg, H. (1995). 'A Grammar of Hunzib (with Texts and Lexicon)'. Ph.D. thesis, University of Leiden.

——(1999). 'Gender and Person Agreement in Akusha Dargi'. *Folia Linguistica* 13/2: 153–68.

Bigalke, R. (1997). *Siciliano* (Languages of the World/Materials 129). Munich: Lincom Europa.

Birk, D. B. W. (1976). *The Malakmalak Language: Daly River (Western Arnhem Land)* (Pacific Linguistics B 45). Canberra: Australian National University.

Blake, B. J. (1988). 'Redefining Pama-Nyungan: Towards the Prehistory of Australian Languages'. *Aboriginal Linguistics* 1: 1–90.

References

Blake, B. J. (1991). 'The Significance of Pronouns in the History of Australian Languages'. In P. Baldi (ed.), *Patterns of Change, Change of Patterns*. Berlin: Mouton de Gruyter, 219–34.

Blake, F. R. (1934). 'The Origin of Pronouns of the First and Second Person'. *American Journal of Philology* 55/219: 244–8.

Blood, C. (1992). 'Subject–Verb Agreement in Kisar'. In D. A. Burquest and W. D. Laidig (eds.), *Descriptive Studies in Languages of Maluku* (NUSA 34). Jakarta: Universitas Atma Jaya, 1–20.

Bloomfield, L. (1942). 'Outline of Ilocano Syntax'. *Language* 18: 193–200.

—— (1946). 'Algonquian'. In H. Hoijer et al., *Linguistic Structures of Native America* (Publications in Anthropology 6). New York: Viking Fund, 85–129.

—— (1956). *Eastern Ojibwa: Grammatical Sketch, Texts and Word List*. Ann Arbor, Mich.: University of Michigan Press.

—— (1962). *Menomini Language*. New Haven, Conn.: Yale University Press.

Boas, F. (1911a). 'Chinook'. In F. Boas (ed.), *Handbook of American Indian Languages*, vol. i. Washington, DC: Bureau of American Ethnology, 559–678.

—— (1911b). 'Introduction'. In F. Boas (ed.), *Handbook of American Indian Languages*, vol. i. Washington, DC: Bureau of American Ethnology, 1–83.

—— (1947). *Kwakiutl Grammar, with a Glossary of the Suffixes* (Transactions of the American Philosophical Society 37: 3). Philadelphia: American Philosophical Society.

Boelaars, J. H. M. C. (1950). *The Linguistic Position of South-Western New Guinea*. Leiden: Brill.

Bohnhoff, L. E. (1986). 'Yag Dii (Duru) Pronouns'. In U. Wiesemann (ed.), *Pronominal Systems*. Tübingen: Narr, 103–30.

Bopp, F. (1974 [1816/20]). *Analytical Comparison of the Sanskrit, Greek, Latin and Teutonic Languages, Showing the Original Identity of their Grammatical Structure* (Amsterdam Classics in Linguistics 3). Amsterdam: Benjamins.

Borgman, D. M. (1990). 'Sanuma'. In D. C. Derbyshire and G. K. Pullum (eds.), *Handbook of Amazonian Languages*, vol. ii. Berlin: Mouton de Gruyter, 15–248.

Boxwell, M. (1967). 'Weri Pronoun System'. *Linguistics* 29: 34–43.

de Bray, R. G. A. (1951). *Guide to the Slavonic Languages*. London: Dent.

Broadbent, S. M. (1964). *The Southern Sierra Miwok Language* (University of California Publications in Linguistics 38). Berkeley, Calif.: University of California Press.

Brockway, E. (1979). 'North Puebla Nahuatl'. In R. W. Langacker (ed.), *Studies in Uto-Aztecan Grammar*, vol. ii: *Modern Aztec Grammatical Sketches* (Summer Institute of Linguistics Publications in Linguistics 56: 2). Arlington, Va.: Summer Institute of Linguistics, 141–98.

Buchler, I. R. (1967). 'The Analysis of Pronominal Systems: Nahuatl and Spanish'. *Anthropological Linguistics* 9/5: 37–43.

—— and R. Freeze (1966). 'The Distinctive Features of Pronominal Systems'. *Anthropological Linguistics* 8/8: 78–105.

Bühler, K. (1934). *Sprachtheorie*. Jena: Fischer.

Bulatova, N., and L. Grenoble (1999). *Evenki* (Languages of the World/Materials 141). Munich: Lincom Europa.

Burling, R. (1970). *Man's Many Voices*. New York: Holt, Rinehart & Winston.

Burquest, D. A. (1986). 'The Pronoun System of Some Chadic Languages'. In U. Wiesemann (ed.), *Pronominal Systems*. Tübingen: Narr, 71–102.

Butt, J., and C. Benjamin (1988). *A New Reference Grammar of Modern Spanish*. London: Arnold.

Bybee, J. L., W. Pagliuca, and R. D. Perkins (1990). 'On the Asymmetries in the Affixation of Grammatical Material'. In W. Croft (ed.), *Studies in Typology and Diachrony*. Amsterdam: Benjamins, 1–42.

Calame-Griaule, G. (1968). *Dictionnaire Dogon* (Langues et Littératures de l'Afrique noire 4). Paris: Klincksieck.

Caldwell, R. (1913 [1856]). *A Comparative Grammar of the Dravidian or South-Indian Family of Languages*. London: Kegan Paul, Trench, Trübner.

Callaghan, C. A. (1965). *Lake Miwok Dictionary* (University of California Publications in Linguistics 39). Berkeley, Calif.: University of California.

Callaghan, C. A. (1974). 'Increase in Morphological Complexity'. In L. Heilmann (ed.), *Proceedings of the Eleventh International Congress of Linguistics*. Bologna: il Mulino, 383–8.

—— (1984). *Plains Miwok Dictionary* (University of California Publications in Linguistics 105). Berkeley, Calif.: University of California Press.

—— (1987). *Northern Sierra Miwok Dictionary* (University of California Publications in Linguistics 110). Berkeley, Calif.: University of California Press.

Callow, J. C. (1962). 'The Apinayé Language: Phonology and Grammar'. Ph.D. thesis, University of London.

Campbell, L. (1985). *The Pipil Language of El Salvador* (Mouton Grammar Library 1). Berlin: Mouton.

—— (1997). *American Indian Languages: The Historical Linguistics of Native America* (Oxford Studies in Anthropological Linguistics 4). Oxford: Oxford University Press.

Capell, A. (1940). 'Language Study for New Guinea Students'. *Oceania* 11/1: 40–74.

—— (1969a). 'Non-Austronesian Languages of the British Solomons'. In *Papers in Linguistics of Melanesia*, vol. ii (Pacific Linguistics A 21). Canberra: Australian National University, 1–16.

—— (1969b). 'The Structure of the Binandere Verb'. In *Papers in New Guinea Linguistics*, vol. ix (Pacific Linguistics A 18). Canberra: Australian National University, 1–32.

—— (1975). 'The "West Papuan Phylum": General, and Timor and Areas Further West'. In S. A. Wurm (ed.), *Papuan Languages and the New Guinea Linguistic Scene* (Pacific Linguistics C38). Canberra: Australian National University, 667–716.

Carstairs-McCarthy, A. (1998). 'Paradigmatic Structure: Inflectional Paradigms and Morphological Classes'. In A. Spencer and A. M. Zwicky (eds.), *The Handbook of Morphology* (Blackwell Handbooks in Linguistics). Oxford: Blackwell, 322–34.

Chafe, W. L. (1976). *The Caddoan, Iroquoian and Siouan Languages* (Trends in Linguistics: State-of-the-art reports 3). The Hague: Mouton.

Chase, W. J. (1926). *The Ars Minor of Donatus: For One Thousand Years the Leading Textbook of Grammar, Translated from the Latin with Introductory Sketch*. Madison, Wis.: University of Wisconsin.

Chelliah, S. L. (1997). *A Grammar of Meithei* (Mouton Grammar Library 17). Berlin: Mouton de Gruyter.

Cherchi, M. (1999). *Georgian* (Languages of the World/Materials 147). Munich: Lincom Europa.
Chlenova, S. F. (1973). 'Kategorija Chisla v Lichnyx Mestoimenijax [Category of Number within Personal Pronouns]'. In *Lingvotipologicheskie Issledovanija, Vypusk 1, Chast' 1*. Moscow: Izdatel'stvo MGU, 164–201.
Chomsky, N. (1981). *Lectures on Government and Binding* (Studies in Generative Grammer). Dordrecht: Foris.
Clairis, C. (1985). *El Qawesqar: Lingüística Fueguina, Teoria y Descriptíon* (Estudios Filológicos, Anejo 12). Valdivia: Universidad Austral de Chile.
Cole, P. (1982). *Imbabura Quechua* (Lingua Descriptive Studies 5). Amsterdam: North-Holland.
Comrie, B. (1980a). 'Inverse Verb Forms in Siberia: Evidence from Chukchee, Koryak and Kamchadal'. *Folia Linguistica Historica* 1/1: 61–74.
——(1980b). Review of *Universals of Human Language*, vol. iii: *Word Structure*, ed. J. H. Greenberg. *Language* 56/4: 834–8.
——(1989). *Language Universals and Linguistic Typology*, 2nd edn. Oxford: Blackwell.
Conklin, H. C. (1962). 'Lexicographical Treatment of Folk Taxonomies'. In F. W. Householder and S. Saporta (eds.), *Problems in Lexicography*. Bloomington: Indiana University Press, 119–42.
Conrad, R. J., and K. Wogiga (1991). *An Outline of Bukiyip Grammar* (Pacific Linguistics C 113). Canberra: Australian National University.
Cook, W. H. (1979). 'A Grammar of North Carolina Cherokee'. Ph.D. thesis, University of Ann Arbor, Michigan.
Cooke, J. R. (1968). *Pronominal Reference in Thai, Burmese, and Vietnamese* (University of California Publications in Linguistics 52). Berkeley, Calif.: University of California Press.
Corbett, G. G. (1979). 'The Agreement Hierarchy'. *Journal of Linguistics* 15: 203–24.
——(1991). *Gender* (Cambridge Textbooks in Linguistics). Cambridge: Cambridge University Press.
——(1994). 'Agreement'. In R. E. Asher (ed.), *The Encyclopedia of Language and Linguistics*. Oxford: Pergamon Press, 54–60.
——(2000). *Number* (Cambridge Textbooks in Linguistics). Cambridge: Cambridge University Press.
——and M. Mithun (1996). 'Associative Forms in a Typology of Number Systems: Evidence from Yup'ik'. *Journal of Linguistics* 32: 1–17.
Cowan, H. K. J. (1965). *Grammar of the Sentani Language* (Verhandelingen van het Koninklijk Instituut voor Taal-, Land- en Volkenkunde 47). The Hague. Martinus Nijhoff.
Crazzolara, J. P. (1955). *A Study of the Acooli Language*. London: Oxford University Press.
——(1960). *A Study of the Logbara (Ma'di) Language*. London: Oxford University Press.
Croft, W. (1990). *Typology and Universals* (Cambridge Textbooks in Linguistics). Cambridge: Cambridge University Press.
Crofts, M. (1973). *Gramática Mundurukú* (Séria Lingüística 2). Brasília: Summer Institute of Linguistics.

Crowell, T. H. (1979). 'A Grammar of Bororo'. Ph.D. thesis, Cornell University.
Crowley, T. (1981). 'The Mpakwithi Dialect of Anguthimri'. In R. M. W. Dixon and B. J. Blake (eds.), *Handbook of Australian Languages*, vol. ii. Amsterdam: Benjamins, 147–94.
——(1982). *The Paamese Language of Vanuatu* (Pacific Linguistics B 87). Canberra: Australian National University.
——(1983). 'Uradhi'. In R. M. W. Dixon and B. J. Blake (eds.), *Handbook of Australian Languages*, vol. iii. Amsterdam: Benjamins, 307–430.
Csúcs, S. (1998). 'Udmurts'. In D. Abondolo (ed.), *The Uralic Languages*. London: Routledge, 276-304.
Culicover, P. W. (ed.) (1997). *Principles and Parameters: An Introduction to Syntactic Theory*. Oxford: Oxford University Press.
Curnow, T. J. (1997). 'A Grammar of Awa Pit (Cuaiquer): An Indigenous Language of South-Western Colombia'. Ph.D. thesis, Australian National University.
Cysouw, M. (2002). 'Interpreting Typological Clusters'. *Linguistic Typology* 6/1: 69–93.
D'Alton, P. A. (1983). 'Esquisse phonologique et grammaticale du Palor, langue Cangin (Senegal)'. Ph.D. thesis, Université de la Sorbonne Nouvelle, Paris.
Dalrymple, M., and R. M. Kaplan (2000). 'Feature Indeterminacy and Feature Resolution'. *Language* 76/4: 759–98.
Davis, H. (2000). 'Remarks on Proto-Salish Subject Inflection'. *International Journal of American Linguistics* 66/4: 499–520.
DeLancey, S. (1987). 'Sino-Tibetan Languages'. In B. Comrie (ed.), *The World's Major Languages*. London: Croom Helm, 797–810.
——(1992). 'The Historical Status of the Conjunct/Disjunct Pattern in Tibeto-Burman'. *Acta linguistica Hafniensia* 25: 39–62.
Derbyshire, D. C. (1999). 'Carib'. In R. M. W. Dixon and A. A. Y. Aikhenvald (eds.), *The Amazonian Languages* (Cambridge Language Surveys). Cambridge: Cambridge University Press, 23–64.
Dibbets, G. R. W. (1995). *De Woordsoorten in de Nederlandse Triviumgrammatica* (Stichting Neerlandistiek VU 18). Münster: Nodus.
Dickinson, C. (1999). 'Semantic and Pragmatic Dimensions of Tsafiki Evidential and Mirative Markers'. *Chicago Linguistic Society*, 35/2: 29–44.
Diessel, H. (1999). *Demonstratives: Form, Function, and Grammaticalisation* (Typological Studies in Language 42). Amsterdam: Benjamins.
Diller, A. (1994). 'Thai'. In C. Goddard and A. Wierzbicka (eds.), *Semantic and Lexical Universals: Theory and Empirical Findings* (Studies in Language Companion Series 25). Amsterdam: Benjamins, 149–70.
Dimmendaal, G. J. (1982). 'The Turkana Language'. Ph.D. thesis, University of Leiden.
——(1983). 'Topics in a Grammar of Turkana'. In M. L. Bender (ed.), *Nilo-Saharan Language Studies*. East Lansing, Mich.: African Studies Center, 239–71.
Dixon, R. M. W. (1972). *The Dyirbal Language of North Queensland*. Cambridge: Cambridge University Press.
——(1977). *A Grammar of Yidiɲ* (Cambridge Studies in Linguistics 19). Cambridge: Cambridge University Press.

Dixon, R. M. W. (1979). 'Ergativity'. *Language* 55: 59–138.
——(1980). *The Languages of Australia*. Cambridge: Cambridge University Press.
——(1981). 'Wargamay'. In R. M. W. Dixon and B. J. Blake (eds.), *Handbook of Australian Languages*, vol. ii. Amsterdam: Benjamins, 1–144.
——(1983). 'Nyawaygi'. In R. M. W. Dixon and B. J. Blake (eds.), *Handbook of Australian Languages*, vol. iii. Amsterdam: Benjamins, 431–525.
——(1997). *The Rise and Fall of Languages*. Cambridge: Cambridge University Press.
——and B. J. Blake (1979). 'Introduction'. In R. M. W. Dixon and B. J. Blake (eds.), *Handbook of Australian Languages*, vol. i. Amsterdam: Benjamins, 1–26.
Doneux, J. L. (1968). *Esquisse grammaticale de Dan* (Documents Linguistiques 15). Dakar: Université de Dakar.
Donohue, M. (1999). *Warembori* (Languages of the World/Materials 341). Munich: Lincom Europa.
——(2000). 'Pronouns and Gender: Exploring Nominal Classification in Northern New Guinea'. *Oceanic Linguistics* 39/2: 339–49.
——and J. C. Smith (1998). 'What's Happened to Us? Some Developments in the Malay Pronoun System'. *Oceanic Linguistics* 37/1: 65–84.
Dorsch, H. (1911). 'Grammatik der Nkosi-Sprache'. *Zeitschrift für Kolonialsprachen* 1: 241–83.
Drabbe, P. (1952). *Spraakkunst van het Ekagi: Wisselmeren Nederlands Nieuw-Guinea*. The Hague: Martinus Nijhoff.
——(1955). *Spraakkunst van het Marind: Zuidkust Nederlands Nieuw-Guinea*. Fribourg: St Paul.
van Driem, G. (1987). *A Grammar of Limbu* (Mouton Grammar Library 4). Berlin: Mouton de Gruyter.
——(1993). *A Grammar of Dumi* (Mouton Grammar Library 10). Berlin: Mouton de Gruyter.
Dryer, M. S. (1997). 'Why Statistical Universals Are Better than Absolute Universals'. *Chicago Linguistic Society* 33/2: 123–45.
Du Feu, V. (1996). *Rapanui*. London: Routledge.
Durie, M. (1985). *A Grammar of Acehnese: On the Basis of a Dialect of North Aceh* (Verhandeligen van het Koninklijk Instituut voor Taal-, Land- en Volkenkunde 112). Dordrecht: Foris.
Dutton, T. E. (1996). *Koiari* (Languages of the World/Materials 10). Munich: Lincom Europa.
Ebermann, E. (1986). 'Die Sprache der Mauka'. Ph.D. thesis, University of Vienna.
Ebert, K. (1997). *Camling (Chamling)* (Languages of the World/Materials 103). Munich: Lincom Europa.
Eisenberg, P. (1994). 'German'. In E. König and J. v. d. Auwera (eds.), *The Germanic Languages*. London: Routledge, 349–87.
Elderkin, E. D. (1988). 'Person and Number Markers in Iragw Verbs'. *Afrikanische Arbeitspapiere* 14: 79–96.
Elson, B. (1960). 'Sierra Popoluca Morphology'. *International Journal of American Linguistics* 26/3: 206–23.
Emeneau, M. B. (1984). *Toda Grammar and Texts*. Philadelphia: American Philosophical Society.

Esser, S. J. (1964). *De Uma-Taal (West Midden-Celebes): Spraakkunstige Schets en Teksten* (Verhandeligen van het Koninklijk Instituut voor Taal-, Land- en Volkenkunde 43). The Hague: Nijhoff.

Everett, D. L. (1986). 'Pirahã'. In D. C. Derbyshire and G. K. Pullum (eds.), *Handbook of Amazonian Languages*, vol. i. Berlin: Mouton de Gruyter, 200–325.

—— (1987). 'Pirahã Clitic Doubling'. *Natural Language and Linguistic Theory* 5: 245–76.

Fabian, G., E. Fabian, and B. Waters (1998). *Morphology, Syntax and Cohesion in Nabak, Papua New Guinea* (Pacific Linguistics C 144). Canberra: Australian National University.

Facundes, S. (2000). 'The Language of the Apurinã People of Brazil (Maipure/Arawak)'. Ph.D. thesis, University of New York at Buffalo.

Farr, J., and C. Farr (1975). 'Some Features of Korafe Morphology'. In T. E. Dutton (ed.), *Studies in Languages of Central and South-East Papua* (Pacific Linguistics C 29). Canberra: Australian National University, 731–70.

Feyerabend, P. (1975). *Against Method: Outline of an Anarchistic Theory of Knowledge.* London: New Left Books.

Foley, W. A. (1986). *The Papuan Languages of New Guinea* (Cambridge Language Surveys). Cambridge: Cambridge University Press.

—— (1991). *The Yimas Language of New Guinea*. Stanford, Calif.: Stanford University Press.

—— (1997). *Anthropological Linguistics: An Introduction*. Oxford: Blackwell.

Forchheimer, P. (1953). *The Category of Person in Language*. Berlin: de Gruyter.

Fortescue, M. (1984). *West Greenlandic* (Croom Helm Descriptive Grammars). London: Croom Helm.

Fortune, R. F. (1942). *Arapesh*. New York: Augustin.

Foster, M. L., and G. M. Foster (1948). *Sierra Popoluca Speech* (Smithsonion Institution Publications 8). Washington, DC: US Govt. Printing Office.

Fox, G. J. (1976). *Big Nambas Grammar* (Pacific Linguistics B 60). Canberra: Australian National University.

Fox, J. J., and C. E. Grimes (1995). 'Roti'. In D. T. Tryon (ed.), *Comparative Austronesian Dictionary*, vol. i, fasc. 1 (Trends in Linguistics: Documentation 10). Berlin: Mouton de Gruyter, 611–22.

Frachtenberg, L. J. (1922a). 'Coos'. In F. Boas (ed.), *Handbook of American Indian Languages*, vol. ii. Washington, DC: Bureau of American Ethnology, 297–430.

—— (1922b). 'Siuslawan (Lower Umpqua)'. In F. Boas (ed.), *Handbook of American Indian Languages*, vol. ii. Washington, DC: Bureau of American Ethnology, 441–629.

Frajzyngier, Z. (2001). *A Grammar of Lele* (Stanford Monographs in African Languages). Stanford: Center for the Study of Language and Information.

—— and E. Shay (2002). *A Grammar of Hdi* (Mouton Grammar Library 21). Berlin: Mouton de Gruyter.

Frank, P. S. (1985). 'A Grammar of Ika'. Ph.D. thesis, University of Pennsylvania.

—— (1990). *Ika Syntax* (Studies in the Languages of Colombia 1). Arlington, Va.: Summer Institute of Linguistics.

Franklin, K. J. (1971). *A Grammar of Kewa, New Guinea* (Pacific Linguistics C 16). Canberra: Australian National University.

References

Fransen, M. A. E. (1995). 'A Grammar of Limbum, a Grassfields Bantu Language Spoken in the North-West Province of Cameroon'. Ph.D. thesis, Free University Amsterdam.

Frantz, C., and H. P. McKaughan (1973). 'Gadsup Independent Verb Affixes'. In H. P. McKaughan (ed.), *The Languages of the Eastern Family of the East New Guinea Highland Stock*. Seattle, Wa.: University of Washington Press, 439–49.

Frantz, D. G. (1991). *Blackfoot Grammar*. Toronto: University of Toronto Press.

Freeland, L. S. (1947). 'Western Miwok Texts with Linguistic Sketch'. *International Journal of American Linguistics* 13: 31–46.

——(1951). *Language of the Sierra Miwok* (Memoir of the International Journal of American Linguistics 6). Baltimore, Md.: Waverly Press.

Gaden, H. (1909). *Essai de grammaire de la langue baguirmienne*. Paris: Leroux.

Gair, J. W. (1970). *Colloquial Sinhalese Clause Structures* (Janua Linguarum, Series Practica 83). The Hague: Mouton.

Garcia, E. C., and F. van Putte (1989). 'Forms are Silver, Nothing is Gold'. *Folia Linguistica Historica* 8/1–2: 365–84.

Garland, R., and S. Garland (1975). 'A Grammar Sketch of Mountain Koiali'. In T. E. Dutton (ed.), *Studies in Languages of Central and South-East Papua* (Pacific Linguistics C 29). Canberra: Australian National University, 413–70.

Garvin, P. L. (1948). 'Kutenai III: Morpheme Distribution (Prefix, Theme, Suffix)'. *International Journal of American Linguistics* 14/3: 171–87.

Gary, J. O., and S. Gamal-Eldin (1982). *Cairene Egyptian Colloquial Arabic* (Lingua Descriptive Studies). Amsterdam: North-Holland.

Geary, E. (1977). *Kunimaipa Grammar* (Workpapers in Papua New Guinea Languages 23). Ukarumpa: Summer Institute of Linguistics.

Geoghegan, R. H. (1944). *The Aleut Language*. Washington, DC: US Dept. of the Interior.

George, K. (1993). 'Cornish'. In M. J. Ball and J. Fife (eds.), *The Celtic Languages*. London: Routledge, 410–68.

Gerzenstein, A. (1994). *Lengua Maká: Estudio descriptivo* (Archivo de Lenguas Indoamericanas). Buenos Aires: University of Buenos Aires.

Gil, D. (2001). 'Creoles, Complexity and Riau Indonesian'. *Linguistic Typology* 5/2–3: 325–70.

Giridhar, P. P. (1994). *Mao Naga Grammar* (Silver Jubilee Publication Series). Mysore: Central Institute of Indian Languages.

Givón, T. (1976). 'Topic, Pronoun and Grammatical Agreement'. In C. N. Li (ed.), *Subject and Topic*. New York: Academic Press, 149–88.

——(1980). *Ute Reference Grammar*. Ignacio: Ute Press.

——(1984). *Syntax: A Functional-Typological Introduction*, vol. i. Amsterdam: Benjamins.

——(1990). *Syntax: A Functional-Typological Introduction*, vol. ii. Amsterdam: Benjamins.

Glasgow, K. (1964). 'Four Principal Contrasts in Burera Personal Pronouns'. In R. Pittman and H. B. Kerr (eds.), *Papers on the Languages of the Australian Aborigines* (Occasional Papers in Aboriginal Studies 3). Canberra: Australian Institute of Aboriginal Studies, 109–17.

—— (1984). 'Burarra Word Classes'. In *Papers in Australian Linguistics*, vol. xvi (Pacifica Linguistics A 68). Canberra: Australian National University, 1–54.
Goddard, C. (1995). 'Who Are We? The Natural Semantics of Pronouns'. *Language Sciences* 17/1: 99–121.
—— (2001). 'Lexico-Semantic Universals: A Critical Overview'. *Linguistic Typology* 5/1: 1–66.
Goddard, I. (1990). 'Algonquian Linguistic Change and Reconstruction'. In P. Baldi (ed.), *Linguistic Change and Reconstruction Methodology* (Trends in Linguistics: Studies and Monographs 45). Berlin: Mouton de Gruyter, 98–114.
Goddard, P. E. (1905). *The Morphology of the Hupa Language* (American Archeology and Ethnology). Berkeley, Calif.: University Press.
—— (1912). *Elements of the Kato Language*. Berkeley, Calif.: University of California Press.
Godfrey, M. (1964). 'A Tentative Outline Grammar of Wik-Munkan'. In *Occasional Papers in Aboriginal Studies*, vol. ii. Canberra: Australian Institute of Aboriginal Studies, 57–78.
—— and H. B. Kerr (1964). 'Personal Pronouns in Wik-Munkan'. In R. Pittman and H. B. Kerr (eds.), *Papers on the Languages of the Australian Aborigines* (Occasional Papers in Aboriginal Studies 3). Canberra: Australian Institute of Aboriginal Studies, 13–34.
Goffman, E. (1979). 'Footing'. *Semiotica* 25/1–2: 1–29.
Gonzales, A. (1981). *Pampangan: Towards a Meaning-Based Description* (Pacific Linguistics C 48). Canberra: Australian National University.
Gonzáles de Pérez, M. S. (1987). *Diccionario y gramática Chibcha: Manuscrito anónimo de la Bibliotheca Nacional de Colombia* (Bibliotheca 'Ezequiel Uricoechea' 1). Bogotá: Instituto Caro y Cuervo.
Gordon, L. (1986). *Maricopa Morphology and Syntax*. Berkeley, Calif.: University of California Press.
Görlach, M. (1997). *The Linguistic History of English: An Introduction*. London: Macmillan.
Gralow, F. L. (1993). *Un Bosquejo del Idioma Koreguaje*. Santafé de Bogotá: Instituto Lingüístico de Verano.
Greenberg, J. H. (1963). 'Some Universals of Grammar with Particular Reference to the Order of Meaningful Elements'. In J. H. Greenberg (ed.), *Universals of Language*. Cambridge, Mass.: MIT Press, 73–113.
—— (1966). *Language Universals, with Special Reference to Feature Hierarchies* (Janua Linguarum, Series Minor 59). The Hague: Mouton.
—— (1969). 'Some Methods of Dynamic Comparison in Linguistics'. In J. Puhvel (ed.), *Substance and Structure of Language*. Berkeley, Calif.: University of California Press, 147–204.
—— (1985). 'Some Iconic Relationship among Place, Time, and Discourse Deixis'. In J. Haiman (ed.), *Iconicity in Syntax* (Typological Studies in Language 6). Amsterdam: Benjamins, 271–88.
—— (1988). 'The First Person Inclusive Dual as an Ambiguous Category'. *Studies in Language* 12/1: 1–18.

Greenberg, J. H. (1989). 'On a Metalanguage for Pronominal Systems: A Reply to McGregor'. *Studies in Language* 13/2: 452–8.

——(1993). 'The Second Person is Rightly so Called'. In M. Eid and G. Iverson (eds.), *Principles and Prediction: The Analysis of Natural Language*. Amsterdam: Benjamins, 9–24.

Griffiths, G., and C. Griffiths (1976). *Aspectos da Língua Kadiwéu* (Série Lingüística 6). Brasília: Summer Institute of Linguistics.

Grimes, B. F. (ed.) (1996). *Ethnologue*, 13th edn. Dallas: Summer Institute of Linguistics.

de Groot, C., and M. J. Limburg (1986). *Pronominal Elements: Diachrony, Typology, and Formalization in Functional Grammar* (Working Papers in Functional Grammer 12). Amsterdam: Instituut voor Functioneel Onderzoek van Taal en Taalgebruik.

Gruzdeva, E. (1998). *Nivkh* (Languages of the World/Materials 111). Munich: Lincom Europa.

Gvozdanović, J. (1985). *Language System and its Change: On Theory and Testability* (Trends in Linguistics: Studies and Monographs 30). Berlin: Mouton de Gruyter.

——(1991). 'Syncretism and the Paradigmatic Patterning of Grammatical Meaning'. In F. Plank (ed.), *Paradigms: The Economy of Inflection* (Empirical Approaches to Language Typology 9). Berlin: Mouton de Gruyter, 133–60.

Haacke, W. H. G. (1977). 'The so-called "Personal Pronoun" in Nama'. In A. Traill (ed.), *Khoisan Linguistic Studies*, vol. iii. Johannesburg: African Studies Institute, 43–62.

Haas, M. R. (1946). 'A Grammatical Sketch of Tunica'. In H. Hoijer et al., *Linguistic Structures of Native America* (Publications in Anthropology 6). New York: Viking Fund, 337–66.

——(1969). ' "Exclusive" and "Inclusive": A Look at Early Usage'. *International Journal of American Linguistics* 35/1: 1–6.

——(1977). 'From Auxiliary Verb Phrase to Inflectional Suffix'. In C. N. Li (ed.), *Mechanisms of Syntactic Change*. Austin, Tx.: University of Texas Press, 525–38.

Hagège, C. (1982). *La Structure des langues* (Que Sais-je? 2006). Paris: Presses Universitaires de France.

Hagman, R. S. (1977). *Nama Hottentot Grammar* (Language Science Monographs 15). Bloomington: Indiana University Press.

Haiman, J. (1980). *Hua: A Papuan Language of the Eastern Highlands of New Guinea* (Studies in Language Companion Series 5). Amsterdam: Benjamins.

Hale, A. (1980). 'Person Markers: Finite Conjunct and Disjunct Verb Forms in Newari'. In R. Trail (ed.), *Papers in South-East Asian Linguistics* (Pacific Linguistics A 53). Canberra: Australian National University, 95–106.

Hale, K. (1973). 'Person Marking in Walbiri'. In P. Kiparski (ed.), *A Festschrift for Morris Halle*. New York: Holt, Rinehart & Winston, 308–44.

——(1976a). 'Tya.Pukay (Djaabugay)'. In P. Sutton (ed.), *Languages of Cape York*. Canberra: Australian Institute of Aboriginal Studies, 236–42.

——(1976b). 'Wik Reflections of Middle Paman Phonology'. In P. Sutton (ed.), *Languages of Cape York*. Canberra: Australian Institute of Aboriginal Studies, 50–60.

Halpern, A. M. (1946). 'Yuma'. In H. Hoijer et al., *Linguistic Structures of Native America* (Publications in Anthropology 6). New York: Viking Fund, 249–88.

Harbert, W. (1995). 'Binding Theory, Control, and Pro'. In G. Webelhuth (ed.), *Government and Binding Theory and the Minimalist Program*. Oxford: Blackwell, 177–240.

Hardman, M. J. (1966). *Jaqaru: Outline of Phonological and Morphological Structure* (Janua Linguarum, Series Practica 22). The Hague: Mouton.

——(1972). 'Early Use of Inclusive/Exclusive'. *International Journal of American Linguistics* 38/2: 145–6.

Harley, H. (1994). 'Hug a Tree: Deriving the Morphosyntactic Feature Hierarchy'. In A. Carnie, H. Harley, and T. Bures (eds.), *Papers on Phonology and Morphology* (MIT Working Papers in Linguistics). Cambridge, Mass.: MIT Press, 289–320.

—— and E. Ritter (2002). 'Structuring the Bundle: A Universal Morphosyntactic Feature Geometry'. In H. Simon and H. Wiese (eds.), *Pronouns: Grammar and Representation*. Amsterdam: Benjamins, 23–39.

Harlow, R. (1996). *Maori* (Languages of the World/Materials 20). Munich: Lincom Europa.

Harms, P. L. (1994). *Epena Pedee Syntax* (Studies in the Languages of Colombia 4). Arlington, Va.: Summer Institute of Linguistics, and in *Linguistics Today*, 52.

Harré, R. (1993). 'Universals Yet Again: A Test of the "Wierzbicka Thesis" '. *Language Sciences* 15/3: 231–8.

Harriehausen, B. (1990). *Hmong Njua: syntaktische Analyse einer gesprochenen Sprache mithilfe datenverarbeitungstechnischer Mittel und sprachvergleichende Beschriebung des südostasiatischen Sprachraums*. Tübingen: Max Niemeyer.

Harrison, C. H. (1971). 'The Morphophonology of Asurini Words'. In D. Bendor-Samuel (ed.), *Tupi Studies*, vol. i (Summer Institute of Linguistics Publications in Lingiustics 29). Oklahoma: Summer Institute of Linguistics.

Hart, H. (1988). *Diccionario Chayahuita–Castellano* (Série Lingüística Peruana 29). Pucallpa: Instituto Lingüístico de Verano.

Haspelmath, M. (1993). *A Grammar of Lezgian* (Mouton Grammar Library 9). Berlin: Mouton de Gruyter.

——(1997). *Indefinite Pronouns* (Oxford Studies in Typology and Linguistic Theory). Oxford: Clarendon Press.

Haviland, J. (1979). 'Guugu-Yimidhirr'. In R. M. W. Dixon and B. J. Blake (eds.), *Handbook of Australian Languages*, vol. i. Amsterdam: Benjamins, 27–180.

Hawkins, J. A. (1983). *Word Order Universals*. New York: Academic Press.

Hawkins, R. E. (1998). 'Wai Wai'. In D. C. Derbyshire and G. K. Pullum (eds.), *Handbook of Amazonian Languages*, vol. iv. Berlin: Mouton de Gruyter, 25–224.

Head, B. F. (1978). 'Respect Degrees in Pronominal Reference'. In J. H. Greenberg (ed.), *Universals of Human Language*, vol. iii: *Word Structure*. Stanford, Calif.: Stanford University Press, 151–212.

Healey, A., A. Isoroembo, and M. Chittleborough (1969). 'Preliminary Notes on Orokaiva Grammar'. In *Papers in New Guinea Linguistics*, vol. ix. Canberra: Australian National University, 33–64.

Heath, J. (1978). *Ngandi Grammar, Texts, and Dictionary*. Canberra: Australian Institute of Aboriginal Studies.

——(1984). *Functional Grammar of Nunggubuyu*. Canberra: Australian Institute of Aboriginal Studies.

——(1991). 'Pragmatic Disguise in Pronominal-Affix Paradigms'. In F. Plank (ed.), *Paradigms: The Economy of Inflection*. Berlin: Mouton de Gruyter, 75–89.

Heath, J. (1998). 'Pragmatic Skewing in 1–2 Pronominal Combination in Native American Languages'. *International Journal of American Linguistics* 64/2: 83–104.
—— (forthcoming). 'Person'. In G. Booij, C. Lehmann, and J. Mugdan (eds.), *Morphology: An International Handbook on Inflection and Word-Formation*, vol. ii (Handbücher zur Sprach- und Kommunikationswissenschaft 17). Berlin: de Gruyter.
Hedlinger, R. (1981). 'Pronouns in Akɔɔse'. *Studies in African Linguistics* 12/3: 277–90.
Helimski, E. (1998). 'Nganasan'. In D. Abondolo (ed.), *The Uralic Languages*. London: Routledge, 480-515.
Helmbrecht, J. (1996). 'The Syntax of Personal Agreement in East Caucasian Languages'. *Sprachtypologie und Universalien Forschung* 49/2: 127–48.
Henderson, T. S. T. (1985). 'Who are We, anyway? A Study of Personal Pronoun Systems'. *Linguistische Berichte* 98: 300–9.
Hengeveld, K. (1997). 'Shifters'. Inaugural speech, University of Amsterdam, 31 October 1997.
Hetzron, R. (1990). 'Semitic Languages'. In B. Comrie (ed.), *The World's Major Languages*. Oxford: Oxford University Press, 654–63.
Hewitt, B. G. (1979). *Abkhaz* (Lingua Descriptive Studies). Amsterdam: North-Holland.
—— (ed.) (1989). *The North West Caucasian Languages* (The Indigenous Languages of the Caucasus 2). Delmar, NY: Caravan Books.
Hoddinott, W. G., and F. M. Kofod (1988). *The Ngankikurungkurr Language* (Pacific Linguistics D 77). Canberra: Australian National University.
Hoffmann, C. (1963). *A Grammar of the Margi Language*. London: Oxford University Press.
Hoffmann, J. (1903). *Mundari Grammar*. Calcutta: Bengal Secreteriat Press.
Höftmann, H. (1993). *Grammatik Des Fon*. Leipzig: Langenscheidt.
Hoijer, H. (1933). *Tonkawa, an Indian Language of Texas*. New York: Columbia University Press.
—— (1946). 'Chiricahua Apache'. In H. Hoijer et al., *Linguistic Structures of Native America* (Publications in Anthropology 6). New York: Viking Fund, 55–84.
Hollenbach, B. E. (1970). 'Inclusive Plural: A Further Look'. *Linguistics* 60: 27–32.
Holm, J. (1988). *Pidgins and Creoles*, vol. i: *Theory and Structure* (Cambridge Language Surveys). Cambridge: Cambridge University Press.
Holmer, N. M. (1946). 'Outline of Cuna Grammar'. *International Journal of American Linguistics* 12/4: 185–97.
Hoogshagen, S. (1984). 'Coatlán Mixe'. In M. S. Edmonson (ed.), *Supplement to the Handbook of Middle American Indians*, vol. ii: *Linguistics*. Austin, Tx.: University of Texas Press, 3–19.
Hopkins, E. B. (1986). 'Pronouns and Pronoun Fusion in Yaouré'. In U. Wiesemann (ed.), *Pronominal Systems*. Tübingen: Narr, 191–204.
Hoskison, J. T. (1983). 'A Grammar and Dictionary of the Gude Language'. Ph.D. thesis, Ohio State University.
Householder, F. W. (1955). Review of *The Category of Person in Language*, by P. Forchheimer. *Language* 31/1–2: 93–100.
Howe, S. (1996). *The Personal Pronouns in the Germanic Languages: A Study of Personal Pronoun Morphology and Change in the Germanic Languages form the First Records to the Present Day* (Studia Linguistica Germanica 43). Berlin: de Gruyter.

Huang, Y. (1995). 'On Null Subject and Null Objects in Generative Grammar'. *Linguistics* 33: 1081–123.
von Humboldt, W. (1994 [1827]). 'Über den Dualis'. In W. von Humboldt, *Über die Sprache: Reden vor der Akademie*. Tübingen: Francke, 143–69.
—— (1830). *Über die Verwandtschaft der Ortsadverbien mit dem Pronomen in einigen Sprachen*. Berlin: Königliche Akademie der Wissenschaften.
Hunt, R. J. (1940). *Mataco Grammar*. Tucuman: Instituto de Antropologia.
Hurd, C., and P. Hurd (1970). 'Nasioi Verbs'. *Oceanic Linguistics* 9/1: 37–78.
Hutchisson, D. (1986). 'Sursurunga Pronouns and the Special Uses of Quadral Number'. In U. Wiesemann (ed.), *Pronominal Systems*. Tübingen: Narr, 1–20.
Huttar, G. L., and M. L. Huttar (1994). *Ndyuka*. London: Routledge.
Hyman, L. M. (1979). 'Phonology and Noun Structure'. In L. M. Hyman (ed.), *Aghem Grammatical Structure* (Southern California Occasional Papers in Linguistics 7). Los Angeles: University of Southern California, 1–72.
—— (1981). *Noni Grammatical Structure: With Special Reference to Verb Morphology* (Southern California Occasional Papers in Linguistics 9). Los Angeles: University of Southern California.
Hymes, D. H. (1955). Review of *The Category of Person in Language*, by P. Forchheimer. *International Journal of American Linguistics* 21/3: 294–300.
—— (1972). 'On Personal Pronouns: "Fourth" Person and Phonesthematic Aspects'. In E. Estellie Smith (ed.), *Studies in Linguistics in Honor of George L. Trager* (Janua Linguarum Series Maior 52). The Hague: Mouton, 100–21.
Ingram, D. (1978). 'Typology and Universals of Personal Pronouns'. In J. H. Greenberg (ed.), *Universals of Human Language*, vol. iii: *Word Structure*. Stanford, Calif.: Stanford University Press, 213–48.
Innes, G. (1966). *An Introduction to Grebo*. London: School of Oriental and African Studies.
Irwin, B. (1974). *Salt-Yui Grammar* (Pacific Linguistics B 35). Canberra: Australian National University.
Jacobsen, W. H., Jr. (1964). 'A Grammar of the Washo Language'. Ph.D. thesis, University of California at Berkeley.
Jaeggli, O., and K. J. Safir (1989). 'The Null Subject Parameter and Parametric Theory'. In O. Jaeggli and K. J. Safir (eds.), *The Null Subject Parameter* (Studies in Natural Language and Linguistic Theory 1–44). Dordrecht: Kluwer, 1–44.
Jakobson, R. (1971 [1957]). 'Shifters, Verbal Categories and the Russian Verb'. In *Selected Writings*, vol. ii: *Word and Language*. The Hague: Mouton, 130–47.
Jelinek, E. (1984). 'Empty Categories, Case, and Configurationality'. *Natural Language and Linguistic Theory* 2/1: 39–76.
Jensen, C. (1990). 'Cross-Referencing Changes in Some Tupí-Guaraní Languages'. In D. L. Payne (ed.), *Amazonian Linguistics*. Austin, Tx.: University of Texas Press, 117–60.
Jespersen, O. (1922). *Language: Its Nature, Development and Origin*. London: Allen & Unwin.
—— (1924). *The Philosophy of Grammar*. London: Allen & Unwin.
Jones, A. A. (1998). *Towards a Lexicogrammar of Mekeo (an Austronesian Language of West Central Papua)* (Pacific Linguistics C 138). Canberra: Australian National University.

Jones, W., and P. Jones (1991). *Barasano Syntax* (Studies in the Languages of Colombia 2). Arlington, Va.: Summer Institute of Linguistics.

Josephs, L. S. (1975). *Palauan Reference Grammar* (PALI Language Texts: Micronesia). Honolulu: University Press of Hawai'i.

Jungraithmayr, H. (1970). *Die Ron-Sprachen: tschadohamitische Studien in Nordnigerien* (Afrikanische Forschungen 3). Glückstadt: Augustin.

Kastenholz, R. (1987). 'Das Koranko'. Ph.D. thesis, University of Cologne.

Keegan, J. M. (1997). *A Reference Grammar of Mbay* (Lincom Studies in African Linguistics 14). Munich: Lincom Europa.

Keesing, R. M. (1985). *Kwaio Grammar* (Pacific Linguistics B 88). Canberra: Australian National University.

Kemp, A. (1987). 'The Tehknè Grammatikè of Dionysius Thrax, Translated into English'. In D. J. Taylor (ed.), *The History of Linguistics in the Classical Period* (Studies in the History of the Language Sciences 46). Amsterdam: Benjamins, 169-89.

Kendall, M. B. (1976). *Selected Problems in Yavapai Syntax*. New York: Garland.

Keraf, G. (1978). *Morfologi Dialek Lamalera*. Ende-Flores: Arnoldus.

Keresztes, L. (1998). 'Mansi'. In D. Abondolo (ed.), *The Uralic Languages*. London: Routledge, 387-427.

van de Kerke, S. (1996). 'Affix Order and Interpretation in Bolivian Quechua'. Ph.D. thesis, University of Amsterdam.

Kießling, R. (1994). *Eine Grammatik des Burunge* (Afrikanistische Forschungen) Hamburg: Research and Progress.

Kimball, G. D. (1985). 'A Descriptive Grammar of Koasati'. Ph.D. thesis, Tulane University, La.

Kirk, J. W. C. (1905). *A Grammar of the Somali Language*. Cambridge: Cambridge University Press.

Kitching, A. L. (1907). *An Outline Grammar of the Acholi Language*. London: Sheldon Press.

van Klinken, C. L. (1999). *A Grammar of the Fehan Dialect of Tetun: An Austronesian Language of West Timor* (Pacific Linguistics C 155). Canberra: Australian National University.

Koch, H. (1994). 'The Creation of Morphological Zeroes'. In G. Booij and J. van Marle (eds.), *Yearbook of Morphology 1994*. Dordrecht: Kluwer, 31-71.

—— (1997). 'Morphological Changes in Arandic Pronouns'. Paper presented at the 13th International Conference on Historical Linguistics, Düsseldorf, 15 Aug. 1997.

Koehn, E., and S. Koehn (1986). 'Apalai'. In D. C. Derbyshire and G. K. Pullum (eds.), *Handbook of Amazonian Languages*, vol. i. Berlin: Mouton de Gruyter, 33-127.

Kuhn, T. S. (1962). *The Structure of Scientific Revolutions*. Chicago: University of Chicago Press.

Kuipers, A. H. (1974). *The Shuswap Language: Grammar, Texts, Dictionary*. The Hague: Mouton.

Kurylowicz, J. (1964). *The Inflectional Categories of Indo-European*. Heidelberg: Winter.

Kutsch Lojenga, C. (1994). *Ngiti: A Central Sudanic Language of Zaire* (Nilo-Saharan Linguistic Analyses and Documentation 9). Hamburg: Köppe.

Lachnitt, G. (1988). *Damreme'uwaimramidzé: Estudos sistemáticos e comparativos de gramática Xavante*. Campo Grande: Missão Salesina de Mato Grosso.

Laidig, W. D., and C. J. Laidig (1990). 'Larike Pronouns: Duals and Trials in a Central Moluccan Language'. *Oceanic Linguistics* 29/2: 87–109.

Langdon, M. (1970). *A Grammar of Diegueño*. Berkeley, Calif.: University of California Press.

Lastra, Y. (1998). *Ixtenco Otomí* (Languages of the World/Materials 19). Munich: Lincom Europa.

Lastra de Suárez, Y. (1984). 'Chichimeco Jonaz'. In M. S. Edmonson (ed.), *Supplement to the Handbook of Middle American Indians*, vol. ii: *Linguistics*. Austin, Tx.: University of Texas Press, 20–42.

Laycock, D. (1977). 'Me and You versus the Rest'. *Irian* 6: 33–41.

Leavitt, R. M. (1996). *Passamaquoddy-Maliseet* (Languages of the World/Materials 27). Munich: Lincom Europa.

Lee, J. (1987). *Tiwi Today: A Study of Language Change in a Contact Situation* (Pacific Linguistics C 96). Canberra: Australian National University.

Lefebvre, C. (1998). *Creole Genesis and the Acquisition of Grammar: The Case of Haitian Creole* (Cambridge Studies in Linguistics 88). Cambridge: Cambridge University Press.

Lehmann, C. (1982). 'Universal and Typological Aspects of Agreement'. In H. Seiler and F. J. Stachowiak (eds.), *Apprehension: das sprachliche Erfassen von Gegenständen*, vol. ii: *Die Techniken und ihr Zusammenhang in Einzelsprachen*. Tübingen: Narr, 201–67.

—— (1983). 'Rektion und syntaktische Relationen'. *Folia Linguistica* 17: 339–78.

Lehmann, T. (1994). *Grammatik des Alttamil unter besonderer Berücksichtigung der Cankam Texte* (Beiträge zur Sdasienforschung 159). Stuttgart: Steiner.

Levin, N. B. (1964). *The Assiniboine Language*. The Hague: Mouton.

Levinson, S. C. (1988). 'Putting Linguistics on a Proper Footing: Explorations in Goffman's Concepts of Participation'. In P. Drew and A. Wootton (eds.), *Erving Goffman: Exploring the Interaction Order*. Oxford: Polity Press, 161–227.

Lewis, E. D., and C. E. Grimes (1995). 'Sika'. In D. T. Tryon (ed.), *Comparative Austronesian Dictionary*, vol. i, fasc. 1 (Trends in Linguistics: Documentation 10). Berlin: Mouton de Gruyter, 601–9.

Lewis, G. L. (1967). *Turkish Grammar*. Oxford: Clarendon Press.

Lichtenberk, F. (2000). 'Inclusory Pronominals'. *Oceanic Linguistics* 39/1: 1–32.

Lindstrom, L., and J. D. Lynch (1994). *Kwamera* (Languages of the World/Materials 2). Munich: Lincom Europa.

Lipkind, W. (1945). *Winnebago Grammar*. New York: King's Crown Press.

Lounsbury, F. G. (1953). *Oneida Verb Morphology* (Yale University Publications in Anthropology 48). New Haven, Conn.: Yale University Press.

Louwerse, J. (1988). *The Morphosyntax of Una in Relation to Discourse Structure: A Descriptive Analysis* (Pacific Linguistics B 100). Canberra: Australian National University.

Loving, R. (1973). 'An Outline of Awa Grammatical Structure'. In H. P. McKaughan (ed.), *The Languages of the Eastern Family of the East New Guinea Highland Stock*. Seattle, Wa.: University of Washington Press, 65–87.

Lowie, R. H. (1941). *The Crow Language: Grammatical Sketch and Analyzed Text*. Berkeley, Calif.: University of California Press.

Luhrman, G. J. (1984). 'C. L. Pasius, T. Linacer, J. C. Scaliger en hun Beschouwing van het Werkwoord: Een Kritisch-Vergelijkende Studie omtrent XVIde Eeuwse Taalkundige Theorievorming'. Ph.D. thesis, University of Groningen.

Lukas, J. (1953). *Die Sprache der Tubu in der zentralen Sahara.* Berlin: Akademie Verlag.

Lupardus, K. J. (1982). 'The Language of the Alabama Indians'. Ph.D. thesis, University of Kansas.

Luraghi, S. (2000). 'Synkretismus'. In G. Booij, C. Lehmann, and J. Mugdan (eds.), *Morphology: An International Handbook on Inflection and Word-Formation*, vol. i (Handbücher zur Sprach- und Kommunikationswissenschaft 17). Berlin: de Gruyter, 638–47.

Lusted, M. (1976). 'Anywa'. In M. L. Bender (ed.), *The Non-Semitic Languages of Ethiopia*. East Lansing, Mich.: African Studies Center, 495–512.

Lynch, J. D. (1967). 'A Comparative Study of the Languages and Dialects of the Island of Tanna, Southern New Hebrides'. Ph.D. thesis, University of Sydney.

—— (1978). *A Grammar of Lenakel* (Pacific Linguistics B 55). Canberra: Australian National University.

—— (1986). 'The Proto-Southern Vanuatu Pronominal System'. In P. Geraghty, L. Carrington, and S. A. Wurm (eds.), *Focal II: Papers from the Fourth International Conference on Austronesian Linguistics* (Pacific Linguistics C 94). Canberra: Australian National University, 259–87.

—— (1998). *Pacific Languages: An Introduction.* Honolulu: University of Hawai'i Press.

Lyons, J. (1968). *Introduction to Theoretical Linguistics.* Cambridge: Cambridge University Press.

—— (1977). *Semantics.* Cambridge: Cambridge University Press.

Macaulay, M. (1996). *A Grammar of Chalcatongo Mixtec* (University of California Publications in Linguistics 127). Berkeley, Calif.: University of California Press.

McElhanon, K. A. (1975). 'North Eastern Trans-New Guinea Phylum Languages'. In S. A. Wurm (ed.), *Papuan Languages and the New Guinea Linguistic Scene* (Pacific Linguistics C 38). Canberra: Australian National University, 527–68.

McGregor, W. (1989). 'Greenberg on the First Person Inclusive Dual: Evidence from some Australian Languages'. *Studies in Language* 13/2: 437–51.

—— (1990). *A Functional Grammar of Gooniyandi* (Studies in Language Companion Series 22). Amsterdam: Benjamins.

—— (1993). *Gunin/Kwini* (Languages of the World/Materials 11). Munich: Lincom Europa.

—— (1994). *Warrwa* (Languages of the World/Materials 89). Munich: Lincom Europa.

—— (1996a). *Nyulnyul* (Languages of the World/Materials 88). Munich: Lincom Europa.

—— (1996b). 'The Pronominal System of Gooniyandi and Bunaba'. In W. McGregor (ed.), *Studies in Kimberley Languages in Honour of Howard Coate*. Munich: Lincom Europa, 159–73.

McIntosh, M. (1984). *Fulfulde Syntax and Verbal Morphology.* Boston, Mass.: Routledge & Kegan Paul.

McKaughan, H. P. (1959). 'Semantic Components of Pronoun Systems: Maranao'. *Word* 15: 101–2.

McKay, G. R. (1978). 'Pronominal Person and Number Categories in Rembarrnga and Djeebbana'. *Oceanic Linguistics* 17: 27–37.
—— (1979). 'Gender and the Category Unit Augmented'. *Oceanic Linguistics* 18/2: 203–10.
—— (1984). 'Ndjébbana (Kunubidji) Grammar: Miscellaneous Morphological and Syntactic Notes'. In *Papers in Australian Linguistics*, vol. xvi (Pacific Linguistics A 68). Canberra: Australian National University, 119–52.
—— (1990). 'The Addressee: Or is the Second Person Singular'. *Studies in Language* 14/2: 429–32.
—— (2000). 'Ndjébbana'. In R. M. W. Dixon and B. J. Blake (eds.), *Handbook of Australian Languages*, vol. v: *Grammatical Sketches of Bunuba, Ndjébbana and Kugu Nganhcara*. Oxford: Oxford University Press, 154–354.
MacLean, E. A. (1986). *North Slope Iñupiaq Grammar*, 3rd edn. Fairbanks: Alaska Native Language Center.
Macuch, R. (1965). *Handbook of Classical and Modern Mandaic*. Berlin: de Gruyter.
Malchukov, A. L. (1995). *Even* (Languages of the World/Materials 12). Munich: Lincom Europa.
Mallinson, G. (1986). *Rumanian* (Croom Helm Descriptive Grammars). London: Routledge.
Malone, T. (1988). 'The Origin and Development of Tuyuca Evidentials'. *International Journal of American Linguistics* 54/2: 119–40.
Mangold, M. (1977). *Wolof Pronoun Verb Patterns and Paradigms* (Forschungen zur Anthropologie und Religionsgeschichte 3). Saarbrücken: Homo et Religio.
Mannheim, B. (1982). 'Person, Number and Inclusivity in Two Andean Languages'. *Acta linguistica Hafniensia* 17/2: 139–56.
Manrique, C. L. (1967). 'Jiliapan Pame'. In R. Wauchope and N. A. McQuown (eds.), *Handbook of Middle American Indians*, vol. v: *Linguistics*. Austin, Tx.: University of Texas Press, 331–48.
Marchese, L. (1978). *Atlas linguistique Kru: Essai de typologie*. Abidjan: University of Abidjan.
Maring, J. M. (1967). 'Grammar of Acoma Keresan'. Ph.D. thesis, Indiana University.
Masica, C. P. (1991). *The Indo-Aryan Languages* (Cambridge Language Surveys). Cambridge: Cambridge University Press.
Matthews, G. H. (1965). *Hidatsa Syntax* (Papers in Formal Linguistics 3). The Hague: Mouton.
Meinhof, C. (1906). *Grundzüge einer vergleichenden Grammatik der Bantusprachen*. Berlin: Dietrich Reimer.
Merlan, F. C. (1982). *Mangarayi* (Lingua Descriptive Studies 4). Amsterdam: North-Holland.
—— (1983). *Ngalakan Grammar, Texts and Vocabulary*. Canberra: Australian National University.
—— (1994). *A Grammar of Wardaman: A Language of the Northern Territory of Australia* (Mouton Grammar Library 11). Berlin: Mouton de Gruyter.
Metcalfe, C. D. (1975). *Bardi Verb Morphology* (Northwestern Australia) (Pacific Linguistics B 30). Canberra: Australian National University.
Milne, L. (1921). *An Elementary Palaung Grammar*. Oxford: Clarendon Press.

Minch, A. S. (1991). 'Essential Elements of Amanab Grammar'. Ph.D. thesis, University of Texas.

Mithun, M. (1986). 'Disagreement: The Case of Pronominal Affixes and Nouns'. In D. Tannen and J. E. Alatis (eds.), *Language and Linguistics: The Interdependence of Theory, Data, and Applications*. Washington, DC: Georgetown University Press, 50–66.

——(1991). 'The Development of Bound Pronominal Paradigms'. In W. P. Lehmann and H.-J. J. Hewitt (eds.), *Language Typology 1988: Typological Models in Reconstruction* (Current Issues in Linguistic Theory 81). Amsterdam: Benjamins, 85–104.

Mixco, M. (1997). *Mandan* (Languages of the World/Materials 159). Munich: Lincom Europa.

Monod-Becquelin, A. (1975). *La Pratique linguistique des indiens Trumai*, vol. i (Langues et Civilisations a Tradition Orale 9). Paris: Société d'Études Linguistiques et Anthropologiques de France.

Moravcsik, E. A. (1978). 'Agreement'. In J. H. Greenberg (ed.), *Universals of Human Language*, vol. iv: *Syntax*. Stanford, Calif.: Stanford University Press, 331–74.

——(1988). 'Agreement and Markedness'. In M. Barlow and C. A. Ferguson (eds.), *Agreement in Natural Language*. Stanford, Calif.: Center for the Study of Language and Information, 89–106.

——(1994). 'Group Plural: Associative Plural or Cohort Plural'. *Linguistlist* 5/681, 11 June 1994 (available at http://linguistlist.org/issues/5/5-681.html).

Morphy, F. (1983). 'Djapu, a Yulngu Dialect'. In R. M. W. Dixon and B. J. Blake (eds.), *Handbook of Australian Languages*, vol. iii. Amsterdam: Benjamins, 1–190.

Mosel, U. (1984). *Tolai Syntax and its Historical Development* (Pacific Linguistics B 92). Canberra: Australian National University.

Mous, M. (in preparation). *Alagwa: Grammar, Texts and Lexicon*.

Mühlhäusler, P. (1986). 'Zur Entstehung von Pronominalsystemen'. In N. Boretzky, W. Enninger, and T. Stolz (eds.), *Beiträge zum 2. essener Kolloquium über 'Kreolsprachen und Sprachkontakte'* (Essener Beiträge zur Sprachwandelforschung 2). Bochum: Brockmeyer, 157–74.

——(2001). 'Personal Pronouns'. In M. Haspelmath, E. König, W. Oesterreicher, and W. Raible (eds.), *Language Typology and Language Universals: An International Handbook*, vol. i (Handbücher zur Sprach- und Kommunikationswissenschaft 20). Berlin: de Gruyter, 741–7.

——and R. Harré (1990). *Pronouns and People: The Linguistic Construction of Social and Personal Identity*. Oxford: Blackwell.

Müller, F. (1876–87). *Grundriss der Sprachwissenschaft*. Vienna: Hölder.

Munro, P. (1976). *Mojave Syntax*. New York: Garland.

Murane, E. (1974). *Daga Grammar: From Morpheme to Discourse* (Summer Institute of Linguistics Publications in Linguistics 43). Oklahoma: Summer Institute of Linguistics.

Muratori, P. C. (1938). *Grammatica Lotuxo*. Verona: Missioni Africane.

Muysken, P. (1977). 'Syntactic Developments in the Verb Phrase of Ecuadorian Quechua'. Ph.D. thesis, University of Amsterdam.

N'diaye-Correard, G. (1970). *Etudes Fca ou Balante (Dialecte Ganja)*. Paris: Société pour l'Étude des Langues Africaines.

Nababan, P. W. J. (1981). *A Grammar of Toba-Batak* (Pacific Linguistics D 37). Canberra: Australian National University.

Najlis, E. L. (1966). *Lengua Abipona*, vol. i (Archivo de Lenguas Precolambinas 1). Buenos Aires: Centro de Estudios Lingüisticos.

Nebel, P. A. (1948). *Dinka Grammar*. Verona: Missioni Africane.

Nettle, D. (1999). *Linguistic Diversity*. Oxford: Oxford University Press.

Newman, S. (1967). 'Classical Nahuatl'. In R. Wauchope and N. A. McQuown (eds.), *Handbook of Middle American Indians*, vol. v: Linguistics. Austin, Tx.: University of Texas Press, 179–200.

——(1980). 'Functional Changes in the Salish Pronominal System'. *International Journal of American Linguistics* 46/3: 155–67.

Nguyen, P. P. (1996). 'Personal Pronouns and Pluralization in Vietnamese'. *Mon-Khmer Studies* 25: 7–14.

Nichols, J. (1992). *Linguistic Diversity in Space and Time*. Chicago: University of Chicago Press.

——(1994). 'Chechen'. In R. Smeets (ed.), *North East Caucasian Languages* (The Indigenous Languages of the Caucasus 4). Delmar, NY: Caravan Books, 1–77.

——and D. A. Peterson (1996). 'The Amerind Personal Pronouns'. *Language* 72/2: 336–71.

Nicklas, T. D. (1974). 'The Elements of Choctaw'. Ph.D. thesis, University of Michigan.

Nikolaeva, I., and M. Tolskaya (2001). *A Grammar of Udihe* (Mouton Grammar Library 22). Berlin: Mouton de Gruyter.

Noonan, M. (1992). *A Grammar of Lango* (Mouton Grammar Library 7). Berlin: Mouton de Gruyter.

Norman, J. (1988). *Chinese* (Cambridge Language Surveys). Cambridge: Cambridge University Press.

Novelli, B. (1985). *A Grammar of the Karimojong Language* (Language and Dialect Studies in East Africa 7). Berlin: Reimer.

Noyer, R. (1992). *Features, Positions and Affixes in Autonomous Morphological Structure* (MIT Working Papers in Linguistics). Cambridge, Mass: MIT.

——(1997). *Features, Positions, and Affixes in Autonomous Morphological Structure* (Outstanding Dissertations in Linguistics). New York: Garland.

Ntage, S., and G. Sop (1972). *Pé ŋké ŋwaʔŋyə ŋə jíʔtɤ Gɔmálá? Manuel de Bamiléké à l'usage de la classe de 6ᵉ*. Douala, Cameroon: Collège Libermann.

Oates, W., and L. Oates (1964). 'Gugu-Yalanji Linguistic and Anthropological Data'. In *Occasional Papers in Aboriginal Studies*, vol. ii. Canberra: Australian Institute of Aboriginal Studies, 1–17.

——(1969). *Kapau Pedagogical Grammar* (Pacific Linguistics C 10). Canberra: Australian National University.

Odden, D. (1983). 'Aspects of Didinga Phonology and Morphology'. In M. L. Bender (ed.), *Nilo-Saharan Language Studies*. East Lansing, Mich.: African Studies Center.

Onishi, M. (1994). 'Semantic Primitives in Japanese'. In C. Goddard and A. Wierzbicka (eds.), *Semantic and Lexical Universals: Theory and Empirical Findings* (Studies in Language Companion Series 25). Amsterdam: Benjamins, 361–85.

Osborne, C. R. (1974). *The Tiwi Language*. Canberra: Australian Institute of Aboriginal Studies.

Palácio, A. P. (1986). 'Aspects of the Morphology of Guató'. In B. F. Elson (ed.), *Language in Global Perspective: Papers in Honor of the 50th Anniversary of the*

Summer Institute of Linguistics 1935–1985. Dallas, Tx.: Summer Institute of Linguistics, 363–72.

Pandharipande, P. V. (1997). *Marathi*. London: Routledge.

Parker, E. (1986). 'Mundani Pronouns'. In U. Wiesemann (ed.), *Pronominal Systems*. Tübingen: Narr, 131–66.

Parker, G. J. (1970). *Southeast Ambrym Dictionary* (Pacific Linguistics C 17). Canberra: Australian National University.

Parks, D. R. (1976). *A Grammar of Pawnee* (Garland Studies in American Indian Linguistics). New York: Garland.

Paton, W. F. (1971). *Ambrym (Lonwolwol) Grammar* (Pacific Linguistics B 19). Canberra: Australian National University.

Payne, D. L. (1981). *The Phonology and Morphology of Axininca Campa* (Summer Institute of Linguistics Publications in Linguistics 66). Arlington, Va.: Summer Institute of Linguistics.

—— (1982). 'Chickasaw Agreement Morphology: A Functional Explanation'. In P. J. Hopper and S. A. Thompson (eds.), *Studies in Transitivity* (Syntax and Semantics 15). New York: Academic Press, 351–78.

Payne, T. E. (1993). *The Twin Stories: Participant Coding in Yagua Discourse* (University of California Publications in Linguistics 120). Berkeley, Calif.: University of California Press.

Pence, A. R. (1968). 'An Analysis of Kunimaipa Pronouns'. *Kivung* 1/2: 109–15.

Pike, K. L. (1954). *Language in Relation to a Unified Theory of the Structure of Human Behaviour*. Glendale, Calif.: Summer Institute of Linguistics.

Plank, F. (1985). 'Die Ordnung der Personen'. *Folia Linguistica* 19: 111–76.

—— (1989). 'On Humboldt on the Dual'. In R. Corrigan, F. Eckman, and M. Noonan (eds.), *Linguistic Categorization* (Current Issues in Linguistics Theory 61). Amsterdam: Benjamins, 293–333.

—— (1996). 'Domains of the Dual, in Maltese and in General'. *Rivista di linguistica* 8/1: 123–40.

—— (2002). 'Ahead of even Greenberg, for once: Paul ("Person") Forchheimer'. *Linguistic Typology* 6/1: 30–47.

—— and W. Schellinger (1997). 'The Uneven Distribution of Genders over Numbers: Greenberg Nos. 37 and 45'. *Linguistic Typology* 1/1: 53–101.

—— (2000). 'Dual Laws in (no) Time'. *Sprachtypologie und Universalien Forschung* 53/1: 46–52.

Plungian, V. (1995). *Dogon* (Languages of the World/Materials 64). Munich: Lincom Europa.

Polak, R. J. E. R. (1894). *A Grammar and a Vocabulary of the Ipuriná Language*. London: Kegan Paul, Trench, Trübner.

Popjes, J., and J. Popjes (1986). 'Canela-Krahô'. In D. C. Derbyshire and G. K. Pullum (eds.), *Handbook of Amazonian Languages*, vol. i. Berlin: Mouton de Gruyter, 128–99.

Popovich, H. (1986). 'The Nominal Reference System of Maxakalí'. In U. Wiesemann (ed.), *Pronominal Systems*. Tübingen: Narr, 351–8.

Poppe, N. (1960). *Buriat Grammar*. Bloomington: Indiana University.

Posner, R. (1996). *The Romance Languages* (Cambridge Language Surveys). Cambridge: Cambridge University Press.

Premsrirat, S. (1987). 'A Khmu Grammar'. In S. Premsrirat (ed.), *Khmu, a Minority Language of Thailand* (Pacific Linguistics A 75). Canberra: Australian National University, 1–143.

Press, M. L. (1979). *A Grammar of Chemehuevi: A Grammar and Lexicon* (University of California Publications in Linguistics 92). Berkeley, Calif.: University of California Press.

Priestly, T. M. S. (1993). 'Slovene'. In C. Bernard and G. G. Corbett (eds.), *The Slavonic Languages*. London: Routledge, 388–451.

Quirk, R., S. Greenbaum, G. Leech, and J. Svartvik (1985). *A Comprehensive Grammar of the English Language*. London: Longman.

Rath, J. C. (1981). 'A Practical Heiltsuk–English Dictionary (with a Grammatical Introduction)'. Ph.D. thesis, University of Leiden.

Reed, J., and D. L. Payne (1986). 'Asheninca (Campa) Pronominals'. In U. Wiesemann (ed.), *Pronominal Systems*. Tübingen: Narr, 323–31.

Reesink, G. P. (1999). *A Grammar of Hatam: Bird's Head Peninsula, Irian Jaya* (Pacific Linguistics C 146). Canberra: Australian National University.

Reh, M. (1985). *Die Krongo Sprache (Nìinó Mó-Dì)* (Kölner Beiträge zur Afrikanistik 12). Berlin: Reimer.

—— (1996). *Anywa Language: Description and Internal Reconstruction* (Nilo-Saharan Linguistic Analyses and Documentation 11). Cologne: Köppe.

Reichard, G. A. (1925). *Wiyot Grammar and Texts*. Berkeley, Calif.: University of California Press.

—— (1951). *Navaho Grammar* (Publications of the American Ethnological Society 11). New York: Augustin.

Reid, L. A. (ed.) (1971). *Philippine Minor Languages: Word Lists and Phonologies* (Oceanic Linguistics Special Publication 8). Honolulu: University of Hawai'i Press.

—— (1979). 'Towards a Reconstruction of the Pronominal Systems of Proto-Cordilleran, Phillines'. In D. N. Liem (ed.), *South-East Asian Linguistic Studies* (Pacific Linguistics C 45). Canberra: Australian National University, 259–75.

Reinisch, L. (1879). *Die Nuba Sprache*, vol. i: *Grammatik und Texte*. Vienna: Braumüller.

—— (1881). *Die Kunama-Sprache in Nord-Ost Afrika*. Vienna: Carl Gerolds Sohn.

Renck, G. L. (1975). *A Grammar of Yagaria* (Pacific Linguistics B 40). Canberra: Australian National University.

Rhodes, R. A. (1997). 'On Pronominal Systems'. In I. Hegedus, P. A. Michalove, and A. Manaster Ramer (eds.), *Indo-European, Nostratic, and Beyond: Festschrift for Vitalij V. Shevoroshkin* (Journal of Indo-European Studies Monographs 22). Washington, DC: Institute for the Study of Man, 293–319.

Rice, K. (1989). *A Grammar of Slave* (Mouton Grammar Library 5). Berlin: Mouton de Gruyter.

Richard, E. L. (1975). 'Sentence Structure of Guhu-Samane'. In T. E. Dutton (ed.), *Studies in Languages of Central and South-East Papua* (Pacific Linguistics C 29). Canberra: Australian National University, 771–816.

Rijkhoff, J., and D. Bakker (1998). 'Language Sampling'. *Linguistic Typology* 2/3: 263–314.

Roberts, J. R. (1987). *Amele*. London: Croom Helm.

Robertson, S., and F. G. Cassidy (1954). *The Development of Modern English*. Englewood Cliffs: Prentice-Hall.

Robinett, F. M. (1955). 'Hidatsa II: Affixes'. *International Journal of American Linguistics* 21/2: 160–77.

Rojas Curieux, T. (1991). 'Las Estructuras de la oracion en Paez'. In T. Rojas Curieux (ed.), *Estudios Gramaticales de la Lengua Paez (Nasa Yuwe)*. Colciencies: Universidad de los Andes, 7–100.

Romero-Figeroa, A. (1997). *A Reference Grammar of Warao* (Lincom Studies in Native American Linguistics 6). Munich: Lincom Europa.

Rood, D. S. (1996). 'Sketch of Wichita, a Caddoan Language'. In I. Goddard (ed.), *Handbook of North American Indians*, vol. xvii: *Languages*. Washington, DC: Smithsonian Institution, 580–608.

—— and A. R. Taylor (1996). 'Sketch of Lakhota, a Siouan Language'. In I. Goddard (ed.), *Handbook of North American Indians*, vol. xvii: *Languages*. Washington, DC: Smithsonian Institution, 440–82.

Ross, M. D., and J. N. Paol (1978). *A Waskia Sketch and Vocabulary* (Pacific Linguistics B 56). Canberra: Australian National University.

Rottland, F. (1982). *Die südnilotischen Sprachen: Beschreibung, Vergleichung und Rekonstruktion* (Kölner Beiträge zur Afrikanistik 7). Berlin: Reimer.

Rowe, J. H. (1974). 'Sixteenth and Seventeenth Century Grammars'. In D. H. Hymes (ed.), *Studies in the History of Linguistics: Traditions and Paradigms*. Bloomington: Indiana University Press, 361–79.

Royen, G. (1929). *Die nominalen Klassifikations-Systeme in den Sprachen der Erde: historisch-kritische Studie, mit besonderer Berücksichtigung des Indogermanischen*. Mödling: Anthropos.

Rude, N. E. (1985). 'Studies in Nez Perce Grammar and Discourse'. Ph.D. thesis, University of Oregon.

Rumsey, A. (1996). 'On Some Relationships among Person, Number, and Mode in Bunaba'. In W. McGregor (ed.), *Studies in Kimberley Languages in Honour of Howard Coate*. Munich: Lincom Europa, 139–48.

—— (2000). 'Bunuba'. In R. M. W. Dixon and B. J. Blake (eds.), *Handbook of Australian Languages*, vol. v: *Grammatical Sketches of Bunuba, Ndjébbana and Kugu Nganhcara*. Oxford: Oxford University Press, 34–152.

Salminen, T. (1998). 'Nenets'. In D. Abondolo (ed.), *The Uralic Languages*. London: Routledge, 516-47.

Santandrea, S. (1963). *A Concise Grammar Outline of the Bongo Language*. Rome: Sodality of St Peter Claver.

de Santo Tomás, F. D. (1560). *Grammatica o arte de la lengua general de los indios de los Reynos del Peru* (facsimile with transcription and comments by R. Cerron-Palomino, 1994). Madrid: Ediciones de Cultura Hispanica.

Sanzheyev, G. D. (1973). *The Modern Mongolian Language* (Languages of Asia and Africa). Moscow: Nauka.

Sapir, E. (1992 [1930]). 'Southern Paiute, a Shoshonean Language'. In W. Bright (ed.), *Southern Paiute and Ute Linguistics and Ethnography* (The Collected Works of Edward Sapir 10). Berlin: Mouton de Gruyter.

Sasse, H.-J. (1993). 'Syntactic Categories and Subcategories'. In J. Jacobs, A. von Stechow, W. Sternefeld, and T. Vennemann (eds.), *Syntax: Ein Internationales Handbuch Zeitgenössischer Forschung*, vol. i (Handbücher zur Sprach- und Kommunikationswissenschaft 9). Berlin: de Gruyter, 646–85.
de Saussure, F. (1916). *Cours de linguistique générale*. Paris: Payot.
Sauvageot, S. (1965). *Desription synchronique d'un dialecte Wolof: Le Parler du Dyolof* (Mémoires de l'Institut Français d'Afrique Noire 73). Dakar: Institut Français d'Afrique Noire.
Saxon, L. A. (1986). 'The Syntax of Pronouns in Dogrib (Athapascan): Some Theoretical Consequences'. Ph.D. thesis, University of California at San Diego.
Schachter, P., and F. T. Otanes (1972). *Tagalog Reference Grammar*. Berkeley, Calif.: University of California Press.
Schadeberg, T. C. (1981). *A Survey of Kordofanian*, vol. i: *The Heiban Group* (Sprache und Geschichte in Africa, Beiheft 1). Hamburg: Buske.
Schaub, W. (1985). *Babungo*. London: Croom Helm.
Schegloff, E. A. (1996). 'Some Practices for Referring to Persons in Talk-in-Interaction: A Partial Sketch of a Systematics'. In B. A. Fox (ed.), *Studies in Anaphora* (Typological Studies in Language 33). Amsterdam: Benjamins, 437–86.
Schenker, A. M. (1993). 'Proto-Slavonic'. In B. Comrie and G. G. Corbett (eds.), *The Slavonic Languages*. London: Routledge, 60–121.
Schmalstieg, W. R. (1998). 'The Baltic Languages'. In A. G. Ramat and P. Ramat (eds.), *The Indo-European Languages*. London: Routledge, 454–79.
Schmidt, W. (1926). *Die Sprachfamilien und Sprachkreise der Erde*. Heidelberg: Winter.
Schönfeld, M. (1959). *Historische Grammatica van het Nederlands*, 6th edn. Zutphen: Thieme.
Schulze-Berndt, E. (2000). 'Simple and Complex Verbs in Jaminjung: A Study of Event Categorisation in an Australian Language'. Ph.D. thesis, University of Nijmegen.
Schuster-Sewc, H. (1996). *Grammar of the Upper Sorbian Language: Phonology and Morphology* (Lincom Studies in Slavic Linguistics 3). Munich: Lincom Europa.
Schwartz, L. J. (1986). 'The Function of Free Pronouns'. In U. Wiesemann (ed.), *Pronominal Systems*. Tübingen: Narr, 405–36.
—— (1988). 'Asymmetric Feature Distribution in Pronominal "Coordinations"'. In M. Barlow and C. A. Ferguson (eds.), *Agreement in Natural Language: Approaches, Theories, Descriptions*. Stanford, Calif.: Center for the Study of Language and Information, 237–49.
—— and T. Dunnigan (1986). 'Pronouns and Pronominal Categories in Southwestern Ojibwe'. In U. Wiesemann (ed.), *Pronominal Systems*. Tübingen: Narr, 285–322.
Schwarze, C. (1988). *Grammatik der italienischen Sprache*. Tübingen: Niemeyer.
Seiler, W. (1985). *Imonda, a Papuan Language* (Pacific Linguistics B 93). Canberra: Australian National University.
Senft, G. (1986). *Kilivila: The Language of the Trobriand Islanders* (Mouton Grammar Library 3). Berlin: Mouton de Gruyter.
Sharma, S. R. (1996). 'Pronouns and Agreement in West Himalayan Tibeto-Burman Languages'. *Indian Linguistics* 57: 81–103.

Sharpe, M. C. (1972). *Alawa Phonology and Grammar* (Australian Aboriginal Studies 37). Canberra: Australian Institute of Aboriginal Studies.
Shelden, H. (1991). 'Galela Pronominal Verb Prefixes'. In T. E. Dutton (ed.), *Papers in Papuan Linguistics*, vol. i (Pacific Linguistics A 73). Canberra: Australian National University, 161–75.
Shibatani, M. (1990). *The Languages of Japan* (Cambridge Language Surveys). Cambridge: Cambridge University Press.
Siewierska, A. (1998). 'On Nominal and Verbal Person Marking'. *Linguistic Typology* 2/1: 1–56.
—— and D. Bakker (1996). 'The Distribution of Subject and Object Agreement and Word Order Type'. *Studies in Language* 20/1: 115–61.
—— (2000). 'Person Asymmetries in the Grammaticalization of Agreement'. Paper presented at the Cognitive Typology conference, Antwerp, 14 April 2000.
Simon, H. (1999). 'Für eine grammatische Kategorie "Respekt" im Deutschen: Synchronie, Diachronie und Typologie der deutschen Anredepronomina'. Ph.D. thesis, Humboldt University, Berlin.
—— (2001). 'Only You? On the Alleged Inclusive–Exclusive Distinction in the Second Person Plural'. Paper presented at the 4th meeting of the Association for Linguistic Typology, Santa Barbara, Calif., 20 July 2001.
Simons, L. (1986). 'The Pronouns of To'abaita'. In U. Wiesemann (ed.), *Pronominal Systems*. Tübingen: Narr, 21–36.
Sims-Williams, N. (1998). 'The Iranian Languages'. In A. G. Ramat and P. Ramat (eds.), *The Indo-European Languages*. London: Routledge, 125–53.
Smith, K. D. (1979). *Sedang Grammar: Phonological and Syntactic Structure* (Pacific Linguistics B 50). Canberra: Australian National University.
Snapp, A., J. Anderson, and J. Anderson (1982). 'Northern Paiute'. In R. W. Langacker (ed.), *Studies in Uto-Aztecan Grammar*, vol. iii: *Uto-Aztecan Grammatical Sketches* (Summer Institute of Linguistics Publications in Linguistics 57.3). Arlington, Va.: Summer Institute of Linguistics, 1–92.
Sneddon, J. N. (1975). *Tondano Phonology and Grammar* (Pacific Linguistics B 38). Canberra: Australian National University.
Sohn, H.-M. (1994). *Korean*. London: Routledge.
Sokolovskaya, N. K. (1980). 'Nekotorye Semanticeskie Universalii v Sisteme Licnyx Mestoimenij [Some Semantic Universals in Systems of Personal Pronouns]'. In I. F. Vardul' (ed.), *Teorija i Tipologija Mestoimenij [Theory and Typology of Pronouns]*. Moscow: Nauka, 84–102. (Translations of the universals are available at the Universals Archive: http://www.ling.uni-konstanz.de:591/Universals/introduction.html.)
Spagnolo, F. L. M. (1933). *Bari Grammar*. Verona: Missioni Africane.
Sridhar, S. N. (1990). *Kannada*. London: Routledge.
Stairs, E. F., and B. E. Hollenbach (1969). 'Huave Verb Morphology'. *International Journal of American Linguistics* 35: 38–53.
Stassen, L. (2000). 'And-Languages and With-Languages'. *Linguistic Typology* 4/1: 1–54.
Stein, P. (1984). *Kreolisch und Französisch* (Romanische Arbeitshefte 25). Tübingen: Niemeyer.
Steinhauer, H. (1985). 'Number in Biak: Counterevidence to Two Alleged Language Universals'. *Bijdragen tot de Taal-, Land- en Volkenkunde* 141: 462–85.

—— (1993). 'Notes on Verbs in Dawanese (Timor)'. In G. P. Reesink (ed.), *Topics in Descriptive Austronesian Linguistics* (Semaian 11). Leiden: Vakgroep Talen en Culturen van Zuidoost-Azië en Oceanië, 130–58.

Stephens, J. (1993). 'Breton'. In M. J. Ball and J. Fife (eds.), *The Celtic Languages*. London: Routledge, 349–409.

Stone, G. (1993). 'Sorbian'. In B. Comrie and G. G. Corbett (eds.), *The Slavonic Languages*. London: Routledge, 593–685.

Streitberg, W. (1920). *Gotisches Elementarbuch*. Heidelberg: Winter.

Strom, C. (1992). *Retuarã Syntax* (Studies in the Languages of Colombia 3). Arlington, Va.: Summer Institute of Linguistics.

Stump, G. T. (2001). *Inflectional Morphology: A Theory of Paradigm Structure* (Cambridge Studies in Linguistics 93). Cambridge: Cambridge University Press.

Suárez, J. A. (1983). *The Mesoamerican Indian Languages* (Cambridge Language Surveys). Cambridge: Cambridge University Press.

Suárez Roca, J. L. (1992). *Lingüística misionera española*. Oviedo: Pentalfa.

Susnik, B. (1961). *Estudio Guayaki, sistema fonético y temático* (Boletin de la Sociedad Cientifica del Paraguay y del Museo Etnográfico 5). Asunción: Museo Etnográfico Andres Barbero.

—— (1968). *Chulupi, esbozo gramatical analitico*. Asunción: Museo Etnográfico Andres Barbero.

—— (1973). *La Lengua de los Ayoweos-Moros: Estructura gramatical y fraseario* (Lenguas Chaqueñas 5). Asunción: Museo Etnográfico Andres Barbero.

—— (1977). *Lengua Maskoy, su hablar, su pensar, su vivencia*. Asunción: Museo Etnográfico Andres Barbero.

—— (1986/7). *Los Aborígenes del Paraguay* (Lenguas Chaqueñas 7/1). Asunción: Museo Etnográfico Andres Barbero.

Swadesh, M. (1936). 'Nootka Internal Syntax'. *International Journal of American Linguistics* 9: 77–102.

—— (1946). 'Chitimacha'. In H. Hoijer et al., *Linguistic Structures of Native America* (Publications in Anthropology 6). New York: Viking Fund, 312–36.

Szemerényi, O. J. L. (1990). *Introduction to Indo-European Linguistics*. Oxford: Clarendon Press.

Tauberschmidt, G. (1999). *A Grammar of Sinaugoro: An Austronesian Language of the Central Province of Papua New Guinea* (Pacific Linguistics C 143). Canberra: Australian National University.

Teeter, K. V. (1964). *The Wiyot Language* (University of California Publications in Linguistics 37). Berkeley, Calif.: University of California Press.

Thelwall, R. (1983). 'Meidob Nubian: Phonology, Grammatical Notes and Basic Vocabulary'. In M. L. Bender (ed.), *Nilo-Saharan Language Studies*. East Lansing, Mich.: African Studies Center, 97–113.

Thomas, D. D. (1955). 'Three Analyses of the Ilocano Pronoun System'. *Word* 11/2: 204–8.

—— (1971). *Chrau Grammar* (Oceanic Linguistics Special Publication 7). Honolulu: University of Hawai'i Press.

Thomson, N. P. (1975). 'Magi Phonology and Grammar—Fifty Years Afterwards'. In T. E. Dutton (ed.), *Studies in Languages of Central and South-East Papua* (Pacific Liguistics C 29). Canberra: Australian National University, 599–666.

Thomason, S. G., and D. L. Everett (forthcoming). 'Borrowed Pronouns in Pirahã'. *Berkeley Linguistic Society* 27.

Thráinsson, H. (1994). 'Icelandic'. In E. König and J. v. d. Auwera (eds.), *The Germanic Languages*. London: Routledge, 142–89.

Tisdall, S. C. (1892). *A Simplified Grammar of the Gujarati Language: Together with a Short Reading Book & Vocabulary*. London: Kegan Paul, Trench, Trübner.

Todd, E. M. (1975). 'The Solomon Language Family'. In S. A. Wurm (ed.), *Papuan Languages and the New Guinea Linguistic Scene* (Pacific Linguistics C 38). Canberra: Australian National University, 805–46.

Tompa, J. (1968). *Ungarische Grammatik* (Janua Linguarum, Series Practica 96). The Hague: Mouton.

Topping, D. M. (1973). *Chamorro Reference Grammar* (PALI Language Texts: Micronesia). Honolulu: University Press of Hawai'i.

Trier, J. (1931). *Der deutsche Wortschatz im Sinnbezirk des Verstandes* (Germanische Bibliothek 31). Heidelberg: Carl Winter.

Troike, R. C. (1996). 'Sketch of Coahuilteco, a Language Isolate of Texas'. In I. Goddard (ed.), *Handbook of North American Indians*, vol. xvii: *Languages*. Washington, DC: Smithsonian Institution, 644–65.

Tryon, D. T. (1970). *An Introduction to Maranungku (Northern Australia)* (Pacific Linguistics B 15). Canberra: Australian National University.

—— (1976). 'The Daly Family'. In R. M. W. Dixon (ed.), *Grammatical Categories in Australian Languages*. Canberra: Australian Institute of Aboriginal Studies, 673–90.

Tsereteli, K. G. (1978). *The Modern Assyrian Language* (Languages of Asia and Africa). Moscow: Nauka.

Tucker, A. N., and M. A. Bryan (1966). *Linguistic Analyses of the Non-Bantu Languages of North-Eastern Africa*. London: Oxford University Press.

—— and J. T. O. Mpaayei (1953). *A Maasai Grammar with Vocabulary*. London: Longmans, Green.

Tuite, K. (1997). *Svan* (Languages of the World/Materials 139). Munich: Lincom Europa.

Turner, P. R. (1966). 'Highland Chontal Grammar'. Ph.D. thesis, University of Chicago.

Tyler, S. A. (1969). *Koya: An Outline Grammar* (University of California Publications in Linguistics 54). Berkeley, Calif.: University of California Press.

Uhlig, G. (1883). *Dionysii Thracis Ars Grammatici* (Grammatici Graeci 1). Leipzig: Teubner.

Urban, G. (1985). 'Ergativity and Accusativity in Shokleng (Gê)'. *International Journal of American Linguistics* 51/2: 164–87.

Uspensky, B. A. (1972). 'Subsystems in Language, their Interrelations and their Correlated Universals'. *Linguistics* 88: 53–71.

Van Valin, R. D., Jr. (1977). 'Aspects of Lakhota Syntax'. Ph.D. thesis, University of California, Berkeley.

Varenne, H. (1984). 'The Interpretation of Pronominal Paradigms: Speech Situation, Pragmatic Meaning, and Cultural Structure'. *Semiotica* 50/3–4: 221–48.

References

Veerman-Leichsenring, A. (2000). 'Popolocan Independent Personal Pronouns: Comparison and Reconstruction'. *International Journal of American Linguistics* 66/3: 318–59.
Versteegh, K. (1997). *The Arabic Language*. Edinburgh: Edinburgh University Press.
Voegelin, C. F. (1937a). 'Tübatulabal Grammar'. *University of California Publications in American Archeology and Ethnology* 34/2: 55–190.
—— (1937b). 'Tübatulabal Texts'. *University of California Publications in American Archeology and Ethnology* 34/3: 191–246.
Voorhoeve, C. L. (1965). 'The Flamingo Bay Dialect of the Asmat Language'. Ph.D. thesis, University of Leiden.
—— (1975). 'Central and Western Trans-New Guinea Phylum Languages'. In S. A. Wurm (ed.), *Papuan Languages and the New Guinea Linguistic Scene* (Pacific Linguistics C 38). Canberra: Australian National University, 345–460.
Voorhoeve, J. (1967). 'Personal Pronouns in Bamileke'. *Lingua* 17: 421–30.
Vorbichler, A. (1971). *Die Sprache der Mamvu* (Afrikanistische Forschungen 5). Hamburg: Augustin.
Vorlat, E. (1975). *The Development of English Grammatical Theory 1568–1737, with Special Reference to the Theory of Parts of Speech*. Leuven: University Press.
de Vries, L. (1989). 'Studies in Wambon and Kombai'. Ph.D. thesis, University of Amsterdam.
Wales, K. (1996). *Personal Pronouns in Present-Day English* (Studies in English Language). Cambridge: Cambridge University Press.
Waterhouse, V. (1967). 'Huameltultec Chontal'. In R. Wauchope and N. A. McQuown (eds.), *Handbook of Middle American Indians*, vol. v: *Linguistics*. Austin, Tx.: University of Texas Press, 349–67.
Webelhuth, G. (ed.) (1995). *Government and Binding Theory and the Minimalist Program*. Oxford: Blackwell.
Weber, D. J. (1986). 'Huallaga Quechua Pronouns'. In U. Wiesemann (ed.), *Pronominal Systems*. Tübingen: Narr, 333–50.
—— (1989). *A Grammar of Huallaga (Huánunco) Quechua* (University of California Publications in Linguistics 112). Berkeley, Calif.: University of California Press.
Weimer, H., and N. Weimer (1975). 'A Short Sketch of Yareba Grammar'. In T. E. Dutton (ed.), *Studies in Languages of Central and South-East Papua* (Pacific Linguistics C 29). Canberra: Australian National University, 667–730.
Wells, M. A. (1979). *Siroi Grammar* (Pacific Linguistics B 41). Canberra: Australian National University.
Welmers, W. E. (1976). *A Grammar of Vai*. Berkeley, Calif.: University of California Press.
Westermann, D. (1911). *A Short Grammar of the Shilluk Language*. Berlin: Reimer.
—— (1924). *Die Kpelle Sprache in Liberia*. Hamburg: Reimer.
Westrum, P. N., and U. Wiesemann (1986). 'Berik Pronouns'. In U. Wiesemann (ed.), *Pronominal Systems*. Tübingen: Narr, 37–46.
Whiteley, W. H. (1958). *A Short Description of Item Categories in Iraqw, with Material on Gorowa, Alagwa and Burunge* (East African Linguistic Studies 3). Kampala: East African Institute of Social Research.
Whorf, B. L. (1946). 'The Milpa Alta Dialect of Aztec'. In H. Hoijer et al., *Linguistic Structures of Native America* (Publications in Anthropology 6). New York: Viking Fund, 367–98.

Wierzbicka, A. (1976). 'In Defense of You and Me'. In W. Girke and H. Jachnow (eds.), *Theoretische Linguistik in Osteuropa: Originalbeiträge Und Erstübersetzungen* (Konzepte der Sprach und Literaturwissenschaft 18). Tübingen: Niemeyer, 1–21.

——(1996). *Semantics: Primes and Universals*. Oxford: Oxford University Press.

Wiesemann, U. (1986a). 'Introduction'. In U. Wiesemann (ed.), *Pronominal Systems*. Tübingen: Narr, vii–ix.

——(1986b). 'The Pronoun Systems of some Je and Macro-Je Languages'. In U. Wiesemann (ed.), *Pronominal Systems*. Tübingen: Narr, 359–80.

Wilkins, D. P. (1989). 'Mparntwe Arrernte (Aranda): Studies in the Structure and Semantics of Grammar'. Ph.D. thesis, Australian National University.

Williams, M. (1976). *A Grammar of Tuscarora* (Garland Studies in American Indian Linguistics 18). New York: Garland.

Willms, A. (1972). *Grammatik der südlichen Beraberdialekte* (Afrikanistische Forschungen 6). Munich: Augustin.

Wilson, D. (1969). 'Suena Grammar Highlights'. In *Papers in New Guinea Linguistics*, vol. ix (Pacific Linguistic A 18). Canberra: Australian National University, 95–110.

Wise, M. R. (1971). *Identification of Participants in Discourse: A Study of Aspects of Form and Meaning in Nomatsiguenga* (Summer Institute of Linguistics Publications in Linguistics 28). Norman, Okla.: Summer Institute of Linguistics.

Wolfart, H. C. (1996). 'Sketch of Cree, an Algonquian Language'. In I. Goddard (ed.), *Handbook of North American Indians*, vol. xvii: *Languages*. Washington, DC: Smithsonian Institution, 390–439.

Wolff, E. (1983). *A Grammar of the Lamang Language (Gwàḍ Làmà)* (Afrikanistische Forschungen 10). Glückstadt: Augustin.

Wolff, J. U. (1966). *Beginning Cebuano*. New Haven, Conn.: Yale University Press.

Woodbury, A. (1981). 'Study of the Chevak Dialect of Central Yup'ic'. Ph.D. thesis, University of California, Berkeley.

Woollams, G. (1996). *A Grammar of Karo Batak, Sumatra* (Pacific Linguistics C 130). Canberra: Australian National University.

Wurm, S. A. (1969). 'The Linguistic Situation in the Reef and Santa Cruz Islands'. In *Papers in Linguistics of Melanesia*, vol. ii (Pacific Linguistics A 21). Canberra: Australian National University, 47–105.

——(1975a). 'The East Papuan Phylum in General'. In S. A. Wurm (ed.), *Papuan Languages and the New Guinea Linguistic Scene* (Pacific Linguistics C 38). Canberra: Australian National University, 783–804.

——(1975b). 'Eastern Central Trans-New Guinea Phylum Languages'. In S. A. Wurm (ed.), *Papuan Languages and the New Guinea Linguistic Scene* (Pacific Linguistics C 38). Canberra: Australian National University, 461–526.

Young, R., and W. Morgan (1987). *The Navaho Language*. Albuquerque, NM: University of New Mexico Press.

Zigmond, M. L., C. G. Booth, and P. Munro (1990). *Kawaiisu: A Grammar and Dictionary with Texts* (University of California Publications in Linguistics 119). Berkeley, Calif.: University of California Press.

de Zwaan, J. D. (1969). *A Preliminary Analysis of Gogo-Yimidjir* (Australian Aboriginal Studies 16). Canberra: Australian Institute of Aboriginal Studies.

Zwicky, A. M. (1977). 'Hierarchies of Person'. *Chicago Linguistic Society* 13/1: 714–33.

List of Languages According to Genetic/Geographical Distribution

African languages

Afro-Asiatic

Berber:	Tamazight
Chadic	
Biu-Mandara:	Gude, Hdi, Margi, Mandara, Lamang, Podoko
East Chadic:	Lele
West Chadic:	Ron, Ngizim
Cushitic	
East Cushitic:	Somali
South Cushitic:	Burunge, Iraqw, Alagwa
Omotic:	Dizi
Semitic	
Arabic:	various Arabic varieties, Maltese
Aramaic:	Mandaic, Neo-Aramaic

Nilo-Saharan languages

Central Sudanic	
East:	Madi, Mamvu, Logbara, Ngiti
West:	Bagirmi, Beli, Bongo, Mbay
Eastern Sudanic	
Eastern:	Didinga, Dongola, Midob
Western:	Temein
Nilotic	
Eastern:	Bari, Karimojong, Maasai, Lango, Lotuho, Teso, Turkana
Southern:	Datooga, Kalenjin, Omotik
Western:	Acholi, Anywa, Dinka, Päri, Shilluk
Kunama:	Kunama
Maban:	Maba
Saharan:	Tubu

Niger-Congo

Bantoid:	
Beboid:	Noni
Narrow Bantu:	Akɔɔse
Grassfields:	
Momo:	Mundani
Ring:	Babungo, Aghem
Mbam-Nkan:	Bamileke, Ghomala', Limbum, Mbili, Ngiembɔɔn
Atlantic:	Bolante, Adamawa Fulfulde, Palor, Wolof
Kru:	Grebo
Mande	
Eastern:	Dan, Yaouré
Western:	Koranko, Kpelle, Northern Looma, Mauka, Vai
Dogon:	Dogon
Kwa:	Fongbe
Adamawa:	Dii
Kordofanian:	Ebang, Krongo, Moro

Khoisan languages

Central Khoisan	Nama
Northern Khoisan	!Xu

European/Asian languages

Indo-European

Baltic:	Lithuanian
Celtic:	Breton, Cornish
Germanic	
East Germanic:	Gothic
North Germanic:	Swedish, Icelandic
West Germanic:	Dutch, English, German
Greek:	Classical Greek
Indo-Aryan:	Gujarati, Marathi, Sinhalese
Italic	
Classical:	Latin
Romance	
Eastern Romance:	Rumanian
Italo-Romance:	Italian, Siciliano
Western Romance:	French, Spanish, Catalan, Portuguese

Slavic
  West Slavic: Sorbian
  South Slavic
    Eastern: Bulgarian, Macedonian, Old Church Slavonic
    Western: Serbo-Croatian, Slovene

Caucasian languages

Nakh-Dagestanian
  Chechen-Ingush: Chechen
  Avar-Andi-Tsez: Akhvakh, Zakatal', Hunzib
  Lak-Dargwa: Gubden, Dargi, Lak, Megeb
  Lezgian: Archi, Lezgian, Tsakhur
Northwest Caucasusian: Abkhaz
South Caucasusian: Upper Bal, Georgian, Svan

Northern Asian languages

Uralic
  Finno-Permic: Estonian, Finnish, Mari, Mordva, Udmurt
  Ugric: Hungarian, Khanti, Mansi
  Samoyedic: Nenets, Nganasan
Altaic
  Turkic: Turkish
  Mongolian: Buriat, Mongolian
  Tungusic: Even, Evenki, Udihe
  Korean: Korean
  Japanese: Japanese
Chukotko-Kamchatkan: Chuckchee, Koryak, Kamchadal
'Siberian' Isolates: Nivkh, Ainu

Southern Asian languages

Dravidian
  South Central: Koya
  Southern: Kannada, Malayalam, Tamil, Toda
Austro-Asiatic
  Munda: Mundari
  Mon-Khmer
    Eastern Mon-Khmer: Chrau, Sedang
    Northern Mon-Khmer: Khmu, Palaung
    Viet-Muong: Vietnamese
Daic: Thai
Miao-Yao: Hmong-Njua

Sino-Tibetan
  Baric: Mao Naga, Meithei
  Bodic
    Tibeto-Kanauri: Bunan, Jiarong, Kanauri, Manchad, Rongpo, Tibetan, Tinan
    East Himalayish: Camling, Limbu, Monpa, Dumi, Thulung, Kham, Bahing, Chepang, Newari
  Burmese-Lolo: Burmese, Akha
  Sinitic: Classical Chinese, Mandarin Chinese, Cantonese

Pacific languages

Austronesian

Western Malayo-Polynesian

Chamorro: Chamorro
Palauan: Palau
Yapese: Yapese
Meso Philippine: Cebuano, Tagalog, Hanunóo
Northern Philippine: Ilocano, Pampangan
Southern Philippine: Maranao
Sulawesi: Uma, Tondano
Sundic: Acehnese, Indonesian, Kawi, Malay, Toba Batak, Karo Batak

Central Malayo-Polynesian

Central Maluku: Larike
Timor: Dawanese, Fehan Tetun, Lamalera, Kisar, Roti, Sika

Eastern Malayo-Polynesian

West New Guinea: Biak
Oceanic
  Western Oceanic
    North New Guinea: Ali, Sera, Sissano, Tumleo, Ulau-Suian
    Meso Melanesian: Gao, Lihir, Mono-Alu, Nakanai, Sursurunga, Tangga, Tolai
    Papuan Tip: Kilivila, Mekeo, Motu, Sinaugoro
  Micronesian: Kiribati, Marshallese, Mokilese, Pulawat, Trukese

Polynesian:	Fijian, Maori, Rapanui, Samoan
Southeast Solomonic:	'Are'are, Kwaio, Langalanga, Lau, Sa'a, To'abaita
Southern Oceanic	
North and Central Vanuatu:	Big Nambas, Lonwolwol Ambrym, Southeast Ambrym, Marina, Nakanamanga, Paamese
Southern Melanesian:	A'jië, Anejom̃, Kwamera, Lenakel

'Papuan' languages

'Trans-New Guinea' languages

Angan:	Baruya, Kapau
Binanderean:	Binandere, Korafe, Orokaiva, Suena, Guhu-Samane
Border:	Morwap, Amanab, Imonda, Manem
Central and Southeastern	
Dagan:	Daga
Goilalan:	Kunimaipa, Weri
Koiarian:	Ömie, Mountain Koiali, Koiari
Mailuan:	Magi
Yareban:	Yareba
Central and South New Guinea	
Asmat-Kamoro:	Asmat
Awyu-Dumut:	Awju, Kombai, Wambon
East Strickland:	Samo
Mombum:	Mombum
Ok:	Kati
East New Guinea Highlands	
Central:	Kuman, Salt-Yui, Golin
Eastern:	Awa, Gadsup, Usarufa, Tairora
Gorokan:	Benabena, Fore, Gahuku, Gende, Kamano, Hua, Siane, Yagaria
Kalam:	Kalam
West Central:	Kewa
Wiru:	Wiru
Eleman:	Elema, Tuaripi
Gogodali-Suki:	Suki
Huon-Finisterre	
Finisterre:	Kewieng, Rawa, Wantoat
Huon:	Kâte, Kovai, Kube, Nabak, Ono, Selepet
Mabuso:	Amele
Marind:	Marind

List of Languages

Mek:	Una
Nimboran:	Nimboran, Kemtuik
Pihom-Isumrud-Mugil:	Waskia
Rai Coast:	Siroi
Sentani:	Sentani
Tor:	Berik, Orya
Trans-Fly:	Jéi, Kiwai, Moraori
Wissel Lakes-Kemandoga:	Ekagi

'East Papuan' languages

Bougainville:	Buin, Nasioi
Reef Island-Santa Cruz:	Reefs, Nanggu, Santa Cruz
Yele-Solomons:	Baniata, Savosavo

Other 'Papuan' languages

Lower Mamberamo:	Warembori
Sepik-Ramu:	Chambri, Murik, Yimas
Sko:	Vanimo
Toricelli:	Arapesh, Bukiyip
West Papuan:	Galela, Hatam
Isolate:	Burmeso

Australian languages

Pama-Nyungan

Arandic:	Alywerre, Mparntwe Arrernte
Dyirbalic:	Dyirbal, Warrgamay
Gumbaynggiric:	Gumbaynggir
Nyawaygic:	Nyawaygi
Paman:	Anguthimri, Umpila, Uradhi, Wik-Munkan
South-West:	Dhalandji, Dhargari, Pitjantjatjara, Walmatjari, Warlbiri, Western Desert
Yalandyic:	Guguyimidjir, Kuku-Yalanji
Yidinic:	Tjapukai, Yidiɲ
Yuulngu:	Djapu Dhuwal, Gupapuyŋu

Non-Pama-Nyungan

Bunaban:	Bunaba, Gooniyandi
Burarran:	Burarra, Ndjébbana
Daly:	Ngankikurungkurr, Malakmalak, Maranungku

Djamindjungan:	Jaminjung
Gunwingguan:	Mangarayi, Ngandi, Ngalakan, Nunggubuyu, Rembarrnga, Wardaman
Maran:	Alawa
Nyulnyulan:	Bardi, Nyikina, Nyulnyul, Warrwa
Tiwian:	Tiwi
Wororan:	Gunin

American languages

North American languages

Eskimo-Aleut:	Aleut, West Greenlandic Inuktitut, North Slope Iñupiaq Inuktitut, Central Yup'ic
Athabascan	
Pacific Coast:	Hupa, Kato
Canadian:	Dogrib, Slave
Apachean:	Chiricahua Apache, Navaho
Wakashan:	Nootka, Kwakiutl, Heiltsuk
Algic	
Ritwan:	Wiyot
Algonquian:	Blackfoot, Cree, Menomini, Passamaquoddy Maliseet, Southwestern Ojibwe, Eastern Ojibwe
Salish:	Shuswap
Caddoan:	Caddo, Pawnee, Wichita
Iroquoian:	Cherokee, Oneida, Tuscarora
Siouan:	
Missouri Valley:	Crow, Hidatsa
Central:	Assiniboine, Lakhota, Mandan, Winnebago
Yuman	
Delta-Californian:	Diegueño
River Yuman:	Maricopa, Mojave, Yuma
Upland Yuman:	Yavapai
Tequistlatecan:	Highland Chontal, Huameltultec Chontal
Miwok	
Eastern:	Southern Sierra Miwok, Plains Miwok, Northern Sierra Miwok
Western:	Bodega Miwok, Lake Miwok
Chinookian:	Chinook

List of Languages

Sahaptin:	Nez Perce
Coahuiltecan:	Coahuilteco
Muskogean	
Eastern:	Chickasaw, Choctaw
Western:	Alabama, Koasati
Keres:	Acoma Keresan
Isolates:	Achumawi, Chitimacha, Coos, Kutenai, Siuslaw, Tunica, Washo

Mesoamerican languages

Uto-Aztecan	
Northern Uto-Aztecan:	Ute, Southern Paiute, Northern Paiute, Kawaiisu, Tübatulabal
Aztecan:	Classical Nahuatl, Huasteca Nahuatl, Milpa Alta Nahuatl, North Puebla Nahuatl, Pipil
Huavean:	Huave
Mixe-Zoque:	Sierra Popoluca, Coatlán Mixe
Oto-Manguean	
Mixtecan:	Chalcatongo Mixtec, Ocotopec Mixtec
Otopamean:	Ixtenco Otomí, Mazahua, Pame, Chichimeco Jonaz

South American languages

Alcalufan:	Qawesqar
Arawakan	
Northern Maipuran:	Bare, Warekena
Southern Maipuran:	Campa, Apurinã
Aymaran:	Jaqaru
Barbacoan-Paezan	
Barbacoan:	Awa-Pit, Tsafiki
Paezan:	Guambino, Paez
Cahuapanan:	Chayahuita
Carib	
Northern:	Kuikúro
Southern:	Apalai, Makushi, Waiwai
Chibchan:	Cuna, Damana, Ika, Muisca
Choco:	Epena Pedee
Macro-Gé	
Bororo:	Bororo
Guato:	Guató
Maxakali:	Maxakali

Kaingang:	Xokleng
Gé	
Central Gé:	Xavante, Xerente
Northwest Gé:	Apinayé, Kayapo, Canela–Krahô
Mascoian:	Lengua
Mataco-Guaicuru	
Guiacuruan:	Abipon, Kadiwéu
Mataco:	Chulupi, Mataco, Maká
Mura:	Mura-Pirahã
Peba-Yaguan:	Yagua
Quechuan	
Quechua I:	Huallage Quechua, Tarma Quechua
Quechua IIb:	Ecuadorian Quechua, Inga
Quechua IIc:	Bolivian Quechua
Tucanoan	
Eastern Tucanoan:	Barasano, Macuna
Western Tucanoan:	Koreguaje, Retuarã, Siona
Tupi	
Munduruku:	Mudurukú
Tupí-Guaraní:	Aché, Asurini, Guarani, Guajajara
Yanomami:	Sanuma
Zamucoan:	Ayoreo
Isolates:	Trumai, Warao, Ticuna

Pidgins/Creoles

English based Creoles:	Ndyuka, Sranan, Tok Pisin
French based Creoles:	Haitian Creole, Mauritius Creole, Seychellois Creole, Réunion Creole
Pidgins:	Chinese Pidgin

Index of Names

Abed, S. B. 14 n.
Abondolo, D. 62 n. 18, 107 n. 4, 207 n. 2
Adelaar, W. F. H. 3 n. 5, 143 n. 39, 149, 254
Aikhenvald, A. A. Y. 129, 257, 265
Alexander, R. M. 149
Allen, E. J. 213
Amaya, M. T. 195
Anceaux, J. C. 150
Andersen, H. 107 n. 3
Andersen, T. 264
Anderson, L. 144
Anderson, S. C. 140 n. 28, 167 n. 1, 174
de Angulo, J. 194, 228
Aquilina, J. 50
Aristeva, Š. K. 75 n.
Asher, R. E. 142 n. 34, 144 n. 40, 264
Austin, P. 14
Austing, J. 46, 134–5
Ayuninjam, F. F. 173

Baerman, M. 58
Baker, M. 14
Bakker, D. 24, 58, 310, 312
Bauman, J. J. 207 n. 3, 218, 225 n. 23, 275
Bavin, E. L. 264
Becker, A. L. 84
Beller, P. 121 n. 22
Beller, R. 121 n. 22
Bender, M. L. 225
Bendor-Samuel, D. 143 n. 39
Benjamin, C. 46, 122
Benveniste, É. 8, 61, 69, 70
Benzing, J. 157 n., 158 n.
van den Berg, B. 41 n. 3
van den Berg, H. 49, 129
Bhat, D. N. S. 76 n. 11
Bigalke, R. 46, 122
Birk, D. B. W. 139 n. 25
Blake, B. J. 139 n. 24, 207, 263, 289 n.
Blake, F. R. 13
Blood, C. 156
Bloomfield, L. 18, 87, 153 n.
Boas, F. 18, 62 n. 23, 73, 86, 145, 225 n. 24
Boelaars, J. H. M. C. 43, 111, 125, 131
Bohnhoff, L. E. 140 n. 28
Bopp, F. 245
Borgman, D. M. 154, 155
Boxwell, M. 235

de Bray, R. G. A. 45, 122, 207, 208
Bresnan, J. 14
Broadbent, S. M. 140 n. 29, 276
Brockway, E. 121 n. 22
Brousseau, A. 125
Bryan, M. A. 16, 58 n., 62 n. 16, 113 n. 12
Buchler, I. R. 73 n. 7
Bühler, K. 5
Bulatova, N. 141 n. 33
Bunn, G. 117, 253
Burling, R. 225 n. 21
Burquest, D. A. 58 n., 140 n. 28, 141, 144, 261
Butt, J. 46, 122
Bybee, J. L. 315–16, 319

Calame-Griaule, G. 135
Caldwell, R. 144 n. 40
Callaghan, C. A. 207 n. 5, 276–7
Callow, J. C. 197 n. 5, 282
Campbell, L. 121 n. 22, 255, 256 n., 286
Capell, A. 94, 111 n., 142 n. 36, 221 n.
Carroll, L. 186
Carstairs-McCarthy, A. 309
Cassidy, F. G. 48, 137
Cerron-Palomino, R. 2 n.
Chafe, W. L. 149
Chase, W. J. 101
Chelliah, S. L. 207 n. 3
Cherchi, M. 114
Chlenova, S. F. 32 n.
Chomsky, N. 14
Clairis, C. 44, 133
Cole, P. 255
Comrie, B. 23, 76 n. 12, 133
Conklin, H. C. 88, 139
Conrad, R. J. 211 n. 15
Cook, W. H. 225 n. 24
Cooke, J. R. 5, 12
Corbett, G. G. 13 n., 16, 69, 70, 188 n., 193, 194, 200 n., 201, 307 n., 319
Cowan, H. K. J. 109
Crazzolara, J. P. 62 n. 16, 115 n. 17, 264 n.
Croft, W. 21, 59, 102 n.
Crofts, M. 143 n. 39
Crowell, T. H. 256
Crowley, T. 140, 199, 289
Csúcs, S. 274
Culicover, P. W. 14

Index of Names

Curnow, T. J. 44, 133
Cysouw, M. 23

Dalrymple, M. 73 n. 7, 88 n. 20, 309
D'Alton, P. A. 141 n. 32
Davis, H. 109
DeLancey, S. 43, 62
Derbyshire, D. C. 158
Dibbets, G. R. W. 101 n. 1
Dickinson, C. 44 n. 5
Diessel, H. 18
Diller, A. 12–13
Dimmendaal, G. J. 113–14, 141 n. 31
Dixon, R. M. W. 6 n., 17, 22 n., 62 n. 22, 63, 139 n. 24, 191, 207, 211, 225 n. 22, 226, 273, 289
Doneux, J. L. 93 n., 140 n. 28
Donohue, M. 16, 140, 142 n. 36, 263
Dorsch, H. 174
Drabbe, P. 120–1
van Driem, G. 43, 228, 275 n.
Dryer, M. S. 23, 57 n.
Du Feu, V. 228
Dunnigan, T. 52, 143 n. 38, 153
Durie, M. 146
Dutton, T. E. 19, 47, 138

Ebermann, E. 107 n. 5
Ebert, K. 228, 275 n.
Eisenberg, P. 135–6
Elderkin, E. D. 59 n. 14
Elson, B. 147 n.
Emeneau, M. B. 143
van Engelenhoven, A. 156
Esser, S. J. 142 n. 35
Everett, D. L. 83

Fabian, E. 272
Fabian, G. 272
Facundes, S. 257
Farr, C. 134, 219
Farr, J. 134, 219
Ferguson 29
Feyerabend, P. 21 n. 20
Foley, W. A. 73 n. 9, 111, 114, 117, 119, 121, 128, 131, 133, 167 n. 2, 198, 201, 207–8, 253, 266, 272, 293
Forchheimer, P. 15, 25–30, 33, 82 n., 87, 90 n., 101, 111 n., 114 n. 14, 166, 167 n. 1, 188 n.
Fortescue, M. 108 n. 8, 183
Fortune, R. F. 211
Foster, G. M. 86, 147
Foster, M. L. 86, 147
Fox, G. J. 120, 142 n. 35
Fox, J. J. 156 n.
Frachtenberg, L. J. 220, 225 n. 24, 286

Frajzyngier, Z. 140 n. 28
Frank, P. S. 47, 48, 62 n. 23, 108 n. 8, 128, 195
Franklin, K. J. 208 n. 9, 212
Fransen, M. A. E. 87, 140 n. 28, 167 n. 1, 176
Frantz, C. 134
Frantz, D. G. 153 n.
Freeland, L. S. 194, 207 n. 5, 228, 275
Freeze, R. 73 n. 7

Gaden, H. 59 n. 15, 135
Gair, J. W. 108
Gamal-Eldin, S. 10 n.
Garcia, E. C. 64
Garland, R. 140
Garland, S. 140
Garvin, P. L. 115 n. 16
Gary, J. O. 10 n.
Geary, E. 91, 235
Geoghegan, R. H. 209, 213
George, K. 62 n. 17, 107 n. 3
Gerzenstein, A. 84, 148 n., 149
Gil, D. 16
Giridhar, P. P. 75–6
Givón, T. 13, 15, 18, 60, 140 n. 29
Glasgow, K. 189, 222, 232 n., 234, 288
Goddard, C. 13, 73 n. 7
Goddard, I. 153 n.
Goddard, P. E. 124 n.
Godfrey, M. 223, 289
Goffman, E. 6, 7
Gonzales, A. 77 n., 90
Gonzáles de Pérez, M. S. 109
Gordon, L. 62 n. 23, 84, 114
Görlach, M. 48
Gould, S. J. 244
Gralow, F. L. 144 n. 41
Greenberg, J. H. 6 n., 13, 24–5, 28–30, 33, 60, 73 n. 7, 75, 77, 80–1, 82 n., 89, 91 n. 23, 190, 193, 196, 247, 252, 262, 263 n. 5, 276, 321
Grenoble, L. 141 n. 33
Griffiths, C. 211
Griffiths, G. 211
Grimes, B. F. 171, 256 n.
Grimes, C. E. 156 n.
de Groot, C. 310
Gruzdeva, E. 140
Gvozdanovic, J. 307 n.

Haacke, W. H. G. 154 n.
Haas, M. R. 3 n. 5, 213
Hagège, C. 166, 307
Hagman, R. S. 154 n.
Haiman, J. 42
Hale, A. 19, 43
Hale, K. 73 n. 8, 211 n. 14, 223, 225 n. 22
Halpern, A. M. 115 n. 15

Index of Names

Harbert, W. 46, 56
Hardman, M. J. 3 n. 5, 148 n., 149
Hargreaves, D. 43
Harley, H. 73 n. 7
Harlow, R. 191, 225
Harms, P. L. 108 n. 8
Harré, R. 9, 13, 15–16, 25, 31–3, 73–4
Harriehausen, B. 207 n. 3
Harrison, C. H. 143 n. 39, 200 n.
Hart, H. 140
Haspelmath, M. 109
Haviland, J. 285
Hawkins, J. A. 57 n.
Hawkins, R. E. 158–9
Head, B. F. 16
Healey, A. 134
Heath, J. 52, 67, 233
Hedlinger, R. 174
Helimski, E. 62 n. 18, 194, 274
Helmbrecht, J. 45, 49, 119, 127, 133
Henderson, T. S. T. 73 n. 7
Hengeveld, K. 5
Hetzron, R. 114 n. 13
Hewitt, B. G. 75
Hoddinott, W. G. 221, 287
Hoffmann, C. 58 n., 140 n. 28, 261
Hoffmann, J. 182
Höftmann, H. 125
Hoijer, H. 62 n. 23, 124 n.
Hollenbach, B. E. 52, 73 n. 7, 73 n. 8, 155
Holm, J. 126, 130
Holmer, N. M. 18
Hoogshagen, S. 115 n. 16
Hopkins, E. B. 93
Hoskison, J. T. 140 n. 28
Householder, F. W. 25, 26, 27, 28, 33
Howe, S. 9, 12 n. 14, 48, 69 n., 118
Huang, Y. 25 n.
von Humboldt, W. 13, 88 n. 18, 188 n., 204, 210 n. 12
Hunt, R. J. 115 n. 16
Hurd, C. 115 n. 17
Hurd, P. 115 n. 17
Hutchisson, D. 200–1
Huttar, G. L. 126
Huttar, M. L. 126
Hyman, L. M. 141 n. 32, 167–9, 172 n., 177
Hymes, D. H. 26–8, 148 n.

Ingram, D. 26, 29–30, 33, 73 n. 7, 82, 141, 206, 225, 307, 309
Innes, G. 60, 63 n.
Irwin, B. 19, 116, 150, 253

Jacobsen, W. H., Jr. 115 n. 16
Jaeggli, O. 57

Jakobson, R. 5
Jelinek, E. 14
Jensen, C. 143
Jespersen, O. 5, 69, 73 n. 8, 102 n., 187
Jones, A. A. 146
Jones, P. 16
Jones, W. 16
Josephs, L. S. 146
Jungraithmayr, H. 140 n. 28

Kaplan, R. M. 73 n. 7, 88 n. 20, 309
Kastenholz, R. 107 n. 5
Keegan, J. M. 114
Keesing, R. M. 199 n. 9
Kemp, A. 38, 101
Kendall, M. B. 115 n. 15
Keraf, G. 156 n.
Keresztes, L. 62 n. 18, 207 n. 2, 213
van de Kerke, S. 255
Kerr, H. B. 207 n. 8, 223, 289
Kibrik, A. E. 16
Kießling, R. 59
Kimball, G. D. 109 n.
Kirk, J. W. C. 141 n. 30
Kitching, A. L. 264 n.
van Klinken, C. L. 125
Koch, H. 17, 58–60
Koehn, E. 85, 145
Koehn, S. 85, 145
Kofod, F. M. 221, 287
Kuhn, T. S. 100
Kuipers, A. H. 143 n. 38, 158
Kumari, T. C. 144 n. 40, 264
Kurylowicz, J. 60, 101
Kusters, W. 255
Kutsch Lojenga, C. 151

Lachnitt, G. 113
Laidig, C. J. 200
Laidig, W. D. 200
Langdon, M. 19, 115 n. 15
Lastra, Y. 115 n. 16
Laycock, D. 25, 32–3, 43 n., 213, 249 n.
Leavitt, R. M. 153 n.
Lee, J. 91–2, 94, 154, 157
Lefebvre, C. 125–6
Lehmann, C. 13 n.
Lehmann, T. 3 n. 4
Levin, N. B. 80, 112
Levinson, S. C. 6, 7
Lewis, E. D. 156 n.
Lewis, G. L. 62 n. 19, 107
Lichtenberk, F. 182
Limburg, M. J. 310
Linacre, T. 101
Lindstrom, L. 230–1

Index of Names

Lipkind, W. 50, 149, 252
Lounsbury, F. G. 73 n. 8, 225 n. 24
Louwerse, J. 136
Loving, R. 124
Lowie, R. H. 115 n. 16
Luhrman, G. J. 101
Lukas, J. 62 n. 16
Lupardus, K. J. 109 n.
Luraghi, S. 40
Lusted, M. 264 n.
Lynch, J. D. 108 n. 6, 142, 143, 156, 197, 199 n., 200, 225, 230–1
Lyons, J. 38, 69, 74–5, 102 n.

Macaulay, M. 149
MacElhanon, K. A. 213 n. 16, 272
MacGregor, W. 75, 77, 80, 81, 93, 139 n. 26, 143 n. 37, 152, 189 n. 2, 227 n., 233, 279, 280
MacIntosh, M. 141 n. 32
MacKaughan, H. P. 134, 139
MacKay, G. R. 89, 189, 192, 232, 233, 281, 288
MacLean, E. A. 207 n. 4
Macuch, R. 62 n. 20
Malchukov, A. L. 141 n. 33
Mallinson, G. 58
Malone, T. 144
Mangold, M. 135
Mannheim, B. 3 n. 5
Manrique, C. L. 50, 115 n. 16
Marchese, L. 60
Maring, J. M. 115 n. 16, 116
Mårtensson, E. 12 n. 14
Masica, C. P. 108, 142
Matthews, G. H. 115 n. 16, 252
Meinhof, C. 167 n. 1
Merlan, F. C. 139 n. 26, 227 n., 233, 281
Metcalfe, C. D. 91, 139 n. 26
Milne, L. 225 n. 21
Minch, A. S. 43 n., 150, 254, 283 n. 8
Mithun, M. 14, 69
Mixco, M. 112, 252
Monod-Becquelin, A. 70–1
Moravcsik, E. A. 13 n., 69, 70, 75, 82 n., 117 n. 19, 221
Morgan, W. 17–18, 124 n.
Morphy, F. 228
Mosel, U. 199 n. 8
Mous, M. 59
Mpaayei, J. T. O. 107 n. 5, 113 n. 12
Mühlhäusler, P. 9, 13, 15, 16, 19, 25, 31–2, 34, 43 n., 73–4, 249 n.
Müller, F. 26
Munro, P. 67–8, 115 n. 15
Murane, E. 60, 62 n. 21, 108 n. 7

Muratori, P. C. 107 n. 5
Muysken, P. 255

N'diaye-Correard, G. 45 n.
Nababan, P. W. J. 142 n. 35
Najlis, E. L. 115 n. 16
Nebel, P. A. 107 n. 5
Nettle, D. 9
Newman, S. 109, 121
Nguyen, P. P. 117
Nichols, J. 9, 141
Nicklas, T. D. 109 n.
Nikolaeva, I. 157, 158 n.
Noonan, M. 114, 264
Norman, J. 83, 107, 117, 141, 258
Novelli, B. 141 n. 31
Noyer, R. 41 n. 2, 73 n. 7, 88 n. 20, 166, 179 n., 180 n. 8, 309
Ntage, S. 180

Oates, L. 51, 215, 218, 285
Oates, W. 51, 215, 218, 285
Odden, D. 62 n. 16
Oka, I. G. N. 84
Onishi, M. 13
Osborne, C. R. 91, 94, 148 n., 154, 157
Otanes, F. T. 183

Pagliuca, W.
Palácio, A. P. 92 n.
Pandharipande, P. V. 142
Paol, J. N. 49–51, 61, 108 n. 7, 126, 137
Parker, E. 17, 167 n. 1, 170, 172
Parker, G. J. 76 n. 12
Parks, D. R. 149
Paton, W. F. 76 n. 12, 199
Pawley, A. 207
Payne, D. L. 62 n. 23, 109, 150, 257
Payne, T. E. 221
Pence, A. R. 91, 94, 235
Peterson, D. A. 9
Piau, J. 111, 208 n. 9, 253
Pike, K. L. 192 n.
Plank, F. 16, 23 n., 28, 73 n. 7, 76 n. 12, 77, 88 n. 18, 107 n. 3, 149, 163, 188 n., 193, 210, 213, 267, 319
Plungian, V. 125
Polak, R. J. E. R. 257
Popjes, J. 71, 118 n., 149, 256, 283
Popovich, H. 146
Poppe, n. 61, 109
Posner, R. 107
Premsrirat, S. 207 n. 3
Press, M. L. 140 n. 29
Priestly, T. M. S. 208
van Putte, F. 64

Index of Names 365

Quirk, R. 73

Rath, J. C. 145 n.
Ray, S. 133, 198
Reed, J. 150, 257
Reesink, G. P. 211
Reh, M. 50, 264 n.
Reichard, G. A. 58 n., 194
Reid, L. A. 77 n., 90, 139
Reinisch, L. 45, 128, 159, 225
Renck, G. L. 62 n. 21, 208
Rhodes, R. A. 9, 153 n.
Rice, K. 17, 18, 124
Richard, E. L. 219
Rijkhoff, J. 24, 312
Ritter, E. 73 n. 7
Roberts, J. R. 208 n. 9
Robertson, S. 48, 137
Robinett, F. M. 115 n. 16, 252
Rojas Curieux, T. 117, 319
Romero-Figeroa, A. 130
Rood, D. S. 91 n. 23, 149
Ross, M. D. 49–51, 61, 108 n. 7, 121, 126, 137
Rottland, F. 107 n. 5, 109
Rowe, J. H. 2 n. 3
Royen, G. 26
Rude, N. E. 50, 127
Rumsey, A. 93

Safir, K. J. 57
Salminen, T. 62 n. 18
Santandrea, S. 59
de Santo Tomás, F. D. 1, 4
Sanzheyev, G. D. 142
Sapir, E. 140 n. 29
Sasse, H. -J. 41 n. 2, 45 n.
de Saussure, F. 8, 100
Sauvageot, S. 130, 135
Saxon, L. A. 14
Scaliger, J. 101 n. 1
Schachter, P. 183
Schadeberg, T. C. 140 n. 28
Schaub, W. 18, 140 n. 28, 172 n., 175
Schegloff, E. A. 17
Schellinger, W. 16, 107 n. 3, 267, 318, 319
Schenker, A. M. 45
Schmalstieg, W. R. 206
Schmidt, W. 26, 27, 82 n., 188 n., 197 n. 6, 201
Schönfeld, M. 48, 51, 135
Schulze-Berndt, E. 227 n.
Schuster-Sewc, H. 208
Schwartz, L. J. 32 n., 52, 143 n. 38, 153, 182, 255
Schwarze, C. 51, 122

Scott, G. 207 n. 8
Seiler, W. 150, 254
Senft, G. 228
Sharma, S. R. 43, 132–3, 136, 209
Sharpe, M. C. 227
Shay, E. 140 n. 28
Shelden, H. 17, 142 n. 36
Shibatani, M. 117 n. 19, 119, 144
Siewierska, A. 58, 310
Silva Lôpez, L. 143 n. 39
Simon, H. 16, 76
Simons, L. 200, 293
Sims-Williams, N. 107 n. 3
Smeets, R. 75 n.
Smith, J. C. 140, 263
Smith, K. D. 228
Snapp, A. 159, 263
Sneddon, J. N. 142 n. 35
Sohn, H.-M. 71, 114 n. 14
Sokolovskaya, N. K. 32 n., 73 n. 7, 96, 210 n. 12
Sop, G. 180
Spagnolo, F. L. M. 182
Sridhar, S. N. 109, 142, 265
Stairs, E. F. 52, 155
Stassen, L. 168
Stein, P. 130
Steinhauer, H. 13, 156 n., 201
Stephens, J. 62 n. 17, 107 n. 3
Stokes, B. 233, 280
Stone, G. 206
Streitberg, W. 212
Strom, C. 143 n. 38
Stump, G. T. 8, 68 n. 2, 121 n. 21
Suárez, J. A. 225 n. 24
Suárez Roca, J. L. 3 n. 5
Susman, A. 252
Susnik, B. 42, 113, 115 n. 16, 132, 143 n. 39
Swadesh, M. 42, 109, 132
Szemerényi, O. J. L. 206

Tauberschmidt, G. 144
Teeter, K. V. 58 n.
Thelwall, R. 136
Thomas, D. D. 87–8, 139, 151
Thomason, S. G. 83
Thomson, N. P. 43, 208 n. 10
Thráinsson, H. 41, 48, 51, 122, 134
Thrax, D. 38, 101
Tisdall, S. C. 142
Todd, E. M. 221
Tolskaya, M. 157, 158 n.
Tompa, J. 62 n. 18
Topping, D. M. 142 n. 35
Trier, J. 9
Troike, R. C. 113
Tryon, D. T. 139 n. 25, 227 n., 287

Tsereteli, K. G. 62 n. 20
Tucker, A. N. 16, 58 n., 62 n. 16, 107 n. 5, 113 n. 12
Tuite, K. 11, 49, 126, 146, 151
Tyler, S. A. 142 n. 34, 144 n. 40

Uhlig, G. 38, 101
Upia, R. 46, 134–5
Urban, G. 113, 118
Uspensky, B. A. 57–8

Van Valin, R. D., Jr. 91 n. 23, 112
Varenne, H. 6
Veerman-Leichsenring, A. 148 n.
Versteegh, K. 14 n., 62 n. 20
Voegelin, C. F. 140 n. 29, 223 n.
Voorhoeve, C. L. 108 n. 7, 109, 117 n. 18, 121, 142 n. 36, 196, 207 n. 5, 207 n. 6, 220, 253
Voorhoeve, J. 166, 167 n. 1, 169 n., 170, 178, 180 n.
Vorbichler, A. 115 n. 17
Vorlat, E. 101 n. 1
de Vries, L. 43, 55, 131
Vydrine, V. 93 n., 140 n. 28

Wales, K. 118
Waterhouse, V. 11 n. 12
Waters, B. 272
Webelhuth, G. 14
Weber, D. J. 62 n. 23, 146, 255
Weimer, H. 215

Weimer, N. 215
Wells, M. A. 43, 62 n. 21, 208
Welmers, W. E. 107 n. 5
Westermann, D. 107 n. 5, 264 n.
Westrum, P. N. 110
Whiteley, W. H. 59
Whorf, B. L. 121 n. 22
Wierzbicka, A. 6, 13
Wiesemann, U. 45 n., 73 n. 8, 110, 113, 117, 118 n., 166, 179–80, 184, 234 n. 32, 256, 282, 283 n. 7
Wilkins, D. P. 17
Williams, M. 225 n. 24
Willms, A. 10 n.
Wilson, D. 230
Winterson, J. 38
Wise, M. R. 150
Wogiga, K. 211 n. 15
Wolfart, H. C. 153 n.
Wolff, E. 140 n. 28
Wolff, J. U. 261
Woodbury, A. 207 n. 4
Woollams, G. 146
Wurm, S. A. 108 n. 7, 140, 207 n., 208, 213, 219

Young, R. 17–18, 124 n.

Zigmond, M. L. 140 n. 29
de Zwaan, J. D. 285
Zwicky, A. M. 73 n. 7, 73 n. 8, 74

Index of Languages

A'jië 225
Abipon 115 n. 16
Abkhaz 75
Acehnese 146
Aché 143 n. 39
Acholi 264 n.
Achumawi 194, 213 n. 17, 228, 230
Acoma Keresan, *see* Keresan
Adamawa Fulfulde, *see* Fulfulde
Aghem 141 n. 32, 167–70, 172, 177, 179, 180, 181
Ainu:
  Classical 119
  Colloquial 144–5
Akha 43, 53
Akhvakh 45, 53
Akoose 172, 174, 175
Alabama 11 n. 11, 109 n.
Alagwa (=Wasi) 59
Alawa 227
Aleut 209, 213–14, 216
Ali (=Yakamul) 108 n. 6
Alywerre (=Alyawarr) 17
Amanab 43 n., 150, 254, 263 n. 4, 283 n. 8
Ambrym:
  Lonwolwol 198–9
  Southeast 76 n. 12
Amele 208 n. 9
Anejoṁ (=Aneityum) 199 n. 8
Anguthimri 140 n. 27
Anywa (=Anuak) 264 n.
Apache, Chiricahua 124 n.
Apalai 85, 145, 146
Apinayé 197 n. 5, 227 n., 281–2
Apurinã 257
Arabic:
  Cairene Colloquial 10 n.
  Classical 213 n. 16
  Southern varieties 213 n. 17
Aramaic, Neo 62 n. 20
Arapesh 211
Archi 16
'Are'are 200
Arrernte, Mparntwe 17
Asmat 108 n. 7, 109, 110
Assiniboine 80, 91 n. 23, 112
Assyrian, *see* Aramaic
Asurini 143 n. 39

Awa 124–5
Awa-Pit (=Cuaiquer) 44, 53, 54, 133
Awju 43, 53, 131
Ayoreo 115 n. 16

Babungo (=Vengo) 18, 140 n. 28, 172, 175, 181, 263 n. 3
Bagirmi 59 n. 15, 135
Bahing 225 n. 23, 275
Bal, *see* Svan
Bamileke 140 n. 28, 169 n., 170, 172, 178, 263 n. 3
Baniata 319 n.
Barasano 16
Bardi (=Baadi) 91–2, 139 n. 26, 263 n. 3
Bare 257, 265
Bari 182–3
Baruya 207 n. 8
Batak:
  Karo 146
  Toba 142 n. 35
Beli 59 n. 15
Benabena 121 n. 21, 266
Berik 110, 148
Biak 201–2
Big Nambas 120, 142 n. 35
Binandere 94–5, 134, 152, 158
Blackfoot 153 n.
Bolante (=Balante) 45 n.
Bolivian Quechua, *see* Quechua
Bongo 59
Bororo 256
Breton 62 n. 17, 107 n. 3
Buin 213
Bukiyip 211 n. 15
Bulgarian 45, 53, 122
Bunaba 93
Bunan 43, 53, 132–3, 225 n. 23
Burarra 157, 222, 232 n., 234, 288
Buriat 61, 62 n. 19, 109
Burmese 12
Burmeso 16
Burunge 59

Caddo 149, 263 n. 4
Camling 228
Campa 150, 257, 263 n. 4

Index of Languages

Canela-Krahô 70, 71, 149, 256, 263 n. 4, 282–3
Cantonese, see Chinese
Catalan 107
Cebuano 261
Chalcatongo Mixtec, see Mixtec
Chambri 293
Chamorro 142 n. 35
Chayahuita 140
Chechen 141 n. 33
Chepang 207 n. 3
Cherokee 225 n. 24
Chichimeco Jonaz 115 n. 16
Chickasaw 11 n. 11, 62 n. 23, 109
Chinese:
    Cantonese (=Yue Chinese) 117
    Classical 83, 117, 258
    Modern Northern (=Mandarin Chinese) 107, 141, 258
    Pidgin, see Pidgin
Chinook 225 n. 24
Chiricahua Apache, see Apache
Chitimacha 42–3, 53–4, 132
Choctaw 11 n. 11, 109 n.
Chontal:
    Highland (=Sierra Chontal) 11 n. 12
    Huameltultec (=Costa Chontal) 11 n. 12
Chrau 151
Chuckchee 45, 53, 133
Chulupi 113
Coahuilteco (=Tonkawa) 62 n. 23, 113
Coatlán Mixe, see Mixe
Coos 220, 286
Cornish 62 n. 17, 107 n. 3
Cree 153 n.
Creole:
    Haitian, Northern 130
    Haitian, Southern 125–6
    Mauritius 130–1
    Réunion 130
    Seychellois 130
    see also Ndyuka; Sranan; Tok Pisin
Crow 115 n. 16
Cuna (=Kuna) 18

Daga 60–1, 62 n. 21, 108 n. 7
Damana (=Malayo) 195
Dan 93 n., 140 n. 28, 263 n. 3
Dargi:
    Colloquial 119
    Literary 119, 129
Datooga 109
Dawanese (=Atoni) 156 n.
Dhalandji 225 n. 22
Dhuwal, Djapu 228–9
Didinga 62 n. 16
Diegueño (=Kumiái) 19, 115 n. 15

Dii 140 n. 28, 263 n. 3
Dinka 107 n. 5
Dizi 213–14
Djapu, see Dhuwal
Dogon:
    Tommo-So 125–6
    Toro 135
Dogrib 14
Dongola, see Kenuzi-Dongola
Dumi 43, 53
Dutch 42–3, 51, 53, 101 n. 1, 118, 137, 247–8, 266
    Middle Dutch 48, 53, 135, 136
Dyirbal 17

Ebang 140 n. 28, 263 n. 3
Ecuadorian Quechua, see Quechua
Ekagi (=Ekari) 121
Elema 19
English 3, 8, 10, 12, 13, 16, 39, 48–9, 53, 55–7, 61, 68 n. 2, 69, 73, 74, 80, 101 n. 1, 118, 137–8, 168
    Old English 48, 53, 137
Epena Pedee (=Embera-Saija) 108 n. 8
Estonian 107 n. 4
Even 141 n. 33
Evenki 141 n. 33

Fehan, see Tetun
Fijian 108 n. 6
    Nadrau 199 n. 9
Finnish 107 n. 4
Fongbe 125
Fore 207 n. 8, 266
French 10, 51–3, 56, 75 n.
Fulfulde, Adamawa 141 n. 32

Gadsup 134
Gahuku 121 n. 21
Galela 17, 142 n. 36
Gao 201 n. 11
Gende 266
Georgian 114
German 48, 53, 57 n., 135, 247–8, 266
Ghomala' 166, 172, 179–81
Golin 116, 117 n. 18, 253
Gooniyandi 93, 189 n. 2, 235 n.
Gothic 48, 53, 212, 216, 247, 266
Grebo 59, 60, 63 n.
Greek, Classical 213 n. 16
Guajajara 143 n. 39
Guambino 44 n. 5, 53
Guarani 143 n. 39
Guató 92 n.
Gubden 119, 120, 129
Gude 140 n. 28, 263 n. 3

Index of Languages   369

Guguyimidjir 285–6, 289 n.
Guhu-Samane 219
Gujarati 142
Gumbaynggir (=Kumbainggar) 225 n. 22
Gunin (=Kwini) 143 n. 37
Gunwingguan 139 n. 26
Gupapuyŋu 225 n. 22

Haitian Creole, *see* Creole
Hanunóo 139, 263 n. 3
Hatam 211
Hdi (=Hedi) 140 n. 28, 263 n. 3
Heiltsuk 145 n.
Hidatsa 115 n. 16, 252–3
Hmong-Njua 207 n. 3
Hua 121 n. 21
Huallaga Quechua, *see* Quechua
Huameltultec Chontal, *see* Chontal
Huasteca Nahuatl, *see* Nahuatl
Huave 52–3, 155–6
Hungarian 62 n. 18, 69
Hunzib 49, 53
Hupa 124 n.

Icelandic 41, 48, 51, 53, 57 n., 122–3, 134
Ika (=Ica) 47–9, 53–4, 62 n. 23, 108 n. 8, 128, 195, 196
Ilocano 77 n., 87–90, 139
Imonda 150, 254, 263 n. 4
Indonesian 13
Inuktitut:
 North Slope Iñupiaq 207 n. 4
 West Greenlandic 108 n. 8, 183
Iñupiaq, *see* Inuktitut
Ipuriná, *see* Apurinã
Iraqw 59 n. 14
Italian 53, 56, 107, 122, 123
Ixtenco Otomí, *see* Otomí

Jaminjung (=Djamindjung) 227 n.
Japanese 117
Jaqaru 149, 263 n. 4
Javanese, Old *see* Kawi
Jéi (=Yéi) 111
Jiarong 218

Kadiwéu 211
Kalam 207, 208
Kalenjin 109
Kamano 266
Kamchadal 45, 53, 133
Kanauri 225 n. 23
Kannada 109, 142, 264–5
Kapau (=Hamtai) 51, 53, 215
Karimojong 141 n. 31

Kâte 272
Kathmandu Newari, *see* Newari
Kati (=Yonggom) 131
Kato 124 n.
Kawaiisu 140 n. 29, 263 n. 3
Kawi (=Old Javanese) 83
Kayapo 234 n. 32, 282–3
Kemtuik 140, 263
Kenuzi-Dongola 45, 53, 128
Keresan, Acoma 115 n. 16, 116
Kewa 208 n. 9, 210 n. 11, 212
Kewieng (=Yopno) 272
Kham 207 n. 3
Khanti 62 n. 18, 207 n. 2
Khmu 207 n. 3
Kilivila 228, 229
Kiribati 108 n. 6
Kisar 152, 156–7
Kiwai 133, 197 n. 6, 198
Koasati 11 n. 11, 109 n.
Koiali, Mountain 140, 263 n. 3
Koiari 46–7, 53–4, 138
Kombai 43, 53, 131, 132
Korafe 134, 219–20
Koranko (=Kuranko) 107 n. 5
Korean 70–1, 114 n. 14
Koreguaje 144 n. 41
Koryak 45, 53, 133
Kovai 272
Koya 142 n. 34, 144 n. 40
Kpelle 107 n. 5
Krongo 50, 53
Kube 272
Kuikúro 158
Kuku-Yalanji 218, 285, 289 n.
Kuman 111–12, 208 n. 9, 253
Kunama 159, 225
Kunimaipa 91–2, 94, 152, 235
Kutenai 115 n. 16
Kwaio 199 n. 9, 200, 293
Kwakiutl 18, 62 n. 23, 145
Kwamera 156, 195, 210 n. 11, 230, 231

Lak 49, 53, 127
Lakhota 91 n. 23, 112
Lamalera 156 n.
Lamang 140 n. 28, 263 n. 3
Langalanga 200, 293
Lango 114, 264
Larike 200
Latin 1, 39, 106–7, 266
Lau 200, 293
Lele 140 n. 28, 263 n. 3
Lenakel 152, 156, 195, 230 n.
Lengua 42–3, 53, 54, 132
Lezgian 109
Lihir 201 n. 11

Index of Languages

Limbu 228
Limbum 87, 140 n. 28, 172, 176, 263 n. 3
Lithuanian 206
Logbara (=Lugbara) 115 n. 17
Lonwolwol, see Ambrym
Looma, Northern (=Loma) 140 n. 28, 263 n. 3
Lotuho (=Otuho) 107 n. 5, 113 n. 12

Maasai 107 n. 5, 113 n. 12
Maba 58 n.
Macedonian 45, 53, 122
Macuna 144
Madi 62 n. 16
Magi (=Mailu) 43, 208 n. 10
Maká (=Maca) 84, 149, 150, 263 n. 4
Makushi (=Macushi) 158
Malakmalak (=Mullukmulluk) 139 n. 25, 263 n. 3
Malay 16
  Classical 13
Malayalam 144 n. 40, 264–5
Maltese 50, 53
Mamvu 115 n. 17
Manchad (=Pattani) 209, 225 n. 23
Manchati, see Manchad
Mandaic 62 n. 20
Mandan 112, 252–3
Mandara (=Wandala) 141, 261
Mandarin, see Chinese
Manem 117 n. 18, 253–4
Mangarayi 233
Mansi 62 n. 18, 207 n. 2, 213
Mao Naga 75, 76
Maori 191, 195, 225–6, 228 n. 26
Maranao 139, 263 n. 3
Maranungku 139 n. 25, 227 n., 263 n. 3, 287–8
Marathi 142
Margi (=Marghi) 58 n., 140 n. 28, 261, 263 n. 3
Mari 107 n. 4
Maricopa 62 n. 23, 83–4, 114–15
Marina (=Tolomako) 201 n. 11
Marind 120
Marshallese 201 n. 11
Mataco (=Wichí) 115 n. 16
Mauka (=Mahou) 107 n. 5
Mauritius Creole, see Creole
Maxakali 146
Mazahua 225 n. 24
Mbay 114
Mbili (=Bambili) 172–3, 181
Megeb 45, 53, 133
Meithei 207 n. 3
Mekeo 146
Menomini 18, 153 n.
Midob 136
Milpa Alta Nahuatl, see Nahuatl

Miwok:
  Bodega (=Coast Miwok) 207 n. 5, 276–8
  Lake 207 n. 5, 276 n.
  Northern Sierra 277–8
  Plains 277–8
  Southern Sierra 140 n. 29, 263 n. 3, 276–8
Mixe, Coatlán 115 n. 16
Mixtec:
  Chalcatongo 149, 263 n. 4
  Ocotepec 149, 263 n. 4
Mojave 67, 68, 115 n. 15
Mokilese 200 n.
Mombum 124
Mongolian 142
Mono-Alu 142 n. 35
Monpa (=Moinba) 43, 53
Moraori 43, 53, 131
Mordva 107 n. 4
Moro 140 n. 28, 263 n. 3
Morwap 43 n.
Motu 142 n. 35
Mountain Koiali, see Koiali
Mparntwe Arrernte, see Arrernte
Mudurukú 143 n. 39
Muisca (=Chibcha) 109
Mundani 17, 170, 172–3, 181, 183
Mundari 182
Mura-Pirahã 83
Murik 293

Nabak 272–3
Nadrau Fijian, see Fijian
Nahuatl:
  Classical 121–2
  Huasteca 121 n. 22
  Milpa Alta 121 n. 22
  North Puebla 121 n. 22
Nakanai 225
Nakanamanga (=North Efate) 142 n. 35
Nama 154 n.
Nanggu 140, 263 n. 3
Nasioi (=Naasioi) 115 n. 17
Navaho 17, 18, 124 n., 194
Ndjébbana (=Djeebbana) 233–4, 288, 319 n.
Ndyuka 126
Nenets 62 n. 18
Neo-Aramaic, see Aramaic
Newari, Kathmandu 43, 53
Nez Perce 50, 53–4, 127–8, 129–30
Ngalakan 227 n., 281
Nganasan 62 n. 18, 194–5, 210 n. 11, 212, 274
Ngandi 233
Ngankikurungkurr (=Nangikurrunggurr) 221, 287
Ngiembɔɔn 172, 174, 175, 176
Ngiti 151
Ngizim 144–5, 261

Index of Languages 371

Nimboran 150, 263 n. 4
Nivkh (=Gilyak) 140
Noni (=Noone) 141 n. 32, 172, 177, 179, 180, 181
Nootka 109–10
Nunggubuyu 233
Nyawaygi 225 n. 22, 273–4, 289 n.
Nyikina (=Nyigina) 233, 280
Nyulnyul 80–1, 139 n. 26, 263 n. 3, 279, 280

Ocotopec Mixtec, *see* Mixtec
Ojibwe 143 n. 38
  Eastern 153 n.
  Southwestern 52, 153, 154
Old Church Slavonic, *see* Slavonic
Ömie 46, 53, 134–5
Omotik 109
Oneida 225 n. 24
Ono 272
Orokaiva 134, 135
Orya 16
Otomí, Ixtenco 115 n. 16

Paamese 199, 200
Paez 117, 319
Paiute:
  Northern 159, 263
  Southern 18, 140 n. 29, 263 n. 3
Palau 146
Palaung 77 n., 225 n. 21
Palor 141 n. 32
Pame 50, 53, 57, 115 n. 16
Pampangan 77 n., 90
Päri (=Lokoro) 264
Passamaquoddy-Maliseet (=Malicite) 153 n.
Pawnee 149, 263 n. 4
Pidgin, Chinese 82 n.
Pipil 121 n. 22
Pirahã, *see* Mura-Pirahã
Pitjantjatjara 207 n. 7
Podoko (=Parkwa) 141 n. 30
Popoluca, Sierra 77 n., 86, 90 n., 147–8, 151, 263 n. 4
Portuguese 106
Puebla Nahuatl, *see* Nahuatl
Pulawat 142 n. 35

Qawesqar (=Kawesqar) 44, 53, 54, 133
Quechua 1–3
  Bolivian 255
  Ecuadorian (=Imbabura Quechua) 255–6
  Huallaga 62 n. 23, 145, 255
  Inga 255–6
  Tarma (=North Junín Quechua), 149, 254–5, 263 n. 4

Rapanui 195, 228–9
Rawa 213 n. 16
Reefs (=Ayiwo) 235–6
Rembarrnga (=Rembarungu) 232–3, 281
Retuarã 143 n. 38
Réunion Creole, *see* Creole
Ron 140 n. 28, 263 n. 3
Rongpo 133, 136
Roti (=Rote) 156 n.
Rumanian 58

Sa'a 200, 293
Salt-Yui 19, 116, 117 n. 18, 150–1, 253, 263 n. 4
Samo 196, 220
Samoan 225
San Fratello, *see* Siciliano
Santa Cruz 140, 263 n. 3
Sanuma 154–5
Savosavo (=Savo) 221–2
Sedang 228
Selepet 272
Sentani 109
Sera 108 n. 6
Serbo-Croatian 45, 53, 122
Seychellois Creole, *see* Creole
Shilluk 264 n.
Shuswap 143 n. 38, 158
Siane 266
Siciliano, San Fratello 46, 53, 122–3
Sierra Popoluca, *see* Popoluca
Sika 156 n.
Sinaugoro 144
Sinhalese 108
Siona 144 n. 41
Siroi 43, 53, 62 n. 21, 208–9
Sissano 108 n. 6
Siuslaw 225 n. 24, 286–7
Slave 17, 18, 124
Slavonic, Old Church 45, 53
Slovene 207
Somali 141 n. 30
Sorbian:
  Lower 206
  Upper 208
Spanish 46, 53, 54, 56, 57, 122, 319
Sranan 126
Suena 230–1
Suki 121
Sursurunga 200–1
Svan 11, 49, 53, 54, 57, 126, 127, 146
  Upper Bal 11–12
Swedish 12 n. 14

Tagalog 182–3, 261, 263 n. 3
Tairora 119

372 Index of Languages

Tamazight 10 n.
Tamil 142 n. 34, 144 n. 40
Tangga 201 n. 11
Tarma Quechua, see Quechua
Temein 62 n. 16
Teso 113 n. 12
Tetun, Fehan 125
Thai 3, 12–13, 31
Thargari (=Dhargari) 225 n. 22
Thulung 275
Tibetan 43, 53
Ticuna 144
Tinan 209
Tiwi 91–2, 94, 154–5, 157, 263 n. 3
Tjapukai (=Dyaabugay) 211 n. 14
To'abaita 293
Toda 143, 144
Tok Pisin 154 n.
Tolai (=Kuanua) 199 n. 8
Tommo-So, see Dogon
Tondano 142 n. 35
Tonkawa, see Coahuilteco
Toro, see Dogon
Trukese (=Chuuk) 142 n. 35
Trumai 70
Tsafiki (=Colorado) 44 n. 5
Tsakhur 45, 53
Tuaripi (=Toaripi) 219
Tübatulabal 140 n. 29, 223 n.
Tubu (=Teda) 62 n. 16
Tumleo 108 n. 6
Tunica 213–14
Turkana 113–14, 141 n. 31
Turkish 62 n. 19, 107
Tuscarora 225 n. 24

Udihe 157
Udmurt 107 n. 4, 274
Ulau-Suian 108 n. 6
Uma 142 n. 35
Umpila 191, 226–7, 289–90
Una 136
Uradhi 140, 263 n. 3, 289–90
Usarufa 119, 128–9
Ute, see Paiute, Southern

Vai 107 n. 5
Vanimo 121, 319 n.
Vietnamese 117

Waiwai 158, 159
Walmatjari 62 n. 22
Wambon 43, 53, 54–7, 131
Wantoat 272
Warao 130
Wardaman 139 n. 26, 263 n. 3
Warekena (=Guarequena) 129–30, 265
Warembori 142 n. 36
Warlbiri 14, 225 n. 22
Warrgamay 207 n. 7, 273, 289 n.
Warrwa 152, 227 n., 279–80
Washo 115 n. 16
Waskia 49, 50, 51, 53, 54, 61, 108 n. 7, 126, 127, 137
Weri 234, 235
West Greenlandic, see Inuktitut
Western Desert 62 n. 22
Wichita 149, 263 n.
Wik-Munkan 217, 223, 289–90
Winnebago (=Hocák) 50, 53, 54, 90 n., 149–50, 252–3, 263 n. 4
Wiru 207 n. 8
Wiyot 58 n.
Wolof 130, 135

Xavante 113
Xerente 113, 117, 256
Xokleng 113, 119
!Xu 319 n.

Yagaria 62 n. 21, 207 n. 8, 208, 215
Yagua 221
Yaouré 93, 235 n.
Yapese 225
Yareba 215
Yavapai 115 n. 15
Yidiɲ 63, 211, 216
Yimas 201–2, 293
Yuma (=Quechan) 115 n. 15
Yup'ic, Central 207 n. 4

Zakatal' (=Avar) 45, 53

Index of Subjects

addressee, *see* second person
agreement 5, 13–14, 83
  direction of 13 n.
  richness of 46, 56; *see also* paradigmatic structure
ambiguity 42, 47, 54, 190–2
areal patterns 142, 171, 197, 224, 263, 293, 297
Aristotelian logic 14 n.
Assiniboine type 80–1, 91 n. 23
associative, *see* plural
augmented, *see* minimal/augmented type

Bell numbers 78 n.
Berik type 110–14, 148, 161

choric 'we', *see* mass speaking
cognate paradigms 246–8, 270, 306
cognitive map 249–50, 268, 291–3; *see also* similarity map
common patterns:
  definition of 23, 105
  generalization about 95–8, 236–41, 298–9
conjunct/disjunct pattern 19, 43–4
cross-linguistic perspective 5, 13, 15, 19, 21–3, 25 n., 26, 30, 31–2, 41 n. 2, 320
crypto-diachronic method 24, 247, 269

debitive 60–1
declension 100
deixis:
  locational 5, 18
  participant 5, 6, 31, 47, 49
  person, *see above* participant
  time 5, 47, 49
diachrony 30, 68 n. 2, 245, 248, 305, 321
disambiguation, *see* ambiguity
discourse structure 56 n.
dual 67, 87–8, 91 n. 25, 169–70, 297
  cognate paradigms 269–94
  paradigmatic variation 204–41
dual-3we type 216–24, 238, 284–91
dual-inclusive/exclusive type 224–6, 237, 273–8, 286–7, 292–3
dual-unified-we type 206–16, 237, 273–4, 285–6, 293
Dutch type 41–5, 52, 58

English type 48–51
ergativity 6 n.
ethnography of speaking 6
etic/emic distinction 31 n., 189 n. 3, 194 n.
Eurocentrism 19, 32–3

first person:
  complex 78–98, 104–5, 298
  definition of 6–8
  different from 'self' 73
  hierarchy 97–8
  universality of 13
  zero marked 58–9
fourth person 148 n.
French type 51–2
frequency 52

gender marking 10 n., 15–16, 62 n. 20, 107 n. 3, 114 n. 13, 318–20
generative grammar 13–14, 25 n.
grammaticalization 5, 7, 12–13, 54, 82, 321
group marking:
  definition of 72–7, 205, 296
  restricted 189–90, 205, 282 n. 6

hierarchy:
  correlation with affixal status 315–17
  dual explicitness 240, 270–1, 304–5
  explicitness 164, 250, 259–67, 270–1, 304–5, 312–15, 318
  first person 97–8
  horizontal homophony 161–2, 250–9, 299, 305, 312–15, 316
  person 210–14; *see also above* horizontal homophony
homonymy 40; *see also* homophony
homophony 40, 103–4
  accidental 40, 309
  diagonal 121–2
  horizontal 104, 108–20, 128–9, 143–52, 210–15, 228–31, 239–40, 299–301
  singular 41–58, 122–3, 126–8, 131–4, 135–6, 137–8, 208–9, 215, 266, 301–2
  systematic 40, 309
  vertical 104, 123–38, 152–9, 202, 207–9, 215, 230–1, 234–5, 239–40, 265–7, 272, 302–3
honorifics, *see* politeness

374 Index of Subjects

imperative 60–1
implication 57 n.
  addressee inclusion 96–7
  dual homophony 301
  reversed 97
  singular homophony 53, 301–2
inclusive/exclusive opposition:
  abbreviations using numbers 73 n. 8
  alike to present/absent 225 n. 21
  development of 169–70
  discovery of 1–4
  errors made in descriptions 19,
    140 nn. 27 and 29, 282 nn. 5 and 6
  implications 96–7
  in second person 74–6, 296
  used for politeness 17
inclusive/exclusive type 85, 95–8, 251, 259,
    261, 264–5, 275–8, 292–3
interlocking pattern 16
intra-genetic comparison 247
item-based approach 9

Kalam type 208, 239
Kombai type 131–3, 162
Kwakiutl type 145–7, 161

Latin type:
  in singular 40, 45 n., 58
  in non-singular 106–8
logophoricity 18

Mandara type 141–3, 161
Maranao type 139–40, 217, 232; *see also*
    minimal/augmented type
Maricopa type 114–19, 161
markedness 58, 61, 193–7
mass speaking 69, 73–4, 77, 296
merger 40, 54
metalanguage 68, 77, 102–3, 188–93
minimal/augmented type 85–90, 91 n. 24, 95–8,
    139–40
  definition of 77, 86
  discovery of 87–9
  morphological transparant marking of 89,
    263
  relation to inclusive/exclusive type 260–2,
    276–8
  relation to only-inclusive type 89, 262–4
  relation to partial-unit-augmented type
    279–83, 289–90
  relation to unit-augmented type 232–3,
    279–83, 289–90
morphological uniformity 57
motherese 4

Natural Semantic Metalanguage 13, 73 n. 7
Nez Perce type 129–31, 162
no-we type 81–4, 95–8, 251, 259
non-configurationality 14
number 186–203, 307–9

Ömie type 134–5, 162
only-inclusive type 84–5, 86 n., 89, 95–8,
    251, 259
other person, *see* third person

parádeigma 100
paradigmatic structure 4, 5
  change of 249–50
  definition of 8–12, 295–6
  history of terminology 100
  impoverished 42, 43, 47, 54, 56
  non-uniform 10–11
  richness of 5, 46, 56–7
partial-unit-augmented type 226–7, 237,
    279–83, 287–90
paucal 67, 199–200, 282 n. 6, 293, 297
person marking:
  by clitics 14, 59, 62 n. 20, 83
  by demonstratives 63
  by full nouns 12, 63
  by proper names 12, 63
  by kin terms 12
  consciousness model of 52
  definition of 5, 27, 295
  feature analysis of 73 n. 7, 309
  for possession 15 n., 59
  hierarchical feature analysis of 73 n. 7, 309
  phonological similarity of 9
  portmanteau forms for transitives
    18–19, 67
  pragmatic model of 52
  set theory analysis of 73 n. 7, 309
  specialized forms for kin reference 17
  speech model of 52
  see also first person; second person; third
    person; fourth person; pure person
persona 38
plural 69–72, 102–3
  additive 175 n.
  associative 69, 117
  cumulative 169–70
  heterogeneous 75–6
  homogeneous 75–6
  incorporative 168–9, 181–3
  morphologically transparent 70
  qualitiative definition 72
  quantitative definition 72
  selective 175 n.
  see also group marking
politeness 12 n. 14, 13, 16–17, 71, 76

Index of Subjects 375

polysemy, 40
possession, *see* person marking, for possession
pro-drop 48, 54–7
projection principle 13–14
pronoun:
    attributes of 101
    complex 167 n. 1
    compound 166–81, 297
    demonstrative 18, 63
    indefinite 17
    interrogative 17
    personal, *see* person marking
    reciprocal 17
    reflexive 17
prósopon 38
pure person 163, 238–9, 303, 320–1

quadral 200–1

rapport associatif 100
rara 23 n.
rare patterns 160, 163, 236, 298
    definition of 23, 105
    of first person complex 90–5
rarissima 23 n., 163

sample 22–4, 29, 52
second person:
    definition of 6–8
    universality of 13
    zero marked 59–61
self 73
self-reference 4–5
shifter 5, 12
Sierra Popoluca type 111, 147–51, 161
similarity map 24, 164, 306–7; *see also* cognitive map
Sinhalese type 108–10, 161
Slave type 124–6, 162
Spanish type 45–8, 52, 57–8
speaker, *see* first person
speech act:
    coordination of 77
    manipulative 60
    participants 3, 4
split patterns:
    definition of 105–6
    with inclusive/exclusive 138–52
    without inclusive/exclusive 106–23
syncretism, 40, 68 n. 2; *see also* homophony
syntagmatic structure 310–11

Tékhne Grammatiké 38, 101
terminology 30, 31, 68–72; *see also* metalanguage
tertium comparationis 21
third person:
    as 'non-person' 8, 61
    definition of 6
    obviative 18
    zero marked 61–4
tolkappyam 3 n. 4
traditional description:
    of Arabic 14 n., 62 n. 20
    of Dravidian languages 3 n. 4
    of Greek 38
    of Ilocano 87
    of Latin 1, 38
    of pronouns 101
transitivity 18–19
trial 67, 197–200, 297
Tupí-Guaraní type 143–5, 161
turn taking 7
typology 21–4, 77 n.

unified-we type 80–1, 95–8, 251, 259, 274
unison speech, *see* mass speaking
unit-augmented type 189, 232–6, 237, 279–83, 288–90, 292
universals 23, 57 n., 82–3; *see also* implication

visibility 18

Wortfeld 9

Yagaria type 208, 239

zero marking 52–3, 57–64